Java™ Performance Tuning

Related titles from O'Reilly

Ant: The Definitive Guide

Building Java™ Enterprise Applications

Database Programming with JDBC and Java™

Developing JavaBeans™

Enterprise JavaBeans™

J2ME™ in a Nutshell

Java™ 2D Graphics

Java™ and SOAP

Java™ & XML

Java™ and XML Data Binding

Java™ and XSLT

Java™ Cookbook

Java™ Cryptography

Java™ Distributed Computing

Java™ Enterprise in a Nutshell

Java™ Examples in a Nutshell

Java™ Foundation Classes in a Nutshell

Java™ I/O

Java™ in a Nutshell

Java™ Internationalization

Java™ Message Service

Java™ Network Programming

Java™ NIO

Java™ Programming with Oracle JDBC

Java™ Programming with Oracle SQLJ

Java™ RMI

Java™ Security

JavaServer™ Pages

Java™ Servlet Programming

Java™ Swing

Java™ Threads

Java™ Web Services

JXTA™ in a Nutshell

Learning Java™

Learning Wireless Java™

Programming Jakarta Struts

NetBeans™: The Definitive Guide

SECOND EDITION

Java™ Performance Tuning

Jack Shirazi

Beijing · Cambridge · Farnham · Köln · Paris · Sebastopol · Taipei · Tokyo

Java™ Performance Tuning, Second Edition
by Jack Shirazi

Copyright © 2003, 2000 O'Reilly & Associates, Inc. All rights reserved.
Printed in the United States of America.

Published by O'Reilly & Associates, Inc., 1005 Gravenstein Highway North, Sebastopol, CA 95472.

O'Reilly & Associates books may be purchased for educational, business, or sales promotional use. Online editions are also available for most titles (*safari.oreilly.com*). For more information, contact our corporate/institutional sales department: (800) 998-9938 or *corporate@oreilly.com*.

Editors:	Mike Loukides and Debra Cameron
Production Editor:	Emily Quill
Cover Designer:	Emma Colby
Interior Designer:	David Futato

Printing History:

September 2000:	First Edition.
January 2003:	Second Edition.

ISBN: 0-596-00377-3
[C]

Table of Contents

Preface . . . . **xi**

1. Introduction **1**

Why Is It Slow?	2
The Tuning Game	3
System Limitations and What to Tune	3
A Tuning Strategy	5
Perceived Performance	6
Starting to Tune	10
What to Measure	15
Don't Tune What You Don't Need to Tune	16
Performance Checklist	17

2. Profiling Tools **19**

Measurements and Timings	20
Garbage Collection	22
Method Calls	27
Object-Creation Profiling	43
Monitoring Gross Memory Usage	51
Client/Server Communications	56
Performance Checklist	62

3. Underlying JDK Improvements **64**

Garbage Collection	64
Tuning the Heap	66
Gross Tuning	66
Fine-Tuning the Heap	68
Sharing Memory	72

Replacing JDK Classes 72
Faster VMs 75
Better Optimizing Compilers 79
Sun's Compiler and Runtime Optimizations 88
Compile to Native Machine Code 94
Native Method Calls 95
Uncompressed ZIP/JAR Files 97
Performance Checklist 98

4. Object Creation **100**
Object-Creation Statistics 101
Object Reuse 102
Reference Objects 115
Avoiding Garbage Collection 122
Initialization 125
Early and Late Initialization 126
Performance Checklist 129

5. Strings **131**
The Performance Effects of Strings 131
Compile-Time Versus Runtime Resolution of Strings 134
Conversions to Strings 135
Strings Versus char Arrays 150
String Comparisons and Searches 162
Sorting Internationalized Strings 164
Performance Checklist 170

6. Exceptions, Assertions, Casts, and Variables **172**
Exceptions 172
Assertions 177
Casts 182
Variables 184
Method Parameters 187
Performance Checklist 188

7. Loops, Switches, and Recursion **190**
Loops 190
Tuning a Loop 194
Exception-Terminated Loops 201
Switches 205

Recursion   211
Recursion and Stacks   215
Performance Checklist   217

8. I/O, Logging, and Console Output **219**
Replacing System.out   221
Logging   223
From Raw I/O to Smokin' I/O   224
Serialization   233
Clustering Objects and Counting I/O Operations   245
Compression   247
NIO   249
Performance Checklist   258

9. Sorting **260**
Avoiding Unnecessary Sorting Overhead   260
An Efficient Sorting Framework   263
Better Than O(nlogn) Sorting   271
Performance Checklist   276

10. Threading **278**
User-Interface Thread and Other Threads   279
Race Conditions   281
Deadlocks   282
Synchronization Overhead   285
Timing Multithreaded Tests   295
Atomic Access and Assignment   296
Thread Pools   299
Load Balancing   301
Threaded Problem-Solving Strategies   312
Performance Checklist   313

11. Appropriate Data Structures and Algorithms **314**
Collections   315
Java 2 Collections   317
Hashtables and HashMaps   320
Optimizing Queries   323
Comparing LinkedLists and ArrayLists   327
The RandomAccess Interface   333
Cached Access   337

Caching Examples   338
Finding the Index for Partially Matched Strings   344
Search Trees   348
Performance Checklist   366

12. Distributed Computing **367**
Tools   369
Message Reduction   371
Comparing Communications Layers   374
Caching   375
Batching I   377
Application Partitioning   378
Batching II   379
Low-Level Communication Optimizations   380
Distributed Garbage Collection   385
Databases   385
Web Services   386
Performance Checklist   394

13. When to Optimize **395**
When Not to Optimize   396
Tuning Class Libraries and Beans   396
Analysis   399
Design and Architecture   403
Tuning After Deployment   418
More Factors That Affect Performance   420
Performance Planning   422
Performance Checklist   426

14. Underlying Operating System and Network Improvements **429**
Hard Disks   430
CPU   435
RAM   436
Network I/O   438
Performance Checklist   442

15. J2EE Performance Tuning **445**
Performance Planning   445
J2EE Monitoring and Profiling Tools   445
Measurements: What, Where, and How   447

Load Testing 451

User Perception 452

Clustering and Load Balancing 455

Tuning JMS 459

Performance Checklist 461

16. Tuning JDBC **463**

Measuring JDBC Performance 463

Tuning JDBC 474

Performance Checklist 499

17. Tuning Servlets and JSPs **501**

Don't Use SingleThreadModel 501

Efficient Page Creation and Output 502

Body Tags 505

Cache Tags 506

HttpSession 506

Compression 509

More Performance Tips 511

Case Study: Ace's Hardware SPECmine Tool 512

Performance Checklist 514

18. Tuning EJBs **516**

Primary Design Guidelines 516

Performance-Optimizing Design Patterns 521

The Application Server 525

More Suggestions for Tuning EJBs 529

Case Study: The Pet Store 529

Case Study: Elite.com 530

Performance Checklist 531

19. Further Resources **533**

The Primary Resource 533

Books 533

Magazines 534

URLs 534

Profilers 536

Optimizers 536

Index **537**

Preface

Performance has been an important issue with Java™ since the first version hit the Web years ago. Making those first interpreted programs run fast enough was a huge challenge for many developers. Since then, Java performance has improved enormously, and any Java program can now be made to run fast enough provided you avoid the main performance pitfalls.

This book provides all the details a developer needs to performance-tune any type of Java program. I give step-by-step instructions on all aspects of the performance-tuning process, from early considerations such as setting goals, measuring performance, and choosing a compiler, to detailed examples on using profiling tools and applying the results to tune the code. This is not an entry-level book about Java, but you do not need any previous *tuning* knowledge to benefit from reading it.

Many of the tuning techniques presented in this book lead to an increased maintenance cost, so they should not be applied arbitrarily. Change your code only when a bottleneck has been identified, and never change the design of your application for minor performance gains.

Contents of This Book

Chapter 1 gives general guidelines on how to tune. If you do not yet have a tuning strategy, this chapter provides a methodical tuning process.

Chapter 2 covers the tools you need to use while tuning. Chapter 3 looks at the SDK, including Virtual Machines (VMs) and compilers.

Chapters 4 through 12 cover various techniques you can apply to Java code. Chapter 12 looks at tuning techniques specific to distributed applications.

Chapter 13 steps back from the low-level code-tuning techniques examined throughout most of the book and considers tuning at all other stages of the development process.

Chapter 14 is a quick look at some operating system–level tuning techniques.

Chapters 15 through 18 are new in this edition, providing the information you need to tune J2EE applications. Chapter 15 describes tuning considerations that are common to all J2EE applications. Chapter 16 looks at specifics for tuning JDBC, including optimizing transactions and SQL, while Chapter 17 provides important information for speeding up servlets and JSPs. Chapter 18 describes performance considerations for Enterprise JavaBeans (EJBs).

Finally, Chapter 19 covers a wide range of additional resources where you can learn more about Java performance tuning.

Substantive chapters include a performance-tuning checklist at the end. Use these lists to ensure that you have not missed any core tuning techniques while you are tuning.

New in the Second Edition

All test results have been updated using the latest versions of the VMs available, including the VMs released with SDK 1.4. The previous edition used Versions 1.1.6, 1.2.0, 1.3.0, and HotSpot 1.0. This edition uses Versions 1.1.8, 1.2.2, 1.3.1_02, and 1.4.0 (which effectively includes HotSpot Version 3.0).

This edition has been thoroughly updated and expanded. Table P-1 provides an overview of material that is new or significantly expanded in this edition.

Table P-1. Second edition highlights

Topic	Covered in
Analyzing garbage-collection statistics	Chapter 2
-Xaprof allocation profiler	Chapter 2
Heap tuning	Chapter 3
Reference types	Chapter 4
SoftReference flushing	Chapter 4
WeakHashMap	Chapter 4
Regular expression tuning	Chapter 5
Assertions	Chapter 6
NIO	Chapter 8
Atomic access	Chapter 10
Optimizing collection queries	Chapter 11
LinkedLists versus ArrayLists	Chapter 11
RandomAccess interface	Chapter 11
Collection classes added in SDK 1.4	Chapter 11
Web services	Chapter 12

Table P-1. Second edition highlights (continued)

Topic	Covered in
Performance planning	Chapter 13
J2EE performance tuning	Chapter 15
JDBC	Chapter 16
Servlets and JSPs	Chapter 17
Enterprise JavaBeans	Chapter 18

Virtual Machine (VM) Versions

I have focused on the Sun VMs, as there is enough variation within these to show interesting results. I have shown the time variation across different VMs for many of the tests. However, your main focus should be on the effects that tuning has on any one VM, as this identifies the usefulness of a tuning technique. Differences between VMs are interesting, but are only indicative and need to be verified for your specific application. Where I have shown the results of timed tests, the VM versions I have used are:

1.1.8

> Version 1.1.x VMs do less VM-level work than later Java 2 VMs, so I have used a 1.1.x VM that includes a just-in-time (JIT) compiler. Version 1.1.8 was the most recently updated 1.1 JVM available for my tests. Version 1.1.8 supports running with and without a JIT. The default is with a JIT, and this is the mode used for all measurements in the book.

1.2.2

> I have used the 1.2.2 JDK for the 1.2 tests. Java 2 VMs have more work to do than prior VMs because of additional features such as Reference objects, and 1.2.2 was the most recently updated 1.2 JVM available for my tests. Version 1.2 supports running with and without a JIT. The default is with a JIT, and this is the mode used for all measurements in the book.

1.3.1_02

> I have used the 1.3.1_02 release for the 1.3 tests. Version 1.3 supports running in interpreted mode, with HotSpot technology for the client (mixed mode) and for the server (server mode). Version 1.3 does not support a pure JIT mode. Tests labeled "1.3.1" use the default client-mode HotSpot technology, and tests labeled "1.3.1 -server" use the server-mode HotSpot technology. For the server-mode tests, I recorded the test times after the JIT generated code, i.e., the second run of tests. These times are more representative of how server-mode JVMs are used.

1.4

> I have used the 1.4.0 release for the 1.4 tests. Tests labeled "1.4" use the default client-mode HotSpot technology, tests labeled "1.4 -server" use the server-mode

HotSpot technology, and tests labeled "1.4 -Xint" use the interpreted mode (i.e., no JIT compilation at all). The 1.4.0 release had a few performance problems with the server mode, and Sun engineering kindly provided me with a 1.4.1 pre-release version of the server-mode JVM on which to run my tests. In addition, I've used the -Xbatch option to ensure that all the HotSpot compilation takes place in the first run through any tests, and I've recorded the second run times. These times are more representative of how server-mode JVMs are used. I do not recommend using -Xbatch in general, unless you know definitely that the first runthrough of the application can be much slower without affecting user expectations.

Conventions Used in This Book

The following font conventions are used in this book:

Italic is used for:

- Pathnames, filenames, and program names
- Internet addresses, such as domain names and URLs
- New terms where they are defined

Constant width is used for:

- All Java code
- Command lines
- Names and keywords in Java programs, including method names, variable names, and class names

Constant width bold is used for:

- Emphasis in some code examples
- Command lines and options that should be typed verbatim

Comments and Questions

The information in this book has been tested and verified, but you may find that features have changed (or even that we have made mistakes!). Please send any errors you find, as well as suggestions for future editions, to:

O'Reilly & Associates, Inc.
1005 Gravenstein Highway North
Sebastopol, CA 95472
800-998-9938 (in the U.S. or Canada)
707-829-0515 (international or local)
707-829-0104 (fax)

There is a web page for this book, which lists errata, examples, and additional information. You can access this page at:

http://www.oreilly.com/catalog/javapt2/

To comment or ask technical questions about this book, send email to:

bookquestions@oreilly.com

For more information about books, conferences, Resource Centers, and the O'Reilly Network, see the O'Reilly web site at:

http://www.oreilly.com

Acknowledgments

A huge thank you to my wonderful wife, Ava, for her unending patience with me. This book would have been considerably poorer without her improvements in clarity and consistency throughout. I am also very grateful to Mike Loukides and Kirk Pepperdine for the enormously helpful assistance I received from them while writing this book. Their many notes have helped to make this book much clearer and more complete.

Thanks also to my reviewers for the first edition, Patrick Killelea, Ethan Henry, Eric Brower, and Bill Venners, who provided many useful comments. They identified several errors and added good advice that makes this book more useful. For the second edition, the J2EE chapters were reviewed by Jim Elliott, Jim Farley, and Ethan Henry.

This edition has benefited from feedback from many, many people, and I'm very grateful to everyone who took the time to give me their opinions and helpful suggestions. Thank you very much.

I am, of course, responsible for the final text of this book, including any erroors tthat rremain.

CHAPTER 1

In this chapter:
- Why Is It Slow?
- The Tuning Game
- System Limitations and What to Tune
- A Tuning Strategy
- Perceived Performance
- Starting to Tune
- What to Measure
- Don't Tune What You Don't Need to Tune

Introduction

The trouble with doing something right the first time is that nobody appreciates how difficult it was.

—Fortune

There is a general perception that Java programs are slow. Part of this perception is pure assumption: many people assume that if a program is not compiled, it must be slow. Part of this perception is based in reality: many early applets and applications *were* slow, because of nonoptimal coding, initially unoptimized Java Virtual Machines (VMs), and the overhead of the language.

In earlier versions of Java, you had to struggle hard and compromise a lot to make a Java application run quickly. More recently, there have been fewer reasons why an application should be slow. The VM technology and Java development tools have progressed to the point where a Java application (or applet, servlet, etc.) is not particularly handicapped. With good designs and by following good coding practices and avoiding bottlenecks, applications usually run fast enough. However, the truth is that the first (and even several subsequent) versions of a program written in any language are often slower than expected, and the reasons for this lack of performance are not always clear to the developer.

This book shows you why a particular Java application might be running slower than expected, and suggests ways to avoid or overcome these pitfalls and improve the performance of your application. In this book I've gathered several years of tuning experiences in one place. I hope you will find it useful in making your Java application, applet, servlet, and component run as fast as you need.

Throughout the book I use the generic words "application" and "program" to cover Java applications, applets, servlets, beans, libraries, and really any use of Java code. Where a technique can be applied only to some subset of these various types of Java programs, I say so. Otherwise, the technique applies across all types of Java programs.

Why Is It Slow?

This question is always asked as soon as the first tests are timed: "Where is the time going? I did not expect it to take this long." Well, the short answer is that it's slow because it has not been performance-tuned. In the same way the first version of the code is likely to have bugs that need fixing, it is also rarely as fast as it can be. Fortunately, performance tuning is usually easier than debugging. When debugging, you have to fix bugs throughout the code; in performance tuning, you can focus your effort on the few parts of the application that are the bottlenecks.

The longer answer? Well, it's true that there is overhead in the Java runtime system, mainly due to its virtual machine layer that abstracts Java away from the underlying hardware. It's also true that there is overhead from Java's dynamic nature. These overheads can cause a Java application to run slower than an equivalent application written in a lower-level language (just as a C program is generally slower than the equivalent program written in assembler). Java's advantages—namely, its platform-independence, memory management, powerful exception checking, built-in multi-threading, dynamic resource loading, and security checks—add costs in terms of an interpreter, garbage collector, thread monitors, repeated disk and network accessing, and extra runtime checks.

For example, hierarchical method invocation requires an extra computation for every method call because the runtime system has to work out which of the possible methods in the hierarchy is the actual target of the call. Most modern CPUs are designed to be optimized for fixed call and branch targets and do not perform as well when a significant percentage of calls need to be computed on the fly. On the other hand, good object-oriented design actually encourages many small methods and significant polymorphism in the method hierarchy. Compiler inlining is another frequently used technique that can significantly improve compiled code. However, this technique cannot be applied when it is too difficult to determine method calls at compile time, as is the case for many Java methods.

Of course, the same Java language features that cause these overheads may be the features that persuaded you to use Java in the first place. The important thing is that none of them slows the system down too much. Naturally, "too much" differs depending on the application, and the users of the application usually make this choice. But the key point with Java is that a good round of performance tuning normally makes your application run as fast as you need it to run. There are already plenty of nontrivial Java applications, applets, and servlets that run fast enough to show that Java itself is not too slow. So if your application is not running fast enough, chances are that it just needs tuning.

The Tuning Game

Performance tuning is similar to playing a strategy game (but happily, you are usually paid to do it!). Your target is to get a better score (lower time) than the last score after each attempt. You are playing with, not against, the computer, the programmer, the design and architecture, the compiler, and the flow of control. Your opponents are time, competing applications, budgetary restrictions, etc. (You can complete this list better than I can for your particular situation.)

I once worked with a customer who wanted to know if there was a "go faster" switch somewhere that he could just turn on and make the whole application go faster. Of course, he was not really expecting one, but checked just in case he had missed a basic option somewhere.

There is no such switch, but very simple techniques sometimes provide the equivalent. Techniques include switching compilers, turning on optimizations, using a different runtime VM, finding two or three bottlenecks in the code or architecture that have simple fixes, and so on. I have seen all of these yield huge improvements to applications, sometimes a 20-fold speedup. Order-of-magnitude speedups are typical for the first round of performance tuning.

System Limitations and What to Tune

Three resources limit all applications:

- CPU speed and availability
- System memory
- Disk (and network) input/output (I/O)

When tuning an application, the first step is to determine which of these is causing your application to run too slowly.

If your application is CPU-bound, you need to concentrate your efforts on the code, looking for bottlenecks, inefficient algorithms, too many short-lived objects (object creation and garbage collection are CPU-intensive operations), and other problems, which I will cover in this book.

If your application is hitting system-memory limits, it may be paging sections in and out of main memory. In this case, the problem may be caused by too many objects, or even just a few large objects, being erroneously held in memory; by too many large arrays being allocated (frequently used in buffered applications); or by the design of the application, which may need to be reexamined to reduce its running memory footprint.

On the other hand, external data access or writing to the disk can be slowing your application. In this case, you need to look at exactly what you are doing to the disks that is slowing the application: first identify the operations, then determine the problems, and finally eliminate or change these to improve the situation.

For example, one program I know of went through web server logs and did reverse lookups on the IP addresses. The first version of this program was very slow. A simple analysis of the activity being performed determined that the major time component of the reverse lookup operation was a network query. These network queries do not have to be done sequentially. Consequently, the second version of the program simply multithreaded the lookups to work in parallel, making multiple network queries simultaneously, and was much, much faster.

In this book we look at the causes of bad performance. Identifying the causes of your performance problems is an essential first step to solving those problems. There is no point in extensively tuning the disk-accessing component of an application because we all know that "disk access is much slower than memory access" when, in fact, the application is CPU-bound.

Once you have tuned the application's first bottleneck, there may be (and typically is) another problem, causing another bottleneck. This process often continues over several tuning iterations. It is not uncommon for an application to have its initial "memory hog" problems solved, only to become disk-bound, and then in turn CPU-bound when the disk-access problem is fixed. After all, the application has to be limited by something, or it would take no time at all to run.

Because this bottleneck-switching sequence is normal—once you've solved the existing bottleneck, a previously hidden or less important one appears—you should attempt to solve only the *main* bottlenecks in an application at any one time. This may seem obvious, but I frequently encounter teams that tackle the main identified problem, and then instead of finding the next real problem, start applying the same fix everywhere they can in the application.

One application I know of had a severe disk I/O problem caused by using unbuffered streams (all disk I/O was done byte by byte, which led to awful performance). After fixing this, some members of the programming team decided to start applying buffering everywhere they could, instead of establishing where the next bottleneck was. In fact, the next bottleneck was in a data-conversion section of the application that was using inefficient conversion methods, causing too many temporary objects and hogging the CPU. Rather than addressing and solving this bottleneck, they instead created a large memory-allocation problem by throwing an excessive number of buffers into the application.

A Tuning Strategy

Here's a strategy I have found works well when attacking performance problems:

1. Identify the main bottlenecks (look for about the top five bottlenecks, but go higher or lower if you prefer).
2. Choose the quickest and easiest one to fix, and address it (except for distributed applications where the top bottleneck is usually the one to attack: see the following paragraph).
3. Repeat from Step 1.

This procedure gets your application tuned the quickest. The advantage of choosing the "quickest to fix" of the top few bottlenecks rather than the absolute topmost problem is that once a bottleneck has been eliminated, the characteristics of the application change, and the topmost bottleneck may not need to be addressed any longer. However, in distributed applications I advise you target the topmost bottleneck. The characteristics of distributed applications are such that the main bottleneck is almost always the best to fix and, once fixed, the next main bottleneck is usually in a completely different component of the system.

Although this strategy is simple and actually quite obvious, I nevertheless find that I have to repeat it again and again: once programmers get the bit between their teeth, they just love to apply themselves to the interesting parts of the problems. After all, who wants to unroll loop after boring loop when there's a nice juicy caching technique you're eager to apply?

You should always treat the actual identification of the cause of the performance bottleneck as a science, not an art. The general procedure is straightforward:

1. Measure the performance by using profilers and benchmark suites and by instrumenting code.
2. Identify the locations of any bottlenecks.
3. Think of a hypothesis for the cause of the bottleneck.
4. Consider any factors that may refute your hypothesis.
5. Create a test to isolate the factor identified by the hypothesis.
6. Test the hypothesis.
7. Alter the application to reduce the bottleneck.
8. Test that the alteration improves performance, and measure the improvement (include regression-testing the affected code).
9. Repeat from Step 1.

Here's the procedure for a particular example:

1. You run the application through your standard profiler (measurement).
2. You find that the code spends a huge 11% of its time in one method (identification of bottleneck).
3. Looking at the code, you find a complex loop and guess this is the problem (hypothesis).
4. You see that it is not iterating that many times, so possibly the bottleneck could be outside the loop (confounding factor).
5. You could vary the loop iteration as a test to see if that identifies the loop as the bottleneck. However, you instead try to optimize the loop by reducing the number of method calls it makes: this provides a test to identify the loop as the bottleneck and at the same time provides a possible solution. In doing this, you are combining two steps, Steps 5 and 7. Although this is frequently the way tuning actually goes, be aware that this can make the tuning process longer: if there is no speedup, it may be because your optimization did not actually make things faster, in which case you have neither confirmed nor eliminated the loop as the cause of the bottleneck.
6. Rerunning the profile on the altered application finds that this method has shifted its percentage time down to just 4%. This method may still be a candidate for further optimization, but nevertheless it's confirmed as the bottleneck and your change has improved performance.
7. (Already done, combined with Step 5.)
8. (Already done, combined with Step 6.)

Perceived Performance

It is important to understand that the user has a particular view of performance that allows you to cut some corners. The user of an application sees changes as part of the performance. A browser that gives a running countdown of the amount left to be downloaded from a server is seen to be faster than one that just sits there, apparently hung, until all the data is downloaded. People expect to see something happening, and a good rule of thumb is that if an application is unresponsive for more than three seconds, it is seen as slow. Some Human Computer Interface authorities put the user patience limit at just two seconds; an IBM study from the early '70s suggested people's attention began to wander after waiting for more than just one second. For performance improvements, it is also useful to know that users are not generally aware of response time improvements of less than 20%. This means that when tuning for user perception, you should not deliver any changes to the users until you have made improvements that add more than a 20% speedup.

A few long response times make a bigger impression on the memory than many shorter ones. According to Arnold Allen,[*] the perceived value of the average response time is not the average, but the 90th percentile value: the value that is greater than 90% of all observed response times. With a typical exponential distribution, the 90th percentile value is 2.3 times the average value. Consequently, as long as you reduce the variation in response times so that the 90th percentile value is smaller than before, you can actually increase the average response time, and the user will still perceive the application as faster. For this reason, you may want to target variation in response times as a primary goal. Unfortunately, this is one of the more complex targets in performance tuning: it can be difficult to determine exactly why response times are varying.

If the interface provides feedback and allows the user to carry on other tasks or abort and start another function (preferably both), the user sees this as a responsive interface and doesn't consider the application as slow as he might otherwise. If you give users an expectancy of how long a particular task might take and why, they often accept this and adjust their expectations. Modern web browsers provide an excellent example of this strategy in practice. People realize that the browser is limited by the bandwidth of their connection to the Internet and that downloading cannot happen faster than a given speed. Good browsers always try to show the parts they have already received so that the user is not blocked, and they also allow the user to terminate downloading or go off to another page at any time, even while a page is partly downloaded. Generally, it is not the browser that is seen to be slow, but rather the Internet or the server site. In fact, browser creators have made a number of tradeoffs so that their browsers appear to run faster in a slow environment. I have measured browser display of identical pages under identical conditions and found browsers that are actually faster at full page display but seem slower because they do not display partial pages, download embedded links concurrently, and so on. Modern web browsers provide a good example of how to manage user expectations and perceptions of performance.

However, one area in which some web browsers have misjudged user expectation is when they give users a momentary false expectation that operations have finished when in fact another is to start immediately. This false expectation is perceived as slow performance. For example, when downloading a page with embedded links such as images, the browser status bar often shows reports like "20% of 34K," which moves up to "56% of 34K," etc., until it reaches 100% and indicates that the page has finished downloading. However, at this point, when the user expects that all the downloading has finished, the status bar starts displaying "26% of 28K" and so on, as the browser reports separately on each embedded graphic as it downloads them. This frustrates users who initially expected the completion time from the first download report and had geared themselves up to do something, only to have to wait

---

[*] *Introduction to Computer Performance Analysis with Mathematica* (Academic Press).

again (often repeatedly). A better practice would be to report on how many elements need to be downloaded as well as the current download status, giving the user a clearer expectation of the full download time.

Where there are varying possibilities for performance tradeoffs (e.g., resolution versus frame rate for animation, compression size versus speed of compression for compression utilities, etc.), the best strategy is to put the user in control. It is better to provide the option to choose between faster performance and better functionality. When users have made the choice themselves, they are often more willing to put up with actions taking longer in return for better functionality. When users do not have this control, their response is usually less tolerant.

This strategy also allows those users who have strong performance requirements to be provided for at their own cost. But it is always important to provide a reasonable default in the absence of any choice from the user. Where there are many different parameters, consider providing various levels of user-controlled tuning parameters, e. g., an easy set of just a few main parameters, a middle level, and an expert level with access to all parameters. This must, of course, be well documented to be really useful.

Threading to Appear Quicker

A lot of time (in CPU cycles) passes while the user is reacting to the application interface. This time can be used to anticipate what the user wants to do (using a background low-priority thread), so that precalculated results are ready to assist the user immediately. This makes an application appear blazingly fast.

Similarly, ensuring that your application remains responsive to the user, even while it is executing some other function, makes it seem fast and responsive. For example, I always find that when starting up an application, applications that draw themselves on screen quickly and respond to repaint requests even while still initializing (you can test this by putting the window in the background and then bringing it to the foreground) give the impression of being much faster than applications that seem to be chugging away unresponsively. Starting different word-processing applications with a large file to open can be instructive, especially if the file is on the network or a slow (removable) disk. Some act very nicely, responding almost immediately while the file is still loading; others just hang unresponsively with windows only partially refreshed until the file is loaded; others don't even fully paint themselves until the file has finished loading. This illustrates what can happen if you do not use threads appropriately.

In Java, the key to making an application responsive is multithreading. Use threads to ensure that any particular service is available and unblocked when needed. Of course, this can be difficult to program correctly and manage. Handling interthread communication with maximal responsiveness (and minimal bugs) is a complex task, but it does tend to make for a very snappily built application.

Streaming to Appear Quicker

When you display the results of some activity on the screen, there is often more information than can fit on a single screen. For example, a request to list all the details on all the files in a particular large directory may not fit on one display screen. The usual way to display this is to show as much as will fit on a single screen and indicate that there are more items available with a scrollbar. Other applications or other information may use a "more" button or have other ways of indicating how to display or move on to the extra information.

In these cases, you initially need to display only a partial result of the activity. This tactic can work very much in your favor. For activities that take too long and for which some of the results can be returned more quickly than others, it is certainly possible to show just the first set of results while continuing to compile more results in the background. This gives the user an apparently much quicker response than if you were to wait for all the results to be available before displaying them.

This situation is often the case for distributed applications. A well-known example is (again!) found in web browsers that display the initial screenful of a page as soon as it is available, without waiting for the whole page to be downloaded. The general case is when you have a long activity that can provide results in a stream so that the results can be accessed a few at a time. For distributed applications, sending all the data is often what takes a long time; in this case, you can build streaming into the application by sending one screenful of data at a time. Also, bear in mind that when there is a really large amount of data to display, the user often views only some of it and aborts, so be sure to build in the ability to stop the stream and restore its resources at any time.

Caching to Appear Quicker

This section briefly covers the general principles of caching. Caching is an optimization technique I return to in several different sections of this book when appropriate to the problem under discussion. For example, in the area of disk access, there are several caches that apply: from the lowest-level hardware cache up through the operating-system disk read and write caches, cached filesystems, and file reading and writing classes that provide buffered I/O. Some caches cannot be tuned at all; others are tuneable at the operating-system level or in Java. Where it is possible for a developer to take advantage of or tune a particular cache, I provide suggestions and approaches that cover the caching technique appropriate to that area of the application. In cases where caches are not directly tuneable, it is still worth knowing the effect of using the cache in different ways and how this can affect performance. For example, disk hardware caches almost always apply a read-ahead algorithm: the cache is filled with the next block of data after the one just read. This means that reading backward through a file (in chunks) is not as fast as reading forward through the file.

Caches are effective because it is expensive to move data from one place to another or to calculate results. If you need to do this more than once to the same piece of data, it is best to hang onto it the first time and refer to the local copy in the future. This applies, for example, to remote access of files such as browser downloads. The browser caches the downloaded file locally on disk to ensure that a subsequent access does not have to reach across the network to reread the file, thus making it much quicker to access a second time. It also applies, in a different way, to reading bytes from the disk. Here, the cost of reading one byte for operating systems is the same as reading a page (usually 4 or 8 KB), as data is read into memory a page at a time by the operating system. If you are going to read more than one byte from a particular disk area, it is better to read in a whole page (or all the data if it fits on one page) and access bytes through your local copy of the data.

General aspects of caching are covered in more detail in the section "Cached Access" in Chapter 11. Caching is an important performance-tuning technique that trades space for time, and it should be used whenever extra memory space is available to the application.

Starting to Tune

Before diving into the actual tuning, there are a number of considerations that will make your tuning phase run more smoothly and result in clearly achieved objectives.

User Agreements

Any application must meet the needs and expectations of its users, and a large part of those needs and expectations is performance. Before you start tuning, it is crucial to identify the target response times for as much of the system as possible. At the outset, you should agree with your users (directly if you have access to them, or otherwise through representative user profiles, market information, etc.) what the performance of the application is expected to be.

The performance should be specified for as many aspects of the system as possible, including:

- Multiuser response times depending on the number of users (if applicable)
- Systemwide throughput (e.g., number of transactions per minute for the system as a whole, or response times on a saturated network, again if applicable)
- The maximum number of users, data, files, file sizes, objects, etc., the application supports
- Any acceptable and expected degradation in performance between minimal, average, and extreme values of supported resources

Agree on target values and acceptable variances with the customer or potential users of the application (or whoever is responsible for performance) before starting to tune. Otherwise, you will not know where to target your effort, how far you need to go, whether particular performance targets are achievable at all, and how much tuning effort those targets may require. But most importantly, without agreed targets, whatever you achieve will tend to become the starting point.

The following scenario is not unusual: a manager sees horrendous performance, perhaps a function that was expected to be quick, but takes 100 seconds. His immediate response is, "Good grief, I expected this to take no more than 10 seconds." Then, after a quick round of tuning that identifies and removes a huge bottleneck, function time is down to 10 seconds. The manager's response is now, "Ah, that's more reasonable, but of course I actually meant to specify 3 seconds—I just never believed you could get down so far after seeing it take 100 seconds. Now you can start tuning." You do not want your initial achievement to go unrecognized (especially if money depends on it), and it is better to know at the outset what you need to reach. Agreeing on targets before tuning makes everything clear to everyone.

Setting Benchmarks

After establishing targets with the users, you need to set benchmarks. These are precise specifications stating what part of the code needs to run in what amount of time. Without first specifying benchmarks, your tuning effort is driven only by the target, "It's gotta run faster," which is a recipe for a wasted return. You must ask, "How much faster and in which parts, and for how much effort?" Your benchmarks should target a number of specific functions of the application, preferably from the user perspective (e.g., from the user pressing a button until the reply is returned or the function being executed is completed).

You must specify target times for each benchmark. You should specify ranges: for example, best times, acceptable times, etc. These times are often specified in frequencies of achieving the targets. For example, you might specify that function A take not more than 3 seconds to execute from user click to response received for 80% of executions, with another 15% of response times allowed to fall in the 3- to 5-second range, and 5% in the 5- to 10-second range. Note that the earlier section on user perceptions indicates that the user will see this function as having a 5-second response time (the 90th percentile value) if you achieve the specified ranges.

You should also have a range of benchmarks that reflect the contributions of different components of the application. If possible, it is better to start with simple tests so that the system can be understood at its basic levels, and then work up from these tests. In a complex application, this helps to determine the relative costs of subsystems and which components are most in need of performance-tuning.

The following point is critical: *Without clear performance objectives, tuning will never be completed.* This is a common syndrome on single or small group projects, where code keeps being tweaked as better implementations or cleverer code is thought up.

Your general benchmark suite should be based on real functions used in the end application, but at the same time should not rely on user input, as this can make measurements difficult. Any variability in input times or any other part of the application should either be eliminated from the benchmarks or precisely identified and specified within the performance targets. There may be variability, but it must be controlled and reproducible.

The Benchmark Harness

There are tools for testing applications in various ways.[*] These tools focus mostly on testing the robustness of the application, but as long as they measure and report times, they can also be used for performance testing. However, because their focus tends to be on robustness testing, many tools interfere with the application's performance, and you may not find a tool you can use adequately or cost-effectively. If you cannot find an acceptable tool, the alternative is to build your own harness.

Your benchmark harness can be as simple as a class that sets some values and then starts the main( ) method of your application. A slightly more sophisticated harness might turn on logging and timestamp all output for later analysis. GUI-run applications need a more complex harness and require either an alternative way to execute the graphical functionality without going through the GUI (which may depend on whether your design can support this), or a screen event capture and playback tool (several such tools exist[†]). In any case, the most important requirement is that your harness correctly reproduce user activity and data input and output. Normally, whatever regression-testing apparatus you have (and presumably are already using) can be adapted to form a benchmark harness.

The benchmark harness should not test the quality or robustness of the system. Operations should be normal: startup, shutdown, and uninterrupted functionality. The harness should support the different configurations your application operates under, and any randomized inputs should be controlled, but note that the random sequence used in tests should be reproducible. You should use a realistic amount of randomized data and input. It is helpful if the benchmark harness includes support for logging statistics and easily allows new tests to be added. The harness should be able to reproduce and simulate all user input, including GUI input, and should test the system across all scales of intended use up to the maximum numbers of users, objects, throughputs, etc. You should also validate your benchmarks, checking some of the values against actual clock time to ensure that no systematic or random bias has crept into the benchmark harness.

---

[*] You can search the Web for "java+perf+test" to find performance-testing tools. In addition, some Java profilers are listed in Chapter 19.

[†] JDK 1.3 introduced a java.awt.Robot class, which provides for generating native system-input events, primarily to support automated testing of Java GUIs.

For the multiuser case, the benchmark harness must be able to simulate multiple users working, including variations in user access and execution patterns. Without this support for variations in activity, the multiuser tests inevitably miss many bottlenecks encountered in actual deployment and, conversely, do encounter artificial bottlenecks that are never encountered in deployment, wasting time and resources. It is critical in multiuser and distributed applications that the benchmark harness correctly reproduce user-activity variations, delays, and data flows.

Taking Measurements

Each run of your benchmarks needs to be under conditions that are as identical as possible; otherwise, it becomes difficult to pinpoint why something is running faster (or slower) than in another test. The benchmarks should be run multiple times, and the full list of results retained, not just the average and deviation or the ranged percentages. Also note the time of day that benchmarks are being run and any special conditions that apply, e.g., weekend or after hours in the office. Sometimes the variation can give you useful information. It is essential that you always run an initial benchmark to precisely determine the initial times. This is important because, together with your targets, the initial benchmarks specify how far you need to go and highlight how much you have achieved when you finish tuning.

It is more important to run all benchmarks under the same conditions than to achieve the end-user environment for those benchmarks, though you should try to target the expected environment. It is possible to switch environments by running all benchmarks on an identical implementation of the application in two environments, thus rebasing your measurements. But this can be problematic: it requires detailed analysis because different environments usually have different relative performance between functions (thus your initial benchmarks could be skewed compared with the current measurements).

Each set of changes (and preferably each individual change) should be followed by a run of benchmarks to precisely identify improvements (or degradations) in the performance across all functions. A particular optimization may improve the performance of some functions while at the same time degrading the performance of others, and obviously you need to know this. Each set of changes should be driven by identifying exactly which bottleneck is to be improved and how much of a speedup is expected. Rigorously using this methodology provides a precise target for your effort.

You need to verify that any particular change does improve performance. It is tempting to change something small that you are sure will give an "obvious" improvement, without bothering to measure the performance change for that modification (because "it's too much trouble to keep running tests"). But you could easily be wrong. Jon Bentley once discovered that eliminating code from some simple loops can actually slow them down.[*] If a change does not improve performance, you should revert to the previous version.

The benchmark suite should not interfere with the application. Be on the lookout for artificial performance problems caused by the benchmarks themselves. This is very common if no thought is given to normal variation in usage. A typical situation might be benchmarking multiuser systems with lack of user simulation (e.g., user delays not simulated, causing much higher throughput than would ever be seen; user data variation not simulated, causing all tests to try to use the same data at the same time; activities artificially synchronized, giving bursts of activity and inactivity; etc.). Be careful not to measure artificial situations, such as full caches with exactly the data needed for the test (e.g., running the test multiple times sequentially without clearing caches between runs). There is little point in performing tests that hit only the cache, unless this is the type of work the users will always perform.

When tuning, you need to alter any benchmarks that are quick (under five seconds) so that the code applicable to the benchmark is tested repeatedly in a loop to get a more consistent measure of where any problems lie. By comparing timings of the looped version with a single-run test, you can sometimes identify whether caches and startup effects are altering times in any significant way.

Optimizing code can introduce new bugs, so the application should be tested during the optimization phase. A particular optimization should not be considered valid until the application using that optimization's code path has passed quality assessment.

Optimizations should also be completely documented. It is often useful to retain the previous code in comments for maintenance purposes, especially as some kinds of optimized code can be more difficult to understand (and therefore to maintain).

It is typically better (and easier) to tune multiuser applications in single-user mode first. Many multiuser applications can obtain 90% of their final tuned performance if you tune in single-user mode, and then identify and tune just a few major multiuser bottlenecks (which are typically a sort of give-and-take between single-user performance and general system throughput). Occasionally, though, there will be serious conflicts that are revealed only during multiuser testing, such as transaction conflicts that can slow an application to a crawl. These may require a redesign or rearchitecting of the application. For this reason, some basic multiuser tests should be run as early as possible to flush out potential multiuser-specific performance problems.

Tuning distributed applications requires access to the data being transferred across the various parts of the application. At the lowest level, this can be a packet sniffer on the network or server machine. One step up from this is to wrap all the external communication points of the application so that you can record all data transfers.

---

[*] Jon Bentley, "Code Tuning in Context," *Dr. Dobb's Journal*, May 1999. An empty loop in C ran slower than one that contained an integer increment operation.

Relay servers are also useful. These are small applications that just reroute data between two communication points. Most useful of all is a trace or debug mode in the communications layer that allows you to examine the higher-level calls and communication between distributed parts.

What to Measure

The main measurement is always wall-clock time. You should use this measurement to specify almost all benchmarks, as it's the real-time interval that is most appreciated by the user. (There are certain situations, however, in which system throughput might be considered more important than the wall-clock time, e.g., for servers, enterprise transaction systems, and batch or background systems.)

The obvious way to measure wall-clock time is to get a timestamp using System.currentTimeMillis( ) and then subtract this from a later timestamp to determine the elapsed time. This works well for elapsed time measurements that are not short.[*] Other types of measurements have to be system-specific and often application-specific. You can measure:

- CPU time (the time allocated on the CPU for a particular procedure)
- The number of runnable processes waiting for the CPU (this gives you an idea of CPU contention)
- Paging of processes
- Memory sizes
- Disk throughput
- Disk scanning times
- Network traffic, throughput, and latency
- Transaction rates
- Other system values

However, Java doesn't provide mechanisms for measuring these values directly, and measuring them requires at least some system knowledge, and usually some application-specific knowledge (e.g., what is a transaction for your application?).

You need to be careful when running tests with small differences in timings. The first test is usually slightly slower than any other tests. Try doubling the test run so that each test is run twice within the VM (e.g., rename main( ) to maintest( ), and call maintest( ) twice from a new main( )).

---

[*] System.currentTimeMillis( ) can take up to half a millisecond to execute. Any measurement including the two calls needed to measure the time difference should be over an interval greater than 100 milliseconds to ensure that the cost of the System.currentTimeMillis( ) calls are less than 1% of the total measurement. I generally recommend that you do not make more than one time measurement (i.e., two calls to System.currentTimeMillis( )) per second.

There are almost always small variations between test runs, so always use averages to measure differences and consider whether those differences are relevant by calculating the variance in the results.

For distributed applications, you need to break down measurements into times spent on each component, times spent preparing data for transfer and from transfer (e.g., marshalling and unmarshalling objects and writing to and reading from a buffer), and times spent in network transfer. Each separate machine used on the networked system needs to be monitored during the test if any system parameters are to be included in the measurements. Timestamps must be synchronized across the system (this can be done by measuring offsets from one reference machine at the beginning of tests). Taking measurements consistently from distributed systems can be challenging, and it is often easier to focus on one machine, or one communication layer, at a time. This is usually sufficient for most tuning.

Don't Tune What You Don't Need to Tune

The most efficient tuning you can do is not to alter what works well. As they say, "If it ain't broke, don't fix it." This may seem obvious, but the temptation to tweak something just because you have thought of an improvement has a tendency to override this obvious statement.

The second most efficient tuning is to discard work that doesn't need doing. It is not at all uncommon for an application to be started with one set of specifications and to have some of the specifications change over time. Many times the initial specifications are much more generic than the final product. However, the earlier generic specifications often still have their stamps in the application. I frequently find routines, variables, objects, and subsystems that are still being maintained but are never used and never will be used because some critical aspect is no longer supported. These redundant parts of the application can usually be chopped without any bad consequences, often resulting in a performance gain.

In general, you need to ask yourself exactly what the application is doing and why. Then question whether it needs to do it in that way, or even if it needs to do it at all. If you have third-party products and tools being used by the application, consider exactly what they are doing. Try to be aware of the main resources they use (from their documentation). For example, a zippy DLL (shared library) that is speeding up all your network transfers is using some resources to achieve that speedup. You should know that it is allocating larger and larger buffers before you start trying to hunt down the source of your mysteriously disappearing memory. Then you can realize that you need to use the more complicated interface to the DLL that restricts resource usage rather than a simple and convenient interface. And you will have realized this before doing extensive (and useless) object profiling because you would have been trying to determine why *your* application is being a memory hog.

When benchmarking third-party components, you need to apply a good simulation of exactly how you will use those products. Determine characteristics from your benchmarks and put the numbers into your overall model to determine if performance can be reached. Be aware that vendor benchmarks are typically useless for a particular application. Break your application down into a hugely simplified version for a preliminary benchmark implementation to test third-party components. You should make a strong attempt to include all the scaling necessary so that you are benchmarking a fully scaled usage of the components, not some reduced version that reveals little about the components in full use.

Performance Checklist

- Specify the required performance.
  - Ensure performance objectives are clear.
  - Specify target response times for as much of the system as possible.
  - Specify all variations in benchmarks, including expected response ranges (e.g., 80% of responses for X must fall within 3 seconds).
  - Include benchmarks for the full range of scaling expected (e.g., low to high numbers of users, data, files, file sizes, objects, etc.).
  - Specify and use a benchmark suite based on real user behavior. This is particularly important for multiuser benchmarks.
  - Agree on all target times with users, customers, managers, etc., before tuning.
- Make your benchmarks long enough: over five seconds is a good target.
  - Use elapsed time (wall-clock time) for the primary time measurements.
  - Ensure the benchmark harness does not interfere with the performance of the application.
  - Run benchmarks before starting tuning, and again after each tuning exercise.
  - Take care that you are not measuring artificial situations, such as full caches containing exactly the data needed for the test.
- Break down distributed application measurements into components, transfer layers, and network transfer times.
- Tune systematically: understand what affects the performance; define targets; tune; monitor and redefine targets when necessary.
  - Approach tuning scientifically: measure performance; identify bottlenecks; hypothesize on causes; test hypothesis; make changes; measure improved performance.
  - Determine which resources are limiting performance: CPU, memory, or I/O.

- Accurately identify the causes of the performance problems before trying to tune them.
- Use the strategy of identifying the main bottlenecks, fixing the easiest, then repeating.
- Don't tune what does not need tuning. Avoid "fixing" nonbottlenecked parts of the application.
- Measure that the tuning exercise has improved speed.
- Target one bottleneck at a time. The application running characteristics can change after each alteration.
- Improve a CPU limitation with faster code, better algorithms, and fewer short-lived objects.
- Improve a system-memory limitation by using fewer objects or smaller long-lived objects.
- Improve I/O limitations by targeted redesigns or speeding up I/O, perhaps by multithreading the I/O.
- Work with user expectations to provide the appearance of better performance.
  - Hold back releasing tuning improvements until there is at least a 20% improvement in response times.
  - Avoid giving users a false expectation that a task will be finished sooner than it will.
  - Reduce the variation in response times. Bear in mind that users perceive the mean response time as the actual 90th percentile value of the response times.
  - Keep the user interface responsive at all times.
  - Aim to always give user feedback. The interface should not be dead for more than two seconds when carrying out tasks.
  - Provide the ability to abort or carry on alternative tasks.
  - Provide user-selectable tuning parameters where this makes sense.
  - Use threads to separate potentially blocking functions.
  - Calculate "look-ahead" possibilities while the user response is awaited.
  - Provide partial data for viewing as soon as possible, without waiting for all requested data to be received.
  - Cache locally items that may be looked at again or recalculated.
- Quality-test the application after any optimizations have been made.
- Document optimizations fully in the code. Retain old code in comments.

In this chapter:
- Measurements and Timings
- Garbage Collection
- Method Calls
- Object-Creation Profiling
- Monitoring Gross Memory Usage
- Client/Server Communications

CHAPTER 2

Profiling Tools

If you only have a hammer, you tend to see
every problem as a nail.
—Abraham Maslow

Before you can tune your application, you need tools that will help you find the bottlenecks in the code. I have used many different tools for performance tuning, and so far I have found the commercially available profilers to be the most useful. You can easily find several of these, together with reviews, by searching the Web using "java+optimi" and "java+profile" as your search term or by checking various computer magazines. I also maintain a list at *http://www.JavaPerformanceTuning.com/ resources.shtml*. These tools are usually available free for an evaluation period, and you can quickly tell which you prefer using. If your budget covers it, it is worth getting several profilers: they often have complementary features and provide different details about the running code. I have included a list of profilers in Chapter 19.

All profilers have some weaknesses, especially when you want to customize them to focus on particular aspects of the application. Another general problem with profilers is that they frequently fail to work in nonstandard environments. Nonstandard environments should be rare, considering Java's emphasis on standardization, but most profiling tools work at the VM level, and there is not currently a VM profiling standard,* so incompatibilities do occur. Even if a VM profiling standard is finalized, I expect there will be some nonstandard VMs you may have to use, possibly a specialized VM of some sort—there are already many of these.

When tuning, I normally use one of the commercial profiling tools, and on occasion when the tools do not meet my needs, I fall back on a variation of one of the custom tools and information-extraction methods presented in this chapter. Where a

---

* The Java Virtual Machine Profiler Interface (JVMPI) was introduced in 1.2, but it is only experimental and subject to change, and looks like it will stay that way officially. There are now two expert groups, JSR 163 and JSR 174, addressing JVM profiling and monitoring issues, and the results of these two expert groups should eventually supersede JVMPI.

particular VM offers extra APIs that tell you about some running characteristics of your application, these custom tools are essential to access those extra APIs. Using a professional profiler and the proprietary tools covered in this chapter, you will have enough information to figure out where problems lie and how to resolve them. When necessary, you can successfully tune without a professional profiler, as the Sun VM contains a basic profiler, which I cover in this chapter. However, this option is not ideal for the most rapid tuning.

 From JDK 1.2, Java specifies a VM-level interface, consisting of C function calls, that allows some external control over the VM. These calls provide monitoring and control over events in the VM, allowing an application to query the VM and to be notified about thread activity, object creation, garbage collection, method call stack, etc. These are the calls required to create a profiler. The interface is intended to standardize the calls to the VM made by a profiler, so any profiler works with any VM that supports the JVMPI standard. However, in JDK 1.2, the JVMPI is experimental and subject to change.

In addition to Java-specific profilers, there are other more generic tools that can be useful for profiling:

- J2EE server-side monitors, useful to monitor server performance both in development and in production
- Network packet sniffers (both hardware and software types, e.g., *netstat*)
- Process and thread-listing utilities (*top* and *ps* on Unix; the task manager and performance monitor on Windows)
- System performance measuring utilities (*vmstat*, *iostat*, *sar*, *top* on Unix; the task manager and performance monitor on Windows)

Measurements and Timings

When looking at timings, be aware that different tools affect the performance of applications in different ways. Any profiler slows down the application it is profiling. The degree of slowdown can vary from a few percent to a few hundred percent. Using System.currentTimeMillis( ) in the code to get timestamps is the only reliable way to determine the time taken by each part of the application. In addition, System. currentTimeMillis( ) is quick and has no effect on application timing (as long as you are not measuring too many intervals or ridiculously short intervals; see the discussion in "What to Measure" in Chapter 1).

Another variation on timing the application depends on the underlying operating system. The operating system can allocate different priorities for different processes, and these priorities determine the importance the operating system applies to a particular process. This in turn affects the amount of CPU time allocated to a particular process compared to other processes. Furthermore, these priorities can change over the lifetime of the process. It is usual for server operating systems to gradually decrease the priority of a process over that process's lifetime. This means that the process has shorter periods of the CPU allocated to it before it is put back in the runnable queue. An adaptive VM (like Sun's HotSpot) can give you the reverse situation, speeding up code shortly after it has started running (see "Faster VMs" in Chapter 3).

Whether or not a process runs in the foreground can also be important. For example, on a machine with the workstation version of Windows (most varieties including NT, 95, 98, and 2000), foreground processes are given maximum priority. This ensures that the window currently being worked on is maximally responsive. However, if you start a test and then put it in the background so that you can do something else while it runs, the measured times can be very different from the results you would get if you left that test running in the foreground. This applies even if you do not actually do anything else while the test is running in the background. Similarly, on server machines, certain processes may be allocated maximum priority (for example, Windows NT and 2000 server version, as well as most Unix server configured machines, allocate maximum priority to network I/O processes).

This means that to get pure absolute times, you need to run tests in the foreground on a machine with no other significant processes running, and use System.currentTimeMillis() to measure the elapsed times. Any other configuration implies some overhead added to timings, and you must be aware of this. As long as you are aware of any extra overhead, you can usually determine whether a particular measurement is relevant or not.

Most profiles provide useful relative timings, and you are usually better off ignoring the absolute times when looking at profile results. Be careful when comparing absolute times run under different conditions, e.g., with and without a profiler, in the foreground versus in the background, on a very lightly loaded server (for example, in the evening) compared to a moderately loaded one (during the day). All these types of comparisons can be misleading.

You also need to take into account cache effects. There will be effects from caches in the hardware, in the operating system, across various points in a network, and in the application. Starting the application for the first time on a newly booted system usually gives different timings as compared to starting for the first time on a system that has been running for a while, and both give different timings compared to an application that has been run several times previously on the system. All these variations need to be considered, and a consistent test scenario used. Typically, you need to manage the caches in the application, perhaps explicitly emptying (or filling) them for each test run to get repeatable results. The other caches are difficult to manipulate, and you should try to approximate the targeted running environment as closely as possible, rather than testing each possible variation in the environment.

Garbage Collection

The Java runtime system normally includes a garbage collector.[*] Some of the commercial profilers provide statistics showing what the garbage collector is doing. You can also use the -verbosegc option with the VM. This option prints out time and space values for objects reclaimed and space recycled as the reclamations occur. The 1.4 VM introduced an additional option to log the output to a file instead of standard error: the -Xloggc:<file> option. Printing directly to a file is slightly more efficient than redirecting the VM output to a file because the direct file write buffering is slightly more efficient than the piped redirect buffering. The printout includes explicit synchronous calls to the garbage collector (using System.gc()) as well as asynchronous executions of the garbage collector, as occurs in normal operation when free memory available to the VM gets low.

 System.gc() does not necessarily force a synchronous garbage collection. Instead, the gc() call is really a hint to the runtime that now is a good time to run the garbage collector. The runtime decides whether to execute the garbage collection at that time and what type of garbage collection to run. In more recent VMs, the effects of calling System.gc() can be completely disabled using the runtime flag XX: +DisableExplicitGC.

Using -verbosegc to Analyze Garbage Collection

It is worth looking at some output from running with -verbosegc. The following code fragment creates lots of objects to force the garbage collector to work, and also includes some synchronous calls to the garbage collector:

```
package tuning.gc;
public class Test {
  public static void main(String[] args)
  {
    int SIZE = 4000;
    StringBuffer s;
    java.util.Vector v;

    //Create some objects so that the garbage collector
    //has something to do
    for (int i = 0; i < SIZE; i++)
    {
      s = new StringBuffer(50);
      v = new java.util.Vector(30);
      s.append(i).append(i+1).append(i+2).append(i+3);
    }
    s = null;
```

---

[*] Some embedded runtimes do not include a garbage collector. All objects may have to fit into memory without any garbage collection for these runtimes.

```
      v = null;
      System.out.println("Starting explicit garbage collection");
      long time = System.currentTimeMillis();
      System.gc();
      System.out.println("Garbage collection took " +
        (System.currentTimeMillis()-time) + " millis");

      int[] arr = new int[SIZE*10];
      //null the variable so that the array can be garbage collected
      time = System.currentTimeMillis();
      arr = null;
      System.out.println("Starting explicit garbage collection");
      System.gc();
      System.out.println("Garbage collection took " +
        (System.currentTimeMillis()-time) + " millis");
  }
}
```

When this code is run in Sun JDK 1.2 with the -verbosegc option,[*] you get:

```
<GC: need to expand mark bits to cover 16384 bytes>
<GC: managing allocation failure: need 1032 bytes, type=1, action=1>
<GC: 0 milliseconds since last GC>
<GC: freed 18578 objects, 658392 bytes in 26 ms, 78% free (658872/838856)>
  <GC: init&scan: 1 ms, scan handles: 12 ms, sweep: 13 ms, compact: 0 ms>
  <GC: 0 register-marked objects, 1 stack-marked objects>
  <GC: 1 register-marked handles, 31 stack-marked handles>
  <GC: refs: soft 0 (age >= 32), weak 0, final 2, phantom 0>
<GC: managing allocation failure: need 1032 bytes, type=1, action=1>
<GC: 180 milliseconds since last GC>
<GC: compactHeap took 15 ms, swap time = 4 ms, blocks_moved=18838>
<GC: 0 explicitly pinned objects, 2 conservatively pinned objects>
<GC: last free block at 0x01A0889C of length 1888>
<GC: last free block is at end>
<GC: freed 18822 objects, 627504 bytes in 50 ms, 78% free (658920/838856)>
  <GC: init&scan: 2 ms, scan handles: 11 ms, sweep: 16 ms, compact: 21 ms>
  <GC: 0 register-marked objects, 2 stack-marked objects>
  <GC: 0 register-marked handles, 33 stack-marked handles>
  <GC: refs: soft 0 (age >= 32), weak 0, final 0, phantom 0>
Starting explicit garbage collection
<GC: compactHeap took 9 ms, swap time = 5 ms, blocks_moved=13453>
<GC: 0 explicitly pinned objects, 5 conservatively pinned objects>
<GC: last free block at 0x019D5534 of length 211656>
<GC: last free block is at end>
<GC: freed 13443 objects, 447752 bytes in 40 ms, 78% free (657752/838856)>
  <GC: init&scan: 1 ms, scan handles: 12 ms, sweep: 12 ms, compact: 15 ms>
  <GC: 0 register-marked objects, 6 stack-marked objects>
  <GC: 0 register-marked handles, 111 stack-marked handles>
  <GC: refs: soft 0 (age >= 32), weak 0, final 0, phantom 0>
Garbage collection took 151 millis
...
```

---

[*] Note that -verbosegc can also work with applets by using this command line:

```
% java -verbosegc sun.applet.AppletViewer <URL>
```

The actual details of the output are not standardized, and are likely to change between different VM versions as well as between VMs from different vendors. As a comparison, this is the output from the later garbage collector version using Sun JDK 1.3:

```
[GC 511K->96K(1984K), 0.0281726 secs]
[GC 608K->97K(1984K), 0.0149952 secs]
[GC 609K->97K(1984K), 0.0071464 secs]
[GC 609K->97K(1984K), 0.0093515 secs]
[GC 609K->97K(1984K), 0.0060427 secs]
Starting explicit garbage collection
[Full GC 228K->96K(1984K), 0.0899268 secs]
Garbage collection took 170 millis
Starting explicit garbage collection
[Full GC 253K->96K(1984K), 0.0884710 secs]
Garbage collection took 180 millis
```

Note the dramatic difference in output from 1.2, stemming from HotSpot technology in 1.3 and later VMs.

As you can see, each time the garbage collector kicks in, it produces a report of its activities. Any one garbage collection reports on the times taken by the various parts of the garbage collector and specifies what the garbage collector is doing. Note that the internal times reported by the garbage collector are not the full time taken for the whole activity. In the examples, you can see the full time for one of the synchronous garbage collections, which is wrapped by print statements from the code fragment (i.e., those lines not starting with a < or [sign). However, these times include the times taken to output the printed statements from the garbage collector and are therefore higher times than those for the garbage collection alone. To see the pure synchronous garbage-collection times for this code fragment, you need to run the program without the -verbosegc option.

In the previous examples, the garbage collector kicks in either because it has been called by the code fragment or because creating an object from the code fragment (or the runtime initialization) encounters a lack of free memory from which to allocate space for that object. This is normally reported as "managing allocation failure."

Some garbage-collector versions appear to execute their garbage collections faster than others. But be aware that this time difference may be an artifact: it can be caused by the different number of printed statements when using the -verbosegc option. When run without the -verbosegc option, the times may be similar. The garbage collector from JDK 1.2 executes a more complex scavenging algorithm than earlier JDK versions to smooth out the effects of garbage collection running in the background. (The garbage-collection algorithm is discussed in Chapter 3 along with tuning the heap. The garbage collection algorithm can be altered a little, and garbage-collection statistics can give you important information about objects being reclaimed, which helps you tune your application.) From JDK 1.2, the VM also handles many types of references that never existed in VM versions before 1.2. Overall,

Java 2 applications do seem to have faster object recycling in application contexts than previous JDK versions did.

It is worthwhile running your application using the -verbosegc option to see how often the garbage collector kicks in. At the same time, you should use all logging and tracing options available with your application so that the output from the garbage collector is set in the context of your application activities. Garbage-collection statistics can be collected and summarized in a useful way. The 1.2 output is relatively easy to understand; the important lines are those summarizing the statistics, e.g.:

```
<GC: freed 18822 objects, 627504 bytes in 50 ms, 78% free (658920/838856)>
```

This line shows that 18822 objects were reclaimed during this garbage collection. The reclamation freed up 627504 bytes, and the time taken to run the garbage collection was 50 milliseconds. After the garbage collection the heap was 78% free, with 658920 bytes available out of a total heap size of 838856 bytes.

The 1.3 (HotSpot) output is a little more concentrated:

```
[GC 609K->97K(1984K), 0.0071464 secs]
[Full GC 253K->96K(1984K), 0.0884710 secs]
```

It consists of two types of output, a "full" or major GC (shown in the second line of the example) that runs through the whole heap, and a minor GC (shown in the first line) that executed in young space (see "Tuning the Heap" in Chapter 3). The numbers before and after the arrow show the amount of space taken by objects before and after the garbage collection. The following number in parentheses is the total available heap space, and the remaining number shows the time taken to execute the garbage collection.

The important items that all -verbosegc output has in common are:

- The size of the heap after the garbage collection
- The time taken to run the garbage collection
- The number of bytes reclaimed by the garbage collection (either listed directly, or deduced by subtracting the before and after used values)

Having the number of objects reclaimed would also be nice, but not all output lists that. Still, these three statistics are extremely useful. First, the heap size gives you a good idea of how much memory the application needs and helps you to tune the heap. Even more useful are the other two options. By running the output through a pattern matcher to extract the GC times and amount freed and totalling those values, you can identify the cost of GC to your application. I like to send some output from the application to indicate when the application finished the initialization stage and started running; then I can filter lines from that point until when I terminate my test.

Let's look at an example now of how to calculate the GC impact on an application. After the application initializes, I start the test running. This particular test is a server application, which I run for 40 minutes, then stop. Taking the logged -verbosegc output, I eliminate any log statements before and after the test run (identified by lines emitted by the application). Then I run a pattern matcher against the -verbosegc logs. The pattern matcher can be Awk, Perl, Java regular expressions, or any pattern matcher you prefer. The matching is very simple; for example, here is a simple matcher in Perl for the 1.2 output:

```
if(/freed\s+(\d+)\s+objects\,\s+(\d+)\s+bytes\s+in\s+(\d+)\s+ms\,/)
{
  $objects += $1;
  $bytes += $2;
  $time_ms += $3;
}
sub END {print "freed $objects objects, $bytes bytes in $time_ms ms\n"}
```

The result from this pattern match shows that over the course of the 40 minutes (or 2400 seconds) of elapsed time, 5654137008 bytes (5392 megabytes) were freed up by garbage collections, taking a total of 717612 milliseconds (or 718 seconds) of GC thread time. With a few simple calculations, we can see that:

- 30% of the time was taken by garbage collection (718 seconds divided by 2400 seconds), which looks excessive. As a guideline, your ultimate target should be under 5% taken by GC, and certainly anything over 15% is an urgent problem.

- 135 megabytes per minute of heap were recycled (5392 megabytes divided by 40 minutes), which for this application looks excessive.

If you don't know the exact number of objects being churned, you can estimate it using a standard average object size of 50 bytes. In this case we have an object churn rate of 2.8 million objects per minute. (5654137008 divided by 50 to get 113 million objects, divided by 40 minutes. For comparison, the actual recorded number of objects churned was 107 million.)

Of course, these values need to be taken in the context of the application. The primary value is the percentage of time taken by the GC, which, again, should be below 15% and ideally below 5%. The other churn values can be considered only in the context of the application, taking into account what you are doing.

The calculation I just made of GC percentage time is actually only partially complete. To be completely accurate, you also need to factor in how much load the application and GC put on the CPU, which would require you to monitor the underlying system for the duration of the test (see Chapter 14 for tools to do that). In this case, the server ran on a single-processor system. The GC utilized the CPU at 100% when running (established in a separate test by correlating GC output to per-second CPU utilization monitoring), and over the course of the 40 minutes of this test, the CPU utilization was 67.5%. Again, a few simple calculations show exactly what is happening:

- The CPU time for the application was 67.5% of 2400 seconds (40 minutes), which makes 1620 seconds.

- The CPU time for the GC was 100% of 718 seconds, which makes 718 seconds.

- Therefore, garbage collection took 718 out of 1620 seconds, or 44% of the application's processing time.

These results reveal that GC is taking way too much time, but at least the metric is accurate. Note that if this were a dual-processor system, GC would probably have utilized the CPU at 50% (i.e., one CPU at 100% and the other unused), which, if everything else was as reported, would have yielded a GC percentage of 22% (as it would have been 50% of 718 seconds of GC CPU time).

The calculation outlined here is fairly simple and can be made with a minimum of tools. It is also easily altered to handle different output formats of -verbosegc.

Tools for Analyzing -verbosegc Output

In addition to performing these calculations yourself, several tools are available to analyze -verbosegc output:

awk script from Ken Gottry
> Ken Gottry's *JavaWorld* article[*] gives a nice description of the HotSpot generational garbage collection and includes an *awk* script for generating an analysis of -verbosegc logs.

GC analyzer from Nagendra Nagarajayya and J. Steven Mayer
> A Sun Wireless Developer article[†] from Nagarajayya and Mayer provides a very detailed discussion of fine-tuning a heap. It includes a GC analyzer tool[‡] for generating reports from -verbosegc logs.

GCViewer from Hendrik Schreiber
> GCViewer is a graphical tool that allows you to visualize GC logging output. GCViewer can also export data in the proper format for further manipulation in a spreadsheet. GCViewer is available from *http://www.tagtraum.com/*.

Method Calls

Most profiling tools provide a profile of method calls, showing where the bottlenecks in your code are and helping you decide where to target your efforts. By showing which methods and lines take the most time, a good profiling tool can quickly pinpoint bottlenecks.

---

[*] Ken Gottry, "Pick up performance with generational garbage collection," *JavaWorld*, January 2002, *http://www.javaworld.com/javaworld/jw-01-2002/jw-0111-hotspotgc.html*.

[†] Nagendra Nagarajayya and J. Steven Mayer, "Improving Java Application Performance and Scalability by Reducing Garbage Collection Times and Sizing Memory," *Sun Wireless Developer*, May 2002, *http://wireless.java.sun.com/midp/articles/garbage/*.

[‡] You can download it directly from *http://wireless.java.sun.com/midp/articles/garbage/gc_analyze.pl*.

Most method profilers work by sampling the call stack at regular intervals and recording the methods on the stack.* This regular snapshot identifies the method currently being executed (the method at the top of the stack) and all the methods below, to the program's entry point. By accumulating the number of hits on each method, the resulting profile usually identifies where the program is spending most of its time. This profiling technique assumes that the sampled methods are representative, i.e., if 10% of stacks sampled show method foo( ) at the top of the stack, then the assumption is that method foo( ) takes 10% of the running time. However, this is a sampling technique, so it is not foolproof: methods can be missed altogether or have their weighting misrecorded if some of their execution calls are missed. But usually only the shortest tests are skewed. Any reasonably long test (i.e., seconds rather than milliseconds) normally gives correct results.

 This sampling technique can be difficult to get right. It is not enough to simply sample the stack. The profiler must also ensure that it has a coherent stack state, so the call must be synchronized across stack activities, possibly by temporarily stopping the thread. The profiler also needs to make sure that multiple threads are treated consistently and that the timing involved in its activities is accounted for without distorting the regular sample time. Also, too short a sample interval causes the program to become extremely slow, while too long an interval results in many method calls being missed and misrepresentative profile results being generated.

The JDK comes with a minimal profiler, obtained by running a program using the java executable with the -Xrunhprof option (-prof before JDK 1.2, -Xprof with HotSpot). This option produces a profile data file called *java.hprof.txt* (*java.prof* before 1.2). The filename can be specified by using the modified option -Xrunhprof: file=<filename> (-prof:<filename> before 1.2).

Profiling Methodology

When using a method profiler, the most useful technique is to target the top five to ten methods and choose the quickest to fix. The reason for this is that once you make one change, the profile tends to be different the next time, sometimes markedly so. This way, you can get the quickest speedup for a given effort.

However, it is also important to consider what you are changing so you know what your results are. If you select a method that is taking 10% of the execution time and then halve the time that method takes, you speed up your application by 5%. On the

---

* A variety of profiling metrics, including the way different metrics can be used, are reported in "A unifying approach to performance analysis in the Java environment" by Alexander, Berry, Levine, and Urquhart, *IBM Systems Journal*, Vol. 39, No. 1, *http://www.research.ibm.com/journal/sj/391/alexander.html*. Specifically, see Table 2-1 in this paper.

other hand, targeting a method that takes up only 1% of execution time gives you a maximum of only 1% speedup to the application, no matter how much effort you put in.

Similarly, if you have a method that takes 10% of the time but is called a huge number of times, with each individual method call being quite short, you are less likely to speed up the method. On the other hand, if you can eliminate some significant fraction of the calling methods (the methods that call the method that takes 10% of the time), you might gain speed that way.

Let's look at the profile output from a short program that repeatedly converts some numbers to strings and inserts them into a hash table:

```java
package tuning.profile;
import java.util.*;

public class ProfileTest
{
  public static void main(String[] args)
  {
    //Repeat the loop this many times
    int repeat = 2000;

    //Two arrays of numbers, eight doubles and ten longs
    double[] ds = {Double.MAX_VALUE, -3.14e-200D,
      Double.NEGATIVE_INFINITY, 567.89023D, 123e199D,
      -0.000456D, -1.234D, 1e55D};
    long[] ls = {2283911683699007717L, -8007630872066909262L,
      4536503365853551745L, 548519563869L, 45L,
      Long.MAX_VALUE, 1L, -9999L, 7661314123L, 0L};

    //Initializations
    long time;
    StringBuffer s = new StringBuffer();
    Hashtable h = new Hashtable();
    System.out.println("Starting test");
    time = System.currentTimeMillis();

    //Repeatedly add all the numbers to a stringbuffer
    //and also put them into a hash table
    for (int i = repeat; i > 0; i--)
    {
        s.setLength(0);
        for (int j = ds.length-1; j >= 0; j--)
        {
            s.append(ds[j]);
            h.put(new Double(ds[j]), Boolean.TRUE);
        }
        for (int j = ls.length-1; j >= 0; j--)
        {
            s.append(ls[j]);
            h.put(new Long(ls[j]), Boolean.FALSE);
```

```
            }
        }
        time = System.currentTimeMillis() - time;
        System.out.println("  The test took " + time + " milliseconds");
    }
}
```

The relevant output from running this program with the JDK 1.2 method profiling option follows. (See "Java 2 cpu=samples Profile Output" later in this chapter for a detailed explanation of the 1.2 profiling option and its output.)

```
CPU SAMPLES BEGIN (total = 15813) Wed Jan 12 11:26:47 2000
rank   self  accum   count trace method
   1 54.79% 54.79%    8664   204 java/lang/FloatingDecimal.dtoa
   2 11.67% 66.46%    1846   215 java/lang/Double.equals
   3 10.18% 76.64%    1609   214 java/lang/FloatingDecimal.dtoa
   4  3.10% 79.74%     490   151 java/lang/FloatingDecimal.dtoa
   5  2.90% 82.63%     458   150 java/lang/FloatingDecimal.<init>
   6  2.11% 84.74%     333   213 java/lang/FloatingDecimal.<init>
   7  1.23% 85.97%     194   216 java/lang/Double.doubleToLongBits
   8  0.97% 86.94%     154   134 sun/io/CharToByteConverter.convertAny
   9  0.94% 87.88%     148   218 java/lang/FloatingDecimal.<init>
  10  0.82% 88.69%     129   198 java/lang/Double.toString
  11  0.78% 89.47%     123   200 java/lang/Double.hashCode
  12  0.70% 90.17%     110   221 java/lang/FloatingDecimal.dtoa
  13  0.66% 90.83%     105   155 java/lang/FloatingDecimal.multPow52
  14  0.62% 91.45%      98   220 java/lang/Double.equals
  15  0.52% 91.97%      83   157 java/lang/FloatingDecimal.big5pow
  16  0.46% 92.44%      73   158 java/lang/FloatingDecimal.constructPow52
  17  0.46% 92.89%      72   133 java/io/OutputStreamWriter.write
```

In this example, I extracted only the top few lines from the profile summary table. The methods are ranked according to the percentage of time they take. Note that the trace does not identify actual method signatures, only method names. The top three methods take, respectively, 54.79%, 11.67%, and 10.18% of the time taken to run the full program.[*] The fourth method in the list takes 3.10% of the time, so clearly you need look no further than the top three methods to optimize the program. The methods ranked first, third, and fourth are the same method, possibly called in different ways. Obtaining the traces for these three entries from the relevant section of the profile output (trace 204 for the first entry, and traces 215 and 151 for the second and fourth entries), you get:

```
TRACE 204:
java/lang/FloatingDecimal.dtoa(FloatingDecimal.java:Compiled method)
java/lang/FloatingDecimal.<init>(FloatingDecimal.java:Compiled method)
```

---

[*] The samples that count toward a particular method's execution time are those where the method itself is executing at the time of the sample. If method foo( ) were calling another method when the sample was taken, that other method would be at the top of the stack instead of foo( ). So you do not need to worry about the distinction between foo( )'s execution time and the time spent executing foo( )'s callees. Only the method at the top of the stack is tallied.

```
java/lang/Double.toString(Double.java:Compiled method)
java/lang/String.valueOf(String.java:Compiled method)
TRACE 214:
java/lang/FloatingDecimal.dtoa(FloatingDecimal.java:Compiled method)
TRACE 151:
java/lang/FloatingDecimal.dtoa(FloatingDecimal.java:Compiled method)
java/lang/FloatingDecimal.<init>(FloatingDecimal.java:Compiled method)
java/lang/Double.toString(Double.java:132)
java/lang/String.valueOf(String.java:2065)
```

In fact, both traces 204 and 151 are the same stack, but trace 151 provides line numbers for two of the methods. Trace 214 is a truncated entry, and is probably the same stack as the other two (these differences highlight the fact that the JDK profiler sometimes loses information).

All three entries refer to the same stack: an inferred call from the StringBuffer to append a double, which calls String.valueOf( ), which calls Double.toString( ), which in turn creates a FloatingDecimal object. (<init> is the standard way to write a constructor call; <clinit> is the standard way to show a class initializer being executed. These are also the actual names for constructors and static initializers in the class file.) FloatingDecimal is private to the java.lang package, which handles most of the logic involved in converting floating-point numbers. FloatingDecimal.dtoa( ) is the method called by the FloatingDecimal constructor that converts the binary floating-point representation of a number into its various parts of digits before the decimal point, after the decimal point, and the exponent. FloatingDecimal stores the digits of the floating-point number as an array of chars when the FloatingDecimal is created; no strings are created until the floating-point number is converted to a string.

Since this stack includes a call to a constructor, it is worth checking the object-creation profile to see whether you are generating an excessive number of objects; object creation is expensive, and a method that generates many new objects is often a performance bottleneck. (I show the object-creation profile and how to generate it later in this chapter under "Object-Creation Profiling.") The object-creation profile shows that a large number of extra objects are being created, including a large number of FDBigInt objects that are created by the new FloatingDecimal objects.

Clearly, FloatingDecimal.dtoa( ) is the primary method to optimize in this case. Almost any improvement in this one method translates directly to a similar improvement in the overall program. However, normally only Sun can modify this method, and even if you want to modify it, it is long and complicated and takes an excessive amount of time to optimize unless you are already familiar with both floating-point binary representation and converting that representation to a string format.

Normally when tuning, the first alternative to optimizing FloatingDecimal.dtoa( ) is to examine the other significant bottleneck method, Double.equals( ), which was second in the summary. Even though this entry takes up only 11.67% compared to over 68% for the FloatingDecimal.dtoa( ) method, it may be an easier optimization target. But note that while a small 10% improvement in the FloatingDecimal.dtoa( )

method translates into a 6% improvement for the program as a whole, the Double.
equals( ) method needs to be speeded up to be more than twice as fast to get a similar 6% improvement for the full program.

The trace corresponding to this second entry in the summary example turns out to be another truncated trace, but the example shows the same method in 14th position, and the trace for that entry identifies the Double.equals( ) call as coming from the Hashtable.put( ) call. Unfortunately for tuning purposes, the Double.equals( ) method itself is already quite fast and cannot be optimized further.

When methods cannot be directly optimized, the next best choice is to reduce the number of times they are called or even avoiding the methods altogether. (In fact, eliminating method calls is actually the better tuning choice, but it is often considerably more difficult to achieve and so is not a first-choice tactic for optimization.) The object-creation profile and the method profile together point to the FloatingDecimal class as being a huge bottleneck, so avoiding this class is the obvious tuning tactic here. In Chapter 5, I employ this technique, avoiding the default call through the FloatingDecimal class for the case of converting floating-point numbers to Strings, and I obtain an order-of-magnitude improvement. Basically, the strategy is to create a more efficient routine to run the equivalent conversion functionality and then replace the calls to the underperforming FloatingDecimal methods with calls to more efficient optimized methods.

 The 1.1 profiling output is quite different and much less like a standard profiler's output. Running the 1.1 profiler with this program (details of this output are described in "JDK 1.1.x -prof and Java 2 cpu=old Profile Output") gives:

```
count callee caller time
21 java/lang/System.gc( )V
    java/lang/FloatingDecimal.dtoa(IJI)V 760
 8 java/lang/System.gc( )V
    java/lang/Double.equals(Ljava/lang/Object;)Z 295
 2 java/lang/Double.doubleToLongBits(D)J
    java/lang/Double.equals(Ljava/lang/Object;)Z 0
```

I have shown only the top four lines from the output. This output actually identifies both the FloatingDecimal.dtoa( ) and the Double.equals( ) methods as taking the vast majority of the time, and the percentages (given by the reported times) are listed as around 70% and 25% of the total program time for the two methods, respectively. Since the "callee" for these methods is listed as System.gc( ), this also indicates that the methods are significantly involved in memory creation, and suggests that the next tuning step might be to analyze the object-creation output for this program.

The best way to avoid the `Double.equals()` method is to replace the hash table with another implementation that stores `double` primitive data types directly rather than requiring the doubles to be wrapped in a `Double` object. This allows the `==` operator to make the comparison in the `put()` method, thus completely avoiding the `Double.equals()` call. This is another standard tuning tactic, replacing a data structure with one more appropriate and faster for the task.

Java 2 cpu=samples Profile Output

The default profile output gained from executing with `-Xrunhprof` in Java 2 is not useful for method profiling. The default output generates object-creation statistics from the heap as the dump (output) occurs. By default, the dump occurs when the application terminates; you can modify the dump time by typing Ctrl-\ on Solaris and other Unix systems, or Ctrl-Break on Windows. To get a useful *method* profile, you need to modify the profiler options to specify method profiling. A typical call to achieve this is:

```
% java -Xrunhprof:cpu=samples,thread=y <classname>
```

(Note that in a Windows command-line prompt, you need to surround the options with double quotes because the equals sign is considered a meta character.) The full list of options available with `-Xrunhprof` can be viewed using the `-Xrunhprof:help` option.

 Note that `-Xrunhprof` has an "h" in it. There seems to be an undocumented feature of the VM in which the option `-Xrun<something>` makes the VM try to load a shared library called `<something>`, for example, using `-Xrunprof` results in the VM trying to load a shared library called *prof*. This can be quite confusing if you are not expecting it. In fact, `-Xrunhprof` loads the *hprof* shared library.

The profiling option in JDKs 1.2/1.3/1.4 can be pretty flaky. Several of the options can cause the runtime to crash (core dump). The output is a large file because huge amounts of trace data are written rather than summarized. Since the profile option is essentially a Sun engineering tool, it is pretty rough, especially since Sun has a separate (not free) profile tool for its engineers. Another tool that Sun provides to analyze the output of the profiler is the Heap Analysis Tool (search *http://www.java.sun.com* for "HAT"). But this tool analyzes only the object-creation statistics output gained with the default profile output, so it is not that useful for method profiling (see "Object-Creation Profiling" for slightly more about this tool).

Nevertheless, I expect the free profiling option to stabilize and be more useful in future versions. The output when run with the options already listed (`cpu=samples`, `thread=y`) already results in fairly usable information. This profiling mode operates by periodically sampling the stack. Each unique stack trace provides a TRACE entry in the second section of the file, describing the method calls on the stack for that trace. Multiple identical samples are not listed; instead, the number of their "hits" is summarized in the third section of the file. The profile output file in this mode has three sections:

Section 1

A standard header section describing possible monitored entries in the file. For example:

```
WARNING!  This file format is under development, and is subject to
change without notice.

This file contains the following types of records:

THREAD START
THREAD END      mark the lifetime of Java threads

TRACE           represents a Java stack trace.  Each trace consists
                of a series of stack frames.  Other records refer to
                TRACEs to identify (1) where object allocations have
                taken place, (2) the frames in which GC roots were
                found, and (3) frequently executed methods.
```

Section 2

Individual entries describing monitored events, i.e., threads starting and terminating, but mainly sampled stack traces. For example:

```
THREAD START (obj=8c2640, id = 6, name="Thread-0", group="main")
THREAD END (id = 6)
TRACE 1:
<empty>
TRACE 964:
java/io/ObjectInputStream.readObject(ObjectInputStream.java:Compiled method)
java/io/ObjectInputStream.inputObject(ObjectInputStream.java:Compiled method)
java/io/ObjectInputStream.readObject(ObjectInputStream.java:Compiled method)
java/io/ObjectInputStream.inputArray(ObjectInputStream.java:Compiled method)
TRACE 1074:
java/io/BufferedInputStream.fill(BufferedInputStream.java:Compiled method)
java/io/BufferedInputStream.read1(BufferedInputStream.java:Compiled method)
java/io/BufferedInputStream.read(BufferedInputStream.java:Compiled method)
java/io/ObjectInputStream.read(ObjectInputStream.java:Compiled method)
```

Section 3

A summary table of methods ranked by the number of times the unique stack trace for that method appears. For example:

```
CPU SAMPLES BEGIN (total = 512371) Thu Aug 26 18:37:08 1999
rank   self  accum   count trace method
   1 16.09% 16.09%   82426  1121 java/io/FileInputStream.read
   2  6.62% 22.71%   33926   881 java/io/ObjectInputStream.allocateNewObject
   3  5.11% 27.82%   26185   918 java/io/ObjectInputStream.inputClassFields
   4  4.42% 32.24%   22671   887 java/io/ObjectInputStream.inputObject
   5  3.20% 35.44%   16392   922 java/lang/reflect/Field.set
```

Section 3 is the place to start when analyzing this profile output. It consists of a table with six fields:

rank

> This column simply counts the entries in the table, starting with 1 at the top and incrementing by 1 for each entry.

self

> The self field is usually interpreted as a percentage of the total running time spent in this method. More accurately, this field reports the percentage of samples that have the stack given by the trace field. Here's a one-line example:

```
rank   self  accum   count trace method
   1 11.55% 11.55%   18382    545 java/lang/FloatingDecimal.dtoa
```

> This example shows that stack trace 545 occurred in 18,382 of the sampled stack traces, and this is 11.55% of the total number of stack trace samples made. It indicates that this method was probably executing for about 11.55% of the application execution time because the samples are at regular intervals. You can identify the precise trace from the second section of the profile output by searching for the trace with identifier 545. For the previous example, this trace was:

```
TRACE 545: (thread=1)
java/lang/FloatingDecimal.dtoa(FloatingDecimal.java:Compiled method)
java/lang/FloatingDecimal.<init>(FloatingDecimal.java:Compiled method)
java/lang/Double.toString(Double.java:Compiled method)
java/lang/String.valueOf(String.java:Compiled method)
```

> This TRACE entry clearly identifies the exact method and its caller. Note that the stack is reported to a depth of four methods. This is the default depth; the depth can be changed using the depth parameter to -Xrunhprof, e.g., -Xrunhprof: depth=6,cpu=samples,....

accum

> This field is a running additive total of all the self field percentages as you go down the table. For the Section 3 example shown previously, the third line lists 27.82% for the accum field, indicating that the sum total of the first three lines of the self field is 27.82%.

count

> This field indicates how many times the unique stack trace that gave rise to this entry was sampled while the program ran.

trace

> This field shows the unique trace identifier from the second section of profile output that generated this entry. The trace is recorded only once in the second section no matter how many times it is sampled; the number of times that this trace has been sampled is listed in the count field.

method

This field shows the method name from the top line of the stack trace referred to from the trace field, i.e., the method that was running when the stack was sampled.

This summary table lists only the method name and not its argument types. Therefore, it is frequently necessary to refer to the stack itself to determine the exact method if the method is an overloaded method with several possible argument types. (The stack is given by the trace identifier in the trace field, which in turn references the trace from the second section of the profile output.) If a method is called in different ways, it may also give rise to different stack traces. Sometimes the same method call can be listed in different stack traces due to lost information. Each of these different stack traces results in a different entry in the third section of the profiler's output, even though the method field is the same. For example, it is perfectly possible to see several lines with the same method field, as in the following table segment:

```
rank   self  accum   count trace method
  95   1.1% 51.55%    110    699 java/lang/StringBuffer.append
 110   1.0% 67.35%    100    711 java/lang/StringBuffer.append
 128   1.0% 85.35%     99    332 java/lang/StringBuffer.append
```

When traces 699, 711, and 332 are analyzed, one trace might be StringBuffer.append(boolean), while the other two traces could both be StringBuffer.append(int), but called from two different methods (and so giving rise to two different stack traces and consequently two different lines in the summary example). Note that the trace does not identify actual method signatures, only method names. Line numbers are given if the class was compiled so that line numbers remain. This ambiguity can be a nuisance at times.

The profiler in this mode (cpu=samples) suffices when you have no better alternative. It does have an effect on real measured times, slowing down operations by variable amounts even within one application run. But it normally indicates major bottlenecks, although sometimes a little extra work is necessary to sort out multiple identical method-name references.

Using the alternative cpu=times mode, the profile output gives a different view of application execution. In this mode, the method times are measured from method entry to method exit, including the time spent in all other calls the method makes. This profile of an application provides a tree-like view of where the application is spending its time. Some developers are more comfortable with this mode for profiling the application, but I find that it does not directly identify bottlenecks in the code.

HotSpot and 1.3 -Xprof Profile Output

HotSpot does not support the standard Java 2 profiler detailed in the previous section; it supports a separate profiler using the -Xprof option. JDK 1.3 supports the

HotSpot profiler as well as the standard Java 2 profiler. The HotSpot profiler has no further options available to modify its behavior; it works by sampling the stack every 10 milliseconds.

The output, printed to standard output, consists of a number of sections. Each section lists entries in order of the number of ticks counted while the method was executed. The various sections include methods executing in interpreted and compiled modes, and VM runtime costs as well:

Section 1

A one-line header. For example:

```
Flat profile of 7.55 secs (736 total ticks): main
```

Section 2

A list of methods sampled while running in interpreted mode. The methods are listed in order of the total number of ticks counted while the method was at the top of the stack. For example:

```
Interpreted + native   Method
   3.7%    23 +    4    tuning.profile.ProfileTest.main
   2.4%     4 +   14    java.lang.FloatingDecimal.dtoa
   1.4%     3 +    7    java.lang.FDBigInt.<init>
```

Section 3

A list of methods sampled while running in compiled mode. The methods are listed in order of the total number of ticks counted while the method was at the top of the stack. For example:

```
Compiled + native   Method
  13.5%    99 +    0    java.lang.FDBigInt.quoRemIteration
   9.8%    71 +    1    java.lang.FDBigInt.mult
   9.1%    67 +    0    java.lang.FDBigInt.add
```

Section 4

A list of external (non-Java) method stubs, defined using the native keyword. Listed in order of the total number of ticks counted while the method was at the top of the stack. For example:

```
Stub + native   Method
   2.6%    11 +    8    java.lang.Double.doubleToLongBits
   0.7%     2 +    3    java.lang.StrictMath.floor
   0.5%     3 +    1    java.lang.Double.longBitsToDouble
```

Section 5

A list of internal VM function calls. Listed in order of the total number of ticks counted while the method was at the top of the stack. Not tuneable. For example:

```
Runtime stub + native   Method
   0.1%    1 +    0    interpreter_entries
   0.1%    1 +    0    Total runtime stubs
```

Section 6

Other miscellaneous entries not included in the previous sections:

```
Thread-local ticks:
   1.4%    10              classloader
```

```
          0.1%    1              Interpreter
         11.7%   86              Unknown code
```

Section 7

A global summary of ticks recorded. This includes ticks from the garbage collector, thread-locking overhead, and other miscellaneous entries:

```
Global summary of 7.57 seconds:
100.0%  754              Received ticks
  1.9%   14              Received GC ticks
  0.3%    2              Other VM operations
```

The entries at the top of Section 3 are the methods that probably need tuning. Any method listed near the top of Section 2 should have been targeted by the HotSpot optimizer and may be listed lower down in Section 3. Such methods may still need to be optimized, but it is more likely that the methods at the top of Section 3 need optimizing. The ticks for the two sections are the same, so you can easily compare the time taken up by the top methods in the different sections and decide which to target.

JDK 1.1.x -prof and Java 2 cpu=old Profile Output

The JDK 1.1.x method-profiling output, obtained by running with the -prof option, is quite different from the normal 1.2 output. This output format is supported in Java 2, using the cpu=old variation of the -Xrunhprof option. This output file consists of four sections:

Section 1

The method profile table showing cumulative times spent in each method executed. The table is sorted on the first count field. For example:

```
callee caller time
29 java/lang/System.gc( )V
        java/io/FileInputStream.read([B)I 10263
1 java/io/FileOutputStream.writeBytes([BII)V
        java/io/FileOutputStream.write([BII)V 0
```

Section 2

One line describing high-water gross memory usage. For example:

```
handles_used: 1174, handles_free: 339046, heap-used: 113960, heap-free: 21794720
```

The line reports the number of handles and the number of bytes used by the heap memory storage over the application's lifetime. A handle is an object reference. The number of handles used is the maximum number of objects that existed at any one time in the application (handles are recycled by the garbage collector, so over its lifetime the application could have used many more objects than are listed). Heap measurements are given in bytes.

Section 3

Reports the number of primitive data type arrays left at the end of the process, just before process termination. For example:

```
sig  count     bytes  indx
[C     174     19060     5
[B       5     19200     8
```

This section has four fields. The first field is the primitive data type (array dimensions and data type given by letter codes listed shortly), the second field is the number of arrays, and the third is the total number of bytes used by all the arrays. This example shows 174 char arrays with a combined space of 19,060 bytes, and 5 byte arrays with a combined space of 19,200 bytes.

The reported data does not include any arrays that may have been garbage-collected before the end of the process. For this reason, the section is of limited use. You could use the -noasyncgc option to try to eliminate garbage collection (if you have enough memory; you may also need -mx with a large number to boost the maximum memory available). If you do, also use -verbosegc so that if garbage collection is forced, you at least know that it has occurred and can get the basic number of objects and bytes reclaimed.

Section 4

The fourth section of the profile output is the per-object memory dump. Again, this includes only objects left at the end of the process just before termination, not objects that may have been garbage-collected before the end of the process. For example:

```
*** tab[267] p=4bba378 cb=1873248 cnt=219 ac=3 al=1103
    Ljava/util/HashtableEntry; 219 3504
    [Ljava/util/HashtableEntry; 3 4412
```

This dump is a snapshot of the actual object table. The fields in the first line of an entry are:

***tab[<index>]

> The entry location as listed in the object table. The index is of no use for performance tuning.

p=<hex value>

> Internal memory locations for the instance and class; of no use for performance tuning.

cb=<hex value>

> Internal memory locations for the instance and class; of no use for performance tuning.

cnt=<integer>

> The number of instances of the class reported on the next line.

ac=<integer>

> The number of instances of arrays of the class reported on the next line.

al=<integer>

> The total number of array elements for all the arrays counted in the previous (ac) field.

This first line of the example is followed by lines consisting of three fields: first, the class name prefixed by the array dimension if the line refers to the array data; next, the number of instances of that class (or array class); and last, the total amount of space used by all the instances, in bytes. So the example reports that there are 219 HashtableEntry instances that comprise (collectively) a total of 3504 bytes,* and three HashtableEntry arrays having 1103 array indexes (which amounts to 4412 bytes total, as each entry is a 4-byte object handle).

Sections 3 and 4 give snapshots of the object table memory and can be used in an interesting way: to run a garbage collection just before termination of your application. That leaves in the object table all the objects that are rooted† by the system and by your application (from static variables). If this snapshot shows significantly more objects than you expect, you may be referencing more objects than you realized.

The first section of the profile output is the most useful. It consists of multiple lines, each specifying a method and its caller, together with the total cumulative time spent in that method and the total number of times it was called from that caller. The first line of this section specifies the four fields in the profile table in this section: count, callee, caller, and time. They are detailed here:

count

The total number of times the callee method was called from the caller method, accumulating multiple executions of the caller method. For example, if foo1( ) calls foo2( ) 10 times every time foo1( ) is executed, and foo1( ) was itself called three times during the execution of the program, the count field should hold the value 30 for the callee-caller pair foo2( )-foo1( ). The line in the table should look like this:

```
30 x/y/Z.foo2( )V x/y/Z.foo1( )V 1263
```

(assuming the foo*( ) methods are in class x.y.Z and they both have a void return). The actual reported numbers may be less than the true number of calls: the profiler can miss calls.

callee

The method that was called count times in total from the caller method. The callee can be listed in other entries as the callee method for different caller methods.

---

* A HashtableEntry has one int and three object handle instance variables, each of which takes 4 bytes, so each HashtableEntry is 16 bytes.

† Objects rooted by the system are objects that the JVM runtime keeps alive as part of its runtime system. Rooted objects generally cannot be garbage-collected because they are referenced in some way from other objects that cannot be garbage-collected. The roots of these non-garbage-collectable objects are normally objects referenced from the stack, objects referenced from static variables of classes, and special objects the runtime system ensures are kept alive.

caller

> The method that called the `callee` method `count` times in total.

time

> The cumulative time (in milliseconds) spent in the `callee` method, including time when the `callee` method was calling other methods (i.e., when the `callee` method was in the stack but not at the top, and so was not the currently executing method).
>
> If each of the `count` calls in one line took exactly the same amount of time, then one call from caller to callee took `time` divided by `count` milliseconds.

This first section is normally sorted into count order. However, for this profiler, the time spent in methods tends to be more useful. Because the times in the `time` field include the total time that the `callee` method was anywhere on the stack, interpreting the output of complex programs can be difficult without processing the table to subtract subcall times. This format is different from the 1.2 output with `cpu=samples` specified, and is similar to a 1.2 profile with `cpu=times` specified.

The lines in the profile output are unique for each callee-caller pair, but any one `callee` method and any one `caller` method can (and normally do) appear in multiple lines. This is because any particular method can call many other methods, and so the method registers as the caller for multiple callee-caller pairs. Any particular method can also be called by many other methods, and so the method registers as the callee for multiple callee-caller pairs.

The methods are written out using the internal Java syntax listed in Table 2-1.

Table 2-1. Internal Java syntax for -prof output format

Internal symbol	Java meaning
/	Replaces the . character in package names (e.g., java/lang/String stands for java.lang.String)
B	byte
C	char
D	double
I	int
F	float
J	long
S	short
V	void
Z	boolean
[	One array dimension (e.g., `[[B` stands for a two-dimensional array of bytes, such as new `byte[3][4]`)
L<classname>;	A class (e.g., Ljava/lang/String; stands for java.lang.String)

There are free viewers, including source code, for viewing this file:

- Vladimir Bulatov's HyperProf (search for HyperProf on the Web)
- Greg White's ProfileViewer (search for ProfileViewer on the Web)

The biggest drawback to the 1.1 profile output is that threads are not shown at all. This means that it is possible to get time values for method calls that are longer than the total time spent in running the application, since all the call times from multiple threads are added together. It also means that you cannot determine from which thread a particular method call was made. Nevertheless, after re-sorting the section on the time field rather than the count field, the profile data is useful enough to suffice as a method profiler when you have no better alternative.

One problem I've encountered is the limited size of the list of methods that can be held by the internal profiler. Technically, this limitation is 10,001 entries in the profile table, and there is presumably one entry per method. There are four methods that help you avoid the limitation by profiling only a small section of your code:

```
sun.misc.VM.suspendJavaMonitor( )
sun.misc.VM.resumeJavaMonitor( )
sun.misc.VM.resetJavaMonitor( )
sun.misc.VM.writeJavaMonitorReport( )
```

These methods also allow you some control over which parts of your application are profiled and when to dump the results.

Java 2 -Xhprof Option

The -Xhprof option seems to be simply an alternative name for the -Xrunhprof option. I believe that originally it was called -Xhprof, and then the option was left in although all subsequent documentation used -Xrunhprof.

Java 2 -Xaprof option

-Xaprof appears to be a simple allocation profiler. It prints the number and total size of instances allocated per class, including array classes, accumulating instances across all threads and creation points. In fact, it seems to be very similar to the tool I describe in the next section. Like other VM profiling tools, it is unfortunately not 100% stable (for example, it core dumps with my 1.4 Windows VM). Nevertheless, it is useful when it works, and it was introduced with 1.3.

Using this profiler to monitor the tuning.profile.ProfileTest class used in the example from the "Profiling Methodology" section results in the following output:

```
Allocation profile (sizes in bytes, cutoff = 0 bytes):

_____Size__Instances__Average__Class_____
 13491592     186025       73  [I
  5634592      86602       65  [C
```

```
2496352      156022      16   java.lang.FDBigInt
 875112       36463      24   java.lang.String
 768000       16000      48   java.lang.FloatingDecimal
 320000       20000      16   java.lang.Long
 256000       16000      16   java.lang.Double
  29832          14    2131   [B
  14256         594      24   java.util.Hashtable$Entry
   8960           6    1493   [S
   8112          25     324   [Ljava.util.Hashtable$Entry;
   2448         102      24   java.lang.StringBuffer
   2312           3     771   [Ljava.lang.FDBigInt;
   1600          24      67   [Ljava.lang.Object;
    584           9      65   [Ljava.util.HashMap$Entry;
    528          22      24   java.util.Locale
    440          11      40   java.util.Hashtable
    432           9      48   java.util.HashMap
    392           4      98   [D
    376           3     125   [J
    320           7      46   [Ljava.lang.String;
    256           4      64   java.lang.Thread
...
23916904      518123     46   --total--
```

The listing has been truncated, but a full listing is output down to objects and arrays with only one instance created. The primitive arrays are listed using the one-character labels from Table 2-1. The listing is fairly clear. All instances created at any time by the VM are included, whether they have been garbage-collected or not. The first column is the total size in bytes taken up by all the instances summed together; the second column provides the number of those instances created; and the third divides the first column by the second column to give an average size per object in bytes.

The only disadvantage seems to be that you cannot take a snapshot. There seems to be no way of registering only those objects created between time 1 (e.g., after initialization) and time 2. Otherwise, this is another useful tool to add to your armory.

Object-Creation Profiling

Unfortunately, the SDK provides only very rudimentary object-creation statistics. Most profile tool vendors provide much better object-creation statistics, determining object numbers and identifying where particular objects are created in the code. My recommendation is to use a better (probably commercial) tool in place of the SDK profiler.

The Heap Analysis Tool, which can analyze the default profiling mode with Java 2, provides a little more information from the profiler output, but if you are relying on this, profiling object creation will require a lot of effort. To use this tool, you must use the binary output option:

```
% java -Xrunhprof:format=b <classname>
```

I have used an alternate trick when a reasonable profiler is unavailable, cannot be used, or does not provide precisely the detail I need. This technique is to alter the java.lang.Object class to catch most nonarray object-creation calls. This is not a supported feature, but it does seem to work on most systems because all constructors chain up to the Object class's constructor, and any explicitly created non-array object calls the constructor in Object as its first execution point after the VM allocates the object on the heap. Objects that are created implicitly with a call to clone( ) or by deserialization do not call the Object class's constructor, and so are missed when using this technique.

Under the terms of the license granted by Sun, it is not possible to include or list an altered Object class with this book. But I can show you the simple changes to make to the java.lang.Object class to track object creation.

The change requires adding a line in the Object constructor to pass this to some object-creation monitor you are using. java.lang.Object does not have an explicitly defined constructor (it uses the default empty constructor), so you need to add one to the source and recompile. For any class other than Object, that is all you need to do. But there is an added problem in that Object does not have a superclass, and the compiler has a problem with this: the compiler cannot handle an explicit super( ) from the Object class, nor the use of this, without an explicit super( ) or this( ) call. In order to get around this restriction, you need to add a second constructor to java.lang.Object: a constructor that does nothing functional but does seem to satisfy the compiler.

 This trick works for the compiler that comes with the JDK; other compilers may be easier or more difficult to satisfy. It is specifically the compiler that has the problem. Generating the bytecodes without the extra constructor is perfectly legal.

Recursive calls to the Object constructor present an additional difficulty. You must ensure that when your monitor is called from the constructor, the Object constructor does not recursively call itself as it creates objects for your object-creation monitor. It is equally important to avoid recursive calls to the Object constructor at runtime initialization. The simplest way to handle all this is to have a flag on which objects are conditionally passed to the monitor from the Object constructor and to have this flag in a simple class with no superclasses so that classloading does not impose extra calls to superclasses.

Essentially, to change java.lang.Object so that it records object creation for each object, you need to add something like the following two constructors to java.lang.Object:

```
public Object( )
{
  this(true);
```

```
    if (tuning.profile.ObjectCreationMonitoringFlag.monitoring)
        tuning.profile.ObjectCreationMonitoring.monitor(this);
}
public Object(boolean b)
{
}
```

This code may seem bizarre, but then this technique uses an unsupported hack. You now need to compile your modified java.lang.Object and any object-monitoring classes (I find that compiling the object-monitoring classes separately before compiling the Object class makes things much easier). You then need to run tests with the new Object class first in your (boot) classpath. The modified Object class[*] must precede the real java.lang.Object in your classpath; otherwise, the real one will be found first and used.

Once you have set the tuning.profile.ObjectCreationMonitoringFlag.monitoring variable to true, each newly created object is passed to the monitor during the creation call. (Actually, the object is passed immediately after it has been created by the runtime system but before any constructors have been executed, except for the Object constructor.) You should not set the monitoring variable to true before the core Java classes have loaded; a good place to set it to true is at the start of the application.

Unfortunately, this technique does not catch any of the arrays that are created: array objects do not chain through the Object constructor (although Object is their superclass) and so do not get monitored. But you typically populate arrays with objects (except for data type arrays such as char arrays), and the objects populating the arrays are caught. In addition, objects that are created implicitly with a call to clone( ) or by deserialization do not call the Object class's constructor, and so these objects are also missed when using this technique. Deserialized objects can be included using a similar technique by redefining the ObjectInputStream class.

When I use this technique, I normally first get a listing of the different object types and how many of each are created. Then I start to focus on a few objects. If you prefer, you can make the technique more focused by altering other constructors to target a specific hierarchy below Object. Or you could focus on particular classes within a more general monitoring class by filtering interesting hierarchies using instanceof. In addition, you can get the stack of the creation call for any object by creating an exception or filling in the stack trace of an existing exception (but not throwing the exception). As an example, I define a monitoring class that provides many of the possibilities you might want to use for analysis. Note that to avoid recursion during the load, I normally keep my actual ObjectCreationMonitoringFlag class very simple,

---

[*] Different versions of the JDK require their Object classes to be recompiled separately; i.e., you cannot recompile the Object class for JDK 1.1.6 and then run that class with the 1.2 runtime.

containing only the flag variable, and put everything else in another class with the `monitor( )` method. The following code defines the flag class:

```
package tuning.profile;
public class ObjectCreationMonitoringFlag
{
  public static boolean monitoring = false;
}
```

The next listed class, `ObjectCreationMonitoring`, provides some of the features you might need in a monitoring class, including those features previously mentioned. It includes a `main( )` method that starts up the real application you wish to monitor and three alternative options. These report every object creation as it occurs (-v), a tally of object creations (-t), or a tally of object-creation stacks (-s; this option can take a long time).

If you run JDK 1.2 and have the recompiled `Object` class in a JAR file with the name *hack.jar* in the current directory, and also copy the *rt.jar* and *i18n.jar* files from under the *JDK1.2/jre/lib* (*JDK1.2\jre\lib*) directory to the current directory, then as an example you can execute the object-creation monitoring class on Windows like this (note that this is one long command line):

```
% java -Xbootclasspath:hack.jar;rt.jar;i18n.jar
  tuning.profile.ObjectCreationMonitoring -t <real class and arguments>
```

You might also need to add a -cp option to specify the location of the various non-core class files that are being run or add to the -classpath list for JDK 1.1. The files listed in the -Xbootclasspath option can be listed with relative or absolute paths; they do not have to be in the current directory.

From JDK 1.3, there is a nicer prepend option to bootclasspath:

```
% java -Xbootclasspath/p:hack.jar tuning.profile.ObjectCreationMonitoring -t <real
  class and arguments>
```

For Unix it looks like this (the main difference is the use of ";" for Windows and ":" for Unix):

```
% java -Xbootclasspath:hack.jar:rt.jar:i18n.jar tuning.profile.
  ObjectCreationMonitoring -t <real class and arguments>
```

For JDK 1.1, the classpath needs to be set instead of the bootclasspath, and the *classes.zip* file from *JDK1.1.x/lib* needs to be used instead, so the command on Windows looks like:

```
% java -classpath hack.jar;classes.zip tuning.profile.ObjectCreationMonitoring -t
  <real class and arguments>
```

For Unix it looks like this (again, the main difference is the use of ";" for Windows and ":" for Unix):

```
% java -classpath hack.jar:classes.zip tuning.profile.ObjectCreationMonitoring -t
  <real class and arguments>
```

Note that classloaders seem to be changed in almost every version of the SDK. Some readers have had problems using the tool described here with Version 1.3. The problems always turned out to be class-path- and classloader-related. If you have problems, try unpacking everything and putting it all in the bootclasspath, including the application classes, for the purposes of running this monitoring tool. That way, there are no issues of classpath or classloading.

Using one of these commands to monitor the tuning.profile.ProfileTest class results in the following output:

```
Starting test
  The test took 3425 milliseconds
java.lang.FloatingDecimal      16000
java.lang.Double               16000
java.lang.StringBuffer         2
java.lang.Long                 20000
java.lang.FDBigInt             156022
java.util.Hashtable            1
java.util.Hashtable$Entry      18
java.lang.String               36002
```

To recap, that program repeatedly (2000 times) appends 8 doubles and 10 longs to a StringBuffer and inserts those numbers wrapped as objects into a hash table. The hash table requires 16,000 Doubles and 20,000 Longs, but beyond that, all other objects created are overheads due to the conversion algorithms used. Even the String objects are overheads: there is no requirement for the numbers to be converted to Strings before they are appended to the StringBuffer. In Chapter 5, I show how to convert numbers and avoid creating all these intermediate objects. The resulting code produces faster conversions in almost every case.

Implementing the optimizations mentioned at the end of the "Profiling Methodology" section allows the program to avoid the FloatingDecimal class (and consequently the FDBigInt class too) and also to avoid the object wrappers for the doubles and longs. This results in a program that avoids all the temporary FloatingDecimal, Double, Long, FDBigInt, and String objects generated by the original version: over a quarter of a million objects are eliminated from the object-creation profile, leaving just a few dozen objects! So the order-of-magnitude improvement in speed attained is now more understandable.

The ObjectCreationMonitoring class is listed here:

```
package tuning.profile;
import java.util.*;
import java.io.*;
import java.lang.reflect.*;

public class ObjectCreationMonitoring
{
  private static int MonitoringMode = 0;
```

```java
    private static int StackModeCount = -1;
    public static final int VERBOSE_MODE = 1;
    public static final int TALLY_MODE = 2;
    public static final int GET_STACK_MODE = 3;

    public static void main(String args[])
    {
      try
      {
        //First argument is the option specifying which type of
        //monitoring: verbose; tally; or stack
        if(args[0].startsWith("-v"))
          //verbose - prints every object's class as it's created
          MonitoringMode = VERBOSE_MODE;
        else if(args[0].startsWith("-t"))
          //tally mode. Tally classes and print results at end
          MonitoringMode = TALLY_MODE;
        else if(args[0].startsWith("-s"))
        {
          //stack mode. Print stacks of objects as they are created
          MonitoringMode = GET_STACK_MODE;
          //support a limited number of stacks being generated
          //so that the running time can be shortened
          if(args[0].length() > 2)
            StackModeCount = Integer.parseInt(args[0].substring(2));
        }
        else
          throw new IllegalArgumentException(
            "First command line argument must be one of -v/-t/-s");

        //Remaining arguments are the class with the
        //main() method, and its arguments
        String classname = args[1];
        String[] argz = new String[args.length-2];
        System.arraycopy(args, 2, argz, 0, argz.length);
        Class clazz = Class.forName(classname);

        //main has one parameter, a String array.
        Class[] mainParamType = {args.getClass()};
        Method main = clazz.getMethod("main", mainParamType);
        Object[] mainParams = {argz};

        //start monitoring
        ObjectCreationMonitoringFlag.monitoring = true;
        main.invoke(null, mainParams);
        //stop monitoring
        ObjectCreationMonitoringFlag.monitoring = false;
        if (MonitoringMode == TALLY_MODE)
          printTally();
        else if (MonitoringMode == GET_STACK_MODE)
          printStacks();
      }
      catch(Exception e)
```

```
    {
      e.printStackTrace( );
    }
  }

  public static void monitor(Object o)
  {
    //Disable object creation monitoring while we report
    ObjectCreationMonitoringFlag.monitoring = false;

    switch(MonitoringMode)
    {
      case 1: justPrint(o); break;
      case 2: tally(o); break;
      case 3: getStack(o); break;
      default:
        System.out.println(
          "Undefined mode for ObjectCreationMonitoring class");
        break;
    }

    //Re-enable object creation monitoring
    ObjectCreationMonitoringFlag.monitoring = true;
  }

  public static void justPrint(Object o)
  {
    System.out.println(o.getClass( ).getName( ));
  }

  private static Hashtable Hash = new Hashtable( );
  public static void tally(Object o)
  {
    //You need to print the tally from printTally( )
    //at the end of the application
    Integer i = (Integer) Hash.get(o.getClass( ));
    if (i == null)
      i = new Integer(1);
    else
      i = new Integer(i.intValue( ) + 1);
    Hash.put(o.getClass( ), i);
  }
  public static void printTally( )
  {
    //should really sort the elements in order of the
    //number of objects created, but I will just print them
    //out in any order here.
    Enumeration e = Hash.keys( );
    Class c;
    String s;
    while(e.hasMoreElements( ))
    {
      c = (Class) e.nextElement( );
      System.out.print(s = c.getName( ));
```

```java
        for (int i = 31-s.length( ); i >= 0; i--)
          System.out.print(' ');
        System.out.print("\t");
        System.out.println(Hash.get(c));
      }
    }

    private static Exception Ex = new Exception( );
    private static ByteArrayOutputStream MyByteStream =
        new ByteArrayOutputStream( );
    private static PrintStream MyPrintStream =
        new PrintStream(MyByteStream);
    public static void getStack(Object o)
    {
      if (StackModeCount > 0)
StackModeCount--;
      else if (StackModeCount != -1)
          return;
      Ex.fillInStackTrace( );
      MyPrintStream.flush( );
      MyByteStream.reset( );
      MyPrintStream.print("Creating object of type ");
      MyPrintStream.println(o.getClass( ).getName( ));
      //Note that the first two lines of the stack will be
      //getStack( ) and monitor( ), and these can be ignored.
      Ex.printStackTrace(MyPrintStream);
      MyPrintStream.flush( );
      String trace = new String(MyByteStream.toByteArray( ));
      Integer i = (Integer) Hash.get(trace);
      if (i == null)
        i = new Integer(1);
      else
        i = new Integer(i.intValue( ) + 1);
      Hash.put(trace, i);
    }

    public static void printStacks( )
    {
      Enumeration e = Hash.keys( );
      String s;
      while(e.hasMoreElements( ))
      {
        s = (String) e.nextElement( );
        System.out.print("Following stack contructed ");
        System.out.print(Hash.get(s));
        System.out.println(" times:");
        System.out.println(s);
        System.out.println( );
      }
    }

}
```

Monitoring Gross Memory Usage

The JDK provides two methods for monitoring the amount of memory used by the runtime system: freeMemory( ) and totalMemory( ) in the java.lang.Runtime class.

totalMemory( ) returns a long, which is the number of bytes currently allocated to the runtime system for this particular VM process. Within this memory allocation, the VM manages its objects and data. Some of this allocated memory is held in reserve for creating new objects. When the currently allocated memory gets filled and the garbage collector cannot allocate sufficiently more memory, the VM requests more memory from the underlying system. If the underlying system cannot allocate any further memory, an OutOfMemoryError error is thrown. Total memory can go up and down; some Java runtimes return sections of unused memory to the underlying system while still running.

freeMemory( ) returns a long, which is the number of bytes available to the VM to create objects from the section of memory it controls (i.e., memory already allocated to the runtime by the underlying system). The free memory increases when a garbage collection successfully reclaims space used by dead objects, and also increases when the Java runtime requests more memory from the underlying operating system. The free memory reduces each time an object is created and when the runtime returns memory to the underlying system.

SDK 1.4 added a new method, Runtime.maxMemory( ). This method simply gives the -Xmx value, and is of no use to monitor heap usage.

It can be useful to monitor memory usage while an application runs: you can get a good feel for the hotspots of your application. You may be surprised to see steady decrements in the free memory available to your application when you were not expecting any change. This can occur when you continuously generate temporary objects from some routine; manipulating graphical elements frequently shows this behavior.

Monitoring memory with freeMemory( ) and totalMemory( ) is straightforward, and I include a simple class that does this graphically. It creates three threads: one to periodically sample the memory, one to maintain a display of the memory usage graph, and one to run the program you are monitoring. Figure 2-1 shows the memory monitor after monitoring a run of the ProfileTest class. The total memory allocation is flat because the class did not hold on to much memory at any one time. The free memory shows the typical sawtooth pattern of an application cycling through temporary objects: each upstroke is where the garbage collector kicked in and freed up the space being taken by the discarded dead objects.

The monitor was run using the command:

```
% java tuning.profile.MemoryMonitor tuning.profile.ProfileTest
```

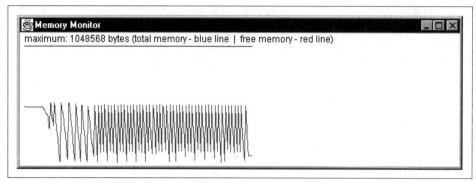

Figure 2-1. Memory monitoring the ProfileTest class

Here are the classes for the memory monitor, together with comments:

```
package tuning.profile;
import java.awt.*;
import java.awt.event.*;
import java.lang.reflect.*;

/*
 * Internal class to periodically sample memory usage
 */
class MemorySampler
  implements Runnable
{
  long[] freeMemory = new long[1000];
  long[] totalMemory = new long[1000];
  int sampleSize = 0;
  long max = 0;
  boolean keepGoing = true;

  MemorySampler()
  {
    //Start the object running in a separate maximum priority thread
    Thread t = new Thread(this);
    t.setDaemon(true);
    t.setPriority(Thread.MAX_PRIORITY);
    t.start();
  }

  public void stop()
  {
    //set to stop the thread when someone tells us
    keepGoing = false;
  }

  public void run()
  {
    //Just a loop that continues sampling memory values every
    //30 milliseconds until the stop() method is called.
    Runtime runtime = Runtime.getRuntime();
```

```
    while(keepGoing)
    {
      try{Thread.sleep(30);}catch(InterruptedException e){ };
      addSample(runtime);
    }
  }

  public void addSample(Runtime runtime)
  {
    //Takes the actual samples, recording them in the two arrays.
    //We expand the arrays when they get full up.
    if (sampleSize >= freeMemory.length)
    {
      //just expand the arrays if they are now too small
      long[ ] tmp = new long[2 * freeMemory.length];
      System.arraycopy(freeMemory, 0, tmp, 0, freeMemory.length);
      freeMemory = tmp;
      tmp = new long[2 * totalMemory.length];
      System.arraycopy(totalMemory, 0, tmp, 0, totalMemory.length);
      totalMemory = tmp;
    }

    freeMemory[sampleSize] = runtime.freeMemory( );
    totalMemory[sampleSize] = runtime.totalMemory( );

    //Keep the maximum value of the total memory for convenience.
    if (max < totalMemory[sampleSize])
      max = totalMemory[sampleSize];
    sampleSize++;
  }
}

public class MemoryMonitor
  extends Frame
  implements WindowListener,Runnable
{
  //The sampler object
  MemorySampler sampler;

  //interval is the delay between calls to repaint the window
  long interval;
  static Color freeColor = Color.red;
  static Color totalColor = Color.blue;
  int[ ] xpoints = new int[2000];
  int[ ] yfrees = new int[2000];
  int[ ] ytotals = new int[2000];

  /*
   * Start a monitor and the graph, then start up the real class
   * with any arguments. This is given by the rest of the commmand
   * line arguments.
   */
  public static void main(String args[ ])
  {
```

```
  try
  {
    //Start the grapher with update interval of half a second
    MemoryMonitor m = new MemoryMonitor(500);

    //Remaining arguments are the class with
    //the main( ) method, and its arguments
    String classname = args[0];
    String[ ] argz = new String[args.length-1];
    System.arraycopy(args, 1, argz, 0, argz.length);
    Class clazz = Class.forName(classname);

    //main has one parameter, a String array.
    Class[ ] mainParamType = {args.getClass( )};
    Method main = clazz.getMethod("main", mainParamType);
    Object[ ] mainParams = {argz};

    //start real class
    main.invoke(null, mainParams);

    //Tell the monitor the application finished
    m.testStopped( );
  }
  catch(Exception e)
  {
    e.printStackTrace( );
  }
}

public MemoryMonitor(long updateInterval)
{
  //Create a graph window and start it in a separate thread
  super("Memory Monitor");
  interval = updateInterval;

  this.addWindowListener(this);
  this.setSize(600,200);
  this.show( );

  //Start the sampler (it runs itself in a separate thread)
  sampler = new MemorySampler( );

  //and put myself into a separate thread
  (new Thread(this)).start( );
}

public void run( )
{
  //Simple loop, just repaints the screen every 'interval' milliseconds
  int sampleSize = sampler.sampleSize;
  for (;;)
  {
    try{Thread.sleep(interval);}catch(InterruptedException e){ };
    if (sampleSize != sampler.sampleSize)
```

```
    {
      //Should just call repaint here
      //this.repaint( );
      //but it doesn't always work, so I'll repaint in this thread.
      //I'm not doing anything else anyway in this thread.
      try{
        this.update(this.getGraphics( ));
      }
      catch(Exception e){e.printStackTrace( );}
      sampleSize = sampler.sampleSize;
    }
  }
}

public void testStopped( )
{
  //just tell the sampler to stop sampling.
  //We won't exit ourselves until the window is explicitly closed
  //so that our user can examine the graph at leisure.
  sampler.stop( );
}

public void paint(Graphics g)
{
  //Straightforward - draw a graph for the latest N points of
  //total and free memory where N is the width of the window.
  try
  {
    java.awt.Dimension d = getSize( );
    int width = d.width-20;
    int height = d.height - 40;
    long max = sampler.max;
    int sampleSize = sampler.sampleSize;
    if (sampleSize < 20)
      return;
    int free, total, free2, total2;
    int highIdx = width < (sampleSize-1) ? width : sampleSize-1;
    int idx = sampleSize - highIdx - 1;
    for (int x = 0 ; x < highIdx ; x++, idx++)
    {
      xpoints[x] = x+10;
      yfrees[x] = height -
        (int) ((sampler.freeMemory[idx] * height) / max) + 40;
      ytotals[x] = height -
        (int) ((sampler.totalMemory[idx] * height) / max) + 40;
    }
    g.setColor(freeColor);
    g.drawPolyline(xpoints, yfrees, highIdx);
    g.setColor(totalColor);
    g.drawPolyline(xpoints, ytotals, highIdx);
    g.setColor(Color.black);
    g.drawString("maximum: " + max +
      " bytes (total memory - blue line  |  free memory - red line)",
      10, 35);
```

```
      }
      catch (Exception e) {
        System.out.println("MemoryMonitor: " + e.getMessage( ));}
    }

    public void windowActivated(WindowEvent e){ }
    public void windowClosed(WindowEvent e){ }
    public void windowClosing(WindowEvent e) {System.exit(0);}
    public void windowDeactivated(WindowEvent e){ }
    public void windowDeiconified(WindowEvent e){ }
    public void windowIconified(WindowEvent e){ }
    public void windowOpened(WindowEvent e) { }
  }
```

Client/Server Communications

To tune client/server or distributed applications, you need to identify all communications that occur during execution. The most important factors to look for are the number of transfers of incoming and outgoing data and the amount of data transferred. These elements affect performance the most. Generally, if the amount of data per transfer is less than about one kilobyte, the number of transfers is the factor that limits performance. If the amount of data being transferred is more than about a third of the network's capacity, the amount of data is the factor limiting performance. Between these two endpoints, either the amount of data or the number of transfers can limit performance, although in general, the number of transfers is more likely to be the problem.

As an example, web surfing with a browser typically hits both problems at different times. A complex page with elements from multiple sites can take longer to display completely than one simple page with 10 times more data. Many different sites are involved in displaying the complex page; each site must have its server name converted to an IP address, which can take many network transfers.* Each site then needs to be connected to and downloaded from. The simple page needs only one name lookup and one connection, and this can make a huge difference. On the other hand, if the amount of data is large compared to the connection bandwidth (the speed of the Internet connection at the slowest link between your client and the server machine), the limiting factor is bandwidth, so the complex page may display more quickly than the simple page.

Several generic tools are available for monitoring communication traffic, all aimed at system and network administrators (and quite expensive). I know of no general-purpose profiling tool targeted at *application*-level communications monitoring;

---

* The DNS name lookup is often hierarchical, requiring multiple DNS servers to chain a lookup request to resolve successive parts of the name. Although there is only one request as far as the browser is concerned, the actual request may require several server-to-server data transfers before the lookup is resolved.

normally, developers put their own monitoring capabilities into the application or use the trace mode in their third-party communications package, if they use one. (*snoop*, *netstat*, and *ndd* on Unix are useful communication-monitoring tools. *tcpdump* and *ethereal* are freeware communication-monitoring tools.)

If you are using a third-party communications package, your first step in profiling is to make sure you understand how to use the full capabilities of its tracing mode. Most communications packages provide a trace mode to log various levels of communication details. Some let you install your own socket layer underlying the communications; this feature, though not usually present for logging purposes, can be quite handy for customizing communications tracing.

For example, RMI (remote method invocation) offers very basic call tracing enabled by setting the `java.rmi.server.logCalls` property to `true`, e.g., by starting the server class with:

```
% java -Djava.rmi.server.logCalls=true <ServerClass> ...
```

The RMI framework also lets you install a custom RMI socket factory. This socket customization support is provided so that the RMI protocol is abstracted away from actual communication details, and it allows sockets to be replaced by alternatives such as nonsocket communications or encrypted or compressed data transfers.

For example, here is the tracing from a small client/server RMI application. The client simply connects to the server and sets three attributes of a server object using RMI. The three attributes are a `boolean`, an `Object`, and an `int`, and the server object defines three remotely callable `set( )` methods for setting the attributes:

```
Sun Jan 16 15:09:12 GMT+00:00 2000:RMI:RMI TCP Connection(3)-localhost/127.0.0.1:
[127.0.0.1: tuning.cs.ServerObjectImpl[0]: void setBoolean(boolean)]
Sun Jan 16 15:09:12 GMT+00:00 2000:RMI:RMI TCP Connection(3)-localhost/127.0.0.1:
[127.0.0.1: tuning.cs.ServerObjectImpl[0]: void setObject(java.lang.Object)]
Sun Jan 16 15:09:12 GMT+00:00 2000:RMI:RMI TCP Connection(3)-localhost/127.0.0.1:
[127.0.0.1: tuning.cs.ServerObjectImpl[0]: void setNumber(int)]
```

If you can install your own socket layer, you may also want to install a customized logging layer to provide details of the communication. An alternative way to trace communications is to replace the sockets (or other underlying communication classes) directly, providing your own logging. In the next section, I provide details for replacing socket-level communication for basic Java sockets.

In addition to Java-level logging, you should be familiar with system- and network-level logging facilities. The most ubiquitous of these is *netstat*, a command-line utility that is normally executed from a Unix shell or Windows command prompt. For example, using *netstat* with the -s option provides a full dump of most network-related structures (cumulative readings since the machine was started). By filtering this, taking differences, and plotting various data, you get a good idea of the network traffic background and the extra load imposed by your application.

Using *netstat* with this application shows that the connection, the resolution of the server object, and the three remote method invocations require four TCP sockets and 39 packets of data (frames) to be transferred. These include a socket pair opened from the client to the registry to determine the server location, then a second socket pair between the client and the server. The frames include several handshake packets required as part of the RMI protocol, and other overhead that RMI imposes. The socket pair between the registry and server are not recorded because the pair lives longer than the interval that measures differences recorded by *netstat*. However, some of the frames are probably communication packets between the registry and the server.

Another useful piece of equipment is a *network sniffer*. This is a hardware device you plug into the network line that views (and can save) all network traffic that is passed along that wire. If you absolutely must know every detail of what is happening on the wire, you may need one of these.

More detailed information on network utilities and tools can be found in system-specific performance tuning books (see Chapter 14 for more about system-specific tools and tuning tips).

Replacing Sockets

Occasionally, you need to be able to see what is happening to your sockets and to know what information is passing through them and the size of the packets being transferred. It is usually best to install your own trace points into the application for all communication external to the application; the extra overhead is generally small compared to network (or any I/O) overhead and can usually be ignored. The application can be deployed with these tracers in place but configured so as not to trace (until required).

However, the sockets are often used by third-party classes, and you cannot directly wrap the reads and writes. You could use a packet sniffer plugged into the network, but this can prove troublesome when used for application-specific purposes (and can be expensive). A more useful possibility I have employed is to wrap the socket I/O with my own classes. You can almost do this generically using the SocketImplFactory, but if you install your own SocketImplFactory, there is no protocol to allow you to access the default socket implementation, so another way must be used. (You could add a SocketImplFactory class into java.net, which then gives you access to the default PlainSocketImpl class, but this is no more generic than the previous possibility, as it too cannot normally be delivered with an application.) My preferred solution, which is also not deliverable, is to wrap the sockets by replacing the java.net.Socket class with my own implementation. This is simpler than the previous alternatives and can be quite powerful. Only two methods from the core classes need changing, namely those that provide access to the input stream and output stream. You need to create your own input stream and output stream wrapper classes to provide logging. The two methods in Socket are getInputStream( ) and getOutputStream( ), and the new versions of these look as follows:

```
public InputStream getInputStream( ) throws IOException {
  return new tuning.socket.SockInStreamLogger(this, impl.getInputStream( ));
}
public OutputStream getOutputStream( ) throws IOException {
  return new tuning.socket.SockOutStreamLogger(this, impl.getOutputStream( ));
}
```

The required stream classes are listed shortly. Rather than using generic classes, I tend to customize the logging on a per-application basis. I even tend to vary the logging implementation for different tests, slowly cutting out more superfluous communications data and headers so that I can focus on a small amount of detail. Usually I focus on the number of transfers, the amount of data transferred, and the application-specific type of data being transferred. For a distributed RMI type communication, I want to know the method calls and argument types and occasionally some of the arguments: the data is serialized and so can be accessed using the Serializable framework.

As with the customized Object class in the "Object-Creation Profiling" section, you need to ensure that your customized Socket class comes first in your (boot) classpath, before the JDK Socket version. The RMI example from the previous section results in the following trace when run with customized socket tracing. The trace is from the client only. I have replaced lines of data with my own interpretation (in bold) of the data sent or read:

```
Message of size 7 written by Socket
Socket[addr=jack/127.0.0.1,port=1099,localport=1092]
client-registry handshake
Message of size 16 read by Socket
Socket[addr=jack/127.0.0.1,port=1099,localport=1092]
client-registry handshake
Message of size 15 written by Socket
Socket[addr=jack/127.0.0.1,port=1099,localport=1092]
client-registry handshake: client identification
Message of size 53 written by Socket
Socket[addr=jack/127.0.0.1,port=1099,localport=1092]
client-registry query: asking for the location of the Server Object
Message of size 210 read by Socket
Socket[addr=jack/127.0.0.1,port=1099,localport=1092]
client-registry query: reply giving details of the Server Object
Message of size 7 written by Socket
Socket[addr=localhost/127.0.0.1,port=1087,localport=1093]
client-server handshake
Message of size 16 read by Socket
Socket[addr=localhost/127.0.0.1,port=1087,localport=1093]
client-server handshake
Message of size 15 written by Socket
Socket[addr=localhost/127.0.0.1,port=1087,localport=1093]
client-server handshake: client identification
```

```
Message of size 342 written by Socket
Socket[addr=localhost/127.0.0.1,port=1087,localport=1093]
```
client-server handshake: security handshake
```
Message of size 283 read by Socket
Socket[addr=localhost/127.0.0.1,port=1087,localport=1093]
```
client-server handshake: security handshake
```
Message of size 1 written by Socket
Socket[addr=jack/127.0.0.1,port=1099,localport=1092]
Message of size 1 read by Socket
Socket[addr=jack/127.0.0.1,port=1099,localport=1092]
Message of size 15 written by Socket
Socket[addr=jack/127.0.0.1,port=1099,localport=1092]
```
client-registry handoff
```
Message of size 1 written by Socket
Socket[addr=localhost/127.0.0.1,port=1087,localport=1093]
Message of size 1 read by Socket
Socket[addr=localhost/127.0.0.1,port=1087,localport=1093]
Message of size 42 written by Socket
Socket[addr=localhost/127.0.0.1,port=1087,localport=1093]
```
client-server rmi: set boolean request
```
Message of size 22 read by Socket
Socket[addr=localhost/127.0.0.1,port=1087,localport=1093]
```
client-server rmi: set boolean reply
```
Message of size 1 written by Socket
Socket[addr=localhost/127.0.0.1,port=1087,localport=1093]
Message of size 1 read by Socket
Socket[addr=localhost/127.0.0.1,port=1087,localport=1093]
Message of size 120 written by Socket
Socket[addr=localhost/127.0.0.1,port=1087,localport=1093]
```
client-server rmi: set Object request
```
Message of size 22 read by Socket
Socket[addr=localhost/127.0.0.1,port=1087,localport=1093]
```
client-server rmi: set Object reply
```
Message of size 45 written by Socket
Socket[addr=localhost/127.0.0.1,port=1087,localport=1093]
```
client-server rmi: set int request
```
Message of size 22 read by Socket
Socket[addr=localhost/127.0.0.1,port=1087,localport=1093]
```
client-server rmi: set int reply

Here is one possible implementation for the stream classes required by the altered Socket class:

```
package tuning.socket;
import java.io.InputStream;
import java.io.OutputStream;
import java.io.IOException;
import java.net.Socket;

public class SockStreamLogger
{
  public static boolean LOG_SIZE = false;
  public static boolean LOG_MESSAGE = false;
```

```java
  public static void read(Socket so, int sz, byte[] buf, int off) {
    log(false, so, sz, buf, off); }
  public static void written(Socket so, int sz, byte[] buf, int off) {
    log(true, so, sz, buf, off); }
  public static void log(boolean isWritten, Socket so,
                         int sz, byte[] buf, int off)
  {
    if (LOG_SIZE)
    {
        System.err.print("Message of size ");
        System.err.print(sz);
        System.err.print(isWritten ? " written" : " read");
        System.err.print(" by Socket ");
        System.err.println(so);
    }
    if (LOG_MESSAGE)
      System.err.println(new String(buf, off, sz));
  }
}

public class SockInStreamLogger extends InputStream
{
  Socket s;
  InputStream in;
  byte[] one_byte = new byte[1];
  public SockInStreamLogger(Socket so, InputStream i){in = i; s = so;}
  public int available() throws IOException {return in.available();}
  public void close() throws IOException {in.close();}
  public void mark(int readlimit) {in.mark(readlimit);}
  public boolean markSupported() {return in.markSupported();}
  public int read() throws IOException {
    int ret = in.read();
    one_byte[0] = (byte) ret;
    //SockStreamLogger.read(s, 1, one_byte, 0);
    return ret;
  }
  public int read(byte b[]) throws IOException {
    int sz = in.read(b);
    SockStreamLogger.read(s, sz, b, 0);
    return sz;
  }
  public int read(byte b[], int off, int len) throws IOException {
    int sz = in.read(b, off, len);
    SockStreamLogger.read(s, sz, b, off);
    return sz;
  }
  public void reset() throws IOException {in.reset();}
  public long skip(long n) throws IOException {return in.skip(n);}
}

public class SockOutStreamLogger extends OutputStream
{
  Socket s;
  OutputStream out;
```

```
byte[ ] one_byte = new byte[1];
public SockOutStreamLogger(Socket so, OutputStream o){out = o; s = so;}
public void write(int b) throws IOException {
  out.write(b);
  one_byte[0] = (byte) b;
  SockStreamLogger.written(s, 1, one_byte, 0);
}
public void write(byte b[ ]) throws IOException {
  out.write(b);
  SockStreamLogger.written(s, b.length, b, 0);
}
public void write(byte b[ ], int off, int len) throws IOException {
  out.write(b, off, len);
  SockStreamLogger.written(s, len, b, off);
}
public void flush( ) throws IOException {out.flush( );}
public void close( ) throws IOException {out.close( );}
}
```

Performance Checklist

- Use system- and network-level monitoring utilities to assist when measuring performance.
- Run tests on unloaded systems with the test running in the foreground.
  - Use `System.currentTimeMillis( )` to get timestamps if you need to determine absolute times. Never use the timings obtained from a profiler as absolute times.
  - Account for performance effects of any caches.
- Get better profiling tools. The better your tools, the faster and more effective your tuning.
  - Pinpoint the bottlenecks in the application: with profilers, by instrumenting code (putting in explicit timing statements), and by analyzing the code.
  - Target the top five to ten methods, and choose the quickest to fix.
  - Speed up the bottleneck methods that can be fixed the quickest.
  - Improve the method directly when the method takes a significant percentage of time and is not called too often.
  - Reduce the number of times a method is called when the method takes a significant percentage of time and is also called frequently.
- Use an object-creation profiler together with garbage-collection statistics to determine which objects are created in large numbers and which large objects are created.
  - See if the garbage collector executes more often than you expect.
  - Determine the percentage of time spent in garbage collection and reduce that if over 15% (target 5% ideally).

— Use the `Runtime.totalMemory( )` and `Runtime.freeMemory( )` methods to monitor gross memory usage.

- Check whether your communication layer has built-in tracing features.
  - Check whether your communication layer supports the addition of customized layers.
- Identify the number of incoming and outgoing transfers and the amounts of data transferred in distributed applications.

CHAPTER 3
Underlying JDK Improvements

In this chapter:
- Garbage Collection
- Tuning the Heap
- Sharing Memory
- Replacing JDK Classes
- Faster VMs
- Better Optimizing Compilers
- Native Method Calls
- Uncompressed ZIP/JAR Files

Throughout the progressive versions of Java, improvements have been made at all levels of the runtime system: in the garbage collector, in the code, in the VM handling of objects and threads, and in compiler optimizations. It is always worthwhile to check your own application benchmarks against each version (and each vendor's version) of the Java system you try out. Any differences in performance need to be identified and explained; if you can determine that a compiler from one version (or vendor) together with the runtime from another version (or vendor) speeds up your application, you may have the option of choosing the best of both worlds. Standard Java benchmarks tend to be of limited use in deciding which VMs provide the best performance for your application. You are always better off creating your own application benchmark suite for deciding which VM and compiler best suit your application.

The following sections identify some points to consider as you investigate different VMs, compilers, and JDK classes. If you control the target Java runtime environment, i.e., with servlet and other server applications, more options are available to you. We will look at these extra options too.

Garbage Collection

The effects of the garbage collector can be difficult to determine accurately. It is worth including some tests in your performance benchmark suite that are specifically arranged to identify these effects. You can do this only in a general way, since the garbage collector is normally not under your control. (Sun does intend to introduce an API that will allow a pluggable garbage collector to replace the one delivered with the VM, but building your own garbage collector is not a realistic tuning option. Using a pluggable third-party garbage collector doesn't give you control over the garbage collector either.) The basic way to see what the garbage collector is up to is to run with the -verbosegc option. This prints out time and space values for objects reclaimed and space recycled. The printout includes explicit synchronous calls to the garbage collector (using System.gc( )) as well as asynchronous executions of the garbage collector, as occurs in normal operation when free memory available to the VM gets low. You can try to force the VM to execute only synchronous garbage collections by using the -noasyncgc option to the Java executable (no longer available from JDK 1.2). The -noasyncgc option does not actually stop the garbage-collector thread from executing; it still executes if the VM runs out of free memory (as opposed to just getting low on memory). Output from the garbage collector running with -verbosegc is detailed in "Garbage Collection" in Chapter 2.

The garbage collector usually works by freeing the memory that becomes available from objects that are no longer referenced or, if this does not free sufficient space, expanding the available memory space by asking the operating system for more memory (up to a maximum specified to the VM with the -Xmx/-mx option). The garbage collector's space-reclamation algorithm tends to change with each version of the JDK.

Sophisticated generational garbage collectors, which smooth out the impact of garbage collection, are now being used; HotSpot uses a state-of-the-art generational garbage collector. Analysis of object-oriented programs has shown that most objects are short-lived, fewer have medium lifespans, and very few objects are long-lived. Generational garbage collectors move objects through multiple spaces, each time copying live objects from one space to the next and reclaiming the space used by objects that are no longer alive. By concentrating on short-lived objects—the early spaces—and spending less time recycling space where older objects live, the garbage collector frees the maximum amount of space for the lowest impact.[*]

Because the garbage collector is different in different VM versions, the output from the -verbosegc option is also likely to change across versions, making it difficult to compare the effects of the garbage collectors across versions (not to mention between different vendors' VMs). But you should still attempt this comparison, as the effect of the garbage collector can make a difference to the application. Looking at garbage-collection output can tell you that parts of your application are causing significantly more work for the garbage collector, suggesting that you may want to alter the flow of objects in those parts. Garbage collection is also affected by the number of threads and whether objects are shared across threads. Expect to see improvements in threaded garbage collection over different VM versions.

Garbage-collection times may be affected by the size of the VM memory. A larger memory implies there will be more objects in the heap space before the garbage collector needs to kick in. This in turn means that the process of sweeping dead objects takes longer, as does the process of running through a larger object table. Different VMs have optimal performance at different sizes, and the optimal size for any particular application-VM pairing must be determined by trial and error.

---

[*] One book giving more details on garbage collection is *Inside the Java 2 Virtual Machine* by Bill Venners (McGraw-Hill). The garbage collection chapter is also available online at *http://www.artima.com*.

Tuning the Heap

Heap size is important to Java application performance. Tuning the heap is a multi-step process. First, we'll look at the big picture, with gross tuning steps that optimize the size of the heap, followed by advice for fine-tuning the heap. Next, we'll look at the impact of shared memory on tuning the heap.

Gross Tuning

The VMs provided by most vendors include the two main heap tuning parameters: -mx/-Xmx and -ms/-Xms. Respectively, these parameters set the maximum and starting sizes of the heap in bytes. They are typically available with every VM.

> VMs vary as to whether they accept the -mx and -ms parameters or the -Xmx and -Xms parameters, or both. They also vary about accepting a space between the number following the parameter and accepting shorthand notations of K and M for kilobytes and megabytes, e.g., -Xmx32M. Check the documentation or simply try the various possibilities for your VM).

Tuning the heap with these two parameters requires trial and error, but is relatively simple. You don't need to consider the exact garbage-collection algorithm or how different parameters might affect each other. Instead, you can identify the cost of garbage collection to the application using the measurement techniques covered in Chapter 2. You can then simply alter the two parameters and remeasure using the same technique. Typically, you might want to use a range of values for the maximum heap size, keeping the starting heap size either absolutely constant (e.g., 1 megabyte) or relatively constant (e.g., half the maximum heap), and graph the result, looking for where garbage collection has the minimum cost.

> Note that GC activity can take hours to settle into a regular pattern. If you are tuning a long-lived application, bear this in mind when looking at the GC output.

Gross heap tuning is fairly stable, in that moving to a different VM or tweaking the application usually won't invalidate the tuning parameters. They may no longer be the most optimal sizes after such changes, but they should still be reasonable. The following sections describe some considerations for heap parameters.

Problems with a Larger Heap

The heap size should not become so large that physical memory is swamped and the system has to start paging. So keep the maximum heap size below the size of the

---

physical memory (RAM) on the machine. Also, subtract from the RAM the amount of memory required for other processes that will be running at the same time as the Java application, and keep the maximum heap size below that value.

A larger heap allows more objects to exist in memory before garbage collection is required to reclaim space for new objects. However, a larger heap also makes the garbage collection last longer, as it needs to work through more objects. In the absence of concurrent garbage collection (see the information about -Xconcgc in "Fine-Tuning the Heap"), a larger heap causes longer individual perceptible pauses, which may be undesirable. You need to balance the pause times against the overall garbage-collection cost. (Using -Xincgc is an alternative that is also described in the section on fine tuning.)

Starting Versus Maximum Heap Size

There are many different suggestions about what the starting heap should be compared to the maximum. The most frequent suggestions include:

- Set the starting heap size the same as the maximum heap size.
- Set the starting heap size to the size needed by the maximum number of live objects (estimated or measured in trials), and set the maximum heap size to about four times this amount.
- Set the starting heap size to half the maximum heap size.
- Set the starting heap size between 1/10 and 1/4 the maximum heap size.
- Use the default initial heap size (1 megabyte).

Although there is no conclusive evidence that any of these suggestions represents the best approach in all situations, each has been shown to be appropriate in different applications. Here are some rationales. Assuming you've worked out what the maximum heap size should be, then growing the JVM memory can be considered as pure overhead, requiring multiple system calls and resulting in segmented system memory allocation. If you figure that you are going to get to the maximum heap anyway, then there is a good argument for simply starting out at the maximum heap (the first suggestion), thus avoiding the growth overhead as well as getting a heap that is less segmented. However, this can mean longer pauses when garbage collection kicks in, so the system load might not be smoothed out as much as you'd want. But a generational garbage collector will not necessarily suffer from this longer pause problem, as it specifically smooths out the GC load.

An alternative view is that there is this lovely garbage-collection system in the JVM, which will grow the JVM to be just as big as needed and no more, so why not let it do its job? This way, despite the overhead in growing the JVM, you will end up using the minimum resources and the GC should be optimizing what it does best, i.e., handling and maintaining memory. With this argument, you set the starting heap to 1MB (the last suggestion) and the maximum as high as reasonable.

A combination of these two rationales might lead you to one of the intermediate recommendations. For example, assuming that the maximum heap is an overestimate of the ultimate JVM size, then half the maximum could be a good starting point to minimize memory allocation and memory segmentation overhead while still giving the GC space to optimize memory usage.

Benchmarking Considerations

When running benchmarks, some engineers try to manipulate the benchmark and heap size so that no garbage collection needs to occur during the run of the benchmark. This is an idealized situation, but it may be appropriate if your application is expected to run for only a short period. In any case, be aware that this may apply to benchmarks presented to you.

The -noclassgc/-Xnoclassgc options prevent classes from being garbage-collected. If you are loading classes indirectly (e.g., through Class.forName() or by J2EE automatic classloading), then classes can be repeatedly garbage-collected and reloaded. Reloaded classes are also reinitialized, so use the -noclassgc/-Xnoclassgc parameter to prevent them from being garbage-collected.

Fine-Tuning the Heap

In addition to the gross heap-tuning factors, a host of other parameters can be used for fine-tuning the VM heap. These other factors are usually strongly dependent on the garbage-collection algorithm being used by the VM, and the parameters vary for different VMs and different versions of VMs. In this section, I'll cover a few examples to give you an idea of the possibilities. Note that every VM and every version of the VM is different, and you need to retune the system with any change for this level of fine-tuning. Fine-tuning is probably worth doing only where every last microsecond is needed or for a really stable deployed system, i.e., one that needs no more development.

Note that the following sections refer to some of the internal heap areas used by the HotSpot generational garbage collector. Generally, the total VM heap consists of permanent space (Perm), old space (Old), young space (Young), and scratch or survivor space (Scratch). Parameters referring to "new" space (New), such as -XX:NewSize, refer to the combination Young+Scratch. The -Xmx parameter sizes Old+New. The full heap is Old+New+Perm.

Expanding the Heap

Most garbage-collection algorithms do not immediately expand the heap if they need space to create more objects, even when the heap has not yet been expanded to the maximum allowable size. Instead, there is usually a series of attempts to free up space by reclaiming objects, compacting objects, defragmenting the heap, and so on. If all these attempts are exhausted, then the heap is expanded. Several GC algorithms try to keep some free space available so that temporary objects can be created and reclaimed without expanding the heap. For example, the Sun 1.3 VM allows the parameter -XX:MinFreeHeapRatio=*num*, where *num* is 0 to 100, to specify that the heap should be expanded if less than *num*% of the heap is free. Similarly, the -XXMaxHeapFreeRatio parameter specifies when the heap should be contracted. The IBM VM uses -Xminf and -Xmaxf with decimal parameters between 0 and 1 (e.g., 20% is 20 for the Sun VM and 0.2 for the IBM VM). The Sun default is to try to keep the proportion of free space to living objects at each garbage collection within the 40%–70% range. That is, if less than 40% of the heap is free after a garbage collection (so more than 60% of the heap is full of objects), then the heap is expanded. Otherwise, the next garbage collection will likely occur sooner than desired. (IBM defaults are 0.3 min and 0.6 max.)

Once an application reaches a steady state, it has a fairly constant churn of objects (created and released). If the minimum free heap ratio is a small value (e.g., 10%), then there is not much space for objects to churn in, and garbage collection occurs frequently. The heap does not expand, because after each garbage collection the free heap ratio is achieved (e.g., 10% is filled, GC runs, and we have 10% available again so no heap expansion occurs). On the other hand, if the minimum free heap ratio is a large value (e.g., 60%), then GC runs much less frequently, but the pause when it runs is longer.

Minimizing Pauses

Garbage collection normally pauses the application. Pauses that last too long create bad user perceptions of performance. The primary technique to eliminate pauses is to identify which objects are being churned, causing the GC to activate, and try to minimize those objects. The secondary option is to reduce the heap size so that garbage collection runs more often, but for shorter periods.

Incremental or "train" GC

As an alternative, -Xincgc changes the garbage-collection algorithm to use an incremental or "train" garbage-collection algorithm. The intention is to minimize individual pause time at the expense of overall GC time. The train algorithm clusters objects that reference each other and collects these clusters individually. The idea is to garbage-collect only a small fraction of the heap at a time, thus causing shorter pauses. But the algorithm is more costly in CPU time and results in longer total GC time.

Concurrent GC

Another alternative is the concurrent garbage collector, -Xconcgc. The concurrent garbage collector tries to avoid stopping the application threads by asynchronously executing as much of the garbage collection algorithm as possible. Once again, this has a higher cost on the CPU, and total GC time is increased. The concurrent garbage collector should be especially effective on multiprocessor machines. Note that the garbage collector has always run in its own thread, but in order to access memory areas to run the garbage collection, it pauses application threads. It is this pausing that the concurrent garbage collector aims to minimize. Note that 1.4.1 provides parameters -XX:+UseParNewGC and -XX:+UseConcMarkSweepGC, which enable concurrent GC separately in the young and old spaces, respectively.

Enlarge the "new" space

Finally, if you need a large heap and want to decrease pause times, you can try altering the size of the "new" space with generational garbage collectors (all Java 2 VMs). The "new" space (also called "Eden" or "the young generation") is the heap space where new objects are created. If the objects are short-lived, they are also garbage-collected rapidly in the new space. The longer pauses are usually caused by the garbage collections that run across the spaces outside the "new" space, i.e., garbage collection of the full heap, so the more objects that are churned in the new space, the better. If you need a large heap, try increasing the new space. For example, in 1.3 and 1.4 VMs, these parameters:

```
-Xms384m -Xmx384m -XX:NewSize=128m -XX:MaxNewSize=128m
```

set the full heap to 384 MB, of which one third is used for the new space, instead of SDK 1.3's default new space of 32 MB on Solaris or 2.5 MB on Windows. SDK 1.4 uses a default dependent on the heap size. Remember that new space is not one space, but internally consists of heap space plus scratch space (working areas for the algorithm). The option XX:SurvivorRatio= sets the ratio of sizes between scratch space and new space (Eden).

1.2 VMs use different parameters. For 1.2, the equivalent parameters would be:

```
-Xgenconfig:64m,64m,semispaces:256m,256m,markcompact -Xmx384m
```

which specify that the new space is a semispace collector of 64 MB, with 256 MB for the "old" space, using a mark-compact GC algorithm. (As you can see, fine-tuning the heap is complex, and changes with every VM.) Here's the complete list of 1.2 genconfig options:

```
-Xgenconfig:<initial young size>,<max young size>,semispaces[,promoteall]:<initial
old size>,<max old size> [,<collector>]
```

where collector can be incmarksweep (producing concurrent GC) or markcompact. The promoteall option forces the GC to move any object that survives a GC in young space to be immediately moved to old space; otherwise, the GC may leave the object in young space for longer. Since young-space garbage collection is faster, you might think that promoteall would decrease performance, but at least one in-depth test found that using promoteall improved performance (see *http://wireless.java.sun.com/midp/articles/garbage/*). In addition, an additional -bestFitFirst option seems to improve concurrent GC. The "best fit" refers to an internal free-list allocation policy that helps to reduce heap fragmentation (see *http://dcb.sun.com/practices/ devnotebook/gc_perspective.jsp*).

Disabling System.gc( ) Calls

Prior to Java 2, explicit calls to System.gc( ) could assist an application. Garbage collection was pretty much an all-or-nothing affair, and often you knew better than the garbage collector when it was a good time to start garbage collecting. But with the introduction of generational garbage collection, explicit calls to System.gc( ) become disruptive, possibly forcing a full mark-sweep of the heap when the generational garbage collector was doing just fine. So Sun has added an option to disable the effect of calling System.gc( ) explicitly: -XX:+DisableExplicitGC.

Tuning RMI Garbage Collection

The frequency of distributed garbage collections can be set with the properties sun.rmi.dgc.client.gcInterval and sun.rmi.dgc.server.gcInterval. The default is one collection per minute (property values of 6000).

Extreme Heap and Intimate Shared Memory

The option -XX:+AggressiveHeap sets the heap to 3850 MB or more, allocates 256K to each thread, defers garbage collection as long as possible, and tries to run some GC activity in parallel (see the earlier discussion of concurrent GC options). This may or may not be a good tuning option; it is intended for very large servers. There is also an option to lock the heap in physical memory (see "RAM" in Chapter 14 and *http://java.sun.com/docs/hotspot/ism.html* for further details).

Loading a Huge Number of Classes

HotSpot stores as Java objects some of its own internal data structures, things like the internal representation of classes, methods, and fields. These are stored in a separate area called the Perm Space. If you are loading a truly huge number of classes, you may need to enlarge this space by using the -XX:MaxPermSize parameter.

Per-Thread Stack Size

Setting the JVM stack and native thread stack size (-oss <Java thread stack size>, -ss <native thread stack size>, -XX:ThreadStackSize=<thread stack size>) too large (e.g., greater than 2MB) can significantly degrade performance.

Eliminate Finalizers

Finalizers force objects to be promoted to old space and degrade the performance of the garbage collector. Finalizers postpone garbage collection until the finalizer is run, adding yet more overhead to the GC algorithm. There is no way to avoid this overhead apart from minimizing the use of finalization methods in the application.

Sharing Memory

If you are running multiple VMs on the same machine, you have the option of sharing some of the memory between them. There is a proposal for VMs to share system memory automatically, and this is likely to happen in the future. But currently (as of the 1.4 release), if you want to share memory between VM processes, you need to run multiple pseudoprocesses within one VM process. The necessary techniques are actually quite complicated, as many subtle problems can arise when trying to run several applications in the same VM while keeping them independent of each other.

Fortunately, there is a free open source library called Echidna (available from *http://www.javagroup.org/echidna/*) that takes care of all the subtleties involved in running multiple applications independently within the same VM system process. The library also provides several management tools to help use Echidna effectively. If you want to know how Echidna works or need to use parts of the library within your project, I have written an article that covers the technology in some detail.[*]

The shared-memory advantages from combining multiple applications into one VM are significant for applications with small memory requirements where the VM memory overhead is significant by comparison. But for applications that require large amounts of memory, there may be little benefit.

A shared-memory VM also provides a faster startup time, as the VM can already be running when the application is started. For example, a VM using the Echidna library can be a running system process with no Java application running (except for the Echidna library). The Echidna library can start any Java application in exactly the same way the VM would have started it, but without all the VM startup overhead.

Replacing JDK Classes

It is possible for you to replace JDK classes directly. Unfortunately, you can't distribute these altered classes with any application or applet unless you have complete control of the target environment. Although you often do have this control with in-house and enterprise-developed applications, most enterprises prefer not to deploy

---

[*] "Catching OutOfMemoryErrors to Preserve Monitoring and Server Processes," *OnJava* magazine, August 2001, *http://www.onjava.com/pub/a/onjava/2001/08/22/optimization.html*.

alterations to externally built classes. The alterations would not be supported by the vendor (Sun in this case) and may violate the license, so contact the vendor if you need to do this. In addition, altering classes in this way can be a significant maintenance problem.*

The upshot is that you can easily alter JDK-supplied classes for development purposes, which can be useful for various reasons including debugging and tuning. But if you need the functionality in your deployed application, you need to provide classes that are used instead of the JDK classes by redirecting method calls to your own classes.

Replacing JDK classes indirectly in this way is a valid tuning technique. Some JDK classes, such as StreamTokenizer (see "Strings Versus char Arrays" in Chapter 5), are inefficient and can be replaced quite easily since you normally use them in small, well-defined parts of a program. Other JDK classes, like Date, BigDecimal, and String, are used all over the place, and it can take a large effort to replace references with your own versions of these classes. The best way to replace these classes is to start from the design stage so that you can consistently use your own versions throughout the application.

 In SDK 1.3, many of the java.lang.Math methods were changed from native to call the corresponding methods in java.lang.StrictMath. StrictMath provides bitwise consistency across platforms; earlier versions of Math used platform-specific native functions that were not identical across all platforms. Unfortunately, StrictMath calculations are somewhat slower than the corresponding native functions. My colleague Kirk Pepperdine, who first pointed out the performance problem to me, puts it this way: "I've now got a bitwise-correct but excruciatingly slow program." The potential workarounds to this performance issue are all ugly: using an earlier JDK version, replacing the JDK class with an earlier version, or writing your own class to manage faster alternative floating-point calculations.

For optimal performance, I recommend developing with your own versions of classes rather than the JDK versions whenever possible. This gives maximum tuning flexibility. However, this recommendation is clearly impractical in most cases. Given that, perhaps the single most significant class to replace with your own version is the String class. Most other classes can be replaced inside identified bottlenecks when required during tuning without affecting other parts of the application. But String is used so extensively that replacing String references in one location tends to have widespread consequences, requiring extensive rewriting in many parts of the application. In fact, this observation also applies to other data type classes you use extensively (Integer,

---

* If your application has its classes localized in one place on one machine, for example with servlets, you might consider deploying changes to the core classes.

Date, etc.). But the String class tends to be used most often. See Chapter 5 for details on why the String class can be a performance problem and why you might need to replace it.

It is often impractical to replace the String classes where their internationalization capabilities are required. Because of this, you should logically partition the application's use of Strings to identify those aspects that require internationalization and those aspects that are really character processing, independent of language dependencies. The latter usage of Strings can be replaced more easily than the former. Internationalization-dependent String manipulation is difficult to tune because you are dependent on internationalization libraries that are difficult to replace.

Many JDK classes provide generic capabilities (as you would expect from library classes), so they are frequently more generic than what is required for your particular application. These generic capabilities often come at the expense of performance. For example, Vector is fine for generic Objects, but if you are using a Vector for only one type of object, then a custom version with an array and accessors of that type is faster, as you can avoid all the casts required to convert the generic Object back into your own type. Using Vector for basic data types (e.g., longs) is even worse, requiring the data type to be wrapped by an object to get it into the Vector. For example, building and using a LongVector class improves performance and readability by avoiding casts, Long wrappers, unwrapping, etc.:

```
public class LongVector
{
  long[ ] internalArray;
  int arraySize
  ...
  public void addElement(long l) {
  ...
  public long elementAt(int i) {
  ...
```

 Note that Generics are due to be introduced in Version 1.5. Generics allow instances of generic classes like Vector to be specified as aggregate objects that hold only specified types of objects. However, the implementation of Generics is to insert casts at all the access points and to analyze the updates to ensure that the update type matches the cast type. There is no specialized class generation, so there is no performance benefit, and there may even be a slight performance degradation from the additional casts.

If you are using your own classes, you can extend them with specific functionality you require, with direct access to the internals of the class. Using Vector as an example, if you want to iterate over the collection (e.g., to select a particular subset based on some criteria), you need to access the elements through the get( ) method for each element, with the significant overhead that implies. If you are using your own (possibly derived) class, you can implement the specific action you want in the class, allowing your loop to access the internal array directly with the consequent speedup:

```
public class QueryVector extends MyVector
{
  public Object[ ] getTheBitsIWant{
    //Access the internal array directly rather than going through
    //the method accessors. This makes the search much faster
    Object[ ] results = new Object[10];
    for(int i = arraySize-1; i >= 0; i--)
      if (internalArray[i] ....
```

Finally, there are often many places where objects (especially collection objects) are used initially for convenience (e.g., using a Vector because you did not know the size of the array you would need, etc.). In a final version of the application, they can be replaced with presized arrays. A known-sized array (not a collection object) is the fastest way in Java to store and access elements of a collection.

Faster VMs

VM runtimes and Java compilers vary enormously over time and across vendors. More and more optimizations are finding their way into both VMs and compilers. Many possible compiler optimizations are considered in later sections of this chapter. In this section I focus on VM optimizations.

VM Speed Variations

Different VMs have different running characteristics. Some VMs are intended purely for development and are highly suboptimal in terms of performance. These VMs may have huge inefficiencies, even in such basic operations as casting between different numeric types, as was the case with one development VM I used. It provided the foundation of an excellent development environment (actually my preferred environment) but was all but useless for performance testing. Any data type manipulation other than with ints or booleans produced highly varying and misleading times.

It is important to run any tests involving timing or profiling in the same VM that will run the application. You should test your application in the current "standard" VMs if your target environment is not fully defined.

There is, of course, nothing much you can do about speeding up any one VM (apart from heap tuning or upgrading the CPUs). But you should be aware of the different VMs available, whether or not you control the deployment environment of your application. If you control the target environment, you can choose your VM appropriately. If you do not control the environment on which your application runs, remember that performance is partly user expectation. If you tell your user that VM "A" gives such and such a performance for your application, but VM "B" gives much slower performance, then you at least inform your user community of the implications of their choice of VM. This might also pressure vendors with slower VMs to improve them.

VMs with JIT Compilers

The basic bytecode interpreter VM executes by decoding and executing bytecode. This is slow and is pure overhead, adding nothing to the functionality of the application. A just-in-time (JIT) compiler in a virtual machine eliminates much of this overhead by doing the bytecode fetch and decode just once. The first time the method is loaded, the decoded instructions are converted into machine code native for the CPU the system is running on. After that, future invocations of a particular method no longer incur the interpreter overhead. However, a JIT must be fast at compiling to avoid slowing the runtime, so extensive optimizations within the compile phase are unlikely. This means that the compiled code is often not as fast as it could be. A JIT also imposes a significantly larger memory footprint to the process.

Without a JIT, you might have to optimize your bytecodes for a particular platform. Optimizing the bytecode for one platform can conceivably make that code run slower on another platform (though a speedup is usually reflected to some extent on all platforms). A JIT compiler can theoretically optimize the same code differently for different underlying CPUs, thus getting the best of all worlds.

In his tests,[*] Mark Roulo found that a good JIT speeded up the overhead of method calls from a best of 280 CPU clock cycles in the fastest non-JIT VM to just 2 clock cycles in the JIT VM. In a direct comparison of method call times for this JIT VM compared to a compiled C++ program, the Java method call time was found to be just one clock cycle slower than C++: fast enough for almost any application. However, object creation is not speeded up by anywhere near this amount, which means that with a JIT VM, object creation is relatively more expensive (and consequently more important when tuning) than with a non-JIT VM.

VM Startup Time

The time your application takes to start depends on a number of factors. First, there is the time taken by the operating system to start the executable process. This time is mostly independent of the VM, though the size of the executable and the size and number of shared libraries needed to start the VM process have some effect. But the main time cost is mapping the various elements into system memory. This time can be shortened by having as much as possible already in system memory. The most obvious way to have the shared libraries already in system memory is to have recently started a VM. If the VM was recently started, even for a short time, the operating system is likely to have cached the shared libraries in system memory, so the next startup is quicker. A better but more complicated way of having the executable elements in memory is to have the relevant files mapped onto a memory-resident filesystem;

[*] "Accelerate Your Java Apps," *JavaWorld*, September 1998, *http://www.javaworld.com/javaworld/jw-09-1998/jw-09-speed.html*.

see the section "Cached Filesystems (RAM Disks, tmpfs, cachefs)" in Chapter 14 for more on how to manage this. Yet another option is to use a prestarted VM; see the earlier section "Sharing Memory." A prestarted VM also partially addresses the startup overhead discussed in the next paragraph.

The second component in the startup time of the VM is the time taken to manage the VM runtime initializations. This is purely dependent on the VM system implementation. Interpreter VMs generally have faster startup times than JIT VMs because the JIT VMs need to manage extra compilations during the startup and initial classloading phases. Starting with SDK 1.3, Sun tried to improve VM startup time. VMs are now already differentiated by their startup times; for example, the 1.3 VM has a deliberately shortened startup time compared to 1.2. HotSpot has the more leisurely startup time acceptable for long-running server processes. In the future you can expect to see VMs differentiated by their startup times even more.

Finally, the application architecture and class file configuration determine the last component of startup time. The application may require many classes and extensive initializations before the application is started, or it may be designed to start up as quickly as possible. It is useful to bear in mind the user perception of application startup when designing the application. For example, if you can create the startup window as quickly as possible and then run any initializations in the background without blocking windowing activity, the user sees this as a faster startup than if you waited for initializations to finish before creating the initial window. This design takes more work but improves startup time.

The number of classes that need to be loaded before the application starts are part of the application initializations, and again the application design affects this time. In the later section "Uncompressed ZIP/JAR Files," I discuss the effects of class file configuration on startup time. The section "Analysis" in Chapter 13 also includes an example of designing an application to minimize startup time.

Other VM Optimizations

On the VM side, improvements are possible using JIT compilers to compile methods to machine code, using algorithms for code caching, applying intelligent analyses of runtime code, etc. Some bytecodes allow the system to bypass table lookups that would otherwise need to be executed. But these bytecodes take extra effort to apply to the VM. Using these techniques, an intelligent VM could skip some runtime steps after parts of the application have been resolved.

Generally, a VM with a JIT compiler gives a huge boost to a Java application and is probably the quickest and simplest way to improve performance. The most optimistic predictions say that using optimizing compilers to generate bytecodes, together with VMs with intelligent JIT (re)compilers, puts Java performance on a par with or even above that of an equivalent natively compiled C++ application. Theoretically, better performance is possible. Having a runtime environment adapt to the running characteristics of a program should, in theory at least, provide better performance than a statically compiled application. A similar argument runs in CPU design circles where dynamic rescheduling of instructions to take pipelining into account allows CPUs to process instructions out of order. But at the time of writing this book, we are not particularly close to proving this theory for the average Java application. The time available for a VM to do something other than the most basic execution and byte-code translation is limited. The following quote about dynamic scheduling in CPUs also applies to adaptive VMs:

> At runtime, the CPU knows almost everything, but it knows everything almost too late to do anything about it. (Tom R. Halfhill quoting Gerrit A. Slavenburg, "Inside IA-64," *Byte*, June 1998)

As an example of an "intelligent" VM, Sun's HotSpot VM is targeted precisely to this area of adaptive optimization. This VM includes some basic improvements (all of which are also present in VMs from other vendors) such as using direct pointers instead of Java handles (which may be a security issue),* improved thread synchronization, a generational garbage collector, speedups to object allocation, and an improved startup time (by not JIT-compiling methods initially). In addition to these basic improvements, HotSpot includes adaptive optimization, which works as follows: HotSpot runs the application initially in interpreted mode (as if there is no JIT compiler present) while a profiler identifies the bottlenecks in the application. Then, an optimizing JIT compiler compiles into native machine code only those hotspots in the application that are causing the bottlenecks. Because only a small part of the application is targeted, the JIT compiler (which might in this case be more realistically called an "after-a-while" compiler rather than a "just-in-time" compiler) can spend extra time compiling those targeted parts of the application, thus allowing more than the most basic compiler optimizations to be applied.

 Consider the example where 20% of the code accounts for 80% of the running application time. Here, a classic JIT compiler might improve the whole application by 30%: the application would now take 70% of the time it originally took.

The HotSpot compiler ignores the nonbottlenecked code, instead focusing on getting the 20% of hotspot code to run twice as fast. The 80% of application time is halved to just 40% of the original time. Adding in the remaining 20% means that the application now runs in 60% of the original time. (These statistics are purely for illustration purposes.)

---

* A handle is a pointer to a pointer. Java uses handles to ensure security so that one object cannot gain direct access to another object without the security capabilities of Java being able to intervene.

Note, however, that HotSpot tries too hard sometimes. For example, HotSpot can speculatively optimize on the basis of guessing the type of particular objects. If that guess turns out to be wrong, HotSpot has to deoptimize the code, which results in some wildly variable timings.

So far, I have no evidence that optimizations I have applied in the past (and detailed in this book) have caused any problems after upgrading compilers and VMs. However, it is important to note that the performance characteristics of your application may change with different VMs and compilers, and not necessarily always for the better. Be on the lookout for any problems a new compiler and VM may bring. The technique of loading classes explicitly from a new thread after application startup can conflict with a particular JIT VM's caching mechanism and actually slow down the startup sequence of your application. I have no evidence for this; I am just speculating on possible conflicts.

Better Optimizing Compilers

Java code compilers that specifically target performance optimizations are increasingly available. (I maintain a list at *http://www.JavaPerformanceTuning.com/resources.shtml*. A list is also included in Chapter 19.) Of course, all compilers try to optimize code, but some are better than others. Some companies put a great deal of effort into making their compiler produce the tightest, fastest code, while others tend to be distracted by other aspects of the Java environment and put less effort into the compile phase.

There are also some experimental compilers around. For example, the JAVAR compiler (*http://www.extreme.indiana.edu/hpjava/*) is a prototype compiler that automatically parallelizes parts of a Java application to improve performance.

It is possible to write preprocessors to automatically achieve many of the optimizations you can get with optimizing compilers; in fact, you can think of an optimizing compiler as a preprocessor together with a basic compiler (though in many cases it is better described as a postprocessor and recompiler). However, writing such a preprocessor is a significant task. Even if you ignore the Java code parsing or bytecode parsing required,[*] any one preprocessor optimization can take months to create and verify. Getting close to the full set of optimizations listed in the following sections could take years of development. Fortunately, it is not necessary for you to make that effort because optimizing-compiler vendors are making the effort for you.

---

[*] Such parsing is a one-off task that can then be applied to any optimization. There are several free packages available for parsing class files, including CFParse from the IBM alphaWorks site, *http://www.alphaworks. ibm.com/tech/cfparse*.

What Optimizing Compilers Cannot Do

Optimizing compilers cannot change your code to use a better algorithm. If you are using an inefficient search routine, there may be a vastly better search algorithm that would give an order-of-magnitude speedup. But the optimizing compiler only tries to speed up the algorithm you are using (probably a small incremental speedup). It is still important to profile applications to identify bottlenecks even if you intend to use an optimizing compiler.

It is important to start using an optimizing compiler from the early stages of development in order to tailor your code to its restrictions. Integrating an optimizing compiler at a late stage of development can mean restructuring core routines and many disparate method calls, and may even require some redesign to work around limitations imposed by being unable to correctly handle reflection and runtime class resolution. Optimizing compilers have difficulty dealing with classes that cannot be identified at compile time (e.g., building a string at runtime and loading a class of that name). Basically, using `Class.forName()` is not (and cannot be) handled in any complete way, though several compilers try to manage as best they can. In short, managers with projects at a late stage of development are often reluctant to make extensive changes to either the development environment or the code. While code tuning can be targeted at bottlenecks and so normally affects only small sections of code, integrating an optimizing compiler can affect the entire project. If there are too many problems in this integration, most project managers decide that the potential risks outweigh the possible benefits and prefer to take the safe route of carrying on without the optimizing compiler.

What Optimizing Compilers Can Do

Compilers can apply many "classic" optimizations and a host of newer optimizations that apply specifically to object-oriented programs and languages with virtual machines. I list many optimizations in the following sections.

You can apply most classic compiler-optimization techniques by hand directly to the source. But usually you should not, as it makes the code more complicated to read and maintain. Individually, each of these optimizations improves performance only by small amounts. Collectively (as applied by a compiler across all the code), they can make a significant contribution to improving performance. This is important to remember: as you look at each individual optimization, in many cases you may think, "Well, that isn't going to make much difference." This is correct. The power of optimizing compilers comes in automatically applying many small optimizations that would be annoying or confusing to apply by hand. The combination of all those small optimizations can add up to a big speedup.

Optimizing-compiler vendors claim to see significant speedups: up to 50% for many applications. Most applications in serious need of optimization are looking for speedups even greater than this, but don't ignore the optimizing compiler for that reason: it may be doubling the speed of your application for a relatively cheap investment. As long as you do not need to restructure much code to take advantage of them, optimizing compilers can give you "the biggest bang for your buck" after JIT VMs in terms of performance improvements.

The next sections list many of the well-known optimizations these compilers may apply. This list can help you when selecting optimizing compilers or applying some of these optimizations by hand.

Remove unused methods and classes

When all application classes are known at compile time, an optimizing compiler can analyze the full runtime code-path tree, identifying all classes that can be used and all methods that can be called. Most method calls in Java necessarily invoke one of a limited set of methods, and by analyzing the runtime path, you can eliminate all but one of the possibilities. The compiler can then remove unused methods and classes, including removing superclass methods that have been overridden in a subclass and are never called in the superclass. The optimization makes for smaller download requirements for programs sent across a network and, more usefully, reduces the impact of method lookup at runtime by eliminating unused alternative methods.

Increase statically bound calls

An optimizing compiler can determine at compile time whether particular method invocations are necessarily polymorphic and so must have the actual method target determined at runtime, or whether the target for a particular method call can be identified at compile time. Many method calls that apparently need to have the target decided at runtime can, in fact, be uniquely identified (see the previous section). Once identified, the method invocation can be compiled as a static invocation, which is faster than a dynamic lookup. Static methods are statically bound in Java. The following example produces "in superclass" if method1( ) and method2( ) are static, but "in subclass" if method1( ) and method2( ) are not static:

```
public class Superclass {
  public static void main(String[ ] args) {(new Subclass()).method1();}
  public static void method1(){method2();}
  public static void method2(){System.out.println("in superclass ");}
}
class Subclass extends Superclass {
  public static void method2(){System.out.println("in subclass ");}
}
```

Cut dead code and unnecessary instructions, including checks for null

Section 14.9 of the Java specification requires compilers to carry out flow analysis on the code to determine the reachability of any section of code. The only valid unreachable code is the consequence of an if statement (see the later section "Dead code branches are eliminated"). Invalid unreachable code must be flagged as a compile error, but the valid code from an if statement is not a compile error and can be eliminated. The if statement test can also be eliminated if the boolean result is conclusively identified at compile time. In fact, this is a standard capability of almost all current compilers.

This flow analysis can be extended to determine if other sections and code branches that are syntactically valid are actually semantically unreachable. A typical example is testing for null. Some null tests can be eliminated by establishing that the variable has either definitely been assigned to or definitely never been assigned to before the test is reached. Similarly, some bytecode instructions that can be generated may be unnecessary after establishing the flow of control, and these can also be eliminated.

Use computationally cheaper alternatives (strength reduction)

An optimizing compiler should determine if there is a computationally cheaper alternative to a set of instructions and replace those slower instructions with the faster alternative.

The classic version of this technique, termed "strength reduction," replaces an operation with an equivalent but faster operation. Consider the following lines of code:

```
x = x + 5;
y = x/2;
z = x * 4;
```

These lines can be replaced by faster operations without altering the meaning of any statements:

```
x += 5;     //Assignment in place is faster
y = x >> 1; //each right shift by one place is equivalent to dividing by 2
z = x << 2; //each left shift by one place is equivalent to multiplying by 2
```

These examples are the most common cases of strength reduction. All the shorthand arithmetic operators (++, --, +=, -=, *=, /=, |=, &=) are computationally faster than the longer versions and should be used (by the coder) or replaced (by the compiler) where appropriate.*

Replace runtime computations with compiled results

An optimizing compiler can identify code that requires runtime execution if byte-codes are directly generated, but can be replaced by computing the result of that code during the compilation phase. The result can then replace the code.

---

* One of the technical reviewers for this book, Ethan Henry, pointed out to me that there is no actual guarantee that these strength reductions are more efficient in Java. This is true. However, they seem to work for at least some VMs. In addition, compilers producing native code (including JIT compilers) should produce faster code, as these techniques do work at the machine-code level.

This technique is applied by most compilers for the simple case of literal folding (see the later sections "Literal constants are folded" and "String concatenation is sometimes folded"). And it can be extended to other structures by adding some semantic input to the compiler. A simple example is:

```
String S_NINETY = "90";
int I_NINETY = Integer.parseInt(S_NINETY);
```

Although it is unlikely that anyone would do exactly this, similar kinds of initializations are used. An optimizing compiler that understood what `Integer.parseInt( )` did could calculate the resulting `int` value and insert that result directly into the compiled file, thus avoiding the runtime calculation.

Remove unused fields

Analysis of the application can identify fields of objects that are never used, and these fields can then be removed. This makes the runtime take less memory and improves the speeds of both the object creation and the garbage collection of these objects. The type of analysis described in the earlier section "Remove unused methods and classes" improves the identification of unused fields.

Remove unnecessary parts of compiled files

Removing some unnecessary parts of compiled files is standard with most optimizing compilers. This option removes line number tables and local variable tables. The Java *.class* file structure allows extra information to be inserted, and some optimizing compilers make an effort to remove everything that is not necessary for runtime execution. This can be useful when it is important to minimize the size of the *.class* files. Frequently, compilers with this capability can remove unnecessary parts of files that are already compiled, e.g., from third-party *.class* files you do not have the source for.

Reduce necessary parts of compiled files

Some optimizing compilers can reduce the necessary parts of compiled files. For example, the *.class* file includes a pool of constants, and an optimizing compiler can minimize the size of the constant pool by combining and reducing entries.

Alter access control to speed up invocations

At least one optimizing compiler (the DashO optimizer by PreEmptive) provides the option to alter the access control to methods. The rationale for this is that any non-`public` method has access control on that method since it is access restricted (i.e., the runtime system must verify at some point that the caller to a method has access to calling that method). However, `public` methods require no such runtime checks. The thinking is that any non-`public` method must have some overhead compared to an identical method declared as `public`.

The result is that the compiler supports normal compilation (so that any incorrect accesses are caught at the compilation stage), and the subsequent compiled class can have all its methods changed to public. This is, of course, a security risk.

Inline calls

Every optimizing compiler supports inlining. However, the degree of inlining supported can vary enormously, as different compilers are more or less aggressive about inlining (see the extended discussion in the later section "Optimizations Performed When Using the -O Option"). Inlining is the technique in which a method call is directly replaced with the code for that method; for example, the code as written may be:

```
private int method1( ) { return method2( ); }
private int method2( ) { return 5; }
```

With inlining operating to optimize method1( ), this code is compiled into the equivalent of:

```
//the call to method2( ) is replaced with the code in method2( )
private int method1( ) { return 5; }
private int method2( ) { return 5; }
```

Remove dynamic type checks

Every compiler removes dynamic type checks when the compiler can establish they are unnecessary. The JDK compiler removes casts that are obviously unnecessary. For example, consider the following two lines of code:

```
Integer i = new Integer(3);
Integer j = (Integer) i;
```

The JDK compiler removes the obviously unnecessary cast here, and the code gets compiled as if the source were:

```
Integer i = new Integer(3);
Integer j = i;
```

This is very basic. A more sophisticated optimizing compiler can analyze a program far more intensively and eliminate further casting operations that the compiler can ascertain are always true. The instanceof operation is similar to casting (the test applied by instanceof differs from a class cast test in that a cast on null always succeeds, but null instanceof SomeClass always returns false), and an optimizing compiler can also remove some tests involving instanceof.

Unroll loops

Loop unrolling makes the loop body larger by explicitly repeating the body statements while changing the amount by which the loop variable increases or decreases. This reduces the number of tests and iterations the loop requires to be completed. This is extensively covered in Chapter 7.

Code motion

Code motion moves calculations out of loops that need calculating only once. Consider the code example:

```
for (int i = 0; i < z.length; i++)
  z[i] = x * Maths.abs(y);
```

The elements of an array are always being assigned the same value, but the assignment expression is still calculating the value each time. Applying code motion, this code is automatically converted to:

```
int t1 = x * Maths.abs(y);
for (int i = 0; i < z.length; i++)
  z[i] = t1;
```

Code motion is also useful in eliminating or reducing redundant tests (though compilers are usually less effective at this). Consider the following method:

```
public String aMethod(String first, String passed)
{
  StringBuffer copy = new StringBuffer(passed);
  if (first == null || first.length() == 0)
   return passed;
  else
  {
    ...//some manipulation of the string buffer to do something
    return copy.toString();
  }
}
```

This method creates an unnecessary new object if the first string is null or zero length. This should be recoded or bytecodes should be generated so that the new object creation is moved to the else clause:

```
public String aMethod(String first, String passed)
{
  if (first == null || first.length() == 0)
   return passed;
  else
  {
    StringBuffer copy = new StringBuffer(passed);
    ...//some manipulation of the string buffer to do something
    return copy.toString();
  }
}
```

It would be nice, but difficult, for a compiler to apply this automatically, but this type of optimization probably needs to be applied manually. For the compiler to apply this sort of optimization, it needs to know that creating a new StringBuffer has no side effects so that the creation can reasonably be moved to a different part of the code.

Both this technique and the next one are good coding practices.

Eliminate common subexpressions

Eliminating common subexpressions is similar to code motion. In this case, though, the compiler identifies an expression that is common to more than one statement and does not need to be calculated more than once. The following example uses the same calculation twice to map two pairs of variables:

```
z1 = x * Maths.abs(y) + x;
z2 = x * Maths.abs(y) + y;
```

After a compiler has analyzed this code to eliminate the common subexpression, the code becomes:

```
int t1 = x * Maths.abs(y);
z1 = t1 + x;
z2 = t1 + y;
```

Eliminate unnecessary assignments

An optimizing compiler should eliminate any unnecessary assignments. The following example is very simplistic:

```
int x = 1;
x = 2;
```

This should obviously be converted into one statement:

```
int x = 2;
```

Although you won't often see this type of example, it is not unusual for chained constructors to repeatedly assign to an instance variable in essentially the same way. An optimizing compiler should eliminate all extra unnecessary assignments.

Rename classes, fields, and methods

Some compilers rename classes, fields, and methods for various reasons, such as to obfuscate the code (making it difficult to understand if it were decompiled). Renaming (especially to one-character names*) can make everything compiled much smaller, significantly reducing classloading times and network download times.

Reorder or change bytecodes

An optimizing compiler can reorder or change bytecode instructions to make methods faster. Normally, this reduces the number of instructions, but sometimes making an activity faster requires increasing the number of instructions. An example is where a switch statement is used with a list of unordered, nearly consecutive values for case statements. An optimizing compiler can reorder the case statements so that the values are in order, insert extra cases to make the values fully consecutive, and

---

* For example, the DashO optimizer renames everything possible to one-character names.

then use a faster switch bytecode to execute the switch statement. The optimization for switch statements is extensively covered in Chapter 7.

Generate information to help a VM

The Java bytecode specification provides support for optional extra information to be included with class files. This information can be VM-specific: any VM that does not understand the codes must ignore them. Consequently, it is possible that a particular compiler may be optimized (in the future) to generate extra information that allows particular VMs to run code faster. For example, it would be possible for the compiler to add extra information that tells the VM the optimal way in which a JIT should compile the code, thus removing some of the JIT workload (and overhead).

A more extreme example might be where a compiler generates optimized native code for several CPUs in addition to the bytecode for methods in the class file. This would allow a VM to execute the native code immediately if it were running on one of the supported CPUs. Unfortunately, this particular example would cause a security loophole, as there would be no guarantee to the VM that the natively compiled method was the equivalent of the bytecode-generated one.

Managing Compilers

All the optimizations previously listed are optimizations that compilers should automatically handle. Unfortunately, you are not guaranteed that any particular compiler actually applies any single optimization. The only way I have found to be certain about the optimizations a particular compiler can make is to compile code with lines such as those shown previously, then decompile the bytecodes to see what comes out. There are several decompilers available on the Net: a web search for "java+decompile" should fetch a few. My personal favorite at the time of this writing is *jad* by Pavel Kouznetsov, which currently resides at *http://kpdus.tripod.com/jad.html*.

Several Java compilers are targeted at optimizing bytecode, and several other compilers (including all mainstream ones) have announced the intention to roll more optimizations into future versions. This highlights another point: ensure that you use the compiler's latest version. It may be that, for robustness, you do not want to go into production with the very latest compiler, as that will have been less tested than an older version, and your own code will have been more thoroughly tested on the classes generated by the older compiler. Nevertheless, you should at least test whether the latest compiler gives your application a boost (using whatever standard benchmarks you choose to assess your application's performance).

Finally, the compiler you select to generate bytecode may not be the same compiler you use while developing code. You may even have different compilers for different parts of development and even for different optimizations (though this is unlikely).

In any case, you need to be sure the deployed application is using the bytecodes generated by the specific compilers you have chosen for the final version. At times in large projects, I have seen some classes recompiled with the wrong compiler. This has occasionally resulted in some of these classes finding their way to the deployed version of the application.

This alternate recompilation does not affect the correctness of the application because all compilers should be generating correct bytecodes, which means that such a situation allows the application to pass all regression test suites. But you can end up with the production application not running as fast as you expect for reasons that are difficult to track down.

Sun's Compiler and Runtime Optimizations

As you can see from the previous sections, knowing how the compiler alters your code as it generates bytecodes is important for performance tuning. Some compiler optimizations can be canceled out if you write your code so that the compiler cannot apply its optimizations. In this section, I cover what you need to know to get the most out of the compilation stage if you are using the JDK compiler (*javac*).

Optimizations You Get for Free

Several optimizations occur at the compilation stage without your needing to specify any compilation options. These optimizations are not necessarily required because of specifications laid down in Java. Instead, they have become standard compiler optimizations. The JDK compiler always applies them, and consequently almost every other compiler applies them as well. You should always determine exactly what your specific compiler optimizes as standard, from the documentation provided or by decompiling example code.

Literal constants are folded

This optimization is a concrete implementation of the ideas discussed in the "Replace runtime computations with compiled results" section earlier. In this implementation, multiple literal constants* in an expression are "folded" by the compiler. For example, in the following statement:

```
int foo = 9*10;
```

the 9*10 is evaluated to 90 before compilation is completed. The result is as if the line read:

```
int foo = 90;
```

---

* Literals are data items that can be identified as numbers, double-quoted strings, and characters, for example, 3, 44.5e-22F, 0xffee, "h", "hello", etc.

This optimization allows you to make your code more readable without having to worry about avoiding runtime overhead.

String concatenation is sometimes folded

With the Java 2 compiler, string concatenations to literal constants are folded. The line:

```
String foo = "hi Joe " + (9*10);
```

is compiled as if it read:

```
String foo = "hi Joe 90";
```

This optimization is not applied with JDK compilers prior to JDK 1.2. Some non-Sun compilers apply this optimization and some don't. The optimization applies where the statement can be resolved into literal constants concatenated with a literal string using the + concatenation operator. This optimization also applies to concatenation of two strings. In this last case, all compilers fold two (or more) strings since that action is required by the Java specification.

Constant fields are inlined

Primitive constant fields (those primitive data type fields defined with the final modifier) are inlined within a class and across classes, regardless of whether the classes are compiled in the same pass. For example, if class A has a public static final field, and class B has a reference to this field, the value from class A is inserted directly into class B, rather than a reference to the field in class A. Strictly speaking, this is not an optimization, as the Java specification requires constant fields to be inlined. Nevertheless, you can take advantage of it.

For instance, if class A is defined as:

```
public class A
{
  public static final int VALUE = 33;
}
```

and class B is defined as:

```
public class B
{
  static int VALUE2 = A.VALUE;
}
```

When class B is compiled, whether or not in a compilation pass of its own, it actually ends up as if it were defined as:

```
public class B
{
  static int VALUE2 = 33;
}
```

with no reference left to class A.

Dead code branches are eliminated

Another type of optimization automatically applied at the compilation stage is to cut code that can never be reached because of a test in an `if` statement that can be completely resolved at compile time. The discussion in the earlier section "Cut dead code and unnecessary instructions, including checks for null" is relevant to this section.

As an example, suppose classes A and B are defined (in separate files) as:

```
public class A
{
  public static final boolean DEBUG = false;
}

public class B
{
  static int foo( )
  {
    if (A.DEBUG)
      System.out.println("In B.foo( )");
    return 55;
  }
}
```

Then when class B is compiled, whether or not on a compilation pass of its own, it actually ends up as if it were defined as:

```
public class B
{
  static int foo( )
  {
    return 55;
  }
}
```

No reference is left to class A, and no `if` statement is left. The consequence of this feature is to allow conditional compilation. Other classes can set a DEBUG constant in their own class the same way, or they can use a shared constant value (as class B used A.DEBUG in the earlier definition).

 A problem is frequently encountered with this kind of code. The constant value is set when the class with the constant, say class A, is compiled. Any other class referring to class A's constant takes the value that is currently set when that class is being compiled, and does not reset the value if A is recompiled. So you can have the situation where A is compiled with A.DEBUG set to false, then B is compiled and the compiler inlines A.DEBUG as false, possibly cutting dead code branches. Then if A is recompiled to set A.DEBUG to true, this does not affect class B; the compiled class B still has the value false inlined, and any dead code branches stay eliminated until class B is recompiled. You should be aware of this possible problem if you compile your classes in more than one pass.

You should use this pattern for debug and trace statements and assertion pre-conditions, postconditions, and invariants. There is more detail on this technique in "Conditional Error Checking" in Chapter 6.

Optimizations Performed When Using the -O Option

The only *standard* compile-time option that can improve performance with the JDK compiler is the -0 option. Note that -0 (for Optimize) is a common option for compilers, and further optimizing options for other compilers often take the form -01, -02, etc. Check your compiler's documentation to find out what other options are available and what they do. Some compilers allow you to make the tradeoff between optimizing the compiled code for speed or minimizing the size.

The standard -0 option does not currently apply a variety of optimizations in the Sun JDK (up to JDK 1.4). In future versions it may do more, though the trend has actually been for it to do less. Currently, the option makes the compiler eliminate optional tables in the class files, such as line number and local variable tables. This gives only a small performance improvement by making class files smaller and therefore faster to load. You should definitely use this option if your class files are sent across a network.

The main performance improvement of using the -0 option used to come from the compiler inlining methods. When using the -0 option with javac prior to SDK 1.3, the compiler considered inlining methods defined with any of the following modifiers: private, static, or final. Some methods, such as those defined as synchronized, are never inlined. If a method can be inlined, the compiler decides whether or not to inline it depending on its own unpublished considerations. These considerations seem mainly to be the simplicity of the method: in JDK 1.2 the compiler inlined only fairly simple methods. For example, one-line methods with no side effects, such as accessing or updating a variable, are invariably inlined. Methods that return just a constant are also inlined. Multiline methods are inlined if the compiler determines they are simple enough (e.g., a System.out.println("blah") followed by a return statement would get inlined). From 1.3, the -0 option does not even inline methods. Instead, inlining is left to the HotSpot compiler, which can speculatively inline and is far more aggressive. The sidebar "Why There Are Limits on Static Inlining" discusses one of the reasons why optimizations such as inlining have been pushed back to the HotSpot compiler.

Choosing simple methods to inline does have a rationale behind it. The larger the method being inlined, the more the code gets bloated with copies of the same code inserted in many places. This has runtime costs in extra code being loaded and extra space taken by the runtime system. A JIT VM would also have the extra cost of compiling more code. At some point, there is a decrease in performance from inlining too much code. In addition, some methods have side effects that can make them quite difficult to inline correctly. All this also applies to runtime JIT compilation.

Why There Are Limits on Static Inlining

The compiler can inline only those methods that can be statically bound at compile time. To see why, consider the following example of class A and its subclass B, with two methods defined, foo1( ) and foo2( ). The foo2( ) method is overridden in the subclass:

```
class A {
  public int foo1( ) {return foo2( );}
  public int foo2( ) {return 5;}
}

public class B extends A {
  public int foo2( ) {return 10;}
}
```

If A.foo2( ) is inlined into A.foo1( ), (new B( )).foo1( ) incorrectly returns 5 instead of 10 because A is compiled incorrectly as if it read:

```
class A {
  public int foo1( ) {return 5;}
  public int foo2( ) {return 5;}
}
```

Any method that can be overridden at runtime cannot be validly inlined (it is a potential bug if it is). The Java specification states that final methods can be non-final at runtime. That is, you can compile a set of classes with one class having a final method, but later recompile that class without the method as final (thus allowing subclasses to override it), and the other classes must run correctly. For this reason, not all final methods can be identified as statically bound at compile time, so not all final methods can be inlined. Some earlier compiler versions incorrectly inlined some final methods, sometimes causing serious bugs.

The static compiler applies its methodology for selecting methods to inline, irrespective of whether the target method is in a bottleneck: this is a machine-gun strategy of many little optimizations in the hope that some inline calls may improve the bottlenecks. A performance tuner applying inlining works the other way around, first finding the bottlenecks, then selectively inlining methods inside bottlenecks. This latter strategy can result in good speedups, especially in loop bottlenecks. This is because a loop can be speeded up significantly by removing the overhead of a repeated method call. If the method to be inlined is complex, you can often factor out parts of the method so that those parts can be executed outside the loop, gaining even more speedup. HotSpot applies the latter rationale to inlining code only in bottlenecks.

I have not found any public document that specifies the actual decision-making process that determines whether or not a method is inlined, whether by static compilation or by the HotSpot compiler. The only reference given is to Section 13.4.21 of the

Java language specification that specifies only that binary compatibility with preexisting binaries must be maintained. It does specify that the package must be guaranteed to be kept together for the compiler to allow inlining across classes. The specification also states that the final keyword does not imply that a method can be inlined since the runtime system may have a differently implemented method. The HotSpot documentation does state that simple methods are inlined, but again no real details are provided.

Prior to JDK 1.2, the -0 option used with the Sun compiler did inline methods across classes, even if they were not compiled in the same compilation pass. This behavior led to bugs.* From JDK 1.2, the -0 option no longer inlines methods across classes, even if they are compiled in the same compilation pass.

Unfortunately, there is no way to specify directly which methods should be inlined rather than relying on some compiler's internal workings. Possibly in the future, some compiler vendors will provide a mechanism that supports specifying which methods to inline, along with other preprocessor options. In the meantime, you can implement a preprocessor (or use an existing one) if you require tighter control. Opportunities for inlining often occur inside bottlenecks (especially in loops), as discussed previously. Selective inlining by hand can give an order-of-magnitude speedup for some bottlenecks, and no speedup at all in others. Relying on HotSpot to detect these kinds of situations is an option.

The speedup obtained purely from inlining is usually only a small percentage: 5% is fairly common. Some static optimizing compilers are very aggressive about inlining code. They apply techniques such as analyzing the entire program to alter and eliminate method calls in order to identify methods that can be coerced into being statically bound. Then these identified methods are inlined as much as possible according to the compiler's analysis. This technique has been shown to give a 50% speedup to some applications.

Performance Effects From Runtime Options

Some runtime options can help your application to run faster. These include:

- Options that allow the VM to have a bigger footprint (-Xmx/-mx is the main one, which allows a larger heap space; but see the comments in the following paragraph).
- -noverify, which eliminates the overhead of verifying classes at classload time (not available from 1.2).

---

* Primarily methods that accessed private or protected variables were incorrectly inlined into other classes, leading to runtime authorization exceptions.

Some options are detrimental to the application performance. These include:

- The -Xrunhprof option, which makes applications run 10% to 1000% slower (-prof in 1.1).
- Removing the JIT compiler (done with -Djava.compiler=NONE in JDK 1.2 and beyond, and with the -nojit option in 1.1).
- -debug, which runs a slower VM with debugging enabled.
- The various alternative garbage-collection strategies like -Xincgc and -Xconcgc are aimed at minimizing some aspect (pause times for these two), but the consequence is that total GC is slower.

Some options can be both detrimental to performance and help make a faster application, depending on how they are used. These include:

- -Xcomp, which forces HotSpot to compile 100% of the code with maximum optimization. This makes the first pass through the code very slow indeed, but subsequent passes should be faster.
- -Xbatch, which forces HotSpot to compile methods in the foreground. Normally methods are compiled in the foreground if they compile quickly. Compilation is moved to the background if it is taking too long (the method carries on executing in interpreted mode until the compilation is finished). This makes the first execution of methods slower, but subsequent executions can be faster if compilation would not have otherwise finished.

Increasing the maximum heap size beyond the default usually improves performance for applications that can use the extra space. However, there is a tradeoff in higher space-management costs to the VM (object table access, garbage collections, etc.), and at some point there is no longer any benefit in increasing the maximum heap size. Increasing the heap size actually causes garbage collection to take longer since it needs to examine more objects and a larger space. Up to now, I have found no better method than trial and error to determine optimal maximum heap sizes for any particular application. This is covered in more detail earlier in this chapter.

Beware of accidentally using VM options detrimental to performance. I once had a customer who had a sudden 40% decrease in performance during tests. Their performance harness had a configuration file that set up how the VM could be run, and this was accidentally set to include the -prof option on the standard tests as well as for the profiling tests. That was the cause of the sudden performance decrease, but it was not discovered until time had been wasted checking software versions, system configurations, and other things.

Compile to Native Machine Code

If you know the target environments of your application, you have the option of taking your Java application and compiling it to a machine-code executable. A variety of these compilers target various platforms, and the list continues to grow. (Check the computer magazines or follow the compiler links on good Java web sites. See also the compilers listed in Chapter 19 and at *http://www.JavaPerformanceTuning.com/ resources.shtml*.) These compilers often work directly from the bytecode (i.e., the *.class* files) without the source code, so any third-party classes and beans you use can normally be included.

If you use this option, a standard technique to remain multiplatform is to start the application from a batch file that checks the platform and installs (or even starts) the application binary appropriate for that platform, falling back to the standard Java runtime if no binary is available. Of course, the batch file also needs to be multiplatform, but then you could build it in Java.

Prepare to be disappointed with the performance of a natively compiled executable compared to the latest JIT-enabled runtime VMs. The compiled executable still needs to handle garbage collection, threads, exceptions, etc., all within the confines of the executable. These runtime features of Java do not necessarily compile efficiently into an executable. The performance of the executable may well depend on how much effort the compiler vendor has made in making those Java features run efficiently in the context of a natively compiled executable. The latest adaptive VMs have been shown to run some applications faster than the equivalent natively compiled executable.

Advocates of the "compile to native executable" approach feel that the compiler optimizations will improve with time so that this approach will ultimately deliver the fastest applications. Luckily, this is a win-win situation for the performance of Java applications: try out both approaches if appropriate to you, and choose the one that works best.

There are also several translators that convert Java programs into C. I only include a mention of these translators for completeness, as I have not tried any of them. They presumably enable you to use a standard C compiler to compile to a variety of target platforms. However, most source code–to–source code translations between programming languages are suboptimal and do not usually generate fast code.

Native Method Calls

For that extra zing in your application (but probably not applet), try out calls to native code. Wave goodbye to 100% pure Java certification, and say hello to added complexity in your development environment and deployment procedure. (If you are already in this situation for reasons other than performance tuning, there is little overhead to taking this route in your project.)

I've seen native method calls used for performance reasons in earlier Java versions when doing intensive number-crunching for a scientific application and parsing large amounts of data in a restricted time. In these and other cases, the runtime application environment at the time could not get to the required speed using Java. I should note that a parsing application would now be able to run fast enough in pure Java, but the original application was built with quite an early version. In addition, some number crunchers find that the latest Java runtimes and optimizing compilers give them sufficient performance in Java without resorting to any native calls.[*]

The JNI interface itself has its own overhead, which means that if a pure Java implementation comes close to the native call performance, the JNI overhead probably cancels any performance advantages from the native call. However, on occasion the underlying system can provide an optimized native call that is not available from Java and cannot be implemented to work as fast in pure Java. In this kind of situation, JNI is useful for tuning.

Another case in which JNI can be useful is reducing the number of objects created, though this should be less common: you should normally be able to do this directly in Java. I once encountered a situation where JNI was needed to avoid excessive objects. This was with an application that originally required the use of a native DLL service. The vendor of that DLL ported the service to Java, which the application developers would have preferred using, but unfortunately the vendor neglected to tune the ported code. This resulted in a native call to a particular set of services producing just a couple dozen objects, but the Java-ported code producing nearly 10,000 objects. Apart from this difference, the speeds of the two implementations were similar.[†] However, the overhead in garbage collection caused a significant degradation in performance, which meant that the native call to the DLL was the preferred option.

If you are following the native function call route, there is little to say. You write your routines in C, plug them into your application using the native keyword, profile the resultant application, and confirm that it provides the required speedup. You can also use C (or C++ or whatever) profilers to profile the native code calls if it is complicated.

Other than this, only a few recommendations apply:

- If you are calling the native routines from loops, you should move the loops down into the native routines and pass the loop parameters to the routine as arguments. This usually produces faster implementations.

---

[*] Serious number crunchers spend a large proportion of their time performance-tuning their code, whatever language it is written in. To gain sufficient performance in Java, they of course need to tune the application intensively. But this is also true if the application is written in C or Fortran. The amount of tuning required is now, apparently, similar for these three languages. Further information can be found at *http://www.javagrande.org*.

[†] This increase in object creation normally results in a much slower implementation. However, in this particular case, the methods required synchronizing to a degree that gave a larger overhead than the object creation. Nevertheless, the much larger number of objects created by the untuned Java implementation needed reclaiming at some point, and this led to greater overhead in the garbage collection.

- In a similar but more generic vein, try to avoid crossing the JNI.

- Avoid passing objects across JNI if possible. Where necessary, try to pass primitive types. If it is necessary to pass objects such as arrays, try to do as much data movement as possible in one transfer to minimize transfer overhead.

- From 1.4, native `ByteBuffer`s (available with the `java.nio` packages) allow you to pass data to native libraries without necessarily passing the data through the JNI, which can be a significant gain. You can allocate a native `ByteBuffer` in the C code and pass the pointer through the JNI, avoiding the JNI data transfer overhead. (At least one animation application has actually allocated memory on the graphics card as a native `ByteBuffer`, and manipulated that `ByteBuffer` from the Java side.)

- If you use JNI `Get` calls (e.g., `GetStringCritical`), you must always use the corresponding `Release` call (e.g., `ReleaseStringCritical`) when you have finished with the data, even if the `isCopy` parameter indicates that no copy was taken.

One other recommendation, which is not performance tuning–specific, is that it is usually good practice to provide a fallback methodology for situations when the native code cannot be loaded. This requires extra maintenance (two sets of code, extra fallback code) but is often worth the effort. You can manage the fallback at the time when the DLL library is being loaded by catching the exception when the load fails and providing an alternative path to the fallback code, either by setting boolean switches or by instantiating objects of the appropriate fallback classes as required.

Uncompressed ZIP/JAR Files

It is better to deliver your classes in a ZIP or JAR file than to deliver them one class at a time over the network or load them individually from separate files in the filesystem. This packaged delivery provides some of the benefits of clustering* (see "Clustering Files" in Chapter 14). The benefits gained from packaging class files come from reducing I/O overhead such as repeated file opening and closing, and possibly improving seek times.† Within the ZIP or JAR file, the classes should not be compressed unless network download time is a factor for the application. The best way to deliver local classes for performance reasons is in an uncompressed ZIP or JAR file. Coincidentally, that's how they're delivered with the SDK.

It is possible to further improve the classloading times by packing the classes into the ZIP/JAR file in the order in which they are loaded by the application. You can

---

* "Clustering" is an unfortunately overloaded word, and is often used to refer to closely linked groups of server machines. In the context here, I use "clustering" to mean the close grouping of files.

† With operating system–monitoring tools, you can see the system temporarily stalling when the operating system issues a disk-cache flush if lots of files are closed around the same time. If you use a single packed file for all classes (and resources), you avoid this potential performance hit.

determine the loading order by running the application with the -verbose option, but note that this ordering is fragile: slight changes in the application can easily alter the loading order of classes. A further extension to this idea is to include your own classloader that opens the ZIP/JAR file itself and reads in all files sequentially, loading them into memory immediately. Perhaps the final version of this performance-improvement route is to dispense with the ZIP/JAR filesystem: it is quicker to load the files if they are concatenated together in one big file, with a header at the start of the file giving the offsets and names of the contained files. This is similar to the ZIP filesystem, but it is better if you read the header in one block, and read in and load the files directly rather than going through the java.util.zip classes.

One further optimization to this classloading tactic is to start the classloader running in a separate (low-priority) thread immediately after VM startup.

Performance Checklist

Many of these suggestions apply only after a bottleneck has been identified:

- Test your benchmarks on each version of Java available to you (classes, compiler, and VM) to identify any performance improvements.
  - Test performance using the target VM or "best practice" VMs.
  - Avoid using VM options that are detrimental to performance.
- Include some tests of the garbage collector appropriate to your application, so that you can identify changes that minimize the cost of garbage collection in your application.
  - Run your application with both the -verbosegc option and with full application tracing turned on to see when the garbage collector kicks in and what it is doing.
  - Vary the -Xmx/-Xms option values to determine the optimal memory sizes for your application.
  - Fine-tuning the heap is possible, but requires knowledge of the GC algorithm and the many parameter options available.
  - Sharing memory between multiple VMs is easy with the Echidna library. This can also provide prestarted VMs for faster startup.
  - Use -noclassgc/-Xnoclassgc to avoid having classes repeatedly reloaded.
- Replace generic classes with more specific implementations dedicated to the data type being manipulated, e.g., implement a LongVector to hold longs rather than using a Vector object with Long wrappers.
  - Extend collection classes to access internal arrays for queries on the class.
  - Replace collection objects with arrays where the collection object is a bottleneck.

- Try various compilers. Look for compilers targeted at optimizing performance: these provide the cheapest significant speedup for all runtime environments.
  - Use the -0 option (but always check that it does not produce slower code).
  - Identify the optimizations a compiler is capable of so that you do not negate the optimizations.
  - Use a decompiler to determine precisely the optimizations generated by a particular compiler.
  - Consider using a preprocessor to apply some standard compiler optimizations more precisely.
  - Remember that an optimizing compiler can only optimize algorithms, not change them. A better algorithm is usually faster than an optimized slow algorithm.
  - Include optimizing compilers from the early stages of development.
  - Make sure that the deployed classes have been compiled with the correct compilers.
- Make sure that any loops using native method calls are converted so that the native call includes the loop instead of running the loop in Java. Any loop iteration parameters should be passed to the native call.
  - Minimize the number of data transfers through the JNI. Native `ByteBuffers` can help.
- Deliver classes in uncompressed format in ZIP or JAR files (unless network download time is significant, in which case files should be compressed).
- Use a customized classloader running in a separate thread to load class files.

CHAPTER 4
Object Creation

In this chapter:
- Object-Creation Statistics
- Object Reuse
- Reference Objects
- Avoiding Garbage Collection
- Initialization
- Early and Late Initialization

*The biggest difference between time and space is that
you can't reuse time.*
—Merrick Furst

"I thought that I didn't need to worry about memory allocation. Java is supposed to handle all that for me." This is a common perception, which is both true and false. Java handles low-level memory allocation and deallocation and comes with a garbage collector. Further, it prevents access to these low-level memory-handling routines, making the memory safe. So memory access should not cause corruption of data in other objects or in the running application, which is potentially the most serious problem that can occur with memory-access violations. In a C or C++ program, problems of illegal pointer manipulations can be a major headache (e.g., deleting memory more than once, runaway pointers, bad casts). They are very difficult to track down and are likely to occur when changes are made to existing code. Java deals with all these possible problems and, at worst, will throw an exception immediately if memory is incorrectly accessed.

However, Java does not prevent you from using excessive amounts of memory nor from cycling through too much memory (e.g., creating and dereferencing many objects). Contrary to popular opinion, you can get memory leaks (or, more accurately, object retention) by holding onto objects without releasing references. This stops the garbage collector from reclaiming those objects, resulting in increasing amounts of memory being used.[*] In addition, Java does not provide for large numbers of objects to be created simultaneously (as you could do in C by allocating a large buffer), which eliminates one powerful technique for optimizing object creation.

Creating objects costs time and CPU effort for an application. Garbage collection and memory recycling cost more time and CPU effort. The difference in object usage

---

[*] For more information, see Ethan Henry and Ed Lycklama's article "How Do You Plug Memory Leaks?", *Dr. Dobb's Journal*, February 2000, *http://www.ddj.com/documents/s=888/ddj0002l/0002l.htm*.

between two algorithms can make a huge difference. In Chapter 5, I cover algorithms for appending basic data types to StringBuffer objects. These can be an order of magnitude faster than some of the conversions supplied with Java. A significant portion of the speedup is obtained by avoiding extra temporary objects used and discarded during the data conversions.[*]

Here are a few general guidelines for using object memory efficiently:

- Avoid creating objects in frequently used routines. Because these routines are called frequently, you will likely be creating objects frequently, and consequently adding heavily to the overall burden of object cycling. By rewriting such routines to avoid creating objects, possibly by passing in reusable objects as parameters, you can decrease object cycling.

- Try to presize any collection object to be as big as it will need to be. It is better for the object to be slightly bigger than necessary than to be smaller than it needs to be. This recommendation really applies to collections that implement size increases in such a way that objects are discarded. For example, Vector grows by creating a new larger internal array object, copying all the elements from the old array, and discarding it. Most collection implementations have similar implementations for growing the collection beyond its current capacity, so presizing a collection to its largest potential size reduces the number of objects discarded.

- When multiple instances of a class need access to a particular object in a variable local to those instances, it is better to make that variable static rather than have each instance hold a separate reference. This reduces the space taken by each object (one fewer instance variable) and can also reduce the number of objects created if each instance creates a separate object to populate that instance variable.

- Reuse exception instances when you do not specifically require a stack trace (see "Exceptions" in Chapter 6).

This chapter presents many other standard techniques to avoid using too many objects and identifies some known inefficiencies when using some types of objects.

Object-Creation Statistics

Objects need to be created before they can be used, and garbage-collected when they are finished with. The more objects you use, the heavier this garbage-cycling impact becomes. General object-creation statistics are actually quite difficult to measure decisively, since you must decide exactly what to measure, what size to pregrow the

---

[*] Up to SDK 1.4, data-conversion and object-lifecycle performance has been targeted by Sun. In 1.4, the core SDK int conversion is faster, but all other data type conversions are still significantly slower.

heap space to, how much garbage collection impacts the creation process if you let it kick in, etc.

For example, on a medium Pentium II, with heap space pregrown so that garbage collection does not have to kick in, you can get around half a million to a million simple objects created per second. If the objects are very simple, even more can be garbage-collected in one second. On the other hand, if the objects are complex, with references to other objects, and include arrays (like Vector and StringBuffer) and nonminimal constructors, the statistics plummet to less than a quarter of a million created per second, and garbage collection can drop way down to below 100,000 objects per second. Each object creation is roughly as expensive as a *malloc* in C, or a *new* in C++, and there is no easy way of creating many objects together, so you cannot take advantage of efficiencies you get using bulk allocation.

There are already runtime systems that use generational garbage collection, minimize object-creation overhead, and optimize native-code compilation. By doing this they reach up to three million objects created and collected per second (on a Pentium II), and it is likely that the average Java system should improve to get closer to that kind of performance over time. But these figures are for basic tests, optimized to show the maximum possible object-creation throughput. In a normal application with varying size objects and constructor chains, these sorts of figures cannot be obtained or even approached. Also bear in mind that you are doing nothing else in these tests apart from creating objects. In most applications, you are doing something with all those objects, making everything much slower but significantly more useful. Avoidable object creation is definitely a significant overhead for most applications, and you can easily run through millions of temporary objects using inefficient algorithms that create too many objects. In Chapter 5, we look at an example that uses the StreamTokenizer class. This class creates and dereferences a huge number of objects while it parses a stream, and the effect is to slow down processing to a crawl. The example in Chapter 5 presents a simple alternative to using a StreamTokenizer, which is 100 times faster: a large percentage of the speedup is gained from avoiding cycling through objects.

Object Reuse

As we saw in the last section, objects are expensive to create. Where it is reasonable to reuse the same object, you should do so. You need to be aware of when not to call new. One fairly obvious situation is when you have already used an object and can discard it before you are about to create another object of the same class. You should look at the object and consider whether it is possible to reset the fields and then reuse the object, rather than throw it away and create another. This can be particularly important for objects that are constantly used and discarded: for example, in graphics processing, objects such as Rectangles, Points, Colors, and Fonts are used and discarded all the time. Recycling these types of objects can certainly improve performance.

Recycling can also apply to the internal elements of structures. For example, a linked list has nodes added to it as it grows, and as it shrinks, the nodes are discarded. Holding onto the discarded nodes is an obvious way to recycle these objects and reduce the cost of object creation.

Pool Management

Most container objects (e.g., Vectors, Hashtables) can be reused rather than created and thrown away. Of course, while you are not using the retained objects, you are holding onto more memory than if you simply discarded those objects, and this reduces the memory available to create other objects. You need to balance the need to have some free memory available against the need to improve performance by reusing objects. But generally, the space taken by retaining objects for later reuse is significant only for very large collections, and you should certainly know which ones these are in your application.

Note that when recycling container objects, you need to dereference all the elements previously in the container so that you don't prevent them from being garbage-collected. Because there is this extra overhead in recycling, it may not always be worth recycling containers. As usual for tuning, this technique is best applied to ameliorate an object-creation bottleneck that has already been identified.

Pooling objects has become slightly controversial recently. In their HotSpot FAQ, Sun engineering states that pooling should definitely no longer be used because it actually gives worse performance with the latest HotSpot engines. This is rather a sweeping statement. Object pools are still useful even with HotSpot, but presumably not as often as before. Certainly for shared resources pooling will always be an option if the overhead associated with creating a shareable resource is expensive. Various recent tests have shown that the efficiency of pooling objects compared to creating and disposing of objects is highly dependent on the size and complexity of the objects. And in some applications where deterministic behavior is important, especially J2ME applications, it is worth noting that object pools have deterministic access and reclamation costs for both CPU and memory, whereas object creation and garbage collection can be less deterministic.

A good strategy for reusing container objects is to use your own container classes, possibly wrapping other containers. This gives you a high degree of control over each collection object, and you can design them specifically for reuse. You can still use a pool manager to manage your requirements, even without reuse-designed classes. Reusing classes requires extra work when you've finished with a collection object, but the effort is worth it when reuse is possible. The code fragment here shows how you could use a vector pool manager:

```
//An instance of the vector pool manager.
public static VectorPoolManager vectorPoolManager =
    new VectorPoolManager(25);
```

```
...

public void someMethod( )
{
  //Get a new Vector. We only use the vector to do some stuff
  //within this method, and then we dump the vector (i.e., it
  //is not returned or assigned to a state variable)
  //so this is a perfect candidate for reusing Vectors.
  //Use a factory method instead of 'new Vector( )'
  Vector v = vectorPoolManager.getVector( );

  ... //do vector manipulation stuff

  //and the extra work is that we have to explicitly tell the
  //pool manager that we have finished with the vector
  vectorPoolManager.returnVector(v);
}
```

Note that nothing stops the application from retaining a handle on a vector after it has been returned to the pool, and obviously that could lead to a classic "inadvertent reuse of memory" bug. You need to ensure that handles to vectors are not held anywhere: these Vectors should be used only internally within an application, not externally in third-party classes where a handle may be retained. The following class manages a pool of Vectors:

```
package tuning.reuse;

import java.util.Vector;

public class VectorPoolManager
{

  Vector[ ] pool;
  boolean[ ] inUse;
  public VectorPoolManager(int initialPoolSize)
  {
    pool = new Vector[initialPoolSize];
    inUse = new boolean[initialPoolSize];
    for (int i = pool.length-1; i>=0; i--)
    {
      pool[i] = new Vector( );
      inUse[i] = false;
    }
  }

  public synchronized Vector getVector( )
  {
    for (int i = inUse.length-1; i >= 0; i--)
      if (!inUse[i])
      {
        inUse[i] = true;
        return pool[i];
      }
```

```
//If we got here, then all the Vectors are in use. We will
//increase the number in our pool by 10 (arbitrary value for
//illustration purposes).
boolean[ ] old_inUse = inUse;
inUse = new boolean[old_inUse.length+10];
System.arraycopy(old_inUse, 0, inUse, 0, old_inUse.length);

Vector[ ] old_pool = pool;
pool = new Vector[old_pool.length+10];
System.arraycopy(old_pool, 0, pool, 0, old_pool.length);

for (int i = old_pool.length; i < pool.length; i++)
{
  pool[i] = new Vector( );
  inUse[i] = false;
}

//and allocate the last Vector
inUse[pool.length-1] = true;
return pool[pool.length-1];
}

public synchronized void returnVector(Vector v)
{
  for (int i = inUse.length-1; i >= 0; i--)
    if (pool[i] == v)
    {
      inUse[i] = false;
      //Can use clear( ) for java.util.Collection objects
      //Note that setSize( ) nulls out all elements
      v.setSize(0);
      return;
    }
  throw new RuntimeException("Vector was not obtained from the pool: " + v);
}
}
```

Because you reset the Vector size to 0 when it is returned to the pool, all objects previously referenced from the vector are no longer referenced (the Vector.setSize( ) method nulls out all internal index entries beyond the new size to ensure no reference is retained). However, at the same time, you do not return any memory allocated to the Vector itself, because the Vector's current capacity is retained. A lazily initialized version of this class simply starts with zero items in the pool and sets the pool to grow by one or more each time.

(Many JDK collection classes, including java.util.Vector, have both a size and a capacity. The capacity is the number of elements the collection can hold before that collection needs to resize its internal memory to be larger. The size is the number of externally accessible elements the collection is actually holding. The capacity is always greater than or equal to the size. By holding spare capacity, elements can be added to collections without having to continually resize the underlying memory. This makes element addition faster and more efficient.)

ThreadLocals

The previous example of a pool manager can be used by multiple threads in a multi-threaded application, although the getVector( ) and returnVector( ) methods first need to be defined as synchronized. This may be all you need to ensure that you reuse a set of objects in a multithreaded application. Sometimes, though, there are objects you need to use in a more complicated way. It may be that the objects are used in such a way that you can guarantee you need only one object per thread, but any one thread must consistently use the same object. Singletons (see the "Canonicalizing Objects" section) that maintain some state information are a prime example of this sort of object.

In this case, you might want to use a ThreadLocal object. ThreadLocals have accessors that return an object local to the current thread. ThreadLocal use is best illustrated using an example like this, which produces:

```
[This is thread 0, This is thread 0, This is thread 0]
[This is thread 1, This is thread 1, This is thread 1]
[This is thread 2, This is thread 2, This is thread 2]
[This is thread 3, This is thread 3, This is thread 3]
[This is thread 4, This is thread 4, This is thread 4]
```

Each thread uses the same access method to obtain a vector to add some elements. The vector obtained by each thread is always the same vector for that thread: the ThreadLocal object always returns the thread-specific vector. As the following code shows, each vector has the same string added to it repeatedly, showing that it is always obtaining the same thread-specific vector from the vector access method. (Note that ThreadLocals are only available from Java 2, but it is easy to create the equivalent functionality using a Hashtable: see the getVectorPriorToJDK12( ) method.)

```
package tuning.reuse;

import java.util.*;

public class ThreadedAccess
  implements Runnable
{
  static int ThreadCount = 0;

  public void run( )
  {
    //simple test just accesses the thread local vector, adds the
    //thread specific string to it, and sleeps for two seconds before
    //again accessing the thread local and printing out the value.
    String s = "This is thread " + ThreadCount++;
    Vector v = getVector( );
    v.addElement(s);
```

```java
      v = getVector( );
      v.addElement(s);
      try{Thread.sleep(2000);}catch(Exception e){ }
      v = getVector( );
      v.addElement(s);
      System.out.println(v);
   }

   public static void main(String[ ] args)
   {
      try
      {
         //Four threads to see the multithreaded nature at work
         for (int i = 0; i < 5; i++)
         {
            (new Thread(new ThreadedAccess( ))).start( );
            try{Thread.sleep(200);}catch(Exception e){ }
         }
      }
      catch(Exception e){e.printStackTrace( );}
   }

   private static ThreadLocal vectors = new ThreadLocal( );
   public static Vector getVector( )
   {
      //Lazily initialized version. Get the thread local object
      Vector v = (Vector) vectors.get( );
      if (v == null)
      {
         //First time. So create a vector and set the ThreadLocal
         v = new Vector( );
         vectors.set(v);
      }
      return v;
   }

   private static Hashtable hvectors = new Hashtable( );
   /* This method is equivalent to the getVector( ) method,
    * but works prior to JDK 1.2 (as well as after).
    */
   public static Vector getVectorPriorToJDK12( )
   {
      //Lazily initialized version. Get the thread local object
      Vector v = (Vector) hvectors.get(Thread.currentThread( ));
      if (v == null)
      {
         //First time. So create a vector and set the thread local
         v = new Vector( );
         hvectors.put(Thread.currentThread( ), v);
      }
      return v;
   }
}
```

Reusable Parameters

Reuse also applies when a constant object is returned for information. For example, the preferredSize( ) of a customized widget returns a Dimension object that is normally one particular dimension. But to ensure that the stored unchanging Dimension value does not get altered, you need to return a copy of the stored Dimension. Otherwise, the calling method accesses the original Dimension object and can change the Dimension values, thus affecting the original Dimension object itself.

Java provides a final modifier to fields that allows you to provide fixed values for the Dimension fields. Unfortunately, you cannot redefine an already existing class, so Dimension cannot be redefined to have final fields. The best solution in this case is that a separate class, FixedDimension, be defined with final fields (this cannot be a subclass of Dimension, as the fields can't be redefined in the subclass). This extra class allows methods to return the same FixedDimension object if applicable, or a new FixedDimension is returned (as happens with Dimension) if the method requires different values to be returned for different states. Of course, it is too late now for java.awt to be changed in this way, but the principle remains.

Note that making a field final does not make an object unchangeable. It only disallows changes to the field:

```
public class FixedDimension {
  final int height;
  final int width;
  ...
}

//Both the following fields are defined as final
public static final Dimension dim = new Dimension(3,4);
public static final FixedDimension fixedDim = new FixedDimension(3,4);

dim.width = 5;           //reassignment allowed
dim = new Dimension(3,5);//reassignment disallowed
fixedDim.width = 5;      //reassignment disallowed
fixedDim = new FixedDimension(3,5); //reassignment disallowed
```

An alternative to defining preferredSize( ) to return a fixed object is to provide a method that accepts an object whose values will be set, e.g., preferredSize(Dimension). The caller can then pass in a Dimension object, which would have its values filled in by the preferredSize(Dimension) method. The calling method can then access the values in the Dimension object. This same Dimension object can be reused for multiple components. This design pattern is beginning to be used extensively within the JDK. Many methods developed with JDK 1.2 and onward accept a parameter that is filled in, rather than returning a copy of the master value of some object. If necessary, backward compatibility can be retained by adding this method as extra, rather than replacing an existing method:

```
public static final Dimension someSize = new Dimension(10,5);
//original definition returns a new Dimension.
```

```
public Dimension someSize( ) {
  Dimension dim = new Dimension(0,0);
  someSize(dim);
  return dim;
}
//New method which fills in the Dimension details in a passed parameter.
public void someSize(Dimension dim) {
  dim.width = someSize.width;
  dim.width = someSize.height;
}
```

Canonicalizing Objects

Wherever possible, you should replace multiple objects with a single object (or just a few). For example, if you need only one VectorPoolManager object, it makes sense to provide a static variable somewhere that holds this. You can even enforce this by making the constructor private and holding the singleton in the class itself; e.g., change the definition of VectorPoolManager to:

```
public class VectorPoolManager
{
  public static final VectorPoolManager SINGLETON =
    new VectorPoolManager(10);
  Vector[ ] pool;
  boolean[ ] inUse;

  //Make the constructor private to enforce that
  //no other objects can be created.
  private VectorPoolManager(int initialPoolSize)
  {
    ...
}
```

An alternative implementation is to make everything static (all methods and both the instance variables in the VectorPoolManager class). This also ensures that only one pool manager can be used. My preference is to have a SINGLETON object for design reasons.[*]

This activity of replacing multiple copies of an object with just a few objects is often referred to as *canonicalizing* objects. The Booleans provide an existing example of objects that should have been canonicalized in the JDK. They were not, and no longer can be without breaking backward compatibility. For Booleans, only two objects need to exist, but by allowing a new Boolean object to be created (by providing public constructors), you lose canonicalization. The JDK should have enforced

---

[*] The VectorPoolManager is really an object with behavior and state. It is not just a related group of functions (which is what class static methods are equivalent to). My colleague Kirk Pepperdine insists that this choice is more than just a preference. He states that holding onto an object as opposed to using statics provides more flexibility should you need to alter the use of the VectorPoolManager or provide multiple pools. I agree.

the existence of only two objects by keeping the constructors private. Note that canonical objects have another advantage in addition to reducing the number of objects created: they also allow comparison by identity. For example:

```
Boolean t1 = new Boolean(true);
System.out.println(t1==Boolean.TRUE);
System.out.println(t1.equals(Boolean.TRUE));
```

produces the output:

```
false
true
```

If Booleans had been canonicalized, all Boolean comparisons could be done by identity: comparison by identity is always faster than comparison by equality, because identity comparisons are simply pointer comparisons.[*]

You are probably better off not canonicalizing all objects that could be canonicalized. For example, the Integer class can (theoretically) have its instances canonicalized, but you need a map of some sort, and it is more efficient to allow multiple instances, rather than to manage a potential pool of four billion objects. However, the situation is different for particular applications. If you use just a few Integer objects in some defined way, you may find you are repeatedly creating the Integer objects with values 1, 2, 3, etc., and also have to access the integerValue( ) to compare them. In this case, you can canonicalize a few integer objects, improving performance in several ways: eliminating the extra Integer creations and the garbage collections of these objects when they are discarded, and allowing comparison by identity. For example:

```
public class IntegerManager
{
  public static final Integer ZERO = new Integer(0);
  public static final Integer ONE = new Integer(1);
  public static final Integer TWO = new Integer(2);
  public static final Integer THREE = new Integer(3);
  public static final Integer FOUR = new Integer(4);
  public static final Integer FIVE = new Integer(5);
  public static final Integer SIX = new Integer(6);
  public static final Integer SEVEN = new Integer(7);
  public static final Integer EIGHT = new Integer(8);
  public static final Integer NINE = new Integer(9);
  public static final Integer TEN = new Integer(10);
}

public class SomeClass
{
```

---

[*] Deserializing Booleans would have required special handling to return the canonical Boolean. All canonicalized objects similarly require special handling to manage serialization. Java serialization supports the ability, when deserializing, to return specific objects in place of the object that is normally created by the default deserialization mechanism.

```
public void doSomething(Integer i)
{
  //Assume that we are passed a canonicalized Integer
  if (i == IntegerManager.ONE)
   xxx();
 else if(i == IntegerManager.FIVE)
   yyy();
 else ...
}
...
}
```

There are various other frequently used objects throughout an application that should be canonicalized. A few that spring to mind are the empty string, empty arrays of various types, and some dates.

String canonicalization

There can be some confusion about whether Strings are already canonicalized. There is no guarantee that they are, although the compiler can canonicalize Strings that are equal and are compiled in the same pass. The String.intern() method canonicalizes strings in an internal table. This is supposed to be, and usually is, the same table used by strings canonicalized at compile time, but in some earlier JDK versions (e.g., 1.0), it was not the same table. In any case, there is no particular reason to use the internal string table to canonicalize your strings unless you want to compare Strings by identity (see "String Comparisons and Searches" in Chapter 5). Using your own table gives you more control and allows you to inspect the table when necessary. To see the difference between identity and equality comparisons for Strings, including the difference that String.intern() makes, you can run the following class:

```
public class Test
{
  public static void main(String[] args)
  {
    System.out.println(args[0]); //see that we have the empty string

    //should be true
    System.out.println(args[0].equals(""));

    //should be false since they are not identical objects
    System.out.println(args[0] == "");

    //should be true unless there are two internal string tables
    System.out.println(args[0].intern() == "");
  }
}
```

This Test class, when run with the command line:

```
% java Test ""
```

gives the output:

```
true
false
true
```

Changeable objects

Canonicalizing objects is best for read-only objects and can be troublesome for objects that change. If you canonicalize a changeable object and then change its state, then all objects that have a reference to the canonicalized object are still pointing to that object, but with the object's new state. For example, suppose you canonicalize a special Date value. If that object has its date value changed, all objects pointing to that Date object now see a different date value. This result may be desired, but more often it is a bug.

If you want to canonicalize changeable objects, one technique to make it slightly safer is to wrap the object with another one, or use your own (sub)class.* You then control all accesses and updates. If the object is not supposed to be changed, you can throw an exception on any update method. Alternatively, if you want some objects to be canonicalized but with copy-on-write behavior, you can allow the updater to return a noncanonicalized copy of the canonical object.

Note that it makes no sense to build a table of millions or even thousands of strings (or other objects) if the time taken to test for, access, and update objects in the table is longer than the time you are saving canonicalizing them.

Weak references

One technique for maintaining collections of objects that can grow too large is the use of WeakReferences (from the java.lang.ref package in Java 2). If you need to maintain one or more pools of objects with a large number of objects being held, you may start coming up against memory limits of the VM. In this case, you should consider using WeakReference objects to hold onto your pool elements. Objects referred to by WeakReferences can be automatically garbage-collected if memory gets low enough (see "Reference Objects" later in this chapter).

Java 2 comes with a java.util.WeakHashMap class that implements a hash table with keys held by weak references.

A WeakReference normally maintains references to elements in a table of canonicalized objects. If memory gets low, any of the objects referred to by the table and not referred to anywhere else in the application (except by other weak references) are garbage-collected. This does not affect the canonicalization because only those objects not referenced anywhere else are removed. The canonical object can be re-created

---

* Beware that using a subclass may break the superclass semantics.

when required, and this new instance is now the new canonical object: remember that no other references to the object exist, or the original could not have been garbage-collected.

For example, a table of canonical Integer objects can be maintained using WeakReferences. This example is not particularly useful: unlike the earlier example, in which Integer objects from 1 to 10 can be referenced directly with no overhead, thus providing a definite speedup for tests, the next example has overhead that probably overshadows any benefits of having canonical Integers. I present it only as a clear and simple example to illustrate the use of WeakReferences.

The example has two iterations: one sets an array of canonical Integer objects up to a value set by the command-line argument; a second loops through to access the first 10 canonical Integers. If the first loop is large enough (or the VM memory is constrained low enough), the garbage collector kicks in and starts reclaiming some of the Integer objects that are all being held by WeakReferences. The second loop then reaccesses the first 10 Integer objects. Earlier, I explicitly held onto five of these Integer objects (integers 3 to 7 inclusive) in variables so that they could not be garbage-collected and so that the second loop would reset only the five reclaimed Integers. When running this test with the VM constrained to 4 MB:

```
% java -Xmx4M  tuning.reuse.Test 100000
```

you get the following output:

```
Resetting integer 0
Resetting integer 1
Resetting integer 2
Resetting integer 8
Resetting integer 9
```

The example is defined here. Note the overhead. Even if the reference has not been garbage-collected, you have to access the underlying object and cast it to the desired type:

```
package tuning.reuse;

import java.util.*;
import java.lang.ref.*;

public class Test
{
  public static void main(String[ ] args)
  {
    try
    {
      Integer ic = null;
      int REPEAT = args.length > 0 ? Integer.parseInt(args[0]) : 10000000;

      //Hang onto the Integer objects from 3 to 7
      //so that they cannot be garbage collected
      Integer i3 = getCanonicalInteger(3);
```

```
    Integer i4 = getCanonicalInteger(4);
    Integer i5 = getCanonicalInteger(5);
    Integer i6 = getCanonicalInteger(6);
    Integer i7 = getCanonicalInteger(7);

    //Loop through getting canonical integers until there is not
    //enough space, and the garbage collector reclaims some.
    for (int i = 0; i < REPEAT; i++)
      ic = getCanonicalInteger(i);

    //Now just re-access the first 10 integers (0 to 9) and
    //the 0, 1, 2, 8, and 9 integers will need to be reset in
    //the access method since they will have been reclaimed
    for (int i = 0; i < 10; i++)
      ic = getCanonicalInteger(i);
    System.out.println(ic);
  }
  catch(Exception e){e.printStackTrace();}
}

private static Vector canonicalIntegers = new Vector();
public static Integer getCanonicalInteger(int i)
{
  //First make sure our collection is big enough
  if (i >= canonicalIntegers.size())
    canonicalIntegers.setSize(i+1);

  //Now access the canonical value.
  //This element contains null if the the value has never been set
  //or a weak reference that may have been garbage collected
  WeakReference ref = (WeakReference) canonicalIntegers.elementAt(i);
  Integer canonical_i;

  if (ref == null)
  {
    //never been set, so create and set it now
    canonical_i = new Integer(i);
    canonicalIntegers.setElementAt(new WeakReference(canonical_i), i);
  }
  else if( (canonical_i = (Integer) ref.get()) == null)
  {
    //has been set, but was garbage collected, so recreate and set it now
    //Include a print to see that we are resetting the Integer
    System.out.println("Resetting integer " + i);
    canonical_i = new Integer(i);
    canonicalIntegers.setElementAt(new WeakReference(canonical_i), i);
  }
  //else clause not needed, since the alternative is that the weak ref was
  //present and not garbage collected, so we now have our canonical integer
  return canonical_i;
}

}
```

Enumerating constants

Another canonicalization technique often used is replacing constant objects with integers. For example, rather than use the strings "female" and "male", you should use a constant defined in an interface:

```
public interface GENDER
{
  public static final int FEMALE=1;
  public static final int MALE=2;
}
```

Used consistently, this enumeration can provide both speed and memory advantages. The enumeration requires less memory than the equivalent strings and makes network transfers faster. Comparisons are faster too, as the identity comparison can be used instead of the equality comparison. For example, you can use:

```
this.gender == FEMALE;
```

instead of:

```
this.gender.equals("female");
```

Reference Objects

In many ways, you can think of Reference objects as normal objects that have a private Object instance variable. You can access the private object (termed the *referent*) using the Reference.get( ) method. However, Reference objects differ from normal objects in one hugely important way. The garbage collector may be allowed to clear Reference objects when it decides space is low enough. Clearing the Reference object sets the referent to null. For example, say you assign an object to a Reference. Later you test to see if the referent is null. It could be null if, between the assignment and the test, the garbage collector kicked in and decided to reclaim space:

```
Reference ref = new WeakReference(someObject);
//ref.get( ) is someObject at the moment
//Now do something that creates lots of objects, making
//the garbage collector try to find more memory space
doSomething( );

//now test if ref is null
if (ref.get( ) == null)
  System.out.println("The garbage collector deleted my ref");
else
 System.out.println("ref object is still here");
```

Note that the referent can be garbage-collected at any time, as long as there are no other strong references referring to it. (In the example, ref.get( ) can become null only if there are no other non-Reference objects referring to someObject.)

The advantage of References is that you can use them to hang onto objects that you want to reuse but are not needed immediately. If memory space gets too low, those objects not currently being used are automatically reclaimed by the garbage collector. This means that you subsequently need to create objects instead of reusing them, but that is preferable to having the program crash from lack of memory. (To delete the reference object itself when the referent is nulled, you need to create the reference with a ReferenceQueue instance. When the reference object is cleared, it is added to the ReferenceQueue instance and can then be processed by the application, e.g., explicitly deleted from a hash table in which it may be a key.)

Reference Types

There are three Reference types in Java 2. WeakReferences and SoftReferences differ essentially in the order in which the garbage collector clears them. Simplistically, the garbage collector does not clear SoftReference objects until all WeakReferences have been cleared. PhantomReferences (not addressed here) are not cleared automatically by the garbage collector and are intended for use in a different way.

Sun's documentation suggests that WeakReferences could be used for canonical tables, whereas SoftReferences would be more useful for caches. In the previous edition, I suggested the converse, giving the rationale that caches take up more space and so should be the first to be reclaimed. But after a number of discussions, I have come to realize that both suggestions are simply misleading. What we have are two reference types, one of which is likely to be reclaimed before the other. So you should use both types of Reference objects in a priority system, using the SoftReference objects to hold higher-priority elements so that they are cleared later than low-priority elements. For both caches and canonical tables, priority would probably be best assigned according to how expensive it is to recreate the object. In fact, you can also add PhantomReferences as a third, even higher-priority element. PhantomReferences would be cleared last of all.

SoftReference Flushing

Prior to Version 1.3.1, SoftReferences and WeakReferences were treated fairly similarly by the VM, simply being cleared whenever they were no longer strongly (and weakly) reachable, with only a slight ordering difference. However, from 1.3.1 on, the Sun VM started treating SoftReferences differently. Now, SoftReferences remain alive for some time after the last time they were referenced. The default length of time value is one second of lifetime per free megabyte in the heap. This provides more of a differentiation between SoftReference and WeakReference behavior.

The initial time-to-live values for SoftReferences can be altered using the -XX: SoftRefLRUPolicyMSPerMB flag, which specifies the lifetime per free megabyte in the heap, in milliseconds. For example, to change the value to 3 seconds per free heap megabyte, you would use:

```
% java -XX:SoftRefLRUPolicyMSPerMB=3000 ...
```

The server mode VM and client mode VM use slightly different methods to calculate the free megabytes in the heap. The server mode VM assumes that the heap can expand to the -Xmx value and uses that as the full heap size to calculate the available free space. The client mode VM simply uses the current heap size, deriving the actual free space in the current heap. This means that the server VM has an increased likelihood of actually growing the heap space rather than clearing SoftReferences, even where there are SoftReferences that could otherwise be reclaimed. This behavior is not part of any specification, so it could change in a future version. But it is likely that some difference in behavior between WeakReferences and SoftReferences will remain, with SoftReferences being longer lived.

The WeakHashMap Class

To complete our picture on references and how they work, we'll look in detail at the implementation and performance effects of the WeakHashMap class. WeakHashMap is a type of Map that differs from other Maps in more than just having a different implementation. WeakHashMap uses weak references to hold its keys, making it one of the few classes able to respond to the fluctuating memory requirements of the JVM. This can make WeakHashMap unpredictable at times, unless you know exactly what you are doing with it.

How WeakHashMap works

The keys in a WeakHashMap are WeakReference objects. The object passed as the key to a WeakHashMap is stored as the referent of the WeakReference object, and the value is the standard Map value. (The object returned by calling Reference.get( ) is termed the *referent* of the Reference object.) A comparison with HashMap can help:

HashMap	WeakHashMap
`Map h = new HashMap( );`	`Map h = new WeakHashMap( );`
`Object key = new Object;` `h.put(key, "xyz");`	`Object key = new Object;` `h.put(key, "xyz");`
`key = null;`	`key = null;`
The key is referenced directly by the HashMap.	The key is not referenced directly by the WeakHashMap. Instead, a WeakReference object is referenced directly by the WeakHashMap, and the key is referenced weakly from the WeakReference object.
	Conceptually, this is similar to inserting a line before the put( ) call, like this: `key = new WeakReferenkey(key);`
The value is referenced directly by the HashMap.	The value is referenced directly by the HashMap.

HashMap	WeakHashMap
The key is not garbage-collectable since the map contains a strong reference to the key. The key could be obtained by iterating over the keys of the HashMap.	The key is garbage-collectable as nothing else in the application refers to it, and the WeakReference only holds the key weakly. Iterating over the keys of the WeakHashMap might obtain the key, but might not if the key has been garbage-collected.
The value is not garbage-collectable.	The value is not directly garbage-collectable. However, when the key is collected by the garbage collector, the WeakReference object is subsequently removed from the WeakHashMap as a key, thus making the value garbage-collectable too.

The 1.2 and 1.3 versions of the WeakHashMap implementation wrap a HashMap for its underlying Map implementation and wrap keys with WeakReferences (actually a WeakReference subclass) before putting the keys into the underlying HashMap. The 1.4 version implements a hash table directly in the class, for improved performance. The WeakHashMap uses its own ReferenceQueue object so that it is notified of keys that have been garbage-collected, thus allowing the timely removal of the WeakReference objects and the corresponding values. The queue is checked whenever the Map is altered. In the 1.4 version, the queue is also checked whenever any key is accessed from the WeakHashMap. If you have not worked with Reference objects and ReferenceQueues before, this can be a little confusing, so I'll work through an example. The following example adds a key-value pair to the WeakHashMap, assumes that the key is garbage-collected, and records the subsequent procedure followed by the WeakHashMap:

1. A key-value pair is added to the Map:

```
aWeakHashMap.put(key, value);
```

This results in the addition of a WeakReference key added to the WeakHashMap, with the original key held as the referent of the WeakReference object. You could do the equivalent using a HashMap like this:

```
ReferenceQueue Queue = new ReferenceQueue( );
MyWeakReference RefKey = new MyWeakReference(key, Queue);
aHashMap.put(RefKey, value);
```

(For the equivalence code, I've used a subclass of WeakReference, as I'll need to override the WeakReference.equals( ) for equal key access in the subsequent points to work correctly.)

Note that at this stage the referent of the WeakReference just created is the original key. That is, the following statement would output true:

```
System.out.println(RefKey.get( ) == key);
```

2. At this point, you could access the value from the WeakHashMap using the original key, or another key that is equal to the original key. The following statements would now output true:

```
System.out.println(aWeakHashMap.get(equalKey) == value);
System.out.println(aWeakHashMap.get(key) == value);
```

In our equivalent code using the HashMap, the following statements would now output true:

```
MyWeakReference RefKey2 = new MyWeakReference(equalKey, Queue);
System.out.println(aHashMap.get(RefKey2) == value);
System.out.println(aHashMap.get(RefKey) == value);
```

Note that in order to get this equivalence, we need to implement equals( ) and hashcode( ) in the MyWeakReference class so that equal referents make equal MyWeakReference objects. This is necessary so that the MyWeakReference wrapped keys evaluate as equal keys in Maps. The equals( ) method returns true if the MyWeakReference objects are identical or if their referents are equal.

3. We now null out the reference to the original key:

```
key = null;
```

After some time, the garbage collector detects that the key is no longer referenced anywhere else in the application and clears the WeakReference key. In the equivalent code using the HashMap from this point on, the WeakReference we created has a null referent. The following statement would now output true:

```
System.out.println(RefKey.get( ) == null);
```

Maintaining a reference to the WeakReference object (in the RefKey variable) does not affect clearing the referent. In the WeakHashMap, the WeakReference object key is also strongly referenced from the map, but its referent, the original key, is cleared.

4. The garbage collector adds the WeakReference that it recently cleared into its ReferenceQueue: that queue is the ReferenceQueue object that was passed in to the constructor of the WeakReference.

5. Trying to retrieve the value using a key equal to the original key would now return null. (To try this, it is necessary to use a key equal to the original key since we no longer have access to the original key; otherwise, it could not have been garbage-collected.) The following statement would now output true:

```
System.out.println(aWeakHashMap.get(equalKey) == null);
```

In our equivalent code using the HashMap, the following statements would now output true:

```
MyWeakReference RefKey3 = new MyWeakReference(equalKey, Queue);
System.out.println(aHashMap.get(RefKey3) == null);
```

6. However, at the moment the WeakReference and the value objects are still strongly referenced by the Map. That is where the ReferenceQueue comes in. Recall that when the garbage collector clears the WeakReference, it adds the WeakReference into the ReferenceQueue. Now that it is in the ReferenceQueue, we need to have it processed. In the case of the 1.2 and 1.3 versions of WeakHashMap, the WeakReference stays in the ReferenceQueue until the WeakHashMap is altered in some way (e.g., by calling put( ), remove( ), or clear( )). Once one of the mutator methods has been called, the WeakHashMap runs through its ReferenceQueue, removing all WeakReference objects from the queue and also removing each WeakReference object as a key in its internal map, thus simultaneously dereferencing the value.

From the 1.4 version, *accessing* any key also causes the WeakHashMap to run through its ReferenceQueue. In the following example, I use a dummy object to force queue processing without making any real changes to the WeakHashMap:

```
aWeakHashMap.put(DUMMY_OBJ, DUMMY_OBJ);
```

The equivalent code using the HashMap does not need a dummy object, but we need to carry out the equivalent queue processing:

```
MyWeakReference aRef;
while ((aRef = (MyWeakReference) Queue.poll( )) != null)
{
  aHashMap.remove(aRef);
}
```

As you can see, we take each WeakReference out of the queue and remove it from the Map. This also releases the corresponding value object, and both the WeakReference object and the value object can now be garbage-collected if there are no other strong references to them.

Reference Objects with String Literal Referents

Note that if you use a string literal as a key to a WeakHashMap or the referent to a Reference object, it will not necessarily be garbage-collected when the application no longer references it. For example, consider the code:

```
String s = "hello ";
WeakHashMap h = new WeakHashMap( );
h.put(s,"xyz");
s = null;
```

You might expect that the string "hello" can now be garbage-collected, since we have nulled the reference to it. However, a string created as a literal is created at compile time and held in a string pool in the class file. The JVM normally holds these strings internally in its own string pool after the class has been loaded. Consequently, the JVM retains a strong reference to the String object, and it will not be garbage-collected until the JVM releases it from the string pool: that may be never, or when the class is garbage-collected, or some other time. If you want to use a String object as a key to a WeakHashMap, ensure that it is created at runtime, e.g.:

```
String s1 = new String("hello");
String s2 = (new StringBuffer( )).append("hello").toString( );
```

This is one of the few times when creating extra copies of an object is better for performance! This string does not get put into the JVM string pool, and so can be garbage-collected when the application no longer holds strong references to it.

Note that calling String.intern( ) on a string will also put it into the internal JVM string pool, giving rise to the same issues as literal strings. Similarly, other objects that the JVM could retain a strong reference to, such as Class objects, may also not be garbage-collected when there are no longer any strong references to them from the application, and so also should not be used as Reference object keys.

Some consequences of the WeakHashMap implementation

1. Reference clearing is atomic. Consequently, there is no need to worry about achieving some sort of corrupt state if you try to access an object and the garbage collector is clearing keys at the same time. You will either get the object or you won't.

2. For 1.2 and 1.3, the values are not released until the WeakHashMap is altered. Specifically, one of the mutator methods, put( ), remove( ), or clear( ), needs to be called directly or indirectly (e.g., from putAll( )) for the values to be released by the WeakHashMap. If you do not call any mutator methods after populating the WeakHashMap, the values and WeakReference objects will never be dereferenced. This does not apply to 1.4 or, presumably, to later versions. However, even with 1.4, the WeakReference keys and values are not released in the background. With 1.4, the WeakReference keys and values are only released when some WeakHashMap method is executed, giving the WeakHashMap a chance to run through the reference queue.

3. The 1.2 and 1.3 WeakHashMap implementation wraps an internal HashMap. This means that practically every call to the WeakHashMap has one extra level of indirection it must go through (e.g., WeakHashMap.get( ) calls HashMap.get( )), which can be a significant performance overhead. This is a specific choice of the implementation. The 1.4 implementation has no such problem.

4. In the 1.2 and 1.3 implementations, every call to get( ) creates a new WeakReference object to enable equality testing of keys in the internal HashMap. Although these are small, short-lived objects, if get( ) is used intensively this could generate a heavy performance overhead. Once again, the 1.4 implementation has no such problem.

Unlike many other collections, WeakHashMap cannot maintain a count of elements, as keys can be cleared at any time by the garbage collector without immediately notifying the WeakHashMap. This means that seemingly simple methods such as isEmpty( ) and size( ) have more complicated implementations than for most collections. Specifically, size( ) in the 1.2 and 1.3 implementations actually iterates through the keys, counting those that have not been cleared. Consequently, size( ) is an operation that takes time proportional to the size of the WeakHashMap. In the 1.4 implementation, size( ) processes the reference queue, then returns the current size. Similarly, in the 1.2 and 1.3 implementations, isEmpty( ) iterates through the collection looking for a non-null key. This produces the perverse result that a WeakHashMap that had all its keys cleared and is therefore empty requires more time for isEmpty( ) to return than a similar WeakHashMap that is not empty. In the 1.4 implementation, isEmpty( ) processes the reference queue and returns whether the current size is 0, thus providing a more consistent execution time, although on average the earlier isEmpty( ) implementation would be quicker.

Avoiding Garbage Collection

The canonicalization techniques I've discussed are one way to avoid garbage collection: fewer objects means less to garbage-collect. Similarly, the pooling technique in that section also tends to reduce garbage-collection requirements, partly because you are creating fewer objects by reusing them, and partly because you deallocate memory less often by holding onto the objects you have allocated. Of course, this also means that your memory requirements are higher, but you can't have it both ways.

Another technique for reducing garbage-collection impact is to avoid using objects where they are not needed. For example, there is no need to create an extra unnecessary Integer to parse a String containing an int value, as in:

```
String string = "55";
int theInt = new Integer(string).intValue( )
```

Instead, there is a static method available for parsing:

```
int theInt = Integer.parseInt(string);
```

Unfortunately, some classes do not provide static methods that avoid the spurious intermediate creation of objects. Until JDK 1.2, there were no static methods that allowed you to parse strings containing floating-point numbers to get doubles or floats. Instead, you needed to create an intermediate Double object and extract the value. (Even after JDK 1.2, an intermediate FloatingDecimal is created, but this is arguably due to good abstraction in the programming design.) When a class does not provide a static method, you can sometimes use a dummy instance to execute instance methods repeatedly, thus avoiding the need to create extra objects.

The primitive data types in Java use memory space that also needs reclaiming, but the overhead in reclaiming data-type storage is smaller: it is reclaimed at the same time as its holding object and so has a smaller impact. (Temporary primitive data types exist only on the stack and do not need to be garbage-collected at all; see "Variables" in Chapter 6.) For example, an object with just one instance variable holding an int is reclaimed in one object reclaim. If it holds an Integer object, the garbage collector needs to reclaim two objects.

Reducing garbage collection by using primitive data types also applies when you can hold an object in a primitive data-type format rather than another format. For example, if you have a large number of objects, each with a String instance variable holding a number (e.g., "1492", "1997"), it is better to make that instance variable an int data type and store the numbers as ints, provided that conversion overhead does not swamp the benefits of holding the values in this alternative format.

Similarly, you can use an int (or long) to represent a Date object, providing appropriate calculations to access and update the values, thus saving an object and the associated garbage overhead. Of course, you have a different runtime overhead instead, as those conversion calculations may take up more time.

A more extreme version of this technique is to use arrays to map objects: for example, see "Search Trees" in Chapter 11. Toward the end of that example, one version of the class gets rid of node objects completely, using a large array to map and maintain all instances and instance variables. This leads to a large improvement in performance at all stages of the object life cycle. Of course, this technique is a specialized one that should not be used generically throughout your application, or you will end up with unmaintainable code. It should be used only when called for (and when it can be completely encapsulated). A simple example is for the class defined as:

```
class MyClass
{
  int x;
  boolean y;
}
```

This class has an associated collection class that seems to hold an array of MyClass objects, but actually holds arrays of instance variables of the MyClass class:

```
class MyClassCollection
{
  int[ ] xs;
  boolean[ ] ys;
  public int getXForElement(int i) {return xs[i];}
  public boolean getYForElement(int i) {return ys[i];}
  //If possible avoid having to declare element access like the
  //following method:
  //public MyClass getElement(int i) {return new MyClass(xs[i], ys[i]);}
}
```

An extension of this technique flattens objects that have a one-to-one relationship. The classic example is a Person object that holds a Name object, consisting of first name and last name (and a collection of middle names), and an Address object, with street, number, etc. This can be collapsed down to just the Person object, with all the fields moved up to the Person class. For example, the original definition consists of three classes:

```
public class Person {
  private Name name;
  private Address address;
}
class Name {
  private String firstName;
  private String lastName;
  private String[ ] otherNames;
}
class Address {
  private int houseNumber;
  private String houseName;
  private String streetName;
  private String town;
  private String area;
```

```
    private String greaterArea;
    private String country;
    private String postCode;
}
```

These three classes collapse into one class:

```
public class Person {
    private String firstName;
    private String lastName;
    private String[ ] otherNames;
    private int houseNumber;
    private String houseName;
    private String streetName;
    private String town;
    private String area;
    private String greaterArea;
    private String country;
    private String postCode;
}
```

This results in the same data and the same functionality (assuming that Addresses and Names are not referenced by more than one Person). But now you have one object instead of three for each Person. Of course, this violates the good design of an application and should be used only when absolutely necessary, not as standard.

Finally, here are some general recommendations that help to reduce the number of unnecessary objects being generated. These recommendations should be part of your standard coding practice, not just performance-related:

- Reduce the number of temporary objects being used, especially in loops. It is easy to use a method in a loop that has side effects such as making copies, or an accessor that returns a copy of some object you need only once.

- Use StringBuffer in preference to the String concatenation operator (+). This is really a special case of the previous point, but needs to be emphasized.

- Be aware of which methods alter objects directly without making copies and which ones return a copy of an object. For example, any String method that changes the string (such as String.trim( )) returns a new String object, whereas a method like Vector.setSize( ) does not return a copy. If you do not need a copy, use (or create) methods that do not return a copy of the object being operated on.

- Avoid using generic classes that handle Object types when you are dealing with basic data types. For example, there is no need to use Vector to store ints by wrapping them in Integers. Instead, implement an IntVector class that holds the ints directly.

Initialization

All chained constructors are automatically called when creating an object with new. Chaining more constructors for a particular object causes extra overhead at object creation, as does initializing instance variables more than once. Be aware of the default values that Java initializes variables to:

- null for objects
- 0 for integer types of all lengths (byte, char, short, int, long)
- 0.0 for float types (float and double)
- false for booleans

There is no need to reinitialize these values in the constructor (although an optimizing compiler should be able to eliminate the redundant statement). Generalizing this point: if you can identify that the creation of a particular object is a bottleneck, either because it takes too long or because a great many of those objects are being created, you should check the constructor hierarchy to eliminate any multiple initializations to instance variables.

You can avoid constructors by unmarshalling objects from a serialized stream because deserialization does not use constructors. However, serializing and deserializing objects is a CPU-intensive procedure and is unlikely to speed up your application. There is another way to avoid constructors when creating objects, namely by creating a clone() of an object. You can create new instances of classes that implement the Cloneable interface using the clone() method. These new instances do not call any class constructor, thus allowing you to avoid the constructor initializations. Cloning does not save a lot of time because the main overhead in creating an object is in the creation, not the initialization. However, when there are extensive initializations or many objects generated from a class with some significant initialization, this technique can help.

If you have followed the factory design pattern,* it is relatively simple to reimplement the original factory method to use a clone. For example, the original factory method can be defined similar to:

```
public static Something getNewSomething()
{
  return new Something();
}
```

---

* The factory design pattern recommends that object creation be centralized in a particular factory method. So instead of directly calling new Something() in the code to create an instance of the Something class, you call a method such as SomethingFactory.getNewSomething(), which creates and returns a new instance of the Something class. This is actually detrimental for performance, as there is the overhead of an extra method call for every object creation, but the pattern does provide more flexibility when it comes to tuning. My inclination is to use the factory pattern. If you identify a particular factory method as a bottleneck when performance tuning, you can relatively easily inline that method using a preprocessor.

The replaced implementation that uses cloning looks like:

```
private static Something MASTER_Something = new Something( );
public static Something getNewSomething( )
{
  return (Something) MASTER_Something.clone( );
}
```

If you have not followed the factory design pattern, you may need to track down all calls that create a new instance of the relevant class and replace those calls. Note that the cloned object is still initialized, but the initialization is not the constructor initialization. Instead, the initialization consists of assigning exactly once to each instance variable of the new (cloned) object, using the instance variables of the object being cloned.

Java arrays all support cloning. This allows you to manage a similar trick when it comes to initializing arrays. But first let's see why you would want to clone an array for performance reasons.

When you create an array in code, using the curly braces to assign a newly created array to an array variable like this:

```
int[ ] array1 = {1,2,3,4,5,6,7,8,9};
```

you might imagine that the compiler creates an array in the compiled file, leaving a nice structure to be pulled into memory. In fact, this is not what happens. The array is still created at runtime, with all the elements initialized then. Because of this, you should specify arrays just once, probably as a static, and assign that array as required. In most cases this is enough, and there is nothing further to improve on because the array is created just once. But sometimes you have a routine for which you want to create a new array each time you execute it. In this case, the complexity of the array determines how efficient the array creation is. If the array is quite complex, it is faster to hold a reference copy and clone that reference than it is to create a new array. For instance, the array example shown previously as array1 is simple and therefore faster to create, as shown in that example. But the following more complex array, array2, is faster to create as a cloned array:

```
static int[ ] Ref_array1 = {1,2,3,4,5,6,7,8,9};
static int[ ][ ] Ref_array2 = {{1,2},{3,4},{5,6},{7,8}};

int[ ] array1 = {1,2,3,4,5,6,7,8,9};           //faster than cloning
int[ ] array1 = (int[ ]) Ref_array1.clone( );  //slower than initializing

int[ ][ ] array2 = {{1,2},{3,4},{5,6},{7,8}}; //slower than cloning
int[ ][ ] array2 = (int[ ][ ]) Ref_array2.clone( );//faster than initializing
```

Early and Late Initialization

The final two sections of this chapter discuss two seemingly opposing tuning techniques. The first section, "Preallocating Objects," presents the technique of creating

---

objects before they are needed. This technique is useful when a large number of objects need to be created at a time when CPU power is needed for other routines and where those objects could feasibly be created earlier, at a time when there is ample spare CPU power.

The second section, "Lazy Initialization," presents the technique of delaying object creation until the last possible moment. This technique is useful for avoiding unnecessary object creation when only a few objects are used even though many possible objects can be created.

In fact, these techniques represent two sides of the same coin: moving object creation from one time to another. Preallocating moves object creation to a time earlier than you would normally create those objects; lazy initialization moves object creation to a later time (or never).

Preallocating Objects

There may be situations in which you cannot avoid creating particular objects in significant amounts: perhaps they are necessary for the application and no reasonable amount of tuning has managed to reduce the object-creation overhead for them. If the creation time has been identified as a bottleneck, it is possible that you can still create the objects, but move the creation time to a part of the application when more spare cycles are available or there is more flexibility in response times.

The idea here is to choose another time to create some or all of the objects (perhaps in a partially initialized stage) and store those objects until they are needed. Again, if you have followed the factory design pattern, it is relatively simple to replace the return new Something( ) statement with an access to the collection of spare objects (presumably testing for a nonempty collection as well). If you have not followed the factory design pattern, you may need to track down all calls that create a new instance of the relevant class and replace them with a call to the factory method. For the real creation, you might want to spawn a background (low-priority) thread to churn out objects and add them into the storage collection until you run out of time, space, or necessity.

This is a variation of the "read-ahead" concept, and you can also apply this idea to:

- Classloading (obviously not for classes needed as soon as the application starts up); see "Uncompressed ZIP/JAR Files" in Chapter 3.
- Distributed objects; see Chapter 12.
- Reading external data files.

Lazy Initialization

Lazy initialization means that you do not initialize objects until the first time they are used. Typically, this comes about when you are unsure of what initial value an instance variable might have but want to provide a default. Rather than initialize explicitly in the constructor (or class static initializer), it is left until access time for the variable to be initialized, using a test for null to determine if it has been initialized. For example:

```
public getSomething( )
{
  if (something == null)
    something = defaultSomething( );
  return something;
}
```

I find this kind of construct quite often in code (too often, in my opinion). I can only rarely see a justifiable reason for using lazy initialization. Not deciding where to initialize a variable correctly is more often a result of lazy design or lazy coding. The result can be many tests for null executing when you access your variables, and these null tests never go away: they are always performed, even after the variable has been initialized. In the worst case, this can impact performance badly, although generally the overhead is small and can be ignored. I always recommend avoiding the use of lazy initialization for general coding.

On the other hand, there are particular design situations in which it is appropriate to use lazy initialization. A good example is classloading, where classes are loaded dynamically as required. This is a specific design situation in which it is clear there will be a performance impact on running applications, but the design of the Java runtime merited this for the features that it brought.

Lazy initialization can be a useful performance-tuning technique. As usual, you should be tuning after functionality is present in your application, so I am not recommending using lazy initialization before the tuning stage. But there are places where you can change objects to be lazily initialized and make a large gain. Specifically, these are objects or variables of objects that may never be used. For example, if you need to make available a large choice of objects, of which only a few will actually be used in the application (e.g., based on a user's choice), then you are better off not instantiating or initializing these objects until they are actually used. An example is the char-to-byte encoding provided by the JDK. Only a few (usually one) of these are used, so you do not need to provide every type of encoding, fully initialized, to the application. Only the required encoding needs to be used.

When you have thousands of objects that need complex initializations but only a few will actually be used, lazy initialization provides a significant speedup to an application by avoiding exercising code that may never be run. A related situation in which lazy initialization can be used for performance tuning is when there are many objects that need to be created and initialized, and most of these objects will be used, but not immediately. In this case, it can be useful to spread out the load of object initialization so you don't get one large hit on the application. It may be better to let a background thread initialize all the objects slowly or to use lazy initialization to take many small or negligible hits, thus spreading the load over time. This is essentially the same technique as for preallocation of objects (see the previous section).

It is true that many of these kinds of situations should be anticipated at the design stage, in which case you could build lazy initialization into the application from the beginning. But this is quite an easy change to make (usually affecting just the accessors of a few classes), and so there is usually little reason to over-engineer the application prior to tuning.

Performance Checklist

Most of these suggestions apply only after a bottleneck has been identified:

- Establish whether you have a memory problem.
- Reduce the number of temporary objects being used, especially in loops.
    - Avoid creating temporary objects within frequently called methods.
    - Presize collection objects.
    - Reuse objects where possible.
    - Empty collection objects before reusing them. (Do not shrink them unless they are very large.)
    - Use custom conversion methods for converting between data types (especially strings and streams) to reduce the number of temporary objects.
    - Define methods that accept reusable objects to be filled in with data, rather than methods that return objects holding that data. (Or you can return immutable objects.)
    - Canonicalize objects wherever possible. Compare canonicalized objects by identity.
    - Create only the number of objects a class logically needs (if that is a small number of objects).
    - Replace strings and other objects with integer constants. Compare these integers by identity.
    - Use primitive data types instead of objects as instance variables.
    - Avoid creating an object that is only for accessing a method.
    - Flatten objects to reduce the number of nested objects.
    - Preallocate storage for large collections of objects by mapping the instance variables into multiple arrays.
    - Use `StringBuffer` rather than the string concatenation operator (+).
    - Use methods that alter objects directly without making copies.
    - Create or use specific classes that handle primitive data types rather than wrapping the primitive data types.

- Consider using a ThreadLocal to provide threaded access to singletons with state.
- Use the final modifier on instance-variable definitions to create immutable internally accessible objects.
- Use WeakReferences to hold elements in large canonical lookup tables. (Use SoftReferences for cache elements.)
- Reduce object-creation bottlenecks by targeting the object-creation process.
  - Keep constructors simple and inheritance hierarchies shallow.
  - Avoid initializing instance variables more than once.
  - Use the clone( ) method to avoid calling any constructors.
  - Clone arrays if that makes their creation faster.
  - Create copies of simple arrays faster by initializing them; create copies of complex arrays faster by cloning them.
- Eliminate object-creation bottlenecks by moving object creation to an alternative time.
  - Create objects early, when there is spare time in the application, and hold those objects until required.
  - Use lazy initialization when there are objects or variables that may never be used, or when you need to distribute the load of creating objects.
  - Use lazy initialization only when there is a defined merit in the design, or when identifying a bottleneck that is alleviated using lazy initialization.

In this chapter:
- The Performance Effects of Strings
- Compile-Time Versus Runtime Resolution of Strings
- Conversions to Strings
- Strings Versus char Arrays
- String Comparisons and Searches
- Sorting Internationalized Strings

CHAPTER 5

Strings

Everyone has a logger and most of them
are string pigs.
—Kirk Pepperdine

`Strings` have a special status in Java. They are the only objects with:

- Their own operators (+ and +=)
- A literal form (characters surrounded by double quotes, e.g., `"hello"`)
- Their own externally accessible collection in the VM and class files (i.e., string pools, which provide uniqueness of `String` objects if the string sequence can be determined at compile time)

Strings are immutable and have a special relationship with `StringBuffer` objects. A `String` cannot be altered once created. Applying a method that looks like it changes the `String` (such as `String.trim()`) doesn't actually do so; instead, it returns an altered copy of the `String`. Strings are also `final`, and so cannot be subclassed. These points have advantages and disadvantages so far as performance is concerned. For fast string manipulation, the inability to subclass `String` or access the internal char array can be a serious problem.

The Performance Effects of Strings

Let's first look at the advantages of the `String` implementation:

- Compilation creates unique strings. At compile time, strings are resolved as far as possible. This includes applying the concatenation operator and converting other literals to strings. So `"hi7"` and `("hi"+7)` both get resolved at compile time to the same string, and are identical objects in the class string pool (see "String concatenation is sometimes folded" in Chapter 3). Compilers differ in their ability to achieve this resolution. You can always check your compiler (e.g., by decompiling some statements involving concatenation) and change it if needed.

- Because String objects are immutable, a substring operation doesn't need to copy the entire underlying sequence of characters. Instead, a substring can use the same char array as the original string and simply refer to a different start point and endpoint in the char array. This means that substring operations are efficient, being both fast and conserving of memory; the extra object is just a wrapper on the same underlying char array with different pointers into that array.*

- Strings have strong support for internationalization. It would take a large effort to reproduce the internationalization support for an alternative class.

- The close relationship with StringBuffers allows Strings to reference the same char array used by the StringBuffer. This is a double-edged sword. For typical practice, when you use a StringBuffer to manipulate and append characters and data types, and then convert the final result to a String, this works just fine. The StringBuffer provides efficient mechanisms for growing, inserting, appending, altering, and other types of String manipulation. The resulting String then efficiently references the same char array with no extra character copying. This is very fast and reduces the number of objects being used to a minimum by avoiding intermediate objects. However, if the StringBuffer object is subsequently altered, the char array in that StringBuffer is copied into a new char array that is now referenced by the StringBuffer. The String object retains the reference to the previously shared char array. This means that copying overhead can occur at unexpected points in the application. Instead of the copying occurring at the toString( ) method call, as might be expected, any subsequent alteration of the StringBuffer causes a new char array to be created and an array copy to be performed. To make the copying overhead occur at predictable times, you could explicitly execute some method that makes the copying occur, such as StringBuffer.setLength( ). This allows StringBuffers to be reused with more predictable performance.

The disadvantages of the String implementation are:

- Not being able to subclass String means that it is not possible to add behavior to String for your own needs.

- The previous point means that all access must be through the restricted set of currently available String methods, imposing extra overhead.

- The only way to increase the number of methods allowing efficient manipulation of String characters is to copy the characters into your own array and manipulate them directly, in which case String is imposing an extra step and extra objects you may not need.

- char arrays are faster to process directly.

---

* Strings are implemented in the JDK as an internal char array with index offsets (actually a start offset and a character count). This basic structure is extremely unlikely to be changed in any version of Java.

- The tight coupling with StringBuffer can lead to unexpectedly high memory usage. When StringBuffer.toString( ) creates a String, the current underlying array holds the string, regardless of the size of the array (i.e., the capacity of the StringBuffer). For example, a StringBuffer with a capacity of 10,000 characters can build a string of 10 characters. However, that 10-character String continues to use a 10,000-char array to store the 10 characters. If the StringBuffer is now reused to create another 10-character string, the StringBuffer first creates a new internal 10,000-char array to build the string with; then the new String also uses that 10,000-char array to store the 10 characters. Obviously, this process can continue indefinitely, using vast amounts of memory where not expected.

The advantages of Strings can be summed up as ease of use, internationalization support, and compatibility to existing interfaces. Most methods expect a String object rather than a char array, and String objects are returned by many methods. The disadvantage of Strings boils down to inflexibility. With extra work, most things you can do with String objects can be done faster and with less intermediate object-creation overhead by using your own set of char array manipulation methods.

For most performance tuning, you pinpoint a bottleneck and make localized changes to objects and methods that speed up that bottleneck. But String tuning often involves converting to char arrays, whereas you rarely come across public methods or interfaces that deal in char arrays. This makes it difficult to switch between Strings and char arrays in any localized way. The consequences are that you either have to switch back and forth between Strings and char arrays, or you have to make extensive modifications that can reach across many application boundaries. I have no easy solution for this problem. String tuning can get messy. Sun recognizes that Strings are not the optimal solution in many cases and has added a CharSequence interface in JDK 1.4 that String and other classes implement. New methods have been added that operate on CharSequence objects rather than requiring Strings. For example, the regular expression classes accept CharSequence objects. This doesn't necessarily help your particular bottleneck, and CharSequences still access the char elements through a charAt( ) method, but it does at least increase the options available for optimizing applications.

It is difficult to handle String internationalization capabilities using raw char arrays. But in many cases, internationalized Strings form a specific subset of String usage in an application, mainly in the user interface, and that subset of Strings rarely causes bottlenecks. You should differentiate between Strings that need internationalization and those that are simply processing characters, independent of language. These latter Strings can be replaced for tuning with char arrays.[*] Internationalization-dependent Strings are more difficult to tune, and I provide some examples of tuning these

---

[*] My editor Mike Loukides summarized this succinctly with the statement, "Avoid using String objects if you don't intend to represent text."

later in the chapter. Note also that internationalized Strings can be treated as char arrays for some types of processing without any problems; see the "Line Filter Example" section later in this chapter.

Compile-Time Versus Runtime Resolution of Strings

For optimized use of Strings, you should know the difference between compile-time resolution of Strings and runtime creation. At compile time, Strings are resolved to eliminate the concatenation operator if possible. For example, the line:

```
String s = "hi " + "Mr. " + " " + "Buddy";
```

is compiled as if it read:

```
String s = "hi Mr. Buddy";
```

However, suppose you defined the String using a StringBuffer:

```
String s = (new StringBuffer()).append("hi ").
        append("Mr. ").append(" ").append("Buddy").toString();
```

Then the compiler cannot resolve the String at compile time. The result is that the String is created at runtime along with a temporary StringBuffer. The version that can be resolved at compile time is more efficient. It avoids the overhead of creating a String and an extra temporary StringBuffer, as well as avoiding the runtime cost of several method calls.

However, when an expression involving String concatenation cannot be resolved at compile time, the concatenation must execute at runtime. This causes extra objects to be generated. For example, consider the following method:

```
public String sayHi(String title, String name)
{
  return "hi " + title + " " + name;
}
```

The String generated by this method cannot be resolved at compile time because the variables can have any value. The compiler is free to generate code to optimize the String creation, but it does not have to. Consequently, the String-creation line could be compiled as:

```
return (new StringBuffer()).append("hi ").
  append(title).append(" ").append(name).toString();
```

This is optimal, creating only two objects. On the other hand, the compiler could also leave the line with the default implementation of the concatenation operator, which is equivalent to:

```
return "hi ".concat(title).concat(" ").concat(name);
```

This last implementation creates two intermediate `String` objects that are then thrown away, and these are generated every time the method is called.

So, when the `String` can be fully resolved at compile time, the concatenation operator is more efficient than using a `StringBuffer`. But when the `String` cannot be resolved at compile time, the concatenation operator is less efficient than using a `StringBuffer`.

One further point is that using the `String` constructor in a `String` definition forces a runtime string creation:

```
String s = new String("hi " + "Mr. " + " " + "Buddy");
```

This is compiled as:

```
String s = new String("hi Mr. Buddy");
```

This line uses the compile-time resolved string as a parameter for the `String` constructor to create a new `String` object at runtime. The new `String` object is equal but not identical to the original string:

```
String s = new String("hi Mr. Buddy");
s == "hi Mr. Buddy";      //is false
s.equals("hi Mr. Buddy"); //is true
```

Conversions to Strings

Generally, the JDK methods that convert objects and data types to strings are suboptimal, both in terms of performance and the number of temporary objects used in the conversion procedure. In this section, we consider how to optimize these conversions.

Converting longs to Strings

Let's start by looking at conversion of `long` values. In the JDK, this is achieved with the `Long.toString( )` method. Bear in mind that you typically add a converted value to a `StringBuffer` (explicitly, or implicitly with the + concatenation operator). So it would be nice to avoid the two intermediate temporary objects created while converting the `long`, i.e., the one `char` array inside the conversion method, and the returned `String` object that is used just to copy the chars into the `StringBuffer`.

Avoiding the temporary `char` array is difficult to do because most fast methods for converting numbers start with the low digits in the number, and you cannot add to the `StringBuffer` from the low to the high digits unless you want all your numbers coming out backwards.

However, with a little work, you can get to a method that is fast and obtains the digits in order. The following code works by determining the magnitude of the number first, then successively stripping off the highest digit, as shown.

```
//Up to radix 36
private static final char[] charForDigit = {
  '0','1','2','3','4','5','6','7','8','9','a','b','c','d','e','f','g','h',
  'i','j','k','l','m','n','o','p','q','r','s','t','u','v','w','x','y','z'
};

public static void append(StringBuffer s, long i)
{
  if (i < 0)
  {
    //convert negative to positive numbers for later algorithm
    if (i == Long.MIN_VALUE)
    {
      //cannot make this positive due to integer overflow,
      //so treat it specially
      s.append("-9223372036854775808");
      return;
    }
    //otherwise append the minus sign, and make the number positive
    s.append('-');
    i = -i;
  }
  //Get the magnitude of the int
  long mag = l_magnitude(i);
  long c;
  while ( mag > 1 )
  {
    //The highest digit
    c = i/mag;
    s.append(charForDigit[(int) c]);
    //remove the highest digit
    c *= mag;
    if ( c <= i )
      i -= c;
    //and go down one magnitude
    mag /= 10;
  }
  //The remaining magnitude is one digit large
  s.append(charForDigit[(int) i]);
}

private static long l_magnitude(long i)
{
    if (i < 10L) return 1;
    else if (i < 100L) return 10L;
    else if (i < 1000L) return 100L;
    else if (i < 10000L) return 1000L;
    else if (i < 100000L) return 10000L;
    else if (i < 1000000L) return 100000L;
    else if (i < 10000000L) return 1000000L;
    else if (i < 100000000L) return 10000000L;
    else if (i < 1000000000L) return 100000000L;
    else if (i < 10000000000L) return 1000000000L;
    else if (i < 100000000000L) return 10000000000L;
```

```
    else if (i < 1000000000000L) return 100000000000L;
    else if (i < 10000000000000L) return 1000000000000L;
    else if (i < 100000000000000L) return 10000000000000L;
    else if (i < 1000000000000000L) return 100000000000000L;
    else if (i < 10000000000000000L) return 1000000000000000L;
    else if (i < 100000000000000000L) return 10000000000000000L;
    else if (i < 1000000000000000000L) return 100000000000000000L;
    else return    1000000000000000000L;
}
```

When compared to executing the plain `StringBuffer.append(long)`, the algorithm listed here is generally quicker (see Table 5-1) and creates two fewer objects. It can be even faster and is quicker for all VMs with further tuning, but I'll leave the more complicated tuning to the next section.

Table 5-1. Time taken to append a long to a StringBuffer

VM	1.1.8	1.2.2	1.3.1	1.3.1 -server	1.4.0	1.4.0 -server	1.4.0 -Xint
JDK long conversion	104%	100%	116%	157%	116%	100%	306%
Optimized long conversion	115%	89%	121%	107%	115%	95%	310%

There are several things to note about possible variations of this algorithm. First, although the algorithm here is specifically radix 10 (decimal), it is easy to change to any radix. To do this, the reduction in magnitude in the loop has to go down by the radix value, and the l_magnitude( ) method has to be altered. For example, for radix 16, hexadecimal, the statement mag = mag/10 becomes mag = mag/16 and the magnitude method for radix 16 looks like:

```
private static long l_magnitude16(long i)
{
    if (i < 16L) return 1;
    else if (i < 256L) return 16L;
    else if (i < 4096L) return 256L;
    else if (i < 65536L) return 4096L;
    else if (i < 1048576L) return 65536L;
    else if (i < 16777216L) return 1048576L;
    else if (i < 268435456L) return 16777216L;
    else if (i < 4294967296L) return 268435456L;
    else if (i < 68719476736L) return 4294967296L;
    else if (i < 1099511627776L) return 68719476736L;
    else if (i < 17592186044416L) return 1099511627776L;
    else if (i < 281474976710656L) return 17592186044416L;
    else if (i < 4503599627370496L) return 281474976710656L;
    else if (i < 72057594037927936L) return 4503599627370496L;
    else if (i < 1152921504606846976L) return 72057594037927936L;
    else return 1152921504606846976L;
}
```

Second, because we are working through the digits in written order, this algorithm is suitable for writing directly to a stream or writer (such as a `FileWriter`) without the need for any temporary objects. This is potentially a large gain, enabling writes to files without generating intermediate temporary strings.

Finally, if you want formatting added in, the algorithm is again suitable because you proceed through the number in written order, and also because you have the magnitude at the start. (You can easily create another method, similar to magnitude( ), that returns the number of digits in the value.) You can put in a comma every three digits as the number is being written (or apply whatever internationalized format is required). This saves you having to write out the number first in a temporary object and then add formatting to it. For example, if you are using integers to fake fixed-place floating-point numbers, you can insert a point at the correct position without resorting to temporary objects.

Converting ints to Strings

While the previous append( ) version is suitable to use for ints by overloading, it is much more efficient to create another version specifically for ints. This is because int arithmetic is optimal and considerably faster than the long arithmetic being used. Although earlier versions of the JDK (before JDK 1.1.6) used an inefficient conversion procedure for ints, from 1.1.6 onward Sun targeted the conversion (for radix 10 integers only) and speeded it up by an order of magnitude. To better this already optimized performance, you need every optimization available.

There are three changes you can make to the long conversion algorithm already presented. First, you can change everything to use ints. This gives a significant speedup (more than a third faster than the long conversion). Second, you can inline the "magnitude" method. And finally, you can unroll the loop that handles the digit-by-digit conversion. In this case, the loop can be completely unrolled since there are at most 10 digits in an int.

The resulting method is a little long-winded:

```
public static void append(StringBuffer s, int i)
{
  if (i < 0)
  {
    if (i == Integer.MIN_VALUE)
    {
      //cannot make this positive due to integer overflow
      s.append("-2147483648");
      return this;
    }
    s.append('-');
    i = -i;
  }
  int mag;
  int c;
  if (i < 10)                        //one digit
    s.append(charForDigit[i]);
```

```
        else if (i < 100)                //two digits
            s.append(charForDigit[i/10])
             .append(charForDigit[i%10]);
        else if (i < 1000)               //three digits
            s.append(charForDigit[i/100])
             .append(charForDigit[(c=i%100)/10])
             .append(charForDigit[c%10]);
        else if (i < 10000)              //four digits
            s.append(charForDigit[i/1000])
             .append(charForDigit[(c=i%1000)/100])
             .append(charForDigit[(c%100)/10])
             .append(charForDigit[c%10]);
        else if (i < 100000)             //five digits
            s.append(charForDigit[i/10000])
             .append(charForDigit[(c=i%10000)/1000])
             .append(charForDigit[(c%1000)/100])
             .append(charForDigit[(c%100)/10])
             .append(charForDigit[c%10]);
        else if (i < 1000000)            //six digits
            ... //I'm sure you get the idea
        else if (i < 10000000)           //seven digits
            ... //so just keep doing the same, but more
        else if (i < 100000000)          //eight digits
            ... //because my editor doesn't like wasting all this space
        else if (i < 1000000000)         //nine digits
            ... //on unnecessary repetitions
        else
        {
            //ten digits
            s.append(charForDigit[i/1000000000]);
            s.append(charForDigit[(c=i%1000000000)/100000000]);
            s.append(charForDigit[(c%=100000000)/10000000]);
            s.append(charForDigit[(c%=10000000)/1000000]);
            s.append(charForDigit[(c%=1000000)/100000]);
            s.append(charForDigit[(c%=100000)/10000]);
            s.append(charForDigit[(c%=10000)/1000]);
            s.append(charForDigit[(c%=1000)/100]);
            s.append(charForDigit[(c%=100)/10]);
            s.append(charForDigit[c%10]);
        }
    }
```

In the first edition of this book, I compared this implementation to executing `StringBuffer.append(int)` with earlier VM versions (1.1.6, 1.2.0, 1.3.0, and HotSpot 1.0). The algorithm listed here ran in less time for all the VMs, and created two fewer objects[*] (see Table 5-2). This algorithm still has a smaller impact on garbage creation, digits are iterated in order so you can write to a stream, and it is easier to alter

---

[*] If the `StringBuffer.append(int)` used the algorithm shown here, it would be faster for all JDK versions measured in this chapter, as the characters could be added directly to the char buffer without going through the `StringBuffer.append(char)` method.

for formatting without using temporary objects. Note that the long conversion method can also be improved using two of the three techniques we used for the int conversion method: inlining the magnitude method and unrolling the loop.

However, the comparison against the latest versions of the various VMs now shows a completely different story (see Table 5-3). Sun has continued to optimize, especially object creation and garbage collection in the VM, as well as the conversion algorithm. The improvement in garbage collection is obvious if you run the comparison test with the -verbosegc parameter. With garbage collection being reported, the much larger volume of garbage slows down the JDK conversion relative to the proprietary algorithm. Without -verbosegc, the extra temporary objects are still overhead, but not as significant as with earlier VMs.

It is also instructive to see what Sun has done to the algorithm to make the conversion faster. The source of the 1.3.1/1.4.0 Integer.toString(int) method is almost unrecognizable from earlier implementations. One optimization is to reduce the number of temporary objects created by using a privileged String constructor that accepts a passed char array rather than creating a new one. But the major algorithmic optimization is that multiplications have been changed to bit-shifts. For example, instead of multiplying by 100, three bit-shifts are used:

```
//These are all equivalent operations
q_times_100 = q * 100;
q_times_100 = (q * 64) + (q * 32) + (q * 4);
q_times_100 = ((q << 6) + (q << 5) + (q << 2));
```

One operation has been replaced with three, but with optimized generated native code on most modern CPUs, the bit-shifts would operate in parallel and are significantly faster than the multiplication. The only VM in Table 5-2 that is slower than the algorithm I presented is the interpreted VM, which supports the analysis that the bit-shifts are crucial. Whether you can produce an algorithm that is even faster than the latest JDK one by also using bit-shifting is best left to another time.

Table 5-2. Time taken to append an int to a StringBuffer (from the first edition)

VM	1.2	1.3	HotSpot 1.0	1.1.6
JDK int conversion	100%	61%	89%	148%
Optimized int conversion	84%	60%	81%	111%

Table 5-3. Time taken to append an int to a StringBuffer (current version)

VM	1.1.8	1.2.2	1.3.1	1.3.1 -server	1.4.0	1.4.0 -server	1.4.0 -Xint
JDK int conversion	148%	100%	51%	45%	58%	40%	498%
Optimized int conversion	172%	107%	96%	122%	94%	83%	402%

Converting bytes, shorts, chars, and booleans to Strings

You can use the int conversion method for bytes and shorts (using overloading). You can make byte conversion even faster using a String array as a lookup table for the 256 byte values. The conversion of bytes and shorts to Strings in the JDK appears not to have been tuned to as high a standard as radix 10 ints (up to JDK 1.4). This means that the int conversion algorithm shown previously, when applied to bytes and shorts, is significantly faster than the JDK conversions and does not produce any temporary objects.

When it comes to using the other data types, there is no need to handle booleans in any special way: the Boolean.toString( ) already uses canonical strings. And there is obviously nothing in particular that needs to be done for chars (apart from making sure you add them to strings as characters, not numbers).

Converting floats to Strings

Converting floating-point numbers to strings turns out to be hideously under-optimized in every version of the JDK up to 1.4 (and maybe beyond). Looking at the JDK code and comments, it seems that no one has yet got around to tuning these conversions. Floating-point numbers can be converted using similar optimizations to the number conversions previously addressed. You need to check for and handle the special cases separately. You then scale the floats into an integer value and use the previously defined int conversion algorithm to convert to characters in order, ensuring that you format the decimal point at the correct position. The case of values between .001 and 10,000,000 are handled differently because they are printed without exponent values; all other floats are printed with exponents. Finally, it would be possible to overload the float and double case, but it turns out that if you do this, the float does not convert as well (in correctness or speed), so it is necessary to duplicate the algorithms for the float and double cases.

Note that the printed values of floats and doubles are, in general, only representative of the underlying value. This is true both for the JDK algorithms and the conversions here. There are times when the string representation comes out differently for the two implementations, and neither is actually more accurate. The algorithm used by the JDK prints the minimum number of digits possible, while maintaining uniqueness of the printed value with respect to the other floating-point values adjacent to the value being printed. The algorithm presented here prints the maximum number of digits (not including trailing zeros) regardless of whether some digits are not needed to distinguish the number from other numbers. For example, the Float.MIN_VALUE is printed by the JDK as "1.4E-45" whereas the algorithm here prints it as "1.4285714E-45". Because of the limitations in the accuracy of numbers, neither printed representation is more or less accurate compared to the underlying floating-point number actually held in Float.MIN_VALUE (e.g., assigning both "1.46e-45F" and "1.45e-45F" to a float results in Float.MIN_VALUE being assigned). Note that the code that follows shortly uses the previously defined append( ) method for appending longs to StringBuffers. Also note that the dot character has been hard-coded as the decimal separator character here for clarity, but it is straightforward to change for internationalization.

This method of converting floats to strings has the same advantages as those mentioned previously for integral types (i.e., it is printed in digit order, no temporary objects are generated, etc.). The double conversion (see the next section) is similar to the float conversion, with all the same advantages. In addition, both algorithms are several times faster than the JDK conversions.

Normally, when you print out floating-point numbers, you print in a defined format with a specified number of digits. The default floating-point toString( ) methods cannot format floating-point numbers; you must first create the string, then format it afterwards. The algorithm presented here could easily be altered to handle formatting floating-point numbers without using any intermediate strings. This algorithm is also easily adapted to handle rounding up or down; it already detects which side of the "half" value the number is on:

```
public static final char[ ] NEGATIVE_INFINITY =
    {'-','I','n','f','i','n','i','t','y'};
public static final char[ ] POSITIVE_INFINITY =
    {'I','n','f','i','n','i','t','y'};
public static final char[ ] NaN = {'N','a','N'};
private static final int floatSignMask = 0x80000000;
private static final int floatExpMask  = 0x7f800000;
private static final int floatFractMask= ~(floatSignMask|floatExpMask);
private static final int floatExpShift = 23;
private static final int floatExpBias = 127;
//change dot to international character where this is used below
public static final char[ ] DOUBLE_ZERO = {'0','.','0'};
public static final char[ ] DOUBLE_ZERO2 = {'0','.','0','0'};
public static final char[ ] DOUBLE_ZEROO = {'0','.'};
public static final char[ ] DOT_ZERO = {'.','0'};
private static final float[ ] f_magnitudes = {
1e-44F, 1e-43F, 1e-42F, 1e-41F, 1e-40F,
1e-39F, 1e-38F, 1e-37F, 1e-36F, 1e-35F, 1e-34F, 1e-33F, 1e-32F, 1e-31F, 1e-30F,
1e-29F, 1e-28F, 1e-27F, 1e-26F, 1e-25F, 1e-24F, 1e-23F, 1e-22F, 1e-21F, 1e-20F,
1e-19F, 1e-18F, 1e-17F, 1e-16F, 1e-15F, 1e-14F, 1e-13F, 1e-12F, 1e-11F, 1e-10F,
1e-9F, 1e-8F, 1e-7F, 1e-6F, 1e-5F, 1e-4F, 1e-3F, 1e-2F, 1e-1F,
1e0F, 1e1F, 1e2F, 1e3F, 1e4F, 1e5F, 1e6F, 1e7F, 1e8F, 1e9F,
1e10F, 1e11F, 1e12F, 1e13F, 1e14F, 1e15F, 1e16F, 1e17F, 1e18F, 1e19F,
1e20F, 1e21F, 1e22F, 1e23F, 1e24F, 1e25F, 1e26F, 1e27F, 1e28F, 1e29F,
1e30F, 1e31F, 1e32F, 1e33F, 1e34F, 1e35F, 1e36F, 1e37F, 1e38F
};

public static void append(StringBuffer s, float d)
{
  //handle the various special cases
  if (d == Float.NEGATIVE_INFINITY)
    s.append(NEGATIVE_INFINITY);
```

```
else if (d == Float.POSITIVE_INFINITY)
  s.append(POSITIVE_INFINITY);
else if (d != d)
  s.append(NaN);
else if (d == 0.0)
{
  //can be -0.0, which is stored differently
  if ( (Float.floatToIntBits(d) & floatSignMask) != 0)
    s.append('-');
  s.append(DOUBLE_ZERO);
}
else
{
  //convert negative numbers to positive
  if (d < 0)
  {
    s.append('-');
    d = -d;
  }
  //handle 0.001 up to 10000000 separately, without exponents
  if (d >= 0.001F && d < 0.01F)
  {
    long i = (long) (d * 1E12F);
    i = i%100 >= 50 ? (i/100) + 1 : i/100;
    s.append(DOUBLE_ZERO2);
    appendFractDigits(s, i,-1);
  }
  else if (d >= 0.01F && d < 0.1F)
  {
    long i = (long) (d * 1E11F);
    i = i%100 >= 50 ? (i/100) + 1 : i/100;
    s.append(DOUBLE_ZERO);
    appendFractDigits(s, i,-1);
  }
  else if (d >= 0.1F && d < 1F)
  {
    long i = (long) (d * 1E10F);
    i = i%100 >= 50 ? (i/100) + 1 : i/100;
    s.append(DOUBLE_ZERO0);
    appendFractDigits(s, i,-1);
  }
  else if (d >= 1F && d < 10F)
  {
    long i = (long) (d * 1E9F);
    i = i%100 >= 50 ? (i/100) + 1 : i/100;
    appendFractDigits(s, i,1);
  }
  else if (d >= 10F && d < 100F)
  {
    long i = (long) (d * 1E8F);
    i = i%100 >= 50 ? (i/100) + 1 : i/100;
    appendFractDigits(s, i,2);
  }
  else if (d >= 100F && d < 1000F)
```

```
    {
      long i = (long) (d * 1E7F);
      i = i%100 >= 50 ? (i/100) + 1 : i/100;
      appendFractDigits(s, i,3);
    }
    else if (d >= 1000F && d < 10000F)
    {
      long i = (long) (d * 1E6F);
      i = i%100 >= 50 ? (i/100) + 1 : i/100;
      appendFractDigits(s, i,4);
    }
    else if (d >= 10000F && d < 100000F)
    {
      long i = (long) (d * 1E5F);
      i = i%100 >= 50 ? (i/100) + 1 : i/100;
      appendFractDigits(s, i,5);
    }
    else if (d >= 100000F && d < 1000000F)
    {
      long i = (long) (d * 1E4F);
      i = i%100 >= 50 ? (i/100) + 1 : i/100;
      appendFractDigits(s, i,6);
    }
    else if (d >= 1000000F && d < 10000000F)
    {
      long i = (long) (d * 1E3F);
      i = i%100 >= 50 ? (i/100) + 1 : i/100;
      appendFractDigits(s, i,7);
    }
    else
    {
      //Otherwise the number has an exponent
      int magnitude = magnitude(d);
      long i;
      if (magnitude < -35)
        i = (long) (d*1E10F / f_magnitudes[magnitude + 45]);
      else
        i = (long) (d / f_magnitudes[magnitude + 44 - 9]);
      i = i%100 >= 50 ? (i/100) + 1 : i/100;
      appendFractDigits(s, i, 1);
      s.append('E');
      append(s,magnitude);
    }
  }
  return this;
}

private static int magnitude(float d)
{
  return magnitude(d,Float.floatToIntBits(d));
}

private static int magnitude(float d, int floatToIntBits)
{
```

```
    int magnitude =
      (int) ((((floatToIntBits & floatExpMask) >> floatExpShift)
                  - floatExpBias) * 0.301029995663981);

    if (magnitude < -44)
      magnitude = -44;
    else if (magnitude > 38)
      magnitude = 38;

    if (d >= f_magnitudes[magnitude+44])
    {
      while(magnitude < 39 && d >= f_magnitudes[magnitude+44])
        magnitude++;
      magnitude--;
      return magnitude;
    }
    else
    {
      while(magnitude > -45 && d < f_magnitudes[magnitude+44])
        magnitude--;
      return magnitude;
    }
}
private static void appendFractDigits(StringBuffer s, long i, int decimalOffset)
{
  long mag = magnitude(i);
  long c;
  while ( i > 0 )
  {
    c = i/mag;
    s.append(charForDigit[(int) c]);
    decimalOffset--;
    if (decimalOffset == 0)
      s.append('.'); //change to use international character
    c *= mag;
    if ( c <= i)
      i -= c;
    mag = mag/10;
  }
  if (i != 0)
    s.append(charForDigit[(int) i]);
  else if (decimalOffset > 0)
  {
    s.append(ZEROS[decimalOffset]); //ZEROS[n] is a char array of n 0's
    decimalOffset = 1;
  }

  decimalOffset--;
  if (decimalOffset == 0)
    s.append(DOT_ZERO);
  else if (decimalOffset == -1)
    s.append('0');
}
```

The conversion times compared to the JDK conversions are shown in Table 5-4. Note that if you are formatting floats, the JDK conversion requires additional steps and so takes longer. However, the method shown here is likely to take even less time, as you normally print fewer digits that require fewer loop iterations.

Table 5-4. Time taken to append a float to a StringBuffer

VM	1.1.8	1.2.2	1.3.1	1.3.1 -server	1.4.0	1.4.0 -server	1.4.0 -Xint
JDK float conversion	128%	100%	85%	60%	117%	66%	472%
Optimized float conversion	55%	62%	47%	44%	49%	29%	144%

Converting doubles to Strings

The double conversion is almost identical to the float conversion, except that the doubles extend over a larger range. The differences are the following constants used in place of the corresponding float constants:

```
private static final long  doubleSignMask = 0x8000000000000000L;
private static final long  doubleExpMask  = 0x7ff0000000000000L;
private static final long  doubleFractMask= ~(doubleSignMask|doubleExpMask);
private static final int  doubleExpShift = 52;
private static final int  doubleExpBias = 1023;
//private static final double[] d_magnitudes = {
   //as f_magnitudes[] except doubles extending
   //from 1e-323D to 1e308D inclusive
   ...
}
```

The last section of the append( ) method is:

```
        int magnitude = magnitude(d);
        long i;
        if (magnitude < -305)
          i = (long) (d*1E18 / d_magnitudes[magnitude + 324]);
        else
          i = (long) (d / d_magnitudes[magnitude + 323 - 17]);
        i = i%10 >= 5 ? (i/10) + 1 : i/10;
        appendFractDigits(s, i, 1);
        s.append('E');
        append(s,magnitude);
```

and the magnitude methods are:

```
    private static int magnitude(double d)
    {
      return magnitude(d,Double.doubleToLongBits(d));
    }
    private static int magnitude(double d, long doubleToLongBits)
    {
      int magnitude =
        (int) (((((doubleToLongBits & doubleExpMask) >> doubleExpShift)
                  - doubleExpBias) * 0.301029995663981);
```

```
    if (magnitude < -323)
      magnitude = -323;
    else if (magnitude > 308)
      magnitude = 308;

    if (d >= d_magnitudes[magnitude+323])
    {
      while(magnitude < 309 && d >= d_magnitudes[magnitude+323])
        magnitude++;
      magnitude--;
      return magnitude;
    }
    else
    {
      while(magnitude > -324 && d < d_magnitudes[magnitude+323])
        magnitude--;
      return magnitude;
    }
  }
```

The conversion times compared to the JDK conversions are shown in Table 5-5. As with floats, formatting doubles with the JDK conversion requires additional steps and would consequently take longer, but the method shown here takes even less time, as you normally print fewer digits that require fewer loop iterations.

Table 5-5. Time taken to append a double to a StringBuffer

VM	1.1.8	1.2.2	1.3.1	1.3.1 -server	1.4.0	1.4.0 -server	1.4.0 -Xint
JDK double conversion	117%	100%	94%	76%	95%	87%	761%
Optimized double conversion	22%	17%	19%	17%	20%	14%	64%

Converting Objects to Strings

Converting Objects to Strings is also inefficient in the JDK. For a generic object, the toString() method is usually implemented by calling any embedded object's toString() method, then combining the embedded strings in some way. For example, Vector.toString() calls toString() on all its elements and combines the generated substrings with the comma character surrounded by opening and closing square brackets.

Although this conversion is generic, it usually creates a huge number of unnecessary temporary objects. If the JDK had taken the "printOn: aStream" paradigm from Smalltalk, the temporary objects used would be significantly reduced. This paradigm basically allows any object to be appended to a stream. In Java, it looks something like:

```
public String toString()
{
  StringBuffer s =new  StringBuffer();
```

```
  appendTo(s);
  return s.toString( );
}

public void appendTo(StringBuffer s)
{
  //The real work of converting to strings. Any embedded
  //objects would have their 'appendTo( )' methods called,
  //NOT their 'toString( )' methods.
  ...
}
```

This implementation allows far fewer objects to be created in converting to strings. In addition, as StringBuffer is not a stream, this implementation becomes much more useful if you use a java.io.StringWriter and change the appendTo( ) method to accept any Writer, for example:

```
public String toString( )
{
  java.io.StringWriter s =new  java.io.StringWriter( );
  appendTo(s);
  return s.getBuffer( ).toString( );
}

public void appendTo(java.io.Writer s)
{
  //The real work of converting to strings. Any embedded
  //objects would have their 'appendTo( )' methods called,
  //NOT their 'toString( )' methods.
  ...
}
```

This implementation allows the one appendTo( ) method to write out any object to any streamed writer object. Unfortunately, this implementation is not supported by the Object class, so you need to create your own framework of methods and interfaces to support this implementation. I find that I can use an Appendable interface with an appendTo( ) method, and then write toString( ) methods that check for that interface:

```
public interface Appendable
{
  public void appendTo(java.io.Writer s);
}

public class SomeClass
  implements Appendable
{
  Object[ ] embeddedObjects;

  ...

  public String toString( )
  {
```

```
        java.io.StringWriter s =new  java.io.StringWriter( );
        appendTo(s);
        return s.getBuffer( ).toString( );
    }
    public void appendTo(java.io.Writer s)
    {
        //The real work of converting to strings. Any embedded
        //objects would have their 'appendTo( )' methods called,
        //NOT their 'toString( )' methods.
        for (int i = 0; i<embeddedObjects.length; i++)
          if (embeddedObjects[i] instanceof Appendable)
            ( (Appendable) embeddedObjects[i]).appendTo(s);
          else
            s.write(embeddedObjects[i].toString( ));
    }
}
```

In addition, you can extend this framework even further to override the appending of
frequently used classes such as Vector, allowing a more efficient conversion mechanism that uses fewer temporary objects:

```
public class AppenderHelper
{
  final static String NULL = "null";
  final static String OPEN = "[";
  final static String CLOSE = "]";
  final static String MIDDLE = ", ";

  public void appendCheckingAppendable(Object o, java.io.Writer s)
  {
    //Use more efficient Appendable interface if possible,
    //and NULL string if appropriate
    if ((o = v.elementAt(0)) == null)
      s.write(NULL);
    else if (o instanceof Appendable)
      ( (Appendable) o).appendTo(s);
    else
      s.write(o.toString( ));
  }

  public void appendVector(java.util.Vector v, java.io.Writer s)
  {
    int size = v.size( );
    Object o;

    //Write the opening bracket
    s.write(OPEN);

    if (size != 0)
    {
      //Add the first element
      appendCheckingAppendable(v.elementAt(0), s);
      //And add in each other element preceded by the MIDDLE separator
      for(int i = 1; i < size; i++)
```

```
        {
            s.append(MIDDLE);
            appendCheckingAppendable(v.elementAt(i), s);
        }
    }

    //Write the closing bracket
    s.append(CLOSE);
  }
}
```

If you add this framework to an application, you can support the notion of converting objects to string representations to a particular depth. For example, a Vector containing another Vector to depth two looks like this:

```
[1, 2, [3, 4, 5]]
```

But to depth one, it looks like this:

```
[1, 2, Vector@4444]
```

The default Object.toString() implementation in the JDK writes out strings for objects as:

```
return getClass().getName() + "@" + Integer.toHexString(hashCode());
```

The JDK implementation is inefficient for two reasons. First, the method creates an unnecessary intermediate string because it uses the concatenation operator twice. Second, the Class.getName() method (which is a native method) also creates a new string every time it is called: the class name is not cached. It turns out that if you reimplement this to cache the class name and avoid the extra temporary strings, your conversion is faster and uses fewer temporary objects. The two are related, of course: using fewer temporary objects means less object-creation overhead.

You can create a generic framework that converts the basic data types while also supporting the efficient conversion of JDK classes (such as Vector, as well as Integer, Long, etc.). With this framework in place, I find that performance is generally improved because the application uses more efficient conversion algorithms and reduces the number of temporary objects. In almost every respect, this framework is better than the simpler framework, which supports only the toString() method.

Strings Versus char Arrays

In one of my first programming courses, in the language C, our instructor made an interesting comment. He said, "C has lightning-fast string handling because it has no string type." He went on to explain this oxymoron by pointing out that in C, any null-terminated sequence of bytes can be considered a string: this convention is supported by all string-handling functions. The point is that since the convention is adhered to fairly rigorously, there is no need to use only the standard string-handling functions. Any string manipulation you want to do can be executed directly on the byte array, allowing you to bypass or rewrite any string-handling functions you need to speed up. Because you are not forced to run through a restricted set of manipulation functions, it is always possible to optimize code using your own hand-crafted functions. Furthermore, some string-manipulating functions operate directly on the original byte array rather than creating a copy of this array. This can be a source of bugs, but is another reason speed can be optimized.

In Java, the inability to subclass String or access its internal char array means you cannot use the techniques applied in C. Even if you could subclass String, this does not avoid the second problem: many other methods operate on or return copies of a String. Generally, there is no way to avoid using String objects for code external to your application classes. But internally, you can provide your own char array type that allows you to manipulate strings according to your needs.

As an example, let's look at a couple of simple text-parsing problems: first, counting the words in a body of text, and second, using a filter to select lines of a file based on whether they contain a particular string.

Word-Counting Example

Let's look at the typical Java approach to counting words in a text. I use the StreamTokenizer for the word count, as that class is tailor-made for this kind of problem.

The word count is fairly easy to implement. The only difficulty comes in defining what a word is and coaxing the StreamTokenizer to agree with that definition. To keep things simple, I define a word as any contiguous sequence of alphanumeric characters. This means that words with apostrophes and numbers with decimal points count as two words, but I'm more interested in the performance than the niceties of word definitions here, and I want to keep the implementation simple. The implementation looks like this:

```
public static void wordcount(String filename)
  throws IOException
{
  int count = 0;
  //create the tokenizer, and initialize it
  FileReader r = new FileReader(filename);
  StreamTokenizer rdr = new StreamTokenizer(r);
  rdr.resetSyntax();
  rdr.wordChars('a', 'z'); //words include any lowercase character
  rdr.wordChars('A', 'Z'); //words include any uppercase character
  rdr.wordChars('0','9');  //words include any digit
  //everything else is whitespace
  rdr.whitespaceChars(0, '0'-1);
  rdr.whitespaceChars('9'+1, 'A'-1);
  rdr.whitespaceChars('z'+1, '\uffff');
  int token;
  //loop getting each token (word) from the tokenizer
```

```
    //until we reach the end of the file
    while( (token = rdr.nextToken()) != StreamTokenizer.TT_EOF)
    {
      //If the token is a word, count it, otherwise it is whitespace
      if ( token == StreamTokenizer.TT_WORD)
        count++;
    }
    System.out.println(count + " words found.");
    r.close();
}
```

Now, for comparison, implement a more efficient version using char arrays. The word-count algorithm is relatively straightforward: test for sequences of alphanumerics and skip anything else. The only slight complication comes when you refill the buffer with the next chunk from the file. You need to avoid counting one word as two if it falls across the junction of the two reads into the buffer, but this turns out to be easy to handle. You simply need to remember the last character of the last chunk and skip any alphanumeric characters at the beginning of the next chunk if that last character was alphanumeric (i.e., continue with the word until it terminates). The implementation looks like this:

```
public static void cwordcount(String filename)
  throws IOException
{
  int count = 0;
  FileReader rdr = new FileReader(filename);
  //buffer to hold read in characters
  char[] buf = new char[8192];
  int len;
  int idx = 0;
  //initialize so that our 'current' character is in whitespace
  char c = ' ';
  //read in each chunk as much as possible,
  //until there is nothing left to read
  while( (len = rdr.read(buf, 0, buf.length)) != -1)
  {
    idx = 0;
    int start;
    //if we are already in a word, then skip the rest of it
    if (Character.isLetterOrDigit(c))
      while( (idx < len) && Character.isLetterOrDigit(buf[idx]) )
        {idx++;}
    while(idx < len)
    {
      //skip non alphanumeric
      while( (idx < len) && !Character.isLetterOrDigit(buf[idx]) )
        {idx++;}
      //skip word
      start = idx;
      while( (idx < len) && Character.isLetterOrDigit(buf[idx]) )
        {idx++;}
      if (start < len)
```

```
        {
            count++; //count word
        }
    }
    //get last character so we know whether to carry on a word
    c = buf[idx-1];
}
System.out.println(count + " words found.");
}
```

You can compare this implementation with the one using the StreamTokenizer. All tests use the same large text file for counting the words. I normalize to 100% the time taken by StreamTokenizer using JDK 1.2.2 with the JIT compiler (see Table 5-6). Interestingly, the test takes a similar amount of time when I run using the StreamTokenizer without the JIT compiler running.

Table 5-6. Word counter timings using wordcount or cwordcount methods

VM	1.1.8	1.2.2	1.3.1	1.3.1 -server	1.4.0	1.4.0 -server	1.2 no JIT
wordcount	153%	100%	232%	230%	11%	9.3%	171%
cwordcount	1.7%	1.6%	2.3%	1.9%	2.3%	1.9%	33%

These results are quite curious. I suspect the curious results and huge differences may have something to do with StreamTokenizer being a severely underoptimized class, as well as being too generic a tool for this particular test.

Looking at object usage,[*] you find that the StreamTokenizer implementation winds through over 1.5 million temporary objects, whereas the char array implementation uses only around 20 objects. Now the results are more explicable. Object-creation differences of this order of magnitude impose a huge overhead on the StreamTokenizer implementation, explaining why the StreamTokenizer is so much slower than the char array implementation. The object-creation overhead also explains why both the JIT and non-JIT tests took similar times for the StreamTokenizer. Object creation requires similar amounts of time in the pre-1.4 VMs, and clearly the performance of the StreamTokenizer is limited by the number of objects it uses (see Chapter 4 for further details). The times also show that the VMs are getting much much better at reducing object creation and garbage collection overhead. The 1.4 test has the advantages of the latest object-creation/garbage-collection techniques, in addition to more optimized byte-to-char conversion from the 1.4 nio package.

---

[*] Object monitoring is easily done using the monitoring tools from Chapter 2, both the object-creation monitor and the -verbosegc option with an explicit System.gc() at the end of the test.

Line Filter Example

For the example of a filter to select lines of a file, I'll use the simple `BufferedReader.readLine()` method. This contrasts with the previous methodology using a dedicated class (`StreamTokenizer`), which turned out to be extremely inefficient. The `readline()` method should present us with more of a performance-tuning challenge, as it is relatively much simpler and so should be more efficient. I'll also add case-independence to the filtering, i.e., the lines will be selected even if the case of the characters in the line do not exactly match the case of the characters in the filter.

The filter using `BufferedReader` and `Strings` is easily implemented. The search phrase is uppercased at the beginning, and each line of text is uppercased so that lines are selected independently of case. I include an option to print only the count of matching lines. The only slightly complex tweak is that I want to avoid any dependence on I/O in the timings, as this is not an I/O test, so I map the file contents into memory and use a `CharArrayReader` rather than a `FileReader`:

```
public static void filter1(String filter, String filename, boolean print)
    throws IOException
  {
    count = 0;
//    BufferedReader rdr = new BufferedReader(new FileReader(filename));
    BufferedReader rdr = new BufferedReader(new CharArrayReader(buf));
    String line;
    String ufilter = filter.toUpperCase();
    while( (line = rdr.readLine()) != null)
    {
      if (line.toUpperCase().indexOf(ufilter) != -1)
      {
        count++;
        if (print)
          System.out.println(line);
      }
    }
    System.out.println(count + " lines matched.");
    rdr.close();
  }
```

Clearly it is not optimal to generate an extra string for every line, as `toUpperCase()` does. `String` doesn't provide any simple case-independent search alternatives, though `regionMatches()` can be used by testing iteratively through each line. For completeness we'll measure that solution too:

```
public static void filter2(String filter, String filename, boolean print)
    throws IOException
  {
    count = 0;
//    BufferedReader rdr = new BufferedReader(new FileReader(filename));
    BufferedReader rdr = new BufferedReader(new CharArrayReader(buf));
    String line;
```

```
    int filterLength = filter.length( );
    while( (line = rdr.readLine( )) != null)
    {
      for(int i = 0; i < line.length( ); i++)
        if (line.regionMatches(true, i, filter, 0, filterLength))
        {
          count++;
          if (print)
            System.out.println(line);
          break;
        }
    }
    System.out.println(count + " lines matched.");
    rdr.close( );
  }
```

Now let's consider how to handle this filter using char arrays. As in the previous
example, you read chunks into your char array. However, this example is a bit more
complicated than the word-count example. Here you need to test for a match against
another char array, look for line endings, and handle reforming lines that are broken
between read( ) calls in a more complete manner than for the word count.

Internationalization doesn't change this example in any obvious way. Both the
readLine( ) implementation and the char array implementation stay the same whatever language the text contains.

This statement about internationalization is slightly disingenuous. In
fact, searches in some languages allow words to match even if they are
spelled differently. For example, when searching for a French word
that contains an accented letter, the user might expect a nonaccented
spelling to match. This is similar to searching for the word "color" and
expecting to match the British spelling "colour."

Such sophistication depends on how extensively the application supports this variation in spelling. The java.text.Collator class has four
"strength" levels that support variations in the precision of word comparisons. Both implementations for the example in this section correspond to matches using the Collator.IDENTICAL strength together with
the Collator.NO_DECOMPOSITION mode.

The full commented listing for the char array implementation is shown shortly.
Looking at the code, it is clearly more complicated than using the BufferedReader.
readLine( ). Obviously you have to work a lot harder to get the performance you
want. The result, though, is that some tests run as much as five times faster using the
char array implementation (see Tables 5-7 and 5-8). The line lengths of the test files
make a big difference, hence the variation in results. In addition, the char array
implementation uses only 1% of the number of objects compared to the
BufferedReader.readLine( ) implementation.

Table 5-7. Filter timings using filter or cfilter method on a short-line file

VM	1.1.8	1.2.2	1.3.1	1.3.1 -server	1.4.0	1.4.0 -server	1.4.0 -Xint
filter1 (uppercased)	168%	100%	49%	40%	49%	31%	626%
filter2 (regionMatches)	140%	88%	53%	48%	60%	49%	1137%
cfilter (proprietary)	17%	17%	19%	17%	20%	15%	337%

Table 5-8. Filter timings using filter or cfilter method on a long-line file

VM	1.1.8	1.2.2	1.3.1	1.3.1 -server	1.4.0	1.4.0 -server	1.4.0 -Xint
filter1 (uppercased)	184%	100%	64%	54%	71%	47%	829%
filter2 (regionMatches)	183%	138%	113%	107%	124%	103%	2332%
cfilter (proprietary)	33%	33%	37%	28%	38%	27%	633%

I have implemented a relatively straightforward class for the char array parsing. If you look in more detail at what you are doing, you can apply further optimizations and make the routine even faster (see, for example, Chapter 7 and Chapter 8).

Tuning like this takes effort, but you can see that it is possible to use char arrays to very good effect for most types of String manipulation. If you are an object purist, you may want to encapsulate the char array access. Otherwise, you may be content to expose external access through static methods. In any case, it is worth investing some time and effort in creating a usable char-handling class. Usually this creation is a single, up-front effort. If the classes are well constructed, you can use them consistently within your applications, and this effort pays off handsomely when it comes to tuning (or, occasionally, the lack of a need to tune).

Here is the commented char array implementation that executes a line-by-line string-matching filter on a file:

```
/** Note that this implementation may have problems with
    text lines longer than 8192 characters.
*/
class MatchReader
{

  public static void filter(String filter, String filename, boolean print)
    throws IOException
  {
//    MatchReader rdr = new MatchReader(new FileReader(filename), filter);
    MatchReader rdr = new MatchReader(new CharArrayReader(FilterComparison.buf),
filter);
    rdr.filter(print);
  }

  static final int BUFFER_SIZE = 8192;
  char[ ] buffer;
  int bufferSize;
```

```
int bufferPos;
char[ ] matchString;
Reader reader;
Writer sysout;

public MatchReader(Reader rdr, String match)
  throws IOException
{
  reader = rdr;
  matchString = new char[match.length( )];
  match.toUpperCase( ).getChars(0, match.length( ), matchString, 0);
  buffer = new char[BUFFER_SIZE];
  bufferSize = 0;
  bufferPos = 0;
  sysout = new OutputStreamWriter(System.out);
  fillBuffer( );
}

/* return true if more characters were read, otherwise false */
private boolean fillBuffer( )
  throws IOException
{
  int len;
  boolean added = false;
  while(bufferSize < buffer.length)
  {
    len = reader.read(buffer, bufferSize, buffer.length-bufferSize);
    if (len <= 0)
      return added;
    else
      bufferSize += len;
    added = true;
  }
  return added;
}

public void filter(boolean print)
  throws IOException
{
  int count = 0;
  while( nextMatchedLine( ) )
  {
    count++;
    if (print)
      printCurrentLine( );
    else
      nextLine( );
  }
  System.out.println(count + " lines matched.");
  close( );
}

public void close( )
  throws IOException
```

```
{
  buffer = null;
  matchString = null;
  reader.close();
}

/* Return true if we matched a line,
 * false if there were no more matches
 */
public boolean nextMatchedLine()
  throws IOException
{
  while(!scrollToNextMatchInCurrentBuffer())
  {
    if (!refillBuffer())
    {
      //No more characters to read, just make sure
      //that no more lines are left in the buffer
      return scrollToNextMatchInCurrentBuffer();
    }
  }
  return true;
}

private boolean scrollToNextMatchInCurrentBuffer()
{
  //Simple linear search
  //No need to try to match beyond the end of the buffer
  int highIdx = bufferSize-matchString.length;
  for (; bufferPos <= highIdx; bufferPos++)
  {
    if (matches())
      return true;
  }
  return false;
}

private boolean matches()
{
  //Assume that this is only called if the match
  //characters can fit into the remaining buffer
  for(int j = 0; j < matchString.length ; j++)
    if(Character.toUpperCase(buffer[bufferPos+j]) != matchString[j])
      return false;
  return true;
}

private boolean refillBuffer()
  throws IOException
{
  return refillBuffer(bufferSize - 1);
}

private boolean refillBuffer(int lastIdx)
  throws IOException
```

```
{
  //Find the start of the last line in the buffer,
  //move that to the start of the buffer,
  //then append some more to the buffer.
  while( (lastIdx > 0) && (buffer[lastIdx] != '\n') && (buffer[lastIdx] != '\r') )
    lastIdx--;
  if ( (buffer[lastIdx] == '\n') || (buffer[lastIdx] == '\r') )
  {
    //Found the most recent newline character
    bufferSize -= lastIdx+1;
    System.arraycopy(buffer, lastIdx+1, buffer, 0, bufferSize);
    bufferPos = 0; //be safe
    return fillBuffer();
  }
  else
  {
    //reached the beginning of the buffer and we still don't have a newline
    return fillBuffer();
  }
}

/* Scroll to just after the next newline character */
public void nextLine()
  throws IOException
{
  while(!scrollToNextLineInCurrentBuffer())
  {
    if (!refillBuffer())
    {
      //No more characters to read, just make sure
      //that no more lines are left in the buffer
      scrollToNextLineInCurrentBuffer();
    }
  }
}

private boolean scrollToNextLineInCurrentBuffer()
{
  //Simple linear search
  //No need to try to match beyond the end of the buffer
  int highIdx = bufferSize-1;
  for (; bufferPos <= highIdx; bufferPos++)
  {
    if ( (buffer[bufferPos] == '\n') || (buffer[bufferPos] == '\r') )
    {
      bufferPos++;
      return true;
    }
  }
  return false;
}

private void printCurrentLine()
  throws IOException
```

```
{
    //Move the start of the current line back to beginning of
    //the buffer, fill it up, and find the next line
    refillBuffer(bufferPos);
    scrollToNextLineInCurrentBuffer( );
    sysout.write(buffer, 0, bufferPos-1);
    sysout.write(FilterComparison.NewLine);
    sysout.flush( );
  }
}
```

The individual methods listed here are fairly basic. As with the JDK methods, I assume a line termination is indicated by a newline or return character. Otherwise, the main effort comes in writing efficient array-matching methods. In this example, I did not try hard to look for the very best array-matching algorithms. Instead, I used straightforward algorithms for clarity, since these are fast enough for the example. There are many sources describing more sophisticated array-matching algorithms; for example, the University of Rouen in France has a nice site listing "Exact String Matching Algorithms" at *http://www-igm.univ-mlv.fr/~lecroq/string/*.

Line Filtering with Regular Expressions

JDK 1.4 includes native support for regular expressions in one of the core packages, java.util.regex. String methods were also added as shortcuts to using the regular-expression objects. For example, the simplest additional new method is String. matches(String regex), which simply returns a boolean if the string can be matched by the regular-expression argument.

 Regular expressions are a pattern-matching language that provides a powerful mechanism to determine if sequences of characters contain particular patterns and to extract those patterns. Almost every type of parsing is much easier and more flexible using regular expressions. For more details about regular expressions, see *Mastering Regular Expressions* by Jeffrey Friedl (O'Reilly & Associates).

However, be aware that the methods in the String class are adequate for one-off uses of regular expressions but are inefficient for repeated application of a regular expression. The String methods both compile (into a java.util.regex.Pattern object) and apply the regular expression on each execution, whereas it is more efficient to compile a regular expression once and apply it repeatedly using the same object. For example, this statement:

```
boolean result = string.matches(regex);
```

executes the equivalent of:

```
Pattern p = Pattern.compile(regex);
Matcher m = p.matcher(string);
boolean result = m.matches( );
```

If the regular expression is to be reapplied to multiple strings, the efficient solution would call the Pattern.compile( ) method only once, but that option is not available if you use the shortcut String.matches(String regex) method.

The line-filtering example in the previous section is a fairly simple problem and doesn't need the full power of regular expressions, but since we have already seen the equivalent functionality in alternative implementations it is worth looking at the cost of using regular expressions to handle the filtering. The method required is straightforward, but I'll walk through it in case you are unused to regular expressions.

First, the regular-expression pattern needs to be compiled into a Pattern object. The pattern itself needs to be wrapped with some characters to indicate that we are searching one line at a time: the ^ character denotes the beginning of a line, and the $ character denotes the end of a line. The .* pattern simply indicates that anything can match between the beginning and the end of the line as long as the filter string is included. In addition, the Pattern object needs to know that we are searching line-by-line, as it also supports searching text while treating line endings simply as any other characters, so we use the MULTILINE flag. We also need the CASE_INSENSITIVE flag to make the match case-insensitive. Next, we will use a java.nio.CharBuffer to wrap the characters, a convenient mechanism to present the text to the Matcher. We could use a String, but if we were actually reading from a file the most efficient mechanism would be to use a CharBuffer on a FileChannel, so I'll stay with the CharBuffer.

Finally, we simply loop, repeatedly matching the regular expression against the text using the Matcher.find( ) method. The Matcher.group( ) method provides us with the previously matched line of text if we need it for printing:

```
public static void filter3(String filter, String filename, boolean print)
      throws IOException
  {
    count = 0;
    Pattern p = Pattern.compile("^.*" + filter + ".*$",
                  Pattern.MULTILINE | Pattern.CASE_INSENSITIVE);
    CharBuffer cbuff = CharBuffer.wrap(buf);
    Matcher m = p.matcher(cbuff);
    while( m.find( ) )
    {
      count++;
      if (print)
        System.out.println(m.group( ));
    }
    System.out.println(count + " lines matched.");
  }
```

The results of testing this method along with the previous methods used to filter lines are shown in Table 5-9. The results show that for our simple line-filtering problem, using regular expressions is slower than the other implementations, but not hugely slower. This shows that the regular-expression implementation in JDK 1.4. is pretty efficient, given how much more it is doing (and can do) compared with the other methods. It certainly looks like you can use regular expressions with some confidence that the implementation is pretty efficient.

Table 5-9. Filter timings using various filter methods in JDK 1.4

VM	1.4.0	1.4.0 -server	1.4.0 -Xint
filter1 (uppercased)	100%	65%	1320%
filter2 (regionMatches)	128%	104%	2390%
cfilter (proprietary)	42%	31%	707%
filter3 (regular expression)	143%	88%	3666%

String Comparisons and Searches

String comparison performance is highly dependent on both the string data and the comparison algorithm (this is really a truism about collections in general). The methods that come with the String class have a performance advantage in being able to directly access the underlying char collection. So if you need to make String comparisons, String methods usually provide better performance than your own methods, provided that you can make your desired comparison fit in with one of the String methods. Another necessary consideration is whether comparisons are case-sensitive or -insensitive, and I will consider this in more detail shortly.

To optimize for string comparisons, you need to look at the source of the comparison methods so you know exactly how they work. As an example, consider the String. equals( ) and String.equalsIgnoreCase( ) methods from the Java 2 distribution.

String.equals(Object) runs in a fairly straightforward way: it first checks for object identity, then for null, then for String type, then for same-size strings, and then character by character, running from the first character to the last. Efficient and complete.

String.equalsIgnoreCase(String) is a little more complex. It checks for null, and then for strings being the same size (the String type check is not needed, since this method accepts only String objects). Then, using a case-insensitive comparison, regionMatches( ) is applied. regionMatches( ) runs a character-by-character test from the first character to the last, converting each character to uppercase before comparing.

Immediately, you see that the more differences there are between the two strings, the faster these methods return. This behavior is common for collection comparisons, and the order of the comparison is crucial. In these two cases, the strings are compared starting with the first character, so the earlier the difference occurs, the faster the methods return. However, equals( ) returns faster if the two String objects are identical. It is unusual to check Strings by identity, but there are a number of situations where it is useful (for example, when you are using a set of canonical Strings; see

Chapter 4). Another example is when an application has enough time during string input to `intern( )`* the strings, so that later comparisons by identity are possible.

In any case, `equals( )` returns immediately if the two strings are identical, but `equalsIgnoreCase( )` does not even check for identity (which may be reasonable given what it does). This results in `equals( )` running an order of magnitude faster than `equalsIgnoreCase( )` if the two strings are identical; identical strings is the fastest test case resolvable for `equals( )`, but the slowest case for `equalsIgnoreCase( )`.

On the other hand, if the two strings are different in size, `equalsIgnoreCase( )` has only two tests to make before it returns, whereas `equals( )` makes four tests before it returns. This can make `equalsIgnoreCase( )` run 20% faster than `equals( )` for what may be the most common difference between strings.

There are more differences between these two methods. In almost every possible case of string data, `equals( )` runs faster (often several times faster) than `equalsIgnoreCase( )`. However, in a test against the words from a particular dictionary, I found that over 90% of the words were different in size from a randomly chosen word. When comparing the performance of these two methods for a comparison of a randomly chosen word against the entire dictionary, the total comparison time taken by each of the two methods was about the same. The many cases in which strings had different lengths compensated almost exactly for the slower comparison of `equalsIgnoreCase( )` when the strings were similar or equal. This illustrates how the data and the algorithm interplay with each other to affect performance.

Even though `String` methods have access to the internal chars, it can be faster to use your own methods if there are no `String` methods appropriate for your test. You can build methods that are tailored to the data you have. One way to optimize an equality test is to look for ways to make the strings identical. An alternative that can actually be better for performance is to change the search strategy to reduce search time. For example, a linear search through a large array of `Strings` is slower than a binary search through the same size array if the array is sorted. This, in turn, is slower than a straight access to a hashed table. Note that when you are able and willing to deploy changes to JDK classes (e.g., for servlets), you can add methods directly to the `String` class. However, altering JDK classes can lead to maintenance problems.†

When case-insensitive searches are required, one standard optimization is to use a second collection containing all the strings uppercased. This second collection is used for comparisons, obviating the need to repeatedly uppercase each character in the search methods. For example, if you have a hash table containing `String` keys,

---

* `String.intern( )` returns the `String` object that is being stored in the internal VM string pool. If two `Strings` are equal, then their `intern( )` results are identical; for example, if `s1.equals(s2)` is true, then `s1.intern( )` `== s2.intern( )` is also true.

† Several of my colleagues have emphasized their view that changes to the JDK sources lead to severe maintenance problems.

you need to iterate over all the keys to match keys case-insensitively. But, if you have a second hash table with all the keys uppercased, retrieving the key simply requires you to uppercase the element being searched for:

```
//The slow version, iterating through all the keys ignoring case
//until the key matches. (hash is a Hashtable)
public Object slowlyGet(String key)
{
  Enumeration e = hash.keys( );
  String hkey;
  while(e.hasMoreElements( ))
  {
    if (key.equalsIgnoreCase(hkey = (String) e.getNext( ))
      return hash.get(hkey);
  }
  return null;
}

//The fast version assumes that a second hashtable was created
//with all the keys uppercased. Access is straightforward.
public Object quicklyGet(String key)
{
  return uppercasedHash.get(key.toUppercase( ));
}
```

However, note that String.toUppercase( ) (and String.toLowercase( )) creates a complete copy of the String object with a new char array. Unlike String.substring( ), String.toUppercase( ) has a processing time that is linearly dependent on the size of the string and also creates an extra object (a new char array). This means that repeatedly using String.toUppercase( ) (and String.toLowercase( )) can impose a heavy overhead on an application. For each particular problem, you need to ensure that the extra temporary objects created and the extra processing overhead still provide a performance benefit rather than causing a new bottleneck in the application.

Sorting Internationalized Strings

One big advantage with Strings is that they are built (almost) from the ground up to support internationalization. This means that the Unicode character set is the lingua franca in Java. Unfortunately, because Unicode uses two-byte characters, many string libraries based on one-byte characters that can be ported into Java do not work so well. Most string-search optimizations use tables to assist string searches, but the table size is related to the size of the character set. For example, a traditional Boyer-Moore string search takes a great deal of memory and a long initialization phase to use with Unicode.

Furthermore, sorting international Strings requires the ability to handle many kinds of localization issues, such as the sorted location for accented characters, characters that can be treated as character pairs, and so on. In these cases, it is difficult (and usually

The Boyer-Moore String-Search Algorithm

The Boyer-Moore string search uses a table of characters to skip comparisons. Here's a simple example with none of the complexities. Assume you are matching "abcd" against a string. The "abcd" is aligned against the first four characters of the string. The fourth character of the string is checked first. If that fourth character is none of a, b, c, or d, the "abcd" can be skipped to be matched against the fifth to eighth characters, and the matching proceeds in the same way. If instead the fourth character of the string is b, the "abcd" can be skipped to align the b against the fourth character, and the matching proceeds as before. For optimum speed, this algorithm requires several arrays giving skip distances for each possible character in the character set. For more detail, see *The Art of Computer Programming* by Donald Knuth (Addison-Wesley) or the paper "Fast Algorithms for Sorting and Searching Strings," by Jon Bentley and Robert Sedgewick, Proceedings of the 8th Annual ACM-SIAM Symposium on Discrete Algorithms, January 1997.

impossible) to handle the general case yourself. It is almost always easier to use the String helper classes Java provides, for example, the java.text.Collator class.[*]

Using the java.text.CollationKey object to represent each string is a standard optimization for repeated comparisons of internationalized Strings. You can use this when sorting an array of Strings, for example. CollationKeys perform more than twice as fast as using java.text.Collator.compare( ). It is probably easiest to see how to use collation keys with a particular example. So let's look at tuning an internationalized String sort.

For this, I use a standard quicksort algorithm (the quicksort implementation can be found in "Finding the Index for Partially Matched Strings" in Chapter 11). The only modification to the standard quicksort is that for each optimization, the quicksort needs to be adjusted to use the appropriate comparison method and the appropriate data type. For example, the generic quicksort that sorts an array of Comparable objects has the signature:

```
public static void quicksort(Comparable[ ] arr, int lo, int hi)
```

and uses the Comparable.compareTo(Object) method when comparing two Comparable objects. On the other hand, a generic quicksort that sorts objects based on a java.util.Comparator has the signature:

```
public static void quicksort(Object[ ] arr, int lo, int hi, Comparator c)
```

---

[*] The code that handles this type of work didn't really start to get integrated in Java until 1.1 and did not start to be optimized until JDK 1.2. An article by Laura Werner of IBM in the February 1999 issue of the *Java Report*, "Efficient Text Searching in Java," covers the optimizations added to the java.text.Collator class for JDK 1.2. There is also a useful StringSearch class available at the IBM alphaWorks site (*http://alphaworks.ibm.com/tech/stringsearch*).

and uses the java.util.Comparator.compare(Object, Object) method when comparing any two objects. (See java.util.Arrays.sort( ) for a specific example.) In each case the underlying algorithm is the same. Only the comparison method changes (and in general the data type too, though not in these examples where the data type was Object).

The obvious first test, to get a performance baseline, is the straightforward internationalized sort:

```
public runsort( ) {
  quicksort(stringArray,0,stringArray.length-1, Collator.getInstance( ));
}
public static void quicksort(String[ ] arr, int lo, int hi, java.text.Collator c)
{
  ...
  int mid = ( lo + hi ) / 2;
  String middle = arr[ mid ]; //String data type
  ...
  //uses Collator.compare(String, String)
  if( c.compare(arr[ lo ], middle) > 0 )
  ...
}
```

I use a large dictionary of words for the array of strings, inserted in random order, and I use the same random order for each of the tests. The first test took longer than expected. Looking at the Collator class, I can see that it does a huge amount of work, and I cannot possibly bypass its internationalized support if I want to support internationalized strings.[*]

However, as previously mentioned, the java.util.CollationKey class is specifically designed to provide for this type of speedup. It is simple to convert the sort in order to use this. You still need the Collator to generate the CollationKeys, so add a conversion method. The sort now looks like:

```
public runsort( ) {
  quicksort(stringArray,0,stringArray.length-1, Collator.getInstance( ));
}
public static void quicksort(String[ ] arr, int lo, int hi, Collator c)
{
  //convert to an array of CollationKeys
  CollationKey keys[ ] = new CollationKey[arr.length];
  for (int i = arr.length-1; i >= 0; i--)
    keys[i] = c.getCollationKey(arr[i]);

  //Run the sort on the collation keys
  quicksort_collationKey(keys, 0, arr.length-1);
```

---

[*] The kind of investment made in building such global support is beyond most projects; it is almost always much cheaper to buy the support. In this case, Taligent put a huge number of man years into the globalization you get for free with the JDK.

```
    //and unwrap so that we get our Strings in sorted order
    for (int i = arr.length-1; i >= 0; i--)
      arr[i] = keys[i].getSourceString();
  }
  public static void quicksort_collationKey(CollationKey[ ] arr, int lo, int hi)
  {
    ...
    int mid = ( lo + hi ) / 2;
    CollationKey middle = arr[ mid ];   //CollationKey data type
    ...
    //uses CollationKey.compareTo(CollationKey)
    if( arr[ lo ].compareTo(middle) > 0 )
    ...
  }
```

Normalizing the time for the first test to 100%, this test is much faster and takes less than half the time (see Table 5-10). This is despite the extra cost imposed by a whole new populated array of CollationKey objects, one for each string. Can it do better? Well, there is nothing further in the java.text package that suggests so. Instead look at the String class, and consider its implementation of the String.compareTo( ) method. This is a simple lexicographic ordering, basically treating the char array as a sequence of numbers and ordering sequence pairs as if there is no meaning to the object being Strings. Obviously, this is useless for internationalized support, but it is much faster. A quick test shows that sorting the test String array using the String. compareTo( ) method takes just 2% of time of the first test, which seems much more reasonable.

But is this test incompatible with the desired internationalized sort? Well, maybe not. Sort algorithms usually execute faster if they operate on a partially sorted array. Perhaps using the String.compareTo( ) sort first might bring the array considerably closer to the final ordering of the internationalized sort, and at a fairly low cost. Testing this is straightforward:

```
  public runsort( ) {
    quicksort(stringArray,0,stringArray.length-1, Collator.getInstance( ));
  }
  public static void quicksort(String[ ] arr, int lo, int hi, Collator c)
  {
    //simple sort using String.compareTo( )
    simple_quicksort(arr, lo, hi);

    //Full international sort on a hopefully partially sorted array
    intl_quicksort(arr, lo, hi, c);
  }
  public static void simple_quicksort(String[ ] arr, int lo, int hi)
  {
    ...
    int mid = ( lo + hi ) / 2;
    String middle = arr[ mid ];   //uses String data type
    ...
    //uses String.compareTo(String)
```

```
    if( arr[ lo ].compareTo(middle) > 0 )
      ...
}
public static void intl_quicksort(String[] arr, int lo, int hi, Collator c)
{
    //convert to an array of CollationKeys
    CollationKey keys[] = new CollationKey[arr.length];
    for (int i = arr.length-1; i >= 0; i--)
      keys[i] = c.getCollationKey(arr[i]);

    //Run the sort on the collation keys
    quicksort_collationKey(keys, 0, arr.length-1);

    //and unwrap so that we get our Strings in sorted order
    for (int i = arr.length-1; i >= 0; i--)
      arr[i] = keys[i].getSourceString();
}
public static void quicksort_collationKey(CollationKey[] arr, int lo, int hi)
{
    ...
    int mid = ( lo + hi ) / 2;
    CollationKey middle = arr[ mid ]; //CollationKey data type
    ...
    //uses CollationKey.compareTo(CollationKey)
    if( arr[ lo ].compareTo(middle) > 0 )
      ...
}
```

This double-sorting implementation reduces the international sort time to a quarter of the original test time (see Table 5-10). Partially sorting the list first using a much simpler (and quicker) comparison test has doubled the speed of the total sort as compared to using only the CollationKeys optimization.

Table 5-10. Timings using different sorting strategies

Sort using:	1.1.8	1.2.2	1.3.1	1.3.1 -server	1.4.0	1.4.0 -server	1.4.0 -Xint
Collator	266%	100%	65%	22%	56%	51%	1235%
CollationKeys	80%	39%	24%	18%	27%	15%	226%
Sorted twice	35%	18%	9.8%	7.9%	12%	8.5%	133%
String.compareTo( )	2.3%	2.3%	1.8%	1.5%	1.9%	1.4%	23%

Of course, these optimizations have improved the situation only for the particular locale I have tested (my default locale is set for US English). However, running the test in a sampling of other locales (European and Asian locales), I find similar relative speedups. Without using locale-specific dictionaries, this locale variation test may not be fully valid, but the speedup will likely hold across all Latinized alphabets. You can also create a simple partial-ordering class-specific sort to some locales, which provides a similar speedup. For example, by duplicating the effect of using String.compareTo( ), you can provide the basis for a customized partial sorter:

```
public class PartialSorter {
  String source;
  char[ ] stringArray;
  public Sorting(String s)
  {
    //retain the original string
    source = s;
    //and get the array of characters for our customized comparison
    stringArray = new char[s.length( )];
    s.getChars(0, stringArray.length, stringArray, 0);
  }
  /* This compare method should be customized for different locales */
  public static int compare(char[ ] arr1, char[ ] arr2)
  {
    //basically the String.compareTo( ) algorithm
    int n = Math.min(arr1.length, arr2.length);
    for (int i = 0; i < n; i++)
    {
      if (arr1[i] != arr2[i])
        return arr1[i] - arr2[i];
    }
    return arr1.length - arr2.length;
  }
  public static void quicksort(String[ ] arr, int lo, int hi)
  {
    //convert to an array of PartialSorters
    PartialSorter keys[ ] = new PartialSorter[arr.length];
    for (int i = arr.length-1; i >= 0; i--)
      keys[i] = new PartialSorter(arr[i]);
    quicksort_mysorter(keys, 0, arr.length-1);
    //and unwrap so that we get our Strings in sorted order
    for (int i = arr.length-1; i >= 0; i--)
      arr[i] = keys[i].source;
  }
  public static void quicksort_mysorter(PartialSorter[ ] arr, int lo, int hi)
  {
    ...
    int mid = ( lo + hi ) / 2;
    PartialSorter middle = arr[ mid ]; //PartialSorter data type
    ...
    //Use the PartialSorter.compare( ) method to compare the char arrays
    if( compare(arr[ lo ].stringArray, middle.stringArray) > 0 )
      ...
  }
}
```

This PartialSorter class works similarly to the CollationKey class, wrapping a string and providing its own comparison method. The particular comparison method shown here is just an implementation of the String.compareTo( ) method. It is pointless to use it exactly as defined here because object-creation overhead means that using the PartialSorter is twice as slow as using the String.compareTo( ) directly. But customizing the PartialSorter.compare( ) method for any particular locale is a reasonable task: remember, we are interested only in a simple algorithm that handles a partial sort, not the full intricacies of completely accurate locale-specific comparison.

Generally, you cannot expect to support internationalized strings and retain the performance of simple one-byte-per-character strings. But, as shown here, you can certainly improve the performance.

Performance Checklist

Most of these suggestions apply only after a bottleneck has been identified:

- Logically partition your strings into those that require internationalization support (i.e., text) and those that don't.
  - — Avoid internationalization where the Strings never require it.
- Avoid using the StreamTokenizer.
- Regular expressions provide acceptable performance compared with using String searching methods and String character iteration tokenizing techniques.
- Create and optimize your own framework to convert objects and primitives to and from strings.
- Use efficient methods of String that do not copy the characters of the string, e.g., String.substring( ).
  - — Avoid using inefficient methods of String that copy the characters of the string, e.g., String.toUppercase( ) and String.toLowercase( ).
  - — Use the string concatenation operator to create Strings at compile time.
  - — Use StringBuffers to create Strings at runtime.
  - — Specify when the underlying char array is copied when reusing StringBuffers.
- Improve access to the underlying String char array by copying the chars into your own array.
  - — Manipulate characters in char arrays rather than using String and StringBuffer manipulation.
  - — Reuse char arrays.
- Optimize the string comparison and search algorithm for the data being compared and searched.
  - — Compare strings by identity.
  - — Convert a comparison task to a (hash) table lookup.

— Handle case-insensitive comparisons differently from case-sensitive comparisons.

— Apply the standard performance optimization for case-insensitive access (maintaining a second collection with all strings uppercased).

— Use `java.text.CollationKeys` rather than a `java.text.Collator` object to sort international strings.

— Use `String.compareTo( )` for string comparison where internationalization is unnecessary.

— Partially sort (international) strings using a simple comparison algorithm before using the full (internationalized) comparison.

CHAPTER 6

Exceptions, Assertions, Casts, and Variables

In this chapter:
- Exceptions
- Assertions
- Casts
- Variables
- Method Parameters

For every complex problem, there is a solution that is simple, neat, and wrong.
—H. L. Mencken

This chapter describes the costs of various programmatic elements, including exceptions, assertions (new in 1.4), casts, and variables. It also describes how to optimize your use of these elements.

Exceptions

In this section, we examine the cost of exceptions and consider ways to avoid that cost. First, we look at the costs associated with try-catch blocks, which are the structures you need to handle exceptions. Then, we go on to optimizing the use of exceptions.

The Cost of try-catch Blocks Without an Exception

try-catch blocks generally use no extra time if no exception is thrown, although some VMs may impose a slight penalty. The following test determines whether a VM imposes any significant overhead for try-catch blocks when the catch block is not entered. The test runs the same code twice, once with the try-catch entered for every loop iteration and again with just one try-catch wrapping the loop. Because we're testing the VM and not the compiler, you must ensure that your compiler has not optimized the test away; use an old JDK version to compile it if necessary. To determine that the test has not been optimized away by the compiler, you need to compile the code, then decompile it:

```
package tuning.exception;

public class TryCatchTimeTest
{
  public static void main(String[] args)
```

```
{
  int REPEAT = (args.length == 0) ? 10000000 : Integer.parseInt(args[0]);
  Object[] xyz = {new Integer(3), new Integer(10101), new Integer(67)};
  boolean res;
  long time = System.currentTimeMillis( );
  res = try_catch_in_loop(REPEAT, xyz);
  System.out.println("try catch in loop took    " +
    (System.currentTimeMillis( ) - time));

  time = System.currentTimeMillis( );
  res = try_catch_not_in_loop(REPEAT, xyz);
  System.out.println("try catch not in loop took " +
    (System.currentTimeMillis( ) - time));

  //Repeat the two tests several more times in this method
  //for consistency checking
  ...
}

public static boolean try_catch_not_in_loop(int repeat, Object[] o)
{
  Integer i[] = new Integer[3];
  try {
    for (int j = repeat; j > 0; j--)
    {
      i[0] = (Integer) o[(j+1)%2];
      i[1] = (Integer) o[j%2];
      i[2] = (Integer) o[(j+2)%2];
    }
    return false;
  }
  catch (Exception e) {return true;}
}

public static boolean try_catch_in_loop(int repeat, Object[] o)
{
  Integer i[] = new Integer[3];
  for (int j = repeat; j > 0; j--)
  {
    try {
      i[0] = (Integer) o[(j+1)%2];
      i[1] = (Integer) o[j%2];
      i[2] = (Integer) o[(j+2)%2];
    }
    catch (Exception e) {return true;}
  }
  return false;
}
}
```

Running this test in various VMs results in increases in the time taken by the looped
try-catch test relative to the nonlooped test for some VMs; however, the latest VMs
show no penalty. See Table 6-1.

Table 6-1. Extra cost of the looped try-catch test relative to the nonlooped try-catch test

VM	1.1.8	1.2.2	1.3.1	1.3.1 -server	1.4.0	1.4.0 -server	1.4.0 -xlnt
Increase in time	~5%	~10%	None	None	None	None	~2%

The Cost of try-catch Blocks with an Exception

Throwing an exception and executing the catch block has a significant overhead. This overhead seems to be due mainly to the cost of getting a snapshot of the stack when the exception is created (the snapshot allows the stack trace to be printed). The cost is large: exceptions should not be thrown as part of the normal code path of your application unless you have factored it in. Generating exceptions is one place where good design and performance go hand in hand. You should throw an exception only when the condition is truly exceptional. For example, an end-of-file condition is not an exceptional condition (all files end) unless the end-of-file occurs when more bytes are expected.[*] Generally, the performance cost of throwing an exception is equivalent to several hundred lines of simple code executions.

If your application is implemented to throw an exception during the normal flow of the program, you must not avoid the exception during performance tests. Any time costs coming from throwing exceptions must be included in performance testing, or the test results will be skewed from the actual performance of the application after deployment.

To find the cost of throwing an exception, compare two ways of testing whether an object is a member of a class: trying a cast and catching the exception if the cast fails, versus using instanceof. In the code that follows, I have highlighted the lines that run the alternative tests:

```
package tuning.exception;

public class TryCatchCostTest
{
  public static void main(String[] args)
  {
    Integer i = new Integer(3);
    Boolean b = new Boolean(true);
    int REPEAT = 5000000;
    int FACTOR = 1000;
    boolean res;
```

---

[*] There are exceptions to the rule. For example, in "Exception-Terminated Loops" in Chapter 7, the cost of one exception thrown is less than the cost of repeatedly making a test in the loop, though this is seen only if the number of loop iterations is large enough.

```
long time = System.currentTimeMillis( );
for (int j = REPEAT*FACTOR; j > 0 ; j--)
  res = test1(i);
time = System.currentTimeMillis( ) - time;
System.out.println("test1(i) took " + time);

time = System.currentTimeMillis( );
for (int j = REPEAT; j > 0 ; j--)
  res = test1(b);
time = System.currentTimeMillis( ) - time;
System.out.println("test1(b) took " + time);

//and the same timed test for test2(i) and test2(b),
//iterating REPEAT*FACTOR times
...
}

public static boolean test1(Object o)
{
  try {
    Integer i = (Integer) o;
    return false;
  }
  catch (Exception e) {return true;}
}

public static boolean test2(Object o)
{
  if (o instanceof Integer)
    return false;
  else
    return true;
}
}
```

The results of this comparison show that if test2( ) (using instanceof) takes one time unit, test1( ) with the ClassCastException thrown takes over 100 time units in JDK 1.4 (see the first line in Table 6-2). The second line in Table 6-2 shows the relative cost of throwing the exception with different parameters passed to test1( ), and also shows that throwing the exception is very costly. The two lines together show that using instanceof is fairly efficient.

Table 6-2. Extra cost of try-catch blocks when exceptions are thrown

Relative times for	1.1.8	1.2.2	1.3.1	1.3.1 -server	1.4.0	1.4.0 -server[a]	1.4.0 -xlnt
test1(b)/test2(b)	~60	~35	~90	~720	~100	N/A	~30
test1(b)/test1(i)	~160	~90	~1000	~40000	~1000	N/A	~200
test2(b)/test2(i)	1	1	~10	~100	~10	N/A	~5

[a] The 1.4 JVM JIT compiler in server mode identified that the test was effectively a repeated constant expression and collapsed the loop to one call, thus eliminating the test. The costs of using exceptions are still present in 1.4.0 server mode, but this test cannot show those costs.

For VMs not running a JIT, or using HotSpot technology, the relative times for test2( ) are different depending on the object passed. test2( ) takes one time unit when returning true but, curiously, two to ten time units when returning false. This difference for a false result indicates that the instanceof operator is faster when the instance's class correctly matches the tested class. A negative instanceof test must also check whether the instance is from a subclass or interface of the tested type before it can definitely return false. Given this, it is actually quite interesting that with a simple JIT, there is no difference in times between the two instanceof tests.

Because it is impossible to add methods to classes that are compiled (as opposed to classes you have the source for and can recompile), there are necessarily places in Java code where you have to test for the type of object. Where this type of code is unavoidable, you should use instanceof, as shown in test2( ), rather than a speculative class cast. There is no maintenance disadvantage in using instanceof, nor is the code any clearer or easier to alter by avoiding its use. I strongly advise you to avoid the use of the speculative class cast, however. It is a real performance hog and ugly as well.

Using Exceptions Without the Stack Trace Overhead

You may decide that you definitely require an exception to be thrown, despite the disadvantages. If the exception is thrown explicitly (i.e., using a throw statement rather than a VM-generated exception such as the ClassCastException or ArrayIndexOutOfBoundsException), you can reduce the cost by reusing an exception object rather than creating a new one. Most of the cost of throwing an exception is incurred in actually creating the new exception, which is when the stack trace is filled in. Reusing an existing exception object without resetting the stack trace avoids the exception-creation overhead. Throwing and catching an existing exception object is two orders of magnitude faster than doing the same with a newly created exception object:

```
public static Exception REUSABLE_EXCEPTION = new Exception( );
...
  //Much faster reusing an existing exception
  try {throw REUSABLE_EXCEPTION;}
  catch (Exception e) {...}

  //This next try-catch is 50 to 100 times slower than the last
  try {throw new Exception( );}
  catch (Exception e) {...}
```

The sole disadvantage of reusing an exception instance is that the instance does not have the correct stack trace, i.e., the stack trace held by the exception object is the one generated when the exception object was created.[*] This disadvantage can be important for some situations when the trace is important, so be careful. This technique can easily lead to maintenance problems.

Conditional Error Checking

During development, you typically write a lot of code that checks the arguments passed into various methods for validity. This kind of checking is invaluable during development and testing, but it can lead to a lot of overhead in the finished application. Therefore, you need a technique for implementing error checks that can optionally be removed during compilation. The most common way to do this is to use an if block:

```
public class GLOBAL_CONSTANTS {
  public static final boolean ERROR_CHECKING_ON = true;
  ...
}

//and code in methods of other classes includes an if block like
if (GLOBAL_CONSTANTS.ERROR_CHECKING_ON)
{
  //error check code of some sort
  ...
```

This technique allows you to turn off error checking by recompiling the application with the ERROR_CHECKING_ON variable set to false. Doing this recompilation actually eliminates all if blocks completely, due to a feature of the compiler (see "Dead code branches are eliminated" in Chapter 3). Setting the value to false without recompilation also works, but avoids only the block, not the block entry test. In this case, the if statement is still executed, but the block is not entered. This still has some performance impact: an extra test for almost every method call is significant, so it is better to recompile.[†]

Assertions

SDK 1.4 added assertions to the Java specification. Assertions allow you to add statements into your code of the form:

```
assert boolean_expression;
```

---

[*] To get the exception object to hold the stack trace that is current when it is thrown, rather than created, you must use the fillInStackTrace( ) method. Of course, this is what causes the large overhead that you are trying to avoid.

[†] However, this technique cannot eliminate all types of code blocks. For example, you cannot use this technique to eliminate try-catch blocks from the code they surround. You can achieve that level of control only by using a preprocessor. My thanks to Ethan Henry for pointing this out.

where `boolean_expression` is any valid Java expression that evaluates to produce a boolean result. If the boolean expression evaluates to `false`, an `AssertionError` is thrown. A second form of the assert statement allows an additional parameter that evaluates to a `String`:

```
assert boolean_expression : String_expression;
```

The second form allows customization of the error message produced when an assertion fails. For example:

```
assert param1 >= 0 :
  "Parameter param1 must be non-negative, but was " + param1;
```

The difference between an `assert` statement and a normal statement is that the `assert` statement can be disabled at runtime. More precisely, assertions can be enabled or disabled at runtime, and you can specify separately for each class whether its assertions are enabled or disabled using the -ea and -da parameters of the java command. Assertions can also be enabled and disabled from code using the various `Classloader.set*AssertionStatus( )` methods. The assertion status of a class is fixed once that class has been loaded. The classloader enables or disables `assert` statements.

The only limitation of the assert keyword is that it must be used in an executable block. An assertion cannot be used with class variable declarations, for instance, but can be placed within any method.

Using assertions generally improves the quality of code and assists in diagnosing problems in an application. Application code should be written so that it is functionally the same when running with assertions disabled. Assertions that cannot be disabled without altering the functionality of the code should not be defined as assertions.

 The assert keyword is not recognized by compilers prior to 1.4. To use assertions with 1.4, you need to specify to the compiler that the Java source file is from SDK 1.4, using the parameters -source 1.4. Unfortunately, the resulting bytecode can not be run under pre-1.4 JVMs.

Assertion Overhead

It is useful to understand how the assertion mechanism works to see how assertion statements can affect performance. When the compiler finds an assertion in a class, it adds a generated `static final` field named `$assertionsDisabled` to the class. The field is left unassigned (this is legal bytecode). The assertion itself is compiled into a statement of the form:

```
if ($assertionsDisabled)
  if (!boolean_expression)
    throw new AssertionError(String_expression);
```

At classloading time, the classloader determines the assertion status of the class using the various rules listed in the assertion specification, and sets the $assertionsDisabled field accordingly. This means that without any further optimizations, every assert imposes a minimum of one runtime boolean test, even if assertions have been disabled.

There are two potential optimizations that could completely eliminate this assertion overhead. First, the classloader itself could strip out the assertion status test and the subsequent if statement when assertions are disabled. As the $assertionsDisabled is a final variable, there is no prospect of the value changing later, so the test is not actually necessary: when assertions are enabled the boolean expression if statement would be executed directly with no assertion status test; when assertions are disabled the boolean expression if statement would be completely eliminated together with the assertion status test. In practice, however, Sun has not enabled the classloader to strip the assertion status test.

As a result, we must consider an alternative optimization. This one uses exactly the same procedure outlined for the classloader optimization but, instead of the classloader, the JIT compiler would strip out the unnecessary statements. In fact, this simply applies the standard compiler optimization of eliminating dead code. This is the approach taken by Sun, which has left the optimization to the HotSpot JIT compiler. This means that, at least for the initial 1.4 release, the overhead of assert statements is dependent on whether a JVM strips those statements. For example, the 1.4 JVM running in client (default) mode is not sufficiently aggressive in JIT compilation optimizations to eliminate assertion overhead. However, when running the same JVM in server mode (with the -server parameter), the JIT compiler effectively eliminates disabled assertion statements.

Tables 6-3 and 6-4 list the results of testing code with assertion statements compared to using an explicit and equivalent if...throw test and to the same code with no tests. As the overhead of the assertion depends on what it is being compared against, I used two separate baselines, comparing assertion cost against a very quick test, essentially just a return statement, and against a more complex, slower test. The test class code is listed shortly after the results.

Table 6-3. Overhead from an assertion statement in a very simple method

Simple method test	java -client	java -server
no check or assert	100%	0%[a]
with assert disabled	235%	57%
with assert enabled	243%	194%
with explicit check	137%	192%

[a] The server mode JIT compiler inlined the quick test into the test loop, resulting in no method call overhead at all and a legible measurement for test time. Interestingly, the server mode fails to do this when the assert is disabled.

Table 6-4. Overhead from an assertion statement in a complex method

Complex method test	java -client	java -server
no check or assert	100%	95%
with assert disabled	100%	95%
with assert enabled	107%	95%
with explicit check	109%	95%

Clearly, assertions can add significant overhead to short methods. You may want to avoid adding assertions willy-nilly to setters, getters, and other short, frequently called methods. However, there is no need to become paranoid about whether or not to add assertions. It is probably better initially to add assertions as desired irrespective of performance considerations, then catch and eliminate any expensive assertions using a profiler. For longer methods, assertions can be added without too much concern.

But do note that when enabled, any assertion takes at least as long to run as its boolean_expression evaluation takes. Consequently, code running with assertions enabled will definitely be slower than code running with assertions disabled, even if only a few percent slower. If possible, you should run the application with as many assertions disabled as possible. Similarly, since assertions can be turned off but explicit checks cannot, you should consider changing all explicit checks for incorrect parameters and state in your code to use assertions instead of explicitly using if... throw statements. For example, IllegalArgumentExceptions often test for documented incorrect conditions, and these tests could be changed to assertions. The decision about whether any particular test can be changed to an assertion ultimately comes down to whether the test should always be present (don't make it an assertion), or whether the test is optional and provides extra robustness, especially during development and testing (definitely an assertion candidate).

Finally, remember to profile the application as it will be run in practice, with the same mixture of assertions turned on or off. Don't make the mistake of profiling the application with all assertions turned off or turned on if that is not the way the application will be run when deployed.

```
package tuning.asserts;

public class AssertTest1 {

  static int sval;
  static int[ ] some_array = {3,5,9,16,5,18,23,66,28,19};

  public static int testWithNoCheck(int val)
  {
//alternative short test
//    return val+2;
    double x = Math.cos(val%Math.PI);
    double y = Math.sin(val%Math.PI);
    double d = x*x + y*y;
```

```
      d = Math.sqrt(d);
      return Math.abs(val - some_array[((int) Math.abs(d))%10]);
    }

  public static int testWithExplicitCheck(int val)
  {
    if (val < 0)
      throw new IllegalArgumentException("parameter val should be positive, but is "
+ val);
//alternative short test
//     return val+2;
    double x = Math.cos(val%Math.PI);
    double y = Math.sin(val%Math.PI);
    double d = x*x + y*y;
    d = Math.sqrt(d);
    return Math.abs(val - some_array[((int) Math.abs(d))%10]);
  }

  public static int testWithAssert(int val)
  {
    assert (val >= 0) : "parameter val should be positive, but is " + val;
//alternative short test
//     return val+2;
    double x = Math.cos(val%Math.PI);
    double y = Math.sin(val%Math.PI);
    double d = x*x + y*y;
    d = Math.sqrt(d);
    return Math.abs(val - some_array[((int) Math.abs(d))%10]);
  }

  public static void main(String[] args)
  {
    test(args);
    test(args);
  }
  public static void test(String[] args)
  {
    try
    {
      testWithAssert(-1);
      System.out.println("Asserts off");
    }
    catch(Throwable t)
    {
      System.out.println("Asserts on");
    }

    int REPEAT = Integer.parseInt(args[0]);

    int v = 0;
    long time = System.currentTimeMillis();
    sval = 0;
    for (int i = 0; i < REPEAT/10; i++)
      v = testWithNoCheck(v);
```

```
v = 0;
sval = 0;
time = System.currentTimeMillis();
for (int i = 0; i < REPEAT; i++)
  v = testWithExplicitCheck(v);
time = System.currentTimeMillis() - time;
System.out.println("testWithExplicitCheck took " + time + " millis, val = " + v +
" sval = " + sval);

v = 0;
sval = 0;
time = System.currentTimeMillis();
for (int i = 0; i < REPEAT; i++)
  v = testWithAssert(v);
time = System.currentTimeMillis() - time;
System.out.println("testWithAssert took " + time + " millis, val = " + v + " sval
= " + sval);

v = 0;
sval = 0;
time = System.currentTimeMillis();
for (int i = 0; i < REPEAT; i++)
  v = testWithNoCheck(v);
time = System.currentTimeMillis() - time;
System.out.println("testWithNoCheck took " + time + " millis, val = " + v + "
sval = " + sval);

  }
}
```

Casts

Casts also have a cost. Casts that can be resolved at compile time can be eliminated by the compiler (and are eliminated by the JDK compiler). Consider the two lines:

```
Integer i = new Integer(3);
Integer j = (Integer) i;
```

These two lines are compiled as if they were written as:

```
Integer i = new Integer(3);
Integer j = i;
```

On the other hand, casts not resolvable at compile time must be executed at runtime. But note that an instanceof test cannot be fully resolved at compile time:

```
Integer integer = new Integer(3);
if (integer instanceof Integer)
  Integer j = integer;
```

The test in the if statement here cannot be resolved by most compilers because instanceof can return false if the first operand (integer) is null. (A more intelligent compiler might resolve this particular case by determining that integer was definitely not null for this code fragment, but most compilers are not that sophisticated.)

Primitive data type casts (ints, bytes, etc.) are quicker than object data type casts because there is no test involved, only a straightforward data conversion. But a primitive data type cast is still a runtime operation and has an associated cost.

Object type casts basically confirm that the object is of the required type. It appears that a VM with a JIT compiler is capable of reducing the cost of some casts to practically nothing. The following test, when run under JDK 1.2 without a JIT, shows object casts having a small but measurable cost. With the JIT compiler running, the cast has no measurable effect (see Table 6-5):

```
package tuning.exception;

public class CastTest
{
  public static void main(String[ ] args)
  {
    Integer i = new Integer(3);
    int REPEAT = 500000000;
    Integer res;

    long time = System.currentTimeMillis( );
    for (int j = REPEAT; j > 0 ; j--)
      res = test1(i);
    time = System.currentTimeMillis( ) - time;
    System.out.println("test1(i) took " + time);

    time = System.currentTimeMillis( );
    for (int j = REPEAT; j > 0 ; j--)
      res = test2(i);
    time = System.currentTimeMillis( ) - time;
    System.out.println("test2(i) took " + time);

    ... and the same test for test2(i) and test1(i)
  }

  public static Integer test1(Object o)
  {
    Integer i = (Integer) o;
    return i;
  }

  public static Integer test2(Integer o)
  {
    Integer i = (Integer) o;
    return i;
  }
}
```

Table 6-5. The extra cost of casts

VM	1.1.8	1.2.2	1.3.1	1.3.1 -server	1.4.0	1.4.0 -server	1.4.0 -xlnt
Increase in time	None	None	>20%	None	>100%	None	>5%

However, the cost of an object type cast is not constant: it depends on the depth of the hierarchy and whether the casting type is an interface or a class. Interfaces are generally more expensive to use in casting, and the further back in the hierarchy (and ordering of interfaces in the class definition), the longer the cast takes to execute. Remember, though: never change the design of the application for minor performance gains.

It is best to avoid casts whenever possible; for example, use type-specific collection classes instead of generic collection classes. Rather than use a standard List to store a list of Strings, you gain better performance with a StringList class. You should always try to type the variable as precisely as possible. In Chapter 9, you can see that by rewriting a sort implementation to eliminate casts, the sorting time can be halved.

If a variable needs casting several times, cast once and save the object into a temporary variable of the cast type. Use that temporary variable instead of repeatedly casting; avoid the following kind of code:

```
if (obj instanceof Something)
    return ((Something)obj).x + ((Something)obj).y + ((Something)obj).z;
...
```

Instead, use a temporary variable:[*]

```
if (obj instanceof Something)
{
    Something something = (Something) obj;
    return something.x + something.y + something.z;
}
...
```

The revised code is also more readable. In tight loops, you may need to evaluate the cost of repeatedly assigning values to a temporary variable (see Chapter 7).

Variables

Local (temporary) variables and method-argument variables are the fastest variables to access and update. Local variables remain on the stack, so they can be manipulated directly; the manipulation of local variables depends on both the VM and the underlying machine implementation. Heap variables (static and instance variables) are manipulated in heap memory through the Java VM-assigned bytecodes that apply to these variables. There are special bytecodes for accessing the first four local variables and parameters on a method stack. Arguments are counted first; then, if there are fewer than four passed arguments, local variables are counted. For non-static methods, this always takes the first slot. longs and doubles each take two slots.

---

[*] This is a special case of common subexpression elimination. See "Eliminate common subexpressions" in Chapter 3.

Theoretically, this means that methods with no more than three parameters and local variables combined (four for static methods) should be slightly faster than equivalent methods with a larger number of parameters and local variables. It also means that any variables allocated the special bytecodes should be slightly faster to manipulate. In practice, I have found any effect to be small or negligible, and it is not worth the effort involved to limit the number of arguments and variables.

Instance and static variables can be up to an order of magnitude slower to operate on when compared to method arguments and local variables. You can see this clearly with a simple test comparing local and static loop counters:

```
package tuning.exception;

public class VariableTest2
{
  static int cntr;
  public static void main(String[ ] args)
  {
    int REPEAT = 500000000;

    int tot = 0;
    long time = System.currentTimeMillis( );
    for (int i = -REPEAT; i < 0; i++)
      tot += i;
    time = System.currentTimeMillis( ) - time;
    System.out.println("Loop local took " + time);

    tot = 0;
    time = System.currentTimeMillis( );
    for (cntr = -REPEAT; cntr < 0; cntr++)
      tot += cntr;
    time = System.currentTimeMillis( ) - time;
    System.out.println("Loop static took " + time);

  }
}
```

Running this test results in the second loop taking significantly longer than the first loop (see Table 6-6).

Table 6-6. The cost of nonlocal loop variables relative to local variables

Times relative to local loop variables	1.1.8	1.2.2	1.3.1	1.3.1 -server	1.4.0	1.4.0 -server[a]	1.4.0 -xlnt
Static variable time/ local variable time	122%	126%	296%	259%	226%	N/A	127%
Static array element/ local variable time	126%	127%	630%	1034%	315%	N/A	211%

[a] The 1.4 JVM JIT compiler in server mode identified that the test was effectively a repeated constant expression and collapsed the loop to one call, thus eliminating the test. Other tests have shown that the costs of static and array elements compared to local variables are still present in 1.4.0 server mode, but this test cannot show those costs.

If you are making many manipulations on an instance or static variable, it is better to execute them on a temporary variable, then reassign to the instance variable at the end. This is true for instance variables that hold arrays as well. Arrays also have an overhead, due to the range checking Java provides. So if you are manipulating an element of an array many times, again you should probably assign it to a temporary variable for the duration. For example, the following code fragment repeatedly accesses and updates the same array element:

```
for(int i = 0; i < Repeat; i++)
    countArr[0]+=i;
```

You should replace such repeated array element manipulation with a temporary variable:

```
int count = countArr[0];
for(int i = 0; i < Repeat; i++)
    count+=i;
countArr[0]=count;
```

This kind of substitution can also apply to an array object:

```
static int[ ] Static_array = {1,2,3,4,5,6,7,8,9};

public static int manipulate_static_array( ) {
    //assign the static variable to a local variable, and use that local
    int[ ] arr = Static_array;
    ...

//or even
public static int manipulate_static_array( ) {
    //pass the static variable to another method that manipulates it
    return manipulate_static_array(Static_array);}
public static int manipulate_static_array(int[ ] arr) {
    ...
```

Array-element access is typically two to three times as expensive as accessing non-array elements.* This expense is probably due to the range checking and null pointer checking (for the array itself) done by the VM. The VM JIT compiler manages to eliminate almost all the overhead in the case of large arrays. But in spite of this, you can assume that array-element access is going to be slower than plain-variable access in almost every Java environment (this also applies to array-element updates). See "Initialization" in Chapter 4 for techniques to improve performance when initializing arrays.

ints are normally the fastest variable type to operate on. longs and doubles can take longer to access and update than other variables because they are twice the basic storage length for Java (which is four bytes). The Java specification allows longs and

---

* Mark Ruolo, "Accelerate Your Java Apps," *JavaWorld*, September 1998, *http://www.javaworld.com/java-world/jw-09-1998/jw-09-speed.html*.

doubles to be stored in more than one action. The specification allows the actual manipulation of longs and doubles to be implementation- and processor-dependent, so you cannot assume that longs and doubles always take longer. If you have one specific target environment, you can test it to determine its implementation. Note that because of the specification, longs and doubles are the only data types that can be corrupted by simultaneous assignment from multiple threads (see "Atomic Access and Assignment" in Chapter 10 for more details).

When executing arithmetic with the primitive data types, ints are undoubtedly the most efficient. shorts, bytes, and chars are all widened to ints for almost any type of arithmetic operation. They then require a cast back if you want to end up with the data type you started with. For example, adding two bytes produces an int and requires a cast to get back a byte. longs are usually less efficient. Floating-point arithmetic seems to be the worst.

Note that temporary variables of primitive data types (i.e., not objects) can be allocated on the stack, which is usually implemented using a faster memory cache local to the CPU. Temporary objects, however, must be created from the heap (the object reference itself is allocated on the stack, but the object must be in the heap). This means that operations on any object are invariably slower than on any of the primitive data types for temporary variables. Also, as soon as variables are discarded at the end of a method call, the memory from the stack can immediately be reused for other temporaries. But any temporary objects remain in the heap until garbage collection reallocates the space. The result is that temporary variables using primitive (non-object) data types are better for performance.

One other way to speed up applications is to access public instance variables rather than use accessor methods (getters and setters). Of course, this breaks encapsulation, so it is bad design in most cases. The JDK uses this technique in a number of places (e.g., Dimension and GridBagConstraints in java.awt have public instance variables; in the case of Dimension, this is almost certainly for performance reasons). Generally, you can use this technique without too much worry if you are passing an object that encapsulates a bunch of parameters (such as GridBagConstraints); in fact, this makes for an extensible design. If you really want to ensure that the object remains unaltered when passed, you can set the instance variables to be final (as long as it is one of your application-defined classes).

Method Parameters

As I said at the beginning of the last section, method parameters are low-cost, and you normally don't need to worry about the cost of adding extra method parameters. But it is worth being alert to situations in which there are parameters that could be added but have not been. This is a simple tuning technique that is rarely considered. Typically, the parameters that could be added are arrays and array lengths. For example, when parsing a String object, it is common not to pass the length of the string to methods because each method can get the length using the String.length( ) method. But parsing tends to be intensive and recursive, with lots of method calls. Most of those methods need to know the length of the string. Although you can eliminate multiple calls within one method by assigning the length to a temporary variable, you cannot do that when many methods need that length. Passing the string length as a parameter is almost certainly cheaper than repeated calls to String. length( ).

Similarly, you typically access the elements of the string one at a time using String. charAt( ). But again, it is better for performance purposes to copy the String object into a char array and pass this array through your methods (see Chapter 5). To provide a possible performance boost, try passing extra values and arrays to isolated groups of methods. As usual, you should do this only when a bottleneck has been identified, not throughout an implementation.

Finally, you can reduce the number of objects used by an application by passing an object into a method, which then fills in the object's fields. This is almost always more efficient than creating new objects within the method. See "Reusable Parameters" in Chapter 4 for a more detailed explanation of this technique.

Performance Checklist

Most of these suggestions apply only after a bottleneck has been identified:

- Include all error-condition checking in blocks guarded by if statements.
- Avoid throwing exceptions in the normal code path of your application.
- Investigate whether a try-catch in the bottleneck imposes any extra cost.
- Use instanceof instead of making speculative class casts in a try-catch block.
- Consider throwing exceptions without generating a stack trace by reusing a previously created instance.
- Include any exceptions generated during the normal flow of the program when running performance tests.
- Assertions add overhead even when disabled, though an optimizing JIT compiler can eliminate the overhead (only HotSpot server mode succeeded in 1.4.0).
- Beware of adding assertions to quick, frequently called methods.
- Minimize casting.
- Avoid casts by creating and using type-specific collection classes.
- Use temporary variables of the cast type, instead of repeatedly casting.
- Type variables as precisely as possible.
- Use local variables rather than instance or static variables for faster manipulation.

- Use temporary variables to manipulate instance variables, static variables, and array elements.
- Use ints in preference to any other data type.
- Avoid long and double instance or static variables.
- Use primitive data types instead of objects for temporary variables.
- Consider accessing instance variables directly rather than through accessor methods. (But note that this breaks encapsulation.)
- Add extra method parameters when that would allow a method to avoid additional method calls.

CHAPTER 7

Loops, Switches, and Recursion

In this chapter:
- Loops
- Tuning a Loop
- Exception-Terminated Loops
- Switches
- Recursion
- Recursion and Stacks

I have made this letter longer than usual because
I lack the time to make it shorter.
—Blaise Pascal

This chapter describes performance-tuning a variety of common code structures: loops, switches, and recursion. Some of the tuning hints here are straightforward (for example, remove code from a loop if it is executed only once), but many are more esoteric, particularly given the subtleties of optimizations performed by HotSpot VMs and JIT compilers. Read on for details.

Loops

Programs spend most of their time in loops. There are many optimizations that can speed up loops, as detailed in the following sections.

Move Code Out of the Loop

Take out of the loop any code that does not need to be executed on every pass. This includes assignments, accesses, tests, and method calls that need to run only once.

Method calls are more costly than the equivalent code without the call, and by repeating method calls again and again, you just add overhead to your application. Move any method calls out of the loop, even if this requires rewriting. Inline method calls in loops when possible.

Use Temporary Variables

Array access (and assignment) always has more overhead than temporary variable access because the VM performs bounds-checking for array-element access. Array access is better done once (and assigned to a temporary) outside the loop rather than repeated at each iteration. For example, consider this next loop:

```
for(int i = 0; i < Repeat; i++)
   countArr[0]+=10;
```

The following loop optimizes the last loop using a temporary variable to execute the addition within the loop. The array element is updated outside the loop. This optimized loop is significantly better (twice as fast) than the original loop:

```
count = countArr[0];
for(int i = 0; i < Repeat; i++)
   count+=10;
countArr[0]=count;
```

Don't Terminate Loops with Method Calls

Avoid using a method call in a loop termination test; the overhead is significant. I often see loops like this when iterating through collections such as Vectors and Strings:

```
for(int i = 0; i < collection.size( ); i++) //or collection.length( )
```

This next loop factors out the maximum iteration value and is faster:

```
int max = v.size( ); //or int max = s.length( );
for(int i = 0; i < max; i++)
```

Use int for Index Variables

Using int data types for the index variable is faster than using any other numeric data types. The VM is optimized to use ints. Operations on bytes, shorts, and chars are normally carried out with implicit casts to and from ints. The loop:

```
for(int i = 0; i < Repeat; i++)
```

is faster than using any of the other numeric data types:

```
for(long i = 0; i < Repeat; i++)
for(double i = 0; i < Repeat; i++)
for(char i = 0; i < Repeat; i++)
```

Use System.arraycopy( )

System.arraycopy( ) is faster than using a loop for copying arrays in any destination VM except where you are guaranteed that the VM has a JIT. In the latter case, using your own for loop may be slightly faster. I recommend using System.arraycopy( ) in either case, since even when the for loop is executing in a JIT VM, it is only slightly faster.

Use Efficient Comparisons

Comparison to 0 is faster than comparisons to most other numbers. The VM has optimizations for comparisons to the integers –1, 0, 1, 2, 3, 4, and 5. So rewriting

loops to make the test a comparison against 0 may be faster.* This alteration typically reverses the iteration order of the loop from counting up (0 to max) to counting down (max to 0). For example, for loops are usually coded:

```
for(int i = 0; i < Repeat; i++)
```

Both of these functionally identical for loops are faster:

```
for(int i = Repeat-1; i >= 0; i--)
for(int i = Repeat; --i >= 0 ; )
```

When tests need to be made within a loop, try to use the fastest tests. For example,
convert equality comparisons to identity comparisons whenever possible. The following uses an equality comparison:

```
Integer one = new Integer(1);
...
 for (...)
  if (integer.equals(one))
```

This comparison is better replaced with an identity comparison:

```
for (...)
  if (integer == CANONICALIZED_INTEGER_ONE)
```

Clearly, for this substitution to work correctly, the objects being compared must be
matched by identity. You may be able to achieve this by canonicalizing your objects
(see "Canonicalizing Objects" in Chapter 4). You can compare Strings by identity if
you String.intern() them to ensure you have a unique String object for every
sequence of characters, but obviously there is no performance gain if you have to do
the interning within the loop or in some other time-critical section of the application. Similarly, the java.util.Comparator and Comparable interfaces provide a nice
generic framework. But they impose a heavy overhead in requiring a method call for
every comparison and may be better avoided in special situations (see Chapter 9).
One test I sometimes see is for a Class:

```
if (obj.getClass().getName().equals("foo.bar.ClassName"))
```

It is more efficient to store an instance of the class in a static variable and test directly
against that instance (there is only one instance of any class):

```
//In class initialization
public static final Class FOO_BAR_CLASSNAME = foo.bar.ClassName.class;
...
//and in the method
if (obj.getClass() == FOO_BAR_CLASSNAME)
```

Note that foo.bar.ClassName.class is a valid construct to refer to the foo.bar.
ClassName class object. However, the compiler generates a static method that calls

---

* The latest VMs try to optimize the standard for(int i = 0; i < Repeat; i++) expression, so rewriting the loop
  may not produce faster code. Only non-JIT VMs and HotSpot showed improvements by rewriting the loop.
  Note that HotSpot does not generate native code for any method executed only once or twice.

`Class.forName()` and replaces the `foo.bar.ClassName.class` construct with a call to that static method. So if the construct will be accessed more than once, it is better to use the `FOO_BAR_CLASSNAME` static variable as suggested, rather than:

```
if (obj.getClass() == foo.bar.ClassName.class)
```

Put the Most Common Case First

When several boolean tests are made together in one expression in the loop, try to phrase the expression so that it "short-circuits" as soon as possible by putting the most likely case first (see the sidebar "Short-Circuit Operators"). Ensure that by satisfying earlier parts of the expression, you do not cause the later expressions to be evaluated. For example, the following expression tests whether an integer is in the range 4 to 8 or is the smallest integer:

```
if (someInt == Integer.MIN_VALUE || (someInt > 3 && someInt < 9))
    ... //condition1
else
    ... //condition2
```

Short-Circuit Operators

The `||` and `&&` boolean operators are "short-circuit" operators. Their left side is evaluated first, and their right side is not evaluated at all if the result of the left side produces a conclusive result for the expression. Specifically, the conditional-And operator, `&&`, evaluates its right side only if the result of its left operand is true. The conditional-Or operator, `||`, evaluates its right side only if the result of its left operand is false.

These operators differ from the logical And and Or operators, `&` and `|`, in that these latter logical boolean operators always evaluate both of their arguments. The following example illustrates the differences between these two types of logical operators by testing both boolean And operators:

```
boolean b, c;
    b = c = true;
    //Left hand side makes the expression true
    if( (b=true) || (c=false) ) //is always true
        System.out.println(b + " " + c);
    b = c = true;
    if( (b=true) | (c=false) ) //is always true
        System.out.println(b + " " + c);
```

Here is the output this code produces:

```
true true
true false
```

The first test evaluates only the left side; the second test evaluates both sides even though the result of the right side is not needed to determine the result of the full boolean expression.

Suppose that the integers passed to this expression are normally in the range of 4 to 8. Suppose also that if they are not in that range, the integers passed are most likely to be values larger than 8. In this case, the given ordering of tests is the worst possible ordering for the expression. As the expression stands, the most likely result (integer in the 4 to 8 range) and the second most likely result (integer larger than 8) both require all three boolean tests in the expression to be evaluated. Let's try an alternative phrasing of the test:

```
if (someInt > 8 || (someInt < 4 && someInt != Integer.MIN_VALUE))
... //condition2
else
... //condition1
```

This rephrasing is functionally identical to the original. But it requires only two tests to be evaluated to process the most likely case, where the integer is in the 4 to 8 range, and only one test to be evaluated for the second most likely case, where the integer is larger than 8.

Avoid Reflection

Avoid the use of reflection within loops (i.e., methods and objects in the `java.lang.reflect` package). Using reflection to execute a method is much slower than direct execution (as well as being bad style). When reflection functionality is necessary within a loop, change any implementation so that you can achieve the same effect using interfaces and type overloading. For the 1.4 VMs, Sun targeted reflection as one of the areas to be speeded up. Some reflection operations are significantly faster than before 1.4, but reflection is still slower than using an interface to call a method. Note that it is not just the resolution of a method that causes overhead when using reflection. Invoking method calls using `Method.invoke( )` is also more expensive than using the plain method call. Handling method references can be complicated, especially with VMs supporting natively compiled code. It can be necessary to manage artificial stack frames that impose overhead to the method calls.

Tuning a Loop

Let's look at an example of tuning a loop. In the `java.io` package, the `Reader` (and `Writer`) classes provide character-based I/O (as opposed to byte-based I/O). The `InputStreamReader` provides a bridge from byte to character streams. It reads bytes and translates them into characters according to a specified character encoding. If no encoding is specified, a default converter class is provided. For applications that spend a significant amount of time reading, it is not unusual to see the `convert( )` method of this encoding class high up on a profile of how the application time is spent.

It is instructive to examine how this particular conversion method functions and to see the effect of a tuning exercise. Examining the bytecodes of the `convert( )`

method* where most of the time is being spent, you can see that the bytecodes correspond to the following method (the Exception used is different; I have just used the generic Exception class):

```
public int convert(byte input[ ], int byteStart, int byteEnd,
                   char output[ ], int charStart, int charEnd)
   throws Exception
{
   int charOff = charStart;
   for(int byteOff = byteStart; byteOff < byteEnd;)
   {
     if(charOff >= charEnd)
       throw new Exception( );
     int i1 = input[byteOff++];
     if(i1 >= 0)
       output[charOff++] = (char)i1;
     else
       output[charOff++] = (char)(256 + i1);
   }

   return charOff - charStart;
}
```

Basically, the method takes a byte array (input) and converts the elements from byteStart to byteEnd of that array into characters. The conversion of bytes to chars is straightforward, consisting of mapping positive byte values to the same char value, and mapping negative byte values to the char with value (byte value + 256). These chars are put into the passed char array (output) from indexes charStart to charEnd.

It doesn't seem that there is too much scope for tuning. There is the obvious first test, which is performed every time through the loop. You can certainly move that. But let's start by trying to tune the data conversion itself. First, be sure that casts on data types are efficient. It's only a quick test to find out. Add a static char array to the class, which contains just char values 0 to 127 at elements 0 to 127 in the array. Calling this array MAP1, test the following altered method:

```
public int convert(byte input[ ], int byteStart, int byteEnd,
                   char output[ ], int charStart, int charEnd)
   throws Exception
{
   int charOff = charStart;
   for(int byteOff = byteStart; byteOff < byteEnd;)
   {
     if(charOff >= charEnd)
       throw new Exception( );
     int i1 = input[byteOff++];
     if(i1 >= 0)
```

---

* The convert method is a method in one of the sun.* packages, so the source code is not available. I have chosen the convert method from the default class used in some ASCII environments, the ISO 8859_1 conversion class.

```
      output[charOff++] = MAP1[i1];
    else
      output[charOff++] = (char)(256 + i1);
  }

  return charOff - charStart;
}
```

On the basis of the original method taking a normalized 100.0 seconds in test runs, this alternative takes an average of 111 seconds over a set of test runs (some VMs, notably the server-mode HotSpot VMs, show even worse performance). Well, that says that casts are not so slow, but it hasn't helped make this method any faster. However, the second cast involves an addition as well, and perhaps you can do better here. Unfortunately, there is no obvious way to use a negative value as an index into the array without executing some offset operation, so you won't gain time. For completeness, test this (with an index offset given by i1+128) and find that the average time is at the 110-second mark. This is not significantly better than the last test, and definitely worse than the original.

 Array-lookup speeds are highly dependent on the processor and the memory-access instructions available from the processor. The lookup speed is also dependent on the compiler taking advantage of the fastest memory-access instructions available. It is possible that other processors, VMs, or compilers will produce lookups faster than the cast.

But we have gained an extra option from these two tests. It is now clear that we can map all the bytes to chars through an array. Perhaps we can eliminate the test for positiveness applied to the byte (i.e., if(i1 >= 0)) and use a char array to map all the bytes directly. And indeed we can. Use the index conversion from the second test (an index offset given by i1+128), with a static char array that contains just char values 128 to 255 at elements 0 to 127 in the array, and char values 0 to 127 at elements 128 to 255 in the array.

The method now looks like:

```
public int convert(byte input[ ], int byteStart, int byteEnd,
                   char output[ ], int charStart, int charEnd)
  throws Exception
{
  int charOff = charStart;
  for(int byteOff = byteStart; byteOff < byteEnd;)
  {
    if(charOff >= charEnd)
      throw new Exception( );
    int i1 = input[byteOff++];
    output[charOff++] = MAP3[128 + i1];
  }

  return charOff - charStart;
}
```

We have eliminated one boolean test each time through the loop at the expense of using a slightly more expensive data-conversion method (array access rather than the cast). The average test result is now slightly faster than the original method. But different VMs show different speedups at this stage: the VMs of 1.1.6, 1.1.8, 1.2.2, 1.3.1, 1.4.1 server, and 1.4.1 interpreted are 5% to 30% faster, whereas 1.2.0, 1.3.1 server, and 1.4.0 client are 5% to 15% slower.

Cleaning up the method slightly, we can see that the temporary variable, i1, which was previously required for the test, is no longer needed. Being assiduous tuners and clean coders, we eliminate it and retest so that we have a new baseline to start from. Astonishingly (to me at least), this speeds up the test measurably in some VMs. The average test time is now even better, though again, a couple of VMs are still slower than the original method. Some VMs incurred a definite overhead from the redundant temporary variable in the loop: a lesson to keep in mind for general tuning.

It may be worth testing to see if an int array performs better than the char array (MAP3) previously used, since ints are the faster data type. And indeed, changing the type of this array and putting a char cast in the loop improves times slightly for some but not all VMs, and on average times are worse. More to the point, after this effort, we have not really managed a speedup consistent enough or good enough to justify the time spent on this tuning exercise.

Now I'm out of original ideas, but one of my readers, Jesper Larsson from Sweden, has thought of a better way to map the chars to bytes. Jesper noticed that the conversion corresponds to a simple bitwise operation, guaranteed by the Java language specification to work. The resulting method uses the following bitwise operator:

```
output[charOff++] = (char)(input[byteOff++] & 0xFF);
```

instead of the previously used array map:

```
output[charOff++] = (char) MAP5[input[byteOff++]+128];
```

All the VMs except the 1.4.0 server mode show Jesper's optimization to be significantly better. And the 1.4.0 server mode is slower only because it has already done a brilliant job of optimizing the earlier changes: in absolute time, the 1.4.0 server mode at this stage is nearly twice as fast as any other VM (probably from loop unrolling; see the later discussion).

Now we will apply the standard optimizations. Start by eliminating expressions from the loop that do not need to be repeatedly called, and move the other boolean test (the one for the out-of-range Exception) out of the loop. The method now looks like this:

```
public int convert(byte input[ ], int byteStart, int byteEnd,
                   char output[ ], int charStart, int charEnd)
  throws Exception
{
  int max = byteEnd;
  boolean throwException = false;
```

```
if ( byteEnd-byteStart > charEnd-charStart )
{
  max = byteStart+(charEnd-charStart);
  throwException = true;
}

int charOff = charStart;
for(int byteOff = byteStart; byteOff < max;)
{
  output[charOff++] = (char)(input[byteOff++] & 0xFF);
}
if(throwException)
  throw new Exception( );

return charOff - charStart;
}
```

I am taking the trouble to make the method functionally identical to the original. The original version filled in the array until the actual out-of-range exception is encountered, so I do the same. If you throw the exception as soon as you establish the index is out of range, the code will be slightly more straightforward. Other than that, the loop is the same as before, but without the out-of-range test and without the temporary assignment. The average test result is now the fastest we've obtained on any tests on all VMs. We've shaved off a third to a half of the time spent in this loop. This is mainly down to eliminating tests that were originally being run on each loop iteration. This speedup applied to all VMs tested.

Loop unrolling is another standard optimization that eliminates some more tests. Let's partially unroll the loop and see what sort of a gain we get. In practice, the optimal amount of loop unrolling corresponds to the way the application uses the convert( ) method, for example, the size of the typical array that is being converted. But in any case, we use a particular example of 10 loop iterations to see the effect.

 Optimal loop unrolling depends on a number of factors, including the underlying operating system and hardware. Loop unrolling is ideally achieved by way of an optimizing compiler rather than by hand. HotSpot interacts with manual loop unrolling in a highly variable way: sometimes HotSpot makes the unoptimized loop faster, sometimes the manually unrolled loop comes out faster. Tables 8-1 and 8-2 show HotSpot producing both faster *and* slower times for the same manually unrolled loop, depending on the data being processed. These two tables show the results from the same optimized program being run against files with long lines (Table 8-1) and files with short lines (Table 8-2). Of all the VMs tested, only the HotSpot VM produces inconsistent results, with a speedup when processing the long-line files but a slowdown when processing the short-line files. (The last two lines of each table show the difference between the original loop and the manually unrolled loop.)

The method now looks like this:

```java
public int convert(byte input[ ], int byteStart, int byteEnd,
                   char output[ ], int charStart, int charEnd)
   throws Exception
{
  //Set the maximum index of the input array to wind to
  int max = byteEnd;
  boolean throwException = false;
  if ( byteEnd-byteStart > charEnd-charStart )
  {
    //If the byte arry length is larger than the char array length
    //then we will throw an exception when we get to the adjusted max
    max = byteStart+(charEnd-charStart);
    throwException = true;
  }

  //charOff is the 'current' index into 'output'
  int charOff = charStart;

  //Check that we have at least 10 elements for our
  //unrolled part of the loop
  if (max-byteStart > 10)
  {
    //shift max down by 10 so that we have some elements
    //left over before we run out of groups of 10
    max -= 10;
    int byteOff = byteStart;
    //The loop test only tests every 10th test compared
    //to the normal loop. All the increments are done in
    //the loop body. Each line increments the byteoff by 1
    //until it's incremented by 10 after 10 lines. Then the test
    //checks that we are still under max - if so then loop again.
    for(; byteOff < max;)
    {
      output[charOff++] = (char) (input[byteOff++] & 0xFF);
      output[charOff++] = (char) (input[byteOff++] & 0xFF);
      output[charOff++] = (char) (input[byteOff++] & 0xFF);
      output[charOff++] = (char) (input[byteOff++] & 0xFF);
      output[charOff++] = (char) (input[byteOff++] & 0xFF);
      output[charOff++] = (char) (input[byteOff++] & 0xFF);
      output[charOff++] = (char) (input[byteOff++] & 0xFF);
      output[charOff++] = (char) (input[byteOff++] & 0xFF);
      output[charOff++] = (char) (input[byteOff++] & 0xFF);
      output[charOff++] = (char) (input[byteOff++] & 0xFF);
    }

    //We exited the loop because the byteoff went over the max.
    //Fortunately we kept back 10 elements so that we didn't go
    //too far past max. Now add the 10 back, and go into the
    //normal loop for the last few elements.
    max += 10;
    for(; byteOff < max;)
    {
```

```
      output[charOff++] = (char) (input[byteOff++] & 0xFF);
    }
  }
  else
  {
    //If we're in this conditional, then there aren't even
    //10 elements to process, so obviously we don't want to
    //do the unrolled part of the method.
    for(int byteOff = byteStart; byteOff < max;)
    {
      output[charOff++] = (char) (input[byteOff++] & 0xFF);
    }
  }
  //Finally if we indicated that the method needed an exception
  //thrown, we do it now.
  if(throwException)
    throw new Exception( );

  return charOff - charStart;
}
```

The average test result is now around 50% of the original method time for almost all the VMs. Only the 1.4.0 server-mode VM has a different result. Though still faster than the original method and almost all the other VMs, the last manual loop unrolling actually slowed down the 1.4.0 VM compared to running it with the earlier optimized method. This is likely to be caused by the 1.4 server VM doing a far better job of unrolling the loop than our handcrafted unroll.

It's good news that this kind of optimization is finally being applied efficiently by the VM. But from a performance-tuning point of view, this means that it is difficult to know whether to unroll the loop manually or not. Obviously, if you know exactly which VM your application runs on, you can establish whether the unrolling optimization produces faster code. But if your application could be used under any VM, the decision is more complex. The slower VMs benefit from manual unrolling, whereas the faster, server-mode VMs still remain faster in absolute terms even after being slowed down by manual loop unrolling. This suggests that, at least for the time being, manual loop unrolling is worth considering.

It is worth repeating that the speedup we have obtained is mainly a result of eliminating tests that were originally run in each loop iteration. For tight loops (i.e., loops that have a small amount of actual work that needs to be executed on each iteration), the overhead of tests is definitely significant.

It is also important during the tuning exercise to run the various improvements under different VMs and determine that the improvements are generally applicable. My tests indicate that these improvements are generally valid for all runtime environments. (One development environment with a very slow VM—an order of magnitude slower than the Sun VM without JIT—showed only a small improvement. However, it is not generally a good idea to base performance tests on development environments.)

For a small Java program that does simple filtering or conversion of data from text files, this convert( ) method could take 40% of the total program time. Improving this one method as shown can shave 20% from the time of the whole program, which is a good gain for a relatively small amount of work (it took me longer to write this section than to tune the convert( ) method).

Exception-Terminated Loops

This is a technique for squeezing out the very last driblet of performance from loops. With this technique, instead of testing on each loop iteration to see whether the loop has reached its normal termination point, you use an exception generated at the end of the loop to halt the loop, thus avoiding the extra test on each run through the loop.

I include this technique here mainly because it is a known performance-tuning technique, but I do not recommend it as I feel it is bad programming practice (the phrase "enough rope to hang yourself" springs to mind). I'll illustrate the technique with some straightforward examples. The full class for testing the examples is listed later, after I discuss the test results. The tests themselves are very simple. Basically, each test runs two varieties of loops. The first variety runs a standard for loop as you normally write it:

```
for (int loopvar = 0; loopvar < someMax; loopvar++)
```

The second variety leaves out the termination test in the for loop, thus making the loop infinite. But these latter loops are put inside a try-catch block so an exception terminates the loop:

```
try
{
  for (int loopvar = 0; ; loopvar++)
  ... //exception is thrown when loop needs to terminate
}
catch(Exception e) { }
```

The three tests I use are:

- A loop that executes integer divisions. The unterminated variety throws an ArithmeticException when a division by zero occurs to terminate the loop.

- A loop that initializes an array of integers. The unterminated variety throws an ArrayIndexOutOfBoundsException when the index of the array grows too large.

- A loop that enumerates a Vector. The unterminated variety throws a NoSuchElementException when there are no more elements to enumerate.

The results of my test runs (summarized in Table 7-1) were variable due to differences in memory allocation, disk paging, and garbage collection. The VMs using HotSpot technology could show quite variable behavior. The plain JDK 1.2 VM had a huge amount of trouble reclaiming memory for the later tests, even when I put in pauses and ran explicit garbage-collection calls more than once. For each set of tests, I tried to increase the number of loop iterations until the timings were over one second. For the memory-based tests, it was not always possible to achieve times of over a second: paging or out-of-memory errors were encountered.

Table 7-1. Speedup using exception-driven loop termination

Speedups	1.1.8	1.2.2	1.3.1	1.3.1 -server	1.4	1.4 -server	1.4 -Xint
Integer division	~2%	~2%	None	~20%	~2%	None	~40%
Assignment to loop	None	None	~15%	None	~20%	~5%	~50%
Vector enumeration	~5%	~7%	~25%	~20%	~25%	~30%	~50%

The 1.3 and 1.4 server-mode VMs were variable, sometimes showing slightly slower times using this technique. In all test cases, I found that the number of iterations for each test was quite important. When I could run the test consistently, there was usually a loop iteration value above which the exception-terminated loop ran faster. One test run output (without JIT) follows:

```
Division loop with no exceptions took 2714 milliseconds
Division loop with an exception took 2604 milliseconds
Division loop with an exception took 2574 milliseconds
Division loop with no exceptions took 2714 milliseconds
Assignment loop with no exceptions took 1622 milliseconds
Assignment loop with an exception took 1242 milliseconds
Assignment loop with an exception took 1222 milliseconds
Assignment loop with no exceptions took 1622 milliseconds
Enumeration loop with no exceptions took 42632 milliseconds
Enumeration loop with an exception took 32386 milliseconds
Enumeration loop with an exception took 31536 milliseconds
Enumeration loop with no exceptions took 43162 milliseconds
```

It is completely conceivable (and greatly preferable) that a compiler or runtime system automatically optimizes loops like this to give the fastest alternative. On some Java systems, try-catch blocks may have enough extra cost associated with them to make this technique slower. Because of the differences in systems, and also because I believe exception-terminated code is difficult to read and likely to lead to bugs and maintenance problems if it proliferates, I prefer to steer clear of this technique.

The actual improvement (if any) in performance depends on the test case that runs in the loop and the code that is run in the body of the loop. The basic consideration is the ratio of the time taken in the loop test compared to the time taken in the body of the loop. The simpler the loop-body execution is compared to the termination test, the more likely that this technique will give a useful effect. This technique works because the termination test iterated many times can have a higher cost than producing and catching an Exception once. Here is the class used for testing, with comments. It is very simple, and the exception-terminated loop technique used is clearly illustrated. Look for the differences between the no_exception methods and the with_ exception methods:

```
package tuning.loop;

public class ExceptionDriven
{
  //Use a default size for the number of iterations
  static int SIZE = 1000000;

  public static void main(String args[ ])
  {
    //Allow an argument to set the size of the loop.
    if (args.length != 0)
      SIZE = Integer.parseInt(args[0]);

    //Run the two tests twice each to ensure there were no
    //initialization effects, reversing the order on the second
    //run to make sure one test does not affect the other.
    no_exception1( ); with_exception1( );
    with_exception1( ); no_exception1( );

    //Execute the array assignment tests only if there is no second
    //argument to allow for large SIZE values on the first test
    //that would give out of memory errors in the second test.
    if (args.length > 1)
      return;
    no_exception2( ); with_exception2( );
    with_exception2( ); no_exception2( );
    no_exception3( ); with_exception3( );
    with_exception3( ); no_exception3( );
  }
  public static void no_exception1( )
  {
    //Standard loop.
    int result;
    long time = System.currentTimeMillis( );
    for (int i = SIZE; i > 0 ; i--)
      result = SIZE/i;
    System.out.println("Division loop with no exceptions took " +
      (System.currentTimeMillis( )-time) + " milliseconds");
  }
  public static void with_exception1( )
  {
    //Non-standard loop with no test for termination using
    //the ArithmeticException thrown at division by zero to
    //terminate the loop.
    int result;
    long time = System.currentTimeMillis( );
    try
    {
      for (int i = SIZE; ; i--)
      result = SIZE/i;
    }
```

```java
    catch (ArithmeticException e) { }
    System.out.println("Division loop with an exception took " +
      (System.currentTimeMillis()-time) + " milliseconds");
  }
  public static void no_exception2()
  {
    //Create the array, get the time, and run the standard loop.
    int array[] = new int[SIZE];
    long time = System.currentTimeMillis();
    for (int i = 0; i < SIZE ; i++)
      array[i] = 3;
    System.out.println("Assignment loop with no exceptions took " +
      (System.currentTimeMillis()-time) + " milliseconds");

    //Garbage collect so that we don't run out of memory for
    //the next test. Set the array variable to null to allow
    //the array instance to be garbage collected.
    array = null;
    System.gc();
  }
  public static void with_exception2()
  {
    //Create the array, get the time, and run a non-standard
    //loop with no test for termination using the
    //ArrayIndexOutOfBoundsException to terminate the loop.
    int array[] = new int[SIZE];
    long time = System.currentTimeMillis();
    try
    {
    for (int i = 0; ; i++)
      array[i] = 3;
    }
    catch (ArrayIndexOutOfBoundsException e) { }
    System.out.println("Assignment loop with an exception took " +
      (System.currentTimeMillis()-time) + " milliseconds");

    //Garbage collect so that we don't run out of memory for
    //the next test. Set the array variable to null to allow
    //the array instance to be garbage collected.
    array = null;
    System.gc();
  }
  public static void no_exception3()
  {
    //Create the Vector, get the time, and run the standard loop.
    java.util.Vector vector = new java.util.Vector(SIZE);
    vector.setSize(SIZE);
    java.util.Enumeration enum = vector.elements();
    Object nothing;
    long time = System.currentTimeMillis();
    for ( ; enum.hasMoreElements(); )
      nothing = enum.nextElement();
    System.out.println("Enumeration loop with no exceptions took " +
      (System.currentTimeMillis()-time) + " milliseconds");
```

```
    //Garbage collect so that we don't run out of memory for
    //the next test. We need to set the variables to null to
    //allow the instances to be garbage collectable.
    enum = null;
    vector = null;
    System.gc();
  }
  public static void with_exception3()
  {
    //Create the Vector, get the time, and run a non-standard
    //loop with no termination test using the
    //java.util.NoSuchElementException to terminate the loop.
    java.util.Vector vector = new java.util.Vector(SIZE);
    vector.setSize(SIZE);
    java.util.Enumeration enum = vector.elements();
    Object nothing;
    long time = System.currentTimeMillis();
    try
    {
      for ( ; ; )
        nothing = enum.nextElement();
    }
    catch (java.util.NoSuchElementException e) { }
    System.out.println("Enumeration loop with an exception took " +
      (System.currentTimeMillis()-time) + " milliseconds");

    //Garbage collect so that we don't run out of memory for
    //the next test. We need to set the variables to null to
    //allow the instances to be garbage collectable.
    enum = null;
    vector = null;
    System.gc();
  }
}
```

Switches

The Java bytecode specification allows a switch statement to be compiled into one of two different bytecodes. One compiled switch type works as follows:

> Given a particular value passed to the switch block to be compared, the passed value is successively compared against the value associated with each case statement in order. If, after testing all cases, no statements match, then the default label is matched. When a case statement that matches is found, the body of that statement and all subsequent case bodies are executed (until one body exits the switch statement, or the last one is reached).

The operation of this switch statement is equivalent to holding an ordered collection of values that are compared to the passed value, one after the other in order, until a match is determined. This means that the time taken for the switch to find the case that matches depends on how many case statements there are and where in the list the matched case is. If no cases match and the `default` must be used, that always takes the longest matching time.

The other `switch` bytecode works for `switch` statements where the case values all lie (or can be made to lie) in a particular range. It works as follows:

> Given a particular value passed to the `switch` block to be compared, the passed value is tested to see if it lies in the range. If it does not, the default label is matched; otherwise, the offset of the case is calculated and the corresponding case is matched directly. The body of that matched label and all subsequent case bodies are executed (until one body exits the `switch` statement, or the last one is reached).

For this latter `switch` bytecode, the time taken for the `switch` statement to match the case is constant. The time is not dependent on the number of cases in the `switch`, and if no cases match, the time to carry out the matching and go to the `default` is still the same. This `switch` statement operates as an ordered collection with the switch value first being checked to see if it is a valid index into the ordered collection, and then that value is used as the index to arrive immediately at the matched location.

Clearly, the second type of `switch` statement is faster than the first. Sometimes compilers can add dummy cases to a `switch` statement, converting the first type of `switch` into the second (faster) kind. (A compiler is not obliged to use the second type of switch bytecode at all, but generally it does if it can easily be used.) You can determine which `switch` a particular statement has been compiled into using `javap`, the disassembler available with the JDK. Using the `-c` option so that the code is disassembled, examine the method that contains the `switch` statement. It contains either a "tableswitch" bytecode identifier or a "lookupswitch" bytecode identifier. The `tableswitch` keyword is the identifier for the faster (second) type of `switch`.

If you identify a bottleneck that involves a `switch` statement, do not leave the decision to the compiler. You are better off constructing `switch` statements that use contiguous ranges of case values, ideally by inserting dummy case statements to specify all the values in the range, or possibly by breaking up the `switch` into multiple switches that each use contiguous ranges. You may need to apply both of these optimizations as in the next example.

Our `tuning.loop.SwitchTest` class provides a repeated test on three methods with switch statements and one other array-access method for comparison. The first method, `switch1( )`, contains some noncontiguous values for the cases, with each returning a particular integer value. The second method, `switch2( )`, converts the single `switch` statement in `switch1( )` into four `switch` statements, with some of those four `switch` statements containing extra dummy cases to make each `switch` statement contain a contiguous set of cases. This second method, `switch2( )`, is functionally identical to `switch1( )`.

The third method, `switch3( )`, replaces the cases with a contiguous set of cases, integers 1 to 13. This method is not directly comparable to the first two methods; it is

---

present as a control test. The fourth method, switch4( ), is functionally identical to switch3( ) but uses an array access instead of the switch statement, essentially doing in Java code what the compiler implicitly does in bytecodes for switch3( ). I run two sets of tests. The first set of tests, labeled "varying," passes in a different integer for each call to the switches. This means that most of the time, the default label is matched. The second set of tests, labeled "constant," alternates between passing in the integers 7 and 8 to the switches. Interestingly, my original test passed in only the integer 8, but HotSpot server mode optimized that to call the method only once and reuse the result, hence the need for the alternation. The results are shown in Table 7-2 for various VMs.

Table 7-2. Speedup using exception-driven loop termination

		1.1.8	1.2.2	1.3.1	1.3.1 -server	1.4.0	1.4.0 -server	1.4.0 -Xint
1	switch1 varying	101%	100%	59%	31%	51%	35%	284%
2	switch2 varying	44%	44%	80%	36%	81%	36%	341%
3	switch3 varying	14%	14%	51%	28%	52%	25%	213%
4	switch4 varying	11%	11%	27%	9%	17%	14%	47%
5	switch1 constant	73%	73%	86%	50%	84%	20%	68%
6	switch2 constant	55%	55%	103%	41%	104%	16%	67%
7	switch3 constant	50%	50%	93%	32%	90%	20%	56%
8	switch4 constant	30%	30%	89%	24%	72%	24%	79%

There is a big difference in optimizations gained depending on whether the VM has a plain JIT or uses HotSpot technology. The times are all relative to the JDK 1.2.2 "switch1 varying" case. From the variation in timings, it is not clear whether the HotSpot technology fails to compile the handcrafted switch in an optimal way or whether it does optimally compile all the switch statements but adds overhead that cancels some of the optimizations. From the first line, it is clear that HotSpot does a great job of compiling the original unoptimized switch. Comparing the times across the different VMs in the second line, for the optimized switch, we can see that client-mode HotSpot does really badly. It appears that the way you optimize your switch statement is heavily dependent on which VM runs your application. This is unfortunate.

For the JIT results, the first and second lines of output show the speedup you can get by recrafting the switch statements. Here, both switch1( ) and switch2( ) are using the default for most of the tests. In this situation, switch1( ) requires 13 failed comparisons before executing the default statement. switch2( ), on the other hand, checks the value against the range of each of its four switch statements, then immediately executes the default statement.

The first and third lines of output show the worst-case comparison for the two types of switch statements. In this test, switch1( ) almost always fails all its comparison tests. On the other hand, switch3( ), with the contiguous range, is much faster than switch1( ) (JIT cases only). This is exactly what is expected, as the average case for switch1( ) here consists of 13 failed comparisons followed by a return statement. The average case for switch3( ) in this test is only a pair of checks followed by a return statement. The two checks are that the integer is smaller than or equal to 13 and larger than or equal to 1. Both checks fail in most of the calls for this "varying" case. Again, the HotSpot values are not so good.

Even when the case statement in switch1( ) is always matched, the fifth and sixth lines show that switch2( ) can be faster (though again, not with HotSpot client mode). In this test, the matched statement is about halfway down the list of cases in switch1( ), so the seven or so failed comparisons for switch1( ) compared to two range checks for switch2( ) should translate into switch2( ) being more than twice as fast as switch1( ).

In each set of tests, switch2( ), which is functionally identical to switch1( ), is faster. The output for switch4( ) is included for comparison, and it turns out to be faster than the functionally identical switch3( ), thus indicating that it is worth considering dispensing with the switch tests completely when you can convert the switch to an array access. In this example, the switch merely returns an integer, so the conversion to an array access is feasible; in general, it may be difficult to convert a set of body statements into an array access and subsequent processing:

```
package tuning.loop;

public class SwitchTest
{
  //Use a default size for the loop of 1 million iterations
  static int SIZE = 10000000;

  public static void main(String args[ ])
  {
    //Allow an argument to set the size of the loop.
    if (args.length != 0)
      SIZE = Integer.parseInt(args[0]);
    int result = 0;
    //run tests looking mostly for the default (switch
    //test uses many different values passed to it)
    long time = System.currentTimeMillis();
    for (int i = SIZE; i >=0 ; i--)
      result += switch1(i);
    System.out.println("Switch1 took " +
      (System.currentTimeMillis()-time) + " millis to get " + result);

    //and the same code to test timings on switch2( ),
    //switch3( ) and switch4( )
    ...
```

```
  //run tests using one particular passed value (8)
  result = 0;
  time = System.currentTimeMillis();
  for (int i = SIZE; i >=0 ; i--)
    result += switch1(i%2==0 ? 7 : 8);
  System.out.println("Switch1 took " +
    (System.currentTimeMillis()-time) + " millis to get " + result);

  //and the same code to test timings on switch2(),
  //switch3() and switch4()
  ...
}

public static int switch1(int i)
{
  //This is one big switch statement with 13 case statements
  //in no particular order.
  switch(i)
  {
    case 318: return 99;
    case 320: return 55;
    case 323: return -1;
    case 14: return 6;
    case 5: return 8;
    case 123456: return 12;
    case 7: return 15;
    case 8: return 29;
    case 9: return 11111;
    case 123457: return 12345;
    case 112233: return 6666;
    case 112235: return 9876;
    case 112237: return 12;
    default: return -1;
  }
}
public static int switch2(int i)
{
  //In this method we break up the 13 case statements from
  //switch1() into four almost contiguous ranges. Then we
  //add in a few dummy cases so that the four ranges are
  //definitely contiguous. This should ensure that the compiler
  //will generate the more optimal tableswitch bytcodes
  switch(i)
  {
    case 318: return 99;
    case 319: break;        //dummy
    case 320: return 55;
    case 321: break;        //dummy
    case 322: break;        //dummy
    case 323: return -1;
  }
  switch(i)
  {
    case 5: return 8;
```

```
    case 6: break;        //dummy
    case 7: return 15;
    case 8: return 29;
    case 9: return 11111;
    case 10: break;       //dummy
    case 11: break;       //dummy
    case 12: break;       //dummy
    case 13: break;       //dummy
    case 14: return 6;
  }
  switch(i)
  {
    case 112233: return 6666;
    case 112234: break;       //dummy
    case 112235: return 9876;
    case 112236: break;       //dummy
    case 112237: return 12;
  }
  switch(i)
  {
    case 123456: return 12;
    case 123457: return 12345;
    default: return -1;
  }
}
public static int switch3(int i)
{
  switch(i)
  {
    //13 contiguous case statements as a kind of fastest control
    case 1: return 99;
    case 2: return 55;
    case 3: return -1;
    case 4: return 6;
    case 5: return 8;
    case 6: return 12;
    case 7: return 15;
    case 8: return 29;
    case 9: return 11111;
    case 10: return 12345;
    case 11: return 6666;
    case 12: return 9876;
    case 13: return 12;
    default: return -1;
  }
}
final static int[ ] RETURNS = {
    99, 55, -1, 6, 8, 12, 15, 29,
    11111, 12345, 6666, 9876, 12
  };
public static int switch4(int i)
{
  //equivalent to switch3( ), but using an array lookup
  //instead of a switch statement.
```

```
      if (i < 1 || i > 13)
        return -1;
      else
        return RETURNS[i-1];
  }
}
```

Recursion

Recursive algorithms are used because they're often clearer and more elegant than the alternatives, and therefore have a lower maintenance cost than the equivalent iterative algorithm. However, recursion often (but not always) has a cost; recursive algorithms are frequently slower. So it is useful to understand the costs associated with recursion and how to improve the performance of recursive algorithms when necessary.

Recursive code can be optimized by a clever compiler (as is done with some C compilers), but only if presented in the right way (typically, it needs to be tail-recursive: see the sidebar "Tail Recursion"). For example, Jon Bentley[*] found that a functionally identical recursive method was optimized by a C compiler if he did not use the ?: conditional operator (using if statements instead). However, it was *not* optimized if he did use the ?: conditional operator. He also found that recursion can be very expensive, taking up to 20 times longer for some operations that are naturally iterative. Bentley's article also looks briefly at optimizing partial-match searching in ternary search trees by transforming a tail recursion in the search into an iteration. See Chapter 11 for an example of tuning a ternary search tree, including an example of converting a recursive algorithm to an iterative one.

Generally, the advice for dealing with methods that are naturally recursive (because that is the natural way to code them for clarity) is to go ahead with the recursive solution. You need to spend time counting the cost (if any) only when your profiling shows that this particular method call is a bottleneck in the application. At that stage, it is worth pursuing alternative implementations or avoiding the method call completely with a different structure.

In case you need to tune a recursive algorithm or convert it into an iterative one, I provide some examples here. I start with an extremely simple recursive algorithm for calculating factorial numbers, as this illustrates several tuning points:

```
public static long factorial1(int n)
{
  if (n < 2) return 1L;
  else return n*factorial1(n-1);
}
```

[*] "The Cost of Recursion," *Dr. Dobb's Journal*, June 1998.

Tail Recursion

A tail-recursive function is a recursive function for which each recursive call to itself is a reduction of the original call. A *reduction* is the situation where a problem is converted into a new problem that is simpler, and the solution of that new problem is exactly the solution of the original problem, with no further computation necessary. This is a subtle concept, best illustrated with a simple example. I will take the factorial example used in the text. The original recursive solution is:

```
public static long factorial1(int n)
{
  if (n < 2) return 1L;
  else return n*factorial1(n-1);
}
```

This is not tail-recursive because each call to itself does not provide the solution to the original problem. Instead, the recursive call provides a partial solution that must be multiplied by a number to get the final result. If you consider the operating stack of the VM, each recursive call must be kept on the stack because each call is incomplete until the next call above on the stack is returned. So factorial1(20) goes on the stack and stays there until factorial1(19) returns. factorial1(19) goes above factorial1(20) on the stack and stays there until factorial1(18) returns, etc.

The tail-recursive version of this function requires two functions: one to set up the recursive call (to keep compatibility) and the recursive call itself. This looks like:

```
public static long factorial1a(int n)
{
  //NOT recursive. Sets up the tail-recursive call to factorial1b( )
  if (n < 2) return 1L;
  else return factorial1b(n, 1L);
}

public static long factorial1b(int n, long result)
{
  //No need to consider n < 2, as factorial1a handles that
  if (n == 2) return 2L*result;
  else return factorial1b(n-1, result*n);
}
```

I have changed the recursive call to add an extra parameter, the partial result, built up as you calculate the answer. The consequence is that each time you return the recursive call, the answer is the full answer to the function since you are holding the partial answer in a variable. Considering the VM stack again, the situation is vastly improved. Because the recursive method returns a call to itself each time, with no further operations needed (i.e., the recursive caller actually exits with the call to recurse), there is no need to keep any calls on the stack except for the current one. factorial1b(20,1) is put on the stack, but this exits with a call to factorial1b(19,20), which replaces the call to factorial1b(20,1) on the stack (since it has exited). This in turn is replaced by the call to factorial1b(18,380), which in turn is replaced by the call to factorial1b(17,6840), and so on, until factorial1b(2, ...) returns just the result.

I have limited the function to long values, which means that you cannot use the function beyond factorial 20, as that overflows the long data type. This keeps the function simple for this illustration.

Since this function is easily converted to a tail-recursive version, it is natural to test the tail-recursive version to see if it performs any better. For this particular function, the tail-recursive version does not perform any better, which is not typical. Here, the factorial function consists of a very simple fast calculation, and the extra function-call overhead in the tail-recursive version is enough of an overhead that it negates the benefit that is normally gained.

Let's look at other ways this function can be optimized. Start with the classic conversion for recursive to iterative and note that the factorial method contains just one value that is successively operated on to give a new value (the result), along with a parameter specifying how to operate on the partial result (the current input to the factorial). A standard way to convert this type of recursive method is to replace the parameters passed to the method with temporary variables in a loop. In this case, you need two variables, one of which is passed into the method and can be reused. The converted method looks like:

```
public static long factorial2(int n)
{
  long result = 1;
  while(n>1)
  {
    result *= n--;
  }
  return result;
}
```

Measuring the performance, you see that this method calculates the result in 92% of the time taken by the original recursive factorial1( ) method (using the JDK 1.2.2 results;[*] see Table 7-3.

Table 7-3. Timings of the various factorial implementations

	1.1.8	1.2.2	1.3.1	1.3.1 -server	1.4.0	1.4.0 -server	1.4.0 -Xint
factoral1 (original recursive)	101%	100%	246%	101%	217%	93%	1084%
factoral1a (tail recursive)	102%	102%	262%	108%	218%	100%	1271%
factorial2 (iterative)	86%	92%	180%	83%	190%	97%	624%
factoral3 (dynamically cached)	56%	56%	101%	60%	100%	52%	559%
factoral4 (statically cached)	44%	44%	90%	37%	77%	37%	416%
factoral5 (dynamically cached with cache size of 21 elements)	8%	8%	12%	13%	86%	13%	130%

[*] The 1.4.0 server HotSpot VM optimized the recursive version sufficiently to make it faster than the iterative version.

The recursion-to-iteration technique as illustrated here is general, and another example in a different domain may help make this generality clear. Consider a linked list, with singly linked nodes consisting of a next pointer to the next node, and a value instance variable holding (in this case) just an integer. A simple linear search method to find the first node holding a particular integer looks like:

```
Node find_recursive(int i)
{
  if (node.value == i)
    return node;
  else if(node.next != null)
    node.next.find_recursive(i);
  else
    return null;
}
```

To convert this to an iterative method, use a temporary variable to hold the "current" node, and reassign that variable with the next node in the list at each iteration. The method is clear, and its only drawback compared to the recursive method is that it violates encapsulation (this one method directly accesses the instance variable of each node object):

```
Node find_iterative(int i)
{
  Node node = this;
  while(node != null)
  {
    if (node.value == i)
      return node;
    else
      node = node.next;
  }
  return null;
}
```

Before looking at general techniques for converting other types of recursive methods to iterative ones, I will revisit the original factorial method to illustrate some other techniques for improving the performance of recursive methods.

To test the timing of the factorial method, I put it into a loop to recalculate factorial(20) many times. Otherwise, the time taken is too short to be reliably measured. When this situation is close to the actual problem, a good tuning technique is to cache the intermediate results. This technique can be applied when some recursive function is repeatedly being called and some of the intermediate results are repeatedly being identified. This technique is simple to illustrate for the factorial method:

```
public static final int CACHE_SIZE = 15;
public static final long[ ] factorial3Cache = new long[CACHE_SIZE];

public static long factorial3(int n)
```

```
{
  if (n < 2) return 1L;
  else if (n < CACHE_SIZE)
  {
    if (factorial3Cache[n] == 0)
      factorial3Cache[n] = n*factorial3(n-1);
    return factorial3Cache[n];
  }
  else return n*factorial3(n-1);
}
```

With the choice of 15 elements for the cache, the factorial3( ) method takes 56% of the time taken by factorial1( ). If you choose a cache with 21 elements, so that all except the first call to factorial3(20) are simply returning from the cache with no calculations at all, the time taken is just 8% of the time taken by factorial1( ) (using the JDK 1.2 results; see Table 7-3).

In this particular situation, you can make one further improvement, which is to compile the values at implementation and hardcode them in:

```
public static final long[] factorial4Cache = {
  1L, 1L, 2L, 6L, 24L, 120L, 720L, 5040L, 40320L, 362880L, 3628800L,
  39916800L, 479001600L, 6227020800L, 87178291200L};
public static final int CACHE_SIZE = factorial4Cache.length;
public static long factorial4(int n)
{
  if (n < CACHE_SIZE)
    return factorial4Cache[n];
  else return n*factorial4(n-1);
}
```

This is a valid technique that applies when you can identify and calculate partial solutions that can be included with the class at compilation time.[*]

Recursion and Stacks

The techniques for converting recursive method calls to iterative ones are suitable only for methods that take a single search path at every decision node when navigating through the solution space. For more complex recursive methods that evaluate multiple paths from some nodes, you can convert a recursive method into an iterative method based on a stack. This is best illustrated with an example. I'll use here the problem of looking for all the files with names ending in some particular string.

---

[*] My editor Mike Loukides points out that a variation on hardcoded values, used by state-of-the-art high-performance mathematical functions, is a partial table of values together with an interpolation method to calculate intermediate values.

The following method runs a recursive search of the filesystem, printing all non-directory files that end in a particular string:

```
public static String FS = System.getProperty("file.separator");
public static void filesearch1(String root, String fileEnding)
{
  File f = new File(root);
  String[] filelist = f.list();
  if (filelist == null)
    return;
  for (int i = filelist.length-1; i >= 0; i--)
  {
    f = new File(root, filelist[i]);
    if (f.isDirectory())
      filesearch1(root+FS+filelist[i], fileEnding);
    else if(filelist[i].toUpperCase().endsWith(fileEnding))
      System.out.println(root+ls+filelist[i]);
  }
}
```

To convert this into an iterative search, it is not sufficient to use an extra variable to hold the current directory. At any one directory, there are several possible directories underneath, all of which must be held onto and searched, and you cannot reference them all from a plain variable. Instead, you can make that variable into a collection object. The standard object to use is a stack. With this hint in mind, the method converts quite easily:

```
public static void filesearch2(String root, String fileEnding)
{
  Stack dirs = new Stack();
  dirs.push(root);
  File f;
  int i;
  String[] filelist;
  while(!dirs.empty())
  {
    f = new File(root = (String) dirs.pop());
    filelist = f.list();
    if (filelist == null)
      continue;
    for (i = filelist.length-1; i >= 0; i--)
    {
      f = new File(root, filelist[i]);
      if (f.isDirectory())
        dirs.push(root+FS+filelist[i]);
      else if(filelist[i].toUpperCase().endsWith(fileEnding))
        System.out.println(root+ls+filelist[i]);
    }
  }
}
```

In fact, the structures of the two methods are almost the same. This second iterative version has the main part of the body wrapped in an extra loop that terminates when the extra variable holding the stack becomes empty. Otherwise, instead of the recursive call, the directory is added to the stack.

In the cases of these particular search methods, the time-measurement comparison shows that the iterative method actually takes 5% longer than the recursive method. This is due to the iterative method having the overhead of the extra stack object to manipulate, whereas filesystems are generally not particularly deep (the ones I tested on were not), so the recursive algorithm is not particularly inefficient. This illustrates that a recursive method is not always worse than an iterative one.

 Note that the methods here were chosen for illustration, using an easily understood problem that could be managed iteratively and recursively. Since the I/O is actually the limiting factor for these methods, there would not be much point in actually making the optimization shown.

For this example, I eliminated the I/O overhead, as it would have swamped the times and made it difficult to determine the difference between the two implementations. To do this, I mapped the filesystem into memory using a simple replacement of the `java.io.File` class. This stored a snapshot of the filesystem in a hash table. (Actually, only the full pathnames of directories as keys, and their associated string array list of files as values, need be stored.)

This kind of trick—replacing classes with another implementation to eliminate extraneous overhead—is quite useful when you need to identify exactly where times are going.

Performance Checklist

Most of these suggestions apply only after a bottleneck has been identified:

- Make the loop do as little as possible.
  - Remove from the loop any execution code that does not need to be executed on each pass.
  - Move any code that is repeatedly executed with the same result, and assign that code to a temporary variable before the loop ("code motion").
  - Avoid method calls in loops when possible, even if this requires rewriting or inlining.
  - Multiple access or update to the same array element should be done on a temporary variable and assigned back to the array element when the loop is finished.
  - Avoid using a method call in the loop termination test.
  - Use `int` data types preferentially, especially for the loop variable.
  - Use `System.arraycopy( )` for copying arrays.
  - Try to use the fastest tests in loops.

— Convert equality comparisons to identity comparisons when possible.

— Phrase multiple boolean tests in one expression so that they "short circuit" as soon as possible.

— Eliminate unneeded temporary variables from loops.

— Try unrolling the loop to various degrees to see if this improves speed.

- Rewrite any switch statements to use a contiguous range of case values.

- Identify whether a recursive method can be made faster.

— Convert recursive methods to use iteration instead.

— Convert recursive methods to use tail recursion.

— Try caching recursively calculated values to reduce the depth of recursion.

— Use temporary variables in place of passed parameters to convert a recursive method using a single search path into an iterative method.

— Use temporary stacks in place of passed parameters to convert a recursive method using multiple search paths into an iterative method.

In this chapter:
- Replacing System.out
- Logging
- From Raw I/O to Smokin' I/O
- Serialization
- Clustering Objects and Counting I/O Operations
- Compression
- NIO

CHAPTER 8

I/O, Logging, and Console Output

I/O, I/O, it's off to work we go.
—Ava Shirazi

I/O to the disk or the network is hundreds to thousands of times slower than I/O to computer memory. Disk and network transfers are expensive activities and are two of the most likely candidates for performance problems. Two standard optimization techniques for reducing I/O overhead are buffering and caching.

For a given amount of data, I/O mechanisms work more efficiently if the data is transferred using a few large chunks of data, rather than many small chunks. Buffering groups of data into larger chunks improves the efficiency of the I/O by reducing the number of I/O operations that need to be executed.

Where some objects or data are accessed repeatedly, caching those objects or data can replace an I/O call with a hugely faster memory access (or replace a slow network I/O call with faster local disk I/O). For every I/O call that is avoided because an item is accessed from a cache, you save a large chunk of time equivalent to executing hundreds or thousands of simple operations.[*]

There are some other general points about I/O at the system level that are worth knowing. First, I/O buffers throughout the system typically use a read-ahead algorithm for optimization. This normally means that the next few chunks are read from disk into a low-level buffer somewhere. Consequently, reading sequentially *forward* through a file is usually faster than other orders, such as reading back to front through a file or random access of file elements.

---

[*] Caching usually requires intercepting a simple attempt to access an object and replacing that simple access with a more complex routine that accesses the object from the cache. Caching is easier to implement if the application has been designed with caching in mind from the beginning, by grouping external data access. If the application is not so designed, you may still be lucky, as there are normally only a few points of external access from an application that allow you to add caching easily.

The next point is that at the system level, most operating systems support mmap( ), memcntl( ), and various shared-memory options. Using these can improve I/O performance dramatically, but they also increase complexity. Portability is also compromised, though not as much as you might think. If you need to use these sorts of features and also maintain portability, you may want to start with the latest Perl distribution. Perl has been ported to a large number of systems, and these features are mapped consistently to system-level features in all ports. Since the Perl source is available, it is possible to extract the relevant system-independent mappings for portability purposes.

In the same vein, when simultaneously using multiple open filehandles to I/O devices (sockets, files, pipes, etc.), Java editions prior to the 1.4 release require you to use either polling across the handles, which is system-intensive; a separate thread per handle, which is also system-intensive; or a combination of these two, which in any case is bad for performance. However, almost all operating systems support an efficient multiplexing function call, often called select( ) or sometimes poll( ). This function provides a way to ask the system in one request if any of the (set of) open handles are ready for reading or writing. SDK 1.4 introduced support for the select( )/poll( ) function under the java.nio package, which I discuss further in the NIO section later in this chapter. For versions prior to 1.4, you could again use Perl, which provides a standardized mapping for this function if you need hints on maintaining portability. For efficient complex I/O performance, select( )/poll( ) functionality was probably the largest single missing piece of functionality in Java.

 SDKs prior to 1.4 do provide nonblocking I/O by means of polling. Polling means that every time you want to read or write, you first test whether there are bytes to read or space to write. If you cannot read or write, you go into a loop, repeatedly testing until you can perform the desired read/write operation. Polling of this sort is extremely system-intensive, especially because in order to obtain good performance, you must normally put I/O into the highest-priority thread. Polling solutions are usually more system-intensive than multithreaded I/O and do not perform as well. Multiplexed I/O, as obtained with the select( ) system call, provides far superior performance to both. Polling does not scale. If you are building a server, you are well advised to add support for the select( ) system call.

Here are some other general techniques to improve I/O performance:

- Execute I/O in the background. Decoupling the application processes from the I/O operations means that, ideally, your application does not spend time waiting for I/O. In practice, it can be difficult to completely decouple the I/O, but usually some reads can be anticipated and some writes can be run asynchronously without the program requiring immediate confirmation of success.

- Avoid executing I/O in loops. Try to replace multiple smaller I/O calls with a few larger I/O calls. Because I/O is a slow operation, executing in a loop means that the loop is normally bottlenecked on the I/O call.

- When actions need to be performed while executing I/O, try to separate the I/O from those actions to minimize the number of I/O operations that need to be executed. For example, if a file needs to be parsed, instead of reading a bit, parsing a bit, and repeating until finished, it can be quicker to read in the whole file and then parse the data in memory.

- If you repeatedly access different locations within the same set of files, you can optimize performance by keeping the files open and navigating around them instead of repeatedly opening and closing the files. This often requires using random-access classes (e.g., RandomAccessFile) rather than the easier sequential-access classes (e.g., FileReader).

- Preallocate files to avoid the operating-system overhead that comes from allocating files. This can be done by creating files of the expected size, filled with any character (0 is conventional). The bytes can then be overwritten (e.g., with the RandomAccessFile class).

- Using multiple files simultaneously can improve performance because of disk parallelism and CPU availability during disk reads and writes. However, this technique needs to be balanced against the cost of extra opens and closes and the extra resources required by multiple open streams. Sequentially opening and closing multiple files is usually bad for performance (e.g., when loading unpacked class files from the filesystem into the Java runtime).

Replacing System.out

Typically, an application generates output to System.out or System.err, if only for logging purposes during development. It is important to realize that this output can affect performance. Any output not present in the final deployed version of the application should be turned off during performance tests; otherwise, your performance results can get skewed. This is also true for any other I/O: to disk, pipes, other processes, or the network.

It is best to include a framework for logging output in your design. You want a framework that centralizes all your logging operations and lets you enable or disable certain logging features (perhaps by setting a "debug level"). You may want to implement your own logging class, which decides whether to send output at all and where to send it. The Unix *syslog* utility provides a good starting point for designing such a framework. It has levels of priority (emergency, alert, critical, error, warning, notice, info, debug) and other aspects that are useful to note. SDK 1.4 introduced a logging API, the java.util.logging package. This includes logging levels and output redirection, as I show briefly in the next section.

If you are already well into development without this kind of framework but need a quick fix for handling unnecessary output, it is still possible to replace System.out and System.err.

It is simple to replace the print stream in System.out and System.err. You need an instance of a java.io.PrintStream or one of its subclasses, and you can use the System.setOut() and System.setErr() methods to replace the current PrintStream instances. It is useful to retain a reference to the original print-stream objects you are replacing, since these retain access to the console. For example, the following class simply eliminates all output sent to System.out and System.err if TUNING is true; otherwise, it sends all output to the original destination. This class illustrates how to implement your own redirection classes:

```
package tuning.console;

public class PrintWrapper
  extends java.io.PrintStream
{
  java.io.PrintStream wrappedOut;
  public static boolean TUNING = false;

  public static void install()
  {
    System.setOut(new PrintWrapper(System.out));
    System.setErr(new PrintWrapper(System.err));
  }

  public PrintWrapper(java.io.PrintStream out)
  {
    super(out);
    wrappedOut = out;
  }

  public boolean checkError() {return wrappedOut.checkError();}
  public void close() {wrappedOut.close();}
  public void flush() {wrappedOut.flush();}
  public void print(boolean x) {if (!TUNING) wrappedOut.print(x);}
  public void print(char x) {if (!TUNING) wrappedOut.print(x);}
  public void print(char[] x) {if (!TUNING) wrappedOut.print(x);}
  public void print(double x) {if (!TUNING) wrappedOut.print(x);}
  public void print(float x) {if (!TUNING) wrappedOut.print(x);}
  public void print(int x) {if (!TUNING) wrappedOut.print(x);}
  public void print(long x) {if (!TUNING) wrappedOut.print(x);}
  public void print(Object x) {if (!TUNING) wrappedOut.print(x);}
  public void print(String x) {if (!TUNING) wrappedOut.print(x);}
  public void println() {if (!TUNING) wrappedOut.println();}
  public void println(boolean x) {if (!TUNING) wrappedOut.println(x);}
  public void println(char x) {if (!TUNING) wrappedOut.println(x);}
  public void println(char[] x) {if (!TUNING) wrappedOut.println(x);}
  public void println(double x) {if (!TUNING) wrappedOut.println(x);}
  public void println(float x) {if (!TUNING) wrappedOut.println(x);}
  public void println(int x) {if (!TUNING) wrappedOut.println(x);}
```

```
   public void println(long x) {if (!TUNING) wrappedOut.println(x);}
   public void println(Object x) {if (!TUNING) wrappedOut.println(x);}
   public void println(String x) {if (!TUNING) wrappedOut.println(x);}
   public void write(byte[] x, int y, int z) {
      if (!TUNING) wrappedOut.write(x,y,z);}
   public void write(int  x) {if (!TUNING) wrappedOut.write(x);}
}
```

Logging

Logging always degrades performance. The penalty you pay depends to some extent on how logging is done. One possibility is using a final static variable to enable logging, as in the following code:

```
public final static boolean LOGGING = true;
...
if (LOGGING)
   System.out.println(...);
```

This code allows you to remove the logging code during compilation. If the LOGGING flag is set to false before compilation, the compiler eliminates the debugging code.[*] This approach works well when you need a lot of debugging code during development but don't want to carry the code into your finished application. You can use a similar technique for when you do want logging capabilities during deployment, by compiling with logging features but setting the boolean at runtime.

An alternative technique is to use a logging object:

```
public class LogWriter {
   public static LogWriter TheLogger = sessionLogger();
   ...
}
...
LogWriter.TheLogger.log(...)
```

This technique allows you to specify various LogWriter objects. Examples include a null log writer that has an empty log( ) method, a file log writer that logs to file, a sysout log writer that logs to System.out, etc. Using this technique allows logging to be turned on after an application has started. It can even install a new type of log writer after deployment, which can be useful for some applications. However, be aware that any deployed logging capabilities should not do too much logging (or even decide whether to log too often), or performance will suffer. The logging framework introduced in 1.4, java.util.logging, provides most of the features you should need. There is also an open source implementation of the logging APIs for JDK Versions 1.2 and 1.3 available from *http://javalogging.sourceforge.net/*. The following is an example of using the 1.4 logging framework.

---

[*] See "Conditional Error Checking" in Chapter 6 and "Dead code branches are eliminated" in Chapter 3.

```
import java.util.logging.*;

...
// Get a Logger object. Use a name to distinguish it.
Logger globalLogger = Logger.getLogger("global");
// Log an INFO level message
globalLogger.info("Starting application.");
try
{
    ... //do something
}
catch(Exception e)
{
    //log a level SEVERE message, including the exception
    globalLogger.log(Level.SEVERE, "Oh dear, this is bad.", e);
    //And a level WARNING message
    globalLogger.warning("Exiting");
    return;
}

//Something went well if we're here, so just send a fairly
//low level message: level FINE message for debugging
globalLogger.fine("Bad things didn't happen.");
...
```

The logging API was designed to minimize overhead when using configurable logging. Given that there are multiple levels of logging, where some levels may be turned off, those logging statements that are turned off should produce negligible overhead to the application, and those that are turned on should impose as small an overhead as possible. In addition, the logging API enables the conversion and output of logging statements to be handled separately, so that overhead from these activities can be minimized. The logging API is covered in more detail in *Learning Java* by Pat Niemeyer and Jonathan Knudsen (O'Reilly), and a basic introduction can be obtained in an *OnJava* article by Brian Gilstrap.[*]

I recommend deploying applications with a simple set of logging features in place. But first ensure that the logging features do not slow down the application.

From Raw I/O to Smokin' I/O

So far we have looked only at general points about I/O and logging. Now we look at an example of tuning I/O performance. The example consists of reading lines from a

---

[*] "An Introduction to the Java Logging API," Brian Gilstrap, *OnJava.com*, June 2002, *http://www.onjava.com/pub/a/onjava/2002/06/19/log.html*.

large file. This section was inspired by an article from Sun Engineering,[*] though I go somewhat further along the tuning cycle.

The initial attempt at file I/O might be to use the FileInputStream to read through a file. Note that DataInputStream has a readLine( ) method (now deprecated because it is byte-based rather than char-based, but ignore that for the moment), so you wrap the FileInputStream with the DataInputStream, and run. The code looks like:

```
DataInputStream in = new DataInputStream(new FileInputStream(file));
while ( (line = in.readLine( )) != null)
{
  doSomethingWith(line);
}
in.close( );
```

For these timing tests, I use two different files, a 1.8 MB file with about 20,000 lines (long lines), and a one-third of a megabyte file with about 34,000 lines (short lines). I test using several VMs to show the variations across VMs and the challenges in improving performance across different runtime environments. To make comparisons simpler, I report the times as normalized to 100% for the JDK 1.2.2 VM with JIT. The long-line case and the short-line case are normalized separately. Tests are averages across at least three test runs. For the baseline test, I have the following chart (see Tables 8-1 and 8-2 for full results). Note that the server mode results show the second run of tests, after HotSpot has had a chance to apply its optimizations.

Short lines	1.1.8	1.2.2[a]	1.3.1	1.3.1 -server	1.4.0	1.4.0 -server	1.4.0 -Xint
Unbuffered input stream	86%	100%	109%	98%	103%	115%	146%

Long lines	1.1.8	1.2.2[a]	1.3.1	1.3.1 -server	1.4.0	1.4.0 -server	1.4.0 -Xint
Unbuffered input stream	83%	100%	108%	95%	95%	110%	170%

[a] The short-line 1.2 and long-line 1.2 cases have been separately normalized to 100%. All short-line times are relative to the short-line 1.2, and all long-line times are relative to the long-line 1.2.

The first test in absolute times is really dreadful because you are executing I/O one byte at a time. This performance is the result of using a plain FileInputStream without buffering the I/O, because the process is completely I/O-bound. For this reason, I expected the absolute times of the various VMs to be similar, since the CPU is not the bottleneck. But curiously, they are varied. Possibly the underlying native call implementation may be different between VM versions, but I am not interested enough to spend time deciding why there should be differences for the unbuffered

[*] "Java Performance I/O Tuning," Java Developer's Journal, Volume 2, Issue 11. See *http://www.JavaDevelopersJournal.com*.

case. After all, no one uses unbuffered I/O. Everyone knows you should buffer your I/O (except when memory is really at a premium, as in an embedded system).

So let's immediately move to wrap the FileInputStream with a BufferedInputStream.[*] The code has only slight changes, in the constructor:

```
//DataInputStream in = new DataInputStream(new FileInputStream(file));
DataInputStream in = new DataInputStream(
    new BufferedInputStream(new FileInputStream(file)));
while ( (line = in.readLine()) != null)
{
  doSomethingWith(line);
}
in.close();
```

However, the times are already faster by an order of magnitude, as you can see in the following charts:

Short lines	1.1.8	1.2.2	1.3.1	1.3.1 -server	1.4.0	1.4.0 -server	1.4.0 -Xint
Unbuffered input stream	86%	100%	109%	98%	103%	115%	146%
Buffered input stream	7%	6%	3%	3%	3%	2%	21%

Long lines	1.1.8	1.2.2	1.3.1	1.3.1 -server	1.4.0	1.4.0 -server	1.4.0 -Xint
Unbuffered input stream	83%	100%	108%	95%	95%	110%	170%
Buffered input stream	6%	5%	3%	3%	3%	2%	24%

The lesson is clear, if you haven't already had it drummed home somewhere else: buffered I/O performs much better than unbuffered I/O. Having established that buffered I/O is better than unbuffered, you renormalize your times on the buffered I/O case so that you can compare any improvements against the normal case.

So far, we have used only the default buffer, which is a 2048-byte buffer (contrary to the JDK 1.1.6 documentation, which states it is 512 bytes; always check the source on easily changeable things like this). Perhaps a larger buffer would be better. Let's try 8192 bytes:

```
//DataInputStream in = new DataInputStream(new FileInputStream(file));
//DataInputStream in = new DataInputStream(
//    new BufferedInputStream(new FileInputStream(file)));
DataInputStream in = new DataInputStream(
    new BufferedInputStream(new FileInputStream(file), 8192));
while ( (line = in.readLine()) != null)
{
```

---

[*] Buffering I/O does not require the use of buffered classes. You can buffer I/O directly from the FileInputStream class and other low-level classes by passing arrays to the read( ) and write( ) methods. This means you need to handle buffer overflows yourself.

```
    doSomethingWith(line);
  }
  in.close( );
```

Short lines	1.1.8	1.2.2	1.3.1	1.3.1 -server	1.4.0	1.4.0 -server	1.4.0 -Xint
Unbuffered input stream	1551%	1808%	1965%	1764%	1872%	2088%	2646%
Buffered input stream	132%	100%	48%	60%	48%	36%	373%
8K buffered input stream	136%	96%	36%	57%	48%	36%	361%

Long lines	1.1.8	1.2.2	1.3.1	1.3.1 -server	1.4.0	1.4.0 -server	1.4.0 -Xint
Unbuffered input stream	1655%	1992%	2169%	1895%	1895%	2201%	3385%
Buffered input stream	123%	100%	65%	59%	57%	37%	487%
8K buffered input stream	123%	99%	64%	59%	56%	37%	484%

The variations are large, but there is a mostly consistent pattern. The 8K buffer doesn't seem to be significantly better than the default.

Let's get back to the fact that we are using a deprecated method, readLine( ). You should really be using Readers instead of InputStreams, according to the Javadoc, for full portability, etc. Let's move to Readers and ascertain what this change costs us:

```
//DataInputStream in = new DataInputStream(new FileInputStream(file));
//DataInputStream in = new DataInputStream(
//     new BufferedInputStream(new FileInputStream(file)));
//DataInputStream in = new DataInputStream(
//     new BufferedInputStream(new FileInputStream(file), 8192));
BufferedReader in = new BufferedReader(new FileReader(file));
while ( (line = in.readLine( )) != null)
{
  doSomethingWith(line);
}
in.close( );
```

Short lines	1.1.8	1.2.2	1.3.1	1.3.1 -server	1.4.0	1.4.0 -server	1.4.0 -Xint
Buffered input stream	132%	100%	48%	60%	48%	36%	373%
8K buffered input stream	136%	96%	36%	57%	48%	36%	361%
Buffered reader	192%	96%	56%	24%	60%	24%	590%

Long Lines	1.1.8	1.2.2	1.3.1	1.3.1 -server	1.4.0	1.4.0 -server	1.4.0 -Xint
Buffered input stream	123%	100%	65%	59%	57%	37%	487%
8K buffered input stream	123%	99%	64%	59%	56%	37%	484%
Buffered reader	53%	43%	43%	20%	52%	24%	582%

These results tell us that someone at Sun spent time optimizing Readers. You can reasonably use Readers in most situations where you would have used an InputStream. Some situations can show a performance decrease, but generally there is a performance increase. Note that if you are running your own versions of these tests, you need to repeat some measurements within the VM, even in plain JIT VMs, to eliminate the JIT compiler overhead.

Now let's get down to some real tuning. So far we have just been working from bad coding to good working practice. The final version so far uses buffered Reader classes for I/O, as recommended by Sun. Can we do better? Well of course, but now let's get down and dirty. You know from general tuning practices that creating objects is overhead you should try to avoid. Up until now, we have used the readLine() method, which returns a string. Suppose you work on that string and then discard it, as is the typical situation. You would do better to avoid the String creation altogether. Also, if you want to process the String, then for performance purposes you are better off working directly on the underlying char array. Working on char arrays is quicker since you can avoid the String method overhead (or, more likely, the need to copy the String into a char array buffer to work on it). See Chapter 5 for more details on this technique.

Basically, this means that you need to implement the readLine() functionality with your own buffer while passing the buffer to the method that does the string processing. The following implementation uses its own char array buffer. It reads in characters to fill the buffer, then runs through the buffer looking for ends of lines. Each time the end of a line is found, the buffer, together with the start and end index of the line in that buffer, is passed to the doSomething() method for processing. This implementation avoids both the String-creation overhead and the subsequent String-processing overhead, but these are not included in any timings here. The only complication comes when you reach the end of the buffer and you need to fill it with the next chunk from the file, but you also need to retain the line fragment from the end of the last chunk. It is unlikely your 8192-char chunk will end exactly on an end of line, so there are almost always some characters left to be carried over to the next chunk. To handle this, simply copy the characters to the beginning of the buffer and read the next chunk into the buffer starting from after those characters. The commented code looks like this:

```
public static void myReader(String string)
    throws IOException
  {
    //Do the processing myself, directly from a FileReader
    //But don't create strings for each line, just leave it
    //as a char array
    FileReader in = new FileReader(string);
    int defaultBufferSize = 8192;
    int nextChar = 0;
    char[] buffer = new char[defaultBufferSize];
```

```
char c;
int leftover;
int length_read;
int startLineIdx = 0;

//First fill the buffer once before we start
int nChars = in.read(buffer, 0, defaultBufferSize);
boolean checkFirstOfChunk = false;

for(;;)
{
  //Work through the buffer looking for end of line characters.
  //Note that the JDK does the eol search as follows:
  //It hardcodes both of the characters \r and \n as end
  //of line characters, and considers either to signify the
  //end of the line. In addition, if the end of line character
  //is determined to be \r, and the next character is \n,
  //it winds past the \n. This way it allows the reading of
  //lines from files written on any of the three systems
  //currently supported (Unix with \n, Windows with \r\n,
  //and Mac with \r), even if you are not running on any of these.
  for (; nextChar < nChars; nextChar++)
  {
    if (((c = buffer[nextChar]) == '\n') || (c == '\r'))
    {
      //We found a line, so pass it for processing
      doSomethingWith(buffer, startLineIdx, nextChar-1);

      //And then increment the cursors. nextChar is
      //automatically incremented by the loop,
      //so only need to worry if 'c' is \r
      if (c == '\r')
      {
        //need to consider if we are at end of buffer
        if (nextChar == (nChars - 1) )
          checkFirstOfChunk = true;
        else if (buffer[nextChar+1] == '\n')
          nextChar++;
      }
      startLineIdx = nextChar + 1;
    }
  }

  leftover = 0;
  if (startLineIdx < nChars)
  {
    //We have some characters left over at the end of the chunk.
    //So carry them over to the beginning of the next chunk.
    leftover = nChars - startLineIdx;
    System.arraycopy(buffer, startLineIdx, buffer, 0, leftover);
  }
  do
  {
    length_read = in.read(buffer, leftover,
```

```
          buffer.length-leftover );
    } while (length_read == 0);
    if (length_read > 0)
    {
      nextChar -= nChars;
      nChars = leftover + length_read;
      startLineIdx = nextChar;
      if (checkFirstOfChunk)
      {
        checkFirstOfChunk = false;
        if (buffer[0] == '\n')
        {
          nextChar++;
          startLineIdx = nextChar;
        }
      }
    }
    else
    { /* EOF */
      in.close( );
      return;
    }
  }
}
```

The following chart shows the new times:

Short lines	1.1.8	1.2.2	1.3.1	1.3.1 -server	1.4.0	1.4.0 -server	1.4.0 -Xint
Buffered input stream	132%	100%	48%	60%	48%	36%	373%
Buffered reader	192%	96%	56%	24%	60%	24%	590%
Custom-built reader	28%	24%	36%	164%	34%	24%	420%

Long lines	1.1.8	1.2.2	1.3.1	1.3.1 -server	1.4.0	1.4.0 -server	1.4.0 -Xint
Buffered input stream	123%	100%	65%	59%	57%	37%	487%
Buffered reader	53%	43%	43%	20%	52%	24%	582%
Custom-built reader	28%	28%	38%	37%	37%	22%	547%

The timings are the best so far, with the single exception of the 1.3.1 server mode VM, and most times are significantly better than before.[*] The 1.3.1 server mode results are quite peculiar and look like a compiler bug of some sort caused the compiler to generate inefficient code. If you were running this code under a 1.3.1 server

---

[*] Note that the HotSpot timings are, once again, for the second run of the repeated tests. No other VMs exhibited consistent variations between the first and second run tests. See Tables 8-1 and 8-2 for the full set of results.

VM, you would need to track down what produced the anomalous times by changing a little bit of the code at a time, until you produced a workaround.

You can try one more thing: performing the byte-to-char conversion. The code comes from Chapter 7, where we looked at this conversion in detail. The changes are straightforward. Change the FileReader to FileInputStream and add a byte array buffer of the same size as the char array buffer:

```
//    FileReader in = new FileReader(string);
//this last line becomes
    FileInputStream in = new FileInputStream(string);
    int defaultBufferSize = 8192;
    //and add the byte array buffer
    byte[ ] byte_buffer = new byte[defaultBufferSize];
```

You also need to change the read( ) calls to read into the byte buffer, adding a convert( ) call after these. The first read( ) is changed like this:

```
//First fill the buffer once before we start
//  this next line becomes a byte read followed by convert( ) call
//  int nChars = in.read(buffer, 0, defaultBufferSize);
    int nChars = in.read(byte_buffer, 0, defaultBufferSize);
    convert(byte_buffer, 0, nChars, buffer, 0, nChars, MAP3);
```

The second read( ) in the main loop is also changed, but the conversion isn't done immediately here. It's done just after the number of characters, nChars, is set, a few lines later:

```
//       length_read = in.read(buffer, leftover,
//               buffer.length-leftover );
//becomes
        length_read = in.read(byte_buffer, leftover,
            buffer.length-leftover);
    } while (length_read == 0);
    if (length_read > 0)
    {
      nextChar -= nChars;
      nChars = leftover + length_read;
      startLineIdx = nextChar;
      //And add the conversion here
      convert(byte_buffer, leftover, nChars, buffer,
          leftover, nChars, MAP3);
```

Measuring the performance with these changes, the times are now significantly better in almost every case:

Short lines	1.1.8	1.2.2	1.3.1	1.3.1 -server	1.4.0	1.4.0 -server	1.4.0 -Xint
Buffered input stream	132%	100%	48%	60%	48%	36%	373%
Custom-built reader	28%	24%	36%	164%	34%	24%	420%
Custom reader and converter	12%	12%	20%	12%	20%	12%	120%

Long lines	1.1.8	1.2.2	1.3.1	1.3.1 -server	1.4.0	1.4.0 -server	1.4.0 -Xint
Buffered input stream	123%	100%	65%	59%	57%	37%	487%
Custom-built reader	28%	28%	38%	37%	37%	22%	547%
Custom reader and converter	9%	10%	19%	29%	17%	14%	125%

Once again, all the VMs produce their best time except for the 1.3.1 server mode long-line case (which was faster with the BufferedReader).* All the times are now under one second, even on a slow machine. Subsecond times are notoriously variable, although in my tests the results were fairly consistent.

We have, however, hardcoded in the ISO 8859_1 type of byte-to-char conversion rather than supporting the generic case (where the conversion type is specified as a property). But this conversion represents a common class of character-encoding conversions, and you could fall back on the method used in the previous test where the conversion is specified differently (in the System property file.encoding). Often, you will read from files you know and whose format you understand and can predict. In those cases, building in the appropriate encoding is not a problem.

Using a buffered reader is adequate for most purposes. But we have seen that it is possible to speed up I/O even further if you're willing to spend the effort. Avoiding the creation of intermediate Strings gives you a good gain. This is true for both reading and writing and allows you to work on the char arrays directly. Working directly on char arrays is usually better for performance, but also more work. In specialized cases, you might want to consider taking control of every aspect of the I/O right down to the byte-to-char encoding, but for this you need to consider how to maintain compatibility with the JDK.

Tables 8-1 and 8-2 summarize all the results from these experiments.

Table 8-1. Timings of the long-line tests normalized to the JDK 1.2.2 buffered input stream test

Long lines	1.1.8	1.2.2	1.3.1	1.3.1 -server	1.4.0	1.4.0 -server	1.4.0 -Xint
Unbuffered input stream	1655%	1992%	2169%	1895%	1895%	2201%	3385%
Buffered input stream	123%	100%	65%	59%	57%	37%	487%
8K buffered input stream	123%	99%	64%	59%	56%	37%	484%
Buffered reader	53%	43%	43%	20%	52%	24%	582%
Custom-built reader	28%	28%	38%	37%	37%	22%	547%
Custom reader and converter	9%	10%	19%	29%	17%	14%	125%

* This shows that HotSpot is quite variable with its optimizations. HotSpot sometimes makes an unoptimized loop faster, and sometimes the manually unrolled loop comes out faster. Tables 8-1 and 8-2 show HotSpot producing both faster *and* slower times for the same manually unrolled loop, depending on the data being processed (i.e., short lines or long lines).

Table 8-2. Timings of the short-line tests normalized to the JDK 1.2.2 buffered input stream test

Short lines	1.1.8	1.2.2	1.3.1	1.3.1 -server	1.4.0	1.4.0 -server	1.4.0 -Xint
Unbuffered input stream	1551%	1808%	1965%	1764%	1872%	2088%	2646%
Buffered input stream	132%	100%	48%	60%	48%	36%	373%
8K buffered input stream	136%	96%	36%	57%	48%	36%	361%
Buffered reader	192%	96%	56%	24%	60%	24%	590%
Custom-built reader	28%	24%	36%	164%	34%	24%	420%
Custom reader and converter	12%	12%	20%	12%	20%	12%	120%

Serialization

Objects are serialized in a number of situations in Java. The two main reasons to serialize objects are to transfer objects and to store them.

There are several ways to improve the performance of serialization and deserialization. First, fields that are transient do not get serialized, saving both space and time. You can consider implementing readObject() and writeObject() (see java.io. Serializable documentation) to override the default serialization routine; it may be that you can produce a faster serialization routine for your specific objects. If you need this degree of control, you are better off using the java.io.Externalizable interface (the reason is illustrated shortly). Overriding the default serialization routine in this way is generally only worth doing for large or frequently serialized objects. The tight control this gives you may also be necessary to correctly handle canonicalized objects (to ensure objects remain canonical when deserializing them).

To transfer objects across networks, it is worth compressing the serialized objects. For large amounts of data, the transfer overhead tends to swamp the costs of compressing and decompressing the data. For storing to disk, it is worth serializing multiple objects to different files rather than to one large file. The granularity of access to individual objects and subsets of objects is often improved as well.

It is also possible to serialize objects in a separate thread for storage and network transfers, letting the serialization execute in the background. For objects whose state can change between serializations, consider using transaction logs or change logs (logs of the differences in the objects since they were last fully serialized) rather than reserializing the whole object. This works much like full and incremental backups. You need to maintain the changes somewhere, of course, so it makes the objects more complicated, but this complexity can have a really good payback in terms of performance: consider how much faster an incremental backup is compared to a full backup.

It is worthwhile to spend some time on a basic serialization tuning exercise. I chose a couple of fairly simple objects to serialize, but they are representative of the sorts of issues that crop up in serialization.

```
class Foo1 implements Serializable
{
  int one;
  String two;
  Bar1[ ] four;

  public Foo1( )
  {
    two = new String("START");
    one = two.length( );
    four = new Bar1[2];
    four[0] = new Bar1( );
    four[1] = new Bar1( );
  }
}

class Bar1 implements Serializable
{
  float one;
  String two;
  public Bar1( )
  {
    two = new String("hello");
    one = 3.14F;
  }
}
```

Note that I have given the objects default initial values for the tuning tests. The defaults assigned to the various String variables are forced to be unique for every object by making them new Strings. Without doing this, the compiler assigns the identical String to every object. That alters the timings: only one String is written on output, and when created on input, all other String references reference the same string by identity. (Java serialization can maintain relative identity of objects for objects that are serialized together.) Using identical Strings would make the serialization tests quicker and would not be representative of normal serializations.

Test measurements are easily skewed by rewriting previously written objects. Previously written objects are not converted and written out again; instead, only a reference to the original object is written. Writing this reference can be faster than writing out the object again. The speed is even more skewed on reading since only one object gets created. All the other references refer to the same uniquely created object.

Early in my career, I was given the task of testing the throughput of an object database. The first tests registered a fantastically high throughput until we realized we were storing just a few objects once, and all the other objects we thought we were storing were only references to those first few.

The Foo objects each contain two Bar objects in an array to make the overall objects slightly more representative of real-world objects. I'll make a baseline using the standard serialization technique:

```
if (toDisk)
    OutputStream ostream = new FileOutputStream("t.tmp");
else
    OutputStream ostream = new ByteArrayOutputStream( );
ObjectOutputStream wrtr = new ObjectOutputStream(ostream);

long time = System.currentTimeMillis( );
//write objects: time only the 3 lines for serialization output
wrtr.writeObject(lotsOfFoos);
wrtr.flush( );
wrtr.close( );
System.out.println("Writing time: " +
        (System.currentTimeMillis( )-time));

if (toDisk)
    InputStream istream = new FileInputStream("t.tmp");
else
    InputStream istream = new ByteArrayInputStream(
      ((ByteArrayOutputStream) ostream).toByteArray( ));
ObjectInputStream rdr = new ObjectInputStream(istream);

time = System.currentTimeMillis( );
//read objects: time only the 2 lines for serialization input
Foo1[ ] allFoos = (Foo1[ ]) rdr.readObject( );
rdr.close( );
System.out.println("Reading time: " +
        (System.currentTimeMillis( )-time));
```

As you can see, I provide for running tests either to disk or purely in memory. This allows you to break down the cost into separate components. The actual values revealed that 95% of the time is spent in the serialization. Less than 5% is the actual write to disk (of course, the relative times are system-dependent, but these results are probably representative).

When measuring, I used a pregrown ByteArrayOutputStream so that there were no effects from allocating the byte array in memory. Furthermore, to eliminate extra memory copying and garbage-collection effects, I reused the same ByteArrayOutputStream, and indeed the same byte array from that ByteArrayOutputStream object for reading. The byte array is accessible by subclassing ByteArrayOutputStream and providing an accessor to the ByteArrayOutputStream.buf instance variable.

The results of this first test for JDK 1.2.2* are shown in the following chart:

	Writing (serializing)	Reading (deserializing)
Standard serialization	100%	164%

I have normalized the baseline measurements to 100% for the byte array output (i.e., serializing the collection of Foos). On this scale, the reading (deserializing) takes 164%. This is not what I expected, because I am used to the idea that "writing" takes longer than "reading." Thinking about exactly what is happening, you can see that for the serialization you take the data in some objects and write that data out to a stream of bytes, which basically accesses and converts objects into bytes. But for the deserializing, you access elements of a byte array and convert these to other object and data types, including creating any required objects. Added to the fact that the serializing procedures are much more costly than the actual (disk) writes and reads, it is now understandable that deserialization is likely to be the more intensive, and consequently slower, activity.

Considering exactly what the ObjectInputStream and ObjectOutputStream must do, I realize that they are accessing and updating internal elements of the objects they are serializing, without knowing beforehand anything about those objects. This means there must be a heavy usage of the java.reflect package, together with some internal VM access procedures (since the serializing can reach private and protected fields and methods).† All this suggests that you should improve performance by taking explicit control of the serializing.

Alert readers might have noticed that Foo and Bar have constructors that initialize the object and may be wondering if deserializing could be speeded up by changing the constructors to avoid the unnecessary overhead there. In fact, the deserialization uses internal VM access to create the objects without going through the constructor, similar to cloning the objects. Although the Serializable interface requires serializable objects to have no-arg constructors, deserialized objects do not actually use that (or any) constructor.

To start with, the Serializable interface supports two methods that allow classes to handle their own serializing. So the first step is to try these methods. Add the following two methods to Foo:

```
private void writeObject(java.io.ObjectOutputStream out)
  throws IOException
{
  out.writeUTF(two);
```

---

* Table 8-3 lists the full results of tests with a variety of VMs. I have used the 1.2 results for discussion in this section, and the results are generally applicable to the other VMs tested.

† The actual code is difficult and time-consuming to work through. It was written in parts as one huge iterated/recursed switch, probably for performance reasons.

```
    out.writeInt(one);
    out.writeObject(four);
}
private void readObject(java.io.ObjectInputStream in)
    throws IOException, ClassNotFoundException
{
    two = in.readUTF( );
    one = in.readInt( );
    four = (Bar2[ ]) in.readObject( );
}
```

Bar needs the equivalent two methods:

```
private void writeObject(java.io.ObjectOutputStream out)
    throws IOException
{
    out.writeUTF(two);
    out.writeFloat(one);
}
private void readObject(java.io.ObjectInputStream in)
    throws IOException, ClassNotFoundException
{
    two = in.readUTF( );
    one = in.readFloat( );
}
```

The following chart shows the results of running the test with these methods added
to the classes:

	Writing (serializing)	Reading (deserializing)
Standard serialization	100%	164%
Customized read/writeObject( ) in Foo and Bar	140%	150%

We have improved the reads but made the writes worse. I expected an improvement
for both, and I cannot explain why the writes are worse (other than perhaps that the
ObjectOutputStream class may have suboptimal performance for this method-overrid-
ing feature; the 1.4 VM does show a speedup for both the writes and reads, suggesting that the class has been optimized in that version). Instead of analyzing what the
ObjectOutputStream class may be doing, let's try further optimizations.

Examining and manipulating objects during serialization takes more time than the
actual conversion of data to or from streams. Considering this, and looking at the
customized serializing methods, you can see that the Foo methods simply pass control back to the default serializing mechanism to handle the embedded Bar objects. It
may be worth handling the serializing more explicitly. For this example, I'll break
encapsulation by accessing the Bar fields directly (although going through accessors
and updators or calling serialization methods in Bar would not make much difference in time here). I redefine the Foo serializing methods as:

```
private void writeObject(java.io.ObjectOutputStream out)
    throws IOException
```

```
{
  out.writeUTF(two);
  out.writeInt(one);
  out.writeUTF(four[0].two);
  out.writeFloat(four[0].one);
  out.writeUTF(four[1].two);
  out.writeFloat(four[1].one);
}
private void readObject(java.io.ObjectInputStream in)
    throws IOException, ClassNotFoundException
{
  two = in.readUTF( );
  one = in.readInt( );
  four = new Bar3[2];
  four[0] = new Bar3( );
  four[1] = new Bar3( );
  four[0].two = in.readUTF( );
  four[0].one = in.readFloat( );
  four[1].two = in.readUTF( );
  four[1].one = in.readFloat( );
}
```

The Foo methods now handle serialization for both Foo and the embedded Bar objects, so the equivalent methods in Bar are now redundant. The following chart illustrates the results of running the test with these altered methods added to the classes (Table 8-3 lists the full results of tests with a variety of VMs):

	Writing (serializing)	Reading (deserializing)
Standard serialization	100%	164%
Customized read/writeObject( ) in Foo and Bar	140%	150%
Customized read/writeObject( ) in Foo handling Bar	38%	58%

Now this gives a clearer feel for the costs of dynamic object examination and manipulation.

Given the overhead the serializing I/O classes incur, it has now become obvious that the more serializing you handle explicitly, the better off you are. This being the case, the next step is to ask the objects explicitly to serialize themselves rather than going through the ObjectInputStream and ObjectOutputStream to have them in turn ask the objects to serialize themselves.

The readObject( ) and writeObject( ) methods must be defined as private according to the Serializable interface documentation, so they cannot be called directly. You must either wrap them in another public method or copy the implementation to another method so you can access them directly. But in fact, java.io provides a third alternative. The Externalizable interface also provides support for serializing objects using ObjectInputStream and ObjectOutputStream. But Externalizable defines two public methods rather than the two private methods required by Serializable. So you can just change the names of the two methods: readObject(ObjectInputStream) becomes readExternal(ObjectInput), and writeObject(ObjectOutputStream) becomes writeExternal(ObjectOutput). You must also redefine Foo as implementing Externalizable instead of Serializable. All of these are simple changes, but to be sure that nothing untoward has happened as a consequence, rerun the tests (as good tuners should for any changes, even minor ones). The following chart shows the new test results:

	Writing (serializing)	Reading (deserializing)
Standard serialization	100%	164%
Customized read/writeObject( ) in Foo handling Bar	38%	58%
Foo made Externalizable, using last methods renamed	28%	44%

Remarkably, the times are significantly faster. This probably reflects the improvement you get from being able to compile and execute a line such as:

```
((Externalizable) someObject).writeExternal(this)
```

in the ObjectOutputStream class, rather than having to go through java.reflect and the VM internals to reach the private writeObject( ) method. This example also shows that you are better off making your classes Externalizable rather than Serializable if you want to control your own serializing.

The drawback to controlling your own serializing is a significantly higher maintenance cost, as any change to the class structure also requires changes to the two Externalizable methods (or the two methods supported by Serializable). In some cases (as in the example presented in this tuning exercise), changes to the structure of one class actually require changes to the Externalizable methods of another class. The example presented here requires that if the structure of Bar is changed, the Externalizable methods in Foo must also be changed to reflect the new structure of Bar. Here, you can avoid the dependency between the classes by having the Foo serialization methods call the Bar serialization methods directly. But the general fragility of serialization, when individual class structures change, still remains.

You changed the methods in the first place to provide public access to the methods in order to access them directly. Let's continue with this task. Now, for the first time, you will change actual test code, rather than anything in the Foo or Bar classes. The new test looks like:

```
if (toDisk)
    OutputStream ostream = new FileOutputStream("t.tmp");
else
    OutputStream ostream = new ByteArrayOutputStream( );
ObjectOutputStream wrtr = new ObjectOutputStream(ostream);
```

```
//The old version of the test just ran the next
//commented line to write the objects
//wrtr.writeObject(lotsOfFoos);

long time = System.currentTimeMillis();
//This new version writes the size of the array,
//then each object explicitly writes itself
//time these five lines for serialization output
wrtr.writeInt(lotsOfFoos.length);
for (int i = 0; i < lotsOfFoos.length ; i++)
  lotsOfFoos[i].writeExternal(wrtr);
wrtr.flush();
wrtr.close();
System.out.println("Writing time: " +
    (System.currentTimeMillis()-time));

if (toDisk)
  InputStream istream = new FileInputStream("t.tmp");
else
  InputStream istream = new ByteArrayInputStream(
    ((ByteArrayOutputStream) ostream).toByteArray());
ObjectInputStream rdr = new ObjectInputStream(istream);

//The old version of the test just ran the next
//commented line to read the objects
//Foo1[ ] allFoos = (Foo1[ ]) rdr.readObject();

time = System.currentTimeMillis();
//This new version reads the size of the array and creates
//the array, then each object is explicitly created and
//reads itself. read objects - time these ten lines to
//the close() for serialization input
int len = rdr.readInt();
Foo[ ] allFoos = new Foo[len];
Foo foo;
for (int i = 0; i < len ; i++)
{
  foo = new Foo();
  foo.readExternal(rdr);
  allFoos[i] = foo;
}
rdr.close();
System.out.println("Reading time: " +
    (System.currentTimeMillis()-time));
```

This test bypasses the serialization overhead completely. You are still using the
ObjectInputStream and ObjectOutputStream classes, but really only to write out basic
data types, not for any of their object-manipulation capabilities. If you didn't require
those specific classes because of the required method signatures, you could have happily used DataInputStream and DataOutputStream classes for this test. The following
chart shows the test results.

	Writing (serializing)	Reading (deserializing)
Standard serialization	100%	164%
Foo made Externalizable, using last methods renamed	28%	44%
Foo as last test, but read/write called directly in test	3.9%	25%

If you test serializing to and from the disk, you find that the disk I/O now takes nearly one-third of the total test times. Because disk I/O is now a significant portion of the total time, the CPU is now underworked, and you can even gain some speedup by serializing in several threads, i.e., you can evenly divide the collection into two or more subsets and have each subset serialized by a separate thread (I leave that as an exercise for you).

Note that since you are now explicitly creating objects by calling their constructors, the instance variables in Bar are being set twice during deserialization, once at the creation of the Bar instance in Foo.readExternal( ), and again when reading in the instance variable values and assigning those values. Normally you should move any Bar initialization out of the no-arg constructor to avoid redundant assignments.

Is there any way of making the deserializing faster? Well, not significantly, if you need to read in all the objects and use them all immediately. But more typically, you need only some of the objects immediately. In this case, you can use lazily initialized objects to speed up the deserializing phase (see also "Lazy Initialization" in Chapter 4). The idea is that instead of combining the read with the object creation in the deserializing phase, you decouple these two operations. So each object reads in just the bytes it needs, but does not convert those bytes into objects or data until that object is actually accessed. To test this, add a new instance variable to Foo to hold the bytes between reading and converting to objects or data. You also need to change the serialization methods. I will drop support for the Serializable and Externalizable interfaces since we are now explicitly requiring the Foo objects to serialize and deserialize themselves, and I'll add a second stream to store the size of the serialized Foo objects. Foo now looks like:

```
class Foo1 implements Serializable
{
  int one;
  String two;
  Bar1[ ] four;
  byte[ ] buffer;

  //empty constructor to optimize deserialization
  public Foo5( ){ }
  //And constructor that creates initialized objects
  public Foo5(boolean init)
  {
    this( );
    if (init)
      init( );
  }
```

```java
public void init()
{
  two = new String("START");
  one = two.length();
  four = new Bar5[2];
  four[0] = new Bar5();
  four[1] = new Bar5();
}

//Serialization method
public void writeExternal(MyDataOutputStream out, DataOutputStream outSizes)
  throws IOException
{
  //Get the amount written so far so that we can determine
  //the extra we write
  int size = out.written();

  //write out the Foo
  out.writeUTF(two);
  out.writeInt(one);
  out.writeUTF(four[0].two);
  out.writeFloat(four[0].one);
  out.writeUTF(four[1].two);
  out.writeFloat(four[1].one);

  //Determine how many bytes I wrote
  size = out.written() - size;

  //and write that out to our second stream
  outSizes.writeInt(size);
}
public void readExternal(InputStream in, DataInputStream inSizes)
  throws IOException
{
  //Determine how many bytes I consist of in serialized form
  int size = inSizes.readInt();

  //And read me into a byte buffer
  buffer = new byte[size];
  int len;
  int readlen = in.read(buffer);

  //be robust and handle the general case of partial reads
  //and incomplete streams
  if (readlen == -1)
    throw new IOException("expected more bytes");
  else
    while(readlen < buffer.length)
    {
      len = in.read(buffer, readlen, buffer.length-readlen);
      if (len < 1)
        throw new IOException("expected more bytes");
      else
```

```
        readlen += len;
      }
    }

    //This method does the deserializing of the byte buffer to a 'real' Foo
    public void convert( )
      throws IOException
    {
      DataInputStream in = new DataInputStream(new ByteArrayInputStream(buffer));
      two = in.readUTF( );
      one = in.readInt( );
      four = new Bar5[2];
      four[0] = new Bar5( );
      four[1] = new Bar5( );
      four[0].two = in.readUTF( );
      four[0].one = in.readFloat( );
      four[1].two = in.readUTF( );
      four[1].one = in.readFloat( );
      buffer = null;
    }
  }
```

As you can see, I have chosen to use DataInputStreams and DataOutputStreams since they are all that's needed. I also use a subclass of DataOutputStream called MyDataOutputStream. The class adds only one method, MyDataOutputStream.written( ), to provide access to the DataOutputStream.written instance variable so that you have access to the number of bytes written. The timing tests are essentially the same as before, except that you change the stream types and add a second stream for the sizes of the serialized objects (e.g., to file *t2.tmp*, or a second pair of byte-array input and output streams). The following chart shows the new times:

	Writing (serializing)	Reading (deserializing)
Standard serialization	100%	164%
Foo as last test, but read/write called directly in test	3.9%	25%
Foo lazily initialized	17%	4%

We have lost out on the writes because of the added complexity, but improved the reads considerably. The cost of the Foo.convert( ) method has not been factored in, but the strategy illustrated here is for cases where you need to run only that convert method on a small subset of the deserialized objects, and so the extra overhead should be small. This technique works well when transferring large groups of objects across a network.

For the case in which you need only a few objects out of many serialized objects that have been stored on disk, another strategy is even more efficient. This strategy uses techniques similar to the example just shown. One file (the data file) holds the serialized objects. A second file (the index file) holds the offset of the starting byte of each serialized object in the first file. For serializing, the only difference to the example is that when writing out the objects, the full `DataOutputStream.written` instance variable is added to the index file as the `writeExternal( )` method is entered, instead of writing the difference between successive values of `DataOutputStream.written`. A moment's thought should convince you that this provides the byte offset into the data file.

With this technique, deserializing is straightforward. You enter the index file and skip to the correct index for the object you want in the data file (e.g., for the object at array index 54, skip 54 × 4 = 216 bytes from the start of the index file). The serialized int at that location holds the byte offset into the data file, so you deserialize that int. Then you enter the data file, skipping to the specified offset, and deserialize the object there. (This is also the first step in building your own database: the next steps are normally to waste time and effort before realizing that you can more easily buy a database that does most of what you want.) This "index file-plus-data file" strategy works best if you leave the two files open and skip around the files, rather than repeatedly opening and closing the files every time you want to deserialize an object. The strategy illustrated in this paragraph does not work as well for transferring serialized objects across a network. For network transfers, a better strategy is to limit the objects being transferred to only those that are needed.* Table 8-3 shows the tunings of the serialization tests, normalized to the JDK 1.2 standard serialization test. Each entry is a pair giving write/read timings. The test name in parentheses refers to the method name executed in the `tuning.io.SerializationTest` class.

Table 8-3. Timings (in write/read pairs) of the serialization tests with various VMs

	1.1.8	1.2.2	1.3.1	1.3.1 -server	1.4.0	1.4.0 -Xint
Standard serialization (test1a)	929%/ 1848%	100%/ 164%	112%/ 120%	68%/ 144%	99%/ 100%	700%/ 593%
Customized write/readObject( ) in Foo and Bar (test2a)	406%/ 612%	140%/ 150%	139%/ 145%	113%/ 178%	91%/ 93%	556%/ 486%
Customized write/readObject( ) in Foo handling Bar (test3a)	43%/ 132%	38%/ 58%	41%/ 53%	37%/ 71%	29%/ 37%	201%/ 234%
Foo made Externalizable, using last methods renamed (test4a)	28%/ 92%	28%/ 44%	25%/ 40%	32%/ 57%	29%/ 39%	187%/ 222%
Foo as last test, but write/read called directly in test (test4c)	2.9%/ 97%	3.9%/ 25%	4.9%/ 19%	19%/ 30%	7.6%/ 18%	75%/ 132%
Foo lazily initialized (test5a)	16%/ 3.4%	17%/ 4%	12%/ 2.6%	61%/ 6.7%	13%/ 2.4%	105%/ 18%

* You could transfer index files across the network, then use those index files to precisely identify the objects required and limit transfers to only those identified objects.

Clustering Objects and Counting I/O Operations

Clustering is a technique that takes advantage of locality (usually on the disk) to improve performance. It is useful when you have objects stored on disk and can arrange where objects are in relation to each other. For example, suppose you store serialized objects on disk, but need to have fast access to some of these objects. The most basic example of clustering is arranging the serialization of the objects in such a way as to selectively deserialize them to get exactly the subset of objects you need, in as few disk accesses, file openings, and object deserializations as possible.

Suppose you want to serialize a table of objects. Perhaps they cannot all fit into memory at the same time, or they are persistent, or there are other reasons for serialization. It may be that of the objects in the table, 10% are accessed frequently while the other 90% are only infrequently accessed and the application can accept slight delays on accessing these less frequently required objects. In this scenario, rather than serializing the whole table, you may be better off serializing the 10% of frequently used objects into one file (which can be deserialized in one long call) and the other 90% into one or more other files with an object table index allowing individual objects to be read in as needed.

Alternatively, it may be that objects are grouped in some way in your application so that whenever one of the table objects is referenced, this also automatically requires certain other related objects. In this case, you want to cluster these groups of objects so they are deserialized together.

If you need to manage objects on disk for persistency, sharing, memory, or whatever reason, you should consider using an object-storage system (such as an object database). The serialization provided with Java is very basic and provides little in the way of simple systemwide customization. For example, if you have a collection of objects on disk, typically you want to read into memory the collection down to one or two levels (i.e., only the collection elements, not any objects held in the instance variables of the collection elements). With serialization, you get the transitive closure* of the collection in general, which is almost certainly much more than you want. Serialization supports reading to certain levels in only a very rudimentary way: basically, it says you have to do the reading yourself, but it gives you the hooks that let you customize on a per-class basis. The ability to tune to this level of granularity is really what you need for any sort of disk-based object storage beyond the most basic. And you usually do get those extra tuning capabilities in various object-storage systems.

---

* The transitive closure is the set of all objects reachable from any one object, i.e., an object and its data variables and their data variables, etc.

At a lower level, you should be aware that the system reads in data from the disk one page at a time (page size is system-dependent, normally 4 or 8 KB). This means that if you cluster data (of whatever type) on the disk so that the data that needs to be together is physically close together on disk, then the reading of that data into memory is also speeded up. Typically, the most control you have over clustering objects is by putting data into the same file near each other and hoping that the filesystem is not too fragmented. Defragmenting the disks on occasion can help.

Clustering should reduce the number of disk I/O operations you need to execute. Consequently, measuring the number of disk I/O operations that are executed is essential to determine if you have clustered usefully.* The simplest technique to measure I/O is to monitor the number of reads, writes, opens, and closes that are performed. This gets complicated by using different I/O classes wrapped one around the other. But you can always find the lowest-level class that is actually doing the I/O (usually one of `FileInputStream`, `FileOutputStream`, and `RandomAccessFile` in the `java.io` package). You can determine all actual methods that execute I/O fairly easily if you have the JDK source: simply find all source files with the word "native." If you look in `java.io` for these and look at the actual method names of the native methods, you will find that in almost every case, the only classes applicable to you are the `FileInputStream`, `FileOutputStream`, and `RandomAccessFile` classes. Now the difficult part is wrapping these calls so that you can monitor them. Native methods that are declared `private` are straightforward to handle: just redefine the `java.io` class to count the times they are called internally. Native methods that are protected or have no access modifier are similarly handled: just ensure you do the same redefinition for subclasses and package members. But the methods defined with the `public` modifier need to be tracked for any classes that call these native methods, which can be difficult and tiresome, but not impossible.

The simplest alternative would be to use the debug interface to count the number of hits on the method. Unfortunately, you cannot set a breakpoint on a `native` method, so this is not possible.

The result is that it takes some effort to identify every I/O call in an application. If you have consistently used your own I/O classes, the `java.io` buffered classes, and the `java.io` `Reader` and `Writer` classes, it may be enough to wrap the I/O calls to `FileOutputStream` and `FileInputStream` from these classes. If you have done nonstandard things, you need to put in more effort.

One other way to determine how many I/O operations you have used is to execute `Runtime.getRuntime().traceMethodCalls(true)` before the test starts, capture the

---

* Ultimately, it is the number of low-level I/O operations that matter. But if you reduce the high-level I/O operations, the low-level ones are generally reduced by the same proportion. The Java read/write/open/close operations at the "native" level are also the OS read/write/open/close operations for all the Java runtimes I've investigated.

method trace, and filter out the native calls you have identified. Unfortunately, this is optional functionality in the JDK (Java specifies that the traceMethodCalls( ) method must exist in Runtime, but it does not have to do anything), so you are lucky if you use a system that supports it. The only one I am aware of is the Symantec development environment, and in that case, you have to be in the IDE and running in debug mode. Running the Symantec VM outside the IDE does not seem to enable this feature. Some profilers may also help to produce a trace of all I/O operations.

I would recommend that all basic I/O calls have logging statements next to them, capable of reporting the amount of I/O performed (both the number of I/O operations and the number of bytes transferred). I/O is typically so costly that one null call or if statement (when logging is not turned on) is not at all significant for each I/O performed. On the other hand, it is incredibly useful to be able to determine at any time whether I/O is causing a performance problem. Typically, I/O performance depends on the configuration of the system and on resources outside the application. So if an unusual configuration causes I/O to be dramatically more expensive, this can be easily missed in testing and difficult to determine (especially remotely) unless you have an I/O-monitoring capability built into your application.

Compression

A colleague of mine once installed a compression utility on his desktop machine that compressed the entire disk. The utility worked as a type of disk driver: accesses to the disk went through the utility, and every read and write was decompressed or compressed transparently to the rest of the system, and to the user. My colleague was expecting the system to run slower, but needed the extra disk space and was willing to put up with a slower system.

What he actually found was that his system ran faster! It turned out that the major bottleneck to his system was disk throughput, and by making most files smaller (averaging half the previous size), everything was moving between memory and disk much quicker. The CPU had plenty of spare cycles necessary to handle the compression-decompression procedures because it was waiting for disk transfers to complete.

This illustrates how the overhead of compression can be outweighed by the benefits of reducing I/O. The system described obviously had a disk that was relatively too slow in comparison to the CPU processing power. But this is quite common. Disk throughput has not improved nearly as fast as CPUs have increased in speed, and this divergent trend is set to continue for some time. The same is true for networks. Although networks do tend to have a huge jump in throughput with each generation, this jump tends to be offset by the much larger volumes of data being transferred. Furthermore, network-mounted disks are also increasingly common, and the double performance hit from accessing a disk over a network is surely a prime candidate for increasing speed using compression.

On the other hand, if a system has a fully loaded CPU, adding compression can make things worse. This means that when you control the environment (servers, servlets, etc.), you can probably specify precisely, by testing, whether or not to use compression in your application to improve performance. When the environment is unknown, the situation is more complex. One suggestion is to write I/O wrapper classes that handle compressed and uncompressed I/O automatically on the fly. Your application can then test whether any particular I/O destination has better performance using compression, and then automatically use compression when called for.

One final thing to note about compressed data is that it is not always necessary to decompress the data in order to work with it. As an example, if you are using 2-Ronnies compression,* the text "Hello. Have you any eggs? No, we haven't any eggs" is compressed into "LO. F U NE X? 9, V FN NE X."

Now, if I want to search the text to see if it includes the phrase "any eggs," I do not actually need to decompress the compressed text. Instead, I compress the search string "any eggs" using 2-Ronnies compression into "NE X", and I can now use that compressed search string to search directly on the compressed text.

When applied to objects or data, this technique requires some effort. You need to ensure that any small data chunk compresses in the same way both on its own and as part of a larger volume of data containing that data chunk. If this is not the case, you may need to break objects and searchable data into fields that are individually compressed.

There are several advantages to this technique of searching directly against compressed data:

- There is no need to decompress a large amount of data.

- Searches are actually quicker because the search is against a smaller volume of data.

- More data can be held in memory simultaneously (since it is compressed), which can be especially important for searching through large volumes of disk-stored data.

It is rarely possible to search for compressed substrings directly in compressed data because of the way most compression algorithms use tables covering the whole dataset. However, this scheme has been used to selectively query for data locations. For this usage, unique data keys are compressed separately from the rest of the data. A pointer is stored next to the compressed key. This produces a compressed index

---

* "The Two Ronnies" was a British comedy show that featured very inventive comedy sketches, many based on word play. One such sketch involved a restaurant scene where all the characters spoke only in letters and numbers, joining the letters up in such a way that they sounded like words. The mapping for some of the words to letters was as follows:

| have = F | you = U | any = NE | eggs = X | hello = LO | no = 9 |
| yes = S | we = V | have = F | haven't = FN | ham = M | and = N |

table that can be searched without decompressing the keys. The compression algorithm is separately applicable for each key. This scheme allows compressed keys to be searched directly to identify the location of the corresponding data.

NIO

SDK 1.4 includes a new set of packages called NIO (New I/O) in the `java.nio` package space. The NIO classes hold I/O functionality that is available from most modern operating systems but that was missing from Java. Much of the NIO functionality is needed for highly scalable efficient server technology, but some aspects are useful for many applications, as we'll see in the next few sections. For a good introduction to NIO, consider *Learning Java* (O'Reilly) as well as a basic introduction in Michael Nygard's excellent article in *JavaWorld*.[*]

Connecting Client Sockets

When you create a client socket to connect to a server, the underlying TCP connection procedure involves a two-phase acknowledgment. The `Socket.connect()` call invokes a blocking procedure, which normally stops the thread from proceeding until the connection is complete.

The NIO package allows you to initiate the socket connection procedure and carry on processing in the thread while the connection is being established. To achieve this, you use a `SocketChannel` set to nonblocking mode. Then, a call to `SocketChannel.connect()` returns immediately, with the connection attempted in the background. You can use the `OP_CONNECT` flag with the `Selector`, or more simply call the `SocketChannel.isConnectionPending()` method at any time to check whether the connection procedure has completed. When the connection is flagged as ready, the connection is finished by calling `SocketChannel.finishConnect()`, which essentially tells you either that the connection is established (by returning normally from the method call), or that the connection attempt failed (by throwing an exception).

Nondirect Buffers: Fast Casts for Primitive Arrays

The NIO package introduces `Buffer` objects, which are essentially collections of primitive data types. For example, `FloatBuffer` holds a collection of `floats`. `Buffer` objects are of two types, direct and nondirect. Direct `Buffer`s are objects that directly wrap a section of system memory. Nondirect buffers essentially wrap a Java array object, e.g., `float[]` arrays for `FloatBuffer`. `Buffer`s are an integral part of the NIO package, and many NIO objects use `Buffer`s in various ways.

---

[*] Michael Nygard, "Master Merlin's new I/O classes," *JavaWorld*, September 2001, *http://www.javaworld. com/javaworld/jw-09-2001/jw-0907-merlin.html*.

In this section we'll look at an example of using nondirect Buffers independently from the rest of NIO. An application I am familiar with needed to send an array of floats across the network to another Java process and did so by looping through the array of floats, writing each float using DataOutput.writeFloat() to the socket and reading each float at the other end. The whole sequence was preceded with the number of floats in the array, like this:

```
dataOut.writeInt(floatArray.length);
for (int i = 0; i < floatArray.length; i++)
  dataOut.writeFloat(floatArray[i]);
dataOut.flush();
dataOut.close();
```

The read at the other end was simply the reverse procedure:

```
int len = dataIn.readInt();
float[] floatArray = new float[len];
for (int i = 0; i < len; i++)
  floatArray[i] = dataIn.readFloat();
dataIn.close();
```

Let's examine this technique for inefficiencies. Using what you have learned from the rest of this chapter, you should immediately see two potential speedups. First, the amount of data written could be compressed. Second, the number of I/O operations is large; fewer I/O operations should make the procedure faster.

Let's deal with compression first. Applying compression would actually slow down the read and write, though the overall transfer might be speeded up if the connection was slow with significant fragmentation. Compression in this situation is heavily network-dependent. I'll assume we are on a LAN, in which case compression would only slow down the transfer.

Next, we can reduce the number of I/O operations. With the current procedure we have one I/O operation executed for every float in the array. The underlying network stack might batch some of the I/O calls, but you cannot rely on that. One obvious way to reduce the number of I/O calls is to treat the array as a single object and use an ObjectInputStream/ObjectOutputStream pair to make the transfer:

```
objectOut.writeObject(floatArray);
objectOut.flush();
objectOut.close();
```

The read at the other end is simply the reverse procedure:

```
float[] floatArray = (float[]) objectIn.readObject();
objectIn.close();
```

Measuring this new procedure, for very large arrays of floats (hundreds of thousands), I obtain times that are more than a hundred times faster—a gain of two orders of magnitude. The gain is due to reducing the number of I/O calls from hundreds of thousands to just one.

Unfortunately for the developers of this application, ObjectStreams cannot be reused. That is, you cannot reset an ObjectStream and start reusing it because of initialization data it writes and reads on the stream. ObjectStreams are fine if you are doing all of your stream I/O looped through one ObjectStream. But if you are using other stream-writing procedures on the same stream as the ObjectStreams, you have to be extremely careful, or you need to create and release ObjectStreams for each group of objects sent. And, unfortunately, ObjectStreams have a high creation overhead. The particular application that was transferring the float arrays could not use ObjectStreams, but needed the speed they could have gained from them.

Next we consider Buffers. Buffer objects allow you to treat arrays of one type of primitive data type as an array of another type. This is equivalent to being able to cast an array of data from one data type to another. In this case, we would like to treat a float[ ] array as a byte[ ] array because we can read and write byte[ ] arrays very efficiently in single I/O operations.

Specifically, you can create a ByteBuffer wrapping a byte[ ] array. The byte[ ] array is going to be used for efficient I/O, using the InputStream.write(byte[ ]) and OutputStream.write(byte[ ]) methods. ByteBuffer provides methods to access the ByteBuffer as another type of Buffer, in this case as a FloatBuffer:

```
//The byte array for output
byte[ ] byteArray = new byte[floatArray.length*4];
//Create a FloatBuffer 'view' on the ByteBuffer that wraps the byte array
FloatBuffer outFloatBuffer = ByteBuffer.wrap(byteArray).asFloatBuffer( );
//Write the array of floats into the byte array. FloatBuffer does this efficiently
outFloatBuffer.put(floatArray, 0, floatArray.length);
//And write the length then the byte array
dataOut.writeInt(floatArray.length);
dataOut.write(byteArray, 0, floatArray.length*4);
dataOut.flush( );
dataOut.close( );
```

The read is very similar:

```
int len = dataIn.readInt( );
//The byte array for input
byte[ ] byteArray = new byte[len*4];
//Create a FloatBuffer 'view' on the ByteBuffer that wraps the byte array
FloatBuffer inFloatBuffer = ByteBuffer.wrap(byteArray).asFloatBuffer( );
float[ ] floatArray = new float[len];
//Read the data into the byte array.
dataIn.readFully(byteArray);
//And copy the array of floats from the byte array. FloatBuffer does this
efficiently
inFloatBuffer.get(floatArray, 0, floatArray.length);
dataIn.close( );
```

As a result, we achieve the same speed as the single I/O object transfer, without the need for ObjectStreams.

Direct Buffers: Optimized I/O Operations

Direct Buffers wrap a portion of system memory. They yield optimal I/O efficiency by allowing system I/O operations to operate directly between system memory and an external medium (e.g., the disk or network). In contrast, nondirect Buffers require an extra copy operation to move the data from the Java heap to and from the external medium. The NIO I/O operations are optimized for dealing with direct Buffers. However, note that the "old" I/O (java.io) classes are also optimized, but for operating on Java arrays. The InputStream and OutputStream classes that operate directly on external media (for example, FileInputStream) also require no extra copy operations to move data to and from Java arrays. So we can see that nondirect Buffers are at a disadvantage when compared to both the other options, but it is not obvious which other combination of data structure and I/O operation is the most efficient.

So let's test out the possibilities. I'll use a simple file-copying operation to test the various options. I've chosen file copying because NIO includes an extra operation for enabling file copies in the FileChannel class, which gives us one further optimization option. First, we have the good old java.io technique of reading chunks from the file into a byte[ ] array buffer and writing those chunks out. You should be fairly familiar with this by now:

```
public static void explicitBufferInputStreamCopy(String f1, String f2)
  throws Exception
{
  long time = System.currentTimeMillis();
  byte[ ] buffer = new byte[1024*16];
  FileInputStream rdr = new FileInputStream(f1);
  FileOutputStream wrtr = new FileOutputStream(f2);
  int readLen;
  while( (readLen = rdr.read(buffer)) != -1)
  {
    wrtr.write(buffer, 0, readLen);
  }
  rdr.close();
  wrtr.close();
  time = System.currentTimeMillis() - time;
  System.out.println(" explicitBufferInputStreamCopy time: " + time);
}
```

Next, we have the equivalent technique using a direct Buffer and FileChannels. This technique may be unfamiliar, but it is straightforward. We allocate a direct Buffer using the ByteBuffer.allocateDirect( ) method, open the file for reading and writing obtaining the FileChannel objects, then simply repeatedly read into the Buffer and write out the Buffer until the file has been copied. Conceptually, this is exactly the same series of operations as the last method we defined, explicitBufferInputStreamCopy( ).

```
public static void directBufferCopy(String f1, String f2)
  throws Exception
{
```

```
    long time = System.currentTimeMillis( );
    ByteBuffer buffer = ByteBuffer.allocateDirect(16*1024);
    FileChannel rdr = (new FileInputStream(f1)).getChannel( );
    FileChannel wrtr = (new FileOutputStream(f2)).getChannel( );
    while( rdr.read(buffer) > 0)
    {
      buffer.flip( );
      wrtr.write(buffer);
      buffer.clear( );
    }
    rdr.close( );
    wrtr.close( );
    time = System.currentTimeMillis( ) - time;
    System.out.println(" directBufferCopy time: " + time);
  }
```

For completeness, I also test using a nondirect `Buffer`. To use a nondirect `Buffer`, the only difference from the last method is that `ByteBuffer.allocate( )` is used instead of `ByteBuffer.allocateDirect( )`.

The `directBufferCopy( )` method we just defined uses `ByteBuffer.allocateDirect( )` to obtain a direct `Buffer`, but NIO gives us another option to get a direct `Buffer`. NIO supports the memory mapping of files. The `FileChannel.map( )` operation uses the operating system to map a portion of a file or the whole file into system memory. Using this method we can obtain a direct `Buffer` containing the entire file. In "old" I/O terms, this is equivalent to creating a byte[ ] array buffer the same size as the file, reading the entire file into that byte[ ] array, then writing it out to the new file copy. For "old" I/O, this procedure would normally be less efficient than using a smaller byte[ ] buffer as we did in the `explicitBufferInputStreamCopy( )` method, but here we are using operating-system memory mapping, which may make a difference.

```
    public static void mappedBufferCopy(String f1, String f2)
      throws Exception
    {
      long time = System.currentTimeMillis( );
      FileChannel rdr = (new FileInputStream(f1)).getChannel( );
      FileChannel wrtr = (new FileOutputStream(f2)).getChannel( );
      ByteBuffer buffer = rdr.map(FileChannel.MapMode.READ_ONLY, 0, (int) rdr.size( ));
      wrtr.write(buffer);
      rdr.close( );
      wrtr.close( );
      time = System.currentTimeMillis( ) - time;
      System.out.println(" mappedBufferCopy time: " + time);
    }
```

Note that the `FileChannel` API documentation indicates that the procedure and efficiency of memory-mapping files is highly system-dependent. The API also states:

> "For most operating systems, mapping a file into memory is more expensive than reading or writing a few tens of kilobytes of data via the usual read and write methods. From the standpoint of performance it is generally only worth mapping relatively large files into memory."

Finally, as I said earlier, FileChannel also provides transferTo( ) and transferFrom( ) methods. Once again, these methods are intended for maximal efficiency in transferring bytes between FileChannels and other Channels, by using the underlying operating system's filesystem cache. The API states that:

> "Bytes can be transferred from a file to some other channel in a way that can be optimized by many operating systems into a very fast transfer directly to or from the filesystem cache."

Using FileChannel.transferTo( ) is relatively simpler than any of the previous methods: you obtain the two FileChannels and then execute transferTo( ). No need for looping, or even reading or writing!

```
public static void directTransferCopy(String f1, String f2)
  throws Exception
{
  long time = System.currentTimeMillis( );
  FileChannel rdr = (new FileInputStream(f1)).getChannel( );
  FileChannel wrtr = (new FileOutputStream(f2)).getChannel( );
  rdr.transferTo(0, (int) rdr.size( ), wrtr);
  rdr.close( );
  wrtr.close( );
  time = System.currentTimeMillis( ) - time;
  System.out.println(" directTransferCopy time: " + time);
}
```

This series of tests is hugely system-dependent. Because NIO operations are much closer to, and more reliant on, the operating system than most other Java classes, we have not only the usual VM variability but also operating-system differences to take into account. Additionally, since we are testing file copying, disk efficiencies also affect these tests. Table 8-4 shows the results of running under one brand of Windows (NT 4), using the 1.4 VM in various modes with various repetitions. I also tested these methods under Windows 98 and Solaris 8. Generally, the NIO results were much more variable than the "old" I/O results. It seems that on average the direct-Buffer copy (directBufferCopy( )) was the fastest operation for the Windows test machines, followed closely by the Stream+byte[ ] copy (explicitBufferInputStreamCopy( )). On Solaris, the FileChannel transfer (directTransferCopy( )) seemed to be the fastest, again followed closely by the Stream+byte[ ] copy (explicitBufferInputStreamCopy( )).

Table 8-4. Time ranges for various file copying techniques

Copy method	Normalized time range
explicitBufferInputStreamCopy	100%-145%
nonDirectBufferCopy	454%-674%
directBufferCopy	67%-241%
MappedBufferCopy	240%-916%
directTransferCopy	238%-514%

Clearly, though, there is no huge advantage to NIO in this situation compared with using the "old" I/O. But bear in mind that the NIO Buffers are not specifically designed to replace the old I/O classes. NIO provides additional capabilities. So, for example, we haven't tested Buffer classes with scatter-gather operations, which work on multiple Buffers simultaneously. For example the ScatteringByteChannel.read(ByteBuffer[ ], int, int) method reads from a Channel directly into multiple Buffers in one I/O operation. Similarly, GatheringByteChannel.write( ) writes the contents of multiple Buffers in one I/O operation. When is this useful? A common example is an HTTP server. When an HTTP server downloads a page (file) to a browser, it writes out a header and then the page. The header itself consists of several different sections that need to be amalgamated. It is efficient to write the parts of the headers to the stream in multiple separate I/O operations, followed by the page body, allowing the network to buffer the response. Unfortunately, this turns out to be suboptimal because you are increasing the I/O operations and allowing the network stack to set the pace. Acme's THTTPD developers ran a series of performance tests of various HTTP servers, and identified that the amount of data sent in the first network packet was crucial to optimal performance:

> "Turns out the change that made the difference was sending the response headers and the first load of data as a single packet, instead of as two separate packets. Apparently this avoids triggering TCP's "delayed ACK," a 1/5th second wait to see if more packets are coming in."[*]

GatheringByteChannel.write( ) is not the only way to optimize this situation, but it is efficient and avoids the requirement for intermediate buffers that would be necessary with stream I/O.

Multiplexing

Possibly the most important features of NIO from a performance standpoint are the nonblocking channels and the ability to multiplex channels. Multiplexing I/O allows you to handle multiple I/O channels from one thread without having the thread block on any one channel. Without NIO, you have no certain way to know that a read or write will block the thread. The InputStream.available( ) method is the only stream method for determining if a read will not block, and it is not reliable; there is no method at all to determine if stream write would not block. NIO provides the Selector class to reliably determine which I/O channels are ready to operate nonblocking I/O. Currently, NIO does not support the multiplexing of FileChannels (though most operating systems do), so multiplexing with JDK 1.4 is primarily for socket communications.

It is useful to understand nonblocking mode in a little more detail. OutputStream.write( ) has a return signature of void. But at the operating-system level, I/O write

---

[*] This quotation can be found at *http://www.acme.com/software/thttpd/benchmarks.html*.

operations *do* return a value, normally the number of bytes that were written by the write call. This is efficient: most calls to an operating-system write send data to some buffer (disk buffer, network stack buffer, filesystem cache, etc.). So any call to write normally fills a buffer. If there are too many bytes being written by the call, then the buffer is filled with those bytes it can take, the remaining bytes are not written, and the number of bytes written is returned. The buffer is then emptied by sending on the data, and it is ready for the next chunk of bytes. The buffer emptying is done at I/O speeds, which is typically several orders of magnitude slower than the write to the in-memory buffer.

Consequently, the Java OutputStream.write( ) doesn't just fill the buffer and return, as it would need to return the number of bytes written. Instead, the buffer is filled, emptied, and so on, until all the bytes have been written. OutputStream.write( ) is actually a looped call to the underlying operating-system write call. Usually this is very convenient. But because the write can block for so long, you need to give it a separate thread of its own until it completes. You are probably familiar with doing this for reads, but it may not have occurred to you that Java writes were in the same category.

NIO writes are much closer to operating-system writes. For example, in all cases, where the data fits into the network buffer, a write to the socket should return immediately. And where there are too many bytes for the buffer, SocketChannel.write( ) still returns immediately if the SocketChannel is in nonblocking mode, returning the number of bytes written to the buffer. The actual network I/O proceeds asynchronously, leaving the Java thread to do other operations. In fact, typically the thread has time for thousands more operations before the buffer is ready to accept more data (i.e., the next write can succeed without blocking). So nonblocking mode gives you asynchronous I/O, and because the thread can execute thousands of operations for each I/O call, this means that one thread can effectively handle thousands of I/O channels simultaneously (in other words, multiplexing). But for effective multiplexing, you also need to know which Channels are ready to be written to or read from. And it is the Selector class that will reliably tell you when any channel is ready to perform its next I/O operation. The Selector class determines from the operating system which subset, from a set of Channels, is ready to perform I/O.

The Selector class differentiates between different types of I/O: there are currently four types. The first two types are where Selector can inform you when any Channel is ready to be read or written to. In addition, client sockets can be trying to connect to a server socket: the Selector can tell you when the connection attempt has completed. And lastly, server sockets can accept new connections: the Selector can tell you when there is a connection pending that will allow the server socket to execute an accept( ) call without blocking.

Note that multiplexed asynchronous I/O does *not* necessarily make I/O any faster. What you get is the ability to handle many I/O channels in one thread. For most Java applications, which have only a few open I/O streams at one time, there is no need to multiplex because a few extra blocked threads are easily managed by the VM. If you have many threads blocked on I/O, then multiplexing your I/O can significantly reduce your resource requirements. Ten I/O threads are probably okay; a hundred is too many. Multiplexed I/O is a definite requirement for scalable high-performance server applications, but most other applications do not need it.

Working with NIO multiplexing takes a little getting used to. You obtain a Selector using Selector.open( ), and the equivalent of new ServerSocket(int port) is to obtain an unbound ServerSocketChannel using ServerSocketChannel.open( ), and then bind it using ServerSocket.bind( ):

```
Selector mySelector = Selector.open( );
ServerSocketChannel serverChannel = ServerSocketChannel.open( );
serverChannel.socket( ).bind(new InetSocketAddress(port));
```

Client SocketChannels are obtained from ServerSocketChannel.accept( ). It is per-fectly possible to multiplex on all client sockets as well as the accept calls of the server socket, but it is also fairly common to have one extra thread dedicated to accepting connections:

```
while(true)
{
  try
  {
    //This is a blocking call, we operate the accepts in its own
    //separate thread to keep the code a bit cleaner.
    SocketChannel client = ServerSocketChannel.accept( );
    addToClientList(client);
  }
  catch (Exception e)
  {
    //If it is a problem with the ServerSocketChannel, we
    //may need to close it and restart the ServerSocketChannel
    //Otherwise we should simply log and ignore the error
    ...
  }
}
```

If you wanted to multiplex the ServerSocketChannel too, it would be:

```
ServerSocketChannel serverChannel = ServerSocketChannel.open( );
serverChannel.configureBlocking(false);
serverChannel.socket( ).bind(new InetSocketAddress(port));
SelectionKey serverChannelAcceptKey =
  serverChannel.register(mySelector, SelectionKey.OP_ACCEPT);
```

And you could accept connections by querying the Selector using Selector.selectedKeys( ) to see when the serverChannelAcceptKey was ready. If the key was in the set returned, the ServerSocketChannel could accept a new connection immedi-ately without blocking. Similarly, the client SocketChannels that were created from the ServerSocketChannel.accept( ) call should be registered with a Selector (it doesn't have to be the same selector; you could use one for reads, one for writes, and one for accepts if you prefer). The `Selector` is then queried for `Channels` ready to perform I/O.

Links to detailed examples, including full code for a high-performance NIO-based HTTP server, can be found at *http://www.JavaPerformanceTuning.com/tips/nio.shtml*.

Performance Checklist

Most of these suggestions apply only after a bottleneck has been identified:

- Ensure that performance tests are run with the same amount of I/O as the expected finished application. Specifically, turn off any extra logging, tracing, and debugging I/O.
- Use `Runtime.traceMethodCalls()`, when supported, to count I/O calls.
  - Redefine the I/O classes to count I/O calls if necessary.
  - Include logging statements next to all basic I/O calls in the application.
- Parallelize I/O by splitting data into multiple files.
- Execute I/O in a background thread.
- Avoid the filesystem file-growing overhead by preallocating files.
- Try to minimize the number of I/O calls.
  - Buffer to reduce the number of I/O operations by increasing the amount of data transfer each I/O operation executes.
  - Cache to replace repeated I/O operations with much faster memory or local disk access.
  - Avoid or reduce I/O calls in loops.
  - Replace `System.out` and `System.err` with customized `PrintStream` classes to control console output.
  - Use logger objects for tight control in specifying logging destinations.
  - Try to eliminate duplicate and unproductive I/O statements.
  - Keep files open and navigate around them rather than repeatedly opening and closing the files.
- Consider optimizing the Java byte-to-char (and char-to-byte) conversion.
- Handle serializing explicitly, rather than using default serialization mechanisms.
  - Use transient fields to avoid serialization.
  - Use the `java.io.Externalizable` interface if overriding the default serialization routines.
  - Use change logs for small changes, rather than reserializing the whole object.
  - Minimize the work done in the no-arg constructor.

— Consider partitioning objects into multiple sets and serializing each set concurrently in different threads.

— Use lazy initialization to move or spread the deserialization overhead to other times.

— Consider indexing an object table for selective access to stored serialized objects.

— Optimize network transfers by transferring only the data and objects needed, and no more.

— Cluster serialized objects that are used together by putting them into the same file.

— Put objects next to each other if they are required together.

— Consider using an object-storage system (such as an object database) if your object-storage requirements are at all sophisticated.

• Use compression when the overhead of compression is outweighed by the benefit of reducing I/O.

— Avoid compression when the system has a heavily loaded CPU.

— Consider using "intelligent" I/O classes that can decide to use compression on the fly.

— Consider searching directly against compressed data without decompressing.

• NIO provides I/O mechanisms mainly targeted at high-performance servers, but is also of use in other situations.

— Use nonblocking SocketChannels to connect asynchronously to servers.

— Nondirect Buffers provide an efficient mechanism for converting arrays of one primitive data type to another primitive data type.

— Direct Buffers provide options for optimizing I/O, especially when using multiple Buffers with scatter-gather I/O operations.

— High-performance scalable servers should use NIO multiplexing and asynchronous I/O.

CHAPTER 9

Sorting

In this chapter:
- Avoiding Unnecessary Sorting Overhead
- An Efficient Sorting Framework
- Better Than O(nlogn) Sorting

Avoiding Unnecessary Sorting Overhead

The JDK system provides sorting methods in java.util.Arrays (for arrays of objects) and in java.util.Collections (for objects implementing the Collection interfaces). These sorts are usually adequate for all but the most specialized applications. To optimize a sort, you can normally get enough improvement by reimplementing a standard sort (such as quicksort) as a method in the class being sorted. Comparisons of elements can then be made directly, without calling generic comparison methods. Only the most specialized applications usually need to search for specialized sorting algorithms.

As an example, here is a simple class with just an int instance variable, on which you need to sort:

```
public class Sortable
  implements Comparable
{
  int order;
  public Sortable(int i){order = i;}
  public int compareTo(Object o){return order - ((Sortable) o).order;}
  public int compareToSortable(Sortable o){return order - o.order;}
}
```

I can use the Arrays.sort() to sort this, but as I want to make a direct comparison with exactly the same sorting algorithm as I tune, I use an implementation of a standard quicksort. (This implementation is not shown here; for an example, see the quicksort implementation in "Finding the Index for Partially Matched Strings" in Chapter 11.) The only modification to the standard quicksort will be that for each optimization, the quicksort is adjusted to use the appropriate comparison method and data type. For example, a generic quicksort that sorts an array of Comparable objects is implemented as:

```
public static void quicksort(Comparable[ ] arr, int lo, int hi)
{
  ...
  int mid = ( lo + hi ) / 2;
```

```
Comparable middle = arr[ mid ]; //Comparable data type
...
//uses Comparable.compareTo(Object)
if(arr[ lo ].compareTo(middle) > 0 )
...
}
```

To start with, I use a quicksort that takes an array of Objects. The comparisons are made using the Comparator.compareTo( ) method, so every Object in the array must implement the Comparable interface. Since every object is a Comparable, why don't I specify a Comparable[ ] instead of an Object[ ] in the quicksort signature? I use an Object[ ] signature initially to illustrate why it is faster to use a Comparable[ ] signature. java.util.Arrays.sort( ) has an Object[ ] as its argument rather than a Comparable[ ] because it needs to support any array type, and Java doesn't let you cast a generic array to a more specific array type. That is, you cannot use:

```
Object[ ] arr = new Object[10];
... //fill the array with Comparable objects
//The following line does not compile
Arrays.sort( (Comparable[ ]) arr); //NOT valid Java code, invalid cast
```

This means that if you specify a sort with the signature that accepts only a Comparable[ ] object array, then you actually have to create a new Comparable array and copy all your objects to that array. And it is often the case that your array is already in an Object array, hence the more generic (but slower) support in the JDK. Another option for the JDK would be to have a second copy of the identical sort method in java.util.Arrays, except that the second sort would specify Comparable[ ] in the signature and have no casts in the implementation. This has not been done in java.util.Arrays up to JDK 1.4, but may be in the future.

Back to the example. The first quicksort with the Object[ ] signature gives a baseline at 100%. I am sorting a randomized array of Sortable objects, using the same randomized order for each test. Switching to a quicksort that specifies an array of Comparable objects (which means you avoid casting every object for each comparison) is faster for every VM I tested (see Table 9-1). You can modify the quicksort even further to cater specifically to Sortable objects, so that you call the Sortable.compareToSortable( ) method directly. This avoids yet another cast, the cast in the Sortable.compareTo( ) method, and therefore reduces the time even further.

Table 9-1. Timings of the various sorting tests normalized to the initial JDK 1.2 test

	1.2.2	1.3.1_02	1.3.1_02 -server	1.4.0	1.4.0 -server	1.4.0 -Xint
Quicksort(Object[ ])	100%	52%	53%	49%	50%	356%
Quicksort(Comparable[ ])	66%	48%	44%	45%	42%	319%
Quicksort(Sortable[ ])	47%	45%	30%	37%	30%	277%
Quicksort(Sortable[ ]) using field access	43%	32%	30%	31%	30%	111%
Arrays.sort( )	152%	63%	62%	59%	56%	267%

The last quicksort accepting a Sortable[ ] array looks like:

```
public static void quicksort(Sortable[ ] arr, int lo, int hi)
{
  ...
  int mid = ( lo + hi ) / 2;
  Sortable middle = arr[ mid ]; //Sortable data type
  ...
  //uses Sortable.compareToSortable(Sortable)
  if(arr[ lo ].compareToSortable(middle) > 0 )
  ...
```

You can make one further improvement, which is to access the Sortable.order fields directly from the quicksort. The final modified quicksort looks like:

```
public static void quicksort(Sortable[ ] arr, int lo, int hi)
{
  ...
  int mid = ( lo + hi ) / 2;
  Sortable middle = arr[ mid ]; //Sortable data type
  ...
  //uses Sortable.order field for direct comparison
  //if(arr[ lo ].order - middle.order > 0 ) -- same as next line
  if(arr[ lo ].order > middle.order )
  ...
```

This last quicksort gives a further improvement in time (see Table 9-1), though clearly the HotSpot server mode inlines the method call, enabling it to achieve the same speed for both the method and field access. Overall, this tuning example shows that by avoiding the casts by implementing a standard sort algorithm and comparison method specifically for a particular class, you can significantly speed up the sort with little effort. For comparison, I have included in Table 9-1 the timings for using the Arrays.sort( ) method, applied to the same randomized list of Sortable objects used in the example. The Arrays.sort( ) method uses a merge sort that performs better on a partially sorted list. Merge sort was chosen for Arrays.sort( ) because, although quicksort provides better performance on average, the merge sort provides sort stability. A stable sort does not alter the order of elements that are equal based on the comparison method used.[*]

For more specialized and optimized sorts, there are books (including Java-specific ones) covering various sort algorithms, and a variety of sort implementations are available on the Web. The computer literature is full of articles providing improved sorting algorithms for specific types of data, and you may need to run a search to find specialized sorts for your particular application. A good place to start is the classic reference *The Art of Computer Programming* by Donald Knuth (Addison-Wesley).

---

[*] The standard quicksort algorithm also has very bad worst-case performance. There are quicksort variations that improve the worst-case performance.

In the case of nonarray elements such as linked-list structures, a recursive merge sort is the best sorting algorithm and can be faster than a quicksort on arrays with the same dataset. Note that the JDK Collections.sort() methods are suboptimal for linked lists. The Collections.sort(List) method converts the list into an array before sorting it, which is the wrong strategy to sort linked lists, as shown in an article by John Boyer.[*] Boyer also shows that a binary search on a linked list is significantly better than a linear search if the cost of comparisons is more than about two or three node traversals, as is typically the case.

If you need your sort algorithm to run faster, optimizing the comparisons in the sort method is a good place to start. This can be done in several ways:

- Eliminating casts by specifying data types more precisely.
- Modifying the comparison algorithm to be quicker.
- Replacing the objects with wrappers that compare faster (e.g., java.text.CollationKeys). These are best used when the comparison method requires a calculation for each object being compared, and that calculation can be cached.
- Eliminating methods by accessing fields directly.
- Partially presorting the array with a faster partial sort, followed by the full sort.

Only when the performance is still short of your target do you need to start looking for alternatives. Several of the techniques listed here have been applied in the earlier example and also in "Sorting Internationalized Strings" in Chapter 5.

An Efficient Sorting Framework

The sorting methods provided by the JDK are perfectly adequate for most situations. When they fall short, the techniques illustrated in the previous section often speed things up as much as is required. However, if you work on a project where varied and flexible sorting capabilities are needed, sorting is one area of performance tuning where it is sensible to create a framework early in the development cycle. A good sorting framework should allow you to change sorting-algorithm and comparison-ordering methods in a generic way, without having to change too much in the application.

Providing support for arbitrary sorting algorithms is straightforward: just use sorting interfaces. There needs to be a sorting interface for each type of object that can be sorted. Arrays and collection objects should be supported by any sorting framework, along with any other objects that are specific to your application. Here are two interfaces that define sorting objects for arrays and collections:

```
import java.util.Comparator;
import java.util.Collection;
```

---

[*] "Sorting and Searching Linked Lists in Java," *Dr. Dobb's Journal*, May 1998.

```
public interface ArraySorter
{
  public void sort(Comparator comparator, Object[] arr);
  public void sort(Comparator comparator, Object[] arr,
      int startIndex, int length);
  public void sortInto(Comparator comparator, Object[] source,
      int sourceStartIndex, int length,
      Object[] target, int targetStartIndex);
}

public interface CollectionSorter
{
  public Object[] sort(Comparator comparator, Collection c);
  public void sortInto(Comparator comparator, Collection c,
      Object[] target, int targetStartIndex);
}
```

Individual classes that implement the interfaces are normally stateless and hence implicitly thread-safe. This allows you to specify singleton sorting objects for use by other objects. For example:

```
public class ArrayQuickSorter
  implements ArraySorter
{
  public static final ArrayQuickSorter SINGLETON = new ArrayQuickSorter();

  //protect the constructor so that external classes are
  //forced to use the singleton
  protected ArrayQuickSorter(){}

  public void sortInto(Comparator comparator, Object[] source,
    int sourceStartIndex, int length, Object[] target, int targetStartIndex)
  {
    //Only need the target - quicksort sorts in place.
    if ( !(source == target && sourceStartIndex == targetStartIndex) )
      System.arraycopy(source, sourceStartIndex, target,
          targetStartIndex, length);
    this.sort(comparator, target, targetStartIndex, length);
  }

  public void sort(Comparator comparator, Object[] arr)
  {
    this.sort(comparator, arr, 0, arr.length);
  }

  public void sort(Comparator comparator, Object[] arr,
      int startIndex, int length)
  {
    //quicksort algorithm implementation using Comparator.compare(Object, Object)
    ...
  }
```

This framework allows you to change the sort algorithm simply by changing the sort object you use. For example, if you use a quicksort but realize that your array is

already partially sorted, simply change the sorter instance from `ArrayQuickSorter.`
`SINGLETON` to `ArrayInsertionSorter.SINGLETON`.

However, we are only halfway to an efficient framework. Although the overall sorting structure is here, you have not supported generic optimizations such as optimized comparison wrappers (e.g., as with `java.text.CollationKey`). For generic support, you need the `Comparator` interface to have an additional method that checks whether it supports optimized comparison wrappers (which I will now call `ComparisonKeys`). Unfortunately, you cannot add a method to the `Comparator` interface, so you have to use the following subinterface:

```
public interface KeyedComparator
  extends Comparator
{
  public boolean hasComparisonKeys();
  public ComparisonKey getComparisonKey(Object o);
}

public interface ComparisonKey
{
  public int compareTo(ComparisonKey target);
  public Object getSource();
}
```

Now you need to support this addition to the framework in each sorter object. Since you don't want to change all your sorter-object implementations again and again, it's better to find any further optimizations now. One optimization is a sort that avoids a call to any method comparison. You can support that with a specific `ComparisonKey` class:

```
public class IntegerComparisonKey
  implements ComparisonKey
{
  public Object source;
  public int order;
  public IntegerComparisonKey(Object source, int order) {
    this.source = source;
    this.order = order;
  }
  public int compareTo(ComparisonKey target){
    return order - ((IntegerComparisonKey) target).order;
  }
  public Object getSource() {return source;}
}
```

Now you can reimplement your sorter class to handle these special optimized cases. Only the method that actually implemented the sort needs to change:

```
public class ArrayQuickSorter
  implements ArraySorter
{
  //everything else as previously
  ...
```

```
public void sort(Comparator comparator, Object[] arr,
                 int startIndex, int length)
{
  //If the comparator is part of the extended framework, handle
  //the special case where it recommends using comparison keys
  if (comparator instanceof KeyedComparator &&
        ((KeyedComparator) comparator).hasComparisonKeys())
  {
    //wrap the objects in the ComparisonKeys
    //but if the ComparisonKey is the special case of
    //IntegerComparisonKey, handle that specially
    KeyedComparator comparer = (KeyedComparator) comparator;
    ComparisonKey first = comparer.getComparisonKey(arr[startIndex]);
    if (first instanceof IntegerComparisonKey)
    {
      //wrap in IntegerComparisonKeys
      IntegerComparisonKey[] iarr = new IntegerComparisonKey[length];
      iarr[startIndex] = (IntegerComparisonKey) first;
      for(int j = length-1, i = startIndex+length-1; j > 0; i--, j--)
        iarr[j] = comparer.getComparisonKey(arr[i]);

      //sort using the optimized sort for IntegerComparisonKeys
      sort_intkeys(iarr, 0, length);

      //and unwrap
      for(int j = length-1, i = startIndex+length-1; j >= 0; i--, j--)
        arr[i] = iarr[j].source;
    }
    else
    {
      //wrap in IntegerComparisonKeys
      ComparisonKey[] karr = new ComparisonKey[length];
      karr[startIndex] = first;
      for(int j = length-1, i = startIndex+length-1; j > 0; i--, j--)
        karr[i] = comparer.getComparisonKey(arr[i]);

      //sort using the optimized sort for ComparisonKeys
      sort_keys(karr, 0, length);

      //and unwrap
      for(int j = length-1, i = startIndex+length-1; j >= 0; i--, j--)
        arr[i] = karr[i].getSource();
    }
  }
  else
    //just use the original algorithm
    sort_comparator(comparator, arr, startIndex, length);
}
public void sort_comparator(Comparator comparator, Object[] arr,
          int startIndex, int length)
{
  //quicksort algorithm implementation using Comparator.compare(Object, Object)
  ...
}
```

```
public void sort_keys(ComparisonKey[ ] arr, int startIndex, int length)
{
  //quicksort algorithm implementation using
  //ComparisonKey.compare(ComparisonKey)
  ...
}
public void sort_intkeys(IntegerComparisonKey[ ] arr,
          int startIndex, int length)
{
  //quicksort algorithm implementation comparing key order directly
  //using access to the IntegerComparisonKey.order field
  //i.e if (arr[i].order > arr[j].order)
  ...
}
}
```

Although the special cases mean that you have to implement the same algorithm three times (with slight changes to data type and comparison method), this is the kind of tradeoff you often have to make for performance optimizations. The maintenance impact is limited by having all implementations in one class, and once you've debugged the sort algorithm, you are unlikely to need to change it.

This framework now supports:

- An easy way to change the sorting algorithm being used at any specific point of the application.

- An easy way to change the pair-wise comparison method, by changing the Comparator object.

- Automatic support for comparison key objects. Comparison keys are optimal to use in sorts where the comparison method requires a calculation for each object being compared, and that calculation could be cached.

- An optimized integer key comparison class, which doesn't require method calls when used for sorting.

This outline should provide a good start to building an efficient sorting framework. Many further generic optimizations are possible, such as supporting a LongComparisonKey class and other special classes appropriate to your application. The point is that the framework should handle optimizations automatically. The most the application builder should do is decide on the appropriate Comparator or ComparisonKey class to build for the object to be sorted.

The last version of our framework supports the fastest sorting implementation from the previous section (the last implementation with no casts and direct access to the ordering field). Unfortunately, the cost of creating an IntegerComparisonKey object for each object being sorted is significant enough to eliminate the speedup from getting rid of the casts. It's worth looking at ways to reduce the cost of object creations for comparison keys. This cost can be reduced using the object-to-array mapping technique from Chapter 4: the array of IntegerComparisonKeys is changed to a pair of Object and int arrays. By adding another interface, you can support the needed mapping:

```
interface RawIntComparator
  //extends not actually necessary, but logically applies
  extends KeyedComparator
{
  public void getComparisonKey(Object o, int[] orders, int idx);
}
```

For the example Sortable class that was defined earlier, you can implement a Comparator class:

```
public class SortableComparator
 implements RawIntComparator
{
  //Required for Comparator interface
  public int compare(Object o1, Object o2){
    return ((Sortable) o1).order -((Sortable) o2).order;}
  //Required for Comparator interface
  public boolean hasComparisonKeys(){return true;}
  public ComparisonKey getComparisonKey(Object o){
    return new IntegerComparisonKey(o, ((Sortable) o).order);}
  //Required for RawIntComparator interface
  public void getComparisonKey(Object s, int[] orders, int index){
    orders[index] = ((Sortable) s).order;}
}
```

Then the logic to support the RawIntComparator in the sorting class is:

```
public class ArrayQuickSorter
  implements ArraySorter
{
  //everything else as previously except rename the
  //previously defined sort(Comparator, Object[], int, int)
  //method as previous_sort
  ...

  public void sort(Comparator comparator, Object[] arr,
                   int startIndex, int length)
  {
    //support RawIntComparator types
    if (comparator instanceof RawIntComparator)
    {
      RawIntComparator comparer = (RawIntComparator) comparator;
      Object[] sources = new Object[length];
      int[] orders = new int[length];

      for(int j = length-1, i = startIndex+length-1; j >= 0; i--, j--)
      {
          comparer.getComparisonKey(arr[i], orders, j);
          sources[j] = arr[i];
      }
```

```java
      //sort using the optimized sort with no casts
      sort_intkeys(sources, orders, 0, length);

      //and unwrap
      for(int j = length-1, i = startIndex+length-1; j >= 0; i--, j--)
        arr[i] = sources[j];
    }
    else
      previous_ sort(comparator, arr, startIndex, length);
}

public void sort_intkeys(Object[ ] sources, int[ ] orders,
          int startIndex, int length)
{
    quicksort(sources, orders, startIndex, startIndex+length-1);
}

public static void quicksort(Object[ ] sources, int[ ] orders, int lo, int hi)
{
    //quicksort algorithm implementation with a pair of
    //synchronized arrays. 'orders' is the array used to
    //compare ordering. 'sources' is the array holding the
    //source objects whicn needs to be altered in synchrony
    //with 'orders'
    if( lo >= hi )
      return;

    int mid = ( lo + hi ) / 2;
    Object tmp_o;
    int tmp_i;
    int middle = orders[ mid ];

    if( orders[ lo ] > middle )
    {
      orders[ mid ] = orders[ lo ];
      orders[ lo ] = middle;
      middle = orders[ mid ];
      tmp_o = sources[mid];
      sources[ mid ] = sources[ lo ];
      sources[ lo ] = tmp_o;
    }

    if( middle > orders[ hi ])
    {
      orders[ mid ] = orders[ hi ];
      orders[ hi ] = middle;
      middle = orders[ mid ];
      tmp_o = sources[mid];
      sources[ mid ] = sources[ hi ];
      sources[ hi ] = tmp_o;

      if( orders[ lo ] > middle)
      {
```

```
        orders[ mid ] = orders[ lo ];
        orders[ lo ] = middle;
        middle = orders[ mid ];
        tmp_o = sources[mid];
        sources[ mid ] = sources[ lo ];
        sources[ lo ] = tmp_o;
      }
    }

    int left = lo + 1;
    int right = hi - 1;

    if( left >= right )
      return;

    for( ;; )
    {
      while( orders[ right ] > middle)
      {
        right--;
      }

      while( left < right && orders[ left ] <= middle )
      {
        left++;
      }

      if( left < right )
      {
        tmp_i = orders[ left ];
        orders[ left ] = orders[ right ];
        orders[ right ] = tmp_i;
        tmp_o = sources[ left ];
        sources[ left ] = sources[ right ];
        sources[ right ] = tmp_o;
        right--;
      }
      else
      {
        break;
      }
    }

    quicksort(sources, orders, lo, left);
    quicksort(sources, orders, left + 1, hi);
  }
}
```

With this optimization, the framework quicksort is now as fast as the fastest hand-crafted quicksort from the previous section for some VMs (see Table 9-2).

Table 9-2. *Timings of the various sorting tests normalized to the initial JDK 1.2 test of Table 9-1*

	1.2.2	1.3.1_02	1.3.1_02 -server	1.4.0	1.4.0 -server	1.4.0 -Xint
Quicksort(Object[ ]) from Table 9-1	100%	52%	53%	49%	50%	356%
Quicksort(Sortable[ ]) using field access from Table 9-1	43%	32%	30%	31%	30%	111%
ArrayQuickSorter using Sortable.field[a]	39%	53%	47%	34%	60%	111%
Arrays.sort( ) from Table 9-1	152%	63%	62%	59%	56%	267%

[a] HotSpot is variable in how well it manages to optimize the framework sort. The 1.4.0 client is almost as fast as the direct field access sort. This indicates that HotSpot technology is theoretically capable of similarly optimizing the framework sort. That it hasn't managed to in some modes of JDK 1.3 and 1.4 indicates that the VM can be improved further.

Better Than O(nlogn) Sorting

Computer-science analysis of sorting algorithms show that, on average, no generic sorting algorithm can scale faster than O(nlogn) (see the sidebar "Orders of Magnitude"). However, many applications don't require a "general" sort. You often have additional information that can help you to improve the speed of a particular sort.

For example, if you have 1000 items to sort and each item can be given a unique ordering value that corresponds to a unique integer between 1 and 1000, the best sort is simply to slot the items directly into their correct locations in an array. No comparisons between the items are necessary.

Of course, typically you can't map your elements so neatly. But if you can map items to integer keys that are more or less evenly distributed, you can still take advantage of improved sorting characteristics. Bear in mind that an array of partially sorted items can be sorted faster than a typical unsorted array.

When you can guess the approximate final position of the items in the collection to be sorted, you can use this knowledge to improve sorting speed. You should specifically look out for sorts where:

- Items can be given an ordering value that can be mapped to integer keys.
- The distribution of the keys is regular, or any one of the following is true:
  - The distribution of the keys is fairly even, so that when mapped into array indexes, ordering is approximately kept.
  - The keys have evenly distributed clusters.
  - The distribution of the keys has a mapping into one of these other distributions.

The distribution of the keys is fairly critical. A regular distribution allows them to be mapped straightforwardly into array indexes. An uneven distribution is difficult to map. But if you have an uneven distribution and can specify a mapping that allows you to flatten out the keys in some way, it may still be possible to apply this

Orders of Magnitude

When discussing the time taken for particular algorithms to execute, it is important to know not just how long the algorithm takes for a particular dataset, but also how long it takes for different-sized datasets, i.e., how it scales. For applications, the problems of handling 10 objects and handling 10 million objects are often completely different problems, not just different-sized versions of the same problem.

One common way to indicate the behavior of algorithms across different scales of datasets is to describe the algorithm's scaling characteristics by the dominant numerical function relating to the scaling behavior. The notation used is "O(*function*)," where *function* is replaced by the dominant numerical scaling function. It is common to use the letter "n" to indicate the number of data items being considered in the function. For example, O(n) indicates that the algorithm under consideration increases in time linearly with the size of the dataset. $O(n^2)$ indicates that the time taken increases according to the square of the size of the dataset.

These orders of magnitude do not indicate absolute times taken by the algorithm. Instead, they indicate how much longer the algorithm takes when the dataset increases in size. If an O(n) algorithm takes 200 seconds for n=10, it will take about 2000 seconds for n=100, i.e., a tenfold increase in the dataset size implies a tenfold increase in the amount of time taken by the algorithm. An $O(n^2)$ algorithm might take 5 seconds for n=10, and about 500 seconds for n=100, i.e., a tenfold increase in the dataset size implies a hundredfold increase in the time taken by the algorithm. Note that the scaled times are approximate; order-of-magnitude statistics include only the dominant scaling function, and there may be other, smaller terms that adjust the actual time taken.

The order of magnitude does not indicate the relative speeds of two different algorithms for any specific dataset size. Instead, order-of-magnitude statistics indicate how expensive one particular algorithm may be as your dataset grows. In the examples of the last paragraph, the time taken for the second $O(n^2)$ algorithm increases much faster than the first O(n) algorithm, but the $O(n^2)$ algorithm is still faster at n=100. However, by n=1000, it would be the slower of the two algorithms (50,000 seconds, compared to 20,000 seconds for the O(n) algorithm).

To take a concrete example, hash tables have an O(1) order of magnitude for accessing elements. This means that the time taken to access elements in a hash table is mostly independent of the size of the hash table. Accessing elements in an array by linearly searching through that array takes O(n). In absolute times, it might be quicker to execute the linear array search on a small array than to access from a hash table. But as the number of elements becomes larger, at some point the hash table will always become quicker.

methodology. For example, if you know that your keys will have a normal (bell-curve) distribution, you can apply an inverse bell-curve function to the keys to flatten them out to array indexes.

For this technique to work, the mapped keys do not need to be unique. Several keys or groups of keys can map to the same value or values. Indeed, it is quite difficult to make the index mapping unique. You need to be aware of this and handle the resulting collisions. Normally, you can map clusters of keys into subsections of the sorted array. These subsections are probably not internally sorted, but they may be correctly sorted against each other (i.e., all elements in subsection 1 are ordered below all elements in subsection 2, all elements in subsection 2 are ordered below all elements in subsection 3, etc.). This way, the problem has been modified to sort multiple smaller subsections (which is faster than sorting the whole array), and hence the array is sorted more quickly.

Note that Object.hashCode( ) provides a mechanism for generating an integer for any object. However, the resulting hash code is not guaranteed to be evenly distributed or even unique, nor is it at all guaranteed to be consistent across different VMs or even over multiple runs of one VM. Consequently, the hash code is of little use for any kind of mapping.

Karl-Dietrich Neubert[*] gives a detailed implementation of this approach, where the algorithm provides O(n) sorting behavior and also minimizes the extra memory needed to manage the sort.

> I also implemented Neubert's sort for a plain int array rather than for an array of objects. The results were the same as for the object array when the JIT was turned off. But with any type of JIT turned on, the two simpler reference-sort algorithms were optimized much better by the native code compiler and were faster for all sizes of arrays I tested (up to several million elements). Their absolute sort times were sufficiently fast that their bad scaling behavior didn't matter. This curious difference in relative speeds applied only to sorting int[ ] arrays, not arrays of objects. For arrays of objects, Neubert's sort seems to be faster both with and without a JIT.

I include here a Java implementation of Neubert's algorithm with comments in the code. I have applied the implementation to an array of objects that have an integer field to specify the sort order, but of course the algorithm can be easily generalized to other cases where object ordering can be mapped to numbers. For a more detailed discussion of the algorithm, refer to Neubert's article. The implementation given here sorts significantly faster than either the sort in java.util.Arrays (in Java 2) or a handcrafted quicksort (the most optimized final version with no casts from the first section of this chapter); see Table 9-3. Note also that this sort is O(n) and thus increases linearly in time, whereas the other sorts are O(nlogn) and so have a superlinear speedup. Notice how the interpreted mode Flashsort time approaches the timings of

---

[*] Algorithm Alley, *Dr. Dobb's Journal*, February 1998.

the compiled JVMs and is actually faster than the pure JIT of 1.2.2 running `Arrays.sort( )`. That's a significant speedup.

Table 9-3. Timings of the various sorting tests normalized to the Flashsort JDK 1.2 test

	1.2.2	1.3.1_02	1.3.1_02 -server	1.4.0	1.4.0 -server	1.4.0 -Xint
Neubert's Flashsort	100%	94%	155%	74%	79%	294%
Handcrafted quicksort	250%	178%	130%	149%	132%	921%
Arrays.sort( )	476%	181%	183%	174%	164%	906%

Note that the sort at the end of the Neubert algorithm is an insertion sort running over the entire array. Insertion sorts provide better performance than quicksorts for partially ordered arrays. This final insertion sort ensures that keys incorrectly classified by the group distribution end up in the right location:

```java
public interface FlashSortable{
    public int sortOrder( );
}

public static void flashsort(FlashSortable[ ] arr)
{
    //Number of groups into which the elements are classified
    //Neubert suggests 0.2 to 0.5 times the number of elements in the array.
    int num_groups = (int) (0.4 * arr.length);

    //Count the number of elements in each group
    int[ ] groups = new int[num_groups];

    flashsort(arr, num_groups, groups);
}

public static void flashsort(FlashSortable[ ] arr, int num_groups, int[ ] groups)
{
    //First get the minimum and maximum values
    int min = arr[0].sortOrder( );
    int max_idx = 0;
    int i;
    for (i = arr.length-1; i > 0; i--)
    {
        if (arr[i].sortOrder( ) < min)
            min = arr[i].sortOrder( );
        if (arr[i].sortOrder( ) > arr[max_idx].sortOrder( ))
            max_idx = i;
    }
    //If they are the same, all elements are identical
    //so the array is already sorted.
    if (min == arr[max_idx].sortOrder( ))
        return;
```

```
//Count the number of elements in each group.
//Take care to handle possible integer overflow by
//casting to larger datatypes where this might occur.
double scaling_constant = (num_groups - 1) /
     ( ((double) arr[max_idx].sortOrder()) - min);
int group;
for (i = arr.length-1; i >= 0; i--)
{
  group = (int) (scaling_constant * (((long) arr[i].sortOrder()) - min));
  groups[group]++;
}

//Set the groups to point to the indexes in the array
//that are the last index for each group.
groups[0]--;
for (i = 1; i < groups.length; i++)
{
  groups[i] += groups[i-1];
}

//Put the biggest element at index 0 so that the swapping
//algorithm below starts on the largest element & max group.
FlashSortable old_value = arr[max_idx];
arr[max_idx] = arr[0];
arr[0] = old_value;

//start with element at index 0
int idx = 0;
//and the maximum group
group = num_groups - 1;

//Start moving elements into their groups.
//We need to make 'arr.length' moves at most,
//but if we have one move left in the outer loop
//then the remaining element is already in the right place,
//so we need test for only 'arr.length-1' moves.
int number_of_moves_left = arr.length - 1;

FlashSortable new_value;
while(number_of_moves_left > 0)
{
  //When the first group fills up, we start scanning
  //for elements left in the wrong groups, and move them.

  //Note that we scan through the whole object array only once.
  while(idx > groups[group])
  {
    idx++;
    group = (int) (scaling_constant * (((long) arr[idx].sortOrder()) - min));
  }

  new_value = arr[idx];
```

```
//We run this loop until the first group fills up.
//Then we run the previous scan loop to get back into this loop.
while( idx != (groups[group]+1) )
{
  group = (int) (scaling_constant * (((long) new_value.sortOrder()) - min));
  old_value = arr[groups[group]];
  arr[groups[group]] = new_value;
  new_value = old_value;
  groups[group]--; //decrement the pointer to the next index
  number_of_moves_left--;
}
}

//Now we have our partially ordered array,
//we do an insertion sort to order the remainder.
for (i = arr.length - 3; i >= 0; i--)
{
  if (arr[i+1].sortOrder() < arr[i].sortOrder())
  {
    old_value = arr[i];
    idx = i;
    while(arr[idx+1].sortOrder() < old_value.sortOrder())
    {
      arr[idx] = arr[idx+1];
      idx++;
    }
    arr[idx] = old_value;
  }
}
}
```

Performance Checklist

Most of these suggestions apply only after a bottleneck has been identified:

- Eliminate casts in the sorting method.
- Reimplement a standard sort (such as quicksort) directly in the class being sorted.
- Make the comparison method faster.
- Directly access fields rather than calling methods.
- Sort linked lists with a merge sort.
- Use comparison keys to replace objects where the comparison method requires a calculation for each object being compared, and that calculation could be cached.
- Partially presort the array with a faster partial sort; then re-sort using the full comparison method.
- Use sorting interfaces to support different sorting algorithms.

- Support generic optimizations within a sorting framework. These optimizations include:
  — Comparison key objects that cache calculations that would otherwise need to be repeatedly executed
  — Comparison key objects that hold the ordering value in a directly accessible public field
  — Improved object creation by mapping arrays of comparison key objects into multiple arrays
- Use specialized sorting algorithms for faster times and better scaling behavior.
- Use specialized sorting algorithms when the sorting order of objects can be mapped directly to integer keys.

CHAPTER 10
Threading

In this chapter:
- User-Interface Thread and Other Threads
- Race Conditions
- Deadlocks
- Synchronization Overhead
- Timing Multithreaded Tests
- Atomic Access and Assignment
- Thread Pools
- Load Balancing
- Threaded Problem-Solving Strategies

Minor Premise: One man can dig a posthole in sixty seconds.
Conclusion: Sixty men can dig a posthole in one second.
—Ambrose Bierce
The Devil's Dictionary

Multithreading allows an application to do multiple things at the same time. While it is often possible to get the same effect with clever programming in a single thread, Java's extensive support of threads makes it easier to use multiple threads. In addition, single-threaded applications cannot take advantage of multiprocessor machines.

However, multithreading can be difficult to implement effectively. Multithreading improves performance in many cases, but it also has drawbacks if the default mechanisms for cooperation between threads are used simplistically. In this chapter, we look at the benefits and the disadvantages threads offer to performance. We examine the likely problems that may be encountered and discuss how to minimize the performance downside while still gaining the benefits of multiple threads.

Multithreading needs more care in coding than single threading. When tuning threads, it is easy to make a little change here, and a little change there, and end up with total confusion, race conditions, and deadlock. Before you start tuning threads, it is important to have a good understanding of how they interact and how to make them cooperate and control each other. This book is not a tutorial on threads, so I don't intend to cover the subject from a non-performance-tuning standpoint in any great detail. Two excellent books on Java threads are *Java Threads* by Scott Oaks and Henry Wong (O'Reilly) and *Concurrent Programming in Java* by Doug Lea (Addison Wesley).

If you are not comfortable with Java synchronization and how it works, I strongly advise you to spend some time studying how to use threads and synchronization. Be sure you understand how race conditions and deadlocks occur (many articles and books on Java go into this in detail, and there are brief examples in the later sections

<div style="border: 1px solid black; padding: 10px;">

Synchronization and Monitors

Synchronization can be confusing, so I felt it was worth including a short reminder of its subtleties here.

Two or more threads accessing and updating the same data variables have no way of knowing when a particular accessor update will occur relative to any other thread accesses. Synchronization ensures that a group of statements (a synchronized block) will execute atomically as far as all synchronized threads are concerned. Synchronization does not address the problem of which thread executes the statements first: it is first come, first served.

Synchronization is achieved using monitors. Every object can have a monitor associated with it, so any object can synchronize blocks. Before a synchronized block can be entered, a thread needs to gain ownership of the monitor for that block. Once the thread has gained ownership of the monitor, no other thread synchronized on the same monitor can gain entry to that block (or any other block or method synchronized on the same monitor). The thread owning the monitor gets to execute all the statements in the block, and then automatically releases ownership of the monitor on exiting the block. At that point, another thread waiting to enter the block can acquire ownership of the monitor.

Note, however, that threads synchronized on different monitors can gain entry to the same block at any time. For example, a block defined with a `synchronized(this)` expression is synchronized on the monitor of the `this` object. If `this` is an object that is different for two different threads, both threads can gain ownership of their own monitor for that block, and both can execute the block at the same time. This won't matter if the block affects only variables specific to its thread (such as instance variables of `this`), but can lead to corrupt states if the block alters variables that are shared between the threads, such as static variables.

of this chapter). Be sure you know how to correctly use the various `wait( )` and `notify( )` methods in the `Object` class as well as the `synchronized` keyword, and understand which monitor objects are used and how they are used when execution reaches a synchronized block or method.

User-Interface Thread and Other Threads

The user's impression of the performance of an application is greatly affected by its responsiveness. Putting the user interface into a separate thread from any other work makes the application feel far more responsive to the user and ensures that an unexpectedly long operation doesn't freeze the application's screen.

This user-interface thread is quite important in applets, where it is simple to use the screen-update thread to execute other tasks because you can easily call code from the paint( ) method. Although more effort is required to spawn a thread to execute other tasks, it is much better to do so, as otherwise you can easily block repainting the screen or other GUI responses. In Figure 10-1, the clock on the left has been resized to a quarter of its original size, but the paint( ) method has been unable to resize the clock drawing, as the paint( ) method is busy keeping the correct time. The clock on the right has been resized to a wide rectangular shape, and it keeps perfect time while also responding to the resize request because its paint( ) method always completes quickly.

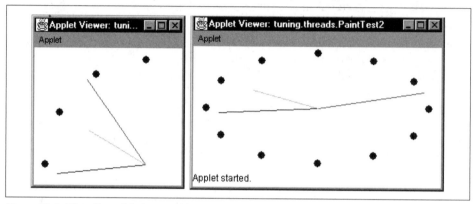

Figure 10-1. The effect of timing on redrawing

If you are able to separate operations that slow processing (such as I/O) into specialized threads, your application will run more smoothly. It can carry on its main work while another thread anticipates the need for data, saves data to disk, etc. However, you should not pass work to another thread while your main thread just sits and waits until that other thread completes. In fact, doing this is likely to hurt performance rather than improve it. You should not use extra threads unless you have good design or performance reasons for doing so.

One useful technique is to use a separate thread to monitor the rest of the application and, when necessary, interrupt threads that are running beyond their expected execution time. This is more often a technique that ensures robustness, but it can apply to performance, too, when a calculation provides successively better approximations to the required result. It may be reasonable to interrupt the calculation after a certain length of time, assuming you have a good approximation calculated. This technique does not specifically require a supervising thread, as the timeout checking could be done within the calculation. It is often used in animation; the frame-display rate can be adjusted according to the time taken to display the frames, which in turn depends on picture resolution and the system environment.

All in all, using multiple threads needs careful consideration, and should be planned for in the design stage. Retrofitting an application to use threads at an intermediate or advanced stage can sometimes be done quite simply in some sections of the application, but is not usually possible throughout the application. In any case, care should be taken when changing the design to use more threads so that the problems illustrated in the next sections are avoided.

Race Conditions

A race condition occurs when two threads attempt to use the same resource at the same time. The following class demonstrates a simple race condition. Two threads simultaneously try to increment a counter. If each thread can complete the increment( ) method in its entirety without the other thread executing, then all is fine, and the counter monotonically increases. Otherwise, the thread context switcher has the opportunity to interrupt one thread in the middle of executing the increment( ) method and let the other thread run through this method. Note that the thread can actually be interrupted anywhere, not necessarily in the middle of the increment( ) method, but I've greatly increased the likelihood of an interruption in the increment( ) method by including a print statement there:

```
package tuning.threads;

public class ThreadRace
    implements Runnable
{
  //global counter
  static int num=0;

  public static void increment( )
  {
    int n = num;
    //This next line gives the context switcher an ideal
    //place to switch context.
    System.out.print(num+" ");
    //And when it switches back, n will still be the old
    //value from the old thread.
    num = n + 1;
  }

  public static void main(String args[ ])
  {
    ThreadRace d1 = new ThreadRace( );
    ThreadRace d2 = new ThreadRace( );

    Thread d1Thread = new Thread(d1);
    Thread d2Thread = new Thread(d2);

    d1Thread.start( );
    d2Thread.start( );
  }

  public void run( )
  {
```

```
    for (int i = 200; i >= 0 ; i--)
    {
      increment( );
    }
  }
}
```

The output from executing this class on a single-processor test machine is:

```
0 1 2 3 4 5 6 7 8 9 10 11 12 13 14 15 16 16 17 18 19 20 21 22 23 24 25 26 27 28 29 30
31 32 17 18 19 20 21 22 23 24 25 26 27 28 29 30 31 32 33 33 34 35 36 37 38 39 40 41
42 43 44 45 46 47 48 49 34 35 36 37 38 39 40 41 42 43 44 45 46 47 48 49
```

You see that after 16, the next number is 16 again, and after the first 32, the next number is 17, as the threads switch back and forth in the middle of the increment( ) method. On a multiprocessor machine, the situation is even more confused.

Synchronizing the increment( ) method ensures the correct behavior of a monotonically increasing counter, as this gives exactly the desired behavior: the method is forced to complete before another call to it from any thread can be started.

In this test, because the counter is static, the increment( ) method needs to be static for synchronization to work correctly. If the increment( ) method is not static, synchronizing it locks the monitor for each this object rather than for the class. In the example I used a different object in each thread. A non-static increment( ) method is synchronized separately on each this object, so the updates remain unsynchronized across the two threads.

It is not simply that the num variable is static (though it needs to be for this particular example to work). The critical point is that the monitor that locks the method must be the same monitor for the two threads; otherwise, each thread gains its own separate lock with no synchronization occurring. Generally, deciding what to synchronize can be quite subtle, and you need to keep in mind which monitor is going to be locked by any particular thread.

Deadlocks

Ensuring that resources are used correctly between threads is easy in Java. Usually, it just takes the use of the synchronized keyword before a method. Because Java makes it seem so easy and painless to coordinate thread access to resources, the synchronized keyword tends to get used liberally. Up to and including Java 1.1, this was the approach taken even by Sun. You can still see in the earlier defined classes (e.g., java.util.Vector) that all methods that update instance variables are synchronized. From JDK 1.2, the engineers at Sun became more aware of performance and are now careful to avoid synchronizing willy-nilly. Instead, many classes are built unsynchronized but are provided with synchronized wrappers (see the later section "Desynchronization and Synchronized Wrappers").

Synchronizing methods liberally may seem like good safe programming, but it is a sure recipe for reducing performance at best, and creating deadlocks at worst. The following Deadlock class illustrates the simplest form of a race condition leading to deadlock. Here, the class Deadlock is Runnable. The run( ) method just has a short half-second delay and then calls hello( ) on another Deadlock object. The problem comes from the combination of the following three factors:

- Both run( ) and hello( ) are synchronized
- There is more than one thread
- The sequence of execution does not guarantee that monitors are locked and unlocked in correct order

The main( ) method accepts one optional parameter to set the delay in milliseconds between starting the two threads. With a parameter of 1000 (one second), there should be no deadlock. Table 10-1 summarizes what happens when the program runs without deadlock.

Table 10-1. Example not deadlocked

d1Thread activity	d1 monitor owned by	d2 monitor owned by	d2Thread activity
Acquire d1 monitor and execute d1.run( )	d1Thread [in d1.run( )]	None	
Sleeping in d1.run( ) for 500 milliseconds	d1Thread [in d1.run( )]	None	
Acquire d2 monitor and execute d2.hello( )	d1Thread [in d1.run( )]	d1Thread [in d2.hello( )]	
Sleeping in d2.hello( ) for 1000 milliseconds	d1Thread [in d1.run( )]	d1Thread [in d2.hello( )]	
Sleeping in d2.hello( ) for 1000 milliseconds	d1Thread [in d1.run( )]	d1Thread [in d2.hello( )]	Try to acquire d2 monitor to execute d2.run( ), but block as d2 monitor is owned by d1Thread
Exit d2.hello( ) and release d2 monitor	d1Thread [in d1.run( )]	None	Blocked until d2 monitor is released
Running final statements in d1.run( )	d1Thread [in d1.run( )]	d2Thread [in d2.run( )]	Finally acquire d2 monitor and execute d2.run( )
Exit d1.run( ) and release d1 monitor	None	d2Thread [in d2.run( )]	Sleeping in d2.run( ) for 500 milliseconds
	d2Thread [in d1.hello( )]	d2Thread [in d2.run( )]	Acquire d1 monitor and execute d1.hello( )
	d2Thread [in d1.hello( )]	d2Thread [in d2.run( )]	Sleeping in d1.hello( ) for 1000 milliseconds
	None	d2Thread [in d2.run( )]	Exit d1.hello( ) and release d1 monitor
	None	None	Exit d2.run( ) and release d2 monitor

With a parameter of 0 (no delay between starting threads), there should be deadlock on all but the most heavily loaded systems. The calling sequence is shown in Table 10-2; Figure 10-2 summarizes the difference between the two cases. The critical difference between the deadlocked and nondeadlocked cases is whether d1Thread can acquire a lock on the d2 monitor before d2Thread manages to acquire a lock on d2 monitor.

Table 10-2. Example deadlocked

d1Thread activity	d1 monitor owned by	d2 monitor owned by	d2Thread activity
Acquire d1 monitor and execute d1.run( )	d1Thread [in d1.run( )]	None	
Sleeping in d1.run( ) for 500 milliseconds	d1Thread [in d1.run( )]	d2Thread [in d2.run( )]	Acquire d2 monitor and execute d2.run( )
Blocked trying to acquire d2 monitor while starting d2.hello( ), as d2Thread owns d2 monitor	d1Thread [in d1.run( )]	d2Thread [in d2.run( )]	Sleeping in d2.run( ) for 500 milliseconds
Blocked until d2 monitor is released	d1Thread [in d1.run( )]	d2Thread [in d2.run( )]	Blocked trying to acquire d1 monitor while starting d1.hello( ), as d1Thread owns d1 monitor
Blocked until d2 monitor is released	d1Thread [in d1.run( )]	d2Thread [in d2.run( )]	Blocked until d1 monitor is released

A heavily loaded system can delay the startup of d2Thread enough that the behavior executes in the same way as the first sequence. This illustrates an important issue when dealing with threads: different system loads can expose problems in the application and also generate different performance profiles. The situation is typically the reverse of this example, with a race condition not showing deadlocks on lightly loaded systems, while a heavily loaded system alters the application behavior sufficiently to change thread interaction and cause deadlock. Bugs like this are extremely difficult to track down.

The Deadlock class is defined as follows:

```
package tuning.threads;

public class Deadlock implements Runnable
{
  String me;
  Deadlock other;

  public synchronized void hello( )
  {
    //print out hello from this thread then sleep one second.
    System.out.println(me + " says hello");
    try {Thread.sleep(1000);}
```

```
    catch (InterruptedException e) { }
  }

  public void init(String name, Deadlock friend)
  {
    //We have a name, and a reference to the other Deadlock object
    //so that we can call each other
    me = name;
    other = friend;
  }

  public static void main(String args[ ])
  {
    //wait as long as the argument suggests (or use 20 ms as default)
    int wait = args.length == 0 ? 20 : Integer.parseInt(args[0]);

    Deadlock d1 = new Deadlock( );
    Deadlock d2 = new Deadlock( );

    //make sure the Deadlock objects know each other
    d1.init("d1", d2);
    d2.init("d2", d1);

    Thread d1Thread = new Thread(d1);
    Thread d2Thread = new Thread(d2);

    //Start the first thread, then wait as long as
    //instructed before starting the other
    d1Thread.start( );
    try {Thread.sleep(wait);}
    catch (InterruptedException e) { }
    d2Thread.start( );
  }

  public synchronized void run( )
  {
    //We say we're starting, then sleep half a second.
    System.out.println("Starting thread " + me);
    try {Thread.sleep(500);}
    catch (InterruptedException e) { }

    //Then we say we're calling the other guy's hello( ), and do so
    System.out.println("Calling hello from " + me + " to " + other.me);
    other.hello( );
    System.out.println("Ending thread " + me);
  }
}
```

Synchronization Overhead

There are two separate costs of synchronization. First, there is the operational cost of managing the monitors. This overhead can be significant: acquiring and testing for

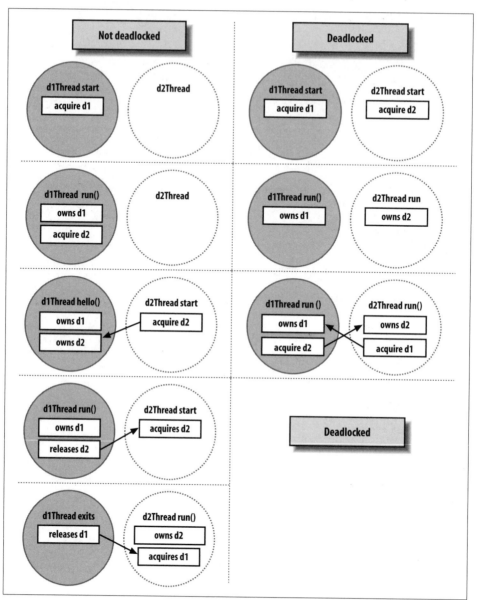

Figure 10-2. The difference between nondeadlocked and deadlocked execution

locks on the monitor for every synchronized method and block can impose a lot of overhead. Attempting to acquire a lock must itself be a synchronized activity within the VM; otherwise, two threads can simultaneously execute the lock-acquisition code. This overhead can be reduced by clever techniques in the VM, but never completely eliminated. The next section addresses this overhead and looks at ways to avoid it whenever possible.

Attempts to lock on different objects in two threads must still be synchronized to ensure that the object identity check and granting of the lock are handled atomically. This means that even attempting to get a lock on any object by two or more threads at the same time can still cause a performance degradation, as the VM grants only one thread at a time access to the lock-acquisition routine.

In some VMs, synchronizing static methods takes significantly longer than synchronizing nonstatic methods, suggesting that code is global in these VMs for the static synchronizations. (This is not strictly speaking a bug, but certainly not optimal for performance.)

The second cost of synchronization is in what it actually does. Synchronization serializes execution of a set of statements so that only one thread at a time executes that set. Whenever multiple threads simultaneously try to execute the same synchronized block, those threads are effectively run together as one single thread. This completely negates the purpose of having multiple threads and is potentially a huge bottleneck in any program. On machines with multiple CPUs, you can leave all but one CPU idle when serialized execution occurs. The later section "Avoiding Serialized Execution" addresses techniques for avoiding serialized execution where possible.

Desynchronization and Synchronized Wrappers

As we just noted, synchronized methods have performance costs. In fact, for short methods, using a synchronized method can mean that the basic time involved in calling the method is significantly larger than the time for actually running it. The overhead of calling an unsynchronized method can be much smaller than that of calling a synchronized method.

You should be aware of when you do not need to synchronize. Read-only objects never need synchronization. Stateless objects (including no-static state) almost never need synchronization on their methods. (There are certain unusual implementations when methods may be altering state directly in another shared object, where synchronization would be required.) Some objects with state may have no need for synchronization because access to the object is highly restricted, and the synchronization is handled by other objects. Some objects can implement a copy-on-write mechanism (StringBuffer uses this; see Chapter 5). You can define copy-on-write in such a way to allow multithreaded updates of that object.

Many multithreaded applications actually use most of their objects in a single-threaded manner. Each individual thread maintains its own references to most objects, with just a few data or utility objects actually being used by multiple threads. From a performance standpoint, it seems a shame to have the overhead of synchronized objects on many classes where synchronization is not needed or used. On the other hand, when you design and build a particular class, it is seldom possible to anticipate that it will never be shared among several threads, so to be on the safe side, typically the class is built with synchronization.

When you have identified a bottleneck that uses synchronized objects, you can sometimes remove synchronization on those objects by giving different threads their own unsynchronized copies of those objects. This is especially easy to achieve when you use objects that have an unsynchronized implementation held in a *synchronized wrapper*.

The idea behind synchronized wrappers is that you build your class completely unsynchronized, as if it is to be used single-threaded. But you also provide a wrapper class with exactly the same interface. The difference in the wrapper class is that all methods that require synchronization are defined with the synchronized modifier. The wrapper could be a subclass with methods reimplemented, but more typically, it is a separate class that holds an internal reference to an instance of the unsynchronized class and wraps all the methods to call that internal object. Using synchronized wrappers allows you the benefits of thread-safe objects by default, while still retaining the capability to selectively use unsynchronized versions of those classes in bottlenecks.

From Java 2, the framework of using synchronized wrappers has become standard. All the new collection classes in java.util are now defined unsynchronized, with synchronized wrappers available. Old collection classes (e.g., Hashtable, Vector) that are already synchronized remain so for backward compatibility. The wrappers are usually generic, so you can actually create wrapped synchronized objects from any object of the right type.

I include a short example of the synchronized-wrapper framework here for clarity. If class UnsyncedAdder is defined as follows:

```
public interface Adder {
  public void add(int aNumber);
}

public class UnsyncedAdder
  implements Adder
{
  int total;
  int numAdditions;
  public void add(int aNumber) {total += aNumber; numAdditions++;}
}
```

Then the synchronized wrapper for this class can be:

```
public class SyncedAdder
  implements Adder
{
  Adder adder;
  public SyncedAdder(Adder a) {adder = a;}
  public synchronized void add(int aNumber) { adder.add(aNumber);}
}
```

Obviously, you refer to Adder objects in your code; don't refer explicitly to concrete implementations of Adder classes (such as UnsyncedAdder and SyncedAdder) except in the constructor or factory classes. Note that the synchronized wrapper is completely generic. It wraps any implementation of Adder, providing synchronization on the add( ) method irrespective of the underlying concrete implementation of the Adder class.

Using unsynchronized classes gives a performance advantage, but it is a maintenance drawback. There is every likelihood that initial implementation of any application will use the unsynchronized classes by default, leading to many subtle threading bugs that can be a debugging and maintenance nightmare. Typical development scenarios then try to identify which objects need to be synchronized for the application, and then wrap those objects in their synchronized wrappers.

Under the stress of project milestones, I know of one project where the developers went through all their code with a recursive routine, chopping out every synchronized keyword in method declarations. This seemed quicker than carefully tuning the code, and did in fact give a performance improvement. They put a few synchronized keywords back in after the regression tests. This type of tuning is exactly the opposite of what I recommend.

Instead, you should use synchronized wrapped objects throughout the application by default, but ensure that you have the capability to easily replace these with the unsynchronized underlying objects. (Remember, tuning is better done after the application works correctly, not at the beginning.) When you come to tune the application, identify the bottlenecks. Then, when you find that a particular class needs to be speeded up, determine whether that class can be used unsynchronized. If so, replace it with its unsynchronized underlying object, and document this thoroughly. Any changes in the application must reexamine these particular tuning changes to ensure that these objects do not subsequently need to become synchronized.*

Be aware, though, that there is no win-win situation here. If you tend toward unsynchronized classes by default, you leave your application open to corruption. If you prefer my recommended "synchronized by default" approach, your application has an increased chance of encountering deadlocks. On the basis that deadlocks are both more obvious and easier to fix than corrupt objects, I prefer the "synchronized by default" option. Implementing with interfaces and synchronized wrappers gives you an easy way to selectively back out of synchronization problems.

The next test gives you an idea of the relative performance of synchronized and unsynchronized methods, and of synchronized wrappers. The test compares synchronized (Vector), unsynchronized (ArrayList), and synchronized wrapper (ArrayList wrapped) classes.

---

* When the design indicates that a class or a set of methods should definitely be synchronized or definitely does not need synchronization, then of course you should apply that design decision. For example, stateless objects can often be specified with no synchronization. However, there are many classes and methods where this decision is uncertain, and this is where my recommendation applies.

```
package tuning.threads;

import java.util.*;

public class ListTesting
{
  public static final int CAPACITY = 100000;
  public static void main(String args[])
  {
    //In order to isolate the effects of synchronization, we make sure
    //that the garbage collector doesn't interfere with the test. So
    //we use a bunch of pre-allocated, pre-sized collections, and
    //populate those collections with pre-existing objects. No objects
    //will be created or released during the timing phase of the tests.
    List[] l = {new Vector(CAPACITY), new Vector(CAPACITY),
      new Vector(CAPACITY), new ArrayList(CAPACITY),
      new ArrayList(CAPACITY), new ArrayList(CAPACITY),
      Collections.synchronizedList(new ArrayList(CAPACITY)),
      Collections.synchronizedList(new ArrayList(CAPACITY)),
      Collections.synchronizedList(new ArrayList(CAPACITY))};
    int REPEAT = (args.length > 0) ? Integer.parseInt(args[0]) : 100;

    //Vary the order.
    test(l[0], REPEAT, "Vector");
    test(l[6], REPEAT, "sync ArrayList" );
    test(l[3], REPEAT, "ArrayList");
    test(l[1], REPEAT, "Vector");
    test(l[4], REPEAT, "ArrayList");
    test(l[7], REPEAT, "sync ArrayList" );
    test(l[2], REPEAT, "Vector");
    test(l[5], REPEAT, "ArrayList");
    test(l[8], REPEAT, "sync ArrayList" );
  }

  public static void test(List l, int REPEAT, String ltype)
  {
    //need to initialize for set() to work. Don't measure this time
    for (int j = 0; j < CAPACITY; j++)
      l.add(Boolean.FALSE);

    long time = System.currentTimeMillis();
    //The test sets elements repeatedly. The set methods are
    //very similar. Apart from synchronization, the Vector.set()
    //is slightly more efficient than the ArrayList.set(), which
    //is in turn more efficient than the wrapped ArrayList because
    //there is one extra layer of method calls for the wrapped object.
    for (int i = REPEAT; i > 0; i--)
      for (int j = 0; j < CAPACITY; j++)
        l.set(j, Boolean.TRUE);
    System.out.println(ltype + " took " +
      (System.currentTimeMillis()-time));
  }
}
```

The normalized results from running this test are shown in Table 10-3.

Table 10-3. Timings of the various array-manipulation tests, normalized to the JDK 1.2 Vector test

	1.2.2	1.3.1_02	1.3.1_02 -server	1.4.0	1.4.0 -server	1.4.0 -Xint
Vector	100%	16%	15%	20%	12%	134%
ArrayList	15%	14%	9%	14%	13%[a]	166%
Wrapped ArrayList	131%	23%	18%	26%	19%	231%

[a] Note that the Vector.set( ) method implementation is slightly more efficient (faster) than the ArrayList.set( ) implementation, so if there were no effect from the synchronization, the Vector test could be slightly faster than the ArrayList test.

There are some reports that the latest VMs have negligible overhead for synchronized methods; however, my own tests show that synchronized methods continue to incur some overhead (VMs up to and including JDK 1.4). The 1.4 server-mode test is the only VM that shows negligible overhead from synchronized methods. This comes from server mode's aggressive inlining together with being able to analyze the requirement for acquiring the lock. In this case, the test is fairly simple, and it looks like the 1.4 server mode is able to establish that the lock does not need acquiring on each pass of the loop and to correctly optimize the situation. In more complex real-world situations, server mode is not always able to optimize away the lock acquisition so well. On the other hand, I shouldn't underplay the fact that the latest 1.3 and 1.4 VMs all do very well in minimizing the synchronization overhead (especially the 1.4 server mode), so much so that synchronization overhead should not be an issue for most applications.

Avoiding Serialized Execution

One way of completely avoiding the requirement to synchronize methods is to use separate objects and storage structures for different threads. Care must be taken to avoid calling synchronized methods from your own methods, or you will lose all your carefully built benefits. For example, Hashtable access and update methods are synchronized, so using one in your storage structure can eliminate any desired benefit. Prior to JDK 1.2, there is no unsynchronized hash table in the JDK, and you have to build or buy your own unsynchronized version. From JDK 1.2, unsynchronized collection classes are available, including Map classes.

As an example of implementing this framework, I look at a simple set of global counters, keyed on a numeric identifier. Basically, the concept is a global counter to which any thread can add a number. This concept is extended slightly to allow for multiple counters, each counter having a different key. String keys are more useful, but for simplicity I use integer keys in this example. To use String keys, an unsynchronized Map replaces the arrays.

The simple, straightforward version of the class looks like this:

```
package tuning.threads;

public class Counter1
{
  //For simplicity make just 10 counters
  static long[ ] vec = new long[10];

  public static void initialize(int key)
  {
    vec[key] = 0;
  }

  //And also just make key the index into the array
  public static void addAmount(int key, long amount)
  {
    //This is not atomically synchronized since we do an array
    //access together with an update, which are two operations.
    vec[key] += amount;
  }

  public static long getAmount(int key)
  {
    return vec[key];
  }
}
```

This class is basic and easy to understand. Unfortunately, it is not thread-safe and leads to corrupt counter values when used. A test run on a particular single-processor system with four threads running simultaneously, each adding the number 1 to the same key 10 million times, gives a final counter value of around 26 million instead of the correct 40 million.* On the positive side, the test is blazingly fast, taking very little time to complete and get the wrong answer.

To get the correct behavior, you need to synchronize the update methods in the class. Here is Counter2, which is just Counter1 with the methods synchronized:

```
package tuning.threads;

public class Counter2
{
  //For simplicity make just 10 counters
  static long[ ] vec = new long[10];

  public static synchronized void initialize(int key)
```

---

* The results discussed are for one particular test run. On other test runs, the final value is different, but it is almost never the correct value (40 million). If I use a faster CPU or a lower total count, the threads can get serialized by the operating system (by finishing quickly enough), leading to consistently correct results for the total count. But those correct results are an artifact of the environment and are not guaranteed. Other system loads and environments generate corrupt values.

```
    {
      vec[key] = 0;
    }

    //And also make the just make key the index into the array
    public static synchronized void addAmount(int key, long amount)
    {
      //Now the method is synchronized, so we will always
      //complete any particular update
      vec[key] += amount;
    }
    public static synchronized long getAmount(int key)
    {
      return vec[key];
    }
  }
```

Now you get the correct answer of 40 million. Unfortunately, the test takes 20 times longer to execute (see Table 10-4). Avoiding the synchronization is going to be more work. To do this, create a set of counters, one for each thread, and update each thread's counter separately.* When you want to see the global total, you need to sum the counters across the threads. The class definition follows:

```
package tuning.threads;

public class Counter3
{
  //support up to 10 threads of 10 counters
  static long vec[ ][ ] = new long[10][ ];

  public static synchronized void initialize(CounterTest t)
  {
    //For simplicity make just 10 counters per thread
    vec[t.num] = new long[10];
  }

  public static void addAmount(int key, long amount)
  {
    //Use our own threads to make the mapping easier,
    //and to illustrate the technique of customizing threads.
    //For generic Thread objects, could use an unsynchronized
    //HashMap or other Map,
    //Or use ThreadLocal if JDK 1.2 is available

    //We use the num instance variable of the CounterTest
    //object to determine which array we are going to increment.
    //Since each thread is different, here is no conflict.
```

---

* ThreadLocal variables might be appropriate here, but not in JDK 1.2, which used an underlying implementation of a synchronized map to allocate pre-thread objects. That implementation would defeat our intention to avoid synchronization completely. JDK 1.3 uses an instance variable in the Thread object to hold an unsynchronized map and would work.

```
    //Each thread updates its own counter.
    long[ ] arr = vec[((CounterTest) Thread.currentThread( )).num];
    arr[key] += amount;
  }
  public static synchronized long getAmount(int key)
  {
    //The current amount must be aggregated across the thread
    //storage arrays. This needs to be synchronized, but
    //does not matter here as I just call it at the end.
    long amount = 0;
    for (int threadnum = vec.length-1; threadnum >= 0 ; threadnum--)
    {
      long[ ] arr = vec[threadnum];
      if (arr != null)
        amount += arr[key];
    }
    return amount;
  }
}
```

Using Counter3, you get the correct answer for the global counter, and the test is quicker than Counter2. The relative timings for a range of VMs are listed in Table 10-4.

Table 10-4. Timings of the various counter tests, normalized to the JDK 1.2 Counter2 test

	1.1.8	1.2.2	1.3.1_02	1.3.1_02 -server	1.4.0	1.4.0 -server	1.4.0 -Xint
Counter2	24.8%	100%	124%	130%	123%	131%	131%
Counter3	1.5%	1.7%	2.2%	2%	2.4%	0.01%	5.7%
Counter1 (incorrect result)	0.2%	0.2%	0.2%	0.01%	0.1%	0.01%	1.9%

The serialized execution avoidance class is a significant improvement on the synchronized case. The Counter2 timings can be extremely variable. This variation is generated from the nature of multithreaded context switching, together with the fact that the activity taking much of the time in this test is lock management. Switching is essentially unpredictable, and the amount of switching and where it occurs affects how often the VM has to release and reacquire locks in different threads. Nevertheless, across a number of measurements, Counter3 was always faster than Counter2, normally orders of magnitude faster.

The listed times were measured on a single-processor machine. Consider what happens on a multiprocessor machine where the threads can run on different CPUs (i.e., where the Java runtime and operating system support preemptive thread scheduling on separate CPUs). Counter3 (the serialized execution avoidance class) is parallelized automatically and scales very nicely. This same test with Counter3 running on a four-CPU machine tends towards one-quarter of the single-CPU time, assuming that the four CPUs have the same power as the single CPU we tested earlier. On the other hand, the synchronized version of the counter, Counter2, always has serialized execution (that's what synchronized does). Consequently, it does not scale and generally performs no better than in the single-CPU test (except for the advantage of running the OS on another CPU).

Timing Multithreaded Tests

I measured timings of the three Counter classes in the previous section using another class, CounterTest. This timing class illustrates some pitfalls you need to avoid when timing multithreaded applications, so I'll go into a little detail about the CounterTest definition.

The first naive implementation of CounterTest is quite simple. Just create a Thread subclass with the run( ) method running timed tests of the classes you are measuring. You need an extra instance variable for the Counter3 class, so the class can be defined as:

```
package tuning.threads;

public class CounterTest
  extends Thread
{
  //instance variable to specify which thread we are.
  int num;

  public CounterTest(int threadnum)
  {
    super( );
    num = threadnum;
  }

  // main forks four threads
  public static void main(String[ ] args)
  {
    int REPEAT = (args.length > 0) ? Integer.parseInt(args[0]) : 10000000;
    for (int i = 0; i < 4; i++)
      (new CounterTest(i)).start( );
  }

  public void run( )
  {
    Counter1.initialize(0);
    long time = System.currentTimeMillis( );
    for (int i = REPEAT; i > 0; i--)
      Counter1.addAmount(0, 1);
    System.out.println("Counter1 count: " + Counter1.getAmount(0)
      + " time: " + (System.currentTimeMillis( )-time));

    Counter2.initialize(0);
    time = System.currentTimeMillis( );
    for (int i = REPEAT; i > 0; i--)
      Counter2.addAmount(0, 1);
```

```
System.out.println("Counter2 count: " + Counter2.getAmount(0)
    + " time: " + (System.currentTimeMillis()-time));

Counter3.initialize(this);
time = System.currentTimeMillis();
for (int i = REPEAT; i > 0; i--)
    Counter3.addAmount(0, 1);
System.out.println("Counter3 count: " + Counter3.getAmount(0)
    + " time: " + (System.currentTimeMillis()-time));
    }
}
```

Unfortunately, this class has two big problems. First, there is no way of knowing that the four threads are running the same test at the same time. With this implementation, it is perfectly possible that one thread is running the Counter1 test while another has already finished that test and is now running the Counter2 test concurrently. This gives incorrect times for both tests because the CPU is being used by another test while you measure the first test. And the synchronization costs are not measured properly because the intention is to test the synchronization costs of running four threads using the same methods at the same time.

The second problem is with the times being measured. The timings are for each thread running its own threaded update to the Counter class. But we should be measuring the time from the first update in any thread to the last update in any thread.

One way to avoid the first pitfall is to synchronize the tests so that they are not started until all the threads are ready. Then all threads can be started at the same time. The second pitfall can be avoided by setting a global time at the start of the first update, then printing the time difference when the last thread finishes.

The full tuning.threads.CounterTest implementation with the correct handling for measurements can be found, along with all the other classes from this book, at *http://www.oreilly.com/catalog/javapt2/*.

Atomic Access and Assignment

Variables shared between multiple threads (e.g., instance variables of objects) have atomic assignment guaranteed by the Java language specification for all data types except longs and doubles. Actually, the storing of a value into a variable takes two primitive operations, a *store* and a *write*. However, the language specification also states that once a store operation occurs on a particular variable, no other store operation is allowed on that variable until the write operation has occurred. The (original[*])

---

[*] The Java memory model specification is being changed. Java Specification Request 133, "Java Memory Model and Thread Specification Revision," addresses the various problems in the existing specification. Chapter 17 of the Java language specification and Chapter 8 of the Java Virtual Machine specification are proposed to be revised substantially. I'm very grateful to Brian Goetz for clarifying several points in this section.

specification allows longs and doubles to be stored in two separate sets of store+write operations, hence their exception to atomicity. A similar atomic specification applies for reading variables.

This means that access and update of individual variables does not need to be synchronized simply to avoid corruption (as long as they are not longs or doubles). If a method consists solely of a single variable access or assignment, there is no need to make it synchronized for thread-safety, and every reason not to do so for performance.

Note that I'm talking about using synchronization for thread-safety here, not synchronization for visibility of updates and accesses of variables. First, read the later "Synchronization Ordering" sidebar to ensure that you understand that synchronization provides no guarantees about the ordering of execution among different threads. Bearing that in mind, atomic access and update once again do not provide any guarantees about ordering of variables. Furthermore, unlike synchronization, atomic access and update do not provide any guarantee about *timely* synchronization between values of a variable held in different threads. When a synchronized block is passed, all the variables in a thread have been updated to the values in the "master" memory: they are *synchronized*. However, that synchronization does not occur with a simple atomic access or update. This means that for a variable that is atomically assigned to outside of a synchronized block, theoretically a thread could see a different value from the "master" memory for that variable for an extended period of time. Some other Java authors have suggested that this is dangerous. And while this book is full of dangerous advice, I don't believe this particular performance-tuning technique is any more dangerous than many other techniques. Specifically, if two or more variables don't need to be consistent with each other or vary consistently among themselves over time, you can trade some delay in propagation between threads for some extra performance. If you have two variables that have to be consistent with each other at all times across threads, such as the X and Y values of a shared point or a variable that has to vary consistently over time between multiple threads, then you need to synchronize. And in the case of variables needing to remain consistent with each other, atomic assignment is still fine for the individual variables, but the combined assignment needs to be synchronized (see the examples discussed shortly).

The concern here is primarily that you might read a variable in one thread, thread1, but meanwhile that variable has been updated in another thread, thread2, and the value has not propagated to thread1. The lack of guarantee of any ordering between threads means that this can occur even with synchronized variables because the read can occur prior to the update. But the difference is that with atomic access, even after thread2 updates its variable, thread1 doesn't necessarily see that updated value until a synchronization takes place. But note that the synchronization does take place as soon as *any* synchronized block is passed in thread1. For the vast majority of programs, there is no issue with using atomic access and update. The only place I have found where atomic access and update might easily be used but could cause a problem is

where a Runnable thread has a stopping condition dependent on a variable being set
from another thread, *and* the thread never enters a synchronized block. For example:

```
class SomeClass implements Runnable
{
  boolean dontStop = true;
  public void run( )
  {
    //dontStop is set to false from another thread
    //when it wants this thread to terminate.
    while(dontStop)
    {
      //Loop body NEVER enters ANY synchronized blocks
      //which is pretty unusual except for animations
    }
  }
}
```

In this situation, you are actually better off declaring the dontStop variable as
volatile rather than changing the test to access a synchronized dontStop( ) method
because that is precisely the appropriate usage for volatile, and you don't incur synchronization overhead.

> The volatile keyword specifies that the variable declared volatile
> must always have its value updated to the "main" memory value. So
> threads are not allowed to have a value for that variable that is differ-
> ent from the main memory value at any time. As a consequence,
> volatile variables can be slower than non-volatile variables because
> of the extra requirement to always synchronize the variable, but faster
> than synchronized access and updates because volatile synchronizes
> only one variable whereas synchronization synchronizes all variables.

The thread-safety of atomic accesses and updates extends further to any set of statements that are accessing or assigning to a variable independently of any other variable values. The exclusion here precludes setting a variable that depends on the value
of another variable being thread-safe; this would be two separate operations, which
is inherently not thread-safe. For example, these methods:

```
public void setMe(Object o) {me = o;}
public Object getMe( ) {return me;}
```

are individually thread-safe, with no need for synchronized modifiers to be added to
the method declaration. On the other hand, this method:

```
public void setMe(Object o) {if(overwrite) me = o;}
```

is not thread-safe: overwrite may be true at the time of checking in the if statement,
but false by the time of the subsequent assignment statement. Anything more complex than simple assignments and accesses is probably not thread-safe: it depends on
whether any particular intermediate state that can be accessed is considered corrupt
by the application. Consider the code being halted before or after any particular

atomic statement, and decide whether or not another thread could now access a corrupt application state.

Combining several calls to methods that atomically assign variables is the same problem as combining several calls to synchronized methods. The individual calls are executed atomically, but the combination is not necessarily atomic:

```
public void setMe1(Object o) {me = o;}
public void setMe2(Object o) {me = o;}
public void setBoth(Object o1, Object o2) {setMe1(o1);setMe2(o2);}
```

For these three methods, it does not matter whether setMe1( ) and setMe2( ) are synchronized. setBoth( ) is not synchronized, so it can be interrupted between the calls to setMe1( ) and setMe2( ), allowing another thread to update one of the instance variables. This can leave the object in a potentially corrupt application state if both instance variables are always supposed to be updated together. Specifically, if two threads call the setBoth( ) method simultaneously, the outcome is not predictable unless setBoth( ) is synchronized. Even the simple example of setInt(getInt( )+1) is not thread-safe; without synchronizing the whole statement you could lose the increment.

A longer discussion about Java's atomicity can be found in an article by Art Jolin,[*] where he discusses unsynchronized thread-safe data structures, including why a binary tree (specifically the AWTEventMulticaster class) can be thread-safe without any synchronized methods.

Thread Pools

The VM is optimized for creating threads, so you can usually create a new thread when you need to without having to worry about performance. But in some circumstances, maintaining a pool of threads can improve performance. For example, in a case where you would otherwise create and destroy many short-lived threads, you are far better off holding onto a (variable-sized) pool of threads. Here, the tasks are assigned to an already created thread, and when a thread completes its task, it is returned to the pool, ready for the next task. This improves performance because thread creation (and, to some extent, destruction) does have a significant overhead that is better avoided for short-lived threads.

A second situation is where you want to limit the number of threads in your application. In this case, your application needs to make all thread requests through a centralized pool manager. Although a pool manager does not prevent other threads from being started, it is a big step toward that goal. (Strictly speaking, limiting threads does not require a pool of threads, just a centralized pool manager, but the

---

[*] "Java's Atomic Assignment," *Java Report*, August 1998.

Synchronization Ordering

It is easy to misunderstand exactly what synchronization does. Synchronization ensures that a set of statements executes exclusively for a particular monitor. Synchronization does not guarantee the relative order of execution of synchronized blocks between threads. If two threads try to execute a synchronized block simultaneously, one succeeds first, but there is no guarantee about which one that is.

Atomic assignment is similar to the case where the set of synchronized statements is one statement, and the synchronization is set by the VM. When considering atomic assignment, you might ask the question, "What if a context switch occurs during the method call setup or tear down? When does the synchronization happen, and what happens with the context switch?" The actual moment when the synchronization occurs does not matter. It does not matter if a context switch happens at any time before or after a set of synchronized statements. Either the synchronized set has not been entered, or it has been completed. Only the actual granting of the lock matters, and that is atomic with respect to all interested threads.

Until you reach an atomic assignment statement, it makes no difference whether another atomic assignment on the same variable occurs. This is purely the ordering of assignments, which is not guaranteed with synchronization anyway. After the atomic assignment is finished, it is complete. A context switch hitting the method tear down does not matter. The usual reason to synchronize a simple updator is to avoid a corrupt assignment (two threads simultaneously updating the same variable, and the resulting value being neither of the updated values). This can indeed occur for doubles and longs, but not for other data types.

For serious number crunching involving doubles and longs, I recommend using separate data structures for each thread or using a VM that guarantees atomic assignment for doubles and longs.

two usually come together.) Every system has a response curve with diminishing returns after a certain number of threads are running on it. This response curve is different for different systems, and you need to identify values for your particular setup. A heavy-duty server needs to show good behavior across a spectrum of loads, and at the high end, you don't want your server crashing when 10,000 requests try to spawn 10,000 threads; instead, you want the server response to degrade (e.g., by queuing requests) and maintain whatever maximum number of threads is optimal for the server system.

When deciding which thread to run next, there may be a slight gain by choosing the available thread that ran most recently. This thread is most likely to have its working set still fully in memory: the longer it has been since a thread was last used, the more likely it is that the thread has been paged or swapped out. Also, any caches (at any level of the system and application) that may apply are more likely to contain elements from the most recently used thread. By choosing the most recently used thread, paging and cache overhead may be minimized.

Thread pools can be completely generic if necessary. By using the `java.lang.reflect` package, you can execute any (public) methods from your threads, thus allowing you to implement a thread pool that can handle general requests that have not been anticipated or specified at implementation time.

Load Balancing

Load balancing is a technique for improving performance when many activities are processed concurrently. These activities could be in separate processes on different machines, in separate processes on the same machine, or in separate threads within the same process. The architecture makes no difference to the basic guidelines.

To support load balancing, a standard design is to have:

- One point of entry for all requests (the request queue)
- One or more request-processor objects behind the queue
- A mechanism for the queue to decide which processor to hand a particular request to

You also need communication lines between the queue and processors and a way to internally identify requests, but this is an obvious part of the infrastructure. The decision mechanism is typically a simple load-balancing system that distributes requests to those available processors. The request processors specify when they are available or busy. When the queue has a request to process, it chooses the first available request processor. Some applications need more complex decision-making, and use a decision mechanism that allocates requests depending on the type of request.

Our main concern with this architecture is that the queue is a potential bottleneck, so it must pass on requests quickly and be ready fairly continually.[*] The pool of request processors behind the queue can be running in one or more threads or processes, usually one request processor per thread. The pool of threaded request processors can be prestarted or started on demand, or you can have a combination of these. Typically for this kind of setup, there are configuration options that specify how many prestarted request processors there should be, the maximum number of request processors to have running simultaneously, and how long to wait before terminating a request processor since it last processed a request.

---

[*] The queue is also a single point of failure. For this reason, an advanced load-balancing design does not rely on a single queue. Instead, any queues in the application are distributed, redundantly copied, and monitored so that any queue failure results in only a small performance degradation at worst. Some designs use persistent queue elements so that a critical failure does not lose queued elements. The Java Messaging Service supports persistent queue elements.

Note that there is always a point of diminishing returns on response time versus the number of threads in a system. If you have too many threads running concurrently, the system's overall response time gets worse. The operating-system thread scheduler (or Java-system thread scheduler, if you're not using OS threads) spends more and more time managing threads, and this overhead takes up the CPU time rather than allowing the threads to run.

You also need to consider whether the queue object handles the responses (collecting them from the request processes and handing them back to the clients) or whether the request-processor objects can hand the responses back directly. The former design has the advantage that the client cannot get any direct access to the request-processor objects, but the disadvantage that you are introducing an unnecessary bottleneck in processing terms. The latter option (handing responses back directly), of course, has the opposite characteristics: no extra bottleneck, but access to client objects is enabled.

Free Load Balancing from TCP/IP

If you use sockets to handle incoming requests within one process, the operating system provides some load-balancing support. If you want, the operating system will provide the queue for free. TCP sockets can have multiple threads reading or accepting on them. A connectionless TCP server (such as a web server) performs the following process:

1. Opens a server socket.

2. Starts however many threads you want.

3. Each thread sits on a ServerSocket.accept( ) call, waiting for the call to return (all threads call accept( ) on the identical ServerSocket object).

4. Whenever a client connects to the server socket, the operating-system TCP stack hands the connection off to only one thread that is blocked on the accept( ) call. This is guaranteed behavior for TCP.

5. The thread that returns from the accept( ) call gets the client connection (Socket object), reads the request, processes it, and writes the request back (directly to the client).

6. The thread goes back into the accept( ) call, waiting for the next connection.

At any time, you can start further threads to scale up the server as long as each thread has access to the previously created ServerSocket object. TCP does not allow more than one ServerSocket object to be bound to the same port on any machine (actually, any one network interface). It is therefore not possible to have multiple separate processes (i.e., independent operating-system processes, rather than threads within one operating-system process) serving on the same server socket. (Strictly speaking, it is possible to fork a process into multiple system processes after the socket has been opened. This is a standard practice on Unix servers. Multiprocess TCP servers have some small disadvantages over multithreaded TCP servers, mainly when they need to communicate between themselves or use other expensive resources. However, multi-process TCP servers do have one big advantage over multithreaded servers, which is that if one server process crashes, the others can continue running independently, unaffected by the crash. Win32 does not support a fork procedure.)

With UDP sockets, the architecture can be slightly different, as you can open a UDP server socket on a port that already has a server socket bound to it. A UDP socket is not connection-oriented but packet-oriented, so there is no accept( ) call to wait on. Instead, all the threads (from potentially multiple system processes) sit on a read( ) call on the UDP socket, and the UDP stack hands off each incoming packet to just one of the threads that are waiting on the read( ). The server then has to use the information from the packet (either at the application level or the protocol level) to determine the return address to send the result of the processed request (again, directly back to the client).

Load-Balancing Classes

If you need to implement your own queuing system, you have to consider whether the queue controls the request processors, or whether the processors access the queue. The latter model is how the socket model works: each request processor sits on the queue and waits for it to pass a request. This looks rather like the following class:

```
public class PassiveRequestQueue
{
  //The queue of requests
  FIFO_Queue queue = new FIFO_Queue( );

  public synchronized void acceptRequest(Request r)
  {
    //Add to the queue, then notify all processors waiting
    //on the releaseRequest( ) method
    queue.add(r);
    notify( );
  }

  public synchronized Request releaseRequest( )
  {
    for(;;)
    {
      //if the queue is empty, just go back into the wait call
      if (queue.isEmpty( ))
        try {wait( );} catch (InterruptedException e){ }
      //Need to check again if the queue is empty, in case
      //we were interrupted
      if (!queue.isEmpty( ))
        return (Request) queue.pop( );
    }
  }
}
```

The former model, in which the request processors are passive and the queue actively manages them, looks more like the following class:

```
public class ActiveRequestQueue
  //subclass the passive queue that holds the behavior
  //needed for managing the queue of requests
  extends PassiveRequestQueue
  //and make us able to run in our own thread
  implements Runnable
{
  int MAXIMUM_NUM_SERVERS=3;

  //Data for the public queue - a list of private servers
  ActiveRequestQueue[] servers;

  //Data for the private (internal) queues
  //the RequestProcessor
  RequestProcessor requestProcessor;
  //Retain a handle on my thread so that we can easily access
  //it if we need control
  Thread myThread;
  //Keep a handle on the 'public' queue - the one that
  //actually holds the objects
  ActiveRequestQueue queueServer;
  //Availability
  boolean isAvailable = true;

  //Internal queue object - processes requests
  private ActiveRequestQueue(ActiveRequestQueue q)
  {
    queueServer = q;
    requestProcessor=new RequestProcessor();
  }

  //External queue object - accepts requests and manages a queue of them
  public ActiveRequestQueue(int num_servers)
  {
    //Create a pool of queue servers and start them in their own threads
    servers = new ActiveRequestQueue[num_servers];
    Thread t;
    for (int i = servers.length-1; i>=0 ; i--)
    {
      servers[i] = new ActiveRequestQueue(this);
      (t = new Thread(servers[i])).start();
      servers[i].myThread = t;
    }
  }

  public synchronized void acceptRequest(Request r)
  {
    //Override the super class accept to increase the number
    //of servers if they are all busy
```

```
    //If we already have the maximum number of threads,
    //just queue the request
    if (servers.length >= MAXIMUM_NUM_SERVERS)
    {
        super.acceptRequest(r);
        return;
    }

    //otherwise, if one of the servers is available, just queue
    //the request
    for (int i = servers.length-1; i>=0 ; i--)
    {
      if (servers[i].isAvailable())
      {
        super.acceptRequest(r);
        return;
      }
    }

    //otherwise, increase the server pool by one, then queue the request
    Thread t;
    ActiveRequestQueue[ ] tmp_servers = servers;
    servers = new ActiveRequestQueue[tmp_servers.length+1];
    System.arraycopy(tmp_servers, 0, servers, 0, tmp_servers.length);
    servers[tmp_servers.length] = new ActiveRequestQueue(this);
    (t = new Thread(servers[tmp_servers.length])).start();
    servers[tmp_servers.length].myThread = t;
    super.acceptRequest(r);
}

public void run()
{
  Request request;
  RequestResult result;

  //Private queues use this method.

  //Basically, we just ask the public server for a request.
  //The releaseRequest() method blocks until one is available.
  //Then we process it and start again.
  for(;;)
  {
    request = queueServer.releaseRequest();
    isAvailable = false;
    result = requestProcessor.processRequest(request);
    returnResult(result);
    isAvailable = true;
  }
}

public boolean isAvailable() { return isAvailable;}
public void returnResult(RequestResult r) { }
}
```

Note that the server classes as they stand can be tested with the following minimal implementations for support classes:

```
class FIFO_Queue {
  java.util.Stack v = new java.util.Stack();
  public void add(Object o){v.push(o);}
  public Object pop(){return v.pop();}
  public boolean isEmpty(){return v.isEmpty();}
}

class RequestProcessor {
  public RequestResult processRequest(Request r)
  {
    System.out.println("Processing request: " + r);
    try{Thread.sleep(2000);}catch(InterruptedException e){ }
    return new RequestResult();
  }
}

class RequestResult { }

class Request { }
```

A Load-Balancing Example

It may help to look at a concrete implementation of load balancing. I'll consider the task of downloading many pages from a web server as quickly as possible.

 It is impolite to batch-download at high speeds from a single web server. Automated programs that download multiple pages from web servers have a voluntary protocol they should adhere to. More information can be found at *http://www.robotstxt.org/wc/robots.html*. One point of the protocol is to avoid overloading web servers by downloading many pages at a high access rate. Automated download programs that are polite specifically stagger downloads over a long period in order to minimize the load on the web server.

The individual page download code is quite simple. Open a URL, read the data, and dump it into a local file:

```
/* Two args, the local file to put the downloaded page into,
 * and the URL where the page to download is.
 */
public static void dowload(String file, String url)
  throws IOException
{
  URL u = new URL(url);
  InputStream in = null;
  //Try repeatedly to get the page opened. Note that catching
  //all exceptions is not such a good idea here. It would be
  //much better to catch individual execption types and handle
  //them separately. Some exceptions should not lead to a repeated
```

```
     //attempt to access the page. But this definition is okay for testing.
     while(in == null)
       try{in = u.openStream( );}
       catch(Exception e){try {Thread.sleep(500);}catch(Exception e2){ }}
     FileOutputStream out = new FileOutputStream(file);
     byte[ ] buffer = new byte[8192];

     //read until the connection terminates (this is not a
     //keep-alive connection), and write to the file.
     int len = in.read(buffer);
     while(len != -1)
     {
       out.write(buffer, 0, len);
       len = in.read(buffer);
     }
     out.close( );
     in.close( );
   }
```

All our tests use this same download( ) method. The most straightforward test implementation is extremely simple. Simply take a list of URLs and corresponding data files, and loop calling download( ) for each URL/file pair:

```
//Use one array to hold alternate file and URL elements
public static void iterativeTest(String[ ] files)
  throws IOException
{
  for (int i = 0; i < files.length; i+=2)
    download(files[i], files[i+1]);
}
```

The opposite to downloading pages one by one is to try to download everything at the same time. Once again, the code is quite straightforward (apart from timing issues: see the earlier section "Timing Multithreaded Tests"). You simply define a Runnable class and loop, starting a thread for every download:

```
public class LoadBalancing
  implements Runnable
{
  String url;
  String localfilename;

  public static void massivelyParallelTest(String[ ] files)
    throws IOException
  {
    for (int i = 0; i < files.length; i+=2)
      (new Thread(new LoadBalancing(files[i], files[i+1]))).start( );
  }

  public LoadBalancing(String f, String u)
  {
    localfilename = f;
    url = s;
  }
```

```
public void run()
{
    try
    {
      download(localfilename, filename);
    }
    catch(Exception e) {e.printStackTrace();}
}
```

The earlier iterative test takes seven times longer than the latter multithreaded test.[*] However, the latter test suffers from significant resource problems. Creating so many threads simultaneously can seriously strain a system. In fact, every system has a limit to the number of threads it can create. If the download requires more threads than the system is capable of supporting, this multithreaded test fails to download many pages. In addition, with so many threads running simultaneously, you are using more of the system's resources than is optimal.

Let's look at a more balanced approach. In fact, you can create a very simple load-balanced test with one small variation to the last test. Simply add a delay between each thread creation to stagger the system load from threads and downloading. This new version of the massivelyParallelTest() method is simple:

```
public static void roughlyParallelTest(String[] files, int delay)
    throws IOException
{
  for (int i = 0; i < files.length; i+=2)
  {
    (new Thread(new LoadBalancing(files[i], files[i+1]))).start();
    try{Thread.sleep(delay);}catch(InterruptedException e){ }
  }
}
```

Now you have a tuning parameter that needs to be optimized. Obviously, a delay of zero is the same test as the previous test, and a very large delay means that the test is spending most of its time simply waiting to create the next thread. Somewhere in between is an optimal range that creates threads fast enough to fully use the system resources, but not so fast that the system is overloaded.

This range is different depending on the full environment, and probably needs to be experimentally determined. But you can make a decent first guess by considering the bottlenecks of the system. In this case, the bottlenecks are CPU, system memory, disk throughput, network-connection latency, server-download rates, and network throughput. In my tests, system memory and CPU limit the number of threads and download speed for the massively parallel case, but you are using a delay specifically

---

[*] For my tests, I downloaded a large number of pages. I validated the tests over the Internet, but not surprisingly, Internet access times are extremely variable. For detailed repeatable tests, I used a small local HTTP server that allowed me to control all the parameters to the tests very precisely. The full test class, tuning.threads.LoadBalancing, is available with the other classes from this book.

to reduce the load on those resources. System memory constrains the number of threads you can use, but again, the delay avoids overloading this resource (provided that the delay is not too short). Disk throughput can be significant, but network and server throughput are far more likely to limit data-transfer rates. So we are left with network-transfer rates and network-connection latency to consider.

Now you can make a good guess as to a starting point for the delay. You can evaluate the average number of bytes to transfer for each download, and work out the amount of time this takes based on the available network throughput. You can also estimate the average time taken to make a connection (by measuring some real connections). A straightforward guess is to set the delay at a value below the higher of these two averages. In my tests, the files being downloaded are not large, and the average connection time is the larger time. I started with a delay of about half the average connection time and ran tests increasing and decreasing the delay in steps of about 10% at a time. Figure 10-3 shows the results of varying the delay times. An optimum choice for the delay in this particular test environment is approximately 70% of the average connection time. The flat line in the middle of the graph shows the relative time taken for the massively parallel test.

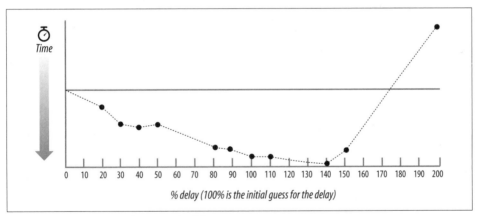

Figure 10-3. The results of varying the delay

The results show that for this environment there are several advantages to running with a delay. A decisive advantage is that you never run out of system resources. There are never so many threads running simultaneously that you run out of memory and completely lose URLs, as occurred with the massively parallel test. In fact, the system doesn't even need to run to full capacity for most of the test.

Another significant advantage is that by tuning the delay, you can run the test faster. The optimum value for the delay, at 70% of the average connection time, executes the full test in 90% of the massively parallel time.

What about our nice load-balancing architecture classes? Let's test these to see how they compare to the last simple optimization you made. You need to add a few support classes so that your load-balancing architecture is running the same download test. Basically, there are three classes to define: Request, RequestProcessor, and RequestResult. They are fairly simple to implement. Request needs to hold only a URL and a local file for storing the downloaded page. RequestProcessor simply needs to call the download( ) method. RequestResult does not need any extra behavior for the test.* The classes are as follows:

```
class RequestProcessor {
  public RequestResult processRequest(Request r)
  {
    try
    {
      LoadBalancing.dowload(r.localfilename, r.url);
    }
    catch(Exception e) {e.printStackTrace( );}
    return new RequestResult( );
  }
}

class Request
{
  String localfilename;
  String url;
  public Request(String f, String u)
  {
    localfilename = f;
    url = u;
  }
}

class RequestResult { }
```

In addition, of course, you need to define the method that kicks off the test itself:

```
public static void loadBalancedTest(String[ ] files, int numThreads)
  throws IOException
{
  ActiveRequestQueue server = new ActiveRequestQueue(numThreads);
  for (int i = 0; i < files.length; i+=2)
    server.acceptRequest(new Request(files[i], files[i+1]));
}
```

I have included a variable to determine the optimum number of threads. As with the earlier test that used a variable delay, the optimum number of threads for this test needs to be experimentally determined. For my test environment, the bottleneck is likely to be my small network throughput. This is easy to see: each thread

---

* RequestResult does need extra state and behavior in order to make timing measurements, and RequestProcessor is similarly a bit more complicated for timing purposes. For full details, see the test class, tuning.threads.LoadBalancing, which is available with the other classes from this book.

corresponds to one download. So for *n* threads to be working at full capacity, they need to be downloading *n* files, which amounts to a throughput of *n* times the average file size. This means that for my test environment, about 10 threads reach capacity. In fact, since files are not all the same size and there are some overheads in the architecture, I would expect the optimum number of threads to be slightly larger than 10.

Running the test with different numbers of threads shows that for 12 or more threads, the time taken is essentially the same (see Figure 10-4). This time is also the same as that achieved with the previous most optimal test. This is not surprising. Both tests optimized the downloads enough that they have reached the same network-throughput bottleneck. This bottleneck cannot be optimized any further by either test.

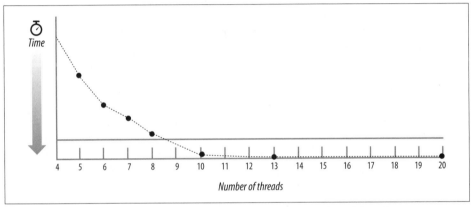

Figure 10-4. Time taken for the load-balanced download versus number of threads

The load-balancing architecture is more complex than adding a delay between threads, but it is much more flexible and far more controlled. If you want to vary your download in a number of ways, such as prioritizing URLs or repeating certain failed ones, it is much easier to do so with the load-balancing architecture. By looking at the CPU utilization graphs for the load-balancing architecture compared to the other tests in Figure 10-5, you can easily see how much more controlled it is and how it uses resources in a far more consistent manner.

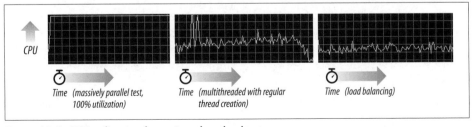

Figure 10-5. CPU utilization for various download tests

Threaded Problem-Solving Strategies

There are many techniques that reduce the time taken to solve intensive problems by using multiple threads to farm out parts of the problem. Here are a few strategies:

- Start multiple threads running to solve the whole of a particular problem, each starting from a different point in the solution space. The first to finish is the winner. This technique has, for instance, been used to speed up a graph-coloring problem. The specific strategy followed* was to run several problem solvers at the same time, one at a higher priority than the others (the main thread). Normally the main thread would win, but on occasion, one of the background threads was lucky due to its starting point and finished quickly. By stopping the main thread if it looked to be far behind in the solution, the problem was solved in one-tenth of the time, on average, compared to the time taken when the main thread was not terminated. This improvement occurred in spite of the fact that this was a single-processor machine. The improvement comes about because the problem can be solved much quicker from some starting points than from others. There would be similar improvements if you also used several different problem-solving strategies in the various threads, where some of the strategies are sometimes quicker than others.

- In the same article, a variation of this strategy was applied to network connections for bypassing congestion. By opening multiple connections to download the same large data source on a highly congested network (the Internet), some connections were less likely than others to be slowed significantly or broken. This resulted in the data being downloaded faster. Of course, if everyone on the network used this technique, downloads would be slower for everyone.

- Break up the search space into logically parallelized search spaces. This does not work too well if the problem is entirely CPU-bound, but if there is any significant I/O or if multiple processors are available, this technique works nicely. An example would be searching a disk-based database for items. If the database is partitioned into multiple segments, then having one thread searching per segment makes the search faster (both on average and in the worst case).

- The classic blackboard architecture approach, in which multiple different solvers work on the parts of a problem in which they have expertise, independently of other solver threads. The threads use a "blackboard" (a sort of globally accessible hash table with published keys) to communicate. The blackboard posts both intermediate and full results. This allows a thread to pick up any (intermediate or full) results other threads may publish that help that particular thread with its own problem-solving routines. JavaSpaces is an implementation of blackboards.

---

* Charles Seife, "A Snail's Pace," *New Scientist*, 21 February 1998. This article reports on the technique used by Bernardo Huberman of Xerox Parc.

Performance Checklist

Many of these suggestions apply only after a bottleneck has been identified:

- Include multithreading at the design stage.
  - Parallelize tasks with threads to speed up calculations.
  - Run slow operations in their own threads to avoid slowing down the main thread.
  - Keep the interface in a separate thread from other work so that the application feels more responsive.
  - Avoid designs and implementations that force points of serialized execution.
  - Use multiple resolution strategies racing in different threads to get quicker answers.
- Avoid locking more resources than necessary.
  - Avoid synchronizing methods of stateless objects.
  - Build classes with synchronized wrappers, and use synchronized versions except when unsynchronized versions are definitely sufficient.
  - Selectively unwrap synchronized wrapped classes to eliminate identified bottlenecks.
  - Avoid synchronized blocks by using thread-specific data structures, combining data only when necessary.
  - Use atomic assignment where applicable.
- Load-balance the application by distributing tasks among multiple threads, using a queue and thread-balancing mechanism for distributing tasks among task-processing threads.
  - Use thread pools to reuse threads if many threads are needed or if threads are needed for very short tasks.
  - Use a thread pool manager to limit the number of concurrent threads used.

CHAPTER 11

Appropriate Data Structures and Algorithms

In this chapter:
- Collections
- Java 2 Collections
- Hashtables and HashMaps
- Optimizing Queries
- Comparing LinkedLists and ArrayLists
- The RandomAccess Interface
- Cached Access
- Caching Examples
- Finding the Index for Partially Matched Strings
- Search Trees

And this is a table ma'am. What in essence it consists of is a horizontal rectilinear plane surface maintained by four vertical columnar supports, which we call legs. The tables in this laboratory, ma'am, are as advanced in design as one will find anywhere in the world.
—Michael Frayn
  The Tin Men

In this chapter, we look at the performance problems that can stem from using an inappropriate or nonoptimal data structure. Of course, I cannot cover every possible structure. Instead, my focus is on how to performance-tune structures and associated algorithms. Those structures I do cover are provided as examples to give you an idea of how the tuning procedure looks.

For performance-tuning purposes, be aware of alternative structures and algorithms, and always consider the possibility of switching to one of these alternatives rather than tuning the structure and algorithm that is already being used. Being aware of alternative data structures requires extensive reading of computer literature.[*] One place to start is with the JDK code. Look at the structures that are provided and make sure that you know all about the available classes. There are already several good books on data structures and algorithms in Java, as well as many packages available from the Web with extensive documentation and often source code too. Some popular computer magazines include articles about structures and algorithms (see Chapter 19).[†]

When tuning, you often need to switch one implementation of a class with a more optimal implementation. Switching data structures is easier because you are in an

---

[*] An interesting analysis of performance-tuning a "traveling salesman" problem is made by Jon Bentley in his article "Analysis of Algorithms," *Dr. Dobb's Journal*, April 1999.

[†] The classic reference is *The Art of Computer Programming* by Donald Knuth (Addison Wesley). A more Java-specific book is *Data Structures and Algorithm Analysis in Java* by Mark Weiss (Peachpit Press).

object-oriented environment, so you can usually replace one or a few classes with different implementations while keeping all the interfaces and signatures the same.

When tuning algorithms, one factor that should pop to the front of your mind concerns the scaling characteristics of the algorithms you use. For example, bubblesort is an $O(n^2)$ algorithm while quicksort is $O(nlogn)$. (The concept of "order of magnitude" statistics is described in "Better Than $O(nlogn)$ Sorting" in Chapter 9.) This tells you nothing about absolute times for using either of these algorithms for sorting elements, but it does clearly tell you that quicksort has better scaling characteristics, and so is likely to be a better candidate as your collections increase in size. Similarly, hash tables have an $O(1)$ searching algorithm where an array requires $O(n)$ searching.

Collections

Collections are the data structures that are most easily altered for performance-tuning purposes. Using the correct or most appropriate collection class can improve performance with little change to code. For example, if a large ordered collection has elements frequently deleted or inserted throughout it, it usually can provide better performance if based on a linked list rather than an array. On the other hand, a static (unchanging) collection that needs to be accessed by index performs better with an underlying implementation that is an array.

If the data is large and insertions are allowed (for example, a text buffer), then a common halfway measure is to use a *linked list of arrays*. This structure copies data within a single array when data is inserted or deleted. When an array gets filled, the collection inserts a new empty array immediately after the full array and moves some data from the full to the empty array so that both old and new arrays have space. A converse structure provides optimized indexed access to a linked-list structure by holding an array of a subset of the link nodes (e.g., every 20th node). This structure allows for quick navigation to the indexed nodes, and then slower nodal access to nodes in between.* The result is a linked-list implementation that is much faster at index access, though it occupies more space.

It is sometimes useful to provide two collections holding the same data so that the data can be accessed using the most appropriate (and fastest) procedure. This is common for indexed data (database-type indexes as opposed to array indexes), but entails extra overhead at the build stage. In a similar way, it may be that a particular data set is best held in two (or more) different collections over its lifetime, but with only one collection being used at any one time. For example, you may use a linked-list implementation of a vector type collection during building because your collection requires many insertions while it is being built. However, this provides

---

* Skip lists are an implementation of this concept. See "The Elegant (and Fast) Skip List" by T. Wenger, *Java Pro*, April-May 1998.

suboptimal random access. After the build is completed, the collection can be converted into one based on an array, thus speeding up access.

It can be difficult to identify optimal algorithms for particular data structures. For example, in the Java 2 java.util.Collections.sort( ) method, a linked list is first converted to an array in order to sort it. This is detrimental to performance, and it would be significantly faster to sort a linked list directly using a merge sort.* In any case, frequently converting between collections and arrays is likely to cause performance problems.

The fastest ordered collections available in Java are plain arrays (e.g., int[ ], Object[ ], etc.). The drawback to using these directly is the lack of object-oriented methodology you can apply. Arrays are not proper classes that can be extended. However, I occasionally find that there are situations when I want to pass these raw arrays directly between several classes rather than wrap the arrays in a class with the behavior required. This is unfortunate in design terms, but does provide speed. An example would be in some communications layers. Here, there are several layers of protocols you need to pass your message through before it is transmitted, for example, a compression layer and an encryption layer. If you use an object as a message being passed through these layers, each layer has to request the message contents (copying it), change the contents, and then assign back the new contents (copying again). An alternative is to implement the content-manipulation methods in the message object itself, which is not a very extensible architecture. Assuming that you use an array to hold the contents, you can allow the message-contents array itself to be passed directly to the other compression and encryption layer objects. This provides a big speedup, avoiding several copies. String objects also illustrate the point. If you want to iterate over the characters in a String, you must either repeatedly call String.charAt( ) or copy the characters into your own array using String.getChars( ), and then iterate over them. Depending on the size of the String and how many times you iterate through the characters, one or the other of these methods is quicker, but if you could iterate directly on the underlying char array, you would avoid the repeated method calls and the copy (see Chapter 5).

A final point is that the collections that come with Java and other packages are usually not type-specific. This generality comes at the cost of performance. For example, if you are using java.util.Vector to hold only String objects, then you have to keep casting to String each time you access elements. If you reimplement the Vector class yourself using an underlying String[ ] array, and then change signature parameters and return types of methods from Object to String, the reimplemented class is faster. It is also clearer to use: you get rid of all those casts from your code. The cost is that you lose the general collection interface (see "Replacing JDK Classes" in Chapter 3 for an example).

---

* See "Sorting and Searching Linked Lists in Java" by John Boyer, *Dr. Dobb's Journal*, May 1998.

It is straightforward to test the performance costs of generalized collections compared to specialized collections. Access that does not involve a cast takes place at essentially the same speed. All the following accesses take the same time:

```
int i =   integerArrayList.get(someIndex);
String s = stringArrayList.get(someIndex);
Object o = objectArrayList.get(someIndex);
```

But the cost of a cast can make the access take 50% longer:

```
//It can take 50% longer to access the string because of the cast
String s = (String) objectArrayList.get(someIndex);
```

Update time can also be significantly faster. Updates to underlying arrays of primitive data types can be 40% faster than updates to object arrays.[*] The biggest difference is when a primitive data type needs to be wrapped and unwrapped in order to store into an array:

```
//Simpler and much faster using a specialized IntArrayList
integerArrayList.set(someIndex, someNum);
int num = integerArrayList.get(someIndex);

//Using a generalized ArrayList requires wrapping, casting & unwrapping
integerArrayList.set(someIndex, new Integer(someNum));
int num = ((Integer) integerArrayList.get(someIndex, someNum)).intValue();
```

For this example, the cost of creating a new Integer object to wrap the int makes setting values take more than ten times longer when using the generalized array. Accessing is not as bad, taking only twice as long after including the extra cast and method access to get to the int.

 Note that Generics are due to be introduced in SDK 1.5. Generics allow instances of generic classes like Vector to be specified as aggregate objects that hold only specified types of objects. However, the implementation of Generics is to insert casts at all the access points and to analyze the updates to ensure that the update type matches the cast type. There is no specialized class generation, so there is no performance benefit, and there may even be a slight performance degradation from the additional casts.

Java 2 Collections

The Java 2 Collections framework provides a set of collection classes. Each class has its own performance strengths and weaknesses, which I cover here. The collection implementations use the synchronized-wrapper framework to provide synchronized

---

[*] Even updating a typed object array with objects of the given type (e.g., Strings into an underlying String[ ] array of an array list) seems to be faster by about 10%. The only reason I can think of for this is that the JIT compiler manages to optimize the update to the specialized array.

classes; otherwise, the implementations are unsynchronized (except for two exceptions noted shortly). Collection classes wrapped in synchronized wrappers are always slower than unwrapped, unsynchronized classes. Nevertheless, my recommendation is generally to use objects within synchronized wrappers. You can selectively "unwrap" objects when they have been identified as part of a bottleneck and when the synchronization is not necessary. (The performance aspects of thread-safe collections are discussed in detail in Chapter 10. Synchronized wrappers are also discussed in that chapter in the "Desynchronization and Synchronized Wrappers" section.)

Table 11-1 summarizes the performance attributes of the collection classes.

Table 11-1. Performance attributes of Java 2 collection classes

Interface	Class	Synchronized?	Performance attributes
Set	HashSet	No	Fastest Set; slower than HashMap but implements the Set interface (HashMap does not).
	LinkedHashSet	No	Available from 1.4. Based on a LinkedHashMap, so provides iteration of elements according to insertion order. Faster than a TreeSet.
	TreeSet	No	Slower than HashSet; provides iteration of keys in order.
Map	IdentityHashMap	No	Available from 1.4. Special-purpose HashMap based on identity ($==$) instead of equality (.equals). Faster than HashMap for high-performance mapping where the identity semantics are acceptable.
	HashMap	No	Fastest general Map.
	Hashtable	Yes	Slower than HashMap, but faster than synchronized HashMap.
	LinkedHashMap	No	Available from 1.4. A hash map implementation that also maintains an ordered linked list of entries. Provides iteration of keys in entry order. Faster than TreeMap but slower than other Maps.
	TreeMap	No	Slower than Hashtable and HashMap; provides iteration of keys in order.
List	ArrayList	No	Fastest List.
	Vector	Yes	Slower than ArrayList, but faster than synchronized ArrayList.
	Stack	Yes	Same speed as Vector; provides LIFO queue functionality.
	LinkedList	No	Slower than other Lists, but may be faster for some types of queues.

Implementations of Set are slower to update than most other collection objects and should be avoided unless you need Set functionality. Of the three available Set implementations, HashSet is definitely faster than TreeSet, with LinkedHashSet, available from SDK 1.4, somewhere in between. HashSet uses an underlying HashMap, so the way HashSet maintains uniqueness is straightforward. Objects are added to the set as the keys to the HashMap, so there is no need to search the set for the elements. This optimizes unique element addition. If you need Set functionality but not specifically a Set implementation, it is faster to use a HashMap directly.

Map has four general-purpose implementations: Hashtable, HashMap, TreeMap, and, added in SDK 1.4, LinkedHashMap. In addition, there are several specialized implementations that provide few performance improvements,* except for IdentityHashMap, added in 1.4. IdentityHashMap is based on identity comparisons rather than equality comparisons (equality comparisons form the basis for all *general*-purpose maps), making it the fastest useful Map. IdentityHashMap has one tuning parameter, the expected maximum size, which can help avoid rehashing by setting the number of buckets in the initial map.

In the case of the general-purpose Maps, TreeMap is significantly slower than the other Maps and should not be used unless you need the extra functionality of iterating ordered keys. LinkedHashMap also provides the ability to iterate its keys in order, with the default order being key-insertion order. LinkedHashMap should normally be faster than TreeMap, but slower than HashMap. Hashtable is a synchronized Map, and HashMap is an unsynchronized Map. Hashtable is present for backward compatibility with earlier versions of the JDK. Nevertheless, if you need to use a synchronized Map, a Hashtable is faster than using a HashMap in a synchronized wrapper.

Hashtable, HashMap, and HashSet are all O(1) for access and update, so they should scale nicely if you have the available memory space. LinkedHashMap is based on a hash table but also maintains a linked list of entries so it can use the linked list to iterate through the entries in a particular order: the default order is the insertion order of keys. LinkedHashMap can be configured to order its entries from most-recently-accessed to least-recently-accessed by passing true as the third argument to the constructor. This mode is specifically provided so that the Map can be used as a least-recently-used (LRU) cache. The class provides a method called removeEldestEntry( ) that is intended to be overriden in a subclass to provide a policy for automatically removing stale mappings when new mappings are added to the Map. The default action is to never remove any entries automatically (removeEldestEntry( ) always returns false). An example implementation for an LRU cache of 100 elements would simply subclass the LinkedHashMap and implement the removeEldestEntry( ) as return size( ) > 100, which would automatically remove entries whenever the collection exceeded 100 elements.

List has four general-purpose implementations: Vector, Stack, ArrayList, and LinkedList. Vector, Stack, and ArrayList have underlying implementations based on arrays. LinkedList has an underlying implementation consisting of a doubly linked list. As such, LinkedList's performance is worse than any of the other three Lists for most operations. For very large collections that you cannot presize to be large

---

* Attributes simply wraps a HashMap, and restricts the keys to be ASCII-character alphanumeric Strings, and values to be Strings. WeakHashMap can maintain a cache of elements that are automatically garbage-collected when memory gets low. RenderingHints is specialized for use within the AWT packages. Properties is a Hashtable subclass specialized for maintaining key-value string pairs in files. UIDefaults is specialized for use within the Swing packages.

enough, LinkedList provides better performance when adding or deleting elements toward the middle of the list, if the array-copying overhead of the other Lists is higher than the linear access time of the LinkedList. Otherwise, LinkedList's only likely performance advantage is as a first-in-first-out queue or double-ended queue. (A circular array-list implementation provides better performance for a FIFO queue.) I discuss the performance differences between LinkedLists and ArrayLists in much more detail later in this chapter. Vector is a synchronized List, and ArrayList is an unsynchronized List. Vector is present for backward compatibility with earlier versions of the JDK. Nevertheless, if you need to use a synchronized List, a Vector is faster than using an ArrayList in a synchronized wrapper. (See the comparison test at the end of "Desynchronization and Synchronized Wrappers" in Chapter 10.) Stack is a subclass of Vector with the same performance characteristics, but with additional functionality as a last-in-first-out queue.

Hashtables and HashMaps

Because Hashtables and HashMaps are the most commonly used nonlist structures, I will spend a little extra time discussing them. Hashtables and HashMaps are pretty fast and provide adequate performance for most purposes. I rarely find that I have a performance problem using Hashtables or HashMaps, but here are some points that will help you tune them or, if necessary, replace them:

- Hashtable is synchronized. That's fine if you are using it to share data across threads, but if you are using it single-threaded, you can replace it with an unsynchronized version to get a small boost in performance. HashMap is an unsynchronized version available from JDK 1.2.

- Hashtables and HashMaps are resized whenever the number of elements reaches the [capacity × loadFactor]. This requires reassigning every element to a new array using the rehashed values. This is not simply an array copy; every element needs to have its internal table position recalculated using the new table size for the hash function. You are usually better off setting an initial capacity that handles all the elements you want to add. This initial capacity should be the number of elements divided by the loadFactor (the default load factor is 0.75).

- Hashtables and HashMaps are faster with a smaller loadFactor, but take up more space. You have to decide how this tradeoff works best for you.

- The hashing function for most implementations should work better with a capacity that is a prime number. However, the 1.4 HashMap implementation (but not the Hashtable implementation) uses a different implementation that requires a power-of-two capacity so that it can use bit shifting and masking instead of the % operator. If you specify a non-power-of-two capacity, the HashMap will automatically find the nearest power-of-two value higher than the specified capacity.

For other hash maps, always use a prime (preferably) or odd number capacity. A useful prime number to remember is 89. The sequence of numbers generated by successively multiplying by two and adding one includes several primes when the sequence starts with 89. But note also that speedups from prime number capacities are small at best.

- Access to the Map requires asking the key for its hashCode( ) and also testing that the key equals( ) the key you are retrieving. You can create a specialized Map class that bypasses these calls if appropriate. Alternatively, you can use specialized key classes that have very fast method calls for these two methods. Note, for example, that Java String objects have hashCode( ) methods that iterate and execute arithmetic over a number of characters to determine the value, and the String. equals( ) method checks that every character is identical for the two strings being compared. Considering that strings are used as the most common keys in Hashtables, I'm often surprised to find that I *don't* have a performance problem with them, even for largish tables. From JDK 1.3, Strings cache their hash code in an instance variable, making them faster and more suited as Map keys.

- If you are building a specialized Hashtable, you can map objects to array elements to preallocate HashtableEntry objects and speed up access as well. The technique is illustrated in the "Search Trees" section later in this chapter.

- The hash function maps the entries to table elements. The fewer entries that map to the same internal table entry, the more efficient the map. There are techniques for creating more efficient hash maps, for instance, those discussed in my article "Optimizing Hash Functions For a Perfect Map" (see *http://www.onjava. com/pub/a/onjava/2001/01/25/hash_functions.html*).

Here is a specialized class to use for keys in a Hashtable. This example assumes that I am using String keys, but all my String objects are nonequal, and I can reference keys by identity. I use a utility class, tuning.dict.Dict, which holds a large array of nonequal words taken from an English dictionary. I compare the access times against all the keys using two different Hashtables, one using the plain String objects as keys, the other using my own StringWrapper objects as keys. The StringWrapper objects cache the hash value of the string and assume that equality comparison is the same as identity comparison. These are the fastest possible equals( ) and hashCode( ) methods. The access speedups are illustrated in the following table of measurements (times normalized to the JDK 1.2 case):

	1.1.8	1.2.2	1.3.1_02	1.3.1_02 -server	1.4.0	1.4.0 -server	1.4.0 -Xint
String keys[a]	112%	100%	40.8%	65.4%	41.2%	60.1%	181%
String-wrapped keys	87.4%	71.1%	40.3%	57.6%	38.4%	58.6%	159%

[a] The limited speedup from JDK 1.3 reflects the improved performance of Strings having their hash code cached in the String instance.

If you create a hash-table implementation specialized for the StringWrapper class, you avoid calling the hashCode( ) and equals( ) methods completely. Instead, the specialized hash table can access the hash-instance variable directly and use identity comparison of the elements. The speedup is considerably larger, and for specialized purposes, this is the route to follow:

```
package tuning.hash;

import java.util.Hashtable;
import tuning.dict.Dict;

public class SpecialKeyClass
{

  public static void main(String[] args)
  {
    //Initialize the dictionary
    try{Dict.initialize(true);}catch(Exception e){ }
    System.out.println("Started Test");

    //Build the two hash tables. Keep references to the
    //StringWrapper objects for later use as accessors.
    Hashtable h1 = new Hashtable( );
    Hashtable h2 = new Hashtable( );
    StringWrapper[ ] dict = new StringWrapper[Dict.DICT.length];
    for (int i = 0; i < Dict.DICT.length; i++)
    {
      h1.put(Dict.DICT[i], Boolean.TRUE);
      h2.put(dict[i] = new StringWrapper(Dict.DICT[i]), Boolean.TRUE);
    }
    System.out.println("Finished building");

    Object o;

    //Time the access for normal String keys
    long time1 = System.currentTimeMillis( );
    for (int i = 0; i < Dict.DICT.length; i++)
      o = h1.get(Dict.DICT[i]);
    time1 = System.currentTimeMillis( ) - time1;
    System.out.println("Time1 = " + time1);

    //Time the access for StringWrapper keys
    long time2 = System.currentTimeMillis( );
    for (int i = 0; i < Dict.DICT.length; i++)
      o = h2.get(dict[i]);
    time2 = System.currentTimeMillis( ) - time2;
    System.out.println("Time2 = " + time2);

  }
}

final class StringWrapper
{
```

```
    //cached hash code
    private int hash;
    private String string;
    public StringWrapper(String str)
    {
      string = str;
      hash = str.hashCode( );
    }
    public final int hashCode( )
    {
      return hash;
    }
    public final boolean equals(Object o)
    {
      //The fastest possible equality check
      return o == this;

  /*
      //This would be the more generic equality check if we allowed
      //access of the same String value from different StringWrapper objects.
      //This is still faster than the plain Strings as keys.
      if(o instanceof StringWrapper)
      {
        StringWrapper s = (StringWrapper) o;
        return s.hash == hash && string.equals(s.string);
      }
      else
        return false;
  */
    }
  }
```

Optimizing Queries

Other than accessing and updating elements of collections, the most common thing you want to do is query the collection. Let's look at some examples of tuning collection queries.

The Query Problem

First, we'll start with a problem. I'll use a list (indexable collection) of strings as my collection. For the query I'll use a simple test that checks whether any particular string includes one of a set of specified substrings, and the query will simply return the count of how many strings include those substrings. For example, the list might be:

```
"code"
"rode"
"load"
"toad"
"road"
```

and the query might be, "How many strings in the list contain the substrings "od" or "lo"?" (The answer for that particular query would be 3 for this example list.)

For my actual collection, I'll generate multicharacter strings using the lowercase characters of the Latin alphabet (a to z). For example, a collection of all four-character strings generated in this way would produce a collection of $26 \times 26 \times 26 \times 26 = 456,976$ four-character strings. I'll simply query this collection for the count of strings that contain any of the substrings "ie" or "xy" or "pq". I've elected to use a Vector object to hold the collection for the start of the tests; I've also chosen to use an easily generated collection for the data and a straightforward query to avoid any application-specific distractions. I want to focus on tuning. The query is representative of the types I've seen in applications.

The simple, straightforward version of the query is:

```
int count = 0;
for(int i = 0; i < collection.size( ); i++)
{
  if(    ( ((String) collection.get(i)).indexOf("ie") != -1 )
       | ( ((String) collection.get(i)).indexOf("xy") != -1 )
       | ( ((String) collection.get(i)).indexOf("pq") != -1 ) )
     count++;
}
return count;
```

Several standard optimizations immediately leap out at me. There's the unnecessarily repeated method call in the loop test (collection.size( )); the use of the normal boolean-OR operator (|) rather than the shortcircuit boolean-OR operator (||); and the repeated String cast in the query. All of these are standard targets for optimization in loops (see Chapter 7). However, just because they are "standard" optimizations doesn't mean we should apply them all immediately without testing their effects. So let's test them.

Applying the Boolean-OR operator optimization

Shortcircuit boolean operators are discussed in more detail in Chapter 7. Basically, these operators avoid evaluating their right-hand side if their left-hand side provides a conclusive result. I change the query block to use the shortcut operator:

```
if(    ( ((String) collection.get(i)).indexOf("ie") != -1 )
    || ( ((String) collection.get(i)).indexOf("xy") != -1 )
    || ( ((String) collection.get(i)).indexOf("pq") != -1 ) )
```

The shortcircuit booleans speed up the test slightly in most cases (see test2 in Table 11-2).

Eliminating the unnecessarily repeated method call

To avoid repeating the method call in the loop test, we can simply replace:

```
for(int i = 0; i < collection.size( ); i++)
```

with:

```
int max = collection.size( );
for(int i = 0; i < max; i++)
```

Again, this optimization speeds up the test slightly in most cases (see test3 in Table 11-2). Combining the two optimizations gives the best results for most of the VMs (see test4 in Table 11-2).

Eliminating casts and extra access calls

Let's push on and try eliminating the unnecessary String casts. This is done simply by holding the first casted object in a variable of the appropriate type:

```
String s;
for(int i = 0; i < max; i++)
{
  if(     ( (s = (String) collection.get(i)).indexOf("ie") != -1 )
      || (                                    s.indexOf("xy") != -1 )
      || (                                    s.indexOf("pq") != -1 ) )
```

Eliminating the cast also naturally eliminates the associated get( ) access call, as the object is held in the extra variable. With this change, all the VMs show their best times yet with significant speedups. I've included the results of testing with all the optimizations together (test5 of Table 11-2) and also without the size( ) call elimination (test6), as that optimization proved ineffective for the 1.2.2 VM.

Avoiding synchronization

We have been using a Vector object to hold the collection so far. In most applications, bottleneck queries tend to be read-only or single-threaded. In either case, you can normally use a nonsynchronized object to hold the collection. To do so here requires using an ArrayList object instead of the Vector object we initially used. The code does not otherwise change. The results of testing the optimizations so far, together with the change to an ArrayList collection object, are listed in test7 of Table 11-2. Once again, we see the best times yet for all the VMs.

Avoiding the method accessor

Another standard optimization is to avoid repeatedly using a method accessor to access elements of a collection if it is possible to access the elements directly in some way. For collection queries, this can be achieved simply by implementing the query in the collection class. For the example here, we could manage this by implementing our own java.util.List class and implementing the query in that class, thus gaining access to the internal collection. There is, however, a quicker possibility. Vector is implemented with its internal element collection defined as protected, so we can subclass Vector to gain access to the internal element collection and implement the query in our subclass as in the following code.

```
class TestList
  extends Vector
{
  public int customQuery( )
  {
    int count = 0;
    String s;
    for(int i = 0; i < elementCount; i++)
    {
      if(     ( (s = (String) elementData[i]).indexOf("ie") != -1 )
          || (                      s.indexOf("xy") != -1 )
          || (                      s.indexOf("pq") != -1 ) )
        count++;
    }
    return count;
  }
}
```

The equivalent of the original test is now:

```
return collection.customQuery( );
```

The results of this test are shown in test9 of Table 11-2. Almost all the VMs show this is now the fastest test.

Tighter typing of the collection elements

Another fairly obvious optimization is to reimplement the collection using an under-lying String[ ] array to hold the elements (see the "Variables" section in Chapter 6 and the "Collections" section earlier in this chapter). The results for this are listed in test12 of Table 11-2, showing the fastest query times for all the VMs.

Optimizing map queries

I've performed a similar optimization exercise for Maps (see *http://www.javaworld. com/javaworld/jw-11-2000/jw-1117-optimize.html*). The results were very similar. Perhaps the only surprise was that the Enumeration implementation for Hashtable was more efficient than the Iterator implementation. Remember, also, that you can iterate the elements just as in this exercise by using a counter loop instead of asking the Enumeration/Iterator whether there are more elements on each loop iteration:

```
Enumeration enumeration = map.keys( );
Object o;
//no need to call Enumeration.hasMoreElements( ) in each iteration
//since we can get the size of the map and use that value to count.
for (int size = map.size( ); size > 0; size--)
{
    o = enumeration.nextElement( );
    ...
}
```

Table 11-2. Optimizing a collection query

	1.2.2[a]	1.3.1_02	1.3.1_02 -server	1.4.0	1.4.0 -server	1.4.0 -Xint
test1: original test	100%	51%	40%	61%	49%	569%
test2: use shortcircuit booleans	99%	50%	39%	73%	48%	565%
test3: replace size( ) call	103%	50%	40%	56%	46%	534%
test4: both test2 and test3 optimizations	102%	48%	39%	55%	47%	531%
test5: test4+eliminate two casts	50%	38%	33%	43%	38%	451%
test6: test2+eliminate two casts	65%	40%	34%	47%	41%	464%
test7: test5 +ArrayList.get( )	25%	35%	32%	39%	36%	423%
test9: query in collection class	24%	34%	31%	37%	37%	397%
test12: query in String collection	24%	33%	31%	36%	36%	362%

[a] Note that some intermediate tests (test8, test10, and test11) are included in the example code but not included in this table.

Comparing LinkedLists and ArrayLists

I'm frequently asked about how LinkedLists compare in performance to ArrayLists. To fully consider the performance ramifications of these two classes, we need to know how they are implemented. So I'll start with brief descriptions of the most important aspects of their implementations from the point of view of performance.

The Vector and ArrayList Implementations

Vector and ArrayList are both implemented with an underlying Object[ ] array that stores the elements. We access the elements in the internal array by index:

```
public Object get(int index) {
    //check the index is valid first .. code not shown here
    return elementData[index];
}
```

The internal array can be bigger than the number of elements held by the Vector/ ArrayList object: the difference is kept as extra capacity for efficiently adding further elements. Adding elements is then very simply achieved by assigning the element to the first empty location in the internal array and incrementing the index (size) for the new empty location.

```
public boolean add(Object o) {
  ensureCapacity(size + 1); //explained soon
  elementData[size++] = o;
  return true;  //List.add(Object) signature support
}
```

Inserting elements into the collection at any location other than the end is slightly more tricky. The array elements above the insertion point must all be moved up by one, then the assignment can occur:

```
public void add(int index, Object element) {
  //check the index is valid first .. code not shown here
  ensureCapacity(size+1); //explained soon
  System.arraycopy(elementData, index, elementData, index + 1,
      size - index);
  elementData[index] = element;
  size++;
}
```

When the spare capacity is used up, the Vector/ArrayList object must replace its internal Object[ ] array with a new larger array when more elements need to be added, copying all the elements to the new array. The new array is 50% to 100% bigger than the old one, depending on the SDK version (the code shown here makes it 100% bigger):

```
public void ensureCapacity(int minCapacity) {
  int oldCapacity = elementData.length;
  if (minCapacity > oldCapacity) {
    Object oldData[ ] = elementData;
    int newCapacity = Math.max(oldCapacity * 2, minCapacity);
    elementData = new Object[newCapacity];
    System.arraycopy(oldData, 0, elementData, 0, size);
  }
}
```

The main difference between the Vector class and the ArrayList class is the use of synchronization. Apart from two methods used only during serialization, none of the ArrayList methods are synchronized; in contrast, most of the Vector methods are synchronized directly or indirectly. Consequently, Vector is thread-safe, while ArrayList is not. This makes ArrayList faster than Vector, though for the latest VMs the difference in speed between the two classes is small.

The Vector and ArrayList implementations have excellent performance for indexed access and update of elements because there is no overhead beyond range checking. Adding elements to or deleting elements from the *end* of the list also gives excellent performance, except when the capacity is exhausted and the internal array has to be expanded. Inserting and deleting elements always requires an array copy (two copies when the internal array must be grown first). The number of elements to be copied is proportional to [size – index], i.e., to the distance between the insertion/ deletion index and the last index in the collection. For insertions, inserting at the front of the collection (index 0) yields the worst performance, and inserting at the end of the collection (after the last element) yields the best performance. The array-copying overhead grows significantly as the size of the collection increases, because the number of elements that need to be copied with each insertion increases.

The LinkedList Implementation

LinkedList is implemented using a list of doubly linked nodes. To access elements by index, you need to traverse all the nodes until the indexed node is reached:

```
public Object get(int index) {
  //check the index is valid first .. code not shown here
  Entry e = header;  //starting node
  //go forwards or backwards depending on which is closer
  if (index < size/2) {
    for (int i = 0; i <= index; i++)
      e = e.next;
  } else {
    for (int i = size; i > index; i--)
      e = e.previous;
  }
  return e;
}
```

Inserting elements into the list is straightforward: traverse to the node at the index and insert a node immediately before that node:

```
public void add(int index, Object element) {
  //check the index is valid first .. code not shown here
  Entry e = header;  //starting node
  //go forwards or backwards depending on which is closer
  if (index < size/2) {
    for (int i = 0; i <= index; i++)
      e = e.next;
  } else {
    for (int i = size; i > index; i--)
      e = e.previous;
  }

  Entry newEntry = new Entry(element, e, e.previous);
  newEntry.previous.next = newEntry;
  newEntry.next.previous = newEntry;
  size++;
}
```

The LinkedList implementation has a performance overhead for indexed access and update of elements, as access to any index requires you to traverse multiple nodes. Adding elements to the collection suffers from the index traversal access performance drawback and has a further overhead in requiring the creation of a node object. On the plus side, there is no further overhead to insertions and deletions, so insertion/deletion overhead is really mostly dependent on how far away the insertion/deletion index is from the ends of the collection.

Performance Tests

There are many different functions of the classes that could be tested. LinkedLists are frequently used because of their supposedly better performance for random index insertion and deletion, so I decided to focus on insertion performance, i.e., building collections. I've tested LinkedList against ArrayList since both are unsynchronized.

The insertion speed is critically dependent on the size of the collection and the position where the element is to be inserted. All the best- and worst-case performances arise when inserting either at one of the ends or at the exact middle point of the collection. Consequently, I've chosen three insertion locations (start, middle, and end of the collection) and three representative collection sizes of medium (100 elements), large (10,000 elements), and very large (1,000,000 elements).

Table 11-3 shows the results for a medium collection.

Table 11-3. Building a medium-sized collection (100 elements)

Insertion point	1.2.2	1.3.1_02	1.3.1_02 -server	1.4.0	1.4.0 -server	1.4.0 -Xint
Start of the ArrayList	100%	115%	96.4%	129%	104%	899%
Start of the LinkedList	100%	82.6%	64.2%	84%	58.7%	548%
Midpoint of the ArrayList	69.2%	101%	67%	114.4%	80.1%	934%
Midpoint of the LinkedList	131%	105%	80.8%	116%	72.2%	872%
End of the ArrayList	45.3%	43.5%	40.8%	47.9%	47.9%	312%
End of the LinkedList	96.2%	65.6%	61.8%	71.2%	60.7%	334%

Table 11-3 shows that for short collections, ArrayList and LinkedList are performance rivals. ArrayLists have the edge when inserting at the end of the collection (appending elements). But then appending elements is the operation that ArrayList is optimized for: if you just want a statically sized collection, a Java array (e.g., Object[ ]) gives better performance than any collection object. Beyond the append operation, measured timings are mixed and reflect various VM optimization capabilities more than anything else.

What I have not measured here are other advantages that ArrayList has over LinkedList, namely the ability to presize collections and the reduced garbage-collection overhead. Specifically, ArrayLists can be created with a particular size (e.g., in this test the ArrayList could be created with a capacity of 100 elements), thus avoiding all the growth overhead. When running this same test with presized ArrayLists, the ArrayLists times are roughly twice as fast as those recorded in the table! LinkedLists (up to SDK 1.4) cannot be presized.

Additionally, the ArrayList generates only a few extra objects for garbage collection, i.e., the internal array object that holds the elements and one extra internal array object each time the ArrayList capacity is exhausted and the ArrayList needs to be grown. The LinkedList generates one node object for every insertion, irrespective of any deletions that might take place. Consequently, LinkedLists can give considerably more work to the garbage collector (many more objects to collect). Taking these added factors into account, my inclination would be to use an ArrayList rather than a LinkedList for any small- to medium-sized collection.

Table 11-4 shows the results for a large collection.

Table 11-4. Building a large collection (10,000 elements)

Insertion point	1.2.2	1.3.1_02	1.3.1_02 -server	1.4.0	1.4.0 -server	1.4.0 -Xint
Start of the ArrayList	6768%	7052%	6612%	7101%	7015%	8125%
Start of the LinkedList	100%	94.2%	52.9%	71.6%	41.2%	682%
Midpoint of the ArrayList	2485%	2923%	2173%	2962%	2882%	3836%
Midpoint of the LinkedList	24152%	14168%	14168%	14064%	14203%	42360%
End of the ArrayList	62.3%	32.4%	34.0%	34.2%	28.5%	254%
End of the LinkedList	84.1%	68.5%	51.4%	56.8%	35.8%	471%

We can see from Table 11-4 that we begin to get a severe performance penalty when we encounter large insertion overhead. The worst case for LinkedList is, as predicted, inserting in the middle of the collection. We can also see that this has worse performance than the ArrayList worst case of insertion at the start of the collection. Insertion at the middle of the ArrayList has significantly better performance than those two worst cases.

Overall, ArrayList again gives better performance for most cases, including index insertion to random locations. If you always need to insert toward the beginning of the collection, LinkedList is a good choice, but you can achieve even better performance using a reversed ArrayList, i.e., either with a dedicated implementation or by flipping indexes using a [size-index] mapping.

The results for very large collections (not shown), indicates very similar conclusions to those of Table 11-4. However, times are so long that they emphasize that very large collections need particularly close matches between data, collection types, and data-manipulation algorithms. Otherwise, you can end up with performance that is essentially unusable. For optimum performance, you should build a dedicated collection class implementation specific to the problem. This is often a necessary step for very large collections.

Querying Performance

Querying is most efficiently achieved by implementing the query inside the class (see the "Optimizing Queries" section). The time needed to iterate over all the elements is the limiting factor for queries on these lists. A query implemented in the ArrayList/

Vector classes iterates over the array elements. The following example counts the number of null elements:

```
int count = 0;
for (int i = 0; i < size; i++)
  if(elementData[i] == null)
    count++;
```

A query implemented in the LinkedList class traverses all the nodes. The following example counts the number of null elements:

```
node = header.next;
count = 0;
for (int i = 0; i < repeat; i++, node = node.next)
  if (node.element == null)
    count++;
```

Table 11-5 shows the ArrayList providing significantly superior performance to that of the LinkedList, once again indicating that ArrayList is the class to use. Table 11-6 shows the time taken to iterate over all the elements using a ListIterator object obtained from the List.listIterator(int) method. These iterators would be necessary if the query could not be implemented in the List class. Once again, ArrayList shows superior performance, though not as dramatically as with Table 11-5. Note that the absolute times in Table 11-6 are about ten times longer than those in Table 11-5; ArrayList internal traversal is about ten times faster than ArrayList iteration using a ListIterator.

Table 11-5. Iterating through all the elements of the collection using internal access

	1.2.2	1.3.1_02	1.3.1_02 -server	1.4.0	1.4.0 -server	1.4.0 -Xint
ArrayList internal traversal	100%	121%	85.9%	159%	86%	962%
LinkedList internal traversal	533%	557%	1576%	565%	436%	1700%

Table 11-6. Iterating through all the elements of the collection using a ListIterator

	1.2.2	1.3.1_02	1.3.1_02 -server	1.4.0	1.4.0 -server	1.4.0 -Xint
ArrayList iteration using ListIterator	100%	119%	63%	101%	72.2%	2021%
LinkedList iteration using ListIterator	112%	189%	159%	167%	144%	1656%

The measurements and the other factors we've considered clearly indicate that ArrayLists and Vectors usually provide better performance than LinkedLists and synchronized wrapped LinkedLists. Even in cases where you might have thought that the LinkedList would provide better performance, you may be able to coax superior performance from ArrayList by altering how elements are added, for example by reversing the collection order.

There are situations where LinkedLists provide better performance, for example with very large collections where many elements need to be added to both the beginning and end of the collection. But in general, I recommend using ArrayList/Vector as the default and using LinkedList only where there is an identified performance problem that a LinkedList improves.

The RandomAccess Interface

SDK 1.4 introduced a java.util.RandomAccess interface for optimizing List performance, but it has no methods. What is the purpose of this interface?

What Does RandomAccess Mean?

RandomAccess is a marker interface, like the Serializable and Cloneable interfaces. All these marker interfaces do not define methods. Instead, they identify a class as having a particular capability. In the case of Serializable, the interface specifies that if the class is serialized using the serialization I/O classes, a NotSerializableException will not be thrown (unless the object contains some other class that cannot be serialized). Cloneable similarly indicates that the use of the Object.clone( ) method for a Cloneable class will not throw a CloneNotSupportedException.

The RandomAccess interface identifies that a particular java.util.List implementation has fast random access. (A more accurate name for the interface would have been "FastRandomAccess.") This interface tries to define an imprecise concept: what exactly is fast? The documentation provides a simple guide: if repeated access using the List.get( ) method is faster than repeated access using the Iterator.next( ) method, then the List has fast random access. The two types of access are shown in the following code examples.

Repeated access using List.get( ):

```
Object o;
for (int i=0, n=list.size( ); i < n; i++)
  o = list.get(i);
```

Repeated access using Iterator.next( ):

```
Object o;
for (Iterator itr=list.iterator( ); itr.hasNext( ); )
  o = itr.next( );
```

A third loop combines the previous two loops to avoid the repeated Iterator.hasNext( ) test on each loop iteration:

```
Object o;
Iterator itr=list.iterator( );
for (int i=0, n=list.size( ); i < n; i++)
  o = itr.next( );
```

This last loop relies on the normal situation where List objects cannot change in size while they are being iterated through without an exception of some sort occurring. So, because the loop size remains the same, you can simply count the accessed elements without testing at each iteration whether the end of the list has been reached. This last loop is generally faster than the previous loop with the Iterator.hasNext() test. In the context of the RandomAccess interface, the first loop using List.get() should be faster than both the other loops that use Iterator.next() for a list to implement RandomAccess.

How Is RandomAccess Used?

So now that we know what RandomAccess means, how do we use it? There are two aspects to using the other marker interfaces, Serializable and Cloneable: defining classes that implement them and using their capabilities via ObjectInput/ObjectOutput and Object.clone(), respectively. RandomAccess is a little different. Of course, we still need to decide whether any particular class implements it, but the possible classes are severely restricted: RandomAccess should be implemented only in java.util.List classes. And most such classes are created outside of projects. The SDK provides the most frequently used implementations, and subclasses of the SDK classes do not need to implement RandomAccess because they automatically inherit the capability where appropriate.

The second aspect, using the RandomAccess capability, is also different. Whether a class is Serializable or Cloneable is automatically detected when you use ObjectInput/ObjectOutput and Object.clone(). But RandomAccess has no such automatic support. Instead, you need to explicitly check whether a class implements RandomAccess using the instanceof operator:

```
if (listObject instanceof RandomAccess)
    ...
```

You must then explicitly choose the appropriate access method, List.get() or Iterator.next(). Clearly, if we test for RandomAccess on every loop iteration, we would be making a lot of redundant calls and probably losing the benefit of RandomAccess as well. So the pattern to follow in using RandomAccess makes the test outside the loop. The canonical pattern looks like this:

```
Object o;
if (listObject instanceof RandomAccess)
{
  for (int i=0, n=list.size(); i < n; i++)
  {
    o = list.get(i);
    //do something with object o
  }

}
else
```

```
{
  Iterator itr = list.iterator();
  for (int i=0, n=list.size(); i < n; i++)
  {
    o = itr.next();
    //do something with object o

  }
}
```

Speedup from RandomAccess

I tested the four code loops shown in this section, using the 1.4 release, separately testing the -client (default) and -server options. To test the effect of the RandomAccess interface, I used the java.util.ArrayList and java.util.LinkedList classes. ArrayList implements RandomAccess, while LinkedList does not. ArrayList has an underlying implementation consisting of an array with constant access time for any element, so using the ArrayList iterator is equivalent to using the ArrayList.get() method but with some additional overhead. LinkedList has an underlying implementation consisting of linked node objects with access time proportional to the shortest distance of the element from either end of the list, whereas iterating sequentially through the list can shortcut the access time by traversing one node after another.

Times shown are the average of three runs, and all times have been normalized to the first table cell, i.e., the time taken by the ArrayList to iterate the list using the List. get() method in client mode.

Loop type (loop test) and access method	ArrayList java -client	LinkedList java -client	ArrayList java -server	LinkedList java -server
loop counter (i<n) and List.get()	100%	too long	77.5%	too long
iterator (Iterator.hasNext()) and Iterator.next()	141%	219%	109%	213%
iterator (i<n) and Iterator.next()	121%	205%	98%	193%
RandomAccess test with loop from row 1 or 3	100%	205%	77.5%	193%

The most important results are in the last two rows. The last line shows the times obtained by making full use of the RandomAccess interface, and the line before that shows the most optimal general technique for iterating lists if RandomAccess is not available. The size of the lists I used for the test (and consequently the number of loop iterations required to access every element) was sufficiently large that the instanceof test had no measurable cost in comparison to the time taken to run the loop. Consequently, we can see that there was no cost (but also no benefit) in adding the instanceof RandomAccess test when iterating the LinkedList, whereas the ArrayList was iterated more than 20% quicker when the instanceof test was included.

Forward and Backward Compatibility

Can you use RandomAccess and maintain backward compatibility with VM versions prior to 1.4? There are three aspects to using RandomAccess:

- You may want to include code referencing RandomAccess without moving to 1.4.

- Many projects need their code to be able to run in any VM, so the code needs to be backward-compatible to run in VMs using releases earlier than 1.4, where RandomAccess does not exist.

- You will want to make your code forward-compatible so that it automatically takes advantage of RandomAccess when running in a 1.4+ JVM.

Making RandomAccess available to your development environment is the first issue, and if you are using an environment prior to 1.4, this can be as simple as adding the RandomAccess interface to your classpath. Any version of the SDK can create the RandomAccess interface. The definition for RandomAccess is:

```
package java.util;
public interface RandomAccess { }
```

We also need to handle RandomAccess in the runtime environment. For pre-1.4 environments, the test:

```
if (listObject instanceof RandomAccess)
```

generates a NoClassDefFoundError at runtime when the JVM tries to load the RandomAccess class (for the instanceof test to be evaluated, the class has to be loaded). However, we can guard the test so that it is executed only if RandomAccess is available. The simplest way to do this is to check whether RandomAccess exists, setting a boolean guard as the outcome of that test:

```
static boolean RandomAccessExists;
...

    //execute this as early as possible after the application starts
    try
    {
      Class c =  Class.forName("java.util.RandomAccess");
      RandomAccessExists = true;
    }
    catch (ClassNotFoundException e)
    {
      RandomAccessExists = false;
    }
```

Finally, we need to change our instanceof tests to use the RandomAccessExists variable as a guard:

```
if (RandomAccessExists && (listObject instanceof RandomAccess) )
```

With the guarded instanceof test, the code automatically reverts to the Iterator loop if RandomAccess does not exist and should avoid throwing a NoClassDefFoundError in

---

pre-1.4 JVMs. And, of course, the guarded `instanceof` test also automatically uses the faster loop branch when `RandomAccess` does exist and the list object implements it.

Cached Access

Caches use local data when present and thus don't need to access nonlocal data. If the data is not present locally, the nonlocal data must be accessed or calculated; it is then stored locally as well as being returned. After the first access, the data is available locally, and access is quicker. How much quicker depends on the type of cache.

Most caches have to maintain the consistency of the data held in the cache: it is usually important for the data in the cache to be up to date. When considering the use of a cache, bear in mind the expected lifetime of the data and any refresh rate or time-to-live values associated with the data. Similarly, for output data, consider how long to keep data in the cache before it must be written out. You may have differing levels of priority for writing out different types of data. For example, some filesystems keep general written data in a write cache, but immediately write critical system data that ensures system consistency in case of crashes. Also, as caches cannot usually hold all the data you would like, a strategy for swapping data out of the cache to overcome cache space limitations is usually necessary. The memory used by the cache is often significant, and it is always better to release the resources used by it explicitly when it is no longer needed, or reduce resources being used by the cache when possible, even if the cache itself is still required.

Caching can apply to data held in single objects or groups of objects. For single objects, it is usual to maintain a structure or instance variable that holds cached values. For groups of objects, there is usually a structure maintained at the point of access to the elements of the group. In addition, caching applies generally to two types of locality of access, usually referred to as *spatial* and *temporal*. Spatial locality refers to the idea that if something is accessed, it is likely that something else nearby will be accessed soon. This is one of the reasons buffering I/O streams works so well. If every subsequent byte read from disk were in a completely different part of the disk, I/O buffering would be no help at all. Temporal locality refers to the idea that if you access something, you are likely to access it again in the near future. This is the principle behind browsers holding files locally once downloaded.

There is a lot of research into the use of caches, but most of it is related to CPU or disk hardware caches. Nevertheless, any good article or book chapter on caches should cover the basics and the pitfalls, and these are normally applicable (with some extra thought) to caches in applications. One thing you should do is monitor cache-hit rates, i.e., the number of times that accessing data retrieves data from the cache, compared to the total number of data accesses. This is important because if the cache-hit rate is too low, the overhead of having a cache may be more than any actual gain in performance. In this case, tune or disable the cache. It is frequently useful to build-in the option of disabling and emptying the cache. This can be very helpful for two reasons. First, you can make direct comparisons of operations with and without the cache, and second, there are times when you want to measure the overhead in filling an empty cache. In this case, you may need to repeatedly fill an empty cache to get a good measurement.

Caching Examples

When accessing elements from sets of data, some elements are accessed much more frequently than others. In these cases, it is possible to apply caching techniques to speed up access to frequently accessed elements. This is best demonstrated with the following example.

Consider a CacheTest class that consists mainly of a Map populated with Integer objects. I use Integer objects for convenience to populate the Map with many elements, but the actual object type is of no significance because you use only the hashCode( ) and equals( ) methods, just as the Map does.

Basically, you provide two ways to access the elements of the Map. The first, plain_ access( ), just calls the Map.get( ) method as usual. The second method, cached_ access( ), uses the lower bits of the hash code of the object to obtain an index value into an array. This index is then checked to see whether the object is there. If it is, the corresponding value in a parallel value array is returned. If it's not, the object is placed there with the value in the corresponding value array.

This is about the simplest example of general cached access. It demonstrates the advantages and pitfalls of cached access. I have selected 10 integers that do not map to the same indexes for the example. Running the class gives a straightforward comparison between the two access methods, and I get the result that the cached access varies significantly depending on the VM used. The access speedups are illustrated in the following table of measurements. Times have been normalized to the JDK 1.2.2 case for using a HashMap. The first time of each entry is the measurement using a HashMap, and the second is the measurement using a Hashtable. For any one VM, cached access is significantly faster.

	1.2.2	1.3.1_02	1.3.1_02 -server	1.4.0	1.4.0 -server	1.4.0 -Xint
Plain access (HashMap/ Hashtable)	100%/ 320%	109%/ 138%	112%/ 152%	82.6%/ 155%	93.2%/ 89.3%	1964%/ 1596%
Cached access (HashMap/ Hashtable)	29.3%/ 29.2%	57.2%/ 57%	36.5%/ 42.3%	60.4%/ 60.2%	38.5%/ 48.1%	1218%/ 1294%

This test is artificial, in that I chose integers where no two map to the same index. If there is more than one integer that maps to the same cache array index, this is called a *collision*. Clearly, with collisions, performance is not as good because you are constantly entering the code that puts the objects into the cache. Collisions are a general problem with cached data, and you need to minimize them for optimal performance. This can be done by choosing an appropriate mapping function to generate indexes that minimize collisions:

```java
package tuning.cache;

import java.util.HashMap;
import java.util.Hashtable;
import java.lang.Math;

public class CacheTest
{
  //The cache array for the keys
  static Object[] cache_keys = new Object[128];
  //The array for the values corresponding to cached keys
  static Object[] cache_values = new Object[128];
  //static Hashtable hash = new Hashtable();
  static HashMap hash = new HashMap();

  public static void main(String[] args)
  {
    try
    {
      System.out.println("started populating");
      populate();
      System.out.println("started accessing");
      access_test();
    }
    catch(Exception e){e.printStackTrace();}
  }

  public static void populate()
  {
    for (int i = 0; i < 100000; i++)
      hash.put(new Integer(i), new Integer(i+5));
  }

  public static Object plain_access(Integer i)
  {
    //simple get() call to the hash table
    return hash.get(i);
  }

  public static Object cached_access(Integer i)
  {
    //First get access index
    int access = Math.abs(i.hashCode()) & 127;
    Object o;
    //if the access index has an object, and that object is equal to key
    //then return the corresponding value in the parallel values array.
    if ( (o = cache_keys[access]) == null || !o.equals(i))
    {
```

```java
        //otherwise, we got a collision. We need to replace the
        //object at that access index with the new one that we
        //get from the hash table using normal Hashtable.get( ),
        //and then return the value retrieved this way
        if (o != null)
          System.out.println("Collsion between " + o + " and " + i);
        o = hash.get(i);
        cache_keys[access] = i;
        cache_values[access] = o;
        return o;
      }
      else
      {
        return cache_values[access];
      }
  }

  public static void access_test( )
  {
    //Ten integers that do not collide under the mapping scheme
    //This gives best performance behavior for illustration purposes
    Integer a0 = new Integer(6767676);
    Integer a1 = new Integer(33);
    Integer a2 = new Integer(998);
    Integer a3 = new Integer(3333);
    Integer a4 = new Integer(12348765);
    Integer a5 = new Integer(9999);
    Integer a6 = new Integer(66665);
    Integer a7 = new Integer(1234);
    Integer a8 = new Integer(987654);
    Integer a9 = new Integer(3121219);
    Object o1,o2,o3,o4,o5,o6,o7,o8,o9,o0;
    long time = System.currentTimeMillis( );
    for (int i = 0; i < 1000000; i++)
    {
      o1 = plain_access(a0);
      o2 = plain_access(a1);
      o3 = plain_access(a2);
      o4 = plain_access(a3);
      o5 = plain_access(a4);
      o6 = plain_access(a5);
      o7 = plain_access(a6);
      o8 = plain_access(a7);
      o9 = plain_access(a8);
      o0 = plain_access(a9);
    }
    System.out.println("plain access took " +
        (System.currentTimeMillis( )-time));

    time = System.currentTimeMillis( );
    for (int i = 0; i < 1000000; i++)
    {
      o1 = cached_access(a0);
      o2 = cached_access(a1);
```

```
      o3 = cached_access(a2);
      o4 = cached_access(a3);
      o5 = cached_access(a4);
      o6 = cached_access(a5);
      o7 = cached_access(a6);
      o8 = cached_access(a7);
      o9 = cached_access(a8);
      o0 = cached_access(a9);
    }
  System.out.println("cached access took " +
      (System.currentTimeMillis( )-time));


  }
}
```

In this example, we add an instance variable to the keys to provide the mapping into the cache. This example uses a circular cache that holds just the most recent 128 keys accessed. Because of more optimal cache access, this has an even larger speedup than the previous example:

```
package tuning.cache;

import java.util.Hashtable;
import java.lang.Math;

public class Test2
{
  //The cache array for the keys
  static Test2[ ] cache_keys = new Test2[128];
  //The array for the values corresponding to cached keys
  static Object[ ] cache_values = new Object[128];
  static Hashtable hash = new Hashtable( );

  //The index to use for the next object added to the cache
  static int freeIndex = 0;

  //The current index in the cache referenced by this object
  int cacheRef = -1;
  //Unique integer for each object, can be used as hash code
  int value;

  public static void main(String[ ] args)
  {
    try
    {
      System.out.println("started populating");
      populate( );
      System.out.println("started accessing");
      access_test( );
    }
    catch(Exception e){e.printStackTrace( );}
  }

  public Test2(int i)
```

```
{
  value = i;
}

public int hashCode( )
{
  return value;
}
public boolean equals(Object obj)
{
  //Equality test requires null check, type check, and value check
  if ((obj != null) && (obj instanceof Test2))
    return value == ((Test2) obj).value;
  else
    return false;
}

public static void populate( )
{
  for (int i = 0; i < 100000; i++)
    hash.put(new Test2(i), new Integer(i+5));
}

public static Object plain_access(Test2 i)
{
  return hash.get(i);
}

public static Object cached_access(Test2 i)
{
  //Access index into the cache is quick and easy to get
  int access = i.cacheRef;
  Object o;

  //If it is -1 then it is not in the cache
  if (access == -1)
  {
    //get the object using the hash table
    o = hash.get(i);
    //Get the next available index in the cache.
    //Wind round to the start of the cache if it is off the end
    if (freeIndex >= cache_keys.length)
      freeIndex = 0;
    //set the cache index; increment the next cache index too
    access = i.cacheRef = freeIndex++;
    //If there was already something in the cache at that location,
    //uncache it
    if (cache_keys[access] != null)
    {
      System.out.println("Collsion between " + cache_keys[access] +
              " and " + i);
      cache_keys[access].cacheRef = -1;
    }
    //And cache our new value.
```

```java
      cache_keys[access] = i;
      cache_values[access] = o;
      return o;
    }
    else
    {
      return cache_values[access];
    }
}

public static void access_test()
{
  Test2 a0 = new Test2(6767676);
  Test2 a1 = new Test2(33);
  Test2 a2 = new Test2(998);
  Test2 a3 = new Test2(3333);
  Test2 a4 = new Test2(12348765);
  Test2 a5 = new Test2(9999);
  Test2 a6 = new Test2(66665);
  Test2 a7 = new Test2(1234);
  Test2 a8 = new Test2(987654);
  Test2 a9 = new Test2(3121219);
  Object o1,o2,o3,o4,o5,o6,o7,o8,o9,o0;
  long time = System.currentTimeMillis();
  for (int i = 0; i < 1000000; i++)
  {
      o1 = plain_access(a0);
      o2 = plain_access(a1);
      o3 = plain_access(a2);
      o4 = plain_access(a3);
      o5 = plain_access(a4);
      o6 = plain_access(a5);
      o7 = plain_access(a6);
      o8 = plain_access(a7);
      o9 = plain_access(a8);
      o0 = plain_access(a9);
  }
  System.out.println("plain access took " +
      (System.currentTimeMillis()-time));

  time = System.currentTimeMillis();
  for (int i = 0; i < 1000000; i++)
  {
      o1 = cached_access(a0);
      o2 = cached_access(a1);
      o3 = cached_access(a2);
      o4 = cached_access(a3);
      o5 = cached_access(a4);
      o6 = cached_access(a5);
      o7 = cached_access(a6);
      o8 = cached_access(a7);
      o9 = cached_access(a8);
      o0 = cached_access(a9);
  }
```

```
        System.out.println("cached access took " +
            (System.currentTimeMillis( )-time));

    }

}
```

These are examples of general data caching. Sometimes you will know beforehand exactly which objects will be frequently accessed. In this case, you can create a specialized class that provides an accessor that optimizes access for just these objects. This can be as simple as a switch statement or multiple if statements. For example:

```
public Object get(Object key)
{
  if (key == FAST_KEY1)
    return value1;
  else if (key.equals(FASTISH_KEY2))
    return value2;
  else if (key.equals(possibly_fast_key_assigned_at_runtime))
    return value3;
  else
    return hash.get(key);
}
```

Finding the Index for Partially Matched Strings

The problem considered here concerns a large number of string keys that need to be accessed by full or partial match. Each string is unique, so the full-match access can easily be handled by a standard hash-table structure (e.g., java.util.HashMap). The partial-match access needs to collect all objects that have string keys starting with a particular substring.

Consider this hash table consisting of keys and values:

```
    "hello"      1
    "bye"        2
    "hi"         3
```

The full match for key "hi" retrieves 3, and the partial match against strings starting with "h" retrieves the collection {1,3}. Using a hash-table structure for the partial-match access is expensive because it requires that all keys be iterated over, and then each key matching the corresponding object needs to be collated.

Of course, I am considering here a large collection of strings. Alternatives are not usually necessary for a few (or even a few thousand) strings. But for large collections, performance-tuning techniques become necessary.

To tune, look for data structures that quickly match any partial string. The task is somewhat simpler than the most generic version of this type of problem because you need to match only the first few consecutive characters. This means that some sort of tree structure is probably ideal. Of the structures available from the JDK, TreeMap looks like it can provide exactly the required functionality; it gives a minimal baseline and, if the performance is adequate, there is no more tuning to do. But TreeMap is 5 to 10 times slower than HashMap for access and update. The target is to obtain HashMap access speed for single-key access.

Don't get carried away searching for the perfect data structure. Thinking laterally, you can consider other possibilities. If you have the strings in a sorted collection, you can apply a binary search to find the index of the string that is greater than or less than the partial string, and then obtain all the strings (and hence corresponding objects) in between.

More specifically, you can construct a sorted array of keys from the hash table. Then, if you want to find all strings starting with "h", you can run a binary search for the strings "h" and "h\uFFFF". This gives all the indexes of the band for all the keys that start with "h". Note that a binary search can return the index where the string would be even if it is not actually in the array. (The correct solution actually goes from "h" inclusive to "i" exclusive, but this solution will do for strings that don't include character \uFFFF.)

Having parallel collections can lead to all sorts of problems in making sure both collections contain the same elements. Solutions that involve parallel collections should hide all accesses and updates to the parallel collections through a separate object to ensure that all accesses and updates are consistent. The solution here is suitable mainly when the collections are updated infrequently, e.g., when they are built once or periodically and read from often. Here is a class implementing this solution:

```
package tuning.struct;

import java.util.Hashtable;
import java.util.Enumeration;

public class PartialSearcher
{
  Hashtable hash;
  String[ ] sortedArray;

  public static void main(String args[ ])
  {
    //Populate a Hashtable with ten strings
    Hashtable h = new Hashtable( );
    h.put("hello", new Integer(1));
    h.put("hell", new Integer(2));
    h.put("alpha", new Integer(3));
    h.put("bye", new Integer(4));
    h.put("hello2", new Integer(5));
    h.put("solly", new Integer(6));
    h.put("sally", new Integer(7));
    h.put("silly", new Integer(8));
```

```java
    h.put("zorro", new Integer(9));
    h.put("hi", new Integer(10));

    //Create the searching object
    PartialSearcher p = new PartialSearcher(h);
    //Match against all string keys given by
    //the first command line argument
    Object[] objs = p.match(args[0]);
    //And print the matches out
    for(int i = 0; i<objs.length; i++)
      System.out.println(objs[i]);

  }

  public PartialSearcher(Hashtable h)
  {
    hash = h;
    createSortedArray();
  }

  public Object[] match(String s)
  {
    //find the start and end positions of strings that match the key
    int startIdx = binarySearch(sortedArray, s,
                                0, sortedArray.length-1);
    int endIdx = binarySearch(sortedArray, s+ '\uFFFF',
                                0, sortedArray.length-1);

    //and return an array of the matched keys
    Object[] objs = new Object[endIdx-startIdx];
    for (int i = startIdx ; i < endIdx; i++)
      objs[i-startIdx] = sortedArray[i];
    return objs;
  }

  public void createSortedArray()
  {
    //Create a sorted array of the keys of the hash table
    sortedArray = new String[hash.size()];
    Enumeration e = hash.keys();
    for (int i = 0; e.hasMoreElements(); i++)
      sortedArray[i] = (String) e.nextElement();
    quicksort(sortedArray, 0, sortedArray.length-1);
  }

  /**
   * Semi-standard binary search returning index of match location or
   * where the location would match if it is not present.
   */
  public static int binarySearch(String[] arr, String elem,
                                 int fromIndex, int toIndex)
  {
    int mid,cmp;
    while (fromIndex <= toIndex)
```

```
  {
    mid =(fromIndex + toIndex)/2;
    if ( (cmp = arr[mid].compareTo(elem)) < 0)
      fromIndex = mid + 1;
    else if (cmp > 0)
      toIndex = mid - 1;
    else
      return mid;
  }
  return fromIndex;
}

/**
 * Standard quicksort
 */
public void quicksort(String[ ] arr, int lo, int hi)
{
  if( lo >= hi )
    return;

  int mid = ( lo + hi ) / 2;
  String tmp;
  String middle = arr[ mid ];

  if( arr[ lo ].compareTo(middle) > 0 )
  {
    arr[ mid ] = arr[ lo ];
    arr[ lo ] = middle;
    middle = arr[ mid ];
  }

  if( middle.compareTo(arr[ hi ]) > 0)
  {
    arr[ mid ] = arr[ hi ];
    arr[ hi ] = middle;
    middle = arr[ mid ];

    if( arr[ lo ].compareTo(middle) > 0)
    {
      arr[ mid ] = arr[ lo ];
      arr[ lo ] = middle;
      middle = arr[ mid ];
    }
  }

  int left = lo + 1;
  int right = hi - 1;

  if( left >= right )
    return;

  for( ;; )
  {
    while( arr[ right ].compareTo(middle ) > 0)
```

```
      {
        right--;
      }

      while( left < right && arr[ left ].compareTo(middle ) <= 0)
      {
        left++;
      }

      if( left < right )
      {
        tmp = arr[ left ];
        arr[ left ] = arr[ right ];
        arr[ right ] = tmp;
        right--;
      }
      else
      {
        break;
      }
    }

    quicksort(arr, lo, left);
    quicksort(arr, left + 1, hi);
  }
}
```

Note that this solution has a wider application than only string keys. Any type of object can be used as a key as long as you can create a methodology to compare the order of the keys. This is a reasonable solution for several types of indexing.

Search Trees

Here's an alternate solution to the problem presented in the last section. I looked for a more obvious solution, another tree structure that would handle the search, provide full keyed access, and give plenty of scope for tuning. Jon Bentley and Bob Sedgewick[*] detail a potential solution that offers an interesting structure and provides a good tuning exercise, so I will use it here.

In a *ternary* tree, each node has three branches. The structure is a halfway point between binary trees of strings (one string per node) and digital tries. A *digital trie* stores strings character by character, and has an *n*-way branching where *n* is the number of possible characters in the string (e.g., 26 if all strings have only lowercase alphabetic characters, 256 if strings can contain any 8-byte character, 34,000 if each node can be any Unicode character). Digital tries are lightning-fast to search, but have exorbitant storage costs that typically rule them out as a solution.

---

[*] "Ternary Search Trees," Jon Bentley and Bob Sedgewick, *Dr. Dobb's Journal*, April 1998.

The ternary tree node searches by comparing the current character with the current node's character. If equal, the next character in the string becomes the current character, and the node at the "equal" pointer becomes the current node. Otherwise, the current character in the string remains the current character, and the node at the "higher" or "lower" pointer becomes the current node. A TernarySearchTreeNode class has the Java class structure given as follows (the extra "value" instance variable is to allow any object to be stored as the value for a particular key):

```java
class TernarySearchTreeNode
{
  char splitchar;
  TernarySearchTreeNode low;
  TernarySearchTreeNode high;
  TernarySearchTreeNode equal;
  Object value;
}
```

Bentley and Sedgewick provide code (in C, but easily ported) to search and insert into the tree. The recursive versions are:

```java
public static Object search(TernarySearchTreeNode p, String str, int strIdx)
{
  //Start from a node
  char c;
  //if the node is null, return null.
  //This means there was no match to the string.
  if (p == null)
    return null;
  //otherwise if the current character is less than
  //the splitchar value, replace the current node with
  //the low node, and carry on searching at this character
  else if ( (c=str.charAt(strIdx)) < p.splitchar)
    return search(p.low, str, strIdx);
  //or if the current character is larger than the
  //splitchar value, replace the current node with the
  //high node, and carry on searching at this character
  else if (c > p.splitchar)
    return search(p.high, str, strIdx);
  else
  {
    //otherwise, we match the current string character with
    //the character at this node. If we have finished the
    //string, then this is the searched for node, and
    //we can return the value stored at this node.
    if (strIdx == (str.length()-1))
      return p.value;
    else
      //or this is not the end of the string, so replace
      //the current node with the equal node, and carry on
      //searching at the next string character
      return search(p.equal, str, strIdx+1);
  }
}
```

```
public static TernarySearchTreeNode insert(TernarySearchTreeNode p, String str,
        int strIdx, Object o)
{
  //Start from a node. If there is no node, then we create a new node
  //to insert into the tree. This could even be the root node.
  char c;
  if (p == null)
  {
    p = new TernarySearchTreeNode(str.charAt(strIdx));
  }

  //Now navigate the tree just as for the search method, inserting
  //nodes as required. For each recursive insert( ) call, the
  //returned node is the one we assign to the current nodes low,
  //high or equal node, depending on the comparison of the
  //current string character and the current node character.
  if ( (c = str.charAt(strIdx)) < p.splitchar)
    p.low = insert(p.low, str, strIdx, o);
  else if (c == p.splitchar)
  {
    //When we finally get to the last node (matched or inserted,
    //doesn't matter), we insert the value, given by Object o
    if (strIdx == (str.length( )-1))
      p.value = o;
    else
      p.equal = insert(p.equal, str, strIdx+1, o);
  }
  else
    p.high = insert(p.high , str, strIdx, o);

  return p;
}

//Simple constructor, just assigns the character.
public TernarySearchTreeNode(char c)
{
  splitchar = c;
}
```

A class to use these methods, with get( ) and put( ) methods such as Map, looks like this:

```
public class TernarySearchTree
{
  TernarySearchTreeNode root;

  public Object get(String key)
  {
    return TernarySearchTreeNode.search(root, key, 0);
  }

  public Object put(String key, Object value)
  {
```

```
//Note there is no need to initialize root. The recursive insert()
//call creates a root object the first time through.
root = TernarySearchTreeNode.insert(root, key, 0, value);
return null; //fake old value for now
    }
}
```

This is fairly straightforward. (Note that the Map.put() should return the old value, if any, at the key being set, but we have not implemented that functionality just yet.) The accessor and updator just follow the described algorithm, comparing the current character to the character at the current node and taking the appropriate next branch unless you have reached the end of the string. In that case, the value is returned or updated according to whether this is a search or insert.

If you compare update and access times against HashMap, you'll find that the Ternary-SearchTree is much slower. We are expecting this slowdown, because the referred article does the same comparison and indicates that many optimizations are necessary to achieve similar times to the HashMap. Since they do achieve similar times after optimizing, assume that you can too, and run through a tuning phase to see what improvements you can make.

The target is always the HashMap times, since you already have TreeMap if you need the partial-matching functionality without HashMap access speed. If TreeMap does not exist, or you tune another structure with no counterpart, you still need a goal for the performance. This goal should be based on the application requirements. In the absence of application requirements, you should aim for the performance of some other existing class that provides similar or partial functionality. For this example, it is still sensible to use HashMap to provide the performance target because the full key-match access time for the structure will probably be compared to HashMap access times by most developers.

The baseline is a large dictionary of words. Knowing that tree access and update are susceptible to the order of keys added, you are testing both for randomized order of insertion and mostly-sorted order, so that you know the near worst case and (probable) average case. Take a HashMap that is presized (i.e., large enough to avoid rehashing after addition of all keys), using the case where the keys are mostly sorted as a baseline. Assign the time taken to build the collection as 100%, and also assign the time taken to access every key in it as 100% (i.e., each of the access and update values, which are different, is separately assigned 100%). If the HashMap is not presized, there is a cost of approximately another 30% to 60% on the HashMap inserts (i.e., 30% to 60% longer in time). The following chart shows the times using Sun VM Version 1.2 with JIT (the ratios vary under other VMs):

	Sorted insert	Random insert	Sorted access	Random access
HashMap	100%	113%	100%	140%
TernarySearchTree	823%	577%	921%	410%

You can see that you need to gain an order of magnitude to catch up to the HashMap performance.

Profiling is not a huge help; it says only that you need to improve the times on these few methods you have. So you need to target basics. First, by using a char array at the beginning, get rid of the overhead of accessing the characters from the string key one at a time through the string accessor. Also, by passing the length as a parameter, remove the overhead of repeatedly accessing the string size through its length() method. At the same time, rather than create a new char array for each string every time you insert or search the tree, repeatedly use the same char buffer. The new classes look like this:

```
public class TernarySearchTree
{
  TernarySearchTreeNode root;
  char[ ] buff = new char[5000];

  public Object get(String key)
  {
    key.getChars(0, key.length( ), buff, 0);
    return TernarySearchTreeNode1.search(root, buff, 0, key.length( )-1);
  }

  public Object put(String key, Object value)
  {
    key.getChars(0, key.length( ), buff, 0);
    root = TernarySearchTreeNode.insert(root, buff, 0, key.length( )-1, value);
    return null; //fake it for now
  }
}

class TernarySearchTreeNode
{
  char splitchar;
  TernarySearchTreeNode low;
  TernarySearchTreeNode high;
  TernarySearchTreeNode equal;
  Object value;

  public static Object search(TernarySearchTreeNode p, char[ ] str,
                              int strIdx, int strMaxIdx)
  {
    char c;
    if (p == null)
      return null;
    else if ( (c=str[strIdx]) < p.splitchar)
      return search(p.low, str, strIdx, strMaxIdx);
    else if (c > p.splitchar)
      return search(p.high, str, strIdx, strMaxIdx);
    else
    {
```

```
        if (strIdx == strMaxIdx)
          return p.value;
        else
          return search(p.equal, str, strIdx+1, strMaxIdx);
    }
  }

  public static TernarySearchTreeNode insert(TernarySearchTreeNode p, char[] str,
                                             int strIdx, int strMaxIdx, Object o)
  {
    char c;
    if (p == null)
    {
      p = new TernarySearchTreeNode(str[strIdx]);
    }
    if ( (c = str[strIdx]) < p.splitchar)
      p.low = insert(p.low, str, strIdx, strMaxIdx, o);
    else if (c == p.splitchar)
    {
      if (strIdx == strMaxIdx)
        p.value = o;
      else
        p.equal = insert(p.equal, str, strIdx+1, strMaxIdx, o);
    }
    else
      p.high = insert(p.high , str, strIdx, strMaxIdx, o);
    return p;
  }

  public TernarySearchTreeNode(char c)
  {
    splitchar = c;
  }
}
```

The algorithms all stay the same; we have applied only the most basic tuning. The following table illustrates the measured values:

	Sorted insert	Random insert	Sorted access	Random access
HashMap	100%	113%	100%	140%
TernarySearchTree	660%	464%	841%	391%
Original implementation	823%	577%	921%	410%

Well, it's a little better, but it should be a lot better. Bentley and Sedgewick suggest one obvious improvement: changing the recursive algorithms to iterative ones. This is a standard tuning technique, but it can be difficult to achieve. You can use the implementations here as a sort of template: look at how the recursion has been converted into iteration by having a "current" node, p, which is changed on each pass.

This is the normal way of moving from recursion to iteration (see also the sections "Recursion" and "Recursion and Stacks" in Chapter 7). The classes now look like:

```java
public class TernarySearchTree
{
  TernarySearchTreeNode root;
  char buff[ ] = new char[5000];

  public Object get(String key)
  {
    if(root == null)
      return null;
    else
    {
      key.getChars(0, key.length( ), buff, 0);
      return root.search(buff, 0, key.length( ) - 1);
    }
  }

  public Object put(String key, Object obj)
  {
    key.getChars(0, key.length( ), buff, 0);
    if(root == null)
      root = new TernarySearchTreeNode(buff[0]);
    return root.insert(buff, 0, key.length( ) - 1, obj);
  }
}

class TernarySearchTreeNode
{
  char splitchar;
  TernarySearchTreeNode low;
  TernarySearchTreeNode high;
  TernarySearchTreeNode equal;
  Object value;

  public Object search(char str[ ], int strIdx, int strMaxIdx)
  {
    char c;
    for(TernarySearchTreeNode p = this; p != null;)
    {
      if((c = str[strIdx]) < p.splitchar)
        p = p.low;
      else if(c == p.splitchar)
      {
        if(strIdx == strMaxIdx)
          return p.value;
        strIdx++;
        p = p.equal;
      }
      else
        p = p.high;
    }
    return null;
```

```
    }

    public Object insert(char str[ ], int strIdx, int strMaxIdx, Object o)
    {
      TernarySearchTreeNode p = this;
      char c;
      while(true)
      {
        if ( (c = str[strIdx]) < p.splitchar)
        {
          if(p.low == null)
            p.low = new TernarySearchTreeNode(c);
          p = p.low;
        }
        else if(c == p.splitchar)
        {
          if(strIdx == strMaxIdx)
          {
            Object old = p.value;
            p.value = o;
            return old;
          }
          strIdx++;
          c = str[strIdx];
          if(p.equal == null)
            p.equal = new TernarySearchTreeNode(c);
          p = p.equal;
        }
        else
        {
          if(p.high == null)
            p.high = new TernarySearchTreeNode(c);
          p = p.high;
        }
      }
    }

    public TernarySearchTreeNode(char c)
    {
      splitchar = c;
    }
  }
```

The iterative implementation of insert( ) allows you to return the old object easily, thus making the implementation of put( ) have correct functionality for a Map. The following table illustrates the resulting measurements (the previous measurements are in parentheses):

	Sorted insert	Random insert	Sorted access	Random access
HashMap	100%	113%	100%	140%
TernarySearchTree	558% (660%)	373% (464%)	714% (841%)	353% (391%)
Original implementation	823%	577%	921%	410%

The performance has improved, but it's still a long way from the HashMap performance. It is worth noting that these simple optimizations have already cut the times by over a third. To get a big boost, you need to target something large. Object creation can be a serious performance problem, as we saw in Chapter 4. Bentley and Sedgewick state that their major performance optimization is to preallocate memory for the tree. So let's change the node creation in the insert call to assign nodes from a precreated pool of nodes, i.e., create a large pool of nodes at the initial creation of TernarySearchTree, and assign these as required in the tree insert( ) method. The code is straightforward, replacing the new TernarySearchTreeNode( ) call with a newNode( ) call, and the pool management is simple:

```
public static TernarySearchTreeNode newNode(char c,
                                  TernarySearchTreeNode pool)
{
  TernarySearchTreeNode p = pool;
  pool = pool.equal;
  p.splitchar = c;
  p.low = p.equal = p.high = null;
  return p;
}

TernarySearchTreeNode static createPool(int size)
{
  TernarySearchTreeNode last;
  TernarySearchTreeNode pool;
  for (int i = size; i > 0; i--)
  {
    last = pool;
    pool = new TernarySearchTreeNode( );
    pool.equal=last;
  }
  return pool;
}
```

The following chart shows the new measurements (previous measurements in parentheses):

	Sorted insert	Random insert	Sorted access	Random access
HashMap	100%	113%	100%	140%
TernarySearchTree	368% (558%)	234% (373%)	654% (714%)	315% (353%)
Original implementation	823%	577%	921%	410%

We are getting closer for the average (random) case. But why is there such a discrepancy between the average and worst (mostly-sorted) case now, and why is there an improvement in the access times when the change should have altered only the insertion times? The discrepancy between the average and worst cases may indicate that the worst times are a result of the time spent in the stack due to the depth of the insert/search loops rather than node creation. The improvement in the access times may be due to internal memory management of the VM: all the nodes being created one after the other may be the reason for the improved access. (Although since everything is in memory, I'm not quite sure why this would be so. Possibly, the heap space is segmented according to requisition from the OS, and you may have paged slightly to disk, which could explain the discrepancy. But I have discarded any timings that had any significant paging, so the discrepancy is not entirely clear.) There is an extra issue now, as you have not been measuring the time taken in creating the tree. The last optimization has increased this time, as the nodes were previously created during the insert, but are now all created at tree creation. Consequently, you might now need to consider this creation time, depending on how the data structure is used.

The creation time is actually rather large. It would be nice if there were a way to create all nodes required in one VM call, but there is none provided in Java (at least up to JDK 1.4). You can finesse this shortcoming by implementing your own memory management using arrays, and it is certainly worth doing so as an exercise to see if the technique gives any advantages. Another possibility is to create objects at initialization in a separate thread, but this requires previous knowledge of many things, so I will not consider that option here.

Fortunately, the node structure is simple, so you can map it into an array of ints. Each node takes five indexes: the first to hold the character, the next three to hold index values for other nodes, and the last to hold an index value into an Object array (which can hold the Object values).

Now you no longer have the separate node class; all management is in the TernarySearchTree class:

```
public class TernarySearchTree
{
    //offsets into the array for each node
    final static int INITIAL_NODE = 1;
    final static int LOW_OFFSET = 1;
    final static int HIGH_OFFSET = 2;
    final static int EQUAL_OFFSET = 3;
    final static int VALUE_OFFSET = 4;
    final static int NODE_SIZE = 5;

    //A buffer for the string
    char[] buff = new char[5000];
    //the array of node 'object's
    int[] nodes;
    //the array of Object values, one for each node
    Object[] objects;
    //The index to the next available unused node.
    //Note that it is at index 1,
    //not zero
    int nextNode = INITIAL_NODE;
    //The index to the next object
    int nextObject = 1;
```

```
//default constructor
public TernarySearchTree( )
{
  this(500000);
}

//Constructor to create a pre-sized Ternary tree
public TernarySearchTree(int size)
{
  //create all the nodes.
  //Each node is five int indexes and one Object index
  nodes = new int[NODE_SIZE*size];
  objects = new Object[size];
}

public Object get(String key)
{
  key.getChars(0, key.length( ), buff, 0);
  return search(buff, 0, key.length( )-1);
}

public Object put(String key, Object value)
{
  key.getChars(0, key.length( ), buff, 0);
  if (nextNode == INITIAL_NODE)
  {
    nodes[INITIAL_NODE] = buff[0];
    nextNode+=NODE_SIZE;
  }
  return insert(buff, 0, key.length( )-1, value);
}

/**
 * The node search and insert methods just map from the previous
 * implementations using the mappings
 *    p.splitchar -> nodes[p]
 *    p.low -> nodes[p+LOW_OFFSET]
 *    p.high -> nodes[p+HIGH_OFFSET]
 *    p.equal -> nodes[p+EQUAL_OFFSET]
 *    p.value -> objects[nodes[p+VALUE_OFFSET]]
 */
public Object search(char[ ] str, int strIdx, int strMaxIdx)
{
  int p = INITIAL_NODE;
  int c;
  while (p != 0)
  {
    if ( (c = str[strIdx]) < nodes[p])
      p = nodes[p+LOW_OFFSET];
    else if (c == nodes[p])
    {
      if (strIdx == strMaxIdx)
        return objects[nodes[p+VALUE_OFFSET]];
      else
```

```
        {
          strIdx++;
          p = nodes[p+EQUAL_OFFSET];
        }
      }
      else
        p = nodes[p+HIGH_OFFSET];
  }
  return null;
}

public Object insert(char[ ] str, int strIdx, int strMaxIdx, Object o)
{
  int p = INITIAL_NODE;
  int c = str[strIdx];
  Object old;
  for(;;)
  {
    if ( c < nodes[p])
    {
      if (nodes[p+LOW_OFFSET] == 0)
      {
        nodes[p+LOW_OFFSET] = nextNode;
        nodes[nextNode] = c;
        nextNode+=NODE_SIZE;
      }
      p = nodes[p+LOW_OFFSET];
    }
    else if (c == nodes[p])
    {
      if (strIdx == strMaxIdx)
      {
        if (nodes[p+VALUE_OFFSET] == 0)
        {
          nodes[p+VALUE_OFFSET] = nextObject;
          nextObject++;
        }
        old = objects[nodes[p+VALUE_OFFSET]];
        objects[nodes[p+VALUE_OFFSET]] = o;
        return old;
      }
      else
      {
        strIdx++;
        c=str[strIdx];
        if (nodes[p+EQUAL_OFFSET] == 0)
        {
          nodes[p+EQUAL_OFFSET] = nextNode;
          nodes[nextNode] = c;
          nextNode+=NODE_SIZE;
        }
        p = nodes[p+EQUAL_OFFSET];
      }
    }
```

```
        else
        {
          if (nodes[p+HIGH_OFFSET] == 0)
          {
            nodes[p+HIGH_OFFSET] = nextNode;
            nodes[nextNode] = c;
            nextNode+=NODE_SIZE;
          }
          p = nodes[p+HIGH_OFFSET];
        }
      }
    }
  }
```

Although the class may look a little complex, it is pretty easy to see what is happening if you bear in mind that nodes[p+HIGH_OFFSET] is equivalent to the p.high in the previous version of the tree (i.e., the tree that had the separate node class). There are only two slightly more complex differences. First, the equivalent of p.value is now objects[nodes[p+VALUE_OFFSET]] because the nodes array holds only ints, and the value can be any Object (hence requiring a separate Object array). Second, a new node is allocated by providing the index of the current high-water mark in the nodes array, held by variable nextNode. This index is then incremented by the size of the node, NODE_SIZE (which is five fields), for the next node allocation.

This alternative implementation does not affect the external interface to the class, so the complexity remains hidden from any other class. This implementation is much closer to the C implementation provided by Bentley and Sedgewick, where nodes were allocated in a similar large chunk. Now the question is, have we improved performance? The next table shows the current measurements (previous measurements in parentheses):

	Sorted insert	Random insert	Sorted access	Random access
HashMap	100%	113%	100%	140%
TernarySearchTree	249% (368%)	200% (234%)	334% (654%)	200% (315%)
Original implementation	823%	577%	921%	410%

Overall, these are the best results so far, and the worst case is much closer to the average case. Also, the object-creation time is much better: it is essentially as fast as possible in a VM since you are creating just two new significant objects (which are very large arrays), and so the limitation is purely down to how quickly the VM can allocate the memory space.

You might be satisfied to stop at this point, even though your structure is slower than a HashMap by a factor of two. It does provide the extra required functionality of partial matching, as well as the full matching that HashMaps provide, and relative performance is acceptable.

But there is one more major change to consider. You know that digital search tries are extremely fast, but inefficient in space. If you are prepared to accept the extra space taken, you can still consider using digital tries to achieve improved performance. If you are using strings that contain mainly the ASCII character set, consider using a digital search trie for the first couple of characters. A two-node digital search trie has 256 nodes for a one-character string, and 256 nodes for the first character in multicharacter strings. For the multicharacter strings, the second node has 256 nodes for each node of the first character, giving $256 \times 257 = 65{,}792$ nodes. With each node using 4 bytes, you would use $65792 \times 4 = 263{,}168$ bytes. So you have a quarter of a megabyte before you even start to use this structure. However, if you use this structure for a large amount of string data, you may find this memory usage small compared to the final overall size. Assuming this is acceptable, let's look at how it is implemented and how it performs.

Basically, you implement a trie for the first two characters, but each two-character node then points to the root of a ternary tree. The two-digit trie needs a parallel Object structure to store the Object values that correspond to one- or two-digit strings. This is, of course, occupying a lot of space, and there are methods for reducing the space requirements (for example, you can optimize for just the alphanumeric characters, mapping them into smaller arrays), but for this exercise, let's keep it simple. The class now looks like this:

```
public class TernarySearchTree
{
  final static int LOW_OFFSET = 1;
  final static int HIGH_OFFSET = 2;
  final static int EQUAL_OFFSET = 3;
  final static int VALUE_OFFSET = 4;
  final static int NODE_SIZE = 5;
  final static int INITIAL_TRIE_NODE = 1 + NODE_SIZE;
  final static int INITIAL_NODE = 1;

  char[ ] buff = new char[5000];
  int[ ] nodes;
  Object[ ] objects;
  int nextNode = INITIAL_TRIE_NODE;
  int nextObject = 0;
  int initial = -1;
  Object[ ] trie1Objects;
  int[ ][ ] trie2;
  Object[ ][ ] trie2Objects;

  public TernarySearchTree( )
  {
    this(500000);
  }

  public TernarySearchTree(int size)
  {
```

```java
    trie1Objects = new Object[256];
    trie2 = new int[256][256];
    trie2Objects = new Object[256][256];
    nodes = new int[NODE_SIZE*size+1];
    objects = new Object[size];
  }

  public Object get(String key)
  {
    int len = key.length( );
    key.getChars(0, len, buff, 0);
    int first = buff[0];
    int second = buff[1];
    if (len == 1 && (first < 256))
    {
      return trie1Objects[first];
    }
    else if (len == 2 && (first < 256) && (second < 256))
    {
      return trie2Objects[first][second];
    }
    else if ((first < 256) && (second < 256))
    {
      int nodep = trie2[first][second];
      if (nodep == 0)
      {
        return null;
      }
      return search(buff, 2, len-1, nodep);
    }
    else
    {
      //Use node[0] as a flag to determine if entered here
      if (nodes[0] == 0)
      {
        return null;
      }
      return search(buff, 0, len-1, INITIAL_NODE);
    }
  }

  public void release( )
  {
    nodes = null;
    objects = null;
  }

  public Object search(char[ ] str, int strIdx, int strMaxIdx, int p)
  {
    int c;
    while (p != 0)
    {
      if ( (c = str[strIdx]) < nodes[p])
```

```
      p = nodes[p+LOW_OFFSET];
    else if (c == nodes[p])
    {
      if (strIdx == strMaxIdx)
        return objects[nodes[p+VALUE_OFFSET]];
      else
      {
        strIdx++;
        p = nodes[p+EQUAL_OFFSET];
      }
    }
    else
      p = nodes[p+HIGH_OFFSET];
  }
  return null;
}

public Object put(String key, Object value)
{
  int len = key.length( );
  key.getChars(0, len, buff, 0);
  int first = buff[0];
  int second = buff[1];
  if (len == 1 && (first < 256))
  {
    Object old = trie1Objects[first];
    trie1Objects[first] = value;
    return old;
  }
  else if (len == 2 && (first < 256) && (second < 256))
  {
    Object old = trie2Objects[first][second];
    trie2Objects[first][second] = value;
    return old;
  }
  else if ((first < 256) && (second < 256))
  {
    int nodep = trie2[first][second];
    if (nodep == 0)
    {
      nodep = trie2[first][second] = nextNode;
      nodes[nextNode] = buff[2];
      nextNode+=NODE_SIZE;
    }
    return insert(buff, 2, len-1, value, nodep);
  }
  else
  {
    //Use node[0] as a flag to determine if entered here
    if (nodes[0] == 0)
    {
      nodes[0] = 1;
      nodes[INITIAL_NODE] = first;
    }
```

```
      return insert(buff, 0, len-1, value, INITIAL_NODE);
   }
}

   public Object insert(char[ ] str, int strIdx, int strMaxIdx,
                        Object value, int p)
{
   int c = str[strIdx];
   int cdiff;
   Object old;
   for(;;)
   {
     if ( (cdiff = c - nodes[p]) < 0)
     {
       if (nodes[p+LOW_OFFSET] == 0)
       {
         nodes[p+LOW_OFFSET] = nextNode;
         nodes[nextNode] = c;
         nextNode+=NODE_SIZE;
       }
       p = nodes[p+LOW_OFFSET];
     }
     else if (cdiff == 0)
     {
       if (strIdx == strMaxIdx)
       {
         if (nodes[p+VALUE_OFFSET] == 0)
         {
           nodes[p+VALUE_OFFSET] = nextObject;
           nextObject++;
         }
         old = objects[nodes[p+VALUE_OFFSET]];
         objects[nodes[p+VALUE_OFFSET]] = value;
         return old;
       }
       else
       {
         strIdx++;
         c=str[strIdx];
         if (nodes[p+EQUAL_OFFSET] == 0)
         {
           nodes[p+EQUAL_OFFSET] = nextNode;
           nodes[nextNode] = c;
           nextNode+=NODE_SIZE;
         }
         p = nodes[p+EQUAL_OFFSET];
       }
     }
     else
     {
       if (nodes[p+HIGH_OFFSET] == 0)
       {
         nodes[p+HIGH_OFFSET] = nextNode;
         nodes[nextNode] = c;
```

```
            nextNode+=NODE_SIZE;
        }
        p = nodes[p+HIGH_OFFSET];
      }
    }
  }
}
```

This table shows the measurements (previous measurements in parentheses):

	Sorted insert	Random insert	Sorted access	Random access
HashMap	100%	113%	100%	140%
TernarySearchTree	103% (249%)	158% (200%)	140% (334%)	205% (200%)
Original implementation	823%	577%	921%	410%

The results are the best yet for all values except the random access, which is roughly the same as before. Perhaps the most interesting aspect is that you now get better times on the mostly-sorted input than on the randomized input (which is also the case for the HashMap). The result is still slower than a HashMap, but has the extra capability to identify partial matches efficiently. For more specialized versions, such as those needed for a particular application, you can make an implementation that is significantly faster (just as for the hash-table structures earlier in this chapter).

All in all, we've taken a particular structure in its initial form, optimized it using various techniques, and made it two to eight times faster accessing and updating elements.

Note that there are also costs beyond the extra space costs for this last hybrid structure. The implementation before this last one is still a pure ternary tree. That pure implementation has some elegant and simple recursive algorithms for iterating through the tree in order and for identifying partial matches. However, implementing the equivalent algorithms for the last hybrid structure is quite a bit more complicated, as you have to jump between the two structures it uses.

There is not much educational value in proceeding further with these classes here. We've covered the uses of different structures and how to reimplement classes to use different underlying structures for the purpose of improving performance. This book is not intended to provide finished components, so if you feel that this structure may be useful to you in some situation, you'll need to complete it yourself.

Just a few final performance notes about the optimized class. Obviously, you want to optimize its use of space. So note that its size is given by the high-water mark, which is easily determined. And if you want to make the class dynamically growable at large sizes, you may be better off catching the exception thrown when the high-water mark grows past the end of the nodes array and then copying to a larger array, rather than making a test on each insertion.

Performance Checklist

Most of these suggestions apply only after a bottleneck has been identified:

- Test using either the target size for collections or, if this is not definite, various sizes of collections.
- Test updating collections using the expected order of the data or, if this is not definite, various orders of data, including sorted data.
- Match the scaling characteristics of the structures against the volumes of data likely to be applied.
- ArrayList is probably a better default list than LinkedList.
- Presize collections to their final sizes when possible.
- Test for the RandomAccess interface where applicable for faster list iteration
- Consider switching to alternative data structures or algorithms.
  - Use the most appropriate collection class available.
  - Consider using two collections with different performance characteristics to hold the same data.
  - Consider using plain arrays, e.g., int[ ], Object[ ].
  - Consider using hybrid data structures.
  - Use specialized collections that avoid casts or unnecessary method calls.
  - Consider wrapping the elements of the collection in a specialized class that improves access times (e.g., Hashtable key class with faster hashCode( ) and equals( ) methods).
  - Add caching or specialized accessors to collections where some elements are accessed more often than others.
- Access the underlying collection structure when iterating over the elements of a collection.
  - Copy the elements into an array rather than access many elements one at a time through the collection element accessors.
- Preallocate memory for element storage rather than allocating at update time.
  - Reuse element-storage objects when they are released.
  - Map elements into one or more arrays of data variables to allocate the whole collection in as few calls as possible.
- Test if changing a recursive algorithm to an iterative one provides a useful speedup.
- Make recursive methods tail-recursive.

In this chapter:
- Tools
- Message Reduction
- Comparing Communications Layers
- Caching
- Batching I
- Application Partitioning
- Batching II
- Low-Level Communication Optimizations
- Distributed Garbage Collection
- Databases
- Web Services

CHAPTER 12
Distributed Computing

> *On a 56K modem, this report will take about half an
> hour to download (for a 30-second download of just
> the information contained in the report, click here).*
> —From a web site that shall remain unnamed

Distributed-application bottlenecks are of two general types. The first type occurs within application subcomponents. This type of bottleneck is essentially independent of the distributed nature of the application, and the other chapters in this book deal with how to tune this type of bottleneck. In this chapter, we deal with the second type of bottleneck, which occurs within the distribution infrastructure. This latter type of bottleneck is specific to the distributed nature of the application, and can be tuned using a number of techniques:

Caching

When an application repeatedly distributes the same data, a significant gain in performance can be obtained by caching the data, thus changing some distributed requests to local ones.

Compression

If the volume of data being transferred is large or causes multiple chunks to be transferred, then compressing the transferred data can improve performance by reducing transfer times.

Reducing messages

Most distributed applications have their performance limited by the latency of the connections. Each distributed message incurs the connection-latency overhead, and so the greater the number of messages, the greater the cumulative performance delay due to latency. Reducing the number of messages transferred by a distributed application can produce a large improvement in the application performance.

Application partitioning

The performance of any distributed function in a distributed application normally has at least two factors involved. These two factors are the location for the function to execute and the location where the data for the function resides. Typically, the application developers are faced with the choice of moving the function to the location of the data, or moving the data to the location of the function. These decisions depend on the volume and nature of the data to be processed, the relative power and availability of the CPUs in the different locations, and how much of the data will be transferred after the function completes. If the function's result is to transfer a relatively small amount of data, it should be located on the machine where the data used by the function resides.

Batching

There are several ways that batching can improve the performance of a distributed application. First, the number of messages can be reduced by combining multiple messages into fewer batched messages. Second, data can be split up and transferred in shorter batches if waiting for all the data is the cause of the delay in response times. Third, data requirements can be anticipated, and extra data can be transferred in batches together with the data that is needed at that moment, in anticipation of the extra data that will be needed soon. Further batching variations can be used by extending these strategies.

Stubbing

When data needs to be transferred across a distributed application, the distribution infrastructure often uses general mechanisms for transfers. This results in transferring more data than is actually required. By selectively "stubbing out" data links, only the data that is needed is transferred. Instance variables of objects can be replaced with "stub" objects that respond to messages by transferring the required data (if the fields are defined using an interface). Java also supports the transient modifier, which can be used to eliminate unnecessary data transfers. Fields defined as transient are not transferred when serialization is used, but this is a rather blunt technique that leads to all-or-nothing transfers of fields.

Asynchronous activities

Distributed systems should make maximum use of asynchronous activities wherever possible. No part of the application should be blocked while waiting for other parts of the application to respond, unless the application logic absolutely requires such blocked activities.

In the following sections, we look at examples of applying some of these techniques to optimize performance.[*]

---

[*] This chapter deals with general distributed application optimizations. Higher-level J2EE optimizations are covered in Chapters 15 through18.

Tools

A number of tools for monitoring distributed applications are listed in the "Client/ Server Communications" section in Chapter 2 as well as in "Network I/O" in Chapter 14. In addition, there is one other monitoring tool I often find useful when dealing with distributed applications: a *relay server*. This is a simple program that accepts incoming socket connections and simply relays all data on to another outgoing socket. Normally, I customize the server to identify aspects of the application being monitored, but having a generic relay server as a template is useful, so I present a simple one here:

```java
package tuning.distrib;

import java.io.*;
import java.net.*;

class RelayServer
  implements Runnable
{
  //Simple input and output sockets
  Socket in_s;
  Socket out_s;

  //A string message to printout for logging identification
  String message;

  //Simple constructor just assigns the three parameters
  public RelayServer(Socket in, Socket out, String msg)
  {
    in_s = in;
    out_s = out;
    message = msg;
  }

  //The required method for Runnable.
  //Simply repeatedly reads from socket input, logs the read data
  //to System.out, and then relays that data on to the socket output
  public void run()
  {
    try
    {
      InputStream in = in_s.getInputStream();
      OutputStream out = out_s.getOutputStream();
      byte[ ] buf = new byte[8192];
      int len;
      for(;;)
      {
        len = in.read(buf);
        System.out.print(message);
        System.out.println(new String(buf, 0, len));
        out.write(buf, 0, len);
      }
    }
```

```
      catch (Exception e)
      {
        System.out.print(message);
        System.out.println(" TERMINATED");
        System.out.flush( );
        try{in_s.close( );}catch(Exception e2){ }
        try{out_s.close( );}catch(Exception e2){ }
      }
    }

    //Basic main( ) takes two arguments, a host and port. All incoming
    //connections will be relayed to the given host and port.
    public static void main(String[ ] args)
    {
      ServerSocket srvr = null;
      try
      {
        //Start a server socket on the localhost at the given port
        srvr = new ServerSocket(Integer.parseInt(args[1]));
        for(;;)
        {
          //Block until a connection is made to us.
          Socket sclient = srvr.accept( );
          System.out.println("Trying to connect to " + args[0]);
          //Connect to the 'real' server
          Socket ssrvr = new Socket(args[0], Integer.parseInt(args[1]));
          System.out.println("Connected to " + args[0]);
          //Start two threads, one to relay client to server comms,
          //and one to relay server to client communications.
          (new Thread(new RelayServer(sclient, ssrvr,
              "CLIENT->SERVER"))).start( );
          (new Thread(new RelayServer(ssrvr, sclient,
              "SERVER->CLIENT"))).start( );
        }
      }
      catch (Exception e)
      {
        System.out.println("SERVER TERMINATED: " + e.getMessage( ));
        try{srvr.close( );}catch(Exception e2){ }
      }
    }
  }
}
```

As listed here, the relay server simply accepts any incoming connections on the given port and relays all communication to the outgoing server, while at the same time printing all communication to System.out. To test the relay server using an HTTP connection, you could start it with the command line:

```
% java tuning.distrib.RelayServer someserver 80
```

Then you could try connecting to *someserver* using a web browser with the URL *http://localhost/some/path/*. This instructs the browser to connect to the relay server, and the relay server acts like a web server at *someserver* (i.e., as if the URL had been *http://someserver/some/path/*).

Message Reduction

Let's look at a simple example of reducing message calls. For later infrastructure comparison, we will use three different distributed-application infrastructures: CORBA, RMI, and a proprietary distribution mechanism using plain sockets and serialization (see the sidebar "Proprietary Communications Infrastructures"). In the example, I present a simple server object that supports only three instance variables and three methods to set those instance variables.

Proprietary Communications Infrastructures

You can easily create your own communication mechanisms by connecting two processes using standard sockets. Creating two-way connections with Sockets and ServerSockets is very straightforward. For basic communication, you decide on your own communication protocol, possibly using serialization to handle passing objects across the communication channel.

However, using proprietary communications is not a wise thing to do and can be a severe maintenance overhead unless your communication and distribution requirements are simple. I occasionally use proprietary communications for testing purposes and for comparison against other communications infrastructures, as I have done in this chapter.

In this chapter, I use a simple, generic communications infrastructure that automatically handles remotely invoking methods: basically, a stripped-down version of RMI. I generate a server skeleton and client proxy using reflection to identify all the public methods of the distributable class. Then I copy the RMI communication protocol (which consists of passing method identifiers and parameters from proxies to server objects identified by their own identifiers). The only other item required is a lookup mechanism, which again is quite simple to add as a remotely accessible table. The whole infrastructure is in one fairly simple class, tuning.distrib.custom.Generate, available from this book's catalog page, *http://www.oreilly.com/catalog/javapt2/*.

CORBA Example

The CORBA IDL definition is quite simple:

```
module tuning {
  module distrib {
    module corba {
      interface ServerObject {
        void setBoolean(in boolean flag);
        void setNumber(in long i);
        void setString(in string obj);
}; }; }; };
```

The server class implementation for this IDL definition is:

```
package tuning.distrib.corba;

public class ServerObjectImpl
  extends _ServerObjectImplBase
{
  boolean bool;
  int num;
  String string;
  public void setBoolean(boolean b) {bool = b;}
  public void setNumber(int i) {num = i;}
  public void setString(String s) {string = s;}
}
```

All the support classes are generated using the *idlj* utility. For JDK 1.3, this generates interfaces ServerObject and ServerObjectOperations; skeleton classes _ServerObjectImplBase and _ServerObjectStub; and server object assistant classes ServerObjectHelper and ServerObjectHolder. In addition, I define a main( ) method that installs an instantiation of the server object in the name service and then remains alive to serve client requests. All classes are defined in the tuning.distrib. corba package.

My client simply resolves the server object from the name service, obtaining a proxy for the server, and then calls the three methods and sets the three instance variables. For the test, I repeat the method calls a number of times to obtain average measurements.

The optimization to reduce the number of method calls is extremely simple. Just add one method, which sets all three instance variables in one call in the following IDL definition:

```
void setAll(in boolean flag, in long i, in string obj);
```

The corresponding method is added to the server class:

```
public void setAll(boolean b, int i, String s)
{
  bool = b; num = i; string = s;
}
```

The result is that the single method call requires one-third of the network transfers and takes one-third of the time, compared to the triple method calls (see the later section "Comparing Communications Layers").

RMI Example

The RMI implementation is essentially the same. The server-object interface (with optimized method) is defined as:

```
package tuning.distrib.rmi;

import java.rmi.Remote;
```

```
import java.rmi.RemoteException;

public interface ServerObject
    extends Remote
{
  public abstract void setBoolean(boolean flag)
    throws RemoteException;
  public abstract void setNumber(int i)
    throws RemoteException;
  public abstract void setString(String obj)
    throws RemoteException;
  public abstract void setAll(boolean flag, int i, String obj)
    throws RemoteException;
}
```

The RMI server-object implementation is the same as the CORBA version, except that it extends UnicastRemoteObject, implements ServerObject, and defines the methods as throwing RemoteException. All the support classes are generated using the *rmic* utility. For JDK 1.3, this generates skeleton classes ServerObjectImpl_Skel and ServerObjectImpl_Stub. In addition, I define a main( ) method that sets a security manager and installs an instantiation of the server object in the name service. All classes are defined in the tuning.distrib.rmi package.

Once again, the result is that the single method call requires one-third of the network transfers and takes one-third of the time, compared to the triple method calls (see "Comparing Communications Layers").

Proprietary Communications Layer

A distributed system can be defined with sockets and serialization. I have implemented a simple generator that provides all the basic stub and skeleton behavior for a distributed application (tuning.distrib.custom.Generate class; see the sidebar "Proprietary Communications Infrastructures"). The server object is defined as before, with the interface:

```
package tuning.distrib.custom;

public interface ServerObject
{
  public abstract void setBoolean(boolean flag);
  public abstract void setNumber(int i);
  public abstract void setString(String obj);
  public abstract void setAll(boolean flag, int i, String obj);
}
```

This server-object implementation is the same as the CORBA version, though without the need to extend any class: it implements only ServerObject.

Yet again, the result is that the single method call requires one-third of the network transfers and takes one-third of the time, compared to the triple method calls (see the next section).

Comparing Communications Layers

In the previous sections, we saw how reducing the number of messages led to a proportional reduction in the time taken by the application to process those messages. Table 12-1 compares the performance between the different communications layers used in those sections.

Table 12-1. Comparison of different communications layers

	Executing three separate methods			Executing one combined method		
	Time taken	Bytes written	Overhead time	Time taken	Bytes written	Overhead time
CORBA	512%	291	194%	175%	106	66%
RMI	356%	136	181%	113%	54	56%
Proprietary	293%	40	80%	100%	20	31%

Here, I detail the measurements made for the three communications layers using the tests defined in the "Message Reduction" section. The first three columns list measurements taken while executing the three updating methods together. The second three columns list the measurements taken when the single updating method updates the server object. Within each set of three columns, the first column lists the round-trip time taken for executing the methods, with all times normalized to the proprietary communications layer time in the combined method case. (The network round-trip overhead is a 10-millisecond ping time in these tests.) The second column lists the number of bytes written from the client to the server to execute one set of methods, and the third column lists the time taken to run the test with no latency (i.e., client and server on the same machine), using the same time scale as the first column.

As you can see, CORBA has more overhead than RMI, which in turn has more overhead than the proprietary system. For simple distributed applications such as those used in the examples, using a proprietary-distribution mechanism is a big win. If you include optimized serialization, which can be easily done only for the proprietary layer, the advantages would be even greater. (See "Serialization" in Chapter 8 for examples of optimizing serialization.) However, the proprietary layer requires more work to support the distribution mechanisms, and the more complicated the application becomes, the more onerous the support is.

There is some evidence that CORBA scales significantly better than RMI as applications grow in any dimension (number of clients, number of servers, number of objects, sizes of objects, etc.). RMI was designed as a relatively simple distributed-application communications layer for Java whereas CORBA has a much more complex architecture, aimed specifically at supporting large enterprise systems. Given this difference, it is probably not surprising that CORBA has the better scaling characteristics. RMI uses significantly more resources to support certain features such as distributed garbage collection, which can impose heavy overhead at large scales. CORBA directly supports asynchronous communications at the method-definition level by allowing methods to be defined as one-way message transfers.

It appears that for simple distributed applications, a proprietary communications layer is most efficient and can be supported fairly easily. For distributed applications of moderate complexity and scale, RMI and CORBA are similar in cost, though it is easier to develop with RMI. For large-scale or very complex distributed applications, CORBA appears to win out in performance.

Caching

To illustrate caching, I extend the server object used in the previous sections. I add three accessor methods to access the three server instance variables:

```
public boolean getBoolean( );
public int getNumber( );
public String getString ( );
```

Now you can add a generic server-object proxy implementation that handles caching. The implementation is essentially the same for all three communications layers:

```
package tuning.distrib.custom;

public class ServerObjectCacher
  implements ServerObject
{
  ServerObject stub;
  boolean b;
  boolean bInit;
  int i;
  boolean iInit;
  String s;
  boolean sInit;

  public ServerObjectCacher(ServerObject stub)
  {
    super ( );
    this.stub = stub;
  }

  public boolean getBoolean( )
  {
    if (bInit)
      return b;
    else
    {
      b = stub.getBoolean( );
      bInit = true;
      return b;
    }
  }
}
```

```
    public int getNumber( )
    {
      if (iInit)
        return i;
      else
      {
        i = stub.getNumber( );
        iInit = true;
        return i;
      }
    }

    public String getString ( )
    {
      if (sInit)
        return s;
      else
      {
        s = stub.getString( );
        sInit = true;
        return s;
      }
    }

    public void setBoolean(boolean flag)
    {
      bInit = false;
      stub.setBoolean(flag);
    }

    public void setNumber (int i)
    {
      iInit = false;
      stub.setNumber(i);
    }

    public void setString(String obj)
    {
      sInit = false;
      stub.setString(obj);
    }

    public void setAll(boolean flag, int i, String obj)
    {
      bInit = iInit = sInit = false;
      stub.setAll(flag, i, obj);
    }
  }
```

As you can see, this is a simple proxy object. Each accessor is lazily initialized, and calling any updating method resets the accessors so that they need to be reinitialized from the server. This ensures that any logic executed on the server is not bypassed. If the server object can be changed by other client programs, you need to add callback support for this caching proxy so that whenever the server object is changed, the client proxy is reset.

Running access tests using this caching proxy is simple. The client code needs to be changed in only one place; once the server object is resolved, the resolved proxy is wrapped in this caching proxy. Then it is used exactly as previously:

```
ServerObject obj = (ServerObject) Naming.lookup("/ServerObj");
//now wrap the server object with the caching proxy
obj = new ServerObjectCacher(obj);
//All the rest of the code is the same
```

The timing results are dependent on how many iterations you test of the uncached versus cached access. After the first access, the cached proxy access is a simple local-variable access, whereas the uncached access requires remote messaging. The difference in timings between these two access mechanisms is more than a factor of 1000, so the more iterations of the tests you make, the bigger the overall relative difference in timings you measure. For example, with accesses repeated 500 times, the average cached access takes about 0.5% of the average uncached access time. Doubling the number of repeated accesses to 1000 times doubles the time taken for the uncached access, but the cached access time is essentially the same, so the time is now 0.25% of the average uncached access time.

Batching I

One form of batching optimization is to combine multiple messages into one message. For the examples we've examined so far, this is easily illustrated. Simply add a method to access all attributes of the server object in one access:[*]

```
class ServerObjectDataCopy
{
  public boolean bool;
  public int number;
  public String string;
}

public class ServerObjectImpl
{
  public ServerObjectDataCopy getAll( );
  ...
```

Using this method to batch the three access methods into one access makes the combined (uncached) access of all the attributes three times faster.

---

[*] The various communications layers handle distributed classes differently. This book is not a tutorial on CORBA or RMI, so I have elected to show a standard Java representation of the required classes.

Application Partitioning

A simple but dramatic example of the benefits of application partitioning is to run two identical queries on a collection. One query runs on the server and returns only the result of the query; the second query runs on the client, requiring the collection to be copied to the client.*

It's pretty obvious that since the only difference between the two queries is the amount of data being copied across the network, the second query that copies much more data is slower. For the example, I use a large array of strings and create a query that returns that subset of strings that includes the query string, e.g., "el" is included in "hello" but not in "hi."

The query method is straightforward:

```
public static String[ ] getQuery(String obj, String[ ] array)
{
  Vector v = new Vector( );
  for (int i = 0; i < array.length; i++)
    if (array[i].indexOf(obj) != -1)
      v.addElement(array[i]);
  String[ ] result = new String[v.size( )];
  for (int i = 0; i < result.length; i++)
    result[i] = (String) v.elementAt(i);
  return result;
}
```

To run the query as a server method, I declare one server method in a server object (i.e., in the ServerObject interface):

```
public String[ ] getServerQuery(String obj);
```

This is also straightforward. The client calls getServerQuery( ) on the server proxy object and receives the results. To run the query on the client, I declare a method (again in the ServerObject interface) giving access to the String array containing the strings to be compared:

```
public String[ ] getQueryArray( );
```

The server implementation of getServerQuery( ) is simple (declared in the class that implements the ServerObject interface):

```
public String[ ]getServerQuery(String obj)
{
  return getQuery(obj, getQueryArray( ));
}
```

* This example is based on a demonstration originally created by GemStone to show the benefits of application partitioning using their application server.

The client query implementation is similarly straightforward (this could be declared in any client class that has access to the proxy object, including the stub class[*]):

```
public String[ ] getClientQuery(ServerObject serverProxy, String obj)
{
  return getQuery(obj, serverProxy.getQueryArray( ));
}
```

In fact, there isn't much difference between the two method definitions. But when a test is run to compare the two different queries, the results are startling. For my test, I used an array of 87,880 four-letter strings. The test result produced five strings. Using RMI, the client query took 35 times longer than the server query, and required the transfer of over 600,000 bytes compared to under 100 bytes for the server query. In absolute times, the server query gave a reasonable response time of well under a second. The client query produced an unacceptable response time of over 15 seconds, which would have users wondering what could possibly be taking so long.

Application partitioning similarly applies to moving some of the "intelligence" of the server to the client to reduce messaging to the server. A simple example is a client form where various fields need to be filled in. Often, some of the fields need to be validated according to data format or ranges. For example, a date field has a particular format, and the parts of the date field must fall in certain ranges (e.g., months from 1 to 12). Any such validation logic should be executed on the client; otherwise, you are generating a lot of unnecessary network transfers. The example of date-field validation is perhaps too obvious. Most applications have a widget customized to handle their date-field entries. But the general area of user-interface presentation logic is one in which the logic should reside mostly on the client.

Batching II

To illustrate a second type of batching, we modify the test query from the last section. The only difference is in the choice of string to pass into the query so that the result of the query is a large set. In this test, the result set is over 25,000 strings. The client query is still significantly longer than the server query, but even the server query now takes several seconds in absolute time.

There is no reason to make the user wait for the whole result set to be transferred before displaying some of the results. Altering the application to send results in batches is quite easy. You need to add an intermediate object to hold the results on the server, which can send the results in batches as required.

```
public class QueryResultHolderImpl
  implements QueryResultHolder
```

---

[*] The client query method is logically defined in the client stub or the client proxy object defined for the application. But technically, it is not forced to be defined in these classes and can be defined in any client class that has access to the server proxy object.

```
{
  String[ ] results;
  int sentSoFar;
  public QueryResultHolderImpl(String[ ] results)
  {
    this.results = results;
    sentSoFar = 0;
  }

  public resultSize( ){return results.length;}
  public nextBatch(int batchSize)
  {
    String[ ] batch = new String[batchSize];
    System.arraycopy(results, sentSoFar, batch, 0, batchSize);
    sentSoFar += batchSize;
    return batch;
  }
}
```

You also need to add methods in the server object to support this batching object:

```
public QueryResultHolder getBatchedServerQuery(String obj)
{
  return new QueryResultHolderImpl(getQuery(obj, getQueryArray( )));
}
```

Now the client has the flexibility to request batches of results. The initial call to the query returns as fast as possible, with minimal network-transfer overhead: only one small proxy object is sent back in reply to the query. Note that the assumption here is that the QueryResultHolder object is not serialized when returned; instead, a proxy to the real object is passed to the client. The actual QueryResultHolder object holding the result set remains on the server. By wrapping the QueryResultHolder proxy, the optimization can be made completely transparent.

Low-Level Communication Optimizations

There are a number of optimizations you can make to the low-level communications infrastructure. These optimizations can be difficult to implement, and it is usually easier to buy these types of optimizations than to build them.

Compression

Where the distributed application is transferring large amounts of data over a network, the communications layer can be optimized to support compression of the data transfers. In order to minimize compression overhead for small data transfers, the compression mechanism should have a filter size below which compression is not used for data packets.

The JDK documentation includes an extended example of installing a compression layer in the RMI communications layer (the main documentation index page leads to

RMI documentation under the "Enterprise Features" heading). The following code illustrates a simple example of adding compression into a communications layer. The bold type shows the extra code required:

```
void writeTransfer(byte[ ] transferbuffer, int offset, int len)
{
  if (len <= 0)
    return;
  int newlen = compress(transferbuffer, offset, len);
  communicationSocket.write(len);
  communicationSocket.write(newlen);
  communicationSocket.write(transferbuffer, offset, newlen);
  communicationSocket.flush( );
}

byte[ ] readTransfer( )
  throws IOException
{
  int len = communicationSocket.read( );
  if (len <= 0)
    throw new IOException("blah blah");
  int newlen = communicationSocket.read( );
  if (newlen <= 0)
    throw new IOException("blah blah");
  int readlen = 0;
  byte[ ] transferbuffer = new byte[len];
  int n;
  while(readlen < newlen)
  {
    //n = communicationSocket.read(transferbuffer, readlen, len-readlen);
    n = communicationSocket.read(transferbuffer, readlen, newlen-readlen);
    if (n >= 0)
      readlen += n;
    else
      throw new IOException("blah blah again");
  }
  int decompresslen = decompress(transferbuffer, 0, newlen);
  if (decompresslen != len)
    throw new IOException("blah blah decompression");
  return transferbuffer;
}
```

Caching

Caching at the low-level communications layer is unusual and often a fallback position where the use of the communications layer is spread too widely within the application to retrofit low-level caching in the application itself. But caching is generally one of the best techniques for speeding up client/server applications and should be used whenever possible, so you could consider low-level caching when caching cannot be added directly to the application. Caching at the low-level communications layer cannot be achieved generically. The following code illustrates an example of adding the simplest low-level caching in the communications layer. The bold type shows the extra code required:

```
void writeTransfer(byte[ ] transferbuffer, int offset, int len)
{
  if (len <= 0)
    return;
  //check if we can cache this code
  CacheObject cacheObj = isCachable(transferbuffer, offset, len);
  if (cacheObj != null)
  {
    //Assume this is simple non-interleaved writes, so we can simply
    //set this cache obj as the cache to be read. The isCachable( )
    //method must have filled in the cache, so it may include a
    //remote transfer if this is the first time we cached this object.
    LastCache = cacheObj;
    return;
  }
  else
  {
    cacheObj = null;
    realWriteTransfer(transferbuffer, offset, len);
  }
}

void realWriteTransfer(byte[ ] transferbuffer, int offset, int len)
{
  communicationSocket.write(len);
  communicationSocket.write(transferbuffer, offset, len);
  communicationSocket.flush( );
}

byte[ ] readTransfer( )
  throws IOException
{
  if (LastCache != null)
  {
    byte[ ] transferbuffer = LastCache.transferBuffer( );
    LastCache = null;
    return transferbuffer;
  }
  int len = communicationSocket.read( );
  if (len <= 0)
    throw new IOException("blah blah");
  int readlen = 0;
  byte[ ] transferbuffer = new byte[len];
  int n;
  while(readlen < newlen)
  {
    n = communicationSocket.read(transferbuffer, readlen, len-readlen);
    if (n >= 0)
      readlen += n;
    else
      throw new IOException("blah blah again");
```

```
    }
    return transferbuffer;
}
```

Transfer Batching

Batching can be useful when your performance analysis indicates there are too many
network transfers occurring. The standard batching technique uses two cutoff values: a timeout and a data limit. The technique is to catch and hold all data transfers
at the batching level (just above the real communication-transfer level) and send all
data transfers together in one transfer. The batched transfer is triggered either when
the timeout is reached or when the data limit (which is normally the batch buffer
size) is exceeded. Most message-queuing systems support this type of batching. The
following code illustrates a simple example of adding batching to the communications layer. The bold type shows the extra code required:

```
//method synchronized since there will be another thread
//which sends the batched transfer if the timeout is reached
void synchronized writeTransfer(byte[ ] transferbuffer, int offset, int len)
{
  if (len <= 0)
    return;
  if (len >= batch.length - 4 - batchSize)
  {
    //batch is too full to take this chunk, so send off the last lot
    realWriteTransfer(batchbuffer, 0, batchSize);
    batchSize = 0;
    lastSend = System.currentTimeMillis( );
  }
  addIntToBatch(len);
  System.arraycopy(transferbuffer, offset, batchBuffer, batchSize, len);
  batchSize += len;
}

void realWriteTransfer(byte[ ] transferbuffer, int offset, int len)
{
  communicationSocket.write(len);
  communicationSocket.write(transferbuffer, offset, len);
  communicationSocket.flush( );
}

//batch timeout thread method
void run( )
{
  int elapsedTime;
  for(;;)
  {
    synchronized(this)
    {
      elapsedTime = System.currentTimeMillis( ) - lastSend;
      if ((elapsedTime >= timeout) && (batchSize > 0))
      {
```

```
        realWriteTransfer(batchbuffer, 0, batchSize);
        batchSize = 0;
        lastSend = System.currentTimeMillis();
      }
    }
    try{Thread.sleep(timeout - elapsedTime);}catch(InterruptedException e){ }
  }
}


realReadTransfer()
  throws IOException
{
  //Don't socket read until the buffer has been completely used
  if (readBatchBufferlen - readBatchBufferOffset > 0)
    return;

  //otherwise read in the next batched communication
  readBatchBufferOffset = 0;
  int readBatchBufferlen = communicationSocket.read();
  if (readBatchBufferlen <= 0)
    throw new IOException("blah blah");
  int readlen = 0;
  byte[] readBatchBuffer = new byte[readBatchBufferlen];
  int n;
  while(readlen < readBatchBufferlen)
  {
    n = communicationSocket.read(readBatchBuffer, readlen,
                                 readBatchBufferlen-readlen);
    if (n >= 0)
      readlen += n;
    else
      throw new IOException("blah blah again");
  }
}


byte[] readTransfer()
  throws IOException
{
  realReadTransfer();
  int len = readIntFromBatch();
  if (len <= 0)
    throw new IOException("blah blah");
  byte[] transferbuffer = new byte[len];
  System.arraycopy(readBatchBuffer, readBatchBufferOffset,
                   transferBuffer, 0, len);
  readBatchBufferOffset += len;
  return transferbuffer;
}
```

Multiplexing

Multiplexing is a technique where you combine multiple pseudo-connections into
one real connection, intertwining the actual data transfers so that they use the same

communications pipe. This reduces the cost of having many communications pipes (which can incur a heavy system load) and is especially useful when you would otherwise be opening and closing connections a lot: repeatedly opening connections can cause long delays in responses. Multiplexing can be managed in a similar way to the transfer-batching example in the previous section.

Distributed Garbage Collection

Distributed systems typically require distributed garbage collection. If a client holds a proxy to an object in the server, it is important that the server does not garbage-collect that object until the client releases the proxy (and it can be validly garbage-collected). Most third-party distributed systems, such as RMI, handle distributed garbage collection, but that does not necessarily mean it will be done efficiently. The overhead of distributed garbage collection and remote reference maintenance in RMI can slow network communications by a significant amount when many objects are involved.

Of course, if you need distributed reference maintenance, you cannot eliminate it, but you can reduce its impact. You can do this by reducing the number of temporary objects that may have distributed references. The issue is considerably more complex in a multiuser distributed environment, and here you typically need to apply special optimizations related to the products you use in order to establish your multiuser environment. However, in all environments, reducing the number and size of the objects being used is typically the most effective optimization.

The techniques described in Chapter 4 are relevant to reducing the number of objects in a distributed system, and should be applied where possible.

Databases

Databases all have particular features that allow performance optimizations. Usually, the database documentation includes a section on optimizing performance, and that is the place to start.

Here are some hints applicable to many databases (note that JDBC optimizations are covered in Chapter 16):

- Object databases are usually faster than relational databases for applications with strongly object-oriented designs, especially when navigating object networks* is a significant part of the application.

---

* By "navigating object networks," I mean the activity of repeatedly accessing objects from one object's instance variables to another's. The structure formed by the graph of objects reachable through nested instance variable access is a network.

- Relational databases are generally faster than object databases when dealing with large amounts of basic data types, e.g., for objects whose object types are easily mapped into relational tables.

- Application partitioning is important for database access. Reducing the amount of data transferred over the network is often the key to good performance with databases.

- Application partitioning applies to accessing relational databases. Most relational-database products have the ability to execute server-side code in the form of stored procedures. Stored procedures are precompiled SQL code that can be executed by the database server. Some relational-database products can now run Java on the server too (e.g., Oracle).

- Database queries are often faster if they are statically defined, i.e., defined and precompiled. For relational databases, these take the form of prepared statements that can usually accept parameters. Many object databases also support statically defined queries that can navigate object networks more quickly using internal nodal access rather than executing methods.

- Many databases support batching queries to reduce the number of network round trips, and these batching features should be used to improve performance.

- Transactional access to databases is slower than nontransactional access, so use the nontransactional form whenever possible.

Web Services

Web Services is yet another distributed computing architecture. As such, all of the general guidelines for efficient client/server systems from previous sections also apply to improving the performance of Web Services.

Table 12-2 lists the equivalent standards for Web Services, CORBA, and Java RMI.

Table 12-2. Equivalent standards for Web Services, CORBA, and Java RMI

Web Services	CORBA	RMI
Simple Object Access Protocol (SOAP)	Remote procedure calling (IIOP)	Remote method invocation (JRMP)
Universal Description, Discovery, and Integration (UDDI)	ORB Name Service plus an IDL data repository	JNDI plus all remote interfaces
Web Services Description Language (WSDL)	CORBA Interface Definition Language (IDL)	None needed (not language-independent)

The simplicity of the Web Services model has both advantages and disadvantages for performance (see Table 12-3). Web Services is too simple for many distributed application requirements. The many additional features in CORBA and RMI are not whimsical; they are there in response to recognized needs. This implies that as these needs are transferred to Web Services, the Web Services standards will evolve to support additional functionality. From a performance point of view, this is problematic. Typically, the more functionality that is added to the standard, the worse performance becomes because the architecture needs to handle more and more options. So consider the performance impact of each function added to the Web Services standards.

Table 12-3. Performance advantages and disadvantages of Web Services

Feature	Advantage	Disadvantage
No distributed garbage collection	Reduces communication overhead and resource management otherwise required to keep track of connected objects and signal reclaimable objects.	Objects have to time out (which means they are around longer than necessary) or are created for each request (which means they are created more often than necessary).
Transactions are not directly supported	Transactional overhead can be one of the highest costs of short, distributed communications, equivalent to the network communication latency. No transaction support improves performance.	If transactions are required, they have to be built on top of Web Services, which means they will be less efficient than transactions supported within Web Services.
Uses HTTP, a stateless protocol	Stateless protocols scale much better than stateful protocols, as the success of the Web proves.	Stateful requests are far more common. Only very simple services can be stateless. State must be maintained in the server, complicating server processes and making them less efficient, or be transferred with every request, increasing the communication cost.
Uses XML for the communication format	Communications can be compressed.	Data bloat means that communication overhead is increased and marshalling/unmarshalling costs are large.
No built-in security	No security overhead makes for faster performance. Security can be efficiently added by wrapping the Web Services server interface with an authentication layer.	None really, as long as security is easy to add when required.

Measuring Web Services Performance

As I write this, there is a market opportunity for Web Services profiling and measurement tools. You can use web measurement tools, such as load-testing tools and web-server monitoring tools, but these provide only the most basic statistics for Web Services, and are not normally sufficient to determine where bottlenecks lie. For developers, this means that you cannot easily obtain a Web Services profiling tool, and consequently breaking down end-to-end performance of a Web Service and finding bottlenecks may be challenging. Currently the best way to measure the component parts of Web Services seems to be to explicitly add logging points (see, for example, Steve Souza's Java Application Monitor at *http://www.JavaPerformanceTuning.com/ tools/jamon/index.shtml*). The major Web Services component times to measure are the time taken by the server service, the time taken by the server marshalling, the time taken by the client marshalling, and the time taken to transport the message. Ideally you would like to measure times:

1. from the client starting the Web Service call
2. to when the SOAP message creation starts
3. to when the SOAP message creation ends (from 2, this is client marshalling time)
4. to when the transport layer starts sending the message
5. to when the server completes reception of the raw message (from 4, this is client-to-server transport time)
6. to when the message starts being decoded
7. to when the message finishes being decoded (from 6, this is server unmarshalling time)
8. to when the server method starts executing
9. to when the server method finishes executing (from 8, this is the time taken to execute the service)
10. to when the return SOAP message creation starts
11. to when the return SOAP message creation ends (from 10, this is server marshalling time)
12. to when the transport layer starts sending the message
13. to when the client completes reception of the raw message (from 12, this is server-to-client transport time)
14. to when the message starts being decoded
15. to when the message finishes being decoded (from 14, this is client unmarshalling time)
16. to when the client finishes the Web Service call

It is important (but difficult to determine) the time taken in marshalling and unmarshalling and the time taken for network transportation, so that you know where to focus your tuning effort. Of course, if you are worried only about the Web Service itself and you have arbitrary Web Service clients connecting to your service, as is the expected scenario, then you are interested in points 4 to 13. Note that I include these points because the client perception of your service is affected not only by how long the server takes to process it but also by any delays in the server receiving the message, and because the time taken to receive the message depends on the size of the returned message. Specifically, if the TCP data has arrived at the server (or starts to arrive at the server if it requires several TCP packets) but the server does not start reading because it is busy, this service wait time is an overhead that adds to the time taken to service the request. In the same way, the larger the size of the returned data, the more time it may take to be assembled on the client side before unmarshalling can begin, which again adds overhead to the total service time.

In practice, what tends to get measured is either the full round-trip time (client to server and back) with no breakdown, or only the server-side method call. But there are a number of different ways to infer some of the intermediate measurements. The following sections detail various ways to directly measure or infer some Web Service request times.

Measuring server-side method execution time

Server-side method execution is the simplest measurement to take. Simply wrap the original method with a timer. For example, if the server method is getBlah(params), then rename it to _getBlah(params) and implement getBlah(params) as:

```
public whatever getBlah(params){
    Thread t;
    Log.start(t = Thread.currentThread( ),"getBlah");
    whatever returnValue = getBlah(params);
    Log.end(t, "getBlah");
    return returnValue;
}
```

Measuring the full round-trip time

To measure the full round-trip time, employ the wrapping technique that we just described, but this time, in the client.

Inferring round-trip overhead

To infer round-trip overhead, simply measure the time taken to execute a call to an "echo" Web Service, i.e., the Web Service implemented as:

```
public String echo(String val) {
    return val;
}
```

Inferring network communication time

You can infer the combined time taken to transfer the data to and from the server by executing the Web Service in two configurations: across the network, and with both client and server executing on the local machine. Be sure to use the numeric IP address in both cases to specify the service (i.e., 10.20.21.22 rather than *myservice. myhost.mycomp.com*) to eliminate DNS lookup costs. Note that since this is likely to be communication over the Internet, you can measure only average times or daily profile times. You should repeat the measurements many times and either take the average or generate a profile of transport times at different times of the day.

Inferring DNS lookup time

To find out how long DNS lookups are taking, compare times using the numeric IP address with time found using the name for the service (i.e., using 10.20.21.22 versus using *myservice.myhost.mycomp.com*). DNS lookup time can vary depending on network congestion and DNS server availability, so averages are helpful.

Inferring marshalling time

From the previous measurements, you can subtract network communication time, DNS time, and server-side method execution time from the total round-trip time to obtain the remaining overhead time, which includes marshalling and other actions such as object resolution, proxy method invocation, etc. The majority of this overhead time is expected to come from marshalling.

If your Web Service is layered behind a web server that runs a Java servlet, you can add logging to the web server layer in the doGet( ) and doPost( ) methods. Since these servlet methods are called before any marshalling is performed, they provide more direct measurements of marshalling and unmarshalling times.

In addition to measuring individual calls, you should also load-test the Web Service, testing it as if multiple, separate clients were making requests. It is not difficult to create a client to run multiple requests to the Web Service, but there are also free load-testing utilities that you can use, such as Load (available from *http://www. pushtotest.com*).

Web Services Versus CORBA

Web Services provides a simple, language-independent client/server communication model. In a sense, this means that Web Services is an alternative to CORBA, which strives for a similar language-independent distributed architecture. At the core, this is true, but Web Services standards target a simpler type of architecture and are already more widely accepted and used. Table 12-2 shows how some of the standards map between Web Services, CORBA, and RMI (note that RMI is not language-independent, so it is not really equivalent to the other two technologies).

A more comprehensive comparison between these technologies as well as DCOM can be found in the article "Web Services and Distributed Component Platforms" in the *Web Services Journal*, Issue 3, Volume 1 (available at *http://www.sys-con.com/ webservices/article.cfm?id=110*).

High-Performance Web Services

It is worth emphasizing that the previous sections of this chapter, as well as other chapters in this book, also apply to performance-tuning Web Services. As with all distributed computing, caching is especially important and should be applied to data and metadata such as WSDL (Web Services Description Language) files. The generation and parsing of XML is a Web Service overhead that you should try to minimize by using specialized XML processors. Additionally, a few techniques are particularly effective for high-performance Web Services:

- Service granularity
- Load balancing
- Asynchronous processing

These techniques are discussed in the following sections.

Service granularity

If you read the "Message Reduction" section, it should come as no surprise that Web Service methods should have a large granularity. A Web Service should provide monolithic methods that do as much work as possible rather than many methods that perform small services. The intention is to reduce the number of client/server requests required to satisfy the client's requirements. For example, the classic example of a Web Service is providing the current share price of a company quoted on a stock exchange:

```
public interface IStockQuoteService {
  public String getQuote(String exchangeSymbol);
  public String getSymbol(String companyName);
}
```

Amusingly, this "classic" example is bad; it is too fine-grained for optimal efficiency. If you wanted to create a Web Service that provides share price quotes, you are far better off providing a service that can return multiple quotes in one request, as it is likely that anyone requesting one share price would also want others. Here is a more efficient interface:

```
public interface IStockQuoteService {
  public String[ ] getQuotes(String[ ] exchangeSymbols);
  public String[ ] getSymbols(String[ ] companyNames);
  public String[ ] getQuotesIfResolved(String[ ] companyNames);
}
```

Note that there are three changes to this interface. First, as already explained, I have changed the methods to accept and return an array of Strings so that multiple prices for multiple companies can be obtained in one request. Second, I have *not* retained the previous interfaces that handle only one company at a time. This is a deliberate attempt to influence the thinking of developers using the service. I want developers of clients using this Web Service to immediately think in terms of multiple companies per request so that they build their client more efficiently. As the server Web Services manager, this benefits me twice over: once by influencing clients to be more efficient, ultimately giving my service a better reputation, and again by reducing the number of requests sent to my Web Service. Note that if a client is determined to be inefficient, he can still send one request per company, but at least I've tried my best to influence his thinking.

The third change I've made is to add a new method. The original interface had two methods: one to get quotes using the company symbol and the other to get the company symbol using the company name. In case you are unfamiliar with stock market exchanges, I should explain that a company may have several recognizable names (for example, Big Comp., Big Company, Big Company Inc., The Big Company). The stock exchange assigns one unique symbol to identify the company (for example, BIGC). The getSymbol( ) method provides a mechanism to get the unique symbol from one of the many alternative company names. With only the two methods, if a client has a company name without the symbol, it needs to make two requests to the server to obtain the share price: a request for the unique symbol and a request for the price. By adding a third method that gives a price directly from one of the various valid company names, I've provided the option to reduce requests for those clients that need this service.

Think through the service you provide, and try to design a service that minimizes client requests. Similarly, if you are writing a Web Services client and the service provides alternative ways to get the information you need, use the methods that minimize the number of requests required. Think in terms of individual methods that do a lot of work and return a lot of information rather than the recommended object-oriented methodology of many small methods that each do a little bit and combine to do a lot. Unfortunately, you also need to be aware that if the interface is too complex, developers may use a competing Web Service provider with a simpler (but less efficient) interface that they can more easily understand.

Load balancing

The most efficient architecture for maximal scalability is a load-balanced server system. This architecture allows the client to connect to a frontend load balancer, which performs the minimum of activity and whose main job is to pass the request onto one of several backend servers (or cluster of servers) that perform the real work. Load balancing is discussed in more detail in Chapter 10.

Since Web Services already leverages the successful HTTP protocol, you can immediately use a web-server load balancer without altering any other aspect of the Web Service. A typical load-balancing Web Service would have the client connect to a frontend load balancer, which is a proxy web server, and have that load balancer pass on requests to a farm of backend Web Services. The main alternative to this architecture is to use round-robin DNS, where the DNS server supplies a different IP address from a list of servers for each request to resolve a hostname. The client automatically connects to a random server in a farm of replicated Web Services.

A different load-balancing scheme is possible by controlling the WSDL document and sending WSDL containing different binding addresses (that is, different URLs for the Web Service location). In fact, all three of the load-balancing schemes mentioned here can be used simultaneously if necessary to scale the load-balancing and reduce failure points in the system.

Where even load balancing is insufficient to provide the necessary throughput to efficiently handle all Web Service requests, priority levels should be added to Web Service requests. Higher-priority requests should be handled first, leaving lower-priority requests queued until server processing power is available.

Asynchronous processing

There are a number of characteristics of Web Services that suggest that asynchronous messaging may be required to use Web Services optimally. HTTP is a best-efforts delivery service. This means that requests can be dropped, typically for network congestion or server overload. The client Web Service will get an error in this situation, but nevertheless needs to handle it and retry.

Traffic on the Internet follows a distinct usage pattern and regularly provides better service at certain times. Web Service usage is likely to follow this pattern, as times of peak congestion are also likely to be peak Web Service usage (unless your service is targeted at an off-peak activity). This means that at peak times the average Web Service gets a double hit of a congested network and a higher number of requests reaching the service.

Many client/server projects over the years have shown that if your application can put up with increased latency, asynchronous messaging maximizes the throughput of the system. Requiring synchronous processing over the Internet is a heavy overhead. Consider that synchronous calls are most likely to fail from congestion when other synchronous calls are also failing. The response for a synchronous protocol, such as TCP, is simply to send more attempts to complete the synchronous call. The repeated attempts only increase congestion, as they occur in addition to all the new synchronous calls that are now starting up.

Consequently, supporting asynchronous requests, especially for large, complicated services, is a good design option. You can do this using an underlying messaging protocol, such as JMS, or independently of the transport protocol using the design of the Web Service. The latter option means that you need to provide an interface that accepts requests and stores the results of processing the request for later retrieval by the client. Similarly, the client of the Web Service should strive to use an asynchronous model where possible.

Finally, some Web Services combine other Web Services in some value-added way to provide what are called *aggregation services*. Aggregation services should try to retrieve the data they require from other services during off-peak hours in large, coarse-grained requests.

Performance Checklist

- Use a relay server to examine data transfers.
- Reduce the number of messages transferred.
  - Cache data and objects to change distributed requests to local ones.
  - Batch messages to reduce the number of messages transferred.
  - Compress large transfers.
  - Partition the application so that methods execute where their data is held.
  - Multiplex communications to reduce connection overhead.
  - Stub out data links to reduce the amount of data required to be transferred.
- Design the various components so that they can execute asynchronously from each other.
  - Anticipate data requirements so that data is transferred earlier.
  - Split up data so that partial results can be displayed.
  - Avoid creating distributed garbage.
- Optimize database communications. Application partitioning is especially important with databases.
  - Use statically defined database queries.
  - Avoid database transactional modes if possible.
  - Use JDBC optimizations such as prepared statements, specific SQL requests, etc.
- Try to break down the time to execute a Web Service into client, server, and network processing times, and extract the marshalling and unmarshalling times from client and server processing.
- Don't forget about DNS resolution time for a Web Service.
- Try to load-balance high-demand Web Services or provide them asynchronously.
- The granularity of a Web Service is important. For more scalable and better performing Web Services, create coarser services that require fewer network requests to complete.

CHAPTER 13

When to Optimize

In this chapter:
- When Not to Optimize
- Tuning Class Libraries and Beans
- Analysis
- Design and Architecture
- Tuning After Deployment
- More Factors That Affect Performance
- Performance Planning

Faster, better, cheaper—choose two of the above.
—Old engineering proverb

When developing an application, it is important to consider performance optimizations and apply them where appropriate in the development cycle. Forgetting these optimizations (or getting them wrong) can be expensive to correct later in development.* In this chapter, we follow the various stages of the full product life cycle and consider when and why you might need to include some performance optimizations.

Performance tuning is frequently a matter of tradeoffs. Occasionally, you have the wonderful situation that a change to the application is better in every way: it provides better performance, cleaner code, and a more maintainable product. But more often, the performance of parts of an application are interrelated. Tuning one part of the application affects other parts, and not necessarily for the better. The more complicated the application, the more often this is true. You should always consider how a particular performance change will affect other parts of the application. This means that tuning can be a lengthy process simply because it must be iterative. The full performance-tuning sequence (identifying the bottleneck, tuning, and then benchmarking) is necessary to make sure that tuning one part of the application is not too detrimental to another part.

Performance tuning at the analysis and design phases differs from performance tuning at the implementation phase. Designing-in a performance problem usually results in a lot of trouble later on, requiring a large effort to correct. On the other hand, coding that results in poor performance simply requires a tuning phase to eliminate bottlenecks and is much simpler (and cheaper) to correct. As a rule of thumb, a performance problem created (or left uncorrected) in one phase requires roughly five times as much effort to correct in the following development phase. Leaving the problem uncorrected means that the effort required to correct it snowballs, growing

---

* When I talk about expense, I mean cost in both time and money.

fivefold through each development phase (planning, analysis, schematic design, technical design, construction, deployment, production).*

Now on to the specifics. Before discussing when to optimize, I'll start with when you should not optimize.

When Not to Optimize

At the code-writing stage, your emphasis should not be on optimizing: it should be entirely on functionality and producing correct bug-free code. Apart from optimizations (such as canonicalizing objects) that are good design, you should normally ignore performance while writing code. Performance tuning should be done after the code is functionally correct. Alan Knight wrote:

> If testing and documentation are inadequate, most people won't notice or care how fast a particular list box updates. They'll have given up on the program before they ever got to that window.†

This is definitely a view to which I subscribe. Many implementation-level optimizations can make code more complicated and difficult to read. Delay optimizing until the program is mostly functionally correct. But make sure you have planned for a tuning phase.

I am not saying that you should create the whole application without considering performance until just before deployment. That would be foolhardy. Performance should be considered and planned for at all phases of the development process (especially design and architecture). You need to rule out designs that lead to a badly performing application. Optimizations that are good design should be applied as early as possible. When parts of the application are complete, they should be tuned. And benchmarks should be run as soon as possible: they give a good idea of where you are and how much effort will be needed for the tuning phase after code writing is mostly complete.

Tuning Class Libraries and Beans

Most code can be categorized into one of two general types:

- *Application-specific code*, normally used for one particular application. If this code is reused, it usually provides only a skeleton that needs reimplementing. Occasionally, application-specific code is generic enough to reuse in another application, but even then it usually needs some rewriting to make it more generic.

---

* The fivefold increase is an average across the phases. Studies of the costs of fixing uncorrected problems have found that some phases have a higher cost than others.

† *Smalltalk Report*, March-April 1996. This is a nice article about when and why to performance-tune.

- Classes written specifically with reusability in mind. This type of code is usually referred to as class libraries, frameworks, components, and beans. I refer to all of these together as *reusable code*.

The first type of code, application-specific code, is considerably easier to tune. You can run the application as it is intended to be used, determine any bottlenecks, and successively tune away those bottlenecks. Typically, 80% of the application time is spent in less than 20% of the code, and only 5% of the application code actually needs to be changed during the tuning process.

The second type of code, reusable code, is much more difficult to tune. This code may be used in many situations that could never be foreseen by the developers. Without knowing how the code will be used, it is very difficult to create tests that appropriately determine the performance of reusable code. There is no truly valid technique that can be applied. Even exhaustively testing every method is of little use (not to mention generally impractical), since you almost certainly cannot identify useful performance targets for every method. Well-tuned reusable code can have 95% of the code altered in some way by the tuning process.[*]

The standard way to tune reusable code is to tune in response to identified problems. Usually the development team releases alpha and beta versions to successively larger groups of testers: other team developers, demo application developers, the quality-assurance team, identified beta testers, general beta testers, and customers of the first released version (some of these groups may overlap). Each of these groups provides feedback in identifying both bugs and performance problems. In fact, as we all know, this feedback process continues throughout the lifetime of any reusable code. But the majority of bugs and performance problems are identified by this initial list of users. This reactive process is hardly ideal, but any alternative makes tuning reusable code very expensive. This is unlike bug testing, in which the quality of the test suite and quality-assessment process makes a big difference to the reliability of the released version, and is fully cost-effective.

There are several consequences to this reactive process. First, from the viewpoint of the developer using reusable components, you need to be aware that first versions frequently have suboptimal performance. Note that this does not imply anything about the quality of the software: it may have wonderfully comprehensive features and be delightfully bug-free. But even in a large beta testing program with plenty of feedback, there is unlikely to be sufficient time to tune the software and repeat the test and release procedures. Getting rid of identified bugs rightfully takes precedence, and developers normally focus on the (next) released version being as bug-free as possible.

---

[*] I have not seen any studies that show this cost. Instead, I base it on my own impression from examining early versions of various class libraries and comparing these classes with later versions. I find that most methods in a random selection of classes are altered in some way that I can identify as giving performance improvements.

Second, for developers *creating* reusable code, the variety of applications testing the reusable code is more important than the absolute number of those applications. Ten people telling you that method X is slow is not as useful as two telling you that method X is slow and two telling you that method Y is slow.

A further consequence when developing reusable code is that to provide greater performance flexibility for the users of those classes, you need to design more flexible method entry points to your classes. Providing performance flexibility unfortunately clashes with the "defensive" programming that is (reasonably) used when creating reusable classes. For example, a defensive developer creating a collection class based on an array (e.g., java.util.Vector) might provide a constructor that accepts an array and copies its elements:

```
public class ArrayBasedCollection
{
  int arraySize;
  Object[ ] array;
  public ArrayBasedCollection(Object[ ] passedArray)
  {
    arraySize = passedArray.length;
    array = new Object[arraySize];
    System.arraycopy(passedArray, 0, array, 0, arraySize);
  }
  ...
```

The defensive developer always ensures that elements are copied into a new array so that no external object retains a reference to the internal array and interrupts the logic of the class. This ensures that the new class cannot be inadvertently corrupted. However, this provides inefficient performance. There will be cases where the application coder has created the array specifically to hold the objects and will discard that array immediately. Developing flexibly with performance in mind directs you to add an extra method that allows the array to be used directly:

```
public class ArrayBasedCollection
{
  int arraySize;
  Object[ ] array;
  public ArrayBasedCollection(Object[ ] passedArray)
  {
    this(passedArray, true);
  }
  /**
   * If <copy> is true, the elements of <passedArray> are
   * copied into the a new underlying array in the collection.
   * If <copy> is false, the <passedArray> is assigned directly
   * as the underlying array. This is potentially dangerous:
   * the collection object can be corrupted if the <passedArray>
   * is altered directly by another object afterwards.
   */
  public ArrayBasedCollection(Object[ ] passedArray, boolean copy)
  {
```

```
arraySize = passedArray.length;
if (copy)
{
  array = new Object[arraySize];
  System.arraycopy(passedArray, 0, array, 0, arraySize);
}
else
  array = passedArray;
}
...
```

This opens the collection object to potential corruption, but by retaining the original one-arg constructor, you have reduced the chance that the two-arg constructor will be used accidentally. A developer looking quickly for a constructor is likely to use the one-arg constructor, whereas a developer desperately searching through the documentation for ways to reduce the number of copies made from several large arrays will be delighted to discover the two-arg constructor.

Finally, perhaps the most significant way to create reusable code that performs well is for developers to be well-versed in performance tuning. After any significant amount of performance tuning, many of the techniques in this book can become second nature. Developers experienced in performance tuning can produce reusable code that is further along the performance curve right from the first cut. Writing reusable code is one of the few situations in which it is sometimes preferable to consider performance when first writing the code.

Analysis

The analysis phase of development encompasses a variety of activities that determine what functionality you are going to build into your application. These activities include:

- Specifying what the application needs to do (e.g., compress files, display graphic files of type, etc.)

- Identifying major functions and business areas (e.g., compression, display; targeted to the area of graphics files)

- Planning generally how the application will work (e.g., read one or more files, use 2-Ronnies compression if possible, etc.)

- Prioritizing subsections (e.g., the compression component must be completed but can use an alternative compression algorithm, the graphics types XYZ must be supported but the graphics types ABC may be dropped until later, etc.)

- Deciding whether to build or buy (e.g., are there available beans or classes to handle compression and display? How much are they? How much will building our own cost? Do the purchasable ones provide all essential features?)

- Documenting the requirements

The analysis phase does not usually specify either the structure of the application or the technology (e.g., you might specify that the application uses a database, but probably not which database or even which type of database). The analysis phase specifies what the application will do (and might do), not how it is done, except in the most general terms.

Here are major performance-tuning considerations during the analysis phase:

- Determining general characteristics of objects, data, and users (e.g., number of objects in the application)
- Specifying expected or acceptable performance boundaries (e.g., functionality X should take less than M seconds)
- Identifying probable performance limitations from the determined specifications (e.g., function Y is an HTTP connection, and so is dependent on the quality of the network path and the availability of the server)
- Eliminating any performance conflicts by extending, altering, or restating the specifications (e.g., the specification states query Z must always respond within N seconds, but this cannot be guaranteed without altering the specification to provide an alternative default result)

Performance goals should be an explicit part of the analysis and should form part of the specification. The analysis phase should include time to analyze the performance impacts of the requirements.

The general characteristics of the application can be determined by asking the following questions about the application:

- How many objects will there be, and what are their sizes (average and distribution)? What is the total amount of data being manipulated, and how are the manipulations expected to be performed (database access, file access, object storage, etc.)?
- What is a transaction for the application? If there are several types of transactions, define each type. Include details such as the number of objects created, deleted, or changed; the duration of the transactions (average and distribution); and expected transaction amounts (transactions per second), both per person and for the system as a whole. Define how data is accessed and queried for, and how often.
- How many simultaneous users will use the application, and what level of concurrency is expected for those simultaneous users? (Are they accessing the same resources, and if so, how many resources and what type of access?)
- What is the expected distribution of the application? This is, of course, mainly relevant for distributed applications. This applies back to the last point, but focuses on the distributed resources that are necessarily used simultaneously.

You can use the answers to these questions to provide an abstract model of the application. Applying this abstract model to a generalized computer architecture allows you to identify any performance problems. For example, if the application is a multiplayer game to be played across a network, a simple model of a network together with the objects (numbers and sizes) that need to be distributed, the number of users and their expected distributions, and possible patterns of play provide the information you need to identify whether the specified application can run over the network. If, after including safety factors, the network can easily cope with the traffic, that section of the application is validated. If the game is unplayable when you put in minimum bandwidths of 56K (typical modem connection) and latency (network communication response time) of 400 milliseconds, you need to reexamine the specifications.

This type of analysis is part of software performance engineering. The general technique for performance tuning prior to actually testing the code (i.e., testing at the analysis and design phases) is to predict the application performance based on the best available data.[*] This technique is covered in detail in the book *High Performance Client/Server* by Chris Loosley and Frank Douglas (John Wiley & Sons).

One of the most significant aspects to examine at the analysis phase is the expected performance gains and drawbacks of distributed computing. Distributing sections of applications always implies some performance drawback. After all, network communication is always slower than interprocess communication on the same machine, and interprocess communication is always slower than component-to-component communication within the same process. Good design usually emphasizes decoupling components, but good performance often requires close coupling. These are not always conflicting requirements, but you do need to bear in mind this potential conflict.

For distributed applications, distributed components should be coupled in such a way as to minimize the communication between those components. The goal is to limit the number of messages that need to be sent back and forth between components, as too many network message transfers can have a detrimental effect on performance. Components engaged in extended conversations over a network spend most of their time sitting idle, waiting for responses. For this type of situation, the network latency tends to dominate the performance.

A simple example, showing the huge difference that distribution performance can make to even a standalone applet, indicates how important this aspect is. You might have thought that a standalone applet does not need much analysis of its distributed components. Table 13-1 shows two development paths that might be followed and illustrates how ignoring performance at the analysis stage can lead to performance problems later.

---

[*] This is a scientific technique referred to as "successive approximation by the application of empirically derived data." Another name for it is "educated guessing."

Table 13-1. Contrasting development processes

Applet1 development	Applet2 development
Distribution analysis: Applet is distributed using a compressed JAR file.	Distribution analysis:
	Applet2 is distributed using one or more compressed JAR files. Because the download time may be significant for the expected number of classes, the analysis indicates that the applet should be engineered from the ground up, with minimizing download time as a high priority. To this end, the specification is altered to state that a small entry point functionality of the applet, with a small isolated set of classes, will be downloaded initially to allow the applet to start as quickly as possible. This initial functionality should be designed to engage the user while the remainder of the applet is downloaded to the browser in the background. The applet could be downloaded in several sections, if necessary, to ensure the user's waiting time is kept to a minimum. A secondary priority is for the user to have no further explicit download waiting time.
Applet1 functional analysis: Similar for both.	Applet2 functional analysis: Similar for both.
Applet1 design: Simple.	Applet2 design: Requires careful thought about which classes require the presence of other classes.
Applet1 coding: Similar for both.	Applet2 coding: Similar for both.
Applet1 performance testing: Applet takes far too long to download. User testing indicates that 99% of users abandon the web page before download is complete and the applet can start. Unpacking the JAR file and having classes download individually makes the situation even worse. Project may be terminated, or a major (and costly) rewrite of the applet design may be undertaken to allow the applet to start faster at the user's desktop.	Applet2 performance testing: Applet downloads and starts in adequate time. Performance within the browser requires some rounds of tuning.

Table 13-1 shows how important performance prediction can be. The analysis on the right saves a huge amount on development costs. Of course, if not identified at the analysis phase, this aspect of performance may be picked up later in some other phase of development, but the further away from the analysis phase it is identified, the more expensive it is to correct.

Another consideration at the analysis stage is the number of features being specified. Sometimes "nice to have" features are thrown into the requirements at the analysis phase. Features seem to have an inverse relationship to performance: the more features there are, the worse the performance or the more effort is required to improve the performance. For good performance, it is always better to minimize the features in the requirements or, at the very least, to specify that the design should be extensible to incorporate certain nice-to-have features rather than to simply go ahead and include the features in the requirements.

One other important aspect that you should focus on during the analysis phase is the application's use of shared resources. Try to identify all shared resources and the performance costs associated with forcing unique access of shared resources. When the performance cost is shown to be excessive, you need to specify alternative mechanisms to allow the efficient use of the shared resource. For example, if several parts of the application may be simultaneously updating a file, then to avoid corruption, the updates may need to be synchronized. If this potentially locks parts of the application for too long, an alternative, such as journaling, might be specified. Journaling allows the different parts of the application to update separate dedicated log files, and these logs are reconciled by another asynchronous part of the application.

Design and Architecture

Many design-stage decisions affect performance. These include how long a transaction will be, how often data or objects need to be updated, where objects will be located, whether they are persistent and how persistency is achieved, how data is manipulated, how components interact, and how tightly coupled subsystems are, as well as determining responses to errors, retry frequencies, and alternative routes for solving tasks.

As I mentioned in the last section, the general technique for performance tuning during the analysis and design phases is to predict performance based on the best available data.[*] During the design phase, a great deal of prototype testing is possible, and all such tests should feed data back to help predict the performance of the application. Any predictions indicating a problem with performance should be addressed at the design phase, prior to coding. If necessary, it is better to revisit the analysis and alter specifications rather than leave any indicated performance issues unresolved.

At each stage, part of the design objective should be to predict the performance of the application. (Note that when I refer to the design phase, I include both logical and physical design; physical design is often called architecture.) The design phase usually includes determining the target platforms, and any predictions must be tailored to the limitations of those platforms. This is especially important for embedded Java systems (e.g., applets and servlets), environments where a specific nonstandard target VM must be used, and where the target VM may be highly variable (i.e., is unknown). In all these cases, the target Java runtime system performance cannot be inferred from using the latest standard VM, and performance prediction must be targeted at the known system or at the worst-performing Java runtime system. (Alternatively, the design phase may rule out some runtime systems as being unsupported by the application.)

---

[*] See Loosley and Douglas.

Any decoupling, indirection, abstraction, or extra layers in the design are highly likely to be candidates for causing performance problems. You should include all these elements in your design if they are called for. But you need to be careful to design using interfaces in such a way that the concrete implementation allows any possible performance optimizations to be incorporated. Design elements that block, copy, queue, or distribute also frequently cause performance problems. These elements can be difficult to optimize, and the design should focus attention on them and ensure that they can either be replaced or that their performance is targeted.* Asynchronous and background events can affect times unpredictably, and their effects need to be clearly identified by benchmark testing.

Shared Resources

Resources that must be shared by several users, processes, or threads are always a potential source of bottlenecks. When a resource is shared, the resource usually requires its various sharers to use it one at a time to avoid a conflict of states and corruption. During the design phase, you should try to identify all shared resources, and predict what performance limitations they impose on the application. Be careful to consider the fully scaled version of the application, i.e., with as many users, objects, files, network connections, etc., as are possible according to the application specifications. Considering fully scaled versions of the application is important because shared resources are highly nonlinear in performance. They usually impose a gently decreasing performance at their bottleneck as the number of sharers increases, up to a point at which there is a sudden and catastrophic decrease in performance as the number of sharers increases further.

If the performance prediction indicates that a particular shared resource is likely to impose too high a performance cost, alternative designs that bypass or reduce the performance cost of that shared resource need to be considered. For example, multiple processes or threads updating a shared collection have to synchronize their updates to avoid corrupting the collection. If this synchronized update is identified as a performance problem, an alternative is to allow each process or thread to update its own collection, and wrap the collections in another collection object that provides global access to all the collections. This solution was illustrated in "Avoiding Serialized Execution" in Chapter 10.

Failing to identify a shared resource at the design phase can be expensive. In some cases, a simple class substitution of a redesigned class can reduce the performance drawback of the shared resource to acceptable performance levels. But in many

---

* For example, in Chapter 10, we considered a load-balancing solution that included a queue. The queue is a potential bottleneck, and care must be taken to ensure that the queue does not unnecessarily delay requests as they pass through.

cases, a complete redesign of part or all of the application may be needed to achieve adequate performance.

Transactions

The purpose of a transaction is to ensure consistency when using shared resources. If there are no possible conflicts across sharers of those resources, there is no need for a transaction. Removing unnecessary transactions is the simplest and most effective performance optimization for applications that include transactions. So, if you do not need a transaction, do not use one. Most systems that provide transactions usually have a "transactionless" mode, i.e., a way to access any shared resources without entering a defined transaction. This mode normally has better performance than the transaction mode.

When transactions are absolutely necessary, your design goal should be to minimize the time spent in the transaction. If transactions extend for too long and cause performance problems, a complete redesign of a significant part of the application is often needed.

You also need to be aware of the shared resources used by the transacting system itself. Any system providing transaction semantics to your application uses an internal set of shared resources: this is necessary to ensure that the transactions are mutually consistent. These transaction-system internal shared resources invariably have some product-specific idiosyncrasies that result in their being used more or less efficiently. These idiosyncrasies can have a large effect on performance. Many products have a performance-tuning section within their documentation, detailing how best to take advantage of idiosyncrasies in their product (more usually termed "features").

Even where short transactions are designed into an application, the application may enter unexpectedly long transactions in two common situations. The first situation is when bugs occur in the transaction, and the second, when the user has control over the transaction. Because unintended long transactions can occur, transactions should always have a timeout imposed on them: this is usually fairly easy to incorporate in Java using a separate high-priority timeout thread.

A standard way to convert naturally long transactions into short ones is to maintain sets of changes, rather like undo/redo logs. In this design pattern, changes are abstracted into separate objects, and ordered lists of these changes can be "played." With this design pattern, the changes that occur in what would be a long transaction are leisurely collected without entering the transaction, and then a short transaction rapidly "plays" all the changes. This pattern cannot be used exactly as described if the precise time of a particular change is important. However, variations of this pattern can be applied to many cases.

Locking

Locking is a technique for ensuring access to a shared resource while maintaining coherence of state within the shared resource. There are a variety of lock types, from exclusive (only one sharer has any type of access) to various types of shared locks (allowing any of a set of sharers simultaneous access, or all sharers access to a restricted set of capabilities of the shared resource, or both of these combined[*]).

Locking can be expensive. Overhead includes the locking and unlocking overhead itself; the fact that locks must be shared resources implying extra shared-resource considerations; the explicit serialization of activities that result from using locks; and the possibility of deadlock when two sharers are simultaneously trying to obtain a lock held by the sharer, causing both sharers to "freeze" activity (see Chapter 10 for a concrete example).

These drawbacks mean you should consider locking only when the design absolutely requires it. For instance, locking must be used when there is a requirement for definite deterministic noncorrupted access to a shared resource. To illustrate: a bank account with no overdraft facilities must serialize access to the account and ensure that each deposit and withdrawal takes place without any other activities legally occurring at the same time. The balance accessed for display also needs to be accurate. You do not want to display a balance of $100 at the ATM window, then have the ATM deny withdrawal of $50 because the actual balance is lower due to a check for $55 being processed at the same time. From the bank's point of view, both transactions might go though, and the bank is owed $5 from someone it did not want to lend to. Or the customer is given the wrong information and suffers frustration. To avoid these two situations, locking is required.

Occasionally, locking improves performance by reducing the conflicts otherwise generated by simultaneous access to a shared resource. Consider the situation in which objects are concurrently added to a collection. You can define the addition operation to provide exclusive updates either by locking the update method or by throwing an exception if the update is not exclusive. The lockable update method can be defined easily with a synchronized method:

```
public synchronized add(Object o)
{
  unsynchronized_add(o);
}
```

The exception-throwing method would be a little more complex:

```
public add(Object o)
  throws InUseException
{
```

---

[*] For example, one type of write-lock allows read access by multiple sharers to the shared resource while restricting write access to just one sharer.

```
    //throws an InUseException if I am currently already in use
    setInUse( );
    unsynchronized_add(o);
    setNotInUse( );
}
```

The advantage of the second definition is that the locking overhead is avoided during the update.* This definition is suitable for cases where there is unlikely to be much concurrent execution of the add( ) method: the exception is not thrown very often. But when there are frequent simultaneous updates to the collection, you will encounter the exception more often than not. For this latter situation, your performance will be better if you use the first synchronized implementation of the add( ) method and explicitly serialize the updates.

Parallelism

For performance reasons, you should try to design parallelism into the application wherever possible. The general guideline is to assume that you parallelize every activity. One of the tasks for the design phase, then, is to identify what cannot be parallelized. This guideline is fairly cost-effective. It is always easy to move from a parallelized design back to the nonparallelized version, since the nonparallelized version is essentially a degenerate case of the more general version. But retrofitting parallelism to the application is often considerably more difficult. Starting with an application designed to work without any parallelism and trying to restructure it to add in parallelism can be extremely difficult and expensive.

Any parallelism designed into the application should take advantage of multiple processors. This can be evaluated in the design phase by predicting the performance of the application on single- and multiple-CPU machines.

Once the application has been designed to run with parallelism, you can decide at the implementation stage, or possibly even at runtime, whether to use the parallelism. A low degree of parallelism (e.g., 5 threads, not 500 threads) almost always improves the performance of an application. But parallelism has overhead that can swamp the advantages. The overhead comes from contention in trying to use shared resources and delays from the communication needed for synchronization. Additional overhead comes from starting extra threads and distributing and coordinating work between the threads (there may also be overhead from caches that deal with twice the data throughput in the same space).

When designing the application to run activities in parallel, you need to focus on shared resources, especially the time spent using these resources. Increasing the time spent exclusively using a shared resource adversely affects all other activities using

---

* In fact, the setInUse( ) method probably needs to be synchronized, so this pattern is useful only for avoiding synchronizing methods that might take a long time. The long synchronization is replaced by a short synchronization and a possible thrown exception.

that resource. For example, the CPU is the most basic shared resource. The more separate threads (and processes) using the CPU, the smaller the time slices allocated to each thread relative to the time spent waiting to acquire the CPU by each thread. Consequently, the time actually taken for computing any particular activity becomes longer, since this is the sum of the time slices allocated to carry out the computation together with the sum of times waiting to gain a time slice.

And the situation is not linear, but exponential. Consider a CPU where 10% is currently used. If there is a computation that normally takes five seconds when this CPU has no work, then as the CPU can currently allocate 90% of its power to that computation, the computation will instead take just over 10% longer: the actual expected time is 5/0.9 = 5.55 seconds.

If instead the CPU were 40% utilized (i.e., 60% available), the expected time for that computation would instead be 5/0.6 = 8.3 seconds. Now look what happens to a 90% utilized CPU (10% available). The expected time for the computation is now 5/0.1 = 50 seconds. And a 99% busy CPU is going to make this computation take 500 seconds (see Table 13-2). You can see the need to keep spare capacity in the CPU to avoid an exponential degradation in performance.

Table 13-2. Theoretical computation time (single-threaded) depending on CPU availability

CPU used	CPU available	Computation time
0% used	100% available	5 seconds
10% used	90% available	5/0.9 = 5.55 seconds
40% used	60% available	5/0.6 = 8.3 seconds
90% used	10% available	5/0.1 = 50 seconds
99% used	1% available	5/0.01 = 500 seconds

You can also predict the effect threading can have if you can parallelize any particular calculation, even on a single-CPU machine. If one thread does the calculation using 10% of the CPU in five seconds, and you can fully parallelize the calculation, then two threads (ideally) each take half the time to do their half of the calculation. Assuming that the calculation does not saturate the CPU when running,* then if the two halves run together, each half takes 2.5 seconds on an unutilized CPU. But since there are two threads and each thread takes 10% of the CPU, each thread sees only 90% availability of the CPU. This means that each half calculation takes 2.5/0.9 = 2.8 seconds. Both calculations run at the same time (that is why the CPU has double the utilization), so this is also the total time taken. Time-slicing adds some additional overhead, but this will leave the expected time well below the three-second mark.

---

* CPU availability is indicated in the example since the calculation loads the CPU only by 10%; presumably, there is some disk activity required by the calculation.

So even on a single-CPU machine, parallelizing this calculation enables it to run faster. This can happen because the calculation considered here is not a pure CPU calculation: it obviously spends time doing some I/O (perhaps a database query), and thus it can be parallelized effectively. If the calculation were number crunching of some sort, the CPU utilization would be 100%, and parallelizing the calculation would actually slow it down.

For example, suppose the number-crunching calculation took five seconds and caused a 100% CPU utilization on an otherwise unworked machine. Running the same calculation on a 50% utilized machine would take 5/0.5 = 10 seconds. So theoretically, if you can parallelize this calculation into two equal halves running together on an otherwise unutilized machine, each half is allocated 50% of the CPU utilization. Each takes half the time of the unparallelized calculation running on a 50% utilized machine (which we just calculated to take 10 seconds), i.e., each parallelized half calculation takes 10/2 = 5 seconds, both running simultaneously. So the total time taken is still five seconds, and there is no overall speedup. If you add in the slight factor due to CPU time-slicing overhead, the total time increases beyond the five-second mark, so it is actually slower to parallelize this calculation. This is what we should intuitively expect for any process that already takes up all the CPU's power.

Now what about the multiple CPU case: do we get a benefit here? Well, for a two-CPU machine, the CPU synchronization overhead may be 5% (this is normally an overestimate). In this case, each part of the parallelized application effectively gets a 5% utilized CPU of its own. For the example, the expected times taken are 2.5/0.95 = 2.63 seconds. And since the two threads are running in parallel, this is also the total expected time taken. See Table 13-3.[*]

Table 13-3. Theoretical computation time depending on number of CPUs and non-CPU-bound threads

	CPU used	CPU available	Computation time
1 CPU, 1 thread	10%	90%	5 seconds
1 CPU, 2 threads serialized	10%/thread	90%/thread	2.5 + 2.5 = 5 seconds
1 CPU, 2 threads parallelized	10%/thread	90%/thread	max(2.5/0.9,2.5/0.9) = 2.8 seconds
2 CPUs, 2 threads parallelized	5%/CPU	95%/CPU	max(2.5/0.95,2.5/0.95) = 2.6 seconds

However, CPU overhead is increased for each additional CPU, as they all have to synchronize with each other. This means that almost another 5% utilization is added to the overhead of each CPU: in fact, Dan Graham of IBM has determined that the

---

[*] In the case of the number-crunching calculation, you have the exact same calculation resulting in 2.63 seconds. So again, as you intuitively expect, the two-CPU machine lets the CPU-swamping parallelized calculation take just over half the time of the original unparallelized version.

overhead is multiplicative, so that if two CPUs each have a 5% utilization (0.95 × 100% free) from CPU parallelism, then three CPUs each have a 9.75% utilization (0.95 × 0.95 × 100% free), and four CPUs each have a 14.26% utilization (0.95 × 0.95 × 0.95 × 100% free), and so on. See Table 13-4.

Table 13-4. Theoretical computation time depending on number of CPUs and threads

	CPU used	CPU available	Computation time
1 CPU, 1 thread	0%	100%	100 seconds
2 CPUs, 2 threads parallelized	5%/CPU	95%/CPU	100/0.95/2 = 52.6 seconds
3 CPUs, 3 threads parallelized	9.75%/CPU	90.25%/CPU	100/0.9025/3 = 36.9 seconds
9 CPUs, 9 threads parallelized	34%/CPU	66%/CPU	100/0.66/9 = 16.8 seconds
10 CPUs, 10 threads parallelized	37%/CPU	63%/CPU	100/0.63/10 = 15.9 seconds
19 CPUs, 19 threads parallelized	60.3%/CPU	39.7%/CPU	100/0.397/19 = 13.26 seconds
20 CPUs, 20 threads parallelized	62.3%/CPU	37.7%/CPU	100/0.377/20 = 13.26 seconds
21 CPUs, 21 threads parallelized	64.2%/CPU	35.8%/CPU	100/0.358/21 = 13.30 seconds
30 CPUs, 30 threads parallelized	64.2%/CPU	22.6%/CPU	100/0.226/30 = 14.75 seconds

Clearly, there are diminishing returns from adding CPUs. In fact, at some point, adding CPUs actually makes performance worse. For example, let's suppose our number-crunching application is fully parallelizable to any number of CPUs, and that on a single unutilized CPU it takes 100 seconds. On a two-CPU machine, it takes 100 seconds divided by 2 (the number of CPUs, which is how many parts you can parallelize the calculation by) and then divided by 0.95 (the factor by which the CPU is utilized by the CPU parallelization overhead), giving 52.6 seconds.

For three CPUs, this time is 100/(0.95 × 0.95 × 3) = 36.9 seconds. So far, so good. Now, let's move on to 20 CPUs. This works out as 100/(0.95^{19} × 20) = 13.26 seconds. But 21 CPUs takes 100/(0.95^{20} × 21) = 13.30 seconds, actually more time. In fact, for this particular sequence, 20 CPUs gives the minimum time. Beyond that, the overhead of parallelizing CPUs makes things successively worse, and each additional CPU makes the fully parallelized calculation take longer.

In addition, well before the 20th CPU was added, you reach a point where each additional CPU is not at all cost-effective: 6 CPUs gave a value of 21.5 seconds for the calculation, 7 CPUs reduced that by only a couple of seconds to 19.4 seconds. A 10% reduction in time does not justify the cost of an extra CPU.

The general calculation presented here applies to other shared resources too. In a similar way, you can determine the performance effects of adding other additional shared resources to the application and predict whether the advantages will outweigh the disadvantages.

Note that these are all general predictions, useful for estimating the benefits of adding shared resources. The actual tested results can sometimes differ dramatically. For example, parallelizing some searches can provide a tenfold speedup on a single CPU because the increased variation in starting points of the solution space means that the probability of one of the searches starting much nearer the solution is greatly increased (see "Threaded Problem-Solving Strategies" in Chapter 10). But this is an exception. The cutoff where adding a shared resource gives a useful speedup is usually quite small, so you can mostly assume that a little parallelizing is good, but a lot of parallelizing is too much of a good thing.

All the calculations we made in this section assumed full load-balancing. Each thread (sharer) took exactly the same share of time to complete its task, and thus the total time was that of any one sharer since they all operated simultaneously. In reality, this is unlikely. If the sharers are unbalanced (as they usually are), the sharer that takes the longest to complete its activity is the one limiting the performance of the system. And the less balanced the various sharers, the worse the performance. This is extremely important as the application scales across different workloads. An unbalanced workload means that one resource is used far more intensively than others. It also means that all other parallel resources are being underutilized, and that the overused resource is highly likely to be a performance bottleneck in the system.

Data parallelism

If you have a large amount of data that needs to reside on disk, a typical strategy for improving access and searches of the data is to split up the data among many different files (preferably on separate disks). This is known as *partitioning* the data. Partitioning the data provides support for parallel access to the data, which takes advantage of I/O and CPU parallelism.

There are many data-partitioning schemes. Some of the more popular are:

Schema partitioning
Separates the data into logically distinct datasets and allocates each dataset to a separate file/disk.

Hash partitioning
Places data in multiple files/disks with location based on a hash function.

Range partitioning
Splits data into ranges, and each range is allocated a separate file/disk; for example, a–c in disk1, d–f in disk2, etc.

Expression partitioning
Uses a logical expression to determine the mapping of data to file/disk. Unbalanced partitioning requires refinement of the expression and repartitioning.

Round-robin partitioning
Allocates data to disks sequentially.

Partitioning schemes work best when used with indexes. Indexes also make searches much faster.

Although your design does not need to support a specific partitioning scheme, it should support partitioning in general if it is relevant to your application.

Scaling

The performance characteristics of an application vary with the number of different factors the application can deal with. These variable factors can include the number of users, the amount of data dealt with, the number of objects used by the application, etc. During the design phase, whenever considering performance, you should consider how the performance scales as the load on the application varies. It is usually not possible to predict (or measure) the performance for all possible variations of these factors. But you should select several representative sets of values for the factors, and predict (and measure) performance for these sets. The sets should include factors for when the application:

- Has a light load
- Has a medium load
- Has a heavy load
- Has a varying load predicted to represent normal operating conditions
- Has spiked loads (where the load is mostly "normal" but occasionally spikes to the maximum supported)
- Consistently has the maximum load the application was designed to support

You need to ensure that your scaling conditions include variations in threads, objects, and users, and variations in network conditions if appropriate. Measure response times and throughput for the various different scenarios and decide whether any particular situation needs optimizing for throughput of the system as a whole or for response times for individual users.

It is clear that many extra factors need to be taken into account during scaling. The tools you have for profiling scaling behavior are fairly basic: essentially, only graphs of response times or throughput against scaled parameters. It is typical to have a point at which the application starts to have bad scaling behavior: the knee or elbow in the response-time curve. At that point, the application has probably reached some serious resource conflict that requires tuning so that "nice" scaling behavior can be extended further. Clearly, tuning for scaling behavior is likely to be a long process, but you cannot shortcut this process if you want to be certain your application scales.[*]

---

[*] By including timer-based delays in the application code, at least one multiuser application has deliberately slowed response times for low-scaled situations. The artificial delay is reduced or cut out at higher scaling values. The users perceive a system with a similar response time under most loads.

Distributed Applications

The essential design points for ensuring good performance of distributed applications are:

- Supporting asynchronous communications
- Decoupling process activities from each other in such a way that no process is forced to wait for others (using queues achieves this)
- Supporting parallelism in the design of the workflows

Determining the bottleneck in a distributed application requires looking at the throughput of every component:

- Client and server processes
- Network transfer rates (peak and average)
- Network interface card throughput
- Router speed, disk I/O
- Middleware/queuing transfer rates
- Database access, update, and transaction rates
- Operating-system loads

Tuning any component other than the current bottleneck gives no improvement. Peak performance of each component is rarely achieved. You need to assume average rates of performance from the underlying resource and expect performance based on those average rates.

Distributed applications tend to exaggerate any performance characteristics. So when performance is bad, the application tends to slow significantly more than in nondistributed applications. The distributed design aspects should emphasize asynchronous and concurrent operations. Typical items to include in the design are:

- Queues
- Asynchronous communications and activities
- Parallelizable activities
- Minimized serialization points
- Balanced workloads across multiple servers
- Redundant servers and automatic switching capabilities
- Activities that can be configured at runtime to run in different locations
- Short transactions

The key to good performance in a distributed application is to minimize the amount of communication necessary. Performance problems tend to be caused by too many messages flying back and forth between distributed components. Bell's rule of networking applies: "Money can buy bandwidth, but latency is forever."[*]

Unfortunately, communication overhead can be incurred by many different parts of a distributed application. There are some general high-level guidelines:

- Allow the application to be partitioned according to the data and processing power. Any particular task should be able to run in several locations, and the location that provides the best performance should be chosen at runtime. Usually the best location for the task is where the data required for the task is stored, as transferring data tends to be a significant overhead.

- Avoid generating distributed garbage. Distributed garbage collection can be a severe overhead on any distributed application.

- Reduce the costs of keeping data synchronized by minimizing the duplication of data.

- Reduce data-transfer costs by duplicating data. This conflicts directly with the last point, so the two techniques must be balanced to find the optimal data duplication points.

- Cache distributed data wherever possible.

- Use compression to reduce the time taken to transfer large amounts of data.

Object Design

My advice for object design is to use interfaces and interface-like patterns throughout the code. Although there are slightly higher runtime costs from using interfaces, that cost is well outweighed by the benefits of being able to easily replace one object implementation with another. Using interfaces means you can design with the option to replace any class or component with a faster one. Consider also where the design requires comparison by identity or by equality and where these choices can be made at implementation time.

The JDK classes are not all designed with interfaces. Those JDK classes and other third-party classes that do not have interface definitions should be wrapped by your own classes so that their use can be made more generic. (Applications that need to minimize download time, such as applets, may need to avoid the extra overhead that wrapping causes.)

Object creation is one significant place where interfaces fall down, since interfaces do not support constructor declarations, and constructors cannot return an object of a different class. To handle object creation in a way similar to interfaces, you should use the *factory pattern*. The factory design pattern recommends that object creation

---

[*] Thomas E. Bell, "Performance of distributed systems," a paper presented at the ICCM Capacity Management Forum 7, San Francisco, October 1993.

be centralized in a particular *factory method*. So rather than calling new Something( ) when you want to create an instance of the Something class, you call a method such as SomethingFactory.getNewSomething( ), which creates and returns a new instance of the Something class. Again, this pattern has performance costs, as there is the overhead of an extra method call for every object creation, but the pattern provides more flexibility when it comes to tuning.

Design for reusable objects: do not unnecessarily throw away objects. The factory design pattern can help, as it supports the recycling of objects. Canonicalize objects where possible (see "Canonicalizing Objects" in Chapter 4). Keep in mind that stateless objects can usually be safely shared, so try to move to stateless objects where appropriate.

Using stateless objects is a good way to support changing algorithms easily by implementing different algorithms in particular types of objects. For example, see "An Efficient Sorting Framework" in Chapter 9, where different sorting algorithms are implemented in various sorting classes. The resulting objects can be interchanged whenever the sorting algorithm needs to be varied.

Consider whether to optimize objects for update or access. For example, a "statistics-calculating" object might update its average and standard deviation each time a value is added to it, thus slowing down updates but making access of those statistics lightning-fast. Or, the object could simply store added values and calculate the average and standard deviation each time those statistics are accessed, making the update as fast as possible, but increasing the time for statistics access.

Techniques for Predicting Performance

Predicting performance is the mainstay of performance tuning at the analysis and design stages. Often it is the experience of the designers that steers design one way or another. Knowing why a particular design element has caused bad performance in another project allows the experienced designer to alter the design in just the right way to get good performance.

Some general guidelines can guide the application designer and avoid bad performance. In the following sections we consider some of these guidelines.

Factor in comparative performance of operations

Different types of operations have widely varying execution times. Some design abstractions decouple the type of intercomponent-communication mechanism from any specific implementation. The design allows the intercomponent communication to be based on a local or remote call, which allows components to be placed very flexibly. However, the performance of different types of calls varies hugely and helps define whether some designs can perform fast enough.

Specifically, if local procedure calls have an average time overhead of one unit, a local interprocess call incurs an overhead of about 100 units. On the same scale, a remote procedure call (RPC) on a local area network takes closer to 1000 time units, and an RPC routed across the Internet likely takes over 10,000 time units.

Applying these variations to the design and factoring the number of messages that components need to send to each other may rule out some distributed architectures. Alternatively, the overhead predictions may indicate that a redesign is necessary to reduce the number of intercomponent messages.

Note also that process startup overhead may need to be considered. For example, Common Gateway Interface (CGI) scripts for HTTP servers typically need to be started for every message sent to the server. For this type of design, the time taken to start up a script is significant, and when many scripts are started together, this can slow down the server considerably. Similarly, if your design allows many thread startups within short intervals, you need to determine whether the architecture can handle this, or if it may be a better option to redesign the applications to use thread pools (see "Thread Pools" in Chapter 10).

Consider the relative costs of different types of accesses and updates

Accesses and updates to system memory are always going to be significantly faster than accesses and updates to other memory media. For example, reads from a local disk can be a thousand times slower than memory access, and disk writes are typically half as fast as disk reads. Random access of disks is significantly slower than sequential access.

Recognizing these variations may steer your design to alternatives you might otherwise not have considered. For example, one application server that supports a shared persistent cache redesigned the persistent cache update mechanism to take account of these different update times (the GemStone application server, *http://www. gemstone. com*). The original architecture performed transactional updates to objects by writing the changes to the objects on the disk, which required random disk access and updates. The modified architecture wrote all changes to shared memory as well as to a sequential journaling log file (for crash recovery). Another asynchronous process handled flushing the changes from shared memory to the objects stored on disk. Because disk navigation to the various objects was significant, this change in architecture improved performance by completely removing that bottleneck from the transaction.

Use simulations and benchmarks

Ideally, you have a detailed simulation of your application that allows you to predict the performance under any set of conditions. More usually, you have a vague simulation that has some characteristics similar to your intended application. It is important to keep striving for the full detailed simulation to be able to predict the performance of the application. But since your resources are limited, you need to project measurements as close as possible to your target application.

You should try to include loads and delays in your simulation that approximate to the expected load of the application. Try to acquire the resources your finished application will use, even if those resources are not used in the simulation. For example, spawn as many threads as you expect the application to use, even if the threads do little more than sleep restlessly.*

Graphing the results from increasing various application-specific parameters allows you to predict the performance of the application under a variety of conditions. It is worth checking vendor or standard benchmarks if you need some really basic statistics, but bear in mind that those benchmarks seldom have much relevance to a particular application.

Consider the total work done and the design overhead

Try stripping your design to the bare essentials or going back to the specification. Consider how to create a special-purpose implementation that handles the specification for a specific set of inputs. This can give you an estimate of the actual work your application will do. Now consider your design and look at the overhead added by the design for each piece of functionality. This provides a good way to focus on the overhead and determine if it is excessive.

Focus on shared resources

Shared resources almost always cause performance problems if they have not been designed to optimize performance. Ensure that any simulation correctly simulates the sharing of resources, and use prediction analyses such as those in the "Parallelism" section earlier in this chapter to predict the behavior of multiple objects using shared resources.

Predict the effects of parallelism

Consider what happens when your design is spread over multiple threads, processes, CPUs, machines, etc. This analysis can be quite difficult without a simulation and test bed, but it can help to identify whether the design limits the use of parallelism.

Assess the costs of data conversions

Many applications convert data between different types (e.g., between strings and numbers). From your design, you should be able to determine the frequency and types of data conversions, and it is fairly simple to create small tests that determine the costs of the particular conversions you are using. Don't forget to include any concurrency or use of shared resources in the tests. Remember that external transfer of

---

* Sleeping restlessly is calling `Thread.sleep()` in a loop, with the sleep time set to some value that requires many loop iterations before the loop terminates. Other activities can be run intermittently in the loop to simulate work.

objects or data normally includes some data conversions. The cost of data conversion may be significant enough to direct you to alter your design.

Determine whether batch processing is faster

Some repeated tasks can be processed as a batch instead of one at a time. Batch processing can take advantage of a number of efficiencies, such as accessing and creating some objects just once, eliminating some tests for shared resources, processing tasks in optimal order, avoiding repeated searches, etc.

If any particular set of tasks could be processed in batch mode, consider the effect this would have on your application and how much faster the processing could be. The simplest conceptual example is that of adding characters one by one to a StringBuffer, as opposed to using a char array to add all the characters together. Adding the characters using a char array is much faster for any significant number of characters.

Tuning After Deployment

Tuning does not necessarily end at the development stage. For many applications such as agent applications, services, servlets and servers, multiuser applications, enterprise systems, etc., there needs to be constant monitoring of the application performance after deployment to ensure that no degradation takes place. In this section, I discuss tuning the deployed application. This is mainly relevant to enterprise systems that are being administered. Shrinkwrapped or similar software is normally tuned the same way as before deployment, using standard profiling tools.

Monitoring the application is the primary tuning activity after deployment. The application should be built with hooks that enable tools to connect to it and gather statistics and response times. The application should be constantly monitored, and all performance logs retained. Monitoring should record as many parameters as possible throughout the system, though clearly you want to avoid monitoring so much that the performance of the running application is compromised by a significant amount. Of course, almost any act of measuring a system affects performance. But the advantage of having performance logs normally pays off enormously, and a few percent decrease in performance should be acceptable.

Individual records in the performance logs should include at least the following six categories:

- Time (including offset time from a reference server)
- User identifier
- Transaction identifier
- Application name, type, class, or group

- Software component or subsystem
- Hardware resource

A standard set of performance logs should be used to give a background system measurement and kept as a reference. Other logs can be compared against that standard. Periodically, the standard should be regenerated, as most enterprise applications change their performance characteristics over time. Ideally, the standard logs can be automatically compared against the current logs, and any significant change in behavior is automatically identified and causes an alert to be sent to the administrators. Trends away from the standard should also trigger a notification; sometimes performance degrades slowly but consistently because of a gradually depleting resource.

Administrators should note every single change to the system: every patch, every upgrade, every configuration change, etc. These changes are the source of most performance problems in production. Patches are cheaper short-term fixes than upgrades, but they usually add to the complexity of the application and increase maintenance costs. Upgrades and rereleases are more expensive in the short term, but cheaper overall.

Administrators should listen to users. Users are the most sensitive barometer of application performance. However, you should double-check users' assertions. A user may be wrong, or might have hit a known system problem or temporary administrative shutdown. Measure the performance yourself. Repeat the measurements several times and take averages and variations. Ensure that caching effects do not skew measurements of a reported problem.

When looking for reasons why performance may have changed, consider any recent changes such as an increase in the number of users, other applications added to the system, code changes on the client or server, hardware changes, etc. In addition to user response time measurements, look at where the distributed code is executing, what volumes of data are being used, and where the code is spending most of its time.

Many factors can easily give misleading or temporarily different measurements to the application. Distributed garbage collection may have cut in, system clocks may become unsynchronized, background processes may be triggered, and relative processor power may change, causing obscure effects. Consider if anyone else is using the processors, and if so, what they are doing and why.

You need to differentiate between:

- Occasional sudden slowness, e.g., from background processes starting up
- General slowness, perhaps reflecting that the application was not tuned for the current load, or that the systems or networks are saturated
- A sudden slowdown that continues, often the result of a change to the system

Each of these characteristic changes in performance indicates a different set of problems.

More Factors That Affect Performance

The following sections discuss some aspects of the application that may not immediately strike you as part of the performance of the application. But they do affect the user's perception of the application performance, and so are relevant.

User Interface Usability

The application's user interface has a significant effect on the user's perception of performance. The time required to navigate through the user interface to execute some functionality is seen by the user as part of the application's response time. If window and menu navigation is difficult, performance is seen to be bad (and, actually, it is bad).

The user interface should support the natural flow of the user's activity; otherwise, you are forcing the user to perform less efficiently. Improving only the navigability of the user interface, even with no other changes to the application, improves the perceived performance of an application.

Training

Training users to use the application is also a performance issue. Without proper training, users may not use the application efficiently and may compare the application unfavorably with another application they are comfortable with. Since they are comparing similar functionality, the user immediately focuses on the differences. The main difference, of course, is the perceived performance.

The user never thinks he is untrained. He simply feels that executing some function in your application takes forever, as he stumbles through menu options trying to find what he wants, fills in forms incorrectly, etc. The result is a perception of bad performance.

Note that making help desks available is an essential part of the training program. Training is seldom so thorough that all parts of the application are covered in enough detail, and it is also common for people to forget some of their training. A help desk keeps the users from getting lost and giving up on the most efficient route to solve their tasks.

Server Downtime

If people can't start a piece of software, they can get frustrated, but they don't normally view this as bad performance. Most people would instead get annoyed at the quality of the software. But when servers are not running, this can be perceived differently. Sometimes a server that isn't running is perceived as bad-quality software, but sometimes it is seen as poor performance. If the server stops responding in the middle of processing, this is invariably seen as slow performance. Consider your own response to a stalled download from an HTTP server.

Avoiding server downtime is a robustness issue as well as a performance issue. Servers should be designed to avoid unnecessary downtime and minimize necessary downtime. One issue when running servers is altering their configuration and patching them. If you need to stop a server from running while you make changes, this affects its perceived performance. You must signal it to stop accepting requests and either wait for current requests to terminate or forcibly terminate all requests; either way, this causes interruptions in service to the clients.[*]

It is possible to design servers that can be reconfigured and patched with no downtime. Designing for reconfiguration on the fly is easier. In this case, you typically have a configuration file. One common solution is for the server to periodically test the timestamp of the configuration file and reread it if the timestamp changes. This solution also provides good security (as presumably, the configuration file can be changed only by authorized persons). Another solution is for the server to recognize and accept a particular signal as a sign to reset its configuration. In most servers using this solution, the signal is an operating-system signal that is trapped. However, Java does not support operating-system signal handling, so if you steer down this path, you need either to install operating-system handlers yourself (using the Java native interface) or use another communication mechanism, such as sockets. If you do use sockets, you need to consider security aspects; you don't want unauthorized persons triggering a server reconfiguration.

Patching a running server is more complex. You need to provide some level of indirection on how the request-processing classes (and all the classes they depend on) are loaded. The most basic solution is to use the configuration file to list names of all classes. Then the server must be built using `Class.forName( )` to access and create any classes and instances. This way, providing a new version requires only changing the class names in the configuration (in an atomic way to avoid corruption).

A more sophisticated solution is to use different `ClassLoaders`. Note that any particular class in Java is identified by its package and class name and by its `ClassLoader`. It is possible to have classes with the same package and class names loaded multiple times in the same VM (whether the implementation is the same or different for those classes) using multiple `ClassLoader` instances. This is easiest in 1.2 and later, where there is a proliferation of `ClassLoaders`. A useful classloader for this type of runtime patching is the `URLClassLoader`:

```
//This method gets a new implementation of a RequestProcessor
//every time.
public RequestProcessor getNewRequestProcessor( )
{
```

---

[*] Load-balancing products often provide features that allow server maintenance with minimum downtime.

```
      URL[ ] urls = {new URL(...)};
      Class c = RequestServerMain.class;
      ClassLoader cl = c.getClassLoader( );
      URLClassLoader xtra_cl = new URLClassLoader(urls , cl);
      c = xtra_cl.loadClass("RequestProcessor");
      RequestProcessor proc = (RequestProcessor) c.newInstance( );
      return proc;
  }

  public void processRequest(Request aRequest, RequestProcessor proc)
  {
    //Signal to get a new implementation of a request processor
    //by passing a null value in the <proc> variable
    if (proc == null)
      proc = getNewRequestProcessor( );
    proc.processRequest(aRequest);
    ...
  }
```

In most cases, you will find that a customized classloader is the best solution, especially because you can include consistency checking within that classloader, as well as ensuring atomicity of changes. You can even provide unloading and loading of classes, which is probably the most sophisticated solution available for runtime patching.

Performance Planning

This chapter has described how to factor in performance at various stages of development. Integrating this advice allows you to create a performance plan, as outlined in this section.

1. **Specify performance requirements.**

   During the specification stage, the performance requirements of the application need to be defined. This is not primarily a developer task. Your customers or business experts need to establish what response time is acceptable for most functions the user will execute. It may be more useful to start by specifying what response times will be unacceptable.

   This task can be undertaken at a later stage of development. In fact, it can be simpler, if a prototype has already been created, to use the prototype and other business information in specifying acceptable responses. But do not neglect to specify these response-time requirements before starting any type of implementation-level performance tuning (code tuning). If code tuning starts without performance requirements, then goals are inadequately defined, and tuning effort will be wasted on parts of the application that do not require tuning.

   If your development environment is layered (e.g., application layer, component layer, technical architecture layer), try to define performance specifications that map to each layer, so that each team has its own set of performance targets to work on. If this is not possible, the performance experts will need to be able to tune across all layers and interact with all teams.

2. **Include a performance focus in the analysis phase.**

During the analysis stage, the main performance focus is to analyze the requirements for shared and limited resources in the application (e.g., a network connection is both a shared and a limited resource; a database table is a shared resource; threads are a limited resource). These are the resources that will cost the most to fix later in development if they are not identified and designed correctly at the outset. Analysis of data volume and load-carrying capacities of the components of the system should also be carried out to determine the limitations of the system.

This task should fit in comfortably as part of the normal analysis stage. To be on the safe side, or to highlight the requirement for performance analysis, you may wish to allocate 10% of planned analysis time for performance analysis in this phase. The analysis team must be aware of the performance impact of different design choices so that they do not miss aspects of the system that need analysis (see the earlier "Analysis" section). The analysis should be made in association with the technical architecture analysis so that you end up with an architectural blueprint that clearly identifies performance aspects.

3. **Require performance predictions from the design team.**

Progressing from the analysis stage, the performance focus in the design phase should be on how shared resources will be used by the application and on the performance consequences of the expected physical architecture of the deployed application.

Ensure that the designers are aware of the performance consequences of different decisions by asking for performance-impact predictions to be included with the normal design aspects. The external design review should either include design experts familiar with the performance aspects of design choices, or a secondary performance expert familiar with design should review the application design. If any significant third-party products will be used (e.g., a middleware or database product), the product vendor should have performance experts who can validate the design and identify any potential performance problems. A 10% budget allocation for performance planning and testing highlights the emphasis on performance. See the earlier "Design and Architecture" section.

The design should include reference to scalability both for users and for data/object volumes, the amount of distribution possible for the application depending on the required level of messaging between distributed components, and the transaction mechanisms and modes (pessimistic, optimistic, required locks, durations of transactions and locks held). The theoretical limitation to the performance of many multiuser applications is the amount and duration of locks held on shared resources. The designers should also include a section on handling queries against large datasets, if that will be significant for your application.

4. **Create a performance-testing environment.**

The performance task for the beginning of the development phase is setting up the performance-testing environment. You need to:

- Specify benchmark functions and required response times based on the specification.
- Ensure that a reasonably accurate test environment for the system is available.
- Buy or build various performance tools for your performance experts to evaluate, including profiling tools, monitoring tools, benchmark harnesses, web loading, GUI capture/playback, or other client emulation tools.
- Ensure that the benchmark/performance-testing harness can drive the application with simulated user and external driver activity.
- Schedule regular, exclusive performance-testing time for the test environment: if the test environment is shared, performance testing should not take place at the same time as other activities.
- Create reusable performance tests with reproducible application activity. Note that this is *not* QA: the tests should not be testing failure modes of the system, only normal, expected activity.
- Prepare the testing and monitoring environment. This is normally system-specific and usually evolves as the testing proceeds. You will ultimately need to have performance-monitoring tools or scripts that monitor the underlying system performance as well as providing statistics on network and application performance (discussed further in Step 8).
- Plan for code versioning and release from your development environment to your performance environment, according to your performance test plan. (Note that this often requires a round of bug-fixing to properly run the tests, and time restrictions usually mean that it is not possible to wait for the full QA release, so plan for some developer support.)

5. **Test a simulation or skeleton system for validation.**

Create a simulation of the system that faithfully represents the main components of the application. The simulation should be implemented so that you can test the scalability of the system and determine how shared resources respond to increased loads and at what stage limited resources start to become exhausted or bottlenecked. The simulation should allow finished components to be integrated as they become available. If budget resources are unavailable, skip the initial simulation, but start testing as soon as sufficient components become available to implement a skeleton version of the system. The targets are to determine response times and scalability of the system for design validation feedback as early as possible.

If you have a "Proof of Concept" stage planned, it could provide the simulation or a good basis for the simulation. Ideally, the validation would take place as part of the "Proof of Concept."

6. **Integrate performance logging.**

   Integrate performance logging into the application. This logging should be deployed with the released application (see Step 8), so performance logging should be designed to be low-impact. Performance logging should be added to all the layer boundaries: servlet I/O and marshalling; JVM server I/O and marshalling; database access/update; transaction boundaries; and so on. Performance logging should not produce more than one line of output to a log file per 20 seconds. It should be designed so that it adds less than 1% of time to all application activity. Logging should be configurable to aggregate variable amounts of statistics so that it can be deployed to produce one summary log line per configurable time unit (e.g., one summary line every minute). Ideally, logging should be designed so that the output can be analyzed in a spreadsheet, allowing for effective and easy-to-read aggregation results. J2EE monitoring products are available that automatically integrate logging into J2EE servers (see *http://www.JavaPerformanceTuning.com/resources.shtml*).

7. **Performance-test and tune using results.**

   During code implementation, unit performance testing should be scheduled along with QA. No unit performance tuning is required until the unit is ready for QA. Unit performance tuning proceeds by integrating the unit into the system simulation and running scaling tests with profiling.

   It is important to test the full system or a simulation of it as soon as is feasible, even if many of the units are incomplete. Simulated units are perfectly okay at an early stage of system performance testing. Initially, the purpose of this system performance test is to validate the design and architecture and identify any parts of the design or implementation that will not scale. Later, the tests should provide detailed logs and profiles that will allow developers to target bottlenecks in the system and produce faster versions of the application.

   To support the later-stage performance testing, the test bed should be configured to provide performance profiles of any JVM processes, including system and network statistics, in addition to performance logging. Your performance experts should be able to produce JVM profiles and obtain and analyze statistics from your target system.

   The performance tests should scale to higher loads of users and data. Scale tests to twice the expected peak load. Test separately:

   - Twice the peak expected throughput, together with the peak expected data volume and the peak expected users.
   - Twice the peak expected data volume, together with the peak expected throughput and the peak expected users.
   - Twice the peak expected users, together with the peak expected data volume and the peak expected throughput.

User activity should be simulated as accurately as possible, but it is most important that data is simulated to produce the expected real data variety; otherwise, cache activity can produce completely misleading results. The numbers of objects should be scaled to reasonable amounts: this is especially important for query testing and batch updates. Do not underestimate the complexity of creating large amounts of realistic data for scalability testing.

8. **Deploy with performance-logging features.**

   Performance-logging features should be deployed with the released application. Such logging provides remote analysis and constant monitoring capabilities for the deployed application. Ideally, you should develop tools that automatically analyze the performance logs. At minimum, the performance-log analysis tools should generate summaries of the logs, compare performance against a set of reference logs, and highlight anomalies.

   Two other useful tools identify long-term trends in the performance logs and generate alerts when particular performance measurements exceed defined ranges. A graphical interface for these tools is also helpful.

Performance Checklist

- Consider performance at each stage of the development cycle. Create a performance plan that anticipates all the various performance issues that regularly crop up.
  - Plan for tuning phases.
  - Leave code tuning until after the code is functional and debugged.
  - Consider how a particular performance change will affect other parts of the application.
  - Identify performance limitations.
  - Eliminate performance conflicts.
  - Consider how the performance scales as the application scales.
  - Consider how the performance scales as the application load varies.
- Determine the general characteristics of the application in the analysis and design phases.
  - Minimize the features in the requirements.
  - Specify performance boundaries and goals.
  - Consider the numbers, sizes, and sources of objects, data, and other parameters of the application.
  - Create an abstract model of the application to identify any performance problems.
  - Design applets to engage the user as soon as possible.

- — Identify and focus on the performance costs of shared resources.
- — Target decoupling, indirection, abstraction, and extra layers in the design.
- — Predict the performance of design elements that block, copy, queue, or distribute.
- — Consider alternative designs that bypass or reduce high-performance costs.
- — Avoid transactions where possible.
- — Minimize transaction time where transactions are necessary.
- — Lock only where the design absolutely requires it.
- — Design parallelism into the application wherever possible. Identify what cannot be parallelized.
- — Watch out for too much parallelism. There are diminishing returns from parallelism overhead.
- — Balance workloads. Unbalanced parallel activities may limit the performance of the system.
- — Split up the data among many different files (preferably on separate disks).
- — Support asynchronous communications.
- — Decouple activities so that no activity is unnecessarily blocked by another activity.
- — Minimize points where parallel activities are forced to converge.
- — Design for redundant servers and automatic switching capabilities.
- — Consider using batch processing.
- — Design more flexible method entry points to your classes to provide greater performance flexibility when developing reusable code.
- Partition distributed applications according to the data and processing power of components.
  - — Minimize the communication between distributed components.
  - — Avoid generating distributed garbage.
  - — Reduce transfer costs by duplicating data.
  - — Cache distributed data wherever possible.
  - — Minimize the synchronization requirements of duplicated data.
  - — Use compression to reduce transfer time.
- Design objects so that they can be easily replaced by a faster implementation.
  - — Use interfaces and interface-like patterns (e.g., the factory pattern).
  - — Design for reusable objects.
  - — Use stateless objects.
  - — Consider whether to optimize objects for update or for access.

— Minimize data conversions.

— Minimize the number and size of developed classes for applications that need to minimize download time.

- Constantly monitor the running application.

  — Retain performance logs. Choose one set as your comparison standard.

  — Monitor as many parameters as possible throughout the system.

  — Note every single change to the system. Changes are the most likely cause of performance variations.

  — Listen to the application users, but double-check any reported problems.

  — Ensure that caching effects do not skew the measurements of a reported problem.

- Make the user interface seem fast.

- Train users to use the application efficiently.

- Minimize server-maintenance downtime.

- Implement a performance plan as an integral part of application design and development.

CHAPTER 14

Underlying Operating System and Network Improvements

If you control the operating system and hardware where the application will be deployed, there are a number of changes you can make to improve performance. Some changes are generic and affect most applications, while some are application-specific. This chapter applies to most server systems running Java applications, including servlets, where you usually specify (or have specified to you) the underlying system, and where you have some control over tuning the system. Client and standalone Java programs are likely to benefit from this chapter only if you have some degree of control over the target system, but some tips in the chapter apply to all Java programs.

I don't cover operating-system and hardware tuning in any great detail, though I give basic tips on monitoring the system. More detailed information on Unix systems can be obtained from the excellent *System Performance Tuning* by Mike Loukides (O'Reilly). Another more specific book on Sun's Solaris operating system is *Sun Performance and Tuning* by Adrian Cockcroft and Richard Pettit (Prentice Hall). A couple of relevant Windows systems books are *Windows NT Performance Monitoring, Benchmarking, and Tuning* by Mark T. Edmead and Paul Hinsberg (New Riders) and *Windows NT Applications: Measuring and Optimizing Performance* by Paul Hinsberg (MacMillan Technical Publishing). Note that Macintoshes running OS X should include the Unix tools I mention in this chapter.

It is usually best to target the operating system and hardware as a last tuning choice. Tuning the application itself generally provides far more significant speedups than tuning the systems on which the application is running. Application tuning also tends to be easier (though buying more powerful hardware components is easier still and a valid choice for tuning). However, application and system tuning are actually complementary activities, so you can get speedups from tuning both the system and the application if you have the skills and resources.

Here are some general tips for tuning systems:

- Constantly monitor the entire system with any monitoring tools available and keep records. This allows you to get a background usage pattern and also lets you compare the current situation with situations previously considered stable.

- You should run offline work during off-hours only. This ensures that there is no extra load on the system when the users are executing online tasks, and enhances performance of both online and offline activities.

- If you need to run extra tasks during the day, try to slot them into times with low user activity. Office activity usually peaks at 9:00 A.M. and 2:30 P.M. and has a low between noon and 1:00 P.M. or at shift changeovers. You should be able to determine the user-activity cycles appropriate to your system by examining the results of normal monitoring. The reduced conflict for system resources during periods of low activity improves performance.

- You should specify timeouts for all processes under the control of your application (and others on the system, if possible) and terminate processes that have passed their timeout value.

- Apply any partitioning available from the system to allocate determinate resources to your application. For example, you can specify disk partitions, memory segments, and even CPUs to be allocated to particular processes.

Hard Disks

In most cases, applications can be tuned so that disk I/O does not cause any serious performance problems. But if, after application tuning, you find that disk I/O is still causing a performance problem, your best bet may be to upgrade the system disks. Identifying whether the system has a problem with disk utilization is the first step. Each system provides its own tools to identify disk usage (Windows has a performance monitor, and Unix has the *sar*, *vmstat*, and *iostat* utilities.) At minimum, you need to identify whether paging is an issue (look at disk-scan rates) and assess the overall utilization of your disks (e.g., performance monitor on Windows, output from iostat -D on Unix). It may be that the system has a problem independent of your application (e.g., unbalanced disks), and correcting this problem may resolve the performance issue.

If the disk analysis does not identify an obvious system problem that is causing the I/O overhead, you could try making a disk upgrade or a reconfiguration. This type of tuning can consist of any of the following:

- Upgrading to faster disks
- Adding more swap space to handle larger buffers
- Changing the disks to be striped (where files are striped across several disks, thus providing parallel I/O, e.g., with a RAID system)

- Running the data on raw partitions when this is shown to be faster
- Distributing simultaneously accessed files across multiple disks to gain parallel I/O
- Using memory-mapped disks or files (see the "Cached Filesystems (RAM Disks, tmpfs, cachefs)" section later in this chapter)

If you have applications that run on many systems and you do not know the specification of the target system, bear in mind that you can never be sure that any particular disk is local to the user. There is a significant possibility that the disk being used by the application is a network-mounted disk. This doubles the variability in response times and throughput. The weakest link, whether it is the network or the disk, is the limiting factor in this case. And this weakest link will probably not even be constant. A network disk is a shared resource, as is the network itself, so performance is hugely and unpredictably affected by other users and network load.

Disk I/O

Do not underestimate the impact of disk writes on the system as a whole. For example, all database vendors strongly recommend that the system swap files* be placed on a separate disk from their databases. The impact of not doing so can decrease database throughput (and system activity) by an order of magnitude. This performance decrease comes from not splitting the I/O of two disk-intensive applications (in this case, OS paging and database I/O).

Identifying that there is an I/O problem is usually fairly easy. The most basic symptom is that things take longer than expected, while at the same time the CPU is not at all heavily worked. The disk-monitoring utilities will also tell you that there is a lot of work being done to the disks. At the system level, you should determine the average and peak requirements on the disks. Your disks will have some statistics that are supplied by the vendor, including:

- The average and peak transfer rates, normally in megabytes (MB) per second, e.g., 5MB/sec. From this, you can calculate how long an 8K page takes to be transferred from disk; for example, 5MB/sec is about 5K/ms, so an 8K page takes just under 2 ms to transfer.
- Average seek time, normally in milliseconds (ms). This is the time required for the disk head to move radially to the correct location on the disk.
- Rotational speed, normally in revolutions per minute (rpm), e.g., 7200 rpm. From this, you can calculate the average rotational delay in moving the disk under the disk-head reader, i.e., the time taken for half a revolution. For example, for 7200 rpm, one revolution takes 60,000 ms (60 seconds) divided by 7200

---

* The disk files for the virtual memory of the operating system; see the later section "RAM."

rpm, which is about 8.3 ms. So half a revolution takes just over 4 ms, which is consequently the average rotational delay.

This list allows you to calculate the actual time it takes to load a random 8K page from the disk, this being seek time + rotational delay + transfer time. Using the examples given in the list, you have 10 + 4 + 2 = 16 ms to load a random 8K page (almost an order of magnitude slower than the raw disk throughput). This calculation gives you a worst-case scenario for the disk-transfer rates for your application, allowing you to determine if the system is up to the required performance. Note that if you are reading data stored sequentially on disk (as when reading a large file), the seek time and rotational delay are incurred less than once per 8K page loaded. Basically, these two times are incurred only at the beginning of opening the file and whenever the file is fragmented. But this calculation is confounded by other processes also executing I/O to the disk at the same time. This overhead is part of the reason why swap and other intensive I/O files should not be put on the same disk.

One mechanism for speeding up disk I/O is to stripe disks. Disk striping allows data from a particular file to be spread over several disks. Striping allows reads and writes to be performed in parallel across the disks without requiring any application changes. This can speed up disk I/O quite effectively. However, be aware that the seek and rotational overhead previously listed still applies, and if you are making many small random reads, there may be no performance gain from striping disks.

Finally, note again that using remote disks adversely affects I/O performance. You should not be using remote disks mounted from the network with any I/O-intensive operations if you need good performance.

Clustering Files

Reading many files sequentially is faster if the files are clustered together on the disk, allowing the disk-head reader to flow from one file to the next. This clustering is best done in conjunction with defragmenting the disks. The overhead in finding the location of a file on the disk (detailed in the previous section) is also minimized for sequential reads if the files are clustered.

If you cannot specify clustering files at the disk level, you can still provide similar functionality by putting all the files together into one large file (as is done with the ZIP filesystem). This is fine if all the files are read-only files or if there is just one file that is writeable (you place that at the end). However, when there is more than one writeable file, you need to manage the location of the internal files in your system as one or more grow. This becomes a problem and is not usually worth the effort. (If the files have a known bounded size, you can pad the files internally, thus regaining the single file efficiency.)

Cached Filesystems (RAM Disks, tmpfs, cachefs)

Most operating systems provide the ability to map a filesystem into the system memory. This ability can speed up reads and writes to certain files in which you control your target environment. Typically, this technique has been used to speed up the reading and writing of temporary files. For example, some compilers (of languages in general, not specifically Java) generate many temporary files during compilation. If these files are created and written directly to the system memory, the speed of compilation is greatly increased. Similarly, if you have a set of external files that are needed by your application, it is possible to map these directly into the system memory, thus allowing their reads and writes to be speeded up greatly.

But note that these types of filesystems are not persistent. In the same way the system memory of the machine gets cleared when it is rebooted, so these filesystems are removed on reboot. If the system crashes, anything in a memory-mapped filesystem is lost. For this reason, these types of filesystems are usually suitable only for temporary files or read-only versions of disk-based files (such as mapping a CD-ROM into a memory-resident filesystem).

Remember that you do not have the same degree of fine control over these filesystems that you have over your application. A memory-mapped filesystem does not use memory resources as efficiently as working directly from your application. If you have direct control over the files you are reading and writing, it is usually better to optimize this within your application rather than outside it. A memory-mapped filesystem takes space directly from system memory. You should consider whether it would be better to let your application grow in memory instead of letting the filesystem take up that system memory. For multiuser applications, it is usually more efficient for the system to map shared files directly into memory, as a particular file then takes up just one memory location rather than being duplicated in each process. Note that from SDK 1.4, memory-mapped files are directly supported from the java. nio package, as discussed in Chapter 8. Memory-mapped *files* are slightly different from memory-mapped *filesystems*. A memory-mapped file uses system resources to read the file into system memory, and that data can then be accessed from Java through the appropriate java.nio buffer. A memory-mapped filesystem does not require the java.nio package and, as far as Java is concerned, files in that filesystem are simply files like any others. The operating system transparently handles the memory mapping.

The creation of memory-mapped filesystems is completely system-dependent, and there is no guarantee that it is available on any particular system (though most modern operating systems do support this feature). On Unix systems, the administrator needs to look at the documentation of the mount command and its subsections on cachefs and tmpfs. Under Windows, you should find details by looking at the documentation on how to set up a RAM disk, a portion of memory mapped to a logical disk drive.

In a similar way, there are products available that precache shared libraries (DLLs) and even executables in memory. This usually means only that an application starts quicker or loads the shared library quicker, and so may not be much help in speeding up a running system (for example, Norton SpeedStart caches DLLs and device drivers in memory on Windows systems).

But you can apply the technique of memory-mapping filesystems directly and quite usefully for applications in which processes are frequently started. Copy the Java distribution and all class files (all JDK, application, and third-party class files) onto a memory-mapped filesystem and ensure that all executions and classloads take place from that filesystem. Since everything (executables, shared libraries, class files, resources, etc.) is already in memory, the startup time is much faster. Because only the startup (and classloading) time is affected, this technique gives only a small boost to applications that are not frequently starting processes, but can be usefully applied if startup time is a problem.

Disk Fragmentation

When files are stored on disk, the bytes in the files are not necessarily stored contiguously: their storage depends on file size and contiguous space available on the disk. This noncontiguous disk storage is called *fragmentation*. Any particular file may have some chunks in one place, and a pointer to the next chunk that may be quite a distance away on the disk.

Hard disks tend to get fragmented over time. This fragmentation delays both reads from files (including loading applications into computer memory on startup) and writes to files. This delay occurs because the disk header must wind on to the next chunk with each fragmentation, and this takes time.

For optimum performance on any system, it is a good idea to periodically defragment the disks. This reunites files that have been split up so that the disk heads do not spend so much time searching for data once the file-header locations have been identified, thus speeding up data access. Defragmenting may not be effective on all systems, however.

Disk Sweet Spots

Most disks have a location from which data is transferred faster than from other locations. Usually, the closer the data is to the outside edge of the disk, the faster it can be read from the disk. Most hard disks rotate at constant angular speed. This means that the linear speed of the disk under a point is faster the farther away the point is from the center of the disk. Thus, data at the edge of the disk can be read from (and written to) at the fastest possible rate commensurate with the maximum density of data storable on disk.

This location with faster transfer rates is usually termed the *disk sweet spot*. Some (commercial) utilities provide mapped access to the underlying disk and allow you to reorganize files to optimize access. On most server systems, the administrator has control over how logical partitions of the disk apply to the physical layout, and how to position files to the disk sweet spots. Experts for high-performance database systems sometimes try to position the index tables of the database as close as possible to the disk sweet spot. These tables consist of relatively small amounts of data that affect the performance of the system in a disproportionately large way, so that any speed improvement in manipulating these tables is significant.

Note that some of the latest operating systems are beginning to include "awareness" of disk sweet spots, and attempt to move executables to sweet spots when defragmenting the disk. You may need to ensure that the defragmentation procedure does not disrupt your own use of the disk sweet spot.

CPU

Java provides a virtual machine runtime system that is just that: an abstraction of a CPU that runs in software. These virtual machines run on a real CPU, and in this section I discuss the performance characteristics of those real CPUs.

CPU Load

The CPU and many other parts of the system can be monitored using system-level utilities. On Windows, the task manager and performance monitor can be used for monitoring. On Unix, a performance monitor (such as *perfmeter*) is usually available, as well as utilities such as *vmstat*. Two aspects of the CPU are worth watching as primary performance points. These are the CPU *utilization* (usually expressed in percentage terms) and the *runnable queue* of processes and threads (often called the load or the task queue). The first indicator is simply the percentage of the CPU (or CPUs) being used by all the various threads. If this is up to 100% for significant periods of time, you may have a problem. On the other hand, if it isn't, the CPU is underutilized, but that is usually preferable. Low CPU usage can indicate that your application may be blocked for significant periods on disk or network I/O. High CPU usage can indicate thrashing (lack of RAM) or CPU contention (indicating that you need to tune the code and reduce the number of instructions being processed to reduce the impact on the CPU).

A reasonable target is 75% CPU utilization. This means that the system is being worked toward its optimum, but that you have left some slack for spikes due to other system or application requirements. However, note that if more than 50% of the CPU is used by system processes (i.e., administrative and operating-system processes), your CPU is probably underpowered. This can be identified by looking at the load of the system over some period when you are not running any applications.

The second performance indicator, the runnable queue, indicates the average number of processes or threads waiting to be scheduled for the CPU by the operating system. They are runnable processes, but the CPU has no time to run them and is keeping them waiting for some significant amount of time. As soon as the run queue goes above zero, the system may display contention for resources, but there is usually some value above zero that still gives acceptable performance for any particular system. You need to determine what that value is in order to use this statistic as a useful warning indicator. A simplistic way to do this is to create a short program that repeatedly does some simple activity. You can then time each run of that activity. You can run copies of this process one after the other so that more and more copies are simultaneously running. Keep increasing the number of copies being run until the run queue starts increasing. By watching the times recorded for the activity, you can graph that time against the run queue. This should give you some indication of when the runnable queue becomes too large for useful responses on your system, and you can then set system threshold monitors to watch for that level and alert the administrator if the threshold is exceeded. (One guideline from Adrian Cockcroft is that performance starts to degrade if the run queue grows bigger than four times the number of CPUs.)

If you can upgrade the CPU of the target environment, doubling the CPU speed is usually better than doubling the number of CPUs. And remember that parallelism in an application doesn't necessarily need multiple CPUs. If I/O is significant, the CPU will have plenty of time for many threads.

Process Priorities

The operating system also has the ability to prioritize the processes in terms of providing CPU time by allocating *process priority levels*. CPU priorities provide a way to throttle high-demand CPU processes, thus giving other processes a greater share of the CPU. If there are other processes that need to run on the same machine but it doesn't matter if they were run more slowly, you can give your application processes a (much) higher priority than those other processes, thus allowing your application the lion's share of CPU time on a congested system. This is worth keeping in mind. If your application consists of multiple processes, you should also consider the possibility of giving your various processes different levels of priority.

Being tempted to adjust the priority levels of processes, however, is often a sign that the CPU is underpowered for the tasks you have given it.

RAM

Maintaining watch directly on the system memory (RAM) is not usually that helpful in identifying performance problems. A better indication that memory might be affecting performance can be gained by watching for paging of data from memory to the swap files. Most current operating systems have a virtual memory that is made up of the actual (real) system memory using RAM chips, and one or more swap files on the system disks. Processes that are currently running are operating in real memory. The operating system can take pages from any of the processes currently in real memory and swap them out to disk. This is known as *paging*. Paging leaves free space in real memory to allocate to other processes that need to bring in a page from disk.*

Obviously, if all the processes currently running can fit into real memory, there is no need for the system to swap out any pages. However, if there are too many processes to fit into real memory, paging allows the system to free up system memory to run more processes. Paging affects system performance in many ways. One obvious way is that if a process has had some pages moved to disk and the process becomes runnable, the operating system has to pull back the pages from the disk before that process can be run. This leads to delays in performance. In addition, both the CPU and the disk I/O subsystem spend time doing the paging, reducing available processing power and increasing the load on the disks. This cascading effect involving both the CPU and I/O can degrade the performance of the whole system in such a way that it may be difficult to even recognize that paging is the problem. The extreme version of too much paging is *thrashing*, in which the system is spending so much time moving pages around that it fails to perform any other significant work. (The next step is likely to be a system crash.)

As with runnable queues (see the "CPU" section), a little paging of the system does not affect performance enough to cause concern. In fact, some paging can be considered good. It indicates that the system's memory resources are being fully used. But at the point where paging becomes a significant overhead, the system is overloaded.

Monitoring paging is relatively easy. On Unix, the utilities *vmstat* and *iostat* provide details as to the level of paging, disk activity, and memory levels. On Windows, the performance monitor has categories to show these details, as well as being able to monitor the system swap files.

If there is more paging than is optimal, the system's RAM is insufficient or processes are too big. To improve this situation, you need to reduce the memory being used by reducing the number of processes or the memory utilization of some processes. Alternatively, you can add RAM. Assuming that it is your application that is causing the paging (otherwise, either the system needs an upgrade, or someone else's processes may also have to be tuned), you need to reduce the memory resources you are using. Chapter 4 provides useful recommendations for improving application-memory usage.

---

* The term *swapping* refers to moving entire processes between main memory and the swap file. Most modern operating systems no longer swap processes; instead, they swap pages from processes.

When the problem is caused by a combination of your application and others, you can partially address the situation by using process priorities (see the "CPU" section). The equivalent to priority levels for memory usage is an all-or-nothing option, where you can lock a process in memory. This option is not available on all systems and is more often applied to shared memory than to processes, but nevertheless it is useful to know. If this option is applied, the process is locked into real memory and is not paged out at all. You need to be aware that using this option reduces the amount of RAM available to all other processes, which can make overall system performance worse. Any deterioration in system performance is likely to occur at heavy system loads, so make sure you extrapolate the effect of reducing the system memory in this way.

Network I/O

At the network level, many things can affect performance. The *bandwidth* (the amount of data that can be carried by the network) tends to be the first culprit checked. Assuming you have determined that bad performance is attributable to the network component of an application, there are more likely causes for the poor performance than network bandwidth. The most likely cause of bad network performance is the application itself and how it is handling distributed data and functionality. I consider distributed-application tuning in several chapters (notably Chapter 12), but this section provides lower-level information to assist you in tuning your application and also considers nonapplication causes of bad performance.

The overall speed of a particular network connection is limited by the slowest link in the connection chain and the length of the chain. Identifying the slowest link is difficult and may not even be consistent: it can vary at different times of the day or for different communication paths. A network communication path can lead from an application through a TCP/IP stack (which adds various layers of headers, possibly encrypting and compressing data as well), then through the hardware interface, through a modem, over a phone line, through another modem, over to a service provider's router, through many heavily congested data lines of various carrying capacities and multiple routers with differing maximum throughputs and configurations, to a machine at the other end with its own hardware interface, TCP/IP stack, and application. A typical web download route is just like this. In addition, there are dropped packets, acknowledgments, retries, bus contention, and so on.

Because so many possible causes of bad network performance are external to an application, one option you can consider including in an application is a network speed-testing facility that reports to the user. This should test the speed of data transfer from the machine to various destinations: to itself, to another machine on the local network, to the Internet service provider, to the target server across the network, and to any other destinations appropriate. This type of diagnostic report can tell your users that they are obtaining bad performance from something other than your application. If you feel that the performance of your application is limited by the actual network communication speed, and not by other (application) factors, this facility will report the maximum possible speeds to your users (and put the blame for poor network performance outside your application, where it belongs).

Latency

Latency is different from the load-carrying capacity (bandwidth) of a network. Bandwidth refers to how much data can be sent down the communication channel for a given period of time (e.g., 64 kilobits per second) and is limited by the link in the communication chain that has the lowest bandwidth. The *latency* is the amount of time a particular data packet takes to get from one end of the communication channel to the other. Bandwidth tells you the limits within which your application can operate before the performance becomes affected by the volume of data being transmitted. Latency often affects the user's view of the performance even when bandwidth isn't a problem. For example, on a LAN, latency might be 10 milliseconds. In this case, you can ignore latency considerations unless your application is making a large number of transmissions. If your application *is* making a large number of transmissions, you need to tune the application to reduce the number of transmissions being made. (That 10 ms overhead added to every transmission can add up if you just ignore it and treat the application as if it were not distributed.)

In most cases, especially Internet traffic, latency is an important concern. You can determine the basic round-trip time for data packets from any two machines using the *ping* utility.[*] This utility provides a measure of the time it takes a packet of data to reach another machine and be returned. However, the time measure is for a basic underlying protocol packet (ICMP packet) to travel between the machines. If the communication channel is congested and the overlying protocol requires retransmissions (often the case for Internet traffic), one transmission at the application level can actually be equivalent to many round trips.

If, for instance, the round-trip time is 400 ms (not unusual for an Internet link), this is the basic overhead time for any request sent to a server and the reply to return, without even adding any processing time for the request. If you are using TCP/IP and retransmissions are needed because some packets are dropped (TCP automatically handles this as needed), each retransmission adds another 400 ms to the request response time. If the application is conversational, requiring many data transmissions to be sent back and forth before the request is satisfied, each intermediate transmission adds a minimum of 400 ms of network delay, again without considering TCP retransmissions. The time can easily add up if you are not careful.

---

[*] *ping* may not always give a good measure of the round-trip time because ICMP has a low priority in some routers.

It is important to be aware of these limitations. It is often possible to tune the application to minimize the number of transfers by packaging data together, caching, and redesigning the distributed-application protocol to aim for a less conversational mode of operation. At the network level, you need to monitor the transmission statistics (using the *ping* and *netstat* utilities and packet sniffers) and consider tuning any network parameters that you have access to in order to reduce retransmissions.

TCP/IP Stacks

The TCP/IP stack is the section of code that is responsible for translating each application-level network request (send, receive, connect, etc.) through the transport layers down to the wire and back up to the application at the other end of the connection. Because the stacks are usually delivered with the operating system and performance-tested before delivery (since a slow network connection on an otherwise fast machine and fast network is pretty obvious), it is unlikely that the TCP/IP stack itself is a performance problem.

Some older versions of Windows TCP/IP stacks, both those delivered with the OS and others, had performance problems, as did some versions of TCP/IP stacks on the Macintosh OS (up to and including System 7.1). Stack performance can be difficult to trace. Because the TCP/IP stack is causing a performance problem, it affects all network applications running on that machine. In the past I have seen isolated machines on a lightly loaded network with an unexpectedly low transfer speed for FTP transfers compared to other machines on the same network. Once you suspect the TCP/IP stack, you need to probe the speed of the stack. Testing the loopback address (127.0.0.0) may be a good starting point, though this address may be optimized by the stack. The easiest way to avoid the problem is to ensure you are using recent versions of TCP/IP stacks.

In addition to the stack itself, stacks include several tuneable parameters. Most of these parameters deal with transmission details beyond the scope of this book. One parameter worth mentioning is the maximum packet size. When your application sends data, the underlying protocol breaks the data into packets that are transmitted. There is an optimal size for packets transmitted over a particular communication channel, and the packet size actually used by the stack is a compromise. Smaller packets are less likely to be dropped, but they introduce more overhead, as data probably has to be broken up into more packets with more header overhead.

If your communication takes place over a particular set of endpoints, you may want to alter the packet sizes. For a LAN segment with no router involved, the packets can be big (e.g., 8KB). For a LAN with routers, you probably want to set the maximum packet size to the size the routers allow to pass unbroken. (Routers can break up the packets into smaller ones; 1500 bytes is the typical maximum packet size and the standard for Ethernet. The maximum packet size is configurable by the router's network administrator.) If your application is likely to be sending data over the Internet and you cannot guarantee the route and quality of routers it will pass through, 500 bytes per packet is likely to be optimal.

Network Bottlenecks

Other causes of slow network I/O can be attributed directly to the load or configuration of the network. For example, a LAN may become congested when many machines are simultaneously trying to communicate over the network. The potential throughput of the network could handle the load, but the algorithms to provide communication channels slow the network, resulting in a lower maximum throughput. A congested Ethernet network has an average throughput approximately one-third the potential maximum throughput. Congested networks have other problems, such as dropped network packets. If you are using TCP, the communication rate on a congested network is much slower as the protocol automatically resends the dropped packets. If you are using UDP, your application must resend multiple copies for each transfer. Dropping packets in this way is common for the Internet. For LANs, you need to coordinate closely with network administrators to alert them to the problems. For single machines connected by a service provider, there are several things you can do. First, there are some commercial utilities available that probe your configuration and the connection to the service provider, suggesting improvements. The phone line to the service provider may be noisier than expected: if so, you also need to speak to the phone line provider. It is also worth checking with the service provider, who should have optimal configurations they can demonstrate.

Dropped packets and retransmissions are a good indication of network congestion problems, and you should be on constant lookout for them. Dropped packets often occur when routers are overloaded and find it necessary to drop some of the packets being transmitted as the router's buffers overflow. This means that the overlying protocol will request the packets to be resent. The *netstat* utility lists retransmission and other statistics that can identify these sorts of problems. Retransmissions may indicate that the maximum packet size is too large.

DNS Lookups

Looking up network addresses is an often-overlooked cause of bad network performance. When your application tries to connect to a network address such as *foo.bar. something.org* (e.g., downloading a web page from *http://foo.bar.something.org*), your application first translates *foo.bar.something.org* into a four-byte network IP address such as 10.33.6.45. This is the actual address that the network understands and uses for routing network packets. The way this translation works is that your system is configured with some seldom-used files that can specify this translation, and a more frequently used Domain Name System (DNS) server that can dynamically provide you with the address from the given string. DNS translation works as follows:

1. The machine running the application sends the text string of the hostname (e.g., *foo.bar.something.org*) to the DNS server.

2. The DNS server checks its cache to find an IP address corresponding to that hostname. If the server does not find an entry in the cache, it asks its own DNS server (usually further up the Internet domain-name hierarchy) until ultimately the name is resolved. (This may be by components of the name being resolved, e.g., first *.org*, then *something.org*, etc., each time asking another machine as the search request is successively resolved.) This resolved IP address is added to the DNS server's cache.

3. The IP address is returned to the original machine running the application.

4. The application uses the IP address to connect to the desired destination.

The address lookup does not need to be repeated once a connection is established, but any other connections (within the same session of the application or in other sessions at the same time and later) need to repeat the lookup procedure to start another connection.[*]

You can improve this situation by running a DNS server locally on the machine, or on a local server if the application uses a LAN. A DNS server can be run as a "caching only" server that resets its cache each time the machine is rebooted. There would be little point in doing this if the machine used only one or two connections per hostname between successive reboots. For more frequent connections, a local DNS server can provide a noticeable speedup to connections. *nslookup* is useful for investigating how a particular system does translations.

Performance Checklist

Some of these suggestions apply only after a bottleneck has been identified:

- Tune the application before tuning the underlying system. This is especially pertinent to network communications.
  - Limit application bandwidth requirements to the network segment with the smallest bandwidth.
  - Consider network latencies when specifying feasible application response times.
  - Aim to minimize the number of network round trips necessary to satisfy an application request.

---

[*] A session can cache the IP address explicitly after the first lookup, but this needs to be done at the application level by holding on to the InetAddress object.

- Constantly monitor the entire system with any monitoring tools available. Monitoring utilities include *perfmeter* (Unix CPU), *vmstat* (Unix CPU, RAM, and disks), *iostat* (Unix disks), performance monitor (Windows CPU, RAM, and disks), *netstat* (network I/O), *ping* (network latency), and *nslookup* (DNS lookup and routing).
  — Keep monitoring records to get a background usage pattern.
  — Use normal monitoring records to get an early warning of changes in the system usage patterns.
  — Watch for levels of paging that decrease system performance.
  — Watch for low CPU activity coupled with high disk activity and delayed responses. This may indicate an I/O problem.
  — Monitor for retransmissions of data packets.
  — Ensure the CPU runnable queue does not get too large.
  — Aim for average CPU utilization of not more than 75%.
- Consider spreading extra computation loads to low activity times.
  — Run offline work in off-peak hours only.
  — Time all processes and terminate any that exceed timeout thresholds.
- Consider upgrading or reconfiguring parts of the system.
  — Doubling the CPU speed is usually better than doubling the number of CPUs.
  — Consider striping the disks (e.g., RAID disks).
  — Add more swap space when there is no other way to increase the memory available to the application (or to reduce the application's memory usage requirements).
  — Test to see if running on raw partitions will be faster.
  — Look at mapping filesystems into memory for speedier startups and accesses. But be aware that this reduces system memory available to applications. For multiuser applications, this is an efficient way of sharing in-memory data.
  — Move components from network-mounted disks to local disks.
  — Ensure that system swap files are on different disks from any intensively used files.
  — Cluster files together at the disk level, if possible, or within one big container file.
  — Defragment disks regularly if applicable to your system.
  — Move executables or index files to disk sweet spots.
  — Consider altering priority levels of processes to tune the amount of CPU time they get.

— Consider locking processes into memory so they do not get paged out.

— Partition the system to allocate determinate resources to your application.

— Consider tuning the maximum packet size specified by the TCP/IP stack.

— Ensure that your TCP/IP stacks have no performance problems associated with them.

— Consider running a local caching DNS server to improve the speed of host-name lookups.

In this chapter:
- Performance Planning
- J2EE Monitoring and Profiling Tools
- Measurements: What, Where, and How
- Load Testing
- User Perception
- Clustering and Load Balancing
- Tuning JMS

CHAPTER 15

J2EE Performance Tuning

J2EE performance tuning builds on lower-level performance-tuning techniques and general architectural considerations described earlier in this book. J2EE-specific considerations are discussed in this chapter and in Chapters 16 through 18. This chapter covers performance aspects of J2EE relevant to all J2EE projects and includes a brief section on tuning JMS.

Performance Planning

The section "Performance Planning" in Chapter 13 is particularly relevant for J2EE projects. Continual load testing, valid test data, appropriate testing environments, good monitoring tools, and well-specified performance targets are all crucial to achieving a high-performing J2EE deployment. In addition, monitoring after deployment is strongly recommended to maintain good performance. Don't let the brevity of this section mislead you—making a performance plan, emphasizing the aspects I've just listed, is the single most important indicator of success for a J2EE project's performance.

J2EE Monitoring and Profiling Tools

J2EE applications and J2SE applications are monitored and profiled differently. J2EE applications include all the bottlenecks that you find in J2SE applications, but they can also have more serious, system-wide resource contention bottlenecks. Contention bottlenecks occur when multiple objects try to use the same resource at the same time and extend across multiple VMs or to outside resources like databases. J2SE profilers essentially monitor and log various aspects of a single VM. To identify performance problems productively, J2EE profilers must monitor and log far more aspects of the overall J2EE system (including potentially multiple VMs).

Features to Look For

Here are some characteristics to look for when evaluating J2EE performance-monitoring tools.

Monitoring and logging components and their interfaces

J2EE tools must monitor and log all the important aspects of the J2EE system. Potential performance bottlenecks come mainly from three generic locations: processing within components, interfaces between components, and communication between components. Intercomponent communication overhead (for example, network transfers) is distinct from interface overhead (such as marshalling) or conversions (such as SQL request generation).

Low overhead

J2EE monitoring should impose only a low overhead on the J2EE system. Less than a 5% overhead is required for useful monitoring; a 1% overhead is ideal. Low-overhead performance monitoring lets you monitor constantly without worrying about how profiling overhead affects server behavior. This means that you can leave monitoring on at all times—in development systems, in test systems, and in production systems—without serious performance degradation. This situation does not occur with J2SE profilers, which have such a large overhead that running with a profiler on at all times would kill a project. J2SE profilers tend to have high overhead because it is considered acceptable, given their usage pattern. J2EE monitors are targeted at production systems as well as development, so they are generally designed to have lower overhead.

Requests mapped to methods

Monitoring should correlate incoming requests with subsequently monitored methods, components, and communications. It should be possible to easily correlate things like request-to-bean-to-db-queries so you can identify which requests are causing which bottlenecks. Without this capability, you can end up targeting many more bottlenecks than necessary or spending significant time trying to determine which requests map to which bottlenecks.

Log storage and granularity

Monitoring should store all data persistently so you can decouple analysis from running the server. Having things happen during a test run with no way to analyze the data later is annoying because one graph or another is displayed only in real time, with no logged data.

Logging is more important than saving performance by not logging. Monitor the resources used by the application. Identify spikes and trends that cause performance problems, and then alter the application to handle those problems. However, too fine a granularity of logging causes too much overhead. Try to keep logging overhead at 1%.

Scalability
The monitoring tool should scale with the application so you can deploy the monitoring with the application in the production environment.

J2EE Monitoring Tools

A separate class of monitoring tools has emerged in the last couple of years, dedicated to monitoring J2EE applications efficiently. These tools improve J2EE performance-tuning productivity significantly, and obtaining one for your project is worthwhile. You can obtain a list of such tools from *http://www.JavaPerformanceTuning.com/resources.shtml*. Should you wish to implement your own tool, you would need to add logging to all the main communication interfaces of the application, the transaction and session boundaries, the life-cycle boundaries (e.g., creation and destruction of EJBs), and request initiation and completion. A freely available logging tool designed to work with J2EE applications, such as Steve Souza's JAMon (see *http://www.JavaPerformanceTuning.com/tools/jamon/index.shtml*), can assist with this task.

Commercial J2EE monitoring products include additional analysis tools that help speed up the most complex part of J2EE tuning: analyzing the monitoring output.

Measurements: What, Where, and How

Measuring performance is the key to improving performance. You need reliable metrics to gauge performance and effectively compare results before you begin tuning and after you make changes. Before getting into the specifics of measurements, let's look at a study that shows where bottlenecks tend to be.

An Instructive Analysis

A Mercury Interactive Corporation analysis of thousands of load tests on company web sites[*] found that enterprise performance problems come from four main areas: databases, web servers, application servers, and the network. Each area typically causes about a quarter of the performance problems.

The most common database problems were insufficient indexing, fragmented databases, out-of-date statistics, and faulty application design. Solutions included tuning the index, compacting the database, updating the database, and rewriting the application so the database server controlled the query process.

---

[*] Drew Robb, "Stopping Web Performance Thieves," *Datamation*, June 24, 2002, *http://itmanagement.earthweb.com/ecom/article/0,,11952_1370691,00.html*.

The most common web-server problems were poor design algorithms, incorrect configurations, poorly written code, memory problems, and overloaded CPUs.

The most common application-server problems were poor cache management, non-optimized database queries, incorrect software configuration, and poor concurrent handling of client requests.

The most common network problems included inadequate bandwidth somewhere along the communication route, and undersized, misconfigured, or incompatible routers, switches, firewalls, and load balancers.

Suggested Measurements

The results from this useful study may help you focus on the most likely problems. However, not all bottlenecks are listed here, and even if yours are, pinpointing their precise location can be difficult. Taking these suggested measurements may help you isolate the main bottlenecks.

Note that different tools take different measurements, and it is not always possible to match one tool's measurements with another or with this list. For example, some tools cannot measure the time from the (simulated) user click, but might start measuring once they send the HTTP request. A typical J2EE monitoring tool either uses the application server's performance-monitoring API to get server-side information or automatically adds a measurement wrapper by using techniques like code injection.

JVM heap size

Eliminate memory leaks before undertaking other tuning to avoid wasted tuning effort. Eliminating memory leaks is absolutely necessary for J2EE applications, and bottlenecks can be changed (eliminated or added) when eliminating these leaks. See "Monitoring Gross Memory Usage" in Chapter 2.

Total response time

Measure the time taken from presentation start to presentation completion—i.e., from when the (simulated) user clicks the button to when the information is displayed.

Total server-side service time

Measure the total time it takes to service the request on the server. Try not to include transfer time to and from the client. You can obtain this measurement by wrapping the doGet( ) and doPost( ) servlet methods or by using a ServletFilter that logs execution times. Here is a simple filter:

```
public void doFilter(ServletRequest request, ServletResponse response,
            FilterChain chain) throws IOException, ServletException {
    long before = System.currentTimeMillis( );
    chain.doFilter(request, response);
    long after = System.currentTimeMillis( );
    ... //log the time in your logger
```

Naturally, this filter should be the first in the filter chain so the time taken for any other filter is included in the total time recorded. The time measured will include some network transfer time, since the server-to-client socket write does not complete on the server until the last portion of data is written to the server's network buffer.

JDBC requests

This measurement is fully covered in the section "Measuring JDBC Performance" in Chapter 16, which explains how to create and use wrappers to measure JDBC performance.

RMI communications

Turn on RMI logging with the `java.rmi.server.logCalls` property:

```
% java -Djava.rmi.server.logCalls=true ...
```

"Client/Server Communications" in Chapter 2 details this technique.

A second technique uses smart proxies to monitor the performance of RMI calls. This technique replaces objects that make a remote call with proxy objects (from `java.lang.reflect.Proxy`) that can wrap the remote call with timing logic.

File descriptors

The number of available file descriptors is limited in each process and in the overall system. Each open file and open socket requires a file descriptor. Use `ulimit` (Unix only) to monitor the number of file descriptors available to the processes, and make sure this number is high enough to service all connections. In Windows, you can monitor open files and sockets from the performance monitor.

Bean life cycle

Essentially, all methods that handle the life cycle of the bean need to be wrapped, including the bean constructor, `setEntityContext( )`, `ejbHome( )`, `ejbCreate( )`, `ejbActivate( )`, `ejbLoad( )`, `ejbStore( )`, `ejbPassivate( )`, `ejbRemove( )`, `ejbFind( )`, and `unsetEntityContext( )`. Look for too many calls to these methods, which can occur with excessive cycling of objects (too many creates) or excessive passivation.

Transaction boundaries

Begin, commit, and abort calls need to be wrapped. Wrapping can be difficult because the container can be responsible for such calls. Relying on the JDBC wrapper to catch transaction boundaries might be easiest. First, you would need to verify that all transaction boundaries correspond to database transaction boundaries.

Cache sizes

Cache sizes—the number of objects held and the physical size used—should be monitored. There is no generic method to do this.

CPU utilization

Use operating-system utilities to measure CPU utilization (no Java API measures CPU utilization of the JVM). Windows has a performance monitor, and Unix has the *sar*, *vmstat*, and *iostat* utilities.

Stack traces

Generate stack dumps on Unix by sending a kill -QUIT signal (kill -3) to the JVM process or by pressing Ctrl-\ in the window where the Java program was started. On Windows, press Ctrl-Break in the window where the Java program is running or (prior to SDK 1.3) click the Close button on the command window. The stack dump lists the state and Java stack of every currently running thread. In the case of a deadlock, two or more threads will be in the "W" (wait) state, indicating that they are waiting for locks to be released. The method at the top of the stack listing is the "current" method—i.e., the method that requested a lock and caused the thread to move into a wait state as it waits for the lock to be granted. Thus, identifying which methods are causing the deadlock is easy.

GC pauses

When garbage collection kicks in, current VMs stop other processing activity. These perceptible pauses in activity can result in unacceptable performance. Use the latest available VMs, and try to tune the garbage collection to minimize "stop the world" pauses. Chapters 2 and 3 discuss garbage-collection algorithms and tuning. Concurrent garbage collection (-Xconcgc in Version 1.4.1 of the Sun VM) allows pause times to be minimized.

Network bandwidth

Use *netperf* (Unix) or the performance monitor (Windows) to measure network bandwidth. See also the "Network I/O" section in Chapter 14.

Symptoms of Performance Problems

Any of the following symptoms can indicate a performance problem:

- Slow response times
- Excessive database table scans
- Database deadlocks
- Pages not available
- Memory leaks
- High CPU usage (consistently over 85%)

Useful Statistics to Analyze from Measurements

After taking the measurements described here, you may want to analyze several statistics, including the number of users, the number of components, throughput (queries per minute), transaction rates, average and maximum response times, and CPU utilization. You should look for trends and anomalies, and try to identify whether any resource is limited in the current system. For example, increasing the number of concurrent users over time may show that throughput flattens out, indicating that the current maximum throughput was reached.

Load Testing

The discussion of load testing in the "Starting to Tune" section of Chapter 1 is relevant to J2EE application tuning. Here's a summary of the steps involved:

1. Specify performance targets and benchmarks, including scaling requirements. Include all user types, such as information-gathering requests and transaction clients, in your benchmarks. Performance requirements should include the required response times for end users, the perceived steady state and peak user loads, the average and peak amount of data transferred per request, and the expected growth in user load over the first or next 12 months.

2. Create a testing environment that mirrors the expected real-world environment as closely as possible. Generally, there will be differences, but the most critical aspects to simulate closely are the expected client activity, the application data, and the peak scaling requirements (amount of data and number of users). The only reliable way to determine a system's scalability is to perform load tests in which the volume and characteristics of the anticipated traffic are simulated as realistically as possible. Characterize the anticipated load as objectively and systematically as possible, use existing log files when possible, and characterize user sessions (such as the number and types of pages viewed or the duration of sessions). Determine the range and distribution of session variation. Don't use averages; use representative profiles.

3. Load-test the system, find bottlenecks, and eliminate them.

Load testing should be repeatable. Use load-test suites and frameworks. Many products are available, including free tools (see *http://www.JavaPerformanceTuning.com/ resources.shtm*). Continuously retest and measure against established benchmarks to ensure that application performance hasn't degraded as changes are made. The server must be designed to handle peak loads, so tests including expected peak loads should be scrutinized. Peak user loads are the number of concurrent sessions managed by the application server, not the number of possible users.

The key elements of a load-test design are the test objective (e.g., can the server handle *N* sessions per hour at peak load level?), pass/fail criteria (e.g., pass if response times stay within a certain range), script description (e.g., user1: page1, page2, ...; user2: page1, page3, start transaction1, etc.), and scenario description (which scripts at which frequency and how the load increases). One stress-test methodology requires the following steps:

1. Determine the maximum acceptable response time for getting a page.

2. Estimate the maximum number of simultaneous users.

3. Simulate user requests, gradually adding simulated users until the application response delay becomes greater than the acceptable response time.

4. Optimize until you reach the desired number of users.

When testing performance, run tests overnight and on weekends to generate longer-term trends. Your tests could generate inaccurate results. Consider these potential pitfalls:

- Testing without a real network connection can give false measures.
- Low user simulation can be markedly different from high user simulation.
- Network throughput may be larger than in the deployed environment.
- Nonpersistent performance depends on processor and memory.
- Disk speed is crucial for persistent messages.

Performance testing should continue even after the application is deployed. For applications expected to perform 24/7, inconsequential issues like database logging can degrade performance. Continuous monitoring is the key to spotting even the slightest abnormality. Set performance capacity thresholds, monitor them, and look for trends. When application transaction volumes reach 40% of maximum expected volumes, you should execute plans to expand the capacity of system. Note that 40% is an arbitrary choice, but it's a good place to start; if you're at 40% and don't see the first hints of more serious problems, like significant spikes in usage profiles, you might relax and set a new, higher threshold. The point is that you should watch for signs that your application is outgrowing the system and make plans for an upgrade well before the upgrade is needed.

User Perception

The user's perception of performance is crucial. The user perception discussion from Chapter 1 applies to J2EE architectures, but there are some additional considerations.

Screen Navigation

Some connections may fail due to a congested network or overloaded server. Users perceive the need to reenter data or return to the last screen as bad performance. Ideally, when a connection is reestablished, the user should find himself back at the same state as before the connection failure. If the session ID is still valid, then you should hold all the session state so the display can be re-created at any point. If the session ID is invalidated by the connection failure, then maintaining state in the client should enable display re-creation.

Page Display

As discussed in Chapter 1, popular browsers try to display screens in a way that seems faster to the user. Nevertheless, certain ways of laying out pages make the display take longer. For example, HTML tables are often not displayed until the contents are available to enable table-cell size calculation. Use size tags to help the browser calculate the display.

Pages constructed from multiple disparate sources (e.g., embedded images) require multiple connections, all of which add to the overall perceived page display time. A poorly designed page could be seen as slow even if the components of the page individually download quickly. You should be able to find multiple sites displaying structures similar to those you wish to display. Compare their performance and choose the best combination for your application.

On the server side, don't rely on the default server buffers to flush the pages. Different buffer sizes and forced flushing of the output at certain points can improve perceived performance by sending displayable parts of a page more quickly.

Priority Service

Different users have different requirements and, more importantly, different value to your business. You should balance the performance provided to your users according to their value to your business. However, doing so is not always a clear-cut matter of giving higher-priority users a faster response at the expense of lower-value users. For example, many web sites provide premium service to paying users, with restricted access to nonpaying users. But if nonpaying users find that the web site is too slow, they may be unlikely to convert to paying users, and converting nonpaying users to paying users may be a business priority. However you may decide to assign priorities, sort incoming requests into different priority queues and service the higher-priority requests first. Priority queuing can be achieved by initially allocating the incoming request a priority level based on your application requirements or according to the priority associated with the session. You can then route the request by priority. To support priorities throughout the J2EE application, requests probably need to be transferred between components at each stage through multiple queues so that queued requests can be accepted in order of priority level.

Internet Congestion

On the Internet, there are inevitably some very long response times and communication failures. This results from the nature of Internet communications, which is liable to variable congestion, spikes, blocked routes, and outages. Even if your server were up 100% of the time and serviced every request with a subsecond response, there would still be some problems due to Internet communication channels. You need to construct your application to handle communication failures gracefully, bearing in mind the issue of user perception. This is discussed in the next section.

Communication Failures

A few long response times from communication failures may not necessarily make a bad impression, especially if handled correctly. Experienced Internet users expect communication failures and don't necessarily blame the server. In any case, if a connection or transaction needs to be reestablished, explain to the user why the outage occurred. Identifying the connection failure can help. For example, the Internet regularly becomes more congested at certain times. By monitoring your server, you should be able to establish whether these congested times result in an increased number of connection retries. If so, you can present a warning to the user explaining that current Internet congestion may result in some connection failures (and perhaps suggest that the user try again later after a certain time if performance is unsatisfactory). Setting the expectation of your users in this way can help reduce the inevitable dissatisfaction that communication failures cause. Including an automated mechanism for congestion reporting could be difficult. The Java API doesn't provide a mechanism to measure connection retries. You could measure download times regularly from some set of reference locations, and use those measurements to identify when congestion causes long download times.

Good Peak Performance

Evaluate performance targets as early as possible (preferably at project specification), and then keep your targets in mind. One million requests per day, 24/7, is equivalent to 12 requests per second. Most servers receive requests unevenly around periodic patterns. Peak traffic can be an order of magnitude higher than the average request rate. For a highly scaled popular server, ideal peak performance targets would probably consist of subsecond response times and hundreds of (e-commerce) transactions per second. You can use these basic guidelines to calculate target response times. Naturally, your application will have its own requirements.

Cumulative Delay and User Impatience

The quickest way to lose user interest is to keep the user waiting for screens to display. Some experts suggest that perceived delays accumulate across multiple screens. It is not sufficient for individual screens to display within the limit of the user's patience (the subject of the earlier "Page Display" section). If the user finds himself waiting for several screens to display slowly, one after the other, the cumulative wait time can exceed a limit (perhaps as low as eight seconds) that induces the user to abandon the transaction (and the site). One of the better ways to keep the cumulative delay low is to avoid making the user go through too many screens to get to his goal.

User Bandwidth

Your users have a characteristic range of bandwidths, from slow modem dialup speeds to broadband. Determine what the range of user bandwidths are and test throughout the range. Different page designs display at different speeds for different bandwidths, and users have different expectations. Users with broadband connections expect pages to appear instantly, and slow pages stand a good chance of never being looked at.

Clustering and Load Balancing

There is a limit to how fast you can make your application run. The application has work to do, and that work takes a minimum number of processor instructions to execute. The faster the machine that runs the application, the faster those instructions execute, but there is a limit to processor speeds. As the number of concurrent requests received by your server increases, your application exceeds the target response times when the workload is too much for the given machine. At this point, you have two options: use a faster machine, or use several machines. The first option is not always available or cost-effective, and ultimately you may use the fastest machine available and still need more power. Any efficient J2EE design should include the possibility that the application will need to be deployed across multiple servers. This is known as horizontal scalability.

Two technologies that enhance the ability to achieve horizontal scalability are clustering and load balancing. Clustering can mean different things in different contexts. In this context, clustering means having a group of machines running the application. Clustering is the mechanism that spreads the application-processing capability across multiple machines; load balancing is the mechanism that ensures that different machines use their various processor capacities efficiently. Currently, scalable web-application architectures consist of many small servers accessed through a load balancer.

Load-Balancing Mechanisms

Generally, the load-balancing mechanism should route requests to the least-busy resource. However, such routing can be difficult to achieve with some load-balancing mechanisms and may be inappropriate for some applications, especially session-based applications. You should determine the load-balancing mechanism that is most appropriate to your application. Load balancing can be achieved in a number of ways, as described in the following sections.

DNS load balancing

The mechanism for obtaining the route to a machine from the machine's name is the Domain Name System (DNS), discussed in the section "DNS Lookups" in Chapter 14. DNS can supply different IP addresses to separate lookups of the same hostname, providing a simple application-independent load-balancing mechanism. For example, *www.oreilly.com* could map to 10.12.14.16 and 10.12.14.17 on each alternate lookup. Many Internet sites use DNS load balancing; it is a common and simple load-balancing technique.

DNS load balancing is achieved by using a round-robin mechanism to send each subsequent DNS lookup request to the next entry for that server name. DNS round-robin has no server load measuring mechanisms, so requests can go to overloaded servers, creating ironically unbalanced load balancing.

The result of a DNS lookup is typically cached at various locations, with caches lasting days (though this is configurable and can be any value down to seconds). Consequently, it is slow to propagate changes when using DNS load balancing, and any one client typically uses the same IP address over multiple connections rather than being directed to alternate servers. These issues can be problematic, but can also be advantageous if transactional or session-based communications are normal for your application.

Also note that DNS load balancing can be used in conjunction with other load-balancing techniques. For example, if you use a load-balancing dispatcher, then you can use DNS to balance multiple load-balancing dispatchers to achieve the optimal case in which the load-balancing mechanism has no single point of failure (DNS lookups are replicated). However, some clients could still see failures due to lookup caching.

Hardware load balancer

A hardware load balancer is a machine at a single IP address that reroutes communications to other machines—for example, it reroutes IP packets by rewriting the IP address in the header and passing the packet to the appropriate machine. This can also be an application-independent load-balancing mechanism. The technique is more complex and more expensive than DNS load balancing, but much more flexible and capable. Multiple hardware load balancers can be used in conjunction with DNS load balancing to achieve application-independent load balancing with no single point of failure (although some clients could see failures if a hardware load balancer fails due to lookup caching).

Hardware load balancers may come with extra features such as the ability to automatically detect unavailable servers and eliminate them from their routing tables; to intelligently reroute packets based on server load, IP address, port number, or other criteria; and to decrypt encrypted communications before rerouting packets.

Load-balancing dispatcher/Proxy load balancing

A cluster can be implemented with a frontend dispatcher that accepts requests and passes them on to other clustered servers. All requests are directed to the dispatcher, either explicitly (the client doesn't know about any machines "behind" the dispatcher) or redirected (as is done when correctly configured browsers have their requests automatically sent to a proxy server).

The dispatcher (or proxy server) services the request in one of three ways:

- The request is satisfied by returning a result (document) cached in the dispatcher. This scenario is common for proxy servers, but unusual for dispatchers.
- The request is redirected to another server that services the request and returns the results to the client, either directly or, more commonly, through the dispatcher.
- The dispatcher redirects the client to send the request to another server. The HTTP protocol supports this option with the Location directive. For example, if a browser connects to a server requesting a particular URL and receives a response like this:

      Location: http://somewhere.else.com/

  then the browser automatically tries to request the new URL.

A dispatcher could also decrypt encrypted requests before handling or forwarding them, thus centralizing security and offloading some processing from the server cluster.

URL-based load balancing

Decide where any particular document or service is best served and specify the appropriate host machine in the URL. This load-balancing mechanism is straightforward. For example, you could retrieve images from the image server and documents from a separate document server.

URL generation can be done statically or dynamically, but generating documents dynamically can add further overhead. In addition, the URL could be retained by the client and used later or reused when the specified host is no longer the optimal server for the request. Where possible, convert dynamic requests into static ones by replacing URLs served dynamically with ones served statically.

Server-pooled objects

Load balancing is possible by varying how pooled objects are handed out. This type of balancing tends to apply at the application level, where you can create and hand out objects from a pool according to your own algorithm.

Client-based load balancing

The connection mechanism in the client can serve as a load-balancing mechanism. The client can even check for an available rerouting server to combine client load balancing with server load balancing. The client connection mechanism should be centrally based, either explicitly by having client objects connect through a connection service, or implicitly using proxy objects in place of server-communicated objects.

One such load-balancing connection mechanism simply selects from a list of available RMI connections sequentially.

Application configuration load balancing

The application itself should be configured for deployments with different usage patterns. Each type of read-only, read-write, and batch-update bean components should be in different application servers so that each application server can be appropriately configured. Transactional and nontransactional sessions and messages should be served from separate servers. Nontransactional server components can be replicated easily for horizontal scaling.

Multiple VMs can be used even within individual server machines to help load-balance the application. Scalable servers usually work best with multiple VMs. Using one thread per user can create a bottleneck with large numbers of concurrent users. Stateless sessions are easily load-balanced; replicating transactional sessions is more involved and carries higher overhead. Pseudo-sessions that encode a session identifier into the URLs and are stored globally are probably the best compromise for load-balancing transactional sessions.

Separate web servers should be used for all static content, which can be served much faster and with much lower overhead than dynamic content. Priority queues can provide higher-priority users with a higher quality of service. The section "Load Balancing" in Chapter 10 discusses queue-based load balancing and network queuing in more detail. The frontend queue can use the network queue as its bottleneck and accept requests only when there are sufficient resources to process the request. Try to balance the workload of the various components so they all work. All components should work at any given time; there should be no idle components.

Database partitioning

The section "Data parallelism" in Chapter 13 discusses database partitioning schemes to assist in load-balancing the application.

Load-Balancing Algorithms

In addition to selecting one or more load-balancing mechanisms, you may need to consider optimal load-balancing algorithms for your application. These algorithms include:

Random
> Randomly allocate requests to servers.

Minimum load
> Allocate requests to the server with the currently minimum load.

Round-robin
> Successively select the next server in a list, starting again from the first server when the list is exhausted.

Weighted round-robin
> Like round-robin, but with some servers listed multiple times.

Performance-based
> Allocate requests based on the performance capability of the server.

Load-based
> Allocate requests based on the servers' total load capability.

Dynamic
> Dynamically allocate to servers based on an application-encoded algorithm.

Nearest IP address
> Allocate requests to the IP address (physically) nearest the client.

Port number
> Allocate requests according to the port number.

HTTP header
> Allocate requests according to a value within the HTTP header, such as the URL or a cookie.

Tuning JMS

Messaging is an important feature for many large J2EE applications. Tuning JMS is an important and relatively straightforward topic. I cover it here rather than dedicating an entire chapter to JMS. For the full details on JMS, I recommend *Java Messaging Service* by Richard Monson-Haefel, David A. Chappell, and Mike Loukides (O'Reilly).

Remember the following points to ensure optimal JMS performance:

- Close resources (e.g., connections, session objects, producers, and consumers) when you finish with them.

- Start the consumer before the producer so the initial messages do not need to queue when waiting for the consumer.

- Nontransactional sessions are faster than transactional ones. If you have transactional sessions, try to separate nontransactional messages and use nontransactional sessions for them.

- Nonpersistent messages are faster than persistent messages.

- Longer messages take longer to deliver and process. You could compress message bodies or eliminate nonessential content to keep the size down.

- The redelivery count should be specified to avoid indefinitely redelivered messages. A higher redelivery delay and lower redelivery limit reduces overhead.

- Set the Delivery TimeToLive value as low as is feasible (the default is for messages to never expire).

- A smaller Delivery capacity increases message throughput. Since fewer messages can sit in the Delivery queue, they have to be moved along more quickly. However, if the capacity is too small, efficiency is reduced because producers have to delay sending messages until the Delivery queue has the spare capacity to accept them.

Some more advanced architectural considerations are also worthy of note. As with most architectures, asynchronous processing is more scalable than synchronous processing. JMS supports the asynchronous reception of messages with the MessageListener interface, which you should use. Similarly, processing in parallel is more scalable, and again, JMS supports parallel-message processing with ConnectionConsumers that manage ServerSessionPools.

When messages are sent in high volumes, delivery can become unpredictable and bursty. Messages can be produced far faster than they can be consumed, causing congestion. When this condition occurs, message sends need to be throttled with flow control. A load-balancing message queue may be needed for a high rate of messages (for example, more than 500 messages per second). In this case, you probably need to use duplicate delivery mode (Session.DUPS_OK_ACKNOWLEDGE). Duplicate delivery mode is the fastest possible delivery mode. In duplicate delivery mode, messages are sent and, if the acknowledgment is delayed long enough, a duplicate message is sent rather than conversing with the server to determine whether the message was received. This mode is more efficient than auto mode (Session.AUTO_ACKNOWLEDGE), which guarantees that messages be sent only once. However, with duplicate delivery mode, you need to identify whether the message has already been processed because it may be sent more than once. The third mode, Session.CLIENT_ACKNOWLEDGE, consists of synchronous message sends with corresponding acknowledgments; it is not recommended for high-performance message delivery.

When dealing with large numbers of active listeners, multicast publish-and-subscribe is more efficient than broadcast or multiple individual (unicast or point-to-point) connections. (Note that JMS does not currently support broadcast messaging, only publish-and-subscribe and point-to-point messaging). When dealing with large numbers of listeners with only a few active, or when dealing with only a few listeners, multicasting publish-and-subscribe is inefficient, and point-to-point communications should be used. Inactive listeners require all missed messages to be re-sent in order when the listener becomes active, which would put too heavy a resource load on the publish-and-subscribe model. For this latter scenario, a unicast-based model of message queuing, organized into a hub-and-spoke model, is more efficient than multicast.

Performance Checklist

- Planning for performance is the single most important indicator of success for a J2EE project's performance.

- J2EE profiling needs more than a J2SE profiler—it needs to be J2EE "aware" so J2EE requests can be followed and logged, and communications, sessions, transactions, and bean life cycles can be monitored.

- Enterprise performance problems tend to come about equally from four main areas: databases, web servers, application servers, and the network.

- Common database problems are insufficient indexing, fragmented databases, out-of-date statistics, and faulty application design. Solutions include tuning the index, compacting the database, updating the database, and rewriting the application so the database server controls the query process.

- Common web-server problems are poor design algorithms, incorrect configurations, poorly written code, memory problems, and overloaded CPUs.

- Common application-server problems are poor cache management, unoptimized database queries, incorrect software configuration, and poor concurrent handling of client requests.

- Common network problems are inadequate bandwidth somewhere along the communication route, and undersized, misconfigured, or incompatible routers, switches, firewalls, and load balancers.

- Monitor JVM heap sizes, request response times, request service times, JDBC requests, RMI communications, file descriptors, bean life cycles, transaction boundaries, cache sizes, CPU utilization, stack traces, GC pauses, and network bandwidth.

- Watch out for slow response times, excessive database table scans, database deadlocks, unavailable pages, memory leaks, and high CPU usage (consistently over 85%).

- Load testing should be repeatable. Tests should include expected peak loads. Tests should be as close to the expected deployed system as possible and should be able to run for a long period of time.

- One testing methodology is to determine the maximum acceptable response time page download, estimate the maximum number of simultaneous users, increase simulated users until the application response delay becomes unacceptable, and tune until you reach a good response time for the desired number of users.

- Page display should be as fast as possible. Use simple pages with static layouts where possible. Let users get to their destination page quickly. Work with the browser's capabilities.

- Use priority queues to provide different levels of service.

- Be prepared to handle network congestion and communication failures.

- High-performance applications probably need clustering and load balancing.

- Close JMS resources when you finish with them.

- Start the consumer before the producer.

- Separate nontransactional and transactional sessions.

- Use nonpersistent messages.

- Use shorter or compressed messages.

- Tune the redelivery count, the `Delivery TimeToLive`, and the `Delivery` capacity.

- Use asynchronous processing (`MessageListener`), parallel processing (`ConnectionConsumers` and `ServerSessionPools`), flow control, load-balancing message queues, and duplicate delivery mode (`Session.DUPS_OK_ACKNOWLEDGE`). Avoid `Session.CLIENT_ACKNOWLEDGE`.

- Use publish-and-subscribe when dealing with many active listeners and point-to-point for only a few active listeners.

CHAPTER 16

Tuning JDBC

JDBC (Java Database Connectivity) consists of a set of APIs and specifications that allow any Java application to connect to any JDBC-enabled data repository that executes SQL statements. Usually, this data repository is a relational database (since that is what JDBC was designed for), but the JDBC protocol does not restrict connections to relational databases.

Connecting to a database with JDBC is essential for many applications. This chapter shows you how to identify the bottlenecks in your communications with the database and how to improve the performance of those communications.

The chapter is divided into two sections. The first section, "Measuring JDBC Performance," provides extensive details on building a tool that allows you to determine whether your JDBC communications cause bottlenecks and, if so, which JDBC statements are to blame. If you have already identified JDBC bottlenecks in your application, you can skip this first section. Note that an open source tool, P6Spy (*http://www.provision6.com/index.htm*), helps identify JDBC bottlenecks by using a similar methodology.

The second section, "Tuning JDBC," provides details on how to tune the JDBC portion of your application. In addition to JDBC-specific issues, this section addresses tuning SQL (Structured Query Language) usage, since optimizing SQL can result in a huge gain in JDBC performance.

Measuring JDBC Performance

As with all other types of tuning, the first step to tuning JDBC usage is to identify bottlenecks. The ease or difficulty of measuring JDBC communications can depend on how you use JDBC and how widespread JDBC calls are in your application. In this section, we'll run through a framework that makes measuring JDBC performance straightforward.

The Core java.sql Interfaces

At the outset, you must identify exactly what you should measure. Effectively profiling distributed applications, such as those that use JDBC, can be difficult. I/O can be significant in profiling simply because of the nature of a distributed application, which normally has threads waiting on I/O. Whether threads blocking on reads and writes are part of a significant bottleneck or simply a side issue can be unclear.

If you look in the java.sql package, three interfaces form the core of JDBC: Connection, Statement, and ResultSet. Normal interaction with a database consists of:

- Obtaining a Connection object from the database driver
- Obtaining from that Connection object some type of Statement object capable of executing a particular SQL statement
- If that SQL statement reads from the database, using the Statement object to obtain a ResultSet object that provides access to the data in question

The following method illustrates standard database interaction by accessing all the columns from every row of a specified database table and storing the data from each row in a String[ ] array, putting all the rows in a vector:

```
public static Vector getATable(String tablename, Connection connection)
  throws SQLException
{
  String sqlQuery = "SELECT * FROM " + tablename;
  Statement statement = connection.createStatement( );
  ResultSet resultSet = statement.executeQuery(sqlQuery);
  int numColumns = resultSet.getMetaData( ).getColumnCount( );
  String[ ] aRow;
  Vector allRows = new Vector( );
  while(resultSet.next( ))
  {
    aRow = new String[numColumns];
    for (int i = 0; i < numColumns; i++)
      //ResultSet access is 1-based, arrays are 0-based
      aRow[i] = resultSet.getString(i+1);
    allRows.addElement(aRow);
  }
  return allRows;
}
```

The SDK does not include implementations of Connection, Statement, or ResultSet to connect to particular databases in java.sql (except for the more generic JDBC-ODBC driver discussed later). Each implementation for these and other JDBC interfaces is created by the producer of the database driver and delivered as part of the database driver package. If you printed out the class name of the Connection object or other objects that you are using, you would probably see something like *XXX*Connection, *XXX*Statement, *XXX*ConnectionImpl, or *XXX*StatementImpl, where *XXX* is the name of the database you are using (Oracle, for example).

To measure the JDBC performance of the getATable( ) method, we could simply put calls to System.currentTimeMillis( ) at the beginning and end of the getATable( ) method and print the time difference to find out how long the process took. That technique works when database interaction is isolated, as it is in this method. However, a Java application usually spreads its database interaction among many methods in many classes, and it is often difficult to isolate the database interaction. You need a way to measure widespread database interactions.

Ideally, the JDBC classes would have built-in measurement capabilities and you could simply turn them on to analyze the performance of database interactions. JDBC classes do not normally provide this feature, but sometimes they do (check the driver documentation). Can we replace the JDBC classes with our own implementations that provide measurements? The replacement classes would have to provide all the current functionality, be able to measure database interactions, require very little change to the application, and be transparent to the rest of the application. That's a tall order.

Fortunately, when a framework is defined almost entirely in terms of interfaces, as JDBC is, it is very simple to replace any class with another implementation. That is, after all, the whole point of interfaces. In particular, you can always replace any implementation of an interface with a wrapper class that simply wraps the original class and forwards (or delegates, in object-oriented terms) all the method calls to that original class. Here, you can replace JDBC classes with wrappers around the original classes. You can embed your measuring capabilities in the wrapper classes and execute those measurements throughout the application.

Wrapping Classes Using Proxy Objects

Wrapping objects of a particular interface by using dedicated wrapper objects is a useful and established technique. The synchronized wrappers of the Collection classes are probably best known, but there are many other examples. The SDK even has a special class to generate wrapper objects at runtime: java.lang.reflect.Proxy. Wrapper objects are also known as proxy objects. I could have used generated proxy objects here, but that would have made the explanation of wrapping JDBC objects more complicated than I wanted, so I stuck with explicitly coded wrapper classes. Proxy classes are also slightly slower than precompiled classes; for measuring JDBC, though, it probably wouldn't make any difference.

Wrapping the Connection class

Start by wrapping the Connection class. The following ConnectionWrapper class implements Connection. The class has one instance variable of Connection type and a constructor that initializes that instance variable with the constructor parameter. Most Connection methods are simply defined to delegate the call to the instance variable:

```
package tuning.jdbc;

import java.sql.*;
```

```
import java.util.Map;

public class ConnectionWrapper implements Connection
{
  protected Connection realConnection;

  public Connection realConnection () {
    return realConnection;
  }

  public ConnectionWrapper (Connection connection) {
    realConnection = connection;
  }

  public void clearWarnings() throws SQLException {
    realConnection.clearWarnings();
  }

  public void close() throws SQLException {
    realConnection.close();
  }

  public boolean isClosed() throws SQLException {
    return realConnection.isClosed();
  }

   public void commit() throws SQLException {
    realConnection.commit();
  }

    ...
```

I have left out most methods, but they follow the template of the ones shown here. Where you would have used a Connection object obtained from the database driver, instead simply wrap that Connection object with the ConnectionWrapper and use the ConnectionWrapper object. Wherever you obtain your Connection object, simply add one extra line such as the one shown here in bold:

```
Connection dbConnection = getConnectionFromDriver();
dbConnection = new ConnectionWrapper(dbConnection);
```

Obtaining connections is really the only part of the application that needs changing, so find and edit calls that obtain a connection. Most applications use a central factory class to provide Connection objects, making it simple to add the ConnectionWrapper. The factory class frequently fronts a pool of connections, and little extra work is necessary to release the connection back into the pool since it first needs to be unwrapped:

```
public static void releaseConnection(Connection conn)
{
  if (conn instanceof ConnectionWrapper)
    conn = ( (ConnectionWrapper) conn).realConnection();
```

```
    //carry on with original release code
    ...
}
```

You haven't actually finished the ConnectionWrapper class yet. Some methods of the ConnectionWrapper class are not simple delegations. These methods provide various types of Statement objects:

```
public Statement createStatement() throws SQLException {
  return new StatementWrapper(realConnection.createStatement(), this);
}

public Statement createStatement(int resultSetType,
            int resultSetConcurrency) throws SQLException {
  return new StatementWrapper(
        realConnection.createStatement(resultSetType,
            resultSetConcurrency), this);
}

public CallableStatement prepareCall(String sql) throws SQLException {
  return new CallableStatementWrapper(
        realConnection.prepareCall(sql), this, sql);
}

public CallableStatement prepareCall(String sql, int resultSetType,
            int resultSetConcurrency) throws SQLException {
  return new CallableStatementWrapper(
        realConnection.prepareCall(sql, resultSetType,
            resultSetConcurrency), this, sql);
}

public PreparedStatement prepareStatement(String sql)
        throws SQLException {
  return new PreparedStatementWrapper(
        realConnection.prepareStatement(sql), this, sql);
}

public PreparedStatement prepareStatement(String sql, int resultSetType,
        int resultSetConcurrency) throws SQLException {
  return new PreparedStatementWrapper(
        realConnection.prepareStatement(sql, resultSetType,
            resultSetConcurrency), this, sql);
}
```

As you can see, you must define three types of Statement wrapper classes. In addition, you need another wrapper class for DatabaseMetaData; this wrapper class is required because DatabaseMetaData can return the Connection object used to create the DatabaseMetaData. Therefore, you need to make sure that the Connection object is wrapped, not the original unwrapped connection:

```
public DatabaseMetaData getMetaData() throws SQLException {
  return new DatabaseMetaDataWrapper(
        realConnection.getMetaData(), this);
}
```

Wrapping the Statement classes

The three statement classes, Statement, PreparedStatement, and CallableStatement, have similar simple wrappers that forward all calls:

```
public class StatementWrapper implements Statement
{
  protected Statement realStatement;
  protected ConnectionWrapper connectionParent;

  public StatementWrapper(Statement statement, ConnectionWrapper parent)
  {
    realStatement = statement;
    connectionParent = parent;
  }

  public void cancel( ) throws SQLException {
    realStatement.cancel( );
  }

  ...
```

You can implement PreparedStatementWrapper as a subclass of StatementWrapper, but it isn't a requirement. You could implement PreparedStatement as a subclass of Object and implement all the required methods rather than inherit the Statement methods:

```
public class PreparedStatementWrapper extends StatementWrapper implements
PreparedStatement
{
  PreparedStatement realPreparedStatement;
  String sql;
  public PreparedStatementWrapper(PreparedStatement statement, ConnectionWrapper
parent, String sql)
  {
    super(statement, parent);
    realPreparedStatement = statement;
    this.sql = sql;
  }

  public void addBatch( ) throws SQLException {
    realPreparedStatement.addBatch( );
  }

  ...
```

Similarly, you can implement the CallableStatementWrapper as a subclass of PreparedStatementWrapper:

```
public class CallableStatementWrapper extends PreparedStatementWrapper implements
CallableStatement
{
  CallableStatement realCallableStatement;
  public CallableStatementWrapper(CallableStatement statement, ConnectionWrapper
parent, String sql)
```

```
{
  super(statement, parent, sql);
  realCallableStatement = statement;
}

public Array getArray(int i) throws SQLException {
  return new SQLArrayWrapper(realCallableStatement.getArray(i), this, sql);
}
```

You still haven't quite finished. Several kinds of methods in these Statement wrapper classes should not be simple delegations. First, there is a method that returns the Connection object. You want to return the ConnectionWrapper instead. Here is the method from StatementWrapper:

```
public Connection getConnection() throws SQLException {
  return connectionParent;
}
```

Second, some methods return ResultSets. These methods need to return ResultSet wrappers. To keep the ResultSetWrapper consistent, I've added a lastSql String instance variable to StatementWrapper, which is passed to the ResultSetWrapper constructor. This instance variable is useful when assigning measurements to particular SQL statements. The methods that return ResultsSets are:

```
//StatementWrapper method
  public ResultSet getResultSet() throws SQLException {
    return new ResultSetWrapper(realStatement.getResultSet(), this, lastSql);
  }

  public ResultSet executeQuery(String sql) throws SQLException {
    return new ResultSetWrapper(realStatement.executeQuery(sql), this, sql);
  }

//PreparedStatementWrapper method
  public ResultSet executeQuery() throws SQLException {
    return new ResultSetWrapper(realPreparedStatement.executeQuery(), this, sql);
  }
```

Third, some methods use java.sql.Array objects. Because these Array objects can return a ResultSet, you again need to provide an Array wrapper so ResultSetWrapper objects rather than plain ResultSets are returned. You also need to handle the case in which an Array object is passed into the setArray() method: if it is an Array wrapper, the object needs to be unwrapped before being passed to the underlying PreparedStatement:

```
public void setArray(int i, Array x) throws SQLException {
  if (x instanceof SQLArrayWrapper)
    realPreparedStatement.setArray(i, ((SQLArrayWrapper) x).realArray);
  else
    realPreparedStatement.setArray(i, x);
}
```

```
public Array getArray(int i) throws SQLException {
  return new SQLArrayWrapper(realCallableStatement.getArray(i), this, sql);
}
```

Finally, the reason why you create all these wrapper classes is to enable measurements to be taken. The methods that execute the SQL statements, reasonably enough, start with execute. You need to add logging to these methods. Note that I delegate responsibility for logging to a JDBCLogger class in the following methods. Essentially, each method has a call to the real execute method wrapped with a logging call. I pass the SQL string and the current thread to the logging call because both are very useful parameters for any type of logging, especially for measuring the time taken for the procedure to run. I also redefine the executeQuery( ) methods that return ResultSets (which were first defined a couple of code fragments back) so they now perform logging:

```
//StatementWrapper methods
  public void addBatch(String sql) throws SQLException {
    realStatement.addBatch(sql);
    lastSql = sql;
  }

  public boolean execute(String sql) throws SQLException {
    Thread t = Thread.currentThread( );
    JDBCLogger.startLogSqlQuery(t, sql);
    boolean b = realStatement.execute(sql);
    JDBCLogger.endLogSqlQuery(t, sql);
    lastSql = sql;
    return b;
  }

  public int[ ] executeBatch( ) throws SQLException {
    Thread t = Thread.currentThread( );
    JDBCLogger.startLogSqlQuery(t, "batch");
    int[ ] i = realStatement.executeBatch( );
    JDBCLogger.endLogSqlQuery(t, "batch");
    return i;
  }

  public ResultSet executeQuery(String sql) throws SQLException {
    Thread t = Thread.currentThread( );
    JDBCLogger.startLogSqlQuery(t, sql);
    ResultSet r = realStatement.executeQuery(sql);
    JDBCLogger.endLogSqlQuery(t, sql);
    lastSql = sql;
    return new ResultSetWrapper(r, this, sql);
  }

  public int executeUpdate(String sql) throws SQLException {
    Thread t = Thread.currentThread( );
    JDBCLogger.startLogSqlQuery(t, sql);
    int i = realStatement.executeUpdate(sql);
    JDBCLogger.endLogSqlQuery(t, sql);
```

```
    lastSql = sql;
    return i;
  }

//PreparedStatementWrapper methods
  public boolean execute( ) throws SQLException {
    Thread t = Thread.currentThread( );
    JDBCLogger.startLogSqlQuery(t, sql);
    boolean b = realPreparedStatement.execute( );
    JDBCLogger.endLogSqlQuery(t, sql);
    return b;
  }

  public ResultSet executeQuery( ) throws SQLException {
    Thread t = Thread.currentThread( );
    JDBCLogger.startLogSqlQuery(t, sql);
    ResultSet r = realPreparedStatement.executeQuery( );
    JDBCLogger.endLogSqlQuery(t, sql);
    return new ResultSetWrapper(r, this, sql);
  }

  public int executeUpdate( ) throws SQLException {
    Thread t = Thread.currentThread( );
    JDBCLogger.startLogSqlQuery(t, sql);
    int i = realPreparedStatement.executeUpdate( );
    JDBCLogger.endLogSqlQuery(t, sql);
    return i;
  }
```

Wrapping the ResultSet class

The ResultSetWrapper class once again consists mainly of delegated methods:

```
public class ResultSetWrapper implements ResultSet
{
  ResultSet realResultSet;
  StatementWrapper parentStatement;
  String sql;

  public ResultSetWrapper(ResultSet resultSet, StatementWrapper statement, String
sql) {
    realResultSet = resultSet;
    parentStatement = statement;
    this.sql = sql;
  }

  public boolean absolute(int row) throws SQLException {
    return realResultSet.absolute(row);
  }

  ...
```

Again, some methods are not plain delegations. The getStatement( ) method returns the statement that generated this ResultSet. You need to return the StatementWrapper:

```
public Statement getStatement( ) throws SQLException {
  return parentStatement;
}
```

The getArray( ) methods need to return a wrapped Array object:

```
public Array getArray(int i) throws SQLException {
  return new SQLArrayWrapper(realResultSet.getArray(i), parentStatement, sql);
}

public Array getArray(String colName) throws SQLException {
  return new SQLArrayWrapper(realResultSet.getArray(colName), parentStatement,
sql);
}
```

Finally, you need to add logging. Many developers erroneously believe that the various Statement.execute methods incur the main cost of the database interaction. This is true for database updates and for database reads that involve only a few rows. However, if more than a few rows of a query are read, then the ResultSet.next( ) method can spend a lot of time fetching rows from the database. If many rows are to be read, ResultSet.next( ) calls can take much more cumulative time than the execution of the SQL statements. Log ResultSet.next( ) calls so you can track them:

```
public boolean next( ) throws SQLException {
  Thread t = Thread.currentThread( );
  JDBCLogger.startLogSqlNext(t, sql);
  boolean b = realResultSet.next( );
  JDBCLogger.endLogSqlNext(t, sql);
  return b;
}
```

You can log other ResultSet calls if needed, such as previous( ), insertRow( ), etc. But most applications need only next( ) logged, and that is how I'll leave the class.

The JDBC wrapper framework

That pretty much covers the classes that need wrapping. I haven't explicitly shown the Array wrapper or the DatabaseMetaData wrapper, but they are straightforward, needing only delegation and ResultSetWrappers and ConnectionWrappers returned instead of ResultSets and Connections. All the classes and wrapper classes for JDBC 2 can be obtained from the web site for this book, *http://www.oreilly.com/catalog/javapt2*. JDBC Versions 1, 2, and 3 are all amenable to using wrapper objects to measure database interaction, though they differ slightly in their interface definitions and thus require different wrapper classes. However, all the wrapper classes for the different versions can be created the same way, following the procedure covered in this chapter.

The class I haven't yet shown you is the JDBCLogger class. A simple implementation of that class would have null calls for the logging methods, providing no logging:

```
package tuning.jdbc;

public class JDBCLogger
{
  public static void startLogSqlQuery(Thread t, String sql) { }
  public static void endLogSqlQuery(Thread t, String sql) { }
  public static void startLogSqlNext(Thread t, String sql) { }
  public static void endLogSqlNext(Thread t, String sql) { }


}
```

Timing the queries would be more useful. The following methods work by holding the start time of the query and finding the elapsed time for the query when it finishes. The methods are kept simple by assuming that SQL queries cannot recurse within the same thread, an assumption that is generally true:

```
private static Hashtable QueryTime = new Hashtable( );

public static void startLogSqlQuery(Thread t, String sql)
{
  if (QueryTime.get(t) != null)
    System.out.println("WARNING: overwriting sql query log time for "
        + sql);
  QueryTime.put(t, new Long(System.currentTimeMillis( )));
}

public static void endLogSqlQuery(Thread t, String sql)
{
  long time = System.currentTimeMillis( );
  time -= ((Long) QueryTime.get(t)).longValue( );
  System.out.println("Time: " + time + " milliseconds for SQL query " + sql);
  QueryTime.remove(t);
}
```

Using these methods in the JDBCLogger class provides output lines similar to the following code for every SQL query execution:

```
Time: 53 milliseconds for SQL query SELECT * FROM JACKTABL
```

This output gives you precise measurements for each SQL query. You can also sum the queries in the JDBCLogger class, retain the maximum half-dozen or so measurements, and then print out a summary statement. The summary measurements I usually like to have are minimum, maximum, average, standard deviation, and the 90th percentile value. Summary values tend to be more useful for a production environment, whereas printing individual lines for each query is more useful when profiling the system during development.

Using the JDBC wrapper framework

Wrappers are very useful for determining the performance of JDBC calls in both development and deployed applications. Because they are simple and robust and require very little alteration to the application, wrappers can be retained in a deployed application. Creating a configurable JDBCLogger class lets you turn logging on and off at will.

During development, these classes enable you to identify individually expensive database interactions and repeated database interactions that are expensive because of their cumulative cost. Identifying these expensive database interactions is the first step toward improving your application's performance. In production, these wrapper classes identify discrepancies between expected performance and reality.

After you use these classes and techniques to pinpoint where JDBC is causing a performance problem, you need to tune the database interactions. The next section addresses performance-tuning techniques for JDBC.

Tuning JDBC

Although JDBC tuning follows general tuning guidelines, specifying that you find the bottlenecks before tuning, it is worth knowing what tuning techniques are available from the outset. You can structure your JDBC usage so it's easier to tune without violating good design and coding practices. Two general principles are:

- Always close or release resources when you are finished with them: Connections, Statements, and ResultSets.

- Use the latest versions. SDK core classes, JVM versions, and JDBC versions improve performance of JDBC with each release. JDBC has not yet matured to the point that I can look back, compare versions, and find operations faster in a previous release. For the foreseeable future, upgrade to new versions as soon as they prove stable.

JDBC Drivers

The JDBC package provides interfaces to standardize the API that allows database connections. However, the JDBC package does not provide concrete implementations of those APIs (except an ODBC driver). Third-party implementations are necessary to make the actual connection to a particular database, and the database vendor usually provides these implementations. These implementations are called *JDBC drivers*, and they fall into four categories or types, which differ in implementation and performance:

Type 1

A JDBC bridge to another driver (e.g., the JDBC-ODBC bridge plus the ODBC driver)

Type 2

A native API, part-Java driver

Type 3

A pure Java driver for database middleware

Type 4

A pure Java driver direct to the database

Type 1: JDBC-bridging driver

Type 1 drivers provide a link to a bridging driver, most commonly to ODBC, that can connect to any ODBC-compatible database (i.e., most databases). Because this type of driver uses a second bridging product, it is usually the slowest type and should be avoided if possible.

Type 2: Native API, part-Java driver

Type 2 drivers connect to a local native binary client. This connection is equivalent to using a native database client library, connecting to it via JNI, and wrapping that connection by using classes implementing the JDBC APIs. This configuration should provide reasonable performance, assuming the driver itself has been through a round of performance tuning (most have by now). If the database is on the local machine and the driver has optimizations to take advantage of that configuration, then a Type 2 driver could provide the fastest performance. The JNI connection adds overhead, and that overhead becomes relatively larger as JVMs get faster. But this type of driver is certainly worth evaluating if you have a choice of available drivers.

Type 3: Pure Java driver for database middleware

Type 3 drivers provide a connection to a middleware product, which in turn connects to a database. In some ways, they are similar to Type 1 drivers. However, Type 1 ODBC drivers are generic. For example, ODBC drivers are limited to using ODBC interfaces to databases, and that type of database interface does not usually provide optimal performance. On the other hand, Type 3 driver middleware can use any interface to the database, including the fastest one. Type 3 drivers have bridging overhead similar to that of Type 1 drivers, but middleware's optimization features and position in the architecture allow it to take full advantage of any spare processing capacity available on the network. Type 3 drivers actually outperform Type 2 drivers in many configurations.

Type 4: Pure Java driver direct to a database

Type 4 drivers connect from Java directly to a database by using network communications (sockets) and the database's network application protocol. As it bypasses every type of intermediate bridging, this type of driver generally provides the fastest communication. However, if the database and the Java code run on the same machine and the database's native client library provides optimizations for that machine's configuration, Type 2 drivers could be faster.

My advice is to use a Type 4 driver when possible, test the performance of Type 2 and Type 3 drivers, if available, and stay away from Type 1 drivers. Type 3 drivers are rarer and tend to be third-party drivers, but this often means that they were built by a company dedicated to building high-performance database drivers. Generally, Type 3 and Type 4 drivers provide the overall best performance, but every configuration is different (i.e., database type, usage, and distribution), so try to test the available alternatives. A list of current drivers is available at *http://industry.java.sun.com/products/jdbc/drivers*, but that page does not provide much information to help select the fastest driver.

Try to use the latest version available, preferably with JDBC 3.0 or higher support. JDBC 3.0 drivers include connection pooling, distributed transaction support, RowSets, and prepared statement pooling.

Connection Pooling

Opening a connection to a database is costly, potentially requiring several network round trips, resources in both the client and database, and setup of several layers of transport and authentication. Once a connection is created, keeping it open is not expensive, even if it is idle. If you make many calls to a database, then repeatedly opening and closing connections can kill the application's performance.

Keeping connections to the database open is an important JDBC performance-tuning technique. However, if you simply open more connections and keep them all open, you quickly reach the database's limit for open connections and probably exceed the number of connections for optimal efficiency. To maintain an efficient number of open database connections, use a *connection pool*: an object pool consisting of Connection objects.

Connection pools are directly supported starting in JDBC 2.0, although earlier drivers may have their own connection pools. Many third-party and open source connection-pool implementations are available, and creating one yourself is also fairly simple. Remember that Connection objects are not *reentrant*: only one client of the pool can use the Connection object at a time. You can even use a Connection wrapper to intercept close( ) requests and deposit the Connection back into the pool, if you want completely transparent connection pooling. The reference page at *http://www.*

JavaPerformanceTuning.com/tips/jdbcconnpool.shtml provides helpful links for finding or building a connection-pool implementation appropriate to your application.

The suggested order of preference for selecting a connection-pool implementation is:

1. `ConnectionPoolDataSource` and `PooledConnection` from JDBC 2.0.
2. The driver implementer's connection pool (the driver implementer has opportunities to optimize its connection pool with database-specific features).
3. A third-party connection pool.

The connection pool itself provides further tuning possibilities. The size of the pool is a tuning parameter. The ideal pool size is just large enough to service requests without forcing the requests for connections to wait a long time. If the pool size is flexible (i.e., connections are created when the pool has no more available connections and destroyed when they are idle for too long), then the goal is to tune the connection-pool size to minimize the creation and destruction of database connections. Timeouts and initial, minimum, and maximum pool sizes all provide parameters to optimize your application's use of the connection pool.

The overall strategy for using pooled connections is to obtain and release pooled connections within each method that requires the connection, if the request is short. However, do not release the connection only to use it again almost immediately in another method. Instead, hold the connection until it is not immediately needed.

Once a connection is obtained from the pool, it is essentially an exclusively locked shared resource. Keeping the connection locked exclusively for the minimum amount of time ensures maximum scalability for the application. You are generally better off obtaining and releasing connections too frequently, and accepting the performance overhead of that strategy, than holding onto connections for too long.

For optimal use of connection pools, you might want to consider using several pools, with each pool supporting a particular connection feature. For example, some databases can optimize read-only operations, which the `Connection` class supports through the `setReadOnly(boolean)` method. Since some proportion of JDBC operations are inevitably read-only, you may want to have a read-only connection pool as well as a general connection pool.

Optimizing SQL

Developers use SQL to interact with databases when using JDBC. SQL is normally used with JDBC, since it provides a standard, well-understood mechanism for database interaction. Drivers can support other syntaxes, such as the database's stored-procedure syntax, but ANSI SQL must be supported.

The SQL used by your application via JDBC can be tuned to create significant gains in overall performance. Tuning SQL is therefore critical for tuning JDBC. Three broad areas to consider when tuning SQL include:

- The nature of set-based database interactions
- The work the database needs to do
- The data transferred via JDBC

These three categories are not completely separate. They overlap slightly, and sometimes produce conflicting optimizations that need to be balanced. We'll look at each category in turn.

Set-Based Processing

When you create a Java application that uses JDBC, you don't tend to think about which procedures are operating on the same tables. Instead, you probably think about which data each method and object needs and which data needs to be updated in the database on a method-by-method and object-by-object basis. The resulting JDBC code tends to use row-by-row operations, with many JDBC-SQL calls inefficiently handling only one row of a table in the database. SQL is designed to process multiple rows in a table simultaneously. Relational-database vendors ensure that operations applied to multiple rows in one table can be executed as efficiently as possible. To take advantage of this, combine SQL statements. Don't query for one row at a time from a table; try to get all the rows you will need. This may require that you restructure objects in your application, but can result in significantly fewer application-to-database round trips.

Even more usefully, SQL consists of more than SELECT and INSERT. Instead of using the database purely as a data store, you can construct sophisticated SQL statements that combine queries, processing, and updates without bringing lots of temporary data back to the Java application for local processing. Combining multiple operations is a good way to take advantage of the efficiencies available in relational databases, and we will discuss batching operations and stored procedures in later sections.

Database Server-Side Processing

On the database side of the JDBC communication, the database needs to process the data and received SQL instructions, execute the accesses and updates required to satisfy the SQL, and return any requested data. The more work the server has to do, the longer the operation takes. The performance-tuning target is to minimize the server's work without disproportionately burdening the Java application.

Some techniques for reducing database work are relatively simple: avoid doing work that doesn't need to be done. This rule seems obvious, but I've seen unnecessary calls to uppercase data (using upper( )) too many times. Examine your SQL and the table structure to decide if the SQL adds unnecessary database-side work. Are those upper-case/count/etc. operations really required? Could you more efficiently uppercase the data on insertion? Sort the data differently? Avoid the count operation by maintaining a separate counter in a dedicated counter table?

Do you really need to access the same table multiple times? Can you change existing rows of data rather than adding or deleting rows? Each time you avoid changing the table by moving, deleting, or adding rows, you've reduced the database workload slightly. If you can construct the application to use existing dummy rows instead of inserting rows, the SQL runs faster.

Some databases can optimize read-only operations. If your connection is read-only, set the connection to read-only with the `Connection.setReadOnly(true)` method. If the database knows a connection is read-only, it does not need to cache new pages, maintain journal entries, or acquire write locks on the data.

Some operations are much more expensive. Multiway joins invariably degrade performance, and performance gets worse as data volume increases. Try working with as few tables as possible within each SQL clause.

Queries of large tables that do not use an index require far more processing than tables with indexes. Further, two checks can help you assess the efficiency of SQL statements. First, the `Connection` class includes a `nativeSQL()` method that converts the SQL you provide into the system's native SQL. This gives the driver an opportunity to convert standard SQL into SQL optimized for the particular database. This method rarely returns anything other than the SQL string you pass to it, but it's always worth checking.

Second, many databases support the `EXPLAIN SQL` command. For databases that support `EXPLAIN`, you can preface a statement with the keyword `EXPLAIN` and the database produces an explanation of how it will execute the SQL, including whether an index is used.

As the Red Hat database manual points out, executing:

```
EXPLAIN SELECT * FROM foo
```

in PostgreSQL on a table with no index produces the plan:

```
Seq Scan on foo  (cost=0.00..2.28 rows=128 width=4)
```

telling you that the query is executed as a sequential scan, produces 128 rows, and requires 2.28 disk pages to execute. Querying the table again with an added index and using an equijoin condition:

```
EXPLAIN SELECT * FROM foo WHERE i = 4
```

produces the plan:

```
Index Scan using fi on foo  (cost=0.00..0.42 rows=1 width=4)
```

telling you that the query is executed with an index, produces 1 row, and requires 0.42 disk pages to execute. Quite a dramatic difference.

Minimizing Transferred Data

Transferring and converting data represents a significant proportion of the cost in many JDBC operations. Parameters that minimize transfer costs are discussed under "Batching," and techniques to minimize data conversion costs are discussed in "Minimizing Data-Conversion Overhead." However, rather than minimize the costs, try to completely avoid transferring the data. Efficient SQL lets you minimize the data that is transferred.

The most glaring example of transferring too much data is the ubiquitous use of the SELECT * query:

```
SELECT * FROM foo ...
```

Using the * character in the SELECT clause asks the database to return all fields in the rows. I recently sampled some applications and found that out of thousands of requests to various databases, fewer than 10 requests needed all the fields in the rows queried. I don't really find the extensive use of SELECT * surprising, though. During development, it is much easier to use the SELECT * query, especially since the required fields can change. Then the fields are accessed from the ResultSet row by field index. Later, converting queries to request only the required fields means changing both the SQL and the indexes of the accessed fields in the ResultSet rows, a bug-prone change in all but the simplest JDBC applications.

It can be difficult to estimate the cost of selecting too many fields without actually comparing the two queries in the context of the application—i.e., comparing:

```
SELECT * FROM foo ...
```

and:

```
SELECT field1,field2 FROM foo ...
```

Several factors come into play; there is no conversion overhead from the unused fields (in most drivers), and the transfer overhead depends on the size of the unused fields, the number of transferred rows, and the transfer batch size, too! There is no doubt that the latter, more precise SELECT is more efficient, but whether the effort to change the queries to the latter SELECT is worthwhile for your application and query is a judgment call. In highly scaled systems, with many queries going to the database, every field counts.

A second type of inappropriate transfer, requesting too many rows, is less frequently a problem. It is easier in development to specify the required rows precisely by using the appropriate clauses. One common technique that results in transferring too many rows is sorting rows with a SORT BY clause, and then using only the top few rows. For example, suppose you want to see the top five URLs hit on your web site.

You might use a SELECT url,hits FROM url_hits SORT BY hits clause, as in the following code:

```
String sqlQuery = "SELECT url,hits FROM url_hits SORT BY hits";
Statement statement = connection.createStatement( );
ResultSet resultSet = statement.executeQuery(sqlQuery);
String[ ] urls = new String[5];
int[ ] hits = new int[5];
//Assume we always have at least 5 urls for simplicity
for(int i= 0; i< 5; i++, resultSet.next( ))
{
  url[i] = resultSet.getString(1);
  hits[i] = resultSet.getInt(2);
}
```

This results in the transfer of all table rows (or actually, the batch size; see the section on "Batching"). At the expense of some costly SQL statements, you can specify the rows you want:

```
select r.url, r.hits from url_hits r
  where 5 >= (select count(*) from url_hits rr
    where rr.hits >= r.hits);
```

This SQL returns only five rows, with the top five URLs and the number of hits for each. It scans through the url_hits table and, for every row, it goes through the whole url_hits table again in an inner loop to see how many URLs have hits that are higher than the current row of the outer scan. This example is probably more useful as an example of how SQL can be made to produce precisely the result you want. It is less useful as a practical example of performance tuning because of the additional overhead such a query would add to the database server and because setting the batch size to 5 for the original query would effectively eliminate the transfer of extra rows.

I saw a more realistic example of transferring too many rows in an application that had been taken over by different developers. Rather than create new queries in the JDBC section of the application, the new developers simply checked data items and discarded those that didn't apply to the new set of criteria. Effectively, they made a SELECT * query, and then executed a WHERE clause in Java by iterating through the ResultSet and collecting the rows that satisfied the new criteria.

Finally, accessing fields by name (e.g., with resultSet.getString("field1")) is inefficient. The driver needs to map the name to the column number, which at best requires one extra round trip for the column mapping, and at worst can result in multiple round trips and significant amounts of extra data transferred from the database. (For example, MySQL and mSQL retrieve all rows from the database before accessing a value by name.) Use the column number to access fields, even though doing so may require extra information about table structures to be maintained in the application.

Caching

Caching data in the client is a highly effective technique for speeding up applications using JDBC. JDBC has the overhead of network communication, data conversion, and server-side processing. Deciding to cache JDBC data is almost a no-brainer. The questions you need to ask are which data, and how to cache it.

Deciding which data to cache is straightforward. Cache small read-only tables and tables that are updated infrequently. Even medium-sized tables are worth considering, though you'll need to test how much space they take up in their final cached form. Large tables and rapidly updated or frequently changing tables are clearly not good candidates, though select rows from large tables may be if they are rarely changed and are used more often than other rows. In some cases, a cache replacement policy, such as least-recently-used, could slowly replace the data being cached so that frequently required data from large tables can settle into the cache.

How to cache the data is more complex. Bearing in mind that any processing through JDBC produces overhead, the best place to cache JDBC-obtained data is after you have processed it (i.e., after it is extracted from the ResultSet and converted into objects or object data). This is an especially good option if you are in the design or early implementation stage of your project, when you can most effectively build in object caching. If you are in a late stage of development, you may be able to modify your application so it caches objects, but that depends on the existing design, considering how the data is used and where it ends up.

The second option is to cache at the ResultSet layer. You cannot use a ResultSet object as the cache object itself because it uses JDBC resources that need to be closed. However, the techniques discussed and used in the first section of the chapter show how to implement wrappers for most kinds of JDBC objects, including ResultSets. You can even create a mostly transparent cache with wrappers. Just add a Hashtable to the ConnectionWrapper that maps SQL query strings to StatementWrappers and ResultSetWrappers. The ResultSetWrapper itself should wrap the original ResultSet accessed from the database and simply iterate through all the rows, obtaining the data to hold locally. All fields can be accessed with the ResultSet.getString() method and converted as required when accessed with other methods. For example, you might read all the data looping through the ResultSet to collect all rows as an array of String fields:

```
public static Vector createCache(ResultSet rs)
{
    //We need to know how many columns there are
    ResultSetMetaData resultSetMetaData = resultSet.getMetaData();
    int numColumns = resultSetMetaData.getColumnCount();
    Vector rowsvector = new Vector();
    //Could use an Object[] and getObject() later in the loop
    //at the cost of more space taken up and more overhead during
    //this create cache routine.
    String[] oneRow = null;
```

```
//Read through the rows one at a time, getting all the fields
//as separate strings, and add them all into the vector
while(resultSet.next())
{
    oneRow = new String[numColumns];
    for (int i = 0; i < numColumns; i++)
      oneRow[i] = resultSet.getString(i+1);
    rowsvector.addElement(oneRow);
}

resultSet.close();
return rowsvector;
}
```

Bear in mind that you do not need to implement a generic framework to handle every possible case. Only the queries that lead to cached data need handling, and only those data types that will be accessed need to have get( ) methods implemented. For example, if you access only Strings and ints, here is a straightforward implementation of a ResultSet:

```
public class ReadOnlyCachedResultSet implements ResultSet
{
  Vector cacheOfRows;
  int currentIndex;
  public ReadOnlyCachedResultSet(Vector rowsCache)
  {
    cacheOfRows = rowsCache;
    currentIndex = -1;
  }

  public int getInt(int columnIndex) throws SQLException {
    String[ ] row = (String[ ]) cacheOfRows.elementAt(currentRow);
    return Integer.parseInt(row[columnIndex-1]);
  }

  public int getString(int columnIndex) throws SQLException {
    String[ ] row = (String[ ]) cacheOfRows.elementAt(currentRow);
    return row[columnIndex-1];
  }

  public boolean next() throws SQLException {
    if (++currentIndex >= cacheOfRows.size())
      return false;
    else
      return true;
  }

  //... All other methods can be implemented as unsupported, e.g.,
  //public Array getArray(String colName) throws SQLException {
  //  throw new UnsupportedOperationException();
  //}
```

The Statement wrapper returns this ResultSet when the application executes the relevant SQL query for the cached data. This framework is relatively easy to implement and understand, and it can be slipped in over the actual JDBC driver, as shown in the first section of this chapter. It has one drawback: the data is vastly expanded as it is held in the form of multiple Strings, one per field. With a little extra work, you can pack all the data into byte arrays and cache it in that form, so even the data size is not an overwhelming problem.

Unfortunately, there is a more serious drawback. This simple mechanism does not support parameterized queries. It is possible to support parameterized queries using similar but considerably more sophisticated wrappers, but the effort is beyond what I can present here.

Finally, an in-memory database product is another reasonable option that can provide relatively transparent database caching, though with a higher overhead. Several commercial versions and an open source product called *hsqldb* (available from *http://hsqldb.sourceforge.net/*) are available. The memory overhead for such products is small, and they work just like a normal relational database, with their own JDBC driver, so you can switch between databases by switching drivers for queries or by redirecting queries with Connection wrappers. Use such products to replicate the tables you want to cache and keep in memory.

An in-memory relational database opens up another interesting performance-tuning option. You can use the database to update cached rows in exactly the same way as you would the proper database. Because the update mechanism is SQL, you can log the SQL statements locally to disk as you execute them on the in-memory database, a process called *journaling*. Then the SQL statements can be applied to the actual database separately and asynchronously, to synchronize it with the in-memory database. Since SQL is standardized, you can use the same SQL easily for both databases.

Prepared Statements

"Use PreparedStatements." You'll hear this refrain again and again when dealing with JDBC performance-tuning tips. Fair enough, but if everyone figures you should use PreparedStatements, what is Statement for? Is it just a redundant interface?

When a database executes an SQL statement, it performs two separate tasks. First, it searches through the data and indexes to determine which data items satisfy the SQL statement. You explicitly direct the database to perform this task.

However, behind the scenes, the database has a second task: to work out exactly how to execute the SQL. The database needs to:

- Parse the SQL to see if it is properly constructed
- Identify whether there are indexes for this search (indexes are not specified in the SQL, nor should they be)
- Identify the location of the indexes
- Identify the location of the tables

- Determine which fields are needed to satisfy the SQL
- Figure out the best way to do the search

These and other tasks combine to form the query plan. When the database "prepares" a statement, it creates a query plan. Now the difference between Statement and PreparedStatement may be clearer: Statement prepares and executes the query plan each time, while PreparedStatement prepares the query plan once and then reuses the query plan. Preparing a statement is also referred to as *precompiling* a statement.

If that were the whole story, then PreparedStatement would always be the statement of choice, and you would avoid Statement objects completely. But it's not quite the whole story. Statement has optimizations that the database can apply; mainly, the database knows that the Statement plan is executed immediately and thrown away. So the database handles Statement queries differently from PreparedStatements. Statement queries can be prepared and executed in one swoop, using the state of the database at the time, without allocating resources to keeping the plan around. PreparedStatements, on the other hand, need to allocate database resources to store and maintain the query plan and to ensure that the query plan is not invalidated by changes to the database. For example, the query plan would need to be updated or re-created in the case of some types of changes to the database, depending on how detailed the query plan is.

Creating and executing a Statement once is faster than creating and executing a PreparedStatement once. But PreparedStatement has a one-off hit in its preparation stage, so after the preparation stage is completed, any single PreparedStatement execution should be faster than a single Statement execution.

Now the options are clearer, though not completely clear-cut. If your application has an initialization phase during which you can create and execute your PreparedStatements, then all subsequent executions of those PreparedStatements provide the fastest query possible. (Note that I say to create *and execute* the PreparedStatement in the initialization phase. Although logically, the PreparedStatement should be prepared when the object is created, the API allows the driver to choose whether to prepare the statement at object-creation time or when the first execution takes place.)

However, if you cannot prepare your statements during an initialization phase, the choice is more difficult. You can choose a Statement or PreparedStatement object, depending on which provides the fastest overall cumulative time for repeated queries. For example, in *Java Programming with Oracle JDBC* (O'Reilly), Donald Bales looks at the cost of table inserts using Oracle drivers and finds that the statement needs to be repeated 65 times before the cumulative time of PreparedStatements is faster than the cumulative time for repeating Statements. Inserts have an overhead different from that of access queries, and different drivers and databases have different overhead, so test your configuration to see where the crossover happens if you need to be precise.

In general, for any particular SQL statement:

- If you have spare time in which a PreparedStatement can be initialized with one execution, use PreparedStatement with this separate initialization.
- If you cannot separately initialize the statement in spare time and you execute the statement only once, use Statement.
- If you cannot separately initialize the statement in spare time and you execute the statement only a few times (say, less than10), use Statement.
- If you cannot separately initialize the statement in spare time and you execute the statement many times, use PreparedStatement.
- If you cannot separately initialize the statement in spare time but it is acceptable for the first execution of the statement to be slower, use PreparedStatement.

Bear in mind two things when using PreparedStatements. First, the SQL needs to be identical for the query plan to be reusable. So:

```
SELECT f1,f2 FROM t1 WHERE f3=4
```

and:

```
SELECT f1,f2 FROM t1 WHERE f3=5
```

are two different statements, and making the first query into a PreparedStatement doesn't help the second query run any faster. Fortunately, PreparedStatements support parameterized queries so you can repeat the same query with different parameters. To get the performance benefit of PreparedStatements, make it a habit to use parameterized statements. This code executes the previous two queries efficiently by using parameterized statements:

```
String query = "SELECT f1,f2 FROM t1 WHERE f3=?";
PreparedStatement ps = conn.prepareStatement(query);
ps.setInt(1, 4);                     //First query with parameter set to 4
ResultSet rs = ps.executeQuery( );   //Execute query
...                                  //Read and process rows
rs.close( );

ps.setInt(1, 5);                     //Second query with parameter set to 5
ResultSet rs = ps.executeQuery( );   //Re-execute query
...                                  //Read and process rows
rs.close( );

ps.close( );
```

The second thing to bear in mind is that the PreparedStatement is associated with a particular connection. Although it may be possible for the driver and database to ensure that any PreparedStatement that uses a particular SQL statement also uses the same query plan, you cannot count on it. Therefore, you need to use the same PreparedStatement object for repeated executions of an SQL statement to ensure that the SQL is executed with precompilations, which requires that you use the same Connection. This is especially important when using pooled connections. With pooled connections, you either hold a separate pool of prepared statements, or implement wrappers, as defined in the first section of this chapter, to hold a cache of SQL statements and their corresponding Connection and PreparedStatement objects and return them. Try to keep the appropriate connections available for the methods needing to reuse the PreparedStatement. This again points to separate connection pools.

JDBC 3.0 supports pooled PreparedStatements that can be used independently of their originating Connection objects. The pooling happens completely under the covers, controlled by the driver. Indeed, a simplistic approach, which assumes that the JDBC/database automatically understands that the same SQL should use the same query plan without worrying about which Connection object and which PreparedStatement are used, can actually work with JDBC 3.0. Unfortunately, the JDBC 3.0 interface does not specify that any particular SQL statement must be cached, and the only parameter available is the maxStatements property of the JDBC 3.0 connection pool, which specifies only how many statements should be kept open. Moving to JDBC 3.0 might solve your particular PreparedStatement reuse issues. However, there isn't sufficient explicit support to determine which PreparedStatements are automatically cached in JDBC 3.0, so if you are a defensive programmer, you may wish to retain control of your pools, even with JDBC 3.0.

Finally, a couple of warnings. First, the JDBC API does not specify how PreparedStatements or Statements should be implemented. The differences in performance between Statements and PreparedStatements are recommendations based on what I've seen, read about, and expect from documented features of various databases. But they are not guaranteed: always check the driver and database documentation and test for expected performance improvements.

Second, the SQL you execute is a String. If you dynamically create the SQL Strings you execute by concatenating various items, you add all the String concatenation and conversion overhead discussed in Chapter 5. This overhead can be costly, especially for repeated or looped executions of SQL statements. Try to avoid extra String overhead. Parameterized SQL statements that are supported by PreparedStatements can help you avoid creating extra strings for repeated SQL statements.

Batching

Relational databases are designed to be operated optimally with SQL, which is a set-processing language. Consequently, relational-database performance is optimized when you combine access of multiple rows of a table and combine multiple updates to a table. Furthermore, operating on one table at a time is normally faster than interleaving operations between multiple tables. This combination of operations is called *batching*.

You can take advantage of batching in JDBC in two ways: on access and on update. These two types of operations are batched very differently, so we'll look at them separately. You may need to check how any particular driver supports batching.

Some have restrictions, such as only supporting update batching with one type of Statement (Oracle batches updates only with PreparedStatement) or one mode of ResultSet (DB2 doesn't batch when used with scrollable ResultSets).

Batching accesses by optimizing row fetching

JDBC includes parameters that support batching accesses from the database by specifying how many rows are fetched in one transfer. Essentially, the amount of data (or, more specifically, the number of rows) read by one call to the database is configurable. Transferring data efficiently is important because network communication time affects performance more than any other factor. For example, if you intend to read 10 rows from a table and each row requires a separate round trip to the database, it takes 10 times longer to access the data than if the 10 rows are read in one network round trip. In practice, JDBC access is already batched, with a typical default number of rows between 10 and 100. For example, Oracle uses a default of 10 and DB2 uses a default of 32. If you access the default number of rows, access is batched automatically. In practice, rather than being critical for performance, for most applications, adjusting access batch size is more like fine-tuning performance.

If you retrieve only a few rows, the default fetch size may be too large. But there is not usually a large cost in having too large a fetch size as long as the data volume of the default fetch size is not so large that the network fragments the data packets. Typical table rows are not large enough to cause fragmenting. Nevertheless, reducing the fetch size to be in line with the number of rows you actually read should improve performance by reducing overhead slightly at both ends of the communication (in the JDBC layer and at the database-access layer).

If you regularly access more than the default fetch size, then you can reduce the number of network trips by increasing the fetch size. This can make a big difference, depending on how much data you retrieve. If you regularly get 33 rows and the fetch size is 32, you incur an extra network call for the 33rd row. If you get 10,000 rows, then a 10-row fetch size requires 1,000 network trips. A 32-row batch reduces that amount by a third, but still requires 313 network trips. A fetch size of 512 requires just 20 network trips. Depending on how the data is processed in the application, this change could alleviate a significant bottleneck. The tradeoff to increasing the fetch size is increased memory use. All fetched data has to be held in the JDBC layer on the client, and this memory can add up excessively if you use a large default batch size that applies to every request.

The fetched data is held in the ResultSet object generated by executing a query. If the fetch size is 10, then accessing the first 10 records simply iterates internally through the ResultSet data held on the client. The 11th access causes a call to the database for another 10 records, and so on for each group of 10 records.

You can set the fetch size in several ways, depending on how widely you want the change to apply. You can set it at the Connection, Statement, or ResultSet level.

However, in all cases, you rely on the database driver supporting the capability to change the fetch size. The database driver can ignore the change. To set the fetch size at the Connection level, use one of the Connection creation methods that accept a Properties object:

```
DriverManager.getConnection(String url, Properties props)
Driver.connect(String url, Properties props)
```

The actual keyword to set the fetch size in the Properties object is driver-dependent. For example, DB2 uses block size, while Oracle uses defaultRowPrefetch:

```
Properties p = new java.util.Properties();
p.put("block size", "512");        //DB2
p.put("defaultRowPrefetch", "512"); //Oracle
Connection c = DriverManager.getConnection("jdbc:dbname:path", p);
```

In addition, some drivers (for example, Oracle) give Connection objects dedicated methods to set the fetch size:

```
public static void setOracleFetchSize(Connection c, int size) {
  ((OracleConnection) c).setDefaultRowPrefetch(size);
}
```

The fetch size can also be set at the Statement or ResultSet level by using their setFetchSize( ) methods:

```
Statement.setFetchSize(int size)
ResultSet.setFetchSize(int size)
```

These setFetchSize( ) methods also depend on the driver supporting the changing of fetch sizes: the API states that the driver can ignore the request.

Batching updates

Batching updates simply means sending multiple update statements in one transaction and one call to the database. JDBC supports this capability with the addBatch( ) and executeBatch( ) methods. The technique is simple and is illustrated here. Remember to explicitly commit the batch transaction:

```
boolean autocommit = connection.getAutoCommit( );
connection.setAutoCommit(false);
Statement s = connection.createStatement( );
s.addBatch("INSERT INTO SOCCER VALUES('Pele    ', '      ', 'Brazil   '));
s.addBatch("INSERT INTO SOCCER VALUES('Charlton', 'Bobby ', 'England  '));
s.addBatch("INSERT INTO SOCCER VALUES('Maradona', 'Diego ', 'Argentina'));
s.addBatch("INSERT INTO SOCCER VALUES('Cruyff  ', 'Johan ', 'Holland  '));
int[ ] results = s.executeBatch( );
//Check the results
if ((results.length != 4) ||
( (results[0] != 1) && (results[0] != -2) ) ||
    ( (results[1] != 1) && (results[1] != -2) )||
    ( (results[2] != 1) && (results[2] != -2) )||
    ( (results[3] != 1) && (results[3] != -2) ) )   {
      throw new java.sql.BatchUpdateException("Something failed.");
}
```

```
        connection.commit( );
        connection.setAutoCommit(autocommit);
```

And similarly using PreparedStatements:

```
        PreparedStatement ps = connection.prepareStatement(
            "INSERT INTO SOCCER VALUES(?, ?, ?) ");
        ps.setString(1, 'Pele    ');
        ps.setString(2, '        ');
        ps.setString(3, 'Brazil   ');
        ps.addBatch( );
        ps.setString(1, 'Charlton');
        ps.setString(2, 'Bobby ');
        ps.setString(3, 'England  ');
        ps.addBatch( );
        ...
        int[ ] results = ps.executeBatch( );
        //Check the results
        if ((results.length != 4) ||
        ( (results[0] != 1) && (results[0] != -2) ) ||
            ( (results[1] != 1) && (results[1] != -2) )||
            ( (results[2] != 1) && (results[2] != -2) )||
            ( (results[3] != 1) && (results[3] != -2) ) )   {
            throw new java.sql.BatchUpdateException("Something failed.");
        }
        connection.commit( );
        connection.setAutoCommit(autocommit);
```

It is easiest to take explicit control when batching updates (i.e., to explicitly collect the data and statements, combine them into SQL calls, and call whichever execute method is most appropriate, normally executeBatch( )). executeBatch( ) is the only standard method for executing batches, but some drivers have additional proprietary methods that optimize batches in different ways, such as with the Oracle sendbatch( ) method. If this is not feasible because of the complexity of changing the existing implementation, you can use an underlying layer to batch the updates. One approach is to use RowSets, available with JDBC 3.0, which can be operated in a disconnected manner. Reading from the RowSet, you can collect the update statements and execute them together.

A more transparent mechanism would use wrappers, constructed in a similar way to the wrappers covered in the first section of this chapter. The wrappers would collect statements and automatically execute them together according to an application-specific triggering mechanism. (For example, Oracle provides this mechanism in its driver as an alternative batching model.)

Data Structures

Databases are designed to hold certain types of data more efficiently than others. The basic data types, such as numeric and string, normally have fixed sizes and often a fixed range of formats. These restrictions are mainly for performance; they enable the database to be efficient in access and update. Dealing with fixed-size data having a known format means that you don't need to search for terminators within the data, and knowing the format reduces the number of branch points necessary to handle many formats. Databases are optimized for these basic data types and formats.

The closer you can come to holding data in your application in the same format required by the database, the more easily you can achieve good JDBC performance. However, this consideration usually compromises your application. Efficiently structured relational-database data is rarely compatible with good object-oriented design.

There are other data-structure considerations. The data you currently use is frequently updated and accessed in the database. Other types of data, such as historic or archived data, are not accessed frequently by the database. However, if you use the same set of tables for both types of data, then the database has no choice but to pull both sets of data into its cache and search through both types of data. So separating tables of frequently and infrequently used data allows the database to optimize its handling of frequently used data. It also reduces the possibility that you will need to search through result sets for data items you need.

Minimizing Data-Conversion Overhead

The data in the database is stored in a different format than the data held in your Java application. Inevitably, this format discrepancy necessitates data conversion. A few techniques are available that minimize conversion overhead.

Use the type-correct get( ) method rather than getObject( ). The ResultSet object has a large number of different get( ) methods. Each method typically accesses the underlying data item and converts the data into the required Java data type or object type. The closer the underlying data is to the resulting Java data type, the more efficient the conversion.

A get( ) method that results in an Object typically costs more than one that converts into a primitive Java data type (e.g., int, float, etc.). Strings, as usual, have special considerations. Strings are usually held in relational databases as single-byte character data (ASCII) and get converted to Unicode two-byte Strings in Java. You can reduce the conversion cost by storing String and char data as Unicode two-byte characters in the database. But bear in mind that doing so will cause your database size to grow—in the worst case, doubling the size of the database.

Finally, if you use data types that are not primitive data types, use the most appropriate data type available from the database. For example, almost every database has a date type, and you should store your dates in that date type and not in the more generic varchar data type. Avoid BLOB and CLOB types whenever possible. But note that relying on database-specific data types, although good for performance, can compromise portability.

Metadata

Metadata is information about how data is structured in the database, such as the size of a column or its numeric precision. There are a number of considerations for dealing with metadata.

First, metadata rarely changes. In fact, unless your application is specifically designed to deal with the possibility that the metadata will change, you can assume that the metadata for a particular table and metadata about database features are constant for the lifetime of a particular JVM. Metadata can be expensive to obtain from the database compared to most other types of queries. Thus, if you use metadata, obtain it once and cache the data. Many DatabaseMetaData methods are quite slow, and executing them repeatedly causes a bottleneck. Methods you should avoid calling include getBestRowIdentifier( ), getColumns( ), getCrossReference( ), getExportedKeys( ), getImportedKeys( ), getPrimaryKeys( ), getTables( ), and getVersionColumns( ). Avoid using null arguments in metadata queries. A null argument has one fewer criterion to restrict a search, which makes the search more intensive.

ResultSetMetaData is more efficient than DatabaseMetaData, so try to use the former. For example, if you want to get column information about a particular table, you are better off getting the ResultSetMetaData object from a query, even a dummy query, on the table, rather than using the more generic DatabaseMetaData.getColumns( ) method.

Avoiding implicit metadata queries can be difficult. For example, Don Bales points out that an Oracle SELECT statement (not a prepared statement) makes two round trips to the database: the first for metadata and the second for data. He suggests using the OracleStatement.defineColumnType( ) method to predefine the SELECT statement, thus providing the JDBC driver with the column metadata it needs. The query can then avoid the first database trip to query for metadata.

Apart from optimizing metadata queries themselves, using metadata information also allows you to optimize standard queries. For example, the DatabaseMetaData. getIndexInfo( ) method allows you to identify which indexes exist for a table. Using this data allows you to optimize your query to use indexes in the query when possible. Another useful example is the DatabaseMetaData.getBestRowIdentifier( ) method, which identifies the optimal set of columns to use in a WHERE clause for updating data. The columns returned by this query can include pseudocolumns not available from the getColumns( ) method. Pseudocolumns can provide the database with a pointer to an internal database location, which allows the database to optimize the operations that include pseudocolumns.

Handling Exceptions

Catching and handling database warnings and exceptions is important. At the very least, record and analyze them for handling in future versions of your application if you cannot handle the exceptions directly. JDBC exceptions are often indicative of incorrectly configured resources, which, if ignored, can result in significant inefficiencies. In addition, not correctly handling JDBC exceptions can leave resources in use but idle, creating resource leakage that inevitably decreases performance over time.

Note that JDBC exceptions often enclose other underlying exceptions, so don't forget to chain through them.

Stored Procedures

Stored procedures are defined in the database and can be executed from a remote call similar to SQL. Stored procedures have some overhead associated with execution, but are precompiled and executed entirely on the database server. This means that they are similar to `PreparedStatements`, but without the preparation and per-call overhead. Stored procedures are more efficient than `PreparedStatements` and `Statements` when the stored procedure is fairly complex, equivalent to many complex SQL statements. Stored procedures are also relatively efficient if they circumvent intermediate round trips between the client and the database—for example, when a procedure would consist of several separate calls to the database while a stored procedure requires only one call.

On the other hand, the procedure-call overhead for stored procedures indicates that they are inefficient compared with any single simple SQL call. Replacing each SQL call in your JDBC application with an equivalent call to a stored procedure with the same functionality, a one-for-one replacement of calls, would probably be inefficient, making performance worse.

Another consideration is the relative processing availability of the database server and the database client. In some cases, the database server may be underutilized compared to the database client, especially when the database client is middleware such as an application server. In this case, stored procedures can move some of the processing to the database server, making better use of the available CPU power on both machines.

Generally, a stored procedure can improve performance if it replaces any of the following:

- A complex series of SQL statements
- Multiple calls to the database with one call to the stored procedure
- Java-side processing when there is spare CPU capacity on the server

Don't use a stored procedure to replace simple SQL calls. Stored procedures are best used to avoid moving data back and forth across the network. And stored procedures are not an option if full database portability needs to be maintained, as they are different for each database.

Stored procedures are executed from JDBC using `CallableStatements`. Stored procedures are not standardized, so use the syntax specific to your database. Here's a simple example of a stored procedure that takes a parameter:

```
String storedProc = "{call doBlah(?)}";
CallableStatement cstmt = connection.prepareCall(storedProc);
cstmt.setString(1, "hello");
if(false == cstmt.execute())
  throw new Exception("No ResultSet Returned");
ResultSet rs = cstmt.getResultSet();
...
rs.close() ;
cstmt.close() ;
```

Transaction Optimization

The very best performance-tuning advice is to avoid doing what doesn't need to be done. Transactions are a lot of work for the database. A database needs to maintain all sorts of different resources to ensure that the ACID properties (Atomicity, Consistency, Isolation, and Durability) apply to a transaction, irrespective of any simultaneous operations and of whether the transaction ends with a commit or rollback. If you can avoid forcing the database to do some of that work, performance improves.

Auto-commit mode

The first way to minimize transaction costs is to combine multiple operations into one transaction. By default, the JDBC connection is in auto-commit mode, which means that every operation sent to the database is automatically its own transaction—that is, as if every Statement.execute() method is preceded with a BEGIN TRANSACTION command and followed by a COMMIT command. Turning off auto-commit and making your transactions explicit requires more work, but pays off if you can combine transactions (see "Batching" earlier in this chapter), especially when you scale the system. On heavily loaded systems, the overhead from transactions can be significant, and the lower that overhead is, the more the system can scale. Turning off auto-commit is done using:

```
Connection.setAutoCommit(false);
```

A Connection.getAutoCommit() method determines the current auto-commit mode. With auto-commit off, you will need to use the two transaction-completion methods: Connection.commit() and Connection.rollback().

Taking manual control over transactions doesn't mean that you should extend the transactions for long periods to catch lots of operations in one transaction. Transactions should be as short as possible. Leaving transactions open keeps locks on rows, which affects other transactions and reduces scalability. If you have several operations that could be executed sequentially, then combine them into one transaction, but otherwise keep transactions as short as possible.

Combining operations into one transaction may require extra conditional logic in the SQL statements and possibly even temporary tables. Even so, this is more efficient than not combining those operations because the database can obtain all the

---

required locks and release them in one step. Multiple transactions result in more communication overhead, more lock-and-release phases, and a greater likelihood of conflict with other sessions.

Transaction levels

Transactions are defined as all-or-nothing operations. Everything occurs in a transaction as if no other operations are occurring in the database during the transaction; that's roughly what the ACID properties mean. As already noted, this gives the database a large amount of work. Thus, most databases have provided other levels of transactions—levels that are not real transactions, as they don't satisfy the ACID properties. Nevertheless, these transaction levels are useful for many types of operations because they provide better performance with acceptable transactional functionality. Transaction levels can be set using the Connection. setTransactionIsolation() method. Not all levels defined in the JDBC Connection interface are supported by all databases. The levels defined in JDBC are:

TRANSACTION_NONE

TRANSACTION_NONE is supposed to be a placeholder, not a valid transaction level. According to the Connection API, you cannot use TRANSACTION_NONE as an argument to the Connection.setTransactionIsolation() method, since TRANSACTION_ NONE supposedly signifies that transactions are not supported. Nevertheless, some database drivers use this level. For example, the DB2 native (Type 2) driver uses TRANSACTION_NONE as its default level. If TRANSACTION_NONE is available as a supported level, TRANSACTION_NONE with auto-commit mode off (false) causes the least overhead to the database. But, of course, no changes can be committed to the database, so it's adequate for read access and temporary row or table creation: any changes are rolled back automatically when the connection is closed. TRANSACTION_NONE with auto-commit mode on (true) causes the next least overhead to the database, and, in the case of DB2, this configuration gives access to triggers and stored procedures that *can* commit work to the database.

TRANSACTION_READ_UNCOMMITTED

This is the fastest properly valid transaction level. TRANSACTION_READ_UNCOMMITTED lets you read changes made by other concurrent transactions that have not yet been committed to the database. The API states that dirty, nonrepeatable, and phantom reads can all occur at this transaction level (see the sidebar "Some Non-ACID Transaction Problems"). Supported by DB2, not by Oracle, this transaction level represents the atomicity of ACID: your changes are treated as if they all happen at the same time if committed, or as if none happen if rolled back.

TRANSACTION_READ_COMMITTED

This level is slower than TRANSACTION_READ_UNCOMMITTED, but is otherwise the fastest properly valid transaction level. TRANSACTION_READ_COMMITTED lets you read changes made by other concurrent transactions that were committed to the database. The API states that dirty reads are prevented with this transaction level, but nonrepeatable and phantom reads can both occur. This level is supported by DB2 and by Oracle, where it is the default level.

TRANSACTION_REPEATABLE_READ

This level is faster than TRANSACTION_SERIALIZABLE, but slower than the other transactions levels. With TRANSACTION_REPEATABLE_READ, reading the same field twice should always result in the same value being read, except when this transaction has changed the value. The API states that dirty and nonrepeatable reads are prevented at this transaction level, but phantom reads can occur. It is technically implemented by placing locks on rows that are read or written and holding the locks until the end of the transaction.

TRANSACTION_SERIALIZABLE

This is the slowest transaction level, but is fully ACID-compliant. At this level, transactions are serialized: your transaction is deemed to have taken place in its entirety as if all other committed transactions have either taken place in entirety before or after this transaction. The API states that dirty, nonrepeatable, and phantom reads are prevented with this transaction. It is supported by any ACID-compliant database.

One transaction level is rarely ideal throughout your application. Look for read queries in the application, and consider for each whether any of the problems outlined in the sidebar adversely affect the query for the given data, data update pattern, and query. Reads of static tables or tables that are updated only by the same transaction that reads them can safely use the lowest transaction level. Basically, in transactions where there is no concurrent update possible, you can use TRANSACTION_NONE or TRANSACTION_READ_UNCOMMITTED safely and efficiently. TRANSACTION_SERIALIZABLE is the truly safe option and should be used unless you determine another acceptable level for any particular transaction. Many drivers are delivered with a default transaction level other than TRANSACTION_SERIALIZABLE because they are faster that way, which means that a simplistic evaluation shows the driver (and database) at its best.

User-controlled transactions

Transactions controlled by the user are another significant JDBC bottleneck. Any transaction that requires a user to execute an action (such as clicking OK or Cancel) to close the transaction (i.e., to commit or abort it) is a problem waiting to happen. Inevitably, one or more users forget to terminate the activity or are forced to leave the activity unfinished. Resources are left open in the application and database, and any concurrent activity can easily conflict with the locked resources, resulting in decreased performance throughout the system. Only single-user applications, or applications that are effectively single-user because they don't share any of the same resources between users, are immune to this problem.

The main alternative to leaving a user in control of a JDBC transaction is to use optimistic transactions. Optimistic transactions collect information for update outside of a JDBC transaction and then use a mechanism to check that the update doesn't conflict with any other update that may have been processed in between. Mechanisms for checking for optimistic conflicts include timestamps, change counters, and checking for differences from an expected state.

For example, when the application gathers user-input data for the update, the data can be sent to the database as a batch set of SQL statements that includes time-stamped safeguards that make sure the original data in the database is the same as the data originally used by the client. A successful transaction updates the rows (including the timestamps) to indicate newly changed data. If another update that invalidates the user's changes is made by another user, the timestamps will have changed, and the current transaction needs to be rolled back instead of committed. Usually, no intermediate conflicting transactions have occurred, so most transactions succeed. When a transaction fails, the application displays the entered data along with the changes that caused the conflict. The user then alters and resubmits the data.

Optimistic transactions are unsuitable for applications that consist of multiple transactions that frequently write data concurrently. This pattern of activity would result in frequently failing optimistic transactions and an increase in overall resource usage.

Savepoints and distributed transactions

JDBC 3.0 introduced *savepoints*, which let you mark a point within a transaction and roll back to that point instead of having to roll back the entire transaction. This feature looks very nice, and I would be surprised if designers using JDBC aren't champing at the bit to use it. Unfortunately, savepoints carry significant overhead. I have not yet been able to test how savepoints may affect performance, but I expect that they should be used sparingly or avoided altogether in any performance-critical sections of code. If you do use them, be sure to release their resources by using the Connection.releaseSavepoint(Savepoint) method.

Some products support distributed transactions across multiple connections. The javax.sql package includes XADataSource and XAConnection interfaces to support distributed transactions. However, distributed transactions are significantly slower than normal transactions because of all the extra communication required to coordinate the connections. Avoid distributed transactions unless they are absolutely required.

Database Location

JDBC is a distributed communications protocol that allows the database to run on a different machine from the process initiating the SQL call—i.e., the JDBC client. It provides you with a tuning option of where to run the database.

Running the database on the same machine as the JDBC client means that the JDBC call has a reduced overhead from avoiding a network call. On the other hand, it also means that all the processes run on the same machine, increasing the load on that machine. The disk I/O impact is even more important. If the client process needs to

Some Non-ACID Transaction Problems

A connection using transaction levels other than the full ACID-compliant TRANSACTION_ SERIALIZABLE level can experience many problems. The following examples use a table called TABLE_SIZES that has two columns, TABLENAME and TABLESIZE. They also use two transactions, T1 and T2, where T1 uses the TRANSACTION_SERIALIZABLE level.

A *dirty read* occurs when a transaction can see uncommitted changes to a row. If another transaction changes a value and your transaction reads that changed value, but then the other transaction rolls back its change, the value becomes invalid or "dirty." For example, suppose T2 uses the transaction level TRANSACTION_READ_UNCOMMITTED:

1. Row TABLENAME=USERS has TABLESIZE=11.
2. T1 and T2 start their transactions.
3. T1 updates row TABLENAME=USERS to TABLESIZE=12.
4. T2 reads T1's uncommitted change, reading row TABLENAME=USERS with TABLESIZE=12 because T2's transaction level means that uncommitted changes can sometimes be read.
5. T1 rolls back the transaction, so row TABLENAME=USERS has TABLESIZE=11.
6. T2 still has the invalid row value for row TABLENAME=USERS with TABLESIZE=12, but can work with the "dirty" table-size value and successfully commit changes that may be based on the dirty value.

A *nonrepeatable read* occurs when a row that is not updated during the transaction is read twice within a transaction with different results. If your transaction reads a value and another transaction commits a change to that value, your transaction can read that changed value even though your transaction has not committed or rolled back. For example, suppose T2 uses transaction level TRANSACTION_READ_COMMITTED:

1. Row TABLENAME=USERS has TABLESIZE=11.
2. T1 and T2 start their transactions.
3. T2 reads row TABLENAME=USERS and sees TABLESIZE=11.
4. T1 updates row TABLENAME=USERS to TABLESIZE=12 and commits the change.
5. T2 rereads row TABLENAME=USERS and sees TABLESIZE=12 because T2's transaction level means that changes committed by other transactions can be seen.

A *phantom read* occurs when a transaction reads a row inserted by another transaction that has been committed. If another transaction inserts a row to a table, when your transaction queries that table, it can read the new row even if a previous query in the transaction did not read that row. For example, here's what happens when T2 uses transaction level TRANSACTION_REPEATABLE_READ, where row tablename=users has tablesize=11:

1. T1 and T2 start their transactions.
2. T2 executes SELECT * FROM table_sizes WHERE tablesize>10 and reads one row, tablename=users with tablesize=11.

—continued—

access the same disks or access through the same disk controller as the database, I/O can be compromised drastically.

Applications that are not too large or complex, that have simple database access and update requirements, and that do not use up most of the machine's processing capacity and memory, are probably better off running the database on the same machine. But make sure that the database uses a dedicated disk controller with dedicated disks, so that database disk I/O is not reduced.

Applications that are large or complex, such as application servers and other multi-user server systems, are usually better off running the database on a separate machine. Beware: testing both configurations at lower scales may show that collocating the database on the same machine as the application provides better performance. However, you can be sure that when the system is scaled up, the system resource requirements of the application and the database will conflict severely, causing reduced system scalability.

Performance Checklist

- I/O can show up as significant in profiling even if I/O is not itself the bottleneck.
- It is worthwhile to have separate measurements available for the JDBC subsystems.
- Use JDBC wrappers to measure the performance of database calls.
- `ResultSet.next()` can spend a significant amount of time fetching rows from the database.
- JDBC wrappers are simple, robust, and low-maintenance.
- Get the JDBC driver right. Using the wrong driver can destroy JDBC performance.
- Use JDBC 3.0 or the latest JDBC version if possible.
- Use connection pooling.
- Optimize the SQL to apply set-based (multi-row) processing rather than one row at a time. Use temporary tables and conditional expressions for extra efficiency. Avoid expensive expressions like `upper()`. Use extra fields, like a COUNT field.

- Avoid moving, deleting, and adding rows where possible: use preinserted and null value rows. Avoid joins, use indexes.
- Use the EXPLAIN statement to examine the SQL operation.
- Don't use `SELECT * ...`, use `SELECT Field1, Field1, ....`
- Access fields by index, not by name (i.e., `resultSet.getString(1)` not `resultSet.getString("field1")`).
- Cache row and field data rather than re-query to access the same data. Using a wrapper, you can transparently cache rows and tables.
- Consider using an in-memory (replicated) database.
- Use parameterized `PreparedStatements` except where a statement will be executed only a few times and there is no spare time to initialize a `PreparedStatement`. Reuse the connection associated with the `PreparedStatement` unless the connection pool supports `PreparedStatement` pooling (as JDBC 3.0 does).
- Create SQL query strings statically, or as efficiently as possible if created dynamically.
- Tune batched row access using fetch sizing.
- Batch updates with `executeBatch()`, explicitly managing the transaction by turning off auto-commit.
- Try to closely match Java data types and database data types. Converting data between badly matching types is slow.
- Avoid using slow metadata calls, particularly `getBestRowIdentifier()`, `getColumns()`, `getCrossReference()`, `getExportedKeys()`, `getImportedKeys()`, `getPrimaryKeys()`, `getTables()`, and `getVersionColumns()`.
- Use metadata queries to reduce the amount of transfers needed in subsequent database communications.
- Consider using stored procedures to move some execution to the database server. Don't use a stored procedure to replace any simple SQL calls. Stored procedures are best used to avoid moving data back and forth across the network.
- Take manual control of transactions with explicit begin and commit calls, turning off auto-commit mode, and combining close transactions to minimize the overall transaction costs.
- Use the lowest transaction isolation level that won't corrupt the application.
- Avoid letting the user control when a transaction terminates.
- Use optimistic transactions when reads predominate over writes.
- Savepoints probably have high overheads.
- Small, lightly used databases can be efficiently located on the same machine as the application server; otherwise, another machine is probably better.

CHAPTER 17

In this chapter:
- Don't Use SingleThreadModel
- Efficient Page Creation and Output
- Body Tags
- Cache Tags
- HttpSession
- Compression
- More Performance Tips
- Case Study: Ace's Hardware SPECmine Tool

Tuning Servlets and JSPs

Most J2EE applications are built around servlets and JSPs. The two types of performance considerations for servlets and JSPs are efficient use of J2SE code (`Strings`, I/O, etc.) and optimizing servlet container-related resources, including the resources provided as part of the Servlet API.

Since JSPs are compiled into servlets, there is usually little difference in performance between them. However, explicitly coding servlets can result in faster applications than JSPs because you have much more control over the fine details of the servlet. This is one of the standard performance tradeoffs: using JSPs results in a better design (separating presentation and logic), but servlets can be tweaked to go faster.

Don't Use SingleThreadModel

`javax.servlet.SingleThreadModel` is a marker interface available to servlet developers that pushes responsibility for thread safety onto the servlet engine. Essentially, if your servlet implements `SingleThreadModel`, the servlet engine creates a separate servlet instance for each concurrent request using the servlet. `SingleThreadModel` does not even guarantee thread safety, since the resulting servlet instances can still access classes and data at the same time. However, `SingleThreadModel` does guarantee that more resources will be used than are needed, as maintaining the multiple instances has some cost to the servlet engine.

Instead of using `SingleThreadModel`, concentrate on writing a thread-safe multithreaded servlet. See "Avoiding Serialized Execution" in Chapter 10 for details on writing efficient thread-safe code. Writing your servlet with big synchronized blocks may be highly thread-safe but won't scale. For example, the following rather extreme implementation synchronizes the entire servlet activity:

```
public class MyVeryThreadSafeServlet extends HttpServlet {
  ...
  public void doGet(HttpServletRequest req, HttpServletResponse res)
      throws ... {
```

```
    synchronized(this)
    {
      //Everything happens in the synchronized block so that
      //we have a thread-safe servlet
      ...
    }
  }
  ...
```

With this servlet implementation, every HTTP request processed by this servlet would have to go through the same synchronized monitor from start to finish, so only one request could be processed at a time, regardless of how many threads you spawned for this servlet. Other concurrent requests would wait until the current request was processed before starting execution. If your servlet received an average of one request per second and the processing took an average of half a second, then this implementation is adequate.

However, if your servlet received an average of one request per second and the processing took an average of two seconds, then your servlet can process an average of only one request every two seconds—i.e., half the requests. This is independent of the CPU capability of the server. You could have plenty of spare CPU power; indeed, if you had eight CPUs, this implementation would leave seven of them mostly idle. The result is that the server listen queue would fill up quickly, and your servlet (actually, the TCP stack) would simply reject half the connections. To sum up:

- Don't use SingleThreadModel.
- Make the servlet thread-safe.
- Try to minimize the amount of time spent in synchronized code while still maintaining a thread-safe servlet.
- Use as many servlet threads as are needed to handle the request throughput.
- Where a limited number of services must be distributed among the servlet threads (for example, database connections), use resource pools (such as database connection pools) to provide optimal service distribution.
- The larger the request service time, the greater the number of threads you need to maintain adequate response times for a given rate of requests.

Efficient Page Creation and Output

The following principles will help you optimize page creation and output and thus improve the performance of your servlet.

Minimize Output and Logging

Output slows down the servlet. Minimize your output as much as possible. If you are logging from your servlet, log only essential data and buffer the output. (Don't turn

---

off logging completely; monitoring servlet performance is essential to maintaining good performance, and eliminating logging is counterproductive. Without logging, it is more difficult to determine if there is a performance problem and where it might be). A dynamically configurable logging framework, such as the `java.util.logging` package briefly covered in Chapter 8, or the open source Log4J, available from *http:// jakarta.apache.org/log4j/docs/index.html*, is very helpful, as you can put in a great deal of logging and selectively turn on those log statements you need at runtime.

For both logging and page output, use the `print( )` methods in preference to the `println( )` methods, where appropriate. `System.out`, `println( )` can cause output to be flushed, prematurely ending the effectiveness of buffer optimization. For HTML output, `println( )` adds only nonsignificant whitespace to the output, adding overhead with no benefit. For JSPs, you can set the output buffer size with the directive `<%@ page buffer="12kb" %>` (or a similar amount).

Use Strings Efficiently

Time spent constructing HTML page output is significant for many servlets. Use efficient `String` manipulation techniques, as described in Chapter 5.

When you need to build strings internally, use `StringBuffers` or other efficient `String` or byte array-building mechanisms. Avoid generating intermediate `Strings` and other objects whenever possible. Avoid the + and += concatenation operators.

Use Bytes Versus Chars

HTML uses bytes, so you don't need to use `chars` unless it is required for your application. Simply using `chars` does not cause any overhead; the conversion between `chars` and bytes creates overhead (i.e., bytes are read and written on the socket).

Use Network Buffers Efficiently

You will output the results, and the output goes to a network buffer. Although the network buffer flushing is not under your control, it will be consistent for any one platform, so try to find its operational capabilities. Use the network buffer by using `print( )` on partial strings rather than building the strings in memory and then writing them. However, the network stack can be suboptimal in flush timing. Tests by Acme Laboratories identified that the amount of data sent in the first network packet was crucial to optimal performance. Sending the response headers and the first load of data as a single packet instead of as two separate packets improved performance significantly (see *http://www.acme.com/software/thttpd/benchmarks.html*). Doing so may require building the data in memory, and then writing it in one chunk.

Display Static Pages Quickly

Static pages display more quickly than dynamic pages. You can gain improved performance by taking advantage of this fact, using static pages and page elements when possible.

Browsers take time to calculate how much space each element should take. Precalculate all formatting that is constant for all generated HTML pages. Use cached in-memory Strings or byte arrays to hold the portions of pages that are common to multiple pages. This should be faster than repeatedly generating the same elements. The headers are usually mostly the same, and most web sites have a look and feel that involves the same elements in many pages. Formatting precalculation is done automatically for JSP pages in the compilation phase.

High-volume web applications pre-render pages that are the same for all users. Those pages can be served directly from a separate web server optimized for serving static pages, taking away a significant load from the servlet.

Some complete or partial pages can become temporarily static. Cache these pages or sections, and regenerate them only when they need to change.

Even more efficient than returning a cached page is to tell the browser to use its own cached page. As part of its request, the browser can send a header telling the server that it has a cached copy of the requested page, including when the copy was cached. The server can reply that the cached copy is valid without resending the page, in which case the browser simply displays the page from its cache. This capability is supported by servlets through the getLastModified( ) method. Implement the getLastModified( ) method in your servlet to return the page's last modified timestamp and allow the browser to use its cached page when possible.

Optimize Data Conversions

Optimize data conversions that you need to make when generating your HTML output. For example, use timestamps instead of formatted Dates, or if you need to format a Date, don't do so from scratch each time. Instead, use a partially cached formatted Date and fill in the changed values. (The date changes only once a day, hours only change once an hour, etc.) There is seldom any requirement to display the current time in a page, and even when it is required, it cannot be accurate to the second because of download time and time differences between machines.

Use ServletOutputStream Directly (Servlets Only)

Use the ServletOutputStream directly to send binary data rather than wrapping the ServletOutputStream in a PrintWriter. JSPs cannot do this; they always use the PrintWriter, which is one of the reasons why a JSP may be slightly slower than the equivalent servlet. A JSP could forward to a plain servlet when binary data needs to be sent.

If you will use a `PrintWriter`, initialize its buffer in the constructor with the optimal size for the pages you write.

Optimize Partial Page Display

Flushing the HTML output in sections lets the browser display partial pages more quickly. As already mentioned, putting more than the header in the first section improves performance. But bear in mind that the browser can display partial pages if it has enough information, so try to send the page sections that help the browser display partial pages quickly. Explicitly flush those sections, rather than waiting for the network buffer to fill and flush the data, to give the user the impression of a faster display.

Body Tags

Various uses of body tags can make a difference in performance.

Use Include Directive, Not Action

The include *directive* `<%@ include file="somefile.html" %>` is a compile-time action, so it doesn't affect runtime performance (it takes effect when the JSP is compiled into a servlet). The include *action* `<jsp:include page="somefile.jsp" flush="true"/>` is a runtime action, so it adds overhead and decreases performance. Use the `include` *directive* whenever possible.

Minimize Scope of useBean Action

The `useBean` action has a scope associated with the bean created by the action. The scope defines the lifetime of the bean. Minimize the scope to minimize the resources taken by the bean—e.g., `<jsp:useBean id="mybean" scope="page" />`. You will need to use a wider scope (`request`, `session`, or `application`) to use beans with pages that are included.

Minimize Custom Tags

Custom tags have a performance cost, but they are useful. Try to minimize custom tags to only those required. `BodyTags` are more costly to performance than simpler custom tags. Using `BodyTags` to iterate on the page section contents makes the page significantly slower. (On the other hand, Jim Elliott wanted me to point out that custom tags are so much better than the alternative of mixing presentation and logic that eliminating custom tags may not be worth the performance gain.)

Use Redirects Versus Forwards

Redirects (using sendRedirect()) are slower than *forwards* (<jsp:forward ...>) because the browser has to make a new request for the redirect. The forward is a simple call that is internal to the servlet, and a redirect tells the browser to make a new request to the redirected target page.

Cache Tags

Caching can improve the responsiveness of a web site significantly. You should cache pages or page sections for a set length of time rather than update the page or section with each request. Cache tags allow pages and sections of pages to be cached. When the page is executed, the cache tag either retrieves the data from its cache or creates the data and caches it. Cache tags can work on a per-user basis, so they are fairly flexible.

An open source cache-tag library, Open Symphony's OSCache, is available from *http://www.opensymphony.com/oscache/*. Serge Knystautas describes how cache tags can improve performance in a *JavaWorld* article.[*] You can also use the application server's caching facility, and the session and application objects' caching facilities with ServletContext and HttpSession's getAttribute()/setAttribute() methods. Note that "context" has a much wider scope than "session," so use the HttpSession methods for session-related resources. Using the context can reduce scalability by having resources open over multiple sessions unnecessarily.

Caching trades CPU for memory. This tradeoff must be balanced correctly for optimal performance. Optimal caching needs tuning of timeout settings and other parameters. Cache elements reused in many pages need to be monitored to ensure that they do not become bottlenecks. On highly personalized web sites, page-level caching can result in low cache-hit rates, as each page can be mostly unique to each user. In this case, cache tags are of limited use (perhaps only for small page fragments).

HttpSession

The HttpSession object associates particular clients with a session. Under the covers, this association is typically done by using a cookie. HttpSession lets you maintain state associated with the session. If you don't need to maintain session state, there is no need to use HttpSession. You can eliminate the creation of session objects with the JSP directive <%@ page session="false"%>. If you *are* maintaining session state, HttpSession seems to provide adequate performance as long as you are aware of the points covered in the following sections.

---

[*] Serge Knystautas, "Cache in on faster, more reliable JSPs," *JavaWorld*, May 2001, *http://www.javaworld.com/javaworld/jw-05-2001/jw-0504-cache.html*.

Timing Out Sessions

Among the HttpSession methods is setMaxinactiveInterval(int interval), which allows you to specify how many seconds the session can be inactive before it is terminated. Try to set this value as low as possible. However, do bear in mind that too low a setting will really annoy your users if it means that they have to reestablish the session state. On the other hand, leaving session objects around too long can be a heavy drain, especially if each session uses anything significant in the way of server resources. Therefore, this method is a classic performance-tuning parameter, requiring optimization on the basis of testing the application to see what value is best.

You can also have pages automatically refresh themselves with embedded page commands, and these pages can keep a session alive indefinitely, even when the page is no longer in use. Each time the page reloads, the session timeout counter is reset. You can explicitly terminate a session yourself at any time by using the HttpSession. invalidate( ) method.

HttpSession Versus Stateful Session Beans

A number of sources recommend that you use HttpSession objects to manage session state rather than using stateful beans. However, in their book *J2EE Performance Testing with BEA WebLogic Server* (Expert Press), Peter Zadrozny, Philip Aston, and Ted Osborne state that there is no real difference in performance between these two options, as long as the beans are explicitly removed from the container when the session expires.[*] The beans are removed automatically by binding the session to a session listener that calls ejbRemove( ) when the session terminates. Removing the beans is critical to achieving comparable performance. Beans not removed are passivated, which imposes a large overhead on the system and causes enormous performance degradation.

The cited test situation was idealized; the sessions were always removed before the test terminated, and the beans were removed when the session terminated. In a production system, lingering sessions can be a problem. Consequently, for optimal performance across the board, use HttpSession rather than stateful session beans to maintain state. If you prefer stateful session beans for design reasons, ensure timely session termination and bean removal.

HttpSession Serialization

HttpSession objects can be serialized by the servlet engine under certain situations: different conditions in different servlet engines cause this to happen. Serialization has costly overheads (see Chapter 8), and you can minimize the chances of and cost

[*] An excerpt is available at *http://www.sys-con.com/weblogic/article.cfm?id=101*.

associated with serialization. Memory conditions and session longevity are the two primary reasons for serialization of HttpSession objects. Longevity can be minimized by timing out sessions; memory usage is best minimized by reducing the number and size of objects stored in the HttpSession.

If your HttpSession is serialized, the smaller the graph of objects reachable from the HttpSession, the faster the serialization will be. Try to avoid storing large object graphs in the HttpSession, use transient variables wherever possible to avoid serializing objects unnecessarily, and bear in mind the costs of serialization when considering what is stored in the HttpSession.

Distributing Sessions for Higher Scalability

Spreading your requests across multiple application servers helps make the application more scalable. If you are maintaining state, you may need to replicate your sessions across the application servers to handle requests that may be distributed across the servers. However, session replication is expensive. If you use a frontend load balancer for your application distribution, then you should ensure that the load balancer can support "sticky" sessions—i.e., that it automatically routes any particular session to the application server handling that session. DNS and hardware load balancers both support this (DNS by virtue of the cached DNS lookup value). A software load balancer may need to be programmed to handle sticky sessions.

If replication of sessions is a definite requirement, then building your own session mechanism is probably better than using HttpSessions. HttpSession identifiers are not unique or consistent across multiple servers. You can build your own session mechanism without too much difficulty to replicate the HttpSession functionality while ensuring that the session mechanism is optimized for distribution. A file-based distributed session mechanism, implemented by altering URLs to encode the session identifier, is described in Budi Kurniawan's article "Pseudo Sessions for JSP, Servlets and HTTP."* Many web sites use this method of session management.

Efficient Resource Management

Optimize your use of HttpSession objects by following these guidelines, some of which summarize earlier tips:

- Remove HttpSession objects explicitly with HttpSession.invalidate( ) when the session is finished, such as when the user logs out.

- Remove HttpSession objects implicitly by timing out the session with HttpSession.setMaxInactiveInterval( ). Set the timeout as low as is reasonable.

---

* Budi Kurniawan, "Pseudo Sessions for JSP, Servlets and HTTP," *ONJava.com*, 3/01/2001, *http://www. onjava.com/pub/a/onjava/2001/03/01/pseudo_sessions.html.*

- Implement the `HttpSessionBindingListener` for resources that need to be cleaned up when sessions terminate, and explicitly release resources in the `valueUnbound()` method.

- Remove stateful session beans as soon as the session terminates; use the `HttpSessionBindingListener` as described in the last point.

- The servlet `init()` and `destroy()` methods are ideal for creating and destroying limited and expensive resources, such as cached objects and database connections.

- The servlet `init()` method is a good place to perform once-only operations.

- You can use the `jspInit()` and `jspDestroy()` methods in the same way as `init()` and `destroy()`.

Compression

Most popular browsers accept GZIP-compressed pages, decompressing them before displaying them to the user without the user knowing that the page was compressed. Google uses this technique to good effect. If the page size is large—or more precisely, the compressed page compared to the uncompressed page is so much smaller that the download time is consistently measurably reduced—then compressing pages is a worthwhile option. To fully determine the potential benefit of compressing pages, you also need to factor in the extra CPU load and time on the server to compress the file (and the extra time to decompress the file on the client, though you can usually ignore this if the download time is significantly improved). In practice, there is a heavier load on the server, but a significantly faster download for limited bandwidth clients.

The mechanics of the HTTP support for compressed pages follows. First, the browser tells the server that it can handle GZIP-compressed pages by including the header `Accept-Encoding: gzip` in the page request. The server can sense that the browser accepts GZIP compression quite easily by looking for the header with code like this:

```
public boolean acceptsGZIP(HttpServletRequest request) {
  //Get any "Accept-Encoding" headers
  String header;
  Enumeration e = ((HttpServletRequest)request).getHeaders(
                          "Accept-Encoding");
  while (e.hasMoreElements())
  {
    String header = (String)e.nextElement();
    //And check that GZIP is supported
    if ( (header != null) && (header.toUpperCase().indexOf("GZIP") > -1) )
      return true;
  }
  return false;
}
```

Next, if you are going to return the page compressed, your server needs to inform the browser that the page sent to it is compressed. Doing so requires a header to be set in the response:

```
public void setGZIPContent(HttpServletResponse response) {
  response.setHeader("Content-Encoding", "gzip");
}
```

Finally, the SDK directly supports GZIP compression in the java.util.zip package. Furthermore, since the GZIPOutputStream is a type of FilterOutputStream, you wrap the servlet output stream and write the data as you normally would:

```
//Write output. First get the output stream
OutputStream out;
if (acceptsGZIP(request))
{
  setGZIPContent(response);
  out = new GZIPOutputStream(response.getOutputStream( ));
}
else
{
  out = response.getOutputStream( );
}
//Now write the page
...
```

This process is simplified here. In practice, you shouldn't waste time compressing small pages, since there is no gain in network transfer time, so you should test to see if the page is big enough to warrant compression.

You could also use a servlet filter instead of building compression support directly into the servlet. In this case, the filter would wrap the HttpServletResponse object with its own wrapper before passing the wrapped response object down the chain. When the servlet requests the output stream, the wrapped HttpServletResponse object then provides a GZIP-compressed output stream that wraps the original output stream. The effect is the same as the code shown earlier. Sun has contributed a servlet compression filter to the examples supplied with the Tomcat application server, and a *JavaWorld* article* by Jason Hunter describes the filter in more detail.

If you can cache the compressed version of the page the first time you write it, or statically compress the page prior to starting the servlet, then you gain the benefits of compression with none of the overhead. Servlet filters add overhead to servlet processing, so the nonfilter solution is slightly more efficient. However, the filter solution is probably much easier to add to existing deployments.

---

* Jason Hunter, "Filter code with Servlet 2.3 model," *JavaWorld*, June 2001, *http://www.javaworld.com/ javaworld/jw-06-2001/jw-0622-filters.html*.

More Performance Tips

I list many performance tips for servlets and JSPs at *http://www. JavaPerformanceTuning.com/tips/j2ee_srvlt.shtml.* Here's a summary of tips we haven't covered yet.

Turn security checks off

Security checks consume CPU resources. You will get better performance if you can turn security checking off.

Optimize the servlet-loading mechanism

Try to optimize the servlet-loading mechanism (for example, by listing the servlet first in loading configurations).

Avoid reverse DNS lookups

Avoid reverse DNS lookups (e.g., ServletRequest.getRemoteHost( )). These lookups take significant time and block the thread. Instead, log the raw IP addresses and use a separate process to execute reverse DNS lookups to supplement the logs.

Precompile JSPs

Precompile your JSPs to avoid giving the first user a slow experience. Either run the page once before making it public (which compiles it), or use the application server's features to precompile the servlet.

Make the servlet event-driven

The Servlet 2.3 specification adds application and session events. Event-driven applications can often be scaled more easily than process-driven applications. Try to make your servlet event-driven.

Servlet filters mean overhead

Servlet filters provide a standardized technique for wrapping servlet calls. However, they have some overhead, which translates to a reduction in performance.

Separate UI logic from business logic

Separate the UI controller logic from the servlet business logic, and let the controllers be mobile so they can execute on the client, if possible.

Validate data at the client

Validate data as close to the data-entry point as possible, preferably on the client. This reduces the network and server load. Business workflow rules should be on the server (or further back than the frontend). You could use invisible applets in a browser to validate data on the client, but the extra time required to download the applet may make this unusable.

Use Keep-Alive for static sites

HTTP 1.1's Keep-Alive feature gives a higher throughput for static sites, but may be extra overhead for dynamic sites.

Increase server listen queues

Increase server listen queues for high-load or high-latency servers. The listen queue is a TCP/IP-level queue for incoming socket accepts and is set with the second argument to the ServerSocket constructor (if you are explicitly creating a server socket). The application server must expose the parameter as a configuration option for you to adjust this.

Disable auto-reloading

Disable the JSP auto-reloading feature. Auto-reloading is a development feature of many application servers that repeatedly reloads servlets and JSPs. Turn this feature off for performance tests and deployed systems.

Tune pool size

Tune pools in the application server (see Chapter 18 for details).

Access data efficiently

Transform your data to minimize the costs of searching it. If your dataset is small enough, read it all into memory or use an in-memory database (keeping the primary copy on disk for recovery). An in-memory database avoids overhead in several ways: it eliminates passing data in from a separate process, reduces memory allocation by avoiding data copies as it passes between processes and layers, eliminates the need for data conversion, and enables fine-tuned sorting and filtering.

Precalculation expedites some results by making the database data more efficient to access (by ordering it in advance, for example), or by setting up extra data in advance, generated from the main data, to simplify result calculations.

Optimize strings

String optimizations tend to be significant in servlets. See Chapter 5 for standard String optimizations.

Case Study: Ace's Hardware SPECmine Tool

At the end of December 2001, Ace's Hardware published a report[*] on how they optimized their SPECmine tool. The procedure they followed to achieve very fast response time is instructive.

The SPECmine tool itself is a JSP that allows a user to query the SPEC database of benchmarks (*http://www.spec.org/*). The query page (at *http://www.aceshardware. com/SPECmine/index.jsp*) allows the user to specify all the parameters for the query, including how to sort the results. The query is so efficient that most of the transaction time is taken by network communication and browser page display.

---

[*] The full report is available from *http://www.aceshardware.com/read.jsp?id=45000251*.

The first issue was the database data. The SPEC database is accessible in a number of different ways, but none provides the full set of data required by the SPECmine tool. In addition, some data items needed cleaning. Querying the SPEC database each time the SPECmine tool was used would have required multiple connections, data transformations, and parsed and cleaned data. Holding the data locally was an obvious solution, but more than that, holding the data locally in a format optimal for the SPECmine tool query was the best solution. This required the SPEC database to be checked periodically for new entries. New entries must be cleaned and transformed for the SPECmine database. To clean and transform the data, parses and regular expression conversions were changed to table maps, which are easier to maintain, cleaner, and faster. The advantages are enormous:

- Data was now held locally, so the SPECmine query was local rather than remote (across the Internet).
- Data was held in an optimal format for the SPECmine query so that only one query was required to obtain the query result, rather than multiple queries together with data processing
- New SPEC entries could be added to the SPECmine database asynchronously, at off-peak time, with no performance degradation to the SPECmine query engine.

The only disadvantage was that the SPECmine tool would occasionally be out of synch with the SPEC database; i.e., the SPEC database would occasionally hold data that was not available from a SPECmine query. This is perfectly acceptable for the application, and the user was warned of this pitfall. The delay between SPEC data entry and SPECmine update could be minimized by increasing the frequency of checking for new data, if this option was ever desired.

Next, the database query itself was considered. The amount of data in the SPECmine database (and the projected future amount of data) was quite small: megabytes rather than hundreds of megabytes or gigabytes. Consequently, mapping the entire database into memory was feasible. Furthermore, rather than simply map in the data directly, Ace's Hardware decided to convert the data into a Java object format when mapping it in instead of converting data for each query. The result was a very fast in-memory query for the SPECmine tool, requiring minimal extra processing when a query was executed. The main disadvantage was that the application was now more complex than it was with a traditional JDBC query: custom querying and sorting capabilities were required. Locking, data integrity, and scaling would have become issues had the database been larger (or had it required concurrent updates). In that case, the in-memory custom solution would have been less practical, and in-memory caching would be used instead (and used for other sections of the web site).

Further optimizations were then applied to the servlet. There were two main types of optimizations: optimizing query requests with precalculation and reducing String manipulation costs. The precalculation optimizations are interesting. One optimization presorts the result set into various orders. You can do this in a small amount of memory by holding an array of sorted elements, with each element pointing to its main entry holding the full data corresponding to that element. Filtering the pre-sorted array for the elements matching the search criteria gives you a sorted result set.

Another optimization used the fact that a list of strings presented to the user in a list selection box can return indexes to the servlet instead of returning the selected strings. This means that you can use the indexes in an array, rather than the strings, as keys to a `Map`. For SPECmine, the indexes were used with a boolean array to determine which strings were "on" in the search filter.

The remaining `String` manipulation optimizations eliminated duplicate `String` objects, avoided unnecessary `String` concatenations, and precalculated HTML `String` elements that do not need to be dynamically generated. The final optimization applied was the GZIP-compression support outlined earlier in this chapter. The application's speed was such that the search itself was the fastest part of the service, HTML generation took significantly more time, and compression, network transfer, and browser display took most of the total time.

The original report also discussed other parts of the web site, including optimizing parts of the site that need disk-based databases. Ace's Hardware goes into the overall architecture of their JSP-based web site in more detail at *http://www.aceshardware.com/read.jsp?id=45000240*. The site serves about 1 million users per month and displays ten times as many pages, illustrating that high performance can be achieved using servlets and JSPs, without excessive resources or tuning.

Performance Checklist

- Don't use `SingleThreadModel`. Make the servlet thread-safe, but try to minimize the amount of time spent in synchronized code while still maintaining a thread-safe servlet.

- Use as many servlet threads as necessary to handle the request throughput. Use resource pools to distribute resources among the servlet threads.

- The amount of data sent in the first network packet is crucial to optimal performance. Send the response headers and the first load of data as a single packet instead of two separate packets.

- Use `StringBuffers` or other efficient `String` or byte array-building mechanisms. Avoid generating intermediate `Strings` and other objects whenever possible. Avoid the + and += concatenation operators.

- Use the browser's caching mechanism to have pages reread by correctly implementing the `getLastModified( )` method.

- Precalculate all static formatting for generated HTML pages. High-volume web applications prerender pages that are the same for all users.

- Use the `include` directive rather than the `include` action.

- Minimize the useBean action's scope to page where possible.
- Remember that redirects (using sendRedirect( )) are slower than forwards (<jsp: forward ...>).
- Use cache tags (see, for example, *http://www.opensymphony.com/oscache/*).
- Avoid creating HttpSession objects if not needed, and time out HttpSessions when they are needed.
- "Context" has a much wider scope than "session." Use HttpSession methods for session resources.
- Avoid having HttpSession objects serialized by the servlet container. Remove HttpSession objects explicitly with HttpSession.invalidate( ) when the session is finished, such as when the user logs out.
- Implement the HttpSessionBindingListener for any resources that need to be cleaned up when sessions terminate, and explicitly release resources in the valueUnbound( ) method.
- The servlet init( ) and destroy( ) or jspInit( ) and jspDestroy( ) methods are ideal for creating and destroying limited and expensive resources, such as cached objects and database connections.
- Compress output if the browser supports displaying compressed pages.
- Avoid reverse DNS lookups.
- Precompile your JSPs.
- Use Servlet 2.3 application and session events to make the application event-driven.
- Remember that servlet filters have overhead associated with the filter mechanism.
- Validate data at the client if it can be done efficiently.
- Increase server TCP/IP listen queues.
- Disable autoreloading features that periodically reload servlets and JSPs.
- Tune the pool sizes in the server.
- Transform your data to minimize the costs of searching it.

CHAPTER 18

Tuning EJBs

In this chapter:
- Primary Design Guidelines
- Performance-Optimizing Design Patterns
- The Application Server
- More Suggestions for Tuning EJBs
- Case Study: The Pet Store
- Case Study: Elite.com

The performance of EJB-based J2EE systems overwhelmingly depends on their design. If you get the design right, tuning the server is similar to tuning a J2SE system: profile and tune the server, targeting object creation as a priority (since the consequences in a multiuser system are an order of magnitude greater). If you get the design wrong, you are unlikely to simply tweak your way to adequate performance. In contrast, a J2SE application can often achieve adequate performance with a non-optimal design after sufficient performance tuning. This design sensitivity is one of the reasons why J2EE design patterns have become so popular: design patterns assist everyone from novices to experienced designers in achieving adequate performance.

This design sensitivity is also the reason for the many stories about badly performing EJB projects. EJBs are a tradeoff, like most standardized APIs. In exchange for the ability to have a standard for components that developers, managers, tool vendors, and other third-party producers all work together to use, there are some overheads and design issues. Make no mistake: using EJBs compared to build-it-completely-your-way almost always incurs more overhead for your runtime system. Chapter 12 compared a proprietary communication layer to RMI (see Table 12-1), and the situation with EJBs is quite similar. Proprietary is almost always faster. It is also usually more difficult to maintain and support. EJBs have third-party support products for development, testing, tuning, deploying, scaling, persisting, clustering, and load balancing. If you don't need standardized components, EJBs may not be the best option for your project. A plain J2SE + JDBC solution has its own advantages.

Primary Design Guidelines

In "Performance-Optimizing Design Patterns" later in this chapter, I describe several design patterns that help EJB systems attain adequate performance. But first, I will discuss some primary design guidelines to consider before you can apply patterns.

Coarse-Grained EJBs Are Faster

EJBs should be designed to have large granularity—one remote invocation to an EJB should perform a large amount of work instead of requiring many remote invocations. This criterion is extremely important for a successful EJB design. Coarse-grained EJBs tend to provide a more efficient application because they minimize the number of remote communications needed to complete the work.

A more refined guideline is that any remotely accessed EJBs should be coarse-grained. Any EJBs that are *always* accessed locally can be fine-grained, if the local access is not treated as a remote access. Bear in mind that prior to the EJB 2.0 specification, *all* EJB access was (theoretically) treated remotely, even with EJBs in the same container. This means that the parameters could always be marshaled and passed through a socket, incurring a significant portion of remote-calling overhead. (Some application servers detect local EJB communication automatically and optimize that communication to avoid remote-calling overhead.) Since EJB 2.0, local entity beans can be defined, allowing optimized communications for local EJBs. But that is not a runtime decision, so it needs to be factored into the design. Local EJBs were added to the EJB specification to address this issue of improving performance among locally collocated EJBs.

The following are some detailed guidelines for achieving this combination design target of coarse-grained remote EJBs and fine-grained local EJBs. In the following list, I consider EJBs either local or remote, but an EJB can implement both interfaces, if appropriate to your application.

- Design the application to access entity beans from session beans. This optimizes the likelihood that an EJB call is local and supports several other design optimizations (listed in the subsequent section covering design patterns).

- Determine which EJBs will be collocated within the same VM. These EJBs can communicate with one another by using optimized local communications.

- Those EJBs that will (always) be collocated should be:
  - Defined as local EJBs (from EJB 2.0); or
  - Defined normally as remote EJBs and collocated within an application server that is capable of optimizing local EJB communications; or
  - Built as normal JavaBeans, and then wrapped in an EJB to provide one coarse-grained EJB (see the `CompositeEntity` pattern).

- EJBs that communicate remotely should combine methods to reduce possible remote invocations. Multiple calls frequently specify various parameters, and these parameters can be combined as a parameter object to be passed for one remote call. "Message Reduction" in Chapter 12 gives a concrete example of how to combine methods to reduce the number of remote calls required to perform an action.

- Don't design EJBs with one access method per data attribute unless they are definitely local EJBs. (More accurately, don't define data attribute accessors and updators as remote, as they have relatively high overheads.)

- Bear in mind that any EJB service could be called remotely if you define a remote interface for it, and try to anticipate the resulting costs to the application.

EJBs Are Not Data Wrappers

EJBs should not be simple wrappers on database table rows. An EJB should be a fully fledged business object that represents and can manipulate underlying database data, applying business logic to provide appropriate refined information to callers of the EJB. If you need to access database data, but not for business-object purposes, use JDBC directly (probably from session beans) without intermediate EJB objects. EJBs can cause multiple per-row database access and updates. While this inefficiency can be justified when the EJB adds information value to the data, it is pure overhead in the absence of such business logic, and plain JDBC could be optimized much better.

Read-Only Data Is Different

Read-only data should be identified and separated from read-write data. When treating read-only data and read-only attributes of objects, a whole host of optimizations are possible. Some optimizations use design patterns, and others are available from the application server. Transactions that consist purely of read-only data are much more efficient than read-write data. Trying to decouple read-only data from read-write data *after* the application has been designed is difficult.

Stateless Session Beans Are Faster

By definition, a stateless session bean has no state. That means that all the services it provides do not depend on what it just did. So a single stateless session bean can serve one client, then another, and then come back to the first, while each client can be in a different or the same state. The stateless session bean doesn't need to worry about which client does what. The result is that one stateless bean instance can serve multiple clients, thereby decreasing the average number of resources required per client. The stateless bean pool doesn't need to grow and shrink according to the number of clients; instead, it can be optimized for the overall rate of requests.

Most application servers support pools of stateless beans. As each bean services multiple clients, the bean pool can be kept smaller, which is more optimal. To optimize the session-bean pool for your application, choose a (maximum) size that minimizes activations and passivations of beans. The container dynamically adjusts the size to optimally handle the current request rate, which may conflict with trying to choose a single size for the pool.

Stateful beans, in contrast, require one instance for each client accessing the bean. The stateful-bean pool grows and shrinks depending on the current number of clients, increasing pool overhead. If you have stateful beans, try to remove any that are finished so that fewer beans are serialized if the container needs to passivate them (see "HttpSession Versus Stateful Session Beans" in Chapter 17, which details how explicitly removing beans can improve performance).

If you have stateful beans in your design, the best technique to reduce their overhead is to convert them to stateless session beans. Primarily, this involves adding parameters that hold the extra state to the bean methods to pass the bean the current client state whenever it needs to execute. An extended example of converting a stateful bean to a stateless bean is available in Brett McLaughlin's *Building Java Enterprise Applications, Volume I: Architecture* (O'Reilly), and online at *http://www.onjava.com/pub/a/onjava/excerpt/bldgjavaent_8/index3.html*. The example even shows that you can retain the stateful-bean interface while using stateless beans by using the Proxy design pattern.

If state needs to be accessible on the server, you can hold it outside session beans, for example, in an HttpSession object, or in a global cache that provides access to the state through a unique session identifier. Converting stateful session beans to stateless session beans adds extra data to the client-server transfers, but the extra data can be minimized by using identifiers and a server data store. For high-performance J2EE systems, the advantages tend to outweigh the disadvantages.

Cache JNDI Lookups

JNDI lookups, like other remote calls, are expensive. The results of JNDI lookups are also easily cached. There is even a dedicated pattern for caching EJBHome objects (the EJBHomeFactory pattern) because it is such a frequently suggested optimization.

CMP or BMP?

Should you use container-managed persistence (CMP) or bean-managed persistence (BMP)? This is one of the most frequently discussed questions about EJBs. BMP requires the developer to add code for persisting the beans. CMP leaves the job of persisting the beans up to the application server. BMP can ultimately be made faster than CMP in almost any situation, but to do so, you would probably need to build a complete generic persistency layer—in effect, your own CMP. So let's get back to reality. (You could build a very fast, simple persistence layer, mainly raw JDBC calls, but it would not be flexible enough for the kinds of development changes constantly made in most J2EE systems. However, if speed is the top priority, this option is viable.)

BMP can be faster for any one bean. You can build in the persistency that is required by the bean, avoiding any generic overhead. That's fine if you have five EJB types in your application. But more realistically, with tens or hundreds of EJB types, writing optimal BMP code for each EJB and *keeping* that code optimal across versions of the application is unachievable (though again, if you can impose the required discipline in your development changes, then it *is* achievable).

With multiple beans and bean types, CMP can apply many optimizations:

- Optimal locking
- Optimistic transactions
- Efficient lazy loading
- Efficient combinations of multiple queries to the same table (i.e., multiple beans of the same type that can be handled together)
- Optimized multi-row deletion to handle deletion of beans and their dependents

I would recommend using CMP by default. However, CMP is not yet mature, which makes the judgment more complex. It may come down to which technique your development team is more comfortable with. If you do use CMP, profile the application to determine which beans cause bottlenecks from their persistency. Implement BMP for those beans. Use the Data Access Object design pattern (described later) to abstract your BMP implementations so you can take advantage of optimizations for multiple beans or database-specific features. (You may also need to use BMP where CMP cannot support the required logic—e.g., if fields use stored procedures, or one bean maps to multiple tables.)

EJB Transactions

Tuning EJB transactions is much like tuning JDBC transactions; you will find "Transaction Optimization" in Chapter 16 very relevant for EJB transactions. There are a few additional considerations. The following list summarizes optimal transaction handling for EJBs:

- Keep transactions short.
- Commit the data after the transaction completes rather than after each method call. That is, if multiple methods are executed close together, each needing to execute a transaction, then combine their transactions into one transaction. The target is to minimize the overall transaction time rather than simplistically targeting each currently defined transaction.
- Try to perform bulk updates to reduce database calls.
- For very large transactions, use the transaction attribute TX_REQUIRED to get all EJB method calls in a call chain to use the same transaction. Use a session façade that provides a high-level entry point so that all the methods called from that point are included in one transaction.
- Optimize read-only EJBs to use read-only transactions. Use read-only in the deployment descriptor to avoid unnecessary calls to ejbStore( ) by the application server (not all application servers support this feature).

- Choose the lowest-cost transaction isolation level that avoids corrupting the data. Transaction levels in order of increasing cost are `TRANSACTION_READ_UNCOMMITTED`, `TRANSACTION_READ_COMMITTED`, `TRANSACTION_REPEATABLE_READ`, and `TRANSACTION_SERIALIZABLE`.

- Don't use client-initiated transactions in the EJB environment because long-running transactions increase the likelihood of conflict, making rows inaccessible to other sessions. If the client controls the duration of the transaction, you may have no way to force the transaction to close from the server, thus allowing long or indefinite transactions. The longer a transaction lasts, the more likely it is to conflict with another transaction.

- If you need client-initiated transactions, set an appropriate transaction timeout in the *ejb-jar.xml* deployment descriptor file. Setting a timeout ensures that the application doesn't start leaking resources from transactions that are opened at the client but not completed. The deployment descriptor should be something like "trans-timeout-seconds," and you should specify a timeout that is long enough for users to reasonably complete their task.

- Declare nontransactional methods of session beans with `NotSupported` or `Never` transaction attributes (in the *ejb-jar.xml* deployment descriptor file).

- Use a dirty flag where supported by the EJB server or in a BMP or DAO implementation to avoid writing unchanged EJBs to the database. Dirty flags are a standard way to avoid writing unchanged data. The write is guarded with the dirty flag and performed only if the flag is dirty. Initially the flag is clean, and any change to the EJB sets the flag to dirty.

Performance-Optimizing Design Patterns

This is not a book on design patterns. However, because of their importance to EJB design, this section lists design patterns that are particularly relevant. You can find articles that detail these performance-optimizing design patterns at *http://www.JavaPerformanceTuning.com/tips/patterns.shtml*.

Reducing the Number of Network Trips: The Value Object Pattern

A Value Object encapsulates a set of data values. Use a Value Object to encapsulate all of a business object's data attributes and access the Value Object remotely rather than accessing individual data attributes one at a time. The Value Object sends all data in one network transfer. "Message Reduction" in Chapter 12 shows how to use the Value Object pattern to reduce the number of network transfers required to access multiple data attributes. The Value Object pattern can be used bidirectionally to improve performance—i.e., to minimize the number of network transfers to transfer data *to* the server as well as *from* the server. One variation, the Value Object Assembler pattern, uses a Session EJB to aggregate all required data from different EJBs as various types of Value Objects.

Using a Value Object may result in very large objects being transferred if too many data attributes are combined into one Value Object. A large Value Object may still be more efficient than separate multiple remote requests, but typically, only a subset of the data held by a large Value Object is needed, in which case the large Value Object should be broken down into multiple smaller Value Objects, each holding the data subset required to satisfy its remote request. This last approach minimizes both the number of network transfers and the amount of transferred data.

Once transferred, the Value Object's data is no longer necessarily up to date. So if you use the Value Object to hold the data locally for a period of time (as a locally cached object), the data could be stale and you might need to refresh it according to your application's requirements.

Optimizing Database Access: The Data Access Object Pattern and the Fast Lane Reader Pattern

Use Data Access Objects to decouple business logic from data-access logic, allowing decoupling of data-access optimizations from other types of optimizations. Data Access Objects usually perform complex JDBC operations behind a simplified interface, providing a platform for optimizing those operations. Data Access Objects allow optimizations in bulk access and update for multiple EJBs, and also allow specialized optimizations by using database-specific optimized access features while keeping complexity low.

For read-only access to a set of data that does not change rapidly, use the Fast Lane Reader pattern, which bypasses the EJBs and uses a (possibly nontransactional) Data Access Object that encapsulates access to the data. The Data Access Object in the Fast Lane Reader pattern accesses the database to get all the required read-only data efficiently, avoiding the overhead of multiple EJB accesses to the database. The resulting data is transferred to the client using a Value Object. The Value Object can also be cached on the server for repeated use, improving performance even further. This means that the Fast Lane Reader pattern efficiently reads unchanging (or slowly changing) data from the server and displays all of the data in one transfer.

Efficiently Transferring Large Datasets: The Page-by-Page Iterator Pattern and the ValueListHandler Pattern

If long lists of data are returned by queries, use the Page-by-Page Iterator pattern. This pattern is used when the result set is large and the client may not need all of the results. It consists of a server-side object that holds data on the server and supplies batches of results to the client. When the client makes a request, the results of the request are held in a stream-like object on the server, and only the first "pageful" of results is returned. The client can control the page size, and when data from the next page needs to be viewed, the whole page is sent. "Batching II" in Chapter 12 shows how to use a Page-by-Page Iterator pattern to reduce the amount of transferred data and improve client display time.

Note that the Page-by-Page Iterator pattern actually increases the number of transfers made. However, it is an essential pattern for any server handling multiple requests that may return large amounts of data to clients. When implementing the Page-by-Page Iterator pattern, you should try to avoid making copies of the data on the server. If the underlying collection data is concurrently altered, care should be taken to ensure the client gets consistent pages. There is no upper limit to the size of a result set that this pattern can handle.

The ValueListHandler pattern combines the Page-by-Page Iterator pattern with the Fast Lane Reader pattern. The ValueListHandler pattern avoids using multiple Entity beans to access the database. Instead, it uses Data Access Objects that explicitly query the database and return the data to the client in batches rather than in one big chunk, as in the Page-by-Page Iterator pattern.

Caching Services: The Service Locator, Verified Service Locator, and EJBHomeFactory Patterns

The Service Locator pattern improves performance by caching service objects with a high lookup cost. For example, EJBHome objects and other JNDI lookups are often costly, but need to be performed regularly. However, many such objects are infrequently changed and thus ideal for caching. The Service Locator pattern simply interposes a Service Locator between the object initiating the lookup and the actual lookup. The Service Locator caches any looked-up object and returns the cached object where possible.

The Verified Service Locator pattern anticipates that objects in the Service Locator cache occasionally become stale and need to be refreshed. The Verified Service Locator periodically and asynchronously tests the cache elements to identify and refresh stale objects. An asynchronous periodic test minimizes the impact of stale objects to callers of the service, which would otherwise require a time-consuming synchronous call to obtain a refreshed service object. The Verified Service Locator pattern is just one variety of cache-element management among many, such as least-recently-used, element timed expiration, etc. The Verified Service Locator pattern element management is appropriate for JNDI lookups, when cache elements need to be refreshed only when the JNDI server is restarted, which should be infrequently.

The EJBHomeFactory pattern is simply a ServiceLocator dedicated to EJBHome objects. It is such a frequently mentioned optimization that it was given its own name.

Combining EJBs: The Session Façade and CompositeEntity Patterns

Use a Session Façade to provide a simple interface to a complex subsystem of enterprise beans and to reduce network communication requirements. The Session

Façade is normally a session bean that encapsulates the interfaces needed to work efficiently with a set of EJBs. The client communicates efficiently with the session bean, which in turn manages all the EJB calls necessary to complete the operation represented by the Session Façade. The Session Façade can communicate with the EJBs by using local calls rather than remote calls, potentially making the whole operation much more efficient. Communication between the client and the Session Façade is often best handled using Value Objects so that EJB remote interfaces are not transferred across the network. The façade can also handle security and logging more efficiently than multiple EJBs, which would each separately require security checks and logging output.

The CompositeEntity pattern reduces the number of actual entity beans by wrapping multiple Java objects (which would each otherwise be an entity bean) into one entity bean. It is used less frequently than the Session Façade pattern.

Reusing Objects: The Factory and Builder Patterns

The Factory pattern allows optimizations to occur at the object-creation stage by redirecting object-creation calls to a factory object. "Object Design" in Chapter 13 discusses this pattern.

Use the Builder pattern to break the construction of complex objects into a series of simpler Builder objects. A Director object combines the Builders to form a complex object. You can then use Recycler (a type of Director) to replace only the broken parts of the complex object, reducing the number of objects that need to be re-created.

Reducing Locking Conflicts: The Optimistic Locking Pattern

The Optimistic Locking pattern checks for data integrity only at update time and uses no locks. This feature increases the scalability of an application compared to pessimistic locking, since lock contention is avoided. The Optimistic Locking pattern is appropriate when concurrent access predominates over concurrent update (i.e., most sessions spend most of their time reading data, and very little time writing data). If sessions are transactional, transactions should be short.

Write-write conflicts with optimistic transactions can be detected using:

Timestamps
> The updated row contains a timestamp field that should not be newer than when the row was accessed or the transaction started.

Version counters
> A simple version counter is maintained and checked to ensure that it matches the version at transaction beginning.

State comparisons
> At update time, all relevant database data is checked to ensure that it matches the "old" data.

Optimistic locking has high rollback costs when conflicts are detected, so it should not be used when conflicts are frequent.

Load Balancing: The Reactor and Front Controller Patterns

The Reactor pattern demultiplexes events and dispatches them to registered object handlers. It is similar to the Observer pattern (not described here), but the Observer handles only a single source of events, whereas the Reactor pattern handles multiple event sources. The Reactor pattern enables efficient load-balancing servers with multiplexing communications. The multiplexing of network I/O using NIO Selectors is an excellent example of the Reactor pattern. See "Multiplexing" in Chapter 8.

The Front Controller pattern centralizes incoming client requests, channeling all client requests through a single decision point that lets you balance the application at runtime (see also "Clustering and Load Balancing" in Chapter 15). This pattern also allows optimizations in aggregating the resulting view.

Optimized Message Handling: The Proxy and Decorator Patterns

Proxy and Decorator objects let you redirect, batch, multiplex, and delay method invocations. They enable application partitioning by intelligently caching data or forwarding method invocations. See "Caching" and "Application Partitioning" in Chapter 12, which show how to use proxies to improve the efficiency of a distributed application. The Proxy pattern differentiates by Proxies often instantiating their real objects, while the Decorator pattern rarely does. A Proxy object is usually created as a wrapper on the "real" object, and other objects only ever get to handle the Proxy. The Decorator is more typically given the "real" object to wrap, allowing access to both the Decorator and the "real" object. Synchronized wrappers are an example of the Decorator pattern: you can pass the original collection object to the wrapper factory and access both the original collection and the wrapped collection.

Optimizing CPU Usage: The Message Façade Pattern

The Message Façade pattern encapsulates a method call into an object that can be executed asynchronously, allowing process flow to continue without blocking. This pattern is ideal for remotely invoked methods that don't need to return a value; remotely invoked methods that do return values can also be accommodated by storing the result for later retrieval.

The Application Server

Considerations other than performance frequently drive the choice of application server. That might not be as serious as it sounds, since all the most popular application servers target good performance as an important feature. I often read about projects in which the application server was exchanged for an alternative, with performance cited as a reason. However, these exchanges seem to be balanced: for each project that moved from application server A to application server B, there seems to be another that moved in the reverse direction.

Nevertheless, I would still recommend that application servers be evaluated with performance and scalability as primary criteria. The ECperf benchmark may help differentiate EJB server performance within your short list of application servers. Performance-optimizing features to look for in an application server include:

Multiple caches
  Application servers should offer multiple caches for session beans, EJBs, JNDI, web pages, and data access. Caching provides the biggest improvement in performance for most enterprise applications.

Load balancing
  Load balancing is absolutely necessary to support clustered systems efficiently.

Clustering
  Clustering is necessary for large, high-performance systems.

Fault-tolerance (hot replacement of failed components)
  If one part of the system goes down, a fault-tolerant system suffers performance degradation. However, a system without fault tolerance has no service until the system is restarted.

Connection pooling
  You can roll your own connection pool, but one should come standard with any application server.

Thread pooling, with multiple users per thread
  Thread pooling should also be a standard feature. It is necessary to efficiently manage system resources if your application uses hundreds or thousands of threads or serves hundreds or thousands of users.

Optimized subsystems
  All subsystems, including RMI, JMS, JDBC drivers, JSP tags, and cacheable page fragments, should be optimized, and the more optimized, the better. Naturally, optimized subsystems provide better performance.

Application distribution over multiple (pseudo) VMs
  Distributing over VMs provides fault tolerance. The latest VMs with threaded garbage collection may not benefit from this option.

Distributed caching with synchronization
  Supported directly by the application server, distributed caching with synchronization lets clustered servers handle sessions without requiring that a particular session always be handled by one particular server, enhancing load balancing.

Optimistic transaction support
  Optimistic transactions reduce contention for most types of applications, enabling the application to handle more users.

Distributed transaction management
> If you need distributed transactions, they are usually handled more efficiently if the application server supports them.

In-memory replication of session state information
> Holding session state information in memory allows clustered servers to handle sessions without requiring that a particular session be handled by one particular server, enhancing load balancing.

No single points of failure
> Eliminating single points of failure helps fault tolerance. Of course, your application may have its own single points of failure.

Hot-deploy and hot-undeploy applications for version management
> You will need to upgrade your application multiple times. Hot-deployment lets you do so with almost no downtime, enhancing 24/7 availability.

Performance-monitoring API
> A performance-monitoring API is useful if you need to monitor internal statistics, and an application server with a performance-monitoring API is more likely to have third-party products that can monitor it.

Performance-monitoring and analysis tools
> More is always better, I say.

Security Layer

A security layer affects response times adversely. Try to dedicate separate application servers to handle secure transactions. Most types of security (SSL, password authentication, security contexts and access lists, and encryption) degrade performance significantly. Many systems use the frontend load balancer to decrypt communications before passing on requests. If using it is feasible, it is worth considering. In any case, try to consider security issues as early as possible in the design.

Gross Configuration

The gross configuration of the system might involve several different servers: application servers, web servers, and database servers. An optimal configuration runs these servers on different machines so each has its own set of specifically tuned resources. This avoids access conflicts with shared resources.

When this separation is not possible, you need to be very careful about how the servers are configured. You must try to minimize resource conflicts. Allocate separate disks, not just separate partitions, to the various servers. Make sure that the operating-system page cache is on yet another disk. Limit memory requirements so it is not possible for any one server to take an excessive amount of memory. Set process priority levels to appropriately allocate CPU availability (see Chapter 14 for more details).

When request rates increase, you should be able to maintain performance by simply adding more resources (for instance, an extra server). This target requires both a well-designed application and correctly configured application servers. Try load-testing the system at higher scales with an extra application server to see how the configuration requirements change.

Tuning Application Servers

Application servers have multiple configuration parameters, and many affect performance: cache sizes, pool sizes, queue sizes, and so on. Some configurations are optimal for read-write beans, and others are for read-only beans, etc. The popular application-server vendors now show how to performance-tune their products (see *http://www.JavaPerformanceTuning.com/tips/appservers.shtml*). Several application servers also come with optional "performance packs." These may include performance-monitoring tools and optimal configurations, and are worth getting if possible.

The single most important tuneable parameter for an application server is the VM heap size. Chapters 2 and 3 cover this topic in detail. For long-lived server VMs, memory leaks (or, more accurately, object retention) are particularly important to eliminate. Another strategy is to distribute the application over several server VMs. This distribution spreads the garbage-collection impact, since the various VMs will most likely collect garbage at different times.

Optimal cache and pool sizing are the next set of parameters to target. Caches are optimized by trying to get a good ratio of hits to misses (i.e., when an attempt is made to access an object or data from the cache, the object or data is probably in the cache). Too small a cache can result in useful objects/data being thrown away to make way for new objects/data. Too large a cache uses up more memory than is required, taking that memory away from other parts of the system. Look at the increase in cache-hit rates as memory is increased, and when the rate of increase starts flattening out, the cache is probably at about the right size.

Each pool has its own criteria that identify when it is correctly sized. Well-sized bean pools minimize activation and passivation costs, as well as bean creation and destruction. A well-sized connection pool minimizes the amount of time requests have to wait for an available connection. If the connection pool can vary in size at runtime, the maximum and minimum sizes should minimize the creation and destruction of database connections. For thread pools, too many threads causes too much context switching; too few threads leaves the CPU underutilized and decreases response times because requests get queued.

Other parameters depend on what the application server makes available for tuning. For example, as connections come into the server, they are queued in the network stack "listen" queue. If many client connections are dropped or refused, the TCP listen queue may be too short. However, not all application servers allow you to alter the listen queue size. (See the backlog parameter, the second parameter of the java. net.ServerSocket constructor.)

More Suggestions for Tuning EJBs

A few additional tuning suggestions for EJBs are listed here:

- Beans.instantiate( ) incurs a filesystem check to create new bean instances in some application servers. You can use the Factory pattern with new to avoid the filesystem check.
- Tune the message-driven beans' pool size to optimize the concurrent processing of messages.
- Use initialization and finalization methods to cache bean-specific resources. Good initialization locations are setSessionContext( ), ejbCreate( ), setEntityContext( ), and setMesssageDrivenContext( ); good finalization locations are ejbRemove( ) and unSetEntityContext( ). Failures to allocate or deallocate resources need to be handled.

Case Study: The Pet Store

Sun created a J2EE tutorial application called the Pet Store.* In the Pet Store, there was no attempt to focus on performance. In a marketing coup in early 2001, Microsoft took the badly performing basic Pet Store application and reimplemented and optimized it in .NET, using the results to "show" that .NET was over 20 times faster than J2EE. (The .NET optimizations appear mostly to have been SQL optimizations together with moving much of the application server logic to database-stored procedures.) A few weeks later, Oracle took the original Pet Store code, keeping it in J2EE, and optimized the application.† The resulting optimized J2EE application performed over 20 times faster than the .NET implementation.

Here's how Oracle optimized the application:

Optimized lazy loading of data
> The original Pet Store didn't try to optimize data handling. All information that might be needed is automatically loaded on the client. This is unrealistic in real-world applications that should minimize data transfers. Oracle changed the application to load only needed information. (Lazy loading is discussed in Chapters 4, 8, and 12.)

SQL query optimization
> The Pet Store made no attempt to optimize the SQL queries. This lack of optimization is appropriate for a tutorial, where the most simple SQL is easier to

---

* See *http://java.sun.com/blueprints/code/index.html#java_pet_store_demo*.

† Oracle's Pet Store benchmark report is available at *http://otn.oracle.com/tech/java/oc4j/pdf/9ias_net_bench.pdf*. You may also want to check out the discussion of the Oracle improvements in the *Server Side* (*http://www.theserverside.com/home/thread.jsp?thread_id=12753*).

understand. Oracle converted some SQL to more optimal statements. (Chapter 16 discusses SQL optimization.)

No unnecessary updates

Oracle changed the EJBs so they use `isModified( )` to avoid unnecessary database updates. It is always good practice to avoid doing what doesn't need to be done. (This is a good example of using a dirty flag, discussed earlier in the "EJB Transactions" section.)

Reduced contention to improve scalability

Some methods opened multiple database connections. These methods were rewritten to use only one connection at a time, reducing contention and increasing scalability. (SQL optimization is discussed in Chapter 16, and contention costs in Chapter 15.)

Limited number of items retrieved by queries

The Pet Store application default settings produced too much unnecessary data. Oracle used the Page-by-Page Iterator pattern with limited page size to improve performance and scalability.

Session data stored in session, not context

Session data was moved from the `ServletContext` to the `HttpSession`, and the JSP was modified to use the session rather than the context. Without this change, multiuser access to the Pet Store application was very limited, as all catalog access to the DB was forced through a single connection. (This topic is discussed briefly in "Cache Tags" in Chapter 17.)

Connections shortened

Connection code was rewritten to keep the DB connections very short, as is optimal with connection pooling. (SQL optimization is discussed in Chapter 16, and transaction optimization in the "EJB Transactions" section.)

String handling optimized

String-handling code was rewritten to use `StringBuffer` instead of `String`, removing unnecessary concatenations. (Chapter 5 discusses string optimizations.)

The combined effect of these optimizations from Oracle produced a greater than 400-fold improvement in performance.

Case Study: Elite.com

Elite.com is a successful Internet startup subsidiary of Elite Information Group, and provides an online time and billing solution. David Essex reviewed the J2EE technology behind the Elite.com web site for *Enterprise Development* magazine.[*] Elite.com's solution is similar to many J2EE implementations, leveraging the full range of J2EE

---

[*] See *http://www.devx.com/upload/free/features/entdev/2000/07jul00/de0007/de0007-1.asp*.

technologies as well as other non-Java technologies. The report covers only a few performance enhancements, but they show some of the most common high-level J2EE performance issues:

Perform work asynchronously whenever possible

Elite.com includes a queueing subsystem that asynchronously accepts external communications, such as email entries. Entries can be batched and run with minimal impact on the online system. (Chapters 12 and 15 discuss asynchronous queuing.)

Concurrency conflicts are the biggest limitation to scalability

Like most enterprise applications, Elite.com experienced conflicting concurrent access to some resources. When this caused severe decreases in performance in one subsystem, Elite.com solved the problem by using a resource pool (an EJB connection pool shared among servlets), improving the subsystem performance. (Contention costs are discussed in Chapter 15.)

Local is much faster than remote

Moving components so they are local to each other can significantly improve performance by eliminating marshalling and remote-transfer overhead. Collocating the EJBs and servlets and converting the communication to local calls can speed performance dramatically. (This topic was discussed earlier in this chapter.)

Performance Checklist

- The performance of EJB-based J2EE systems overwhelmingly depends on getting the design right. Use performance-optimizing design patterns: Value Object, Page-by-Page Iterator, ValueListHandler, Data Access Object, Fast Lane Reader, Service Locator, Verified Service Locator, EJBHomeFactory, Session Façade, CompositeEntity, Factory, Builder, Director, Recycler, Optimistic Locking, Reactor, Front Controller, Proxy, Decorator, and Message Façade.

- Explicitly remove beans from the container when a session is expired. Leaving beans too long will get them serialized by the container, which can dramatically decrease performance.

- Coarse-grained EJBs are faster. Remote EJB calls should be combined to reduce the required remote invocations.

- Design the application to access entity beans from session beans.

- Collocated EJBs should be defined as Local EJBs (from EJB 2.0), collocated within an application server that can optimize local EJB communications, or built as normal JavaBeans and then wrapped in an EJB to provide one coarse-grained EJB (CompositeEntity design pattern).

- EJBs should not be simple wrappers on database data rows; they should have business logic. To simply access data, use JDBC directly.

- Stateless session beans are faster than stateful session beans. If you have stateful beans in your design, convert them to stateless session beans by adding parameters that hold the extra state to the bean methods.

- Optimize read-only EJBs to use their own design, their own application server, read-only transactions, and their own optimal configuration.

- Cache JNDI lookups.

- Use container-managed persistence (CMP) by default. Profile the application to determine which beans cause bottlenecks from their persistency, and implement bean-managed persistence (BMP) for those beans.

- Use the Data Access Object design pattern to abstract your BMP implementations so you can take advantage of optimizations possible when dealing with multiple beans or database-specific features.

- Minimize the time spent in any transaction, but don't shorten transactions so much that you are unnecessarily increasing the total number of transactions. Combine transactions that are close in time to minimize overall transaction time. This may require controlling the transaction manually (i.e., turning off auto-commit for JDBC transactions or using TX_REQUIRED for EJBs).

- J2EE transactions are defined with several isolation modes. Choose the lowest-cost transaction isolation level that avoids corrupting the data. Transaction levels in order of increasing cost are: TRANSACTION_READ_UNCOMMITTED, TRANSACTION_READ_COMMITTED, TRANSACTION_REPEATABLE_READ, and TRANSACTION_SERIALIZABLE.

- Don't leave transactions open, relying on the user to close them. There will inevitably be times when the user does not close the transaction, and the consequent long transaction will decrease the performance of the system significantly.

- Bulk or batch updates are usually more efficiently performed in larger transactions.

- Lock only where the design absolutely requires it.

- Beans.instantiate() incurs a filesystem check to create new bean instances in some application servers. Use the Factory pattern with new to avoid the filesystem check.

- Tune the message-driven beans' pool size to optimize the concurrent processing of messages.

- Use initialization and finalization methods to cache bean-specific resources. Good initialization locations are setSessionContext(), ejbCreate(), setEntityContext(), and setMesssageDrivenContext(); good finalization locations are ejbRemove() and unSetEntityContext().

- Tune the application server's JVM heap, pool sizes, and cache sizes.

In this chapter:
- The Primary Resource
- Books
- Magazines
- URLs
- Profilers
- Optimizers

CHAPTER 19

Further Resources

The Primary Resource

The *JavaPerformanceTuning.com* web site contains abundant resources relevant to Java performance, including over 3,000 performance tips, references to hundreds of articles, a newsletter providing all the latest Java performance news, lists of tools and descriptions, Java performance discussion group roundups, and basically anything relevant to Java performance. Be sure to visit *http://www.javaperformancetuning.com/*.

Books

- *Algorithms in C++*, Robert Sedgewick (Addison Wesley)
- *The Art of Computer Programming*, Donald Knuth (Addison Wesley)
- *Building Java Enterprise Applications, Volume I: Architecture*, Brett McLaughlin (O'Reilly)
- *Concurrent Programming in Java*, Doug Lea (Addison Wesley)
- *Data Structures and Algorithm Analysis in Java*, Mark Weiss (Peachpit Press)
- *High Performance Client/Server*, Chris Loosley and Frank Douglas (John Wiley & Sons)
- *Inside the Java 2 Virtual Machine*, Bill Venners (McGraw-Hill) (see *http://www.artima.com/insidejvm/resources/*)
- *Introduction to Computer Performance Analysis with Mathematica*, Arnold O. Allen (Academic Press)
- *J2EE Performance Testing*, Peter Zadrozny and Philip Aston (Expert Press)
- *Java Distributed Computing*, Jim Farley (O'Reilly)
- *Java Threads*, Scott Oaks and Henry Wong (O'Reilly)
- *Learning Java*, Pat Niemeyer and Jonathan Knudsen (O'Reilly)
- *Performance Engineering of Software Systems*, Connie Smith (Addison Wesley)

- *Sun Performance and Tuning*, Adrian Cockcroft and Richard Pettit (Prentice Hall)
- *System Performance Tuning*, Mike Loukides (O'Reilly)
- *Windows NT Applications: Measuring and Optimizing Performance*, Paul Hinsberg (MacMillan Technical Publishing)
- *Windows NT Performance Monitoring, Benchmarking, and Tuning*, Mark T. Edmead and Paul Hinsberg (New Riders)
- *Writing Efficient Programs*, Jon Louis Bentley (Prentice Hall)

Magazines

- *OnJava* (*http://www.onjava.com*)
- *Dr. Dobb's Journal* (*http://www.ddj.com*)
- *Java Developer's Journal* (*http://www.sys-con.com/java*)
- *JavaWorld* (*http://www.javaworld.com*)
- *Java Pro* (*http://www.fawcette.com/javapro*)
- *Byte* (*http://www.byte.com*)
- *New Scientist* (*http://www.newscientist.com*)
- *IBM Systems Journal* (*http://www.research.ibm.com/journal*) (see Volume 39, No. 1, 2000 — Java Performance)
- *Java Report* (*http://www.adtmag.com/java/index.asp*)

URLs

- O'Reilly (*http://www.oreilly.com*)
- Java (*http://www.java.sun.com*)
- Perl (*http://www.perl.com*)
- Pavel Kouznetsov's jad decompiler (*http://kpdus.tripod.com/jad.html*)
- IBM alphaWorks site (*http://www.alphaworks.ibm.com*)
- Vladimir Bulatov's HyperProf (*http://www.physics.orst.edu/~bulatov/HyperProf/*)
- Greg White and Ulf Dittmer's ProfileViewer (*http://www.capital.net/~dittmer/profileviewer/index.html*)
- JAVAR experimental compiler (*http://www.extreme.indiana.edu/hpjava/*)
- Jalapeño server JVM (*http://www.research.ibm.com/journal/sj/391/alpern.html*)
- Java supercomputing (*http://www.javagrande.org*)
- Java supercomputing (*http://www.research.ibm.com/journal/sj/391/moreira.html*)

- Web robot guidelines (*http://www.robotstxt.org/wc/robots.html*)
- GemStone application server (*http://www.gemstone.com*)
- Profiling metrics (*http://www.research.ibm.com/journal/sj/391/alexander.html*)
- Bill Venner's discussion of optimization (*http://www.artima.com/designtechniques/hotspot.html*)
- Doug Bell's article discussing optimization techniques (*http://www.javaworld.com/jw-04-1997/jw-04-optimize.html*)
- Classic but old Java optimization site (*http://www.cs.cmu.edu/~jch/java/optimization.html*)
- Rouen University String Matching Algorithms site (*http://www-igm.univ-mlv.fr/~lecroq/string*)
- Generic Java (*http://www.cs.bell-labs.com/~wadler/gj*)
- The Logging API (*http://www.onjava.com/pub/a/onjava/2002/06/19/log.html*)
- The NIO packages (*http://www.javaworld.com/javaworld/jw-09-2001/jw-0907-merlin.html*)
- Echidna multiprocessing library (*http://www.javagroup.org/echidna/*)
- Article covering Multiprocess JVM technology (*http://www.onjava.com/lpt/a//onjava/2001/09/25/optimization.html*)
- Garbage collection analysis articles (*http://wireless.java.sun.com/midp/articles/garbage/*; *http://dcb.sun.com/practices/devnotebook/gc_perspective.jsp*; *http://www.javaworld.com/javaworld/jw-01-2002/jw-0111-hotspotgc.html*)
- Hendrik Schreiber's GCViewer tool, which visualizes the output of GC logging generated from the -verbosegc option, available from (*http://www.tagtraum.com/*)
- "Optimizing Hash Functions For a Perfect Map" (*http://www.onjava.com/pub/a/onjava/2001/01/25/hash_functions.html*)
- "Optimizing a query on a Map" (*http://www.javaworld.com/javaworld/jw-11-2000/jw-1117-optimize.html*)
- Example of converting a stateful bean to a stateless bean (*http://www.onjava.com/pub/a/onjava/excerpt/bldgjavaent_8/index3.html*)
- "Cache in on faster, more reliable JSPs," Serge Knystautas, *JavaWorld*, May 2001 (*http://www.javaworld.com/javaworld/jw-05-2001/jw-0504-cache.html*)
- Open Symphony's OSCache open source cache-tag library (*http://www.opensymphony.com/oscache/*)
- "Filter code with Servlet 2.3 model," Jason Hunter, *JavaWorld*, June 2001 (*http://www.javaworld.com/javaworld/jw-06-2001/jw-0622-filters.html*)

Profilers

Many of these profilers have been reviewed in the various magazines listed previously. You can usually search the magazine web sites to identify which issue of the magazine provides a review. Often the reviews are available online. The profiler vendors should also be happy to provide pointers to reviews. The annual "best of Java" awards includes a section for profilers (see the *Java Developer's Journal*).

- Borland's OptimizeIt! (*http://www.borland.com/optimizeit*)
- Sitraka's JProbe (*http://www.klgroup.com*)
- PureLoad from Minq Software (*http://www.minq.se/products/pureload/index.html*)
- SockPerf from IBM alphaWorks (*http://www.alphaworks.ibm.com/tech/sockperf*)
- DevPartner Java Edition from Compuware Corporation (*http://www.compuware.com/numega/*)

Optimizers

- PreEmptive's DashO optimizer (*http://www.preemptive.com*)
- TowerJ environment (compiler & runtime) from Tower Technology Corporation (*http://www.towerj.com*)
- TowerJ review (*http://www.javaworld.com/javaworld/jw-10-1999/jw-10-volano_p.html*)
- JOVE (*http://www.instantiations.com/jove/*)
- Condensity from Plumb Design (*http://www.condensity.com*)
- JAX size optimizer from IBM alphaWorks (*http://www.alphaworks.ibm.com/tech/jax/*)
- jres resource manager and compressor from IBM alphaWorks (*http://www.alphaworks.ibm.com/jres/*)
- Jshrink size optimizer from Eastridge Technology (*http://www.e-t.com/jshrink.html*)

Index

Symbols

& (ampersand)
  && (boolean And) operator, 193
  & (logical And) operator, 193
  &= (shorthand arithmetic) operator, 82
<< (left shift) operator, 140
*= (shorthand arithmetic) operator, 82
{ }, assigning newly created array to array
    variable, 126
^ beginning of line indicator in regular
    expressions, 161
$ end of line indicator in regular
    expressions, 161
- (minus sign)
  -- (shorthand arithmetic) operator, 82
  -= (shorthand arithmetic) operator, 82
+ (plus sign)
  + and += string concatenation
    operators, 131, 503
  ++ operator, 82
  += (shorthand arithmetic) operator, 82
  string concatenation operator, replacing
    with StringBuffer, 124
?: (conditional) operator, 211
" in string literals, 131
/= (shorthand arithmetic) operator, 82
| (vertical bar)
  | (boolean-OR) operator, 324
  || (shortcircuit boolean-OR)
    operator, 193, 324
  |= (shorthand arithmetic) operator, 82

A

accept( )
  ServerSocket class, 302
  ServerSocketChannel class, 257
access control, 108
  avoiding, 83
  avoiding use of accessor methods with
    public instance variables, 187
  batching access methods, 377
  batching database accesses, 488
  cached access, 337–344
    examples, 338–344
  canonicalizing objects and, 112
  collection queries, directly accessing
    elements, 325
  costs of, 416
  Data Access Objects in EJB, 522
  direct access to class internals, 74
  eliminating extra access calls, 325
  load balancing and, 302
  locking shared resources, 406
  optimizing objects for access, 415
  to parallel collections, 345–348
  queues, 303
  serialization and, 236, 239, 243
  sorting and, 262
  thread synchronization and, 279
  threads, 106
  variables and, 187
Ace Hardware SPECmine tool, case study on
    optimization, 512–514

We'd like to hear your suggestions for improving our indexes. Send email to *index@oreilly.com*.

ACID properties of transactions, 495
    problems with non-ACID
        transactions, 498
actions, directives vs., 505
adaptive optimization (HotSpot VM), 78
addBatch( ), 489
aggregation services, 393
algorithms
    array matching, 160
    Boyer-Moore string search, 164
    collection comparisons, 162
    compression, 248
    conversion, overhead of, 47
    for data structures, 314–366
        identifying optimal, 316
        scaling behavior, 315
        performance checklist, 366
    dependency on data, 163
    inefficient, causing excess object
        creation, 102
    load-balancing, 459
    network access, 441
    Neubert's flashsort, 273
    optimizing compilers and, 80
    quicksort, 165, 260
    read-ahead, 9
    recursion, converting to iteration, 353
    recursive, 211
    scaling behavior, 272
    scavenging, 24
    sorting, 260, 271
    stateless algorithm objects, 415
allocate( ) (ByteBuffer), 253
allocateDirect( ) (ByteBuffer), 252
analysis phase of development, 399–403
    focusing on performance, 423
    performance checklist, 426
    performance goals, setting, 400
    performance-tuning considerations, 400
analysis tools for performance-monitoring,
        EJB application server, 527
analyzing performance statistics, 450
And operators
    && (Boolean And), 193
    & (logical And), 193
append( ) (StringBuffer), 137
Appendable interface, 148
appendTo( ), 148
applets
    design of, 414
    standalone, distribution analysis for, 401
    user interface thread in, 279

application servers, EJB, 525–528
    gross configuration of, 527
    performance tuning, 528
    performance-optimizing features, 526
    security layer, 527
applications
    caching, effects on timings, 21
    configuration for load balancing, 458
    discarding unneeded parts of, 16
    distributed (see distributed applications)
    measurements for benchmarking and
        tuning, 15
    monitoring, 280
        performance checklist, 428
    multiuser, tuning, 14
    network components, performance
        of, 438
    partitioning (see partitioning)
    timing, 20
application-specific code, 396
    analysis phase of development, 399–403
        features, reducing, 402
        performance goals, setting, 400
        tuning considerations, 400
    tuning, 397
arithmetic operators, 82
arraycopy( ) (System), 191
ArrayList class, 318, 319
    comparing with LinkedList, 330–333
        building a large collection, 331
        building a medium collection, 330
        queries, 331
    implementation, 327
    RandomAccess, testing effect of, 335
    synchronized wrapper vs. unsynchronized
        class, 289
ArrayQuickSorter class, 264, 268
arrays
    byte, conversion to char, 195
    cloning, 126
    collection class based on, writing, 398
    converting switches to array
        access, 208–211
    cost of accessing elements, 186
    cost of element manipulation, 186
    initialization of, 126
    linked lists of, 315
    List class and, 319
    mapping objects with, 123
    order of magnitude for accessing
        elements, 272

primitive types
  fast casts of, 249–251
  objects vs., 317
  replacing collections with, 75
  sorting interfaces for, 263
Arrays class
  sort( ), 166, 261
    timings for, 262
  sorting methods, 260
ArraySorter class, 264
assert keyword, 178
AssertionError class, 178
assertions, 91, 177–182
  enabling/disabling at runtime, 178
  overhead of, 178–182
  performance checklist, 188
assignment
  eliminating unnecessary, 86
  variables shared between multiple
    threads, 296–300
asynchronous processing
  communications, 374
    designing distributed applications
      for, 413
    distributed applications, performance
      checklist, 394
  in distrubuted systems, 368
  I/O, multiplexed, 256
  JMS (Java Messaging Service), 460
  scalability, synchronous vs., 460
  in Web Services, 393
atomic access to variables shared between
  multiple threads, 296–300
auto mode for message delivery, 460
auto-commit mode for transactions, 494
awk script for analyzing verbosegc logs, 27
AWTEventMulticaster class, 299

B

background processes
  executing I/O in, 220
  serialization, 233
backups, full and incremental, 233
bandwidth, 401
  limiting browser performance, 56
  measuring for networks, 450
  network latency vs., 439
  perceived performance and, 7
  user, page display and, 455

batching, 15
  data transfers in low-level communication
    optimization, 383–384
  database queries, 386
  determining whether it's faster, 418
  in distributed applications, 377, 379
    data transfers, 368
  in JDBC, 487–490
    accesses, batching by optimizing row
      fetches, 488
    updates, 489
bean-managed persistence (BMP) in
  EJBs, 519
Beans class, 529
beans (see EJBs)
Bell's rule of networking, 414
benchmarks
  asynchronous and background events,
    effects of, 404
  checking against JDK versions, 64
  harness for, 12
  measurements for, 13, 15
  performance checklists for, 17, 98
  performance problems, causing, 14
  predicting performance with, 416
  preventing garbage collection during, 68
  setting, 10, 11
  third-party components, 17
Bentley, Jon, 348
BigDecimal class, replacing with your own
  version, 73
binary output option (-Xrunhprof), 43
bind( ) (ServerSocket), 257
binding, static, 81
bit-shifting, replacing multiplication
  with, 140
blackboard architecture for solving threading
  problems, 312
BMP (bean-managed persistence), 519
body tags
  custom tags, minimizing, 505
  include directive, include action vs., 505
  minimizing scope of useBean action, 505
  redirects vs. forwards, 506
boolean data types, converting to
  strings, 141
boolean objects, object canonicalization
  and, 109
boolean operators, 193
  | (OR) operator vs. || (shortcircuit OR)
    operator, 324

boolean_expression evaluation
    (assertions), 177
bottlenecks, 2
  contention for system-wide resource, 445
  CPU, 3
  disk throughput, 247
  in distributed applications, 367
    identifying, 56–58
  generic locations for in J2EE systems, 446
  identifying, 5, 47
    in memory, 51
    with profilers, 27
  inefficient algorithms, excess object
    creation from, 102
  I/O, 4
    disk, 431
    network, 438
    network, configuration and load, 441
  JDBC, identifying, 463
  memory, 3
  memory leaks, eliminating, 448
  object creation, 127
    reducing and eliminating, 129
  paging, 437
  queues, 301
  requests, correlating with methods, 446
  scaling and, 412
  serialized execution, 287, 291
  shared resources, 404
  strings, 133
  system (load balancing example), 308
Boyer-Moore string search algorithm, 164
broadcast messaging, 460
browsers
  caching pages, 504
  redirecting to different page, 506
BufferedInputStream class, 226
BufferedReader class, 154, 155
buffering
  I/O, 219, 225–233
    bigger buffers, 226
    byte arrays and char arrays, 231
    network, using efficiently for servlet
      output, 503
    profiling output and, 31
    server-side, page flushing and, 453
buffers, NIO
  direct, 252–258
  nondirect, 249–251
Builder pattern in EJB design, 524
business logic in EJBs, 518
byte arrays, conversion to char, 195

ByteArrayOutputStream class, 235
ByteBuffer class, 97, 251
  allocate( ), 253
  allocateDirect( ), 252
bytecodes
  for heap variable manipulation, 184
  reordering in compiler optimizations, 86
  switch statements, versions of, 205
bytes
  changing to ints in arithmetic
    operations, 187
  converting to chars, 231
  converting to strings, 141
  HTML, using for, 503

C

cachefs, 433
caching, 9
  access, cached, 337–344
    data retrieval rates, monitoring, 337
    examples, 338–344
  cache tags for servlets, 506
  circular cache, 341
  code, 77
  in dispatchers, 457
  in distributed applications, 367, 375–377
  distributed data, 414
  DLLs, 434
  DNS lookups, 442, 456
  effects of, 21
    startup, 14
  in EJB
    application servers, capabilities of, 526
    bean-specific resources, 529
    services, 523
  filesystems, 433
  InetAddress class, 442
  intermediate results, 214
  I/O, 219
  JDBC data, 482–484
    in-memory database products, 484
  JNDI lookups, 519
  low-level communication layer
    optimization, 381
  operating system
    filesystem cache, 254
    page cache, 527
  perceived performance and, 9
  shared persistent caches, 416
  static pages, 504
CallableStatement class, defining wrapper
    class for, 468–471

canonicalizing objects, 109–115, 192, 396
    changeable objects, 112
    enumerating constants, 115
    Integer class instances, 110
    serialization and deserialization, 233
    weak references, using, 112–114
canonicalizing strings, 111
    boolean to string conversions, use in, 141
    comparing strings for identity, 162
capacity of collection classes, 105
case
    case-insensitive searches, 163
    converting string to uppercase, 154
    in regular expression matching, 161
    in string comparisons, 162
    in string searches, 154
    in strings, converting to upper or lower
        case, 164
case statements, 205
    contiguous sets of cases, 206
    non-contiguous values for, 206
    reordering for switch statements with
        optimizing compiler, 86
casts
    arrays of primitive types, 249–251
    avoiding, 74
        with collection classes, 316
    avoiding in comparisons, 261
        for sort methods, 263
        implementing standard sort algorithm
            and comparison method for
            class, 262
    costs of, 182–184
        avoiding with collections, 184
        object type, 183
    efficiency of, 195
    eliminating in queries, 325
    instanceof vs., 174
    performance checklist, 188
    removing unnecessary, 84
    throwing exceptions, cost of, 174, 175
C/C++
    compile time compared to JIT VM, 76
    converting Java to C, 95
    illegal pointer manipulations and, 100
    object creation, 102
    string handling and, 150
CGI (Common Gateway Interface) scripts,
        process startup overhead, 416
chaining constructors, 45
    multiple initializations to instance
        variables, 125
    unnecessary assignments in, 86

changeable objects, canonicalizing, 112
channels (I/O), multiplexing, 255–258
char arrays, 188
    converting byte arrays to, 195
    I/O string processing, using for, 228
    strings vs., 150–162
        line filter example, 154–160
        line filtering with regular
            expressions, 160–162
        word-counting (example), 151–153
characters, encoding, 194, 232
CharArrayReader class, 154
charAt( ) (String), 188, 316
CharBuffer class, 161
chars
    changing to ints in arithmetic
        operations, 187
    converting to strings, 141
CharSequence interface, 133
Class class
    forName( ), 193
    getName( ), 150
class libraries, 397
ClassCastException class, 175
classes
    casts of objects, 184
    delivering in uncompressed ZIP or JAR
        files, 97
    JDK, replacing, 72–75
    load-balancing, 303–306
    loading
        class files, 434
        large numbers of, 71
        lazy object initialization and, 128
        preallocating objects, 127
    preventing garbage collection of, 68
    removing unused with compiler, 81
    renaming in compiler optimization, 86
    reusing, 103
    testing for instances of, 192
ClassLoader class, 421
    set*AssertionStatus( ), 178
classloaders, 97
    changes in SDK versions, 47
    runtime server patching with, 421
client mode for message delivery, 460
client requests, centralizing with Front
        Controller pattern, 525
client SocketChannels, obtaining, 257
client-based load balancing, 458
client-initiated transactions in EJB, 521

client/server communications,
        profiling, 56–62
    sockets, replacing, 58–62
    third-party communications packages,
        using, 57
clone( ) (Object), 334
Cloneable interface, 334
cloning objects to avoid using
        constructors, 125
clustering, 455–459
    defined, 455
    EJB application server, 526
    files, 97, 432, 443
    load-balancing dispatcher, using
        with, 457
CMP (container-managed persistence), 519
code
    moving out of loops, 190
    reusable, 397
    unreachable, 90
code motion, 85, 197
CollationKey class, 165, 166, 263
Collator class, 165, 166
    compare( ), 165
    word comparison, varying precision
        of, 155
Collection interface, 263
Collections class, sorting methods, 263
Collections framework, 315–333
    arrays
        advantages/disadvantages of, 316
        collection class based on, 398
        replacing collections with, 75
        (see also arrays)
    casts, avoiding with, 184
    comparing LinkedLists and
        ArrayLists, 327–333
        building a large collection, 331
        building a medium collection, 330
        querying performance, 331
    comparisons, 162
    concurrently adding objects, 406
    Hashtables and HashMaps, 320–323
    Java 2, 317–320
        performance attributes of classes, 318
    parallel collections, accesses and
        updates, 345–348
    performance checklist, 366
    presizing collections, 101
    queries, optimizing, 323–327
        avoiding method accessor, 325
        avoiding synchronization, 325

casts and extra access calls,
        eliminating, 325
    lighter typing of elements, 326
    map queries, 326
    method call in loop test, avoiding
        repetition of, 324
    shortcircuit boolean operators, 324
    reusing collection objects, 103
    shared collections, updating by multiple
        threads, 404
    size and capacity of collection
        classes, 105
    sorting, 316
        interfaces for, 263
    synchronized classes and wrappers, 288
collisions in cache array indexes, 338
    minimizing, 339–341
commit( ) (Connection), 494
Common Gateway Interface (CGI), 416
Common Object Request Broker
        Architecture (see CORBA)
communications
    asynchronous, 374, 413
    failures in, user perceptions of, 454
    monitoring tools, 56
communications layers
    comparison of, 374
    CORBA, message reduction in, 371
    low-level optimizations, 380
        batching transfers, 383–384
        caching, 381
        compression, 380
        multiplexing, 384
    proprietary, 371, 373
    RMI, message reduction in, 372
Comparable interface, 192, 260, 261
    compareTo( ), 165
    quicksort for array of Comparable
        objects, 260
Comparator interface, 165, 192
    compareTo( ), 261
    defining sorting objects for arrays, 263
    optimized comparison wrappers, checking
        for support, 265
compare( )
    Collator class, 165
    Comparator class, 166
    PartialSorter class (example), 169
compareTo( )
    Comparable interface, 165
    Comparator interface, 261

Sortable class, 261
String class, 167
compareToSortable( ) (Sortable), 261
ComparisonKey class, 265
comparisons
 avoiding casts, 262
 identity
  canonical objects, 110
  IdentityHashMap class, 319
  strings, 111
 numeric, efficiency in, 191
 optimizing in sorting, 263
 strings, 162–164
compile( ) (Pattern), 160
compilers
 array initialization and, 126
 assert statements, stripping, 179
 casts, eliminating, 182
 inlining, 2
 javac, runtime optimizations and, 88–94
 JIT (just-in-time), 76
  loops and, 207
  VMs with, 95
 listing of, 95
 optimizing, 79–88
  access control to methods, altering, 83
  assignments, eliminating
   unnecessary, 86
  code motion, 85
  computationally cheaper alternatives,
   using, 82
  cutting dead code and unnecessary
   instructions, 81
  dynamic type checks, removing, 84
  generating helpful information for
   VM, 87
  increasing statically bound calls, 81
  inlining calls, 84
  managing, 87
  reducing necessary parts of compiled
   files, 83
  removing unused methods and
   classes, 81
  removing unused object fields, 83
  renaming classes, fields, and
   methods, 86
  reordering or changing bytecodes, 86
  replacing runtime computations with
   compiled results, 82
  subexpressions, eliminating
   common, 86

 unrolling loops, 84
 what they can't do, 80
 performance checklist, 99
 profiling, object creation, 44
 recursion and, 211
 switches, 206
compile-time resolution of strings, 134
components, analyzing statistics on, 450
CompositeEntity pattern in EJB design, 524
compression, 247
 communication layer optimization, 380
 distributed computing, use in, 367
 performance checklist, 259
 reducing data transfer time with, 414
 searching directly in compressed
  data, 248
 serialized objects, 233
 servlet tuning, use in, 509
 uncompressed ZIP/JAR files, 97
concatenating strings, 90
 + and += operators, 131, 503
 at runtime, extra object generation
  by, 134
concurrency conflicts in EJB, reducing, 531
concurrent execution, 7
concurrent garbage collection, 69, 70, 450
conditional operator (?:), 211
configuration
 applications, for load balancing, 458
 EJB application servers, 527
 network, bottlenecks from, 441
 optimal, for servers, 527
 for service providers, 441
congested networks, 441
connect( )
 Socket class, 249
 SocketChannel class, 249
Connection interface, 464
 commit( ), 494
 getAutoCommit( ), 494
 releaseSavepoint( ), 497
 rollback( ), 494
 setTransactionIsolation( ), 495
 wrapper classes, defining, 465–467
ConnectionConsumer interface, 460
connections
 database
  pooling, 476
  shortening in Pet Shop code, 530
 network, overall speed of, 438
 pooling with EJB application server, 526
ConnectionWrapper class, 465–467

constants, enumerating as string
    replacements, 115
constructors
    array-based collection class, 398
    avoiding use of, 125
    chaining, 45
        multiple initializations to instance
            variables, 125
        unnecessary assignments in, 86
    making private for SINGLETON
        object, 109
    Object class and, 44
    profiling calls to, 31
    serialization and, 236
    string, 135
consumers (JMS), load balancing, 459
container objects, reusing, 103
container-managed persistence (CMP) in
    EJBs, 519
contention for resources
    bottlenecks caused by, 445
    reducing to improve scalability, 530
conversions
    byte to character, 230
    bytes, shorts, chars, and booleans to
        strings, 141
    byte-to-char, with NIO package, 153
    data types, 187
        costs of, 417
    doubles to strings, 146
    floats to strings, 141–146
    ints to strings, 138–140
    JDBC data, minimizing, 480, 491
    longs to strings, 135–138
        avoiding temporary objects, 137
    objects to strings, 147–150
    optimizing in servlets, 504
    stateful bean to stateless, 519
convert( ), 231
copies of objects, reducing generation by
    methods, 124
copy-on-write
    allowing multithreaded updates of
        object, 287
    behavior in canonicalized objects, 112
CORBA (Common Object Request Broker
    Architecture)
    comparison with other communication
        layers, 374
    reducing messges in applications, 371
    scaling, 374
    Web Services vs., 390

counters, unsynchronized vs.
    synchronized, 291
cpu=old option (-Xrunhprof), 38–42
CPUs, 435
    computation time (single-threaded) based
        on availibility, 408
    dynamic method calls and, 2
    limitations on performance, 3
    multiprocessor
        threading and, 294
    optimizing usage of in EJB, 525
    parallelism, 294
    parallelization, 409–411
    predicting performance on for
        parallelism, 407
    process priorities, 436
    time allocated to processes, 20
    time measurements for procedures, 15
    upgrading, 436
    utilization, 435
        analyzing statistics on, 450
        checklist, 443
        measuring, 449
cpu=samples option (-Xrunhprof), 33
cpu=times mode (-Xrunhprof), 36
currentTimeMillis( ) (System), 15, 20, 465
custom tags, BodyTags vs., 505

D

data
    compressing (see compression)
    duplication in distributed
        applications, 414
    parallelism, 411
Data Access Object design pattern, 520
data structures, 314–366
    collections, 315–333
        arrays, advantages/disadvantages
            of, 316
        Java 2 framework, 317–320
        presizing, 101
        specialized for primitives, 124
    in JDBC, 490
    performance checklist, 366
    replacing with faster, 33
data types
    collection elements, lighter typing of, 326
    conversions between, costs of, 417
    converting to strings, 135–147
    dynamic checks, eliminating, 84, 86
    Java, closely matching with database
        types, 500

numeric, using ints for, 191
primitive
    arrays of, fast casts, 249–251
    reducing garbage collection with, 122
    replacing others with ints, 186
    using instead of Object types, 124
    (see also primitive data types)
references, 115–121
types of, 116
DatabaseMetaData class, 467, 492
databases
    JDBC (see JDBC)
    location of, 497
    object, 245
    optimizations, 385
        access with Data Access Objects in
            EJB, 522
        communications, performance
            checklist for, 394
    partitioning, 458
    performance problems with, 447, 461
    server-side processing, minimizing, 478
DataInputStream class, 225, 240
DataOutputStream class, 240
Date class, replacing with your own
        version, 73
Deadlock class (example), 284–286
deadlocks, 282–286, 406
    identifying in stack traces, 450
    unsynchronized classes and, 289
debug statements, 91
debugging code, logging and, 223
decompilers, 87
Decorator objects in EJB, 525
decoupling I/O from application
        processes, 220
defensive programming, 398
defineColumnType( )
        (OracleStatement), 492
defragmenting disks, 434
delays (cumulative), user impatience
        and, 454
delivery of messages
    load balancing and, 460
    modes, 460
deployment descriptors (EJB), setting
        transaction timeouts in, 521
deserialization, 85
    constructors, avoiding use of, 125
    (see also serialization)

design, EJBs
    performance checklist for, 531
    performance-optimizing, 521–525
        caching services, 523
        combining EJBs, 523
        CPU usage, 525
        Data Access Objects, 522
        efficient transfer of large datasets, 522
        load balancing, 525
        message handling, 525
        reducing locking conflicts, 524
        reusing objects, 524
        Value Objects, 521
    primary guidelines, 516–521
        business logic, representing, 518
        caching JNDI lookups, 519
        container-managed or bean-managed
            persistence, 519
        granularity, 517
        read-only data, 518
        stateless session beans for speed, 518
        transactions, 520
design phase of development, 403–412
    distributed applications, 413
    object design, 414
    performance checklist, 426
    predicting performance, 415–418
        batch processing, 418
        comparative performance of
            operations, 415
        data conversions, costs of, 417
        focusing on shared resources, 417
        parallelism, effects of, 417
        relative costs of different access and
            update types, 416
        simulations and benchmarks,
            using, 416
        total work done and design
            overhead, 417
    requiring performance predictions from
        designers, 423
    scaling, 412
    shared resources, 404–412
        locking, 406
        parallelism, 407–412
        transactions, 405
destroy( ) (Servlet), 509
desynchronization, 287–291
    (see also synchronization)

development
    analysis phase, 399–403
        performance-tuning
            considerations, 400
    design and architecture (see design phase
        of development)
    performance checklist for analysis and
        design phases, 426
digital search tries, 348
    ternary search tree, using with, 361–365
dirty flags, using to avoid writing unchanged
    EJBs to database, 521
disks
    I/O, 416, 430
    network, 431
    pages on, 246
    throughput, 247
    (see also hard disks)
distributed applications
    analysis phase of development, 400
    bottlenecks, 367
    client/server communications,
        monitoring, 56–58
    designing for good performance, 413
    measurements of, 16
    performance checklists, 17
    performance tuning, 14, 367, 413
        batching, 377, 379
        caching, 375–377
        message reduction, 371–373
        partitioning applications, 378
    proxies, use in, 525
    streaming, use in, 9
    targeting topmost bottleneck, 5
distributed computing, 367–394
    caching with synchronization (EJB
        application server), 526
    comparing communication layers, 374
    database
        location of, 497
        optimizations of, 385
    garbage collection, 385
    low-level communication
        optimizations, 380
        batching transfers, 383–384
        caching, 381
        compression, 380
        multiplexing, 384
    objects, preallocating, 127
    performance checklist, 394
    tools for application monitoring, 369
        relay servers, 369

    transactions, 527
    Web Services, 386–393
        measuring performance, 387
DLLs (dynamic link libraries), caching, 434
DNS (Domain Name System)
    load balancing, 456
        hardware load balancer, using
            with, 456
    looking up network addresses, 441
    lookup times, measuring for Web
        Services, 389
doGet( ) and doPost( ) methods, getting
    execution times, 448
Domain Name System (see DNS)
double data type
    converting to strings, 146
    Double class, profiling calls to
        equals( ), 31
    parsing doubles from strings with
        floating-point numbers, 122
    replacing with ints for performance
        gains, 186
downloading many pages from a web
    server, 306–311
downtime for servers, performance and, 420
drivers, JDBC, 474–476
    connection pools, 476
    optimized, for EJB application server, 526
dropped packets on congested
    networks, 441
dummy objects, 122
duplicate delivery mode, 460
duplication of data in distributed
    applications, 414
dynamic class loading, lazy initialization
    and, 128
dynamic link libraries (DLLs), caching, 434
dynamic method calls, effect on CPUs, 2
dynamic type checks, eliminating, 84
dynamic URL generation, 457

E

early initialization, 126
ejbCreate( ), 529
EJBHomeFactory pattern, 523
ejbRemove( ), 529
EJBs
    application server, 525–528
        gross configuration of, 527
        performance tuning, 528
        performance-optimizing features, 526
        security layer, 527

bean life cycle methods, monitoring for excessive use, 449
design guidelines, performance-optimizing, 521–525
  caching services, 523
  combining EJBs, 523
  CPU usage, 525
  Data Access Objects, 522
  efficient transfer of large datasets, 522
  load balancing, 525
  message handling, 525
  reducing locking conflicts, 524
  reusing objects, 524
  Value Objects, 521
design guidelines, primary, 516–521
  business logic, representing, 518
  caching JNDI lookups, 519
  container-managed or bean-managed persistence, 519
  granularity, 517
  read-only data, 518
  stateless session beans for speed, 518
  transactions, 520
tuning
  Elite.com case study, 530
  Pet Store case study, 529
  suggestions, additional, 529
elapsed time measurements, 15
Elite.com case study of EJB performance tuning, 530
encapsulation, voiding, 187
enterprise performance problems, sources of, 461
entity beans
  accessing from session beans, 517
  local, 517
environments, specifying in application design, 403
equality comparisons
  converting to identity comparisons for efficiency, 192
  strings, 111
equals( )
  Double class, 31
  Object class, 321
  String class, 162, 321
equalsIgnoreCase( ) (String), 162
error checking, conditional, 177
error messages, customizing for assertion failures, 178
ethereal (communication-monitoring tool), 57

Ethernet packet sizes, 440
event handling, EJB design patterns for, 525
exceptions, 172–177
  conditional error checking, 177
  handling in JDBC, 492
  performance checklist, 188
  reusing, 101, 176
  terminating loops with, 201–205
    speedup for various VMs, 207
  try-catch blocks with, 174–176
  try-catch blocks without, 172–174
  using without stack trace overhead, 176
execute( ) (Statement), 494
executeBatch( ), 489, 490
executeQuery( ), 470
execution
  atomic, 279
  concurrent, 7, 296, 406, 413
  serialized, 287, 291–295
expressions
  eliminating common subexpressions, 86
  partitioning, 411
external data files, reading, 127
Externalizable interface, 233, 238, 258

F

factory design pattern, 125, 127
Factory pattern in EJB design, 524
Fast Lane Reader pattern in EJB design, 522
fault-tolerance in EJB application servers, 526
  single point of failure, eliminating, 527
fields
  constant, inlining, 89
  object, removing unused, 83
  renaming in compiler optimization, 86
  transient, 368
    avoiding serialization of, 233
File class, 217
file descriptors, monitoring available number of, 449
FileChannel class, 252
  map( ), 253
  transferTo( ) and transferFrom( ) methods, 254
FileInputStream class, 225
  using without buffering, 225
  wrapping with BufferedInputStream, 226
FileReader class, 154

files
  class
    delivering in uncompressed ZIP/JAR
      files, 97
    loading, 434
    shrinking, 83
  clustering, 432, 443
  copying with NIO, 252
  memory mapping of, 253
  optimizing I/O for, 221
  preallocating for I/O, 221
  striping, 430
filesystems
  cached, 433
  memory-mapped, 443
fillInStackTrace( ) (Throwable), 177
filtering
  lines from a file, 154–160
    char arrays, using, 155
    regular expressions, using, 160–162
    strings, using, 154
  logging execution times for servlet
    method, 448
FilterOutputStream class, 510
final modifier, 108
finalization methods (EJB), caching
    bean-specific resources with, 529
finalizers, eliminating, 72
find( ) (Matcher), 161
finishConnect( ) (SocketChannel), 249
FixedDimension class (example), 108
FlashSortable interface (example), 274–276
flattening objects, 123
FloatingDecimal class, 47
floating-point numbers
  doubles, converting to strings, 146
  floats, converting to strings, 141–146
  parsing floats and doubles from
    strings, 122
  (see also double data type)
foreground processes, time measurements
  and, 21
forName( ) (Class), 193
forwards, redirects vs., 506
fragmentation, disk, 434
freeMemory( ) (Runtime), 51
Front Controller pattern in EJB design, 525

G

garbage collection, 24
  ArrayList vs. LinkedList, 330
  avoiding, 122–124

flattening objects, 123
  general guidelines to limit object
    generation, 124
  mapping objects with arrays, 123
  primitive data types, using, 122
  temporary variables using primitive
    data types, 187
  distributed, 385
    overhead of, 414
  improvements in, 64–65
  object creation statistics and, 101
  object pool management and, 103
  object references, failure to release, 100
  pauses for, minimizing, 69–71, 450
    concurrent GC, 69, 70
    incremental or train algorithm, 69
    "new" space, enlarging, 70
  preventing during benchmarking and
    heap tuning, 68
  Reference objects, 115
  statistics provided by profilers, 22–27
    -verbosegc option, 22–27
  weak references and, 112
GatheringByteChannel class, 255
gc( ) (System), 22, 32
  disabling, 71
GC analyzer tool, 27
GCViewer tool, 27
GemStone application server, 416
Generate class (example), 371
Generics, 74
get( )
  ArrayList class, 335
  List class, 333
  List interface, 335
  Reference class, 117
getArray( ) (Array), 472
getAutoCommit( ) (Connection), 494
getBestRowIdentifier( )
    (DatabaseMetaData), 492
getChars( ) (String), 316
getColumns( ) (DatabaseMetaData), 492
getIndexInfo( ) (DatabaseMetaData), 492
getInputStream( ) (Socket), 59
getLastModified( ), 504
getName( ) (Class), 150
getOutputStream( ) (Socket), 59
getStatement( ), 472
getString( ) (ResultSet), 482
getVectorPriorToJDK12( ), 106

granularity
  of EJBs, 517
    remote access and, 517
  log storage and, 446
  of Web Services methods, 391, 394
graphics processing, reusing objects in, 102
group( ) (Matcher), 161
GZIP compression, using on web pages, 509
GZIPOutputStream class, 510

H

handles to vectors, memory leak caused
      by, 104
hard disks, 430–435
  cached filesystems, 433
  clustering files, 432
  disk I/O, 431
    striping, 432
  fragmentation, 434
  performance checklist, 443
  sweet spots, transferring data from, 434
hardware load balancing mechanisms, 456
hash partitioning, 411
hash tables, 272
  synchronized and unsynchronized, 291
hashCode( ) (Object), 273, 321
HashMap class, 318, 319, 320–323
  access and update times, comparing with
      TernarySearchTree, 351
  access, plain vs. cached, 338
  wrapped in WeakHashMap
      implementation, 121
HashSet class, 318
Hashtable class, 318, 319, 320–323
  access, plain vs. cached, 338
  specialized class for keys
      (example), 321–323
  synchronization, 288
HashtableEntry class, 40
hasNext( ) (Iterator), 333
Heap Analysis Tool (HAT), 33
heap, tuning, 66–72
  benchmarking considerations, 68
  fine-tuning, 68–72
    disabling System.gc( ) calls, 71
    eliminating finalizers, 72
    expanding the heap, 68
    extreme heap and intimate shared
        memory, 71
    loading huge number of classes, 71
    minimizing pauses, 69–71
    per-thread stack size, 71
    RMI garbage collection, 71
  for EJB application server, 528
  gross tuning, 66
  measuring JVM heap size, 448
  monitoring size of, 461
  problems with larger heap, 66
  starting vs. maximum heap size, 67
heap variables, 184
hierarchical method invocation, overhead
      involved in, 2
horizontal scalability, 455
hostnames, DNS lookups of IP
      addresses, 456
hot replacement of failed components in EJB
      application server, 526
hot-deploy/undeploy applications for version
      management, 527
HotSpot, 21
  assert statements, stripping, 179
  garbage collection and, 65
  loops
    exception-terminated, 201
    unrolling, 198
  object pooling and, 103
  optimizations and, 232
  profiler, 37
  timings, 230
  VM optimizations in, 78
  VM startup times and, 77
HTTP servers, writing contents of multiple
      buffers in one I/O operation, 255
HttpServletResponse class, 510
HttpSession class, 506–509
  caching, 506
  invalidate( ), 507
  optimizing use of, 508
  serialization, 507
  session data, storing in, 530
  setMaxinactiveInterval( ), 507
  stateful session beans vs., 507
HttpSessionBindingListener class, 509
HyperProf program, 42

I

identity comparisons
  canonical objects, 110
  replacing equality comparisons with, 192
  strings, 111, 162
IdentityHashMap class, 318, 319
idlj utility, 372

if statements, conditional error
    checking, 177
include directive, 505
increment( ) (ThreadRace), 282
incremental backups, 233
incremental or "train" garbage collection
    algorithm, 69
index tables, 243
indexes
    cache array, minimizing
        collisions, 339–341
    collections and, 315
    finding for partially matched
        strings, 344–348
    int data types for variables, 191
    partitioning and, 411
InetAddress class, 442
init( ) (Servlet), 509
initialization, 14, 125–126
    early/late, 126
    lazy, 127, 376
    preallocating objects, 127
initialization methods, caching bean-specific
    resources with, 529
inlining, 2, 84
    constant fields, 89
    limits on, 92
    with -O option, 91
input/output (I/O)
    buffering, 219
    caching, 219
    caching output, 337
    counting operations, 246
    disk, 430, 431
        fragmentation, 434
        limitations from, 3
    filesystems, cached, 433
    logging, 223
    network, 438–442
        DNS lookups, 441
        latency, 439
        limitations from, 3
        priority of processes, 21
        TCP/IP stacks, 440
    new I/O packages (see NIO)
    performance checklist, 258
    performance improvement
        techniques, 220
    replacing System.out, 221–223
    servlet output, tuning, 502
    ServletOutputStream class, 504
    system level, 219

threaded, 280
    tuning performance (example), 224–233
        buffering, 225–233
InputStreamReader class, 194
insertion sorts, 274
insertRow( ) (ResultSet), 472
instance variables, 184
    public, avoiding accessor method use
        with, 187
    static vs., 101
instanceof operator, 176
    casts vs., 174
    checking classes for RandomAccess
        implementation, 334
    RandomAccess, guarded test for, 336
    resolution at compile time, 182
instantiate( ) (Beans), 529
int data types
    converting to strings, 138–140
    generating integers for any object, 273
    index variables, use for, 191
    Integer class, canonicalizing instances
        of, 110
    replacing other primitive types with, 186
interfaces
    in casting, cost of, 184
    J2EE systems, performance
        bottlenecks, 446
    java.sql, 464
    performance benefits of, 414
intern( ) (String), 111, 120, 163, 192
internationalization
    filtering lines and, 155
    sorting internationalized strings, 164–170
    strings and, 132
        replacing strings, 74
        tuning strings, 133
Internet
    congestion, performance perception
        and, 453
    dropped packets, 441
    latency and, 439
invalidate( ) (HttpSession), 507
invariants, 91
invoke( ) (Method), 194
I/O (see input/output)
IP addresses
    DNS lookups for hostnames, 456
    DNS lookups for networks, 441
isConnectionPending( )
    (SocketChannel), 249
isEmpty( ) (WeakHashMap), 121

isolation levels for transactions, choosing lowest-cost, 521
iteration
    converting recursive algorithms to, 353
    converting recursive searches to, 215–217
Iterator class
    hasNext( ), 333
    next( ), 333

J

J2EE
    performance tuning, 445–462
        analyzing statistics, 450
        clustering and load balancing, 455–459
        JMS (Java Messaging Service), 459–461
        load testing, 451
        load-balancing algorithms, 459
        monitoring and profiling tools, 445–447
        performance planning, 445
        user perception of performance, 452–455
    Pet Store tutorial application, 529
    server-side monitors, 20
    (see also EJBs; JDBC; JSP; servlets)
JAR files (uncompressed), for class delivery, 97
Java
    advantages of, 2
    converting programs to C, 95
Java Application Monitor, 387
Java Messaging Service (see JMS)
Java Naming and Directory Interface (JNDI), caching lookups, 519
Java Native Interface (JNI)
    avoiding data transfers through, 97
    overhead of, 96
javac compiler, runtime optimizations and, 88–94
    (see also compilers)
java.io package, 194
javap disassembler, 206
JavaPerformanceTuning.com (web site), 533
JAVAR compiler, 79
JavaServer Pages (see JSP)
JavaSpaces, as implementation of blackboards, 312
java.sql interfaces, 464
java.util.zip package, 510

javax.sql package, 497
JDBC (Java Database Connectivity), 463–500
    bottlenecks, identifying, 463
    drivers, optimized for EJB application server, 526
    measuring performance, 463–474
        core java.sql interfaces, 464
        wrapping classes with proxy objects, 465–474
    performance checklist, 499
    requests, measuring, 449
    tuning, 474–500
        batching, 487–490
        caching data, 482–484
        connection pooling, 476
        data conversions, minimizing, 491
        data structures, 490
        database location, 497
        database server-side processing, 478
        handling exceptions, 492
        JDBC drivers, 474–476
        metadata, 492
        optimizing SQL, 477
        prepared statements, 484–487
        set-based processing, 478
        stored procedures, 493
        transactions, 494–497
        transferred data, minimizing, 480
JDBCLogger class, 473
JDK (Java Development Kit)
    improvements in, 64–99
        better optimizing compilers, 79–88
        compiling to native machine code, 94
        faster VMs, 75–79
        garbage collection, 64–65
        native method calls, 95
        performance checklists, 98
        replacing classes, 72–75
        sharing memory, 72
        Sun's javac compiler, 88–94
        tuning the heap, 66–72
        uncompressed ZIP/JAR files, 97
    Logging framework (Version 1.4), 223
    -prof option (Version 1.1.x), 38–42
    -verbosegc option
        Version 1.2, 23
        Version 1.3, 24
    -Xprof option (Version 1.3), 36
JIT compilers, 76
    assert statements, stripping, 179
    Neubert's sorting algorithm and, 273

JMS (Java Messaging Service)
   optimized for EJB application server, 526
   performance checklist, 462
   persistent queue elements, 301
   tuning, 459–461
JNDI (Java Naming and Directory Interface),
     caching lookups, 519
JNI (Java Native Interface)
   avoiding data transfers through, 97
   overhead of, 96
journaling, 484
JSP (JavaServer Pages)
   optimized tags for EJB application
     server, 526
   tuning, 501–515
     case study on Ace Hardware
       SPECmine tool, 512–514
     compression, use in, 509
     efficient page creation and
       output, 502–505
     more performance tips, 511
     performance checklist, 514
jspDestroy( ), 509
jspInit( ), 509
just-in-time compilers (see JIT compilers)
JVM (see VMs)

K

keywords
   assert, 178
   synchronized, 279, 282, 288
   volatile, 298
kill -QUIT signal, 450

L

late initialization, 126
latency, 401
   network, 439
lazy initialization, 127
   accessor methods for proxy server, 376
lazy loading (code optimization
     example), 529
least-recently-used (LRU) cache
     (LinkedHashMap), 319
left shift (<<) operator, 140
length( ) (String), 188
levels for transactions, 495
   choosing lowest-cost, 521
levels of logging, 224
line endings in regular expression pattern
     matching, 161

line filtering
   regular expressions, using, 160–162
   strings vs. char arrays, 154–160
linked lists
   of arrays, 315
   collections and, 315
   recursive search method, changing to
     iterative, 214
   sorting, 316
LinkedHashMap class, 318, 319
LinkedHashSet class, 318
LinkedList class, 318, 319
   comparing with ArrayList, 330–333
     building a large collection, 331
     building a medium collection, 330
     queries, 331
   implementation, 329
   RandomAccess, testing effect of, 335
List interface, 318
   get( ), 333, 335
lists of Strings, avoiding casts for, 184
literals, string, 131
load balancing, 301–311, 455–459
   algorithms for, 459
   classes for, 303–306
   CPU computation time and, 411
   in distributed application design, 413
   EJB application server, 526
   EJB design patterns for, 525
   example of, 306–311
   mechanisms for, 455–458
     application configuration, 458
     client-based, 458
     database partitioning, 458
     dispatching requests or redirecting to
       proxies, 457
     DNS, 456
     hardware, 456
     server-pooled objects, 457
     URL-based, 457
   performance checklist, 313
   TCP/IP, using, 302
   Web Services, 392
load testing
   J2EE applications, steps in, 451
   performance checklist for, 461
   Web Services, 390
loading classes
   large numbers of, 71
   lazy initialization and, 128
   preallocating objects for, 127

thread, starting separate for, 98
uncompressed ZIP/JAR files, using, 97
local EJBs, 517, 531
local procedure calls, time overhead of, 416
local variables, 184
locales, internationalized string sorting
   and, 168
localization, internationalized string sorting
   and, 164
locking
   methods, 282
   optimizations and, 406
   reducing conflicts with Optimistic
      Locking pattern, 524
logging, 223
   change logs, 233
   client/server communications, 57
   garbage collection output, 27
   granularity, 446
   integrating for performance, 425
   I/O calls, 247
   J2EE applications, tool for, 447
   JDBC, 470
   JDBCLogger class, 473
   JDK 1.4 framework (example of
      using), 223
   open source implementation of JDK 1.2
      and 1.3 logging APIs, 223
   performance monitoring tools, 446
   performance-logging features in
      applications, 426
   RMI, enabling, 449
   from servlets, minimizing, 502
   sockets, providing for, 59
   web server layer, adding to, 390
logical And (&) operator, 193
logical Or (|) operator, 193
LogWriter class, 223
long data types
   converting to strings, 135–138
   replacing with ints for performance
      gains, 186
LongVector class (example), 74
loop counters (local and static), comparing
      costs of, 185
loops, 190–205
   copying arrays with arraycopy( )
      (System), 191
   efficient comparisons in, 191
   int data types, using for index
      variables, 191
   I/O, avoiding execution in, 221
   moving code out of, 190
   moving one-time calculations out of, 85
   moving to native routines, 96
   performance checklist, 99, 217
   putting most common case first, 193
   reducing temporary objects in, 124
   reflection, avoiding in, 194
   temporary variables, use of, 190
   terminating with exceptions, 201–205
      speedup for various VMs using, 207
   termination tests, avoiding method calls
      in, 191
   threads, sleeping restlessly in, 417
   unrolling, 84, 198
LRU (least-recently-used) cache
      (LinkedHashMap), 319

M

machine code (native), compiling to, 94
Macintosh, TCP/IP stacks, 440
main( ) (ObjectCreationMonitoring), 46
map( ) (FileChannel), 253
Map interface, 318
   implementations of, 319
   optimizing queries, 326
marshalling time, inferring for Web
      Services, 390
Matcher class
   find( ), 161
   group( ), 161
matches( ) (String), 160
MatchReader class (example), 156–160
Math class, replacing with StrictMath, 73
maxMemory( ) (Runtime), 51
measurements
   analyzing statistics from, 450
   application response times and
      throughput, 412
   benchmarks, 13
   checklist for, 17
   communication layers, 374
   for distributed applications, 16
   of I/O operations, 246
      disk I/O, 431
   multithreading, timing, 295
   network speeds, 438
   profilers and, 20
   serialization and, 235
   skewing by rewriting previously written
      objects, 234
   timing exceptions, 174
   transmission statistics, 440

measurements (*continued*)
    what to measure, 15
    what, where, and how, 447
memcntl( ), 220
memory
    cycling through, 100
    freeing with garbage collection, 65, 112
        (see also garbage collection)
    in-memory database products, 484
    leaks in, 100
        caused by vector handles, 104
    physical, locking heap in, 71
    profiling usage by runtime system, 51–56
    RAM, 436
    reusing objects, balancing against free
        memory needs, 103
    runtime, reducing, 115
    session state information, holding in, 527
    shared, 72
        I/O performance and, 220
    size of, 94, 100
    system, 3
        updates to, 416
    VM startup time and, 76
    (see also heap, tuning)
memory mapping of files, 253
memory-mapped filesystems, 433, 443
MemoryMonitor class (example), 53
MemorySampler class (example), 52
Mercury Interactive Corporation analysis of
    enterprise performance, 447
message calls, reducing, 367, 371–373
    CORBA example, 371
    performance checklist, 394
    proprietary communications layer, 373
    remote invocations of EJBs, 517
    RMI example, 372
Message Façade pattern in EJB design, 525
message-driven beans in EJB, pooling, 529
MessageListener interface, 460
messaging
    broadcast, point-to-point, and
        unicast, 460
    Java Messaging Service (see JMS)
    multicast publish-and-subscribe, 460
metadata, 492
    performance checklist, 500
method calls
    eliminating for performance gains, 32
    inlining with compiler, 84
    in loop termination tests, avoiding, 191
    moving out of loops, 190

    to native code, 95
    profiling tools for, 27–43
        HotSpot and 1.3 -Xprof, 36
        Java 2 cpu=samples output, 33–36
        Java 2 -Xaprof option, 42
        JDK 1.1.x -prof and Java 2
            cpu=old, 38–42
        -Xhprof option, 42
    reflection, avoiding use of, 194
    RMI (see RMI)
method parameters, 187
methods
    access control for, altering to speed up
        calls, 83
    bean life cycle, monitoring for excessive
        use, 449
    entry points, 398
    granularity of, 391
    hierarchical invocation, overhead involved
        in, 2
    inlining by compiler, 2
    mapping requests to, 446
    remote method invocation (see RMI)
    removing unused with compiler, 81
    renaming in compiler optimization, 86
    static, 109
        avoiding creation of objects, 122
    synchronized, 287
    tail-recursive, 212
        (see also recursion)
Microsoft,
    reimplementation and optimization of Pet
        Store application in .NET, 529
    Windows systems (see Windows)
mmap( ), 220
monitoring performance
    applications, 280, 418
        performance checklist for, 428
    J2EE tools for, 445–447
        downloading from web site, 447
        features to look for, 446
    operating systems, 435
monitors
    locking methods, 282
    locking/unlocking, 283
    synchronization and, 279
mount command (Unix), 433
multicast publish-and-subscribe
    messaging, 460
multiplexing, 384
    I/O channels with NIO, 255–258

multiplication, replacing with
  bit-shifting, 140
multithreading
  for application responsiveness, 8
  performance checklist, 313
  timing, 295
  (see also threads)
multiuser applications, tuning, 14

N

native code
  calls to, 95
  compiler optimization of, 87
  compiling to, 94
  fallbacks for failures to load, 97
.NET Pet Store application
  implementation, 529
netstat utility, 440
  profiling and, 57
network sniffers, 58
networks
  analyzing capabilities of in application
    development, 401
  application components, performance
    of, 438
  bandwidth, measuring, 450
  caching, effects on timings, 21
  I/O, 438–442
    DNS lookups, performance problems
      with, 441
    latency, 439
    network bottlenecks, 441
    speed-testing facility, 438
    TCP/IP stacks, 440
  latency of, 414
  packet sniffers, 20
  performance checklist, 442
  performance problems with, 447, 448,
    461
  throughput, 247
  transfer rates and connection latency (load
    balancing example), 309
  transfer times, measuring for
    benchmarks, 17
Neubert's flashsort, 273
new I/O (see NIO)
new operator, calling chained constructors
    during object creation, 125
"new" space, 70
next( )
  Iterator class, 333
  ResultSet interface, 472

NIO, 249–258
  byte-to-char conversion, 153
  connecting client sockets, 249
  direct buffers, 252–258
  multiplexing, 255–258
  nondirect buffers, 249–251
  performance checklist, 259
nonblocking I/O, 220, 256
non-static methods, synchronization of, 282
nontransactional methods of session
    beans, 521
notify( ) (Object), 279
nslookup utility, 442
null values
  avoiding unnecessary checks for, 82
  references, 115
numbers
  efficient comparisons of, 191
  formatting
    floating-point conversions to
      strings, 142
    in long to string conversion, 138

O

Object class, 279
  changing to record object creation, 44
  clone( ), 334
  hashCode( ), 273
  toString( ), 150
  wait( ) and notify( ) methods, 279
object creation, 100–130
  garbage collection, avoiding, 122–124
    flattening objects, 123
    general guidelines to limit object
      generation, 124
    mapping objects with arrays, 123
    primitive data types, using, 122
  guidelines for efficient memory
      usage, 101
  initialization, 125–126
    early and late, 126
  lazy initialization, 127
  performance checklists, 129
  preallocating objects, 127
    ternary search tree optimization, 356
  profiling, 43–50
  Reference objects, 115–121
    SoftReference flushing, 116
    types, 116
  reusing objects, 102–115
    canonicalizing objects, 109–115
    pool management, 103–106

object creation, reusing objects (*continued*)
  reusable parameters, 108
  ThreadLocal objects, 106
statistics on, 101
StreamTokenizer vs. char array word
    counters, 153
ObjectCreationMonitoring class
    (example), 46, 47–50
ObjectInput interface, 334
ObjectInputStream class, 236
ObjectOutput interface, 334
ObjectOutputStream class, 236
objects
  canonicalizing, 192, 396
  casts of, 183
  converting to strings, 147–150
  creation of (see object creation)
  databases of, relational databases vs., 385
  designing, 414
    optimizing for update or access, 415
    performance checklist, 427
    reusability, 415
  field, removing unused with optimizing
    compiler, 83
  heap space for creating new, 70
  passing into methods which fill in object
    fields, 188
  pooling, load balancing with, 457
  references to (see references)
  reusing in EJB, 524
  root, 40
  serialization of, 233–244
  temporary (see temporary objects)
  unnecessary, avoiding with JNI, 96
Observer pattern, 525
open( )
  Selector class, 257
  ServerSocketChannel class, 257
Open Symphony, OSCache, 506
operating systems
  caching, effects on timings, 21
  disk-cache flush, avoiding performance
    hit, 97
  memory-mapping files, 253
  NIO operations and, 254
  page cache, 527
  performance checklist, 442
  signal handling, 421
  timing applications and, 20
operators
  arithmetic, shorthand versions of, 82

instanceof, 176
  casts vs., 174
  resolution at compile time, 182
logical And, 193
logical Or, 193
short-circuit, 193
string, 131
Optimistic Locking pattern in EJB
    design, 524
optimistic transactions, 496
  EJB application server, support of, 526
  write-write conflicts with, detecting, 524
optimizations, 395–428
  analysis phase of development, 399–403
    considerations, 400
    features, reducing, 402
  assertion overhead, eliminating, 179
  collection queries, 323–327
  compiler, 79–88
    access control to methods, altering, 83
    assignments, avoiding unnecessary, 86
    code motion, 85
    computationally cheaper alternatives,
      using, 82
    cutting dead code and unnecessary
      instructions, 81
    dynamic type checks, removing, 84
    eliminating common
      subexpressions, 86
    generating helpful information for
      VM, 87
    increasing statically bound calls, 81
    inlining calls, 84
    javac and, 88–94
    managing compilers, 87
    reducing necessary parts of compiled
      files, 83
    removing unused methods and
      classes, 81
    removing unused object fields, 83
    renaming classes, fields, and
      methods, 86
    reordering or changing bytecodes, 86
    runtime computations, replacing with
      compiled results, 82
    unrolling loops, 84
  container-managed persistence in
    EJBs, 520
  databases, 385
  design and architecture, 403–412
    distributed applications, 413
    object design, 414

predicting performance, 415–418
scaling, 412
shared resources, 404–412
EJBS, design patterns for, 521–525
    caching services, 523
    combining EJBs, 523
    CPU usage, 525
    Data Access Objects, 522
    efficient transfer of large datasets, 522
    load balancing, 525
    message handling, 525
    reducing locking conflicts, 524
    reusing objects, 524
    Value Objects, 521
I/O operations, with NIO direct
        buffers, 252–258
loops, 190–205
    copying arrays with System.arraycopy(
        ), 191
    efficient comparisons, 191
    int data types for index variables, 191
    moving code out of, 190
    putting most common case first, 193
    reflection, avoiding, 194
    temporary variables, using, 190
    terminating with exception, 201–205
more factors affecting
        performance, 420–422
    server downtime, 420
    training users, 420
    user interface usability, 420
with -O option, 91
performance checklist, 426
performance planning, 422–426
    deploy with performance-logging
        features, 426
    designers, requiring performance
        predictions from, 423
    focus on performance in analysis
        phase, 423
    integrating performance logging, 425
    specifying performance
        requirements, 422
    test environment for performance,
        creating, 424
    test performance and use results, 425
    testing simulation or skeleton
        system, 424
repeated comparisons of internationalized
        strings, 165
runtime, 91
string equality tests, 163

ternary search tree, creating node pool
        for, 356
testing and documenting, 18
tuning after deployment, 418–419
tuning class libraries and beans, 396
    application-specific code, 397
VM, 77
when to avoid, 396
when to make, 395
optimizers, listing of resources on, 536
options (runtime), performance and, 93
Or operator (logical Or), 193
Oracle, optimization of Pet Store
        application, 529
orders of magnitude, 272, 315
OutOfMemoryError class, 51
OutputStream class, 256
overhead
    of array initialization, 126
    of assertions, 178–182
    of communications in distributed
        applications, 414
        proprietary communication layer, 37
    of CPU parallelization, 409
    of data conversions, 47
        in JDBC, 491
    of design, 417
    of disk/file seeking, 432
    of dynamic URL generation, 457
    of exceptions, 174
    of files, 221
    of hierarchical method invocation, 2
    of Java Native Interface (JNI), 96
    of locks, 406
    of longs and doubles, 186
    of method polymorphism, 2
    of paging, 437
    of parallelism, 407
    of performance monitoring in J2EE, 446
    of process startup, 416
    of recursion, 211
    of remote calling of EJBs, 517
    runtime, 2
    of serialization, 239
        bypassing, 240
    of stack trace, 176
    of startup, reducing with thread
        pooling, 416
    of strings
        concatenating at runtime, 134
        in SQL statement execution, 487

overhead (*continued*)
    of synchronous processing over the
        Internet, 393
    of tests in loops, 200
    of thread synchronization, 285–295
    of transaction savepoints, 497
    of Web Services, round-trip, 389

P

packet sizes (TCP/IP), 440
packet sniffers, 20, 440
packets
    dropped, 441
    resending on congested networks, 441
page cache (operating system), 527
page display
    partial display, optimizing, 505
    perceived performance and, 452
    performance checklist for, 462
Page-by-Page Iterator pattern
    in EJB design, 522
    Pet Store application otpimization, use
        in, 530
pages
    browser caching of, 504
    caching with cache tags, 506
    compressing, 509
    JavaServer Pages (see JSP)
    static, displaying quickly, 504
paging, 437
parallelism
    CPU load and, 436
    distributed applications, designing to
        support, 413
    effects on performance, predicting, 417
    JMS message processing, 460
    optimizations and, 407–412
        data parallelism, 411
    performance checklist, 427
    of search spaces, 312
parameters
    method, 187
    reusable, in object creation, 108
    tuneable, in TCP/IP stacks, 440
PartialSorter class (example), 169
partitioning, 414
    applications
        distributed, 368, 378
        EJB message handling design, 525
        performance checklist, 427
    data, 411

databases, 386, 394
    load balancing with, 458
    expressions, 411
    raw partitions, 431
patching a running server, 421
Pattern class, 160
pattern matching
    verbosegc logs, using with, 26
    (see also regular expressions)
pauses for garbage collection,
        minimizing, 69–71
peak performance targets, 454
perceived performance, 6–10
    caching, 9
    checklist for user expectations, 18
    J2EE applications, 452–455
        communication failures, 454
        cumulative delay and user
            impatience, 454
        good peak performance, 454
        Internet congestion, 453
        page display, 452
        priority service, 453
        screen navigation, 452
        user bandwidths, range of, 455
    network latency, effects on, 439
    startup times, 77
    streaming to appear quicker, 9
    threading to appear quicker, 8
performance
    checklists for, 17
    planning (see planning for performance)
    predicting (see predicting performance)
    targets, 10
performance checklists (see under individual
        topic listings)
performance goals, 400
performance monitor (on Windows), 20
performance problems
    application and web servers, 461
    caused by benchmarking, 14
    four main areas of, 447
    network, 447, 448, 461
    with network I/O, 441
    sources of, 461
    symptoms of, 450
performance tuning
    resources
        books, 533
        JavaPerformanceTuning.com (web
            site), 533
        magazines, 534

optimizers, 536
profilers, 536
URLs, 534
strategy for, 5
identifying bottlenecks, 5
(see also optimizations; related entries
under individual topics)
performance-monitoring API for EJB
application server, 527
Perm Space, 71
persistence in EJBs, 519
bean-managed, 519
container-managed, optimizations
for, 520
design guidelines for, 519
pessimistic locking, 524
Pet Store tutorial application (Sun), 529
PhantomReference class, 116
ping utility, 439
planning for performance, 422–426, 461
deployment with performance-logging
features, 426
focusing on performance in analysis
phase, 423
integrating performance logging, 425
J2EE performance tuning, 445
requiring performance predictions from
designers, 423
specifying performance
requirements, 422
test environment, creating, 424
test performance and use results, 425
testing simulation or skeleton, 424
point-to-point messaging, 460
poll( ), 220
polling, 220
polymorphism of methods, overhead
involved in, 2
pooling
connections with EJB application
server, 526
database connections, 476
prepared statements and, 486
message-driven beans in EJB, 529
objects, 103–106
load balancing with, 457
node pool for ternary search tree, 356
reducing garbage collection, 122
VectorPoolManager class
(example), 104
server sessions, 460
stateful EJBs, 519

stateless EJBs, 518
threads, 299
EJB application server, 526
reducing startup overhead with, 416
preallocating objects, 127
precompiling a statement, 485
preconditions, 91
predicting performance, 403
CPU parallelism, 407
techniques for, 415–418
batch processessing, 418
comparative performance of
operations, 415
data conversions, costs of, 417
focusing on shared resources, 417
parallelism, effects of, 417
relative costs of different access and
update types, 416
simulations and benchmarks,
using, 416
total work done and design
overhead, 417
preferredSize( ), 108
prepared statements in JDBC, 484–487
PreparedStatement interface
batching updates, 490
Statement vs., 485
when to use, 486
wrapper class, defining, 468–471
preprocessors
eliminating code blocks with, 177
inlining and, 93
optimizing compilers and, 79
previous( ) (ResultSet), 472
primitive data types
arrays of
fast casts for, 249–251
updates to, 317
casts of, 183
garbage collecting, 122
replacing others with ints, 186
using instead of Object types, 124
PrintWriter class, 504
priorities
queues, load balancing with, 458
user service, assigning to, 453
private objects (referents), 115
processes
forking, 302
listing, utilities for, 20
performance checklist, 443

processes (*continued*)
 priorities, 436, 438
  allocated by operating systems, timing
   and, 20
 runnable queue of, 435
producers (JMS), load balancing, 459
-prof option, 28, 38–42
 internal Java syntax for output, 41
profilers
 further resources, 536
 methodology, 28, 33
 output, 30
 sampling techniques, 28
 scaling behavior, 412
ProfileTest class (example), 29
 memory monitoring, 51
 -Xaprof profiler, using with, 42
ProfileViewer program, 42
profiling
 assertions, enabling/disabling, 180
 J2EE, 461
profiling tools, 19–63
 client/server communications, 56–62
  sockets, replacing, 58–62
  third-party communications packages,
   using, 57
 commercially available profilers, 19
 garbage collection, statistics on, 22–27
  -verbosegc option, 22–27
 generic, 20
 HAT (Heap Analysis Tool), 33
 J2EE, 445–447
 measurements and timings, 20
 memory usage, monitoring, 51–56
 method calls, 27–43
  HotSpot and 1.3 -Xprof output, 36
  Java 2 -Xaprof option, 42
  Java2 cpu=samples output, 33–36
  JDK 1.1.x -prof and Java 2
   cpu=old, 38–42
  -Xhprof option, 42
 object-creation, 43–50
 performance checklists for, 62
 -Xrunhprof option for JDK, 28
proprietary communication layers,
  comparison with other types, 374
proprietary communications
  infrastructures, 371, 373
proxies
 load balancing with proxy servers, 457
 monitoring performance of RMI
  calls, 449

Proxy class, 465
proxy objects
 use in EJB message handling, 525
 wrapping JDBC objects, 465–474
ps utility, 20
pseudo VMs, application distrubution
  over, 526
pseudocolumns (database), 492
public instance variables, avoiding accessor
  method use with, 187
publish-and-subscribe messaging, 460

Q

queries
 comparing LinkedLists and
  ArrayLists, 331
 database
  batching, 386
  statically defined, 386
 JDBC, timing, 473
 optimizing for collections, 323–327
  casts and extra access calls,
   eliminating, 325
  lighter typing of elements, 326
  map queries, 326
  method accessor, avoiding, 325
  method call in loop test, avoiding
   repetition of, 324
  shortcircuit boolean operators, 324
  synchronization, avoiding, 325
 SQL, limiting number of items
  retrieved, 530
QueryVector class (example), 75
queues
 actively managing requests
  (example), 304–306
 in distributed application design, 413
 messages, load balancing with, 460
 prioritizing for load balancing, 458
 processing for references,
  WeakHashMap, 119
 request processors accessing, 303
 runnable queue of processes and
  threads, 435
quicksort algorithm, 165, 260

R

race conditions, 281, 282
 deadlocks, system load and, 284
RAID (redundant array of independent
  disks), striping files and, 430

RAM, 436
RandomAccess interface, 333–337
    forward and backward compatibility, 336
    performance improvements in loop
        tests, 335
    uses of, 334
RandomAccessFile class, 221
range partitioning, 411
raw partitions, 431
RawIntComparator interface, 268
Reactor pattern in EJB design, 525
read( ), 231
    ScatteringByteChannel class, 255
    Socket class, 303
read-ahead algorithm for I/O buffers, 219
Reader class, 194, 227
readExternal (Externalizable), 238
readLine( )
    BufferedReader class, 154, 155
    DataInputStream class (deprecated
        method), 225, 227
readObject( ) (Serializable), 233, 238
read-only data in EJBs, 518
    Data Access Objects, using for, 522
    optimizing read-only EJBs for read-only
        transactions, 520
recursion, 211–217
    caching intermediate results, 214
    converting recursive method to
        iterative, 211, 214
    performance checklist, 218
    recursive merge sort for nonarray
        elements, 263
    stacks and, 215–217
    tail recursion, 212
    ternary search tree, converting to
        iteration, 353
    ternary search tree node, 349
redelivery of messages, limiting, 460
redirecting requests to proxy servers, 457
redirects, forwards vs., 506
reduction, 212
redundant array of independent disks
        (RAID), striping files, 430
references, 115–121
    garbage collection, 115
    Reference class, 117
    skewing test measurements with, 234
    SoftReference flushing, 116
    types of, 116
    weak, 112–114
    WeakHashMap class, 117–121

referents, 115, 117
    string literals as, 120
reflection, avoiding in loops, 194
regionMatches( ), 154, 162
regular expressions, 160–162
relay servers, 369
releaseSavepoint( ) (Connection), 497
remote access to EJBs, granularity and, 517
remote disks, adverse effect on I/O, 432
remote EJBs, 531
remote method invocation (see RMI)
remote procedure call (RPC), time
        measurement on a LAN, 416
removeEldestEntry( )
        (LinkedHashMap), 319
removing beans for performance gains, 519
request queue, 301
requesting too many rows in database data
        transfers, 480
requests
    centralizing client requests with Front
        Controller pattern, 525
    dispatchers or proxy servers for, 457
    JDBC, measuring, 449
    mapping to methods, 446
requirements for performance,
        specifying, 422
resources
    allocation/deallocation in EJB, 529
    concurrency conflicts in EJB,
        reducing, 531
    JDBC, closing or releasing, 474
    limitations of, 3
    partitioning, 430
    shared (see shared resources)
response times, 412
    measuring total response time, 448
    monitoring applications for, 418
    statistics on, analyzing, 450
    variation, 7
ResultSet interface, 464
    caching data with
        ReadOnlyCachedResultSet, 483
    getString( ), 482
    wrapper class, defining, 471
ResultSetMetaData class, 492
reusing code, 397
    exceptions, 176
    method entry points, 398
    method parameters, 187
    objects, 102–115, 415
        canonicalizing, 109–115

reusing code, objects (*continued*)
   in EJB, 524
      pool management, 103–106
      reusable paramaters, 108
      ThreadLocal objects, 106
RMI (remote method invocation)
   comparison with other communication
      layers, 374
   compression layer, adding, 380
   garbage collection and, 385
   garbage collection, tuning, 71
   message reduction example, 372
   monitoring performance of, 449
   optimized for EJB application server, 526
   profiling, 57
   scaling, 374
   standards equivalent to CORBA and Web
      Services, 390
rmic utility, 373
Robot class, 12
rollback( ) (Connection), 494
root objects, 40
rounding numbers in floating-point to string
      conversions, 142
round-robin partitioning, 411
routers
   dropping packets, 441
   packet sizes and, 440
RowSet interface, batching updates, 490
run( ) (Thread), 295
runnable queue of processes and
      threads, 435
runtime as overhead, 2
Runtime class
   freeMemory( ), 51
   maxMemory( ), 51
   totalMemory( ), 51
runtime optimizations, 91
runtime options, performance and, 93
runtime resolution of strings, 134

S

sampling techniques, profilers and, 28
savepoints, 497
scalability
   asynchronous vs. synchronous
      processing, 460
   concurrency conflicts in EJB
      application, 531
   horizontal, 455
   monitoring tools, 447

reducing resource contention to
      improve, 530
sessions, distributing for, 508
testing in simulation or skeleton
      system, 424
scaling, 412
   CORBA vs RMI, 374
   load balancing, importance of, 411
   of algorithms, 272, 315
   optimizations and, 404
   performance tests, 425
scatter-gather operations, NIO buffer
      classes, 255
schema partitioning, 411
screen navigation in reestablished
      connections, 452
search trees, 348–365
   digital tries, 348
      using with ternary, 361–365
   ternary, 348
      converting recursion to iteration, 354
      precreated pool of nodes, using, 356
      recursive ternary tree node, 349
      TernarySearchTree class, 350
      tuning, 352
searches
   case-insensitive, 163
   recursive, converting to iterative, 214,
      215–217
   search spaces, breaking up into logically
      parallelized spaces, 312
   in strings, 162–164
      Boyer-Moore algorithm, 164
security
   dispatcher decryption of requests, 457
   EJB application server, 527
Sedgewick, Bob, 348
seek time, 431
select( ), 220
SELECT statement (Oracle), optimizing, 492
selectedKeys( ) (Selector), 257
selecting too many fields in database
      queries, 480
Selector class, 256
   open( ), 257
   selectedKeys( ), 257
Serializable interface, 233, 236, 334
serialization, 233–244
   change logs, using, 233
   constructors, avoiding use of, 125
   HttpSession objects, 507

overhead of, 239
performance checklist, 258
ServerObject class, 373
servers
    application
        EJB, evaluating for performance and
            scalability, 525–528
        performance problems with, 447, 461
        performance-monitoring API, 448
        persistent cache update mechanism,
            design of, 416
    application, web, and database, optimal
        configuration of, 527
    CORBA, 372
    DNS, running locally, 442
    downtime, 420
    J2EE monitors for, 20
    measuring total server-side service
        time, 448
    relay, 369
    RMI, enabling call tracing, 57
    ServerObjectCacher class
        (example), 375–377
    TCP/IP, 302
    web servers
        performance problems caused by, 447,
            461
    Web Services, method execution
        time, 389
ServerSessionPool interface, 460
ServerSocket class, 302
    bind( ), 257
ServerSocketChannel class
    accept( ), 257
    open( ), 257
Service Locator pattern in EJB design, 523
service providers, probing configuration and
        connection to, 441
ServletContext class
    caching, 506
    moving session data to HttpSession, 530
ServletOutputStream class, 504
servlets
    doGet( ) and doPost( ) methods,
        execution times, 448
    logging capabilities for web server
        layer, 390
    network improvements, 429
    tuning, 501–515
        body tags, use of, 505
        cache tags, 506

case study (Ace Hardware SPECmine
        tool), 512–514
    compression, using, 509
    efficient page creation and
        output, 502–505
    HttpSession, 506–509
    more performance tips, 511
    performance checklist, 514
    SingleThreadModel, avoiding use
        of, 501
session beans
    accessing entity beans from, 517
    nontransactional methods, declaring, 521
    stateless, speediness of, 518
Session Façade in EJB design, 523
sessions, 506
    distributing for higher scalability, 508
    HttpSession vs. stateful session
        beans, 507
    optimizing use of HttpSession
        objects, 508
    screen navigation in reestablished
        connections, 452
    serialization of HttpSession objects, 508
    state information, in-memory replication
        of, 527
    storing data in HttpSession instead of
        ServletContext, 530
    terminating, 507
    timing out, 507
Set interface, 318
set*AssertionStatus( ) methods
        (Classloader), 178
set-based processing in JDBC, 478
setEntityContext( ), 529
setErr( ) (System), 222
setLength( ) (StringBuffer), 132
setMaxinactiveInterval( ) (HttpSession), 507
setMesssageDrivenContext( ), 529
setOut( ) (System), 222
setSessionContext( ), 529
setSize( ) (Vector), 105
setTransactionIsolation( ) (Connection), 495
shared resources, 404–412
    connection pools, 477
    DLLs, caching, 434
    focusing on in performance
        prediction, 417
    locking, 406
    memory, 72
        heap tuning and, 71
        I/O performance and, 220

shared resources (*continued*)
  parallelism, 407–412
    data parallelism, 411
    persistent caches, 416
    testing in simulation or skeleton
        system, 424
    transactions, 405
short data type
  changing to ints in arithmetic
      operations, 187
  converting to strings, 141
short-circuit operators for loops, 193
signals, handling for operating systems, 421
simulations of applications, 416
  testing, 424
single point of failure, elimination in EJB
      application server, 527
SingleThreadModel interface, 501
singleton sorting objects, 264
size of collection classes, 105
size( ) (WeakHashMap), 121
skeleton classes, 373
skeleton version of system, testing for
      performance, 424
Socket class, 302
  connect( ), 249
  customizing for logging, 59
SocketChannel class, 249, 256
sockets
  client, connecting with NIO package, 249
  client/server communications
    providing information on, 57
    tracing, 58–62
  load balancing and, 302
  UDP, 303
SockInStreamLogger class (example), 61
SockOutStreamLogger class (example), 61
SockStreamLogger class (example), 60
SoftReference objects, flushing, 116
Solaris, file copying tests with old and new
      I/O, 254
sort( )
  Arrays class, 166, 260, 261
    timings for, 262
  Collections class, 263, 316
Sortable class
  compareTo( ), 261
  compareToSortable( ), 261
  order fields, accessing directly in
      quicksort, 262
SortableComparator class (example), 268

sorting, 260–277
  casts, avoiding with standard sort
      algorithm and comparison method
      for a class, 262
  comparisons, optimizing in, 263
  database rows, resulting in excessive
      transfers, 480
  faster than O(nlogn), 271–276
  framework for efficient, 263–271
  generic vs specific, 271
  internationalized strings, 164–170
  merge sort, 316
  performance checklist, 276
  quicksort, 348
spatial locality of access, 337
SPECmine tool (Ace Hardware), case study
      on optimization, 512–514
SpeedStart program, 434
SQL
  database execution of statements, 484
  eliminating unnecessary data
      transfers, 481
  limiting query returns, 530
  optimizing, 477
  performance checklist, 499
  query optimization in Pet Store
      application, 529
  Statement vs. PreparedStatement, when to
      use, 486
  statements combining multiple
      operations, 478
Stack class, 318, 319
stack traces, 450
  exception overhead and, 174
  exceptions, using without, 176
  sampling with -Xrunhprof, 34
stacks
  recursion and, 215–217
  size per thread, setting, 71
  TCP/IP, performance of, 440
startup
  of applets, 401
  of caches, 14
  from disk sweet spots, 434
  overhead for processes, 416
  responsiveness of, 8
  timings and, 21
  of VMs, 76
  with threaded class loading, 98
stateful beans
  converting to stateless, 519
  pooling, 519

session beans
    HttpSession vs., 507
    prompt removal of, 509
stateless beans
    converting stateful to, 519
    speediness of, 518
stateless objects, benefits of, 415
Statement classes, wrapping, 468–471
Statement interface, 464
    execute( ), 494
    PreparedStatement vs., 485
    when to use, 486
statements, assert statements vs. others, 178
static binding, methods, 81
static methods, 109
    avoiding creation of intermediate
        objects, 122
    synchronization of, 282, 287
static pages, displaying quickly, 504
static URL generation, 457
static variables, 101, 109, 184
    class instance, storing in, 192
    enabling logging with, 223
statically defined database queries, 386
statistics
    analyzing from performance
        measurements, 450
    CPU utilization, 450
    object creation, 101
        garbage collection and, 101
    (see also profiling tools)
stock quoting service (Web Services), 391
stored procedures, 493
    performance checklist, 500
storing of a value into a variable, 296
strategy for performance tuning, 5
stream classes for socket logging, 60
streaming, for partial results, 9
streams
    appending objects to, 147
    object, I/O optimization and, 250
StreamTokenizer class, 102, 151
    replacing for efficiency, 73
    word counter, char array vs., 153
strength reduction, 82
StrictMath class, 73
String class
    charAt( ), 188
    compareTo( ), 167
    equals( ), 162
    equalsIgnoreCase( ), 162
    intern( ), 120, 163, 192

    iterating directly on underlying char
        array, 316
    length( ), 188
    matches( ), 160
    replacing with your own version, 73
    substring( ), 164
    toLowercase( ), 164
    toUppercase( ), 164
string literal referents, 120
StringBuffer class
    advantages of, 132
    appending ints, 140
    disadvantages of, 133
    using instead of concatenation (+)
        operator, 124
strings, 131–171
    C language, 150
    canonicalizing, 111
    char arrays vs., 150–162
        line filter example, 154–160
        line filtering with regular
            expressions, 160–162
        word-counting example, 151–153
    comparisons and searches, 162–164
    compilation, 131
    compile-time vs. runtime resolution, 134
    concatenating, 89, 90, 131, 503
        at runtime, 134
    conversions to, 135–150
        bytes, shorts, chars and booleans, 141
        doubles, 146
        floats, 141–146
        ints, 138–140
        longs, 135–138
        objects, 147–150
    immutability of, 131
    internationalized, sorting, 164–170
    lists of, avoiding casts with, 184
    optimization of string-handling in Pet
        Shop code, 530
    partially matched, finding index
        for, 344–348
    performance checklist, 170
    performance effects of, 131–134
        advanatages, 131
        disadvantages, 132
    processing in I/O, 228
    replacing with enumerated constants, 115
    in servlet output, using efficiently, 503
    SQL statement execution, 487
    substring operation, 132
StringWriter class, 148

striping, disk, 432
stubs, replacing object instance variables with, 368
subexpressions, eliminating common, 86
substring( ) (String), 164
subsystems, optimized for EJB application server, 526
super( ), 44
swap files, 431, 437, 443
swap space, increasing, 430
switches, 205–211
    array access, converting to, 207
    case statement reordering by optimizing compiler, 86
    contiguous sets of cases, 206
    converting to array access, 208–211
    non-contiguous values for cases, 206
    performance checklist, 218
    speedup for VMs using exception-driven loop termination, 207
    SwitchTest class (example), 206–211
Symantec development environment, I/O operations, 247
synchronization
    ArrayList and Vector classes, 328
    atomic access and assignment, 296–300
        ordering, 300
    collection queries, avoiding in, 325
    desynchronization and synchronized wrappers, 287–291
    distributed caching with, EJB application server, 526
    increment( ), 282
    lockable update method, 406
    multithreaded tests, timing, 295
    overhead of, 285–295
        serialized execution, avoiding, 291–295
    performance checklist for, 313
    servlet activities, 501
    threads, 278
        counter incrementation, 282
        monitors and, 279
    unnecessary, avoiding, 287
synchronized keyword, 279, 282, 288
System class
    arraycopy( ), 191
    currentTimeMillis( ), 15, 20, 465
    gc( ), 22
        disabling, 71
    setErr( ), 222
    setOut( ), 222

system level I/O, 219
System.out, replacing, 221–223
systems
    bottlenecks in load balancing example, 308
    limitations of, 3
    noting changes to, 419
    throughput, measuring in benchmarking, 15
    (see also operating systems)

T

tail recursion, 212
task manager (Windows), 20
task queue, 435
tcpdump (communication-monitoring tool), 57
TCP/IP
    communication rate on congested networks, 441
    load balancing with, 302
    servers, 302
    stacks, 438
        network I/O and, 438, 440
    tuneable parameters, 440
temporal locality of access, 337
temporary objects
    avoiding creation of
        appending objects to streams, 147
        char array vs. StreamTokenizer, 153
        in long to string conversion, 137
    reducing number of, 124
    temporary variables of primitive data types vs., 187
temporary variables
    avoiding repeated casts with, 184
    frequently manipulated array elements, assigning to, 186
    local variables as, 184
    loops, speeding up with, 190
    primitive data types, using instead of object types, 187
terminating loops with exceptions, 201–205
    speedup for various VMs using, 207
termination tests for loops, avoiding method calls in, 191
ternary search trees, 348
    digital trie, using with, 361–365
    recursion, converting to iteration, 354

TernarySearchTree class, 350
    access and update times compared with
        HashMap, 351
    tuning, 352
TernarySearchTreeNode class, 349
test environment for performance,
        creating, 424
testing
    inacurrate results from, 452
    performance and tuning using
        results, 425
    simulation or skeleton system, 424
    with small differences in timings, 15
this( ), 44
thread safety (SingleThreadModel), 501
threaded class loading, 98
ThreadedAccess class (example), 106
ThreadLocal class, 106
threads, 278–313
    atomic access and assignment, 296–300
    deadlocked, 282–286
    listing, utilities for, 20
    load balancing, 301–311
        classes for, 303–306
        example of, 306–311
        TCP/IP, using, 302
    locking, 286
    multithreaded tests, timing, 295
    object local to current thread, 106
    perceived performance and, 8
    performance checklist, 313
    pooling, 299
        EJB application server, 526
        startup overhead, reducing, 416
    problem-solving strategies, 312
    race conditions, 281
    runnable queue of, 435
    sleeping restlessly, 417
    stack size, setting, 71
    synchronization, 278
        monitors and, 279
        overhead of, 285–295
    user-interface and other, 279–281
thread=y option (-Xrunhprof), 33
throughput
    applications, 412
    disk, 247
    statistics on, analyzing, 450
    system, measuring in benchmarking, 15
tight loops, 200
time
    exceptions, cost of, 174
    measurements for benchmarks, 15, 17

measurements for distributed
    applications, 16
timeouts
    setting for client-initiated transactions in
        EJB, 521
    specifying, 430
timestamps, 15
time-to-live values for SoftReferences, 116
timing out sessions, 508
timings
    caching, effects on, 21
    profilers and, 20
tmpfs, 433
toLowercase( ) (String), 164
top utility, 20
toString( )
    Boolean class, 141
    Integer class, 140
    Long class, 135
    Object class, 150
    StringBuffer class, 133
    Vector class, 147
totalMemory( ) (Runtime), 51
toUpperCase( ) (String), 154, 164
trace statements, 91
traceMethodCalls( ) (Runtime), 258
"train" garbage collection algorithm, 69
training users, 420
transaction logs, 233
transactional access to databases, 386
transactions
    analyzing in application
        development, 400
    design-stage decisions about, 403
    distributed, management by EJB
        application server, 527
    EJB
        performance checklist, 531
        tuning, 520
    JDBC, optimizing in, 494–497
        auto-commit mode, 494
        non-ACID transaction problems, 498
        performance checklist, 500
        savepoints and distributed
            transactions, 497
        transaction levels, 495
        user-controlled transactions, 496
    JMS messages, transactional and
        nontransactional, 460
    optimistic, 496
        EJB application server, support of, 526
        write-write conflicts with,
            detecting, 524

transactions *(continued)*
   optimizing, 405
   rates of, analyzing statistics on, 450
transfer layers, measuring performance
      of, 17
transfer rates, disks, 431, 435
transferFrom( ) (FileChannel), 254
transferring data
   minimizing in JDBC operations, 480
   Page-by-Page Iterator pattern in EJB, 522
   reducing costs with data duplication, 414
   reducing network transfers with Value
      Objects in EJB, 521
   ValueListHandler pattern in EJB, 523
transferTo( ) (FileChannel), 254
transient fields, avoiding serialization of, 233
transient modifier, 368
translations between programming
      languages, 95
tree structures (search trees), 348–365
TreeMap class, 318, 319
TreeSet class, 318
trie structures, 348
try-catch blocks, 202
   with exceptions, cost of, 174–176
   without exceptions, cost of, 172–174
tuning performance
   avoiding unneeded, 16
   benchmarks, setting, 11
   distributed applications, 14
   EJB application servers, 528
   EJBs
      additional suggestions for, 529
      Elite.com case study, 530
      Pet Store case study, 529
   measurements, 15
   multiuser applications, 14
   strategy for, 5, 28
      identifying bottlenecks, 5
   systematically, 17
   user expectations for performance, 10
   (see also related entries under individual
      topics)
tutorial application (Pet Store), 529

U

UDP
   network bottlenecks and, 441
   resending packets on congested
      networks, 441
   sockets, 303

unicast messaging, 460
UnicastRemoteObject class, 373
Unicode, 164
Unix
   communication-monitoring tools, 57
   CPU monitoring, 435
   disk usage, 430, 449
   file descriptors, monitoring availability
      of, 449
   forking processes on, 302
   generating stack dumps, 450
   measuring network bandwidth, 450
   memory-mapped filesystem, 433
   netstart utility, 57
   paging, monitoring, 437
   priority of processes, 21
   process and thread-listing utiilities, 20
   profiling object creation, 46
unmarshalling objects, 125
unrolling loops, 84, 198
unSetEntityContext( ), 529
updates
   arrays of primitive types vs. object
      arrays, 317
   costs of different types, 416
   database
      batching in JDBC, 489
      eliminating unnecessary
         (example), 530
   optimizing objects for, 415
URLClassLoader class, 421
URLs
   Java performance tuning resources, 534
   load balancing based on, 457
useBean action, 505
User Datagram Protocol (see UDP)
user interface usability, 420
user-controlled transactions, 496
user-interface thread and others, 279–281
users
   expectations for performance, 10
   multiple, benchmarking and, 13
   number simultaneously using
      application, 400
   performance perception of
      latency and, 439
   statistics on, analyzing, 450
   training, 420
utilization, CPU
   analyzing statistics on, 450
   measuring, 449

V

Value Object Assembler pattern in EJB design, 521
Value Objects in EJB design, 521
ValueListHandler pattern in EJB, 523
valueUnbound( ) (HttpSessionBinderListener), 509
variables, 184–187
  array element access vs., cost of, 186
  casting repeatedly, 184
  class, static vs. instance, 101
  corrupt, 292, 300, 398
    unsynchronized classes and, 289
  default initialization values in Java, 125
  heap, 184
  local, 184
  multithreaded, atomic access and assignment, 296–300
  performance checklist, 188
  primitive types, replacing with ints, 186
  public instance variables, accessing, 187
  shared between threads, corruption of, 279
  static, 109, 184
    enabling logging with, 223
    storing class instances in, 192
  volatile, 298
Vector class, 318, 319
  appending to streams, 149
  generic capabilities of, performance and, 74
  implementation, 327
    with underlying String[ ] array, 316
  setSize( ), 105
  synchronization, 288
  toString( ), 147
  unsynchronized, synchronized wrapper vs., 289
  (see also ArrayList class)
VectorPoolManager class (example), 104
vectors
  handles to, memory reuse caused by, 104
  pool management and, 104
  for threads, 106
verbose option, 97
-verbosegc option, 22
  analyzing output of, 22–27
    common items for all versions, 25
    pattern matching, using with logs, 26
    tools for, 27
Verified Service Locator pattern in EJB design, 523

version management, hot-deploy and hot-undeploy applications for, 527
virtual memory, 437
VMs (virtual machines)
  application distribution over, 526
  client/server modes, calculation of free space in heap, 117
  EJBs located within, local communications among, 517
  eliminating disabled assertion statements, 179
  faster, 75–79
    other optimizations, 77
    startup time, 76
    variations in speed, 75
  generating helpful information for, 87
  heap size
    tuning for EJB application servers, 528
    (see also heap, tuning)
  HotSpot, speeding up code, 21
  multiple, using for load balancing, 458
  optimizations for number comparisons, 191
  RandomAccess, compatibility with, 336
  runtime initializations, 77
  speedup using exception-driven loop termination, 207
  synchronized methods, overhead of, 291
  -verbosegc option, 22
    Sun JDK 1.2 output with, 23
  -Xloggc:<file> option, 22
  (see also -verbosegc option)
vmstat utility, 20
volatile keyword, 298

W

wait( ) (Object), 279
weak references, canonicalized objects and, 112–114
WeakHashMap class, 117–121
WeakReference class, 116
  object canonicalization and, 112
web browsers
  perceived performance and, 7
  profiling data transfers, 56
web pages (see page display; pages)
web servers
  downloading many pages from, 306–311
  overloading by downloading many pages at high access rate, 306
  performance problems with, 447, 461

Web Services, 386–393
   asynchronous processing, 393
   CORBA vs., 390
   granularity of methods, 391
   high-performance, 390
   load balancing, 392
   measuring performance, 387, 394
      DNS lookup time, 389
      marshalling time, 390
      network communication time, 389
      round-trip overhead, inferring, 389
      round-trip time, 389
      server-side method execution, 389
   performance advantages and
      disadvantages, 387
Web Services Description Language
      (WSDL), 390
Windows
   CPU monitoring, 435
   file copying tests, 254
   fork procedures on, 302
   measuring network bandwidth, 450
   memory-mapped filesystem, 433
   monitoring open files and sockets, 449
   netstart utility, 57
   ObjectCreationMonitoring class,
      executing, 46
   paging, monitoring, 437
   profiling object creation, 46
   stack dumps, generating, 450
   task manager and performance monitor
      utilities, 20
   TCP/IP stacks, 440
words, counting (example), 151–153
wrappers
   ConnectionWrapper class, 465–467
   JDBC, 465–474
      caching with, 482

Proxy and Decorator patterns, wrapping
      objects with, 525
   synchronized, 287–291, 317
write( )
   GatheringByteChannel, 255
   OutputStream class, 256
   SocketChannel class, 256
writeExternal (Externalizable), 238
writeObject( ) (Serializable), 233, 238
Writer class, 194
   appendTo( ), 148
WSDL (Web Services Description
      Language), 390

X

XAConnection interface, 497
XADataSource interface, 497
-Xaprof option, 42
-Xbootclasspath option, 46
-Xconcgc option (concurrent garbage
      collector), 69
-Xhprof option, 42
-Xincgc option, 69
-Xloggc:<file> option for the VM, 22
-Xprof option, 36
Xrun option, Xrunhprof option and, 33
-Xrunhprof option, 28, 33
   cpu=old variation, 38–42
   format=b (binary output option), 43
-XX:MaxPermSize parameter, 71

Z

ZIP files (uncompressed), for class
      delivery, 97

About the Author

Jack Shirazi is the director of JavaPerformanceTuning.com. He was an early adopter of Java, quickly focusing on Java performance, and has since been providing consulting services across a diverse range of business sectors.

Jack's early career involved research in theoretical physics and bioinformatics. Jack has many published articles on Java performance and also has publications in the field of protein science. He is also proud to have contributed to some of the core Perl5 modules.

Colophon

Our look is the result of reader comments, our own experimentation, and feedback from distribution channels. Distinctive covers complement our distinctive approach to technical topics, breathing personality and life into potentially dry subjects.

The animal on the cover of *Java Performance Tuning* is a serval (*Leptailurus serval*). This long-legged cat is found in most parts of Africa, except for very dry areas of the continent, such as the northern regions around the Sahara Desert. Servals range in color from light brown to a darker reddish brown (some servals are entirely black); their coats are covered with dark spots that merge into stripes along the upper part of their backs. The pattern of their markings varies geographically; servals from wetter areas have smaller, finer spots, while those from drier areas have larger marks. Servals can grow up to 3 feet long and 20 inches tall at the shoulder, making their legs very long in proportion to their bodies. They use this height to their advantage, as they are able to see movement in the tall grass in which they hunt for the hares, rodents, and small birds they like to eat. Their big ears and highly developed auditory systems enable them to hear the high-pitched, ultrasonic sounds made by rodents—they are even able to hear them tunneling underground—and they can also leap up to 10 feet into the air to catch birds.

Emily Quill was the production editor and proofreader for *Java Performance Tuning*, Second Edition. Ann Schirmer was the copyeditor. Linley Dolby and Philip Dangler provided quality control. Ellen Troutman wrote the index.

Emma Colby designed the cover of this book, based on a series design by Edie Freedman. The cover image is a 19th-century engraving from the Couvier Pictorial Archive. Emma Colby produced the cover layout with QuarkXPress 4.1 using Adobe's ITC Garamond font.

David Futato designed the interior layout. This book was converted to FrameMaker 5.5.6 by Joe Wizda and Judy Hoer with a format conversion tool created by Erik Ray, Jason McIntosh, Neil Walls, and Mike Sierra that uses Perl and XML technologies. The text font is Linotype Birka; the heading font is Adobe Myriad Condensed; and the code font is LucasFont's TheSans Mono Condensed. The illustrations that appear in the book were produced by Robert Romano and Jessamyn Read using Macromedia FreeHand 9 and Adobe Photoshop 6. The tip and warning icons were drawn by Christopher Bing. This colophon was written by Leanne Soylemez.

Related Titles Available from O'Reilly

Java

Ant: The Definitive Guide

Enterprise JavaBeans, *3rd Edition*

Head First Java

Head First EJB

J2EE Design Patterns

J2ME in a Nutshell

Java and SOAP

Java & XML Data Binding

Java & XML

Java Cookbook

Java Data Objects

Java Database Best Practices

Java Enterprise Best Practices

Java Enterprise in a Nutshell, *2nd Edition*

Java Examples in a Nutshell, *2nd Edition*

Java Extreme Programming Cookbook

Java in a Nutshell, *4th Edition*

Java Management Extensions

Java Message Service

Java Network Programming, *2nd Edition*

Java NIO

Java RMI

Java Security, *2nd Edition*

Java ServerPages, *2nd Edition*

Java Servlet Programming, *2nd Edition*

Java Swing, *2nd Edition*

Java Web Services in a Nutshell

JXTA in a Nutshell

Learning Java, *2nd Edition*

Mac OS X for Java Geeks

NetBeans: The Definitive Guide

Programming Jakarta Struts

Tomcat: The Definitive Guide

Keep in touch with O'Reilly

1. Download examples from our books

To find example files for a book, go to:

www.oreilly.com/catalog

select the book, and follow the "Examples" link.

2. Register your O'Reilly books

Register your book at *register.oreilly.com*

Why register your books?
Once you've registered your O'Reilly books you can:

- Win O'Reilly books, T-shirts or discount coupons in our monthly drawing.
- Get special offers available only to registered O'Reilly customers.
- Get catalogs announcing new books (US and UK only).
- Get email notification of new editions of the O'Reilly books you own.

3. Join our email lists

Sign up to get topic-specific email announcements of new books and conferences, special offers, and O'Reilly Network technology newsletters at:

elists.oreilly.com

It's easy to customize your free elists subscription so you'll get exactly the O'Reilly news you want.

4. Get the latest news, tips, and tools

www.oreilly.com

- "Top 100 Sites on the Web"—PC Magazine
- CIO Magazine's Web Business 50 Awards

Our web site contains a library of comprehensive product information (including book excerpts and tables of contents), downloadable software, background articles, interviews with technology leaders, links to relevant sites, book cover art, and more.

5. Work for O'Reilly

Check out our web site for current employment opportunities:

jobs.oreilly.com

6. Contact us

O'Reilly & Associates, Inc.
1005 Gravenstein Hwy North
Sebastopol, CA 95472 USA

TEL: 707-827-7000 or 800-998-9938
      (6am to 5pm PST)

FAX: 707-829-0104

order@oreilly.com
For answers to problems regarding your order or our products. To place a book order online, visit:

www.oreilly.com/order_new

catalog@oreilly.com
To request a copy of our latest catalog.

booktech@oreilly.com
For book content technical questions or corrections.

corporate@oreilly.com
For educational, library, government, and corporate sales.

proposals@oreilly.com
To submit new book proposals to our editors and product managers.

international@oreilly.com
For information about our international distributors or translation queries. For a list of our distributors outside of North America check out:

international.oreilly.com/distributors.html

adoption@oreilly.com
For information about academic use of O'Reilly books, visit:

academic.oreilly.com

O'REILLY®

Our books are available at most retail and online bookstores.
To order direct: 1-800-998-9938 • order@oreilly.com • www.oreilly.com
Online editions of most O'Reilly titles are available by subscription at *safari.oreilly.com*